D1593812

THE HISTORY OF MODERN JAPANESE EDUCATION

THE HISTORY OF MODERN JAPANESE EDUCATION

Constructing the National

School System, 1872–1890

BENJAMIN DUKE

RUTGERS UNIVERSITY PRESS
New Brunswick, New Jersey, and London

Library of Congress Cataloging-in-Publication Data

Duke, Benjamin C.
    The history of modern Japanese education : constructing the national school system, 1872–1890 / Benjamin Duke.
        p. cm.
    Includes bibliographical references and index.
        ISBN 978-0-8135-4403-8 (alk. paper)
    1. Education—Japan—History—19th century.   2. Education and state—Japan—History—19th century.   I. Title.
    LA1311.7.D85 2009
    370.952'09034—dc22   2008007748

A British Cataloging-in-Publication record for this book is available from the British Library.

Visit our Web site: http://rutgerspress.rutgers.edu

Manufactured in the United States of America

To the Japanese samurai who led their nation into the modern era

Contents

Illustrations

Tables

Acknowledgments

Among the many individuals who greatly assisted me in collecting and analyzing the massive amount of material necessary for this book, I want to especially acknowledge Dr. Yoshiie Sadao who teaches the history of Japanese education at the distinguished Keio University. He graciously devoted countless numbers of hours over a ten-year period with me at the National Diet Library and at his home discussing my interpretation, as a non-Japanese, of Japanese education during the early Meiji Period. He then countered with his interpretation as a recognized Japanese scholar and teacher on the subject. He was as interested in the non-Japanese perspective as I was in the Japanese perspective. He also carefully read many of the chapters extending his stamp of approval which proved highly gratifying coming from a Japanese scholar.

The other individual who proved so important was my long-time senior graduate assistant at the International Christian University in Tokyo, Arai Hajime. His dedicated service began when he was appointed as my undergraduate assistant when I was elected to the Chairmanship of the Graduate Division of Education. Shortly thereafter I began to collect the material for this book. Arai san spent many hours sifting through old documents and publications searching for pertinent material and assisting me in the interpretation of the contents. Even after I retired from the university and began writing the manuscript in the United States, Arai san faithfully assisted me when I returned to the ICU campus each spring to fill in the missing links. I wish him well in his future endeavors.

I am also indebted to the staff of the ICU library and especially Mrs. Nagano Yuki who was the Head Librarian during most of the period of this research. Although the ICU Library contains impressive holdings of materials and books on the 1872–1890 period under review, there were naturally materials needed that were not internally available. The staff went to extraordinary measures to obtain them through interlibrary loans and personal contacts that proved most helpful. I also want to recognize the cooperation and encouragement of my divisional colleague and campus neighbor of many years, Dr. David Rackham from Canada. He assisted with the preparation of the pictures, many old and faded from the 1800s, that I felt would add a great deal to the book. My gratitude is additionally extended to Dr. Fred Notehelfer and Dr. Thomas Havens, two distinguished American scholars on Japanese culture and society, who read various chapters near the end of the writing period and offered encouragement to complete the work.

My wife June deserves recognition for her support and patience when I spent so much time on this project during the decade that it took to complete this manuscript, including the times when she accompanied me on library visits not only in Japan but also in Britain and the United States.

And finally I am greatly appreciative for a financial grant from the United States–Japan Foundation whose president, Dr. David Packard, took a personal interest in assuring that my lengthy manuscript would be published in its entirety.

THE HISTORY OF
MODERN JAPANESE
EDUCATION

Introduction

THE AIMS OF EDUCATION
FOR MODERN JAPAN

Japanese historians invariably designate the beginning of modernism in their country with the restoration of imperial rule in 1868, which ended the 250-year era of the feudal Tokugawa regime. Japanese educational historians, by contrast, date the beginning of the modern era in education with the issuance in 1872 of the Gakusei, literally the "education plan." Since the Gakusei was specifically designed by the newly formed Ministry of Education as a national system of public education, a more appropriate reading renders it the First National Plan for Education. Regardless of the name, the Gakusei of 1872 represents the single most important document in modern Japanese educational history.

The proclamation of the Gakusei provoked a discussion of profound importance to the future of Japan: what are the aims of education in a modern nation? Never before in the long history of the Japanese people had this issue been addressed. Within two decades, a solution emerged in the form of the 1890 Imperial Rescript on Education, which was deemed suitable for Japan to enter the twentieth century as a modern state. In the process, a bitter debate between the modernists and the traditionalists transpired that extended far beyond the schools. It marks the 1870s and 1880s as one of the most decisive as well as controversial periods in the history of Japanese education, when leaders of the Imperial Restoration struggled valiantly to determine the aims of education for a modern country.

This historical analysis is devoted to the first two decades of modern Japanese public education, tracing the fate of the 1872 Gakusei to the 1890 Imperial Rescript on Education. Because the development of education in every country reflects the social and cultural traits of its people, the First National Plan for Education can best be understood in its social and cultural milieu. A brief description of the historical environment in which the Gakusei originated may serve as a sufficient introduction to the primary document that governed the opening of the modern period of education in Japan.

When the Gakusei was formulated in 1872, government leaders were haunted by a crisis of international proportions. Powerful western nations were expanding trading posts throughout the world. European colonial empires had spread into the Far East, threatening the very existence of Japan as a sovereign state. During the years of self-imposed isolation by the Tokugawa regime from the early 1600s, the country had fallen dangerously behind the West as the industrial revolution got under way. The rise of western capitalism and international colonialism posed a pervasive threat to Japan, as perceived by the new leaders. They were determined to use any means necessary to transform their country into a modern state in order to to preserve the political order and national sovereignty. Education on the western model was envisioned as an instrument to achieve that goal.

In spite of hundreds of years under feudalism, the Japanese people had already achieved a remarkable literary standard and level of sophistication by 1872. Three rather well-defined cultural influences or schools of thought produced those results. The first, Kangaku, was based on Chinese culture and learning. Its origin dates back to the seventh century, when the powerful and somewhat overwhelming influence of China reached Japan. Kangaku as a school of thought, however, reached its zenith during the Tokugawa period from the early 1600s to the late 1800s. The second, Wagaku, incorporated indigenous Japanese cultural elements in existence before the entry of Chinese cultural influences. And the final influence, Yōgaku, referred to all things western then in the early stages of influence upon Japan. The history of modern Japanese education revolves around the interplay among these three broad cultural influences.

Each of the three schools of thought that vied for cultural, and therefore educational, supremacy contained a particular feature that symbolized its uniqueness. Wagaku, the Japanese school of thought, was centered on the institution of the emperor and all that accompanied the long imperial tradition with its inextricable relationship to the beliefs of Shintō. Kangaku, the Chinese school of thought, particularly during the Tokugawa era, focused on Confucius classics, with primary concern for interpersonal hierarchical relationships and behavior undergirding social harmony. Yōgaku, the western school of thought, primarily although not exclusively meant science and technology in the later half of the 1800s.

The first two, Wagaku and Kangaku, from Japan and China respectively, had coexisted for centuries in a symbiotic relationship. It was the introduction of secular western science with its basis in mathematical and rationalistic thought that deviated significantly from the two cultural patterns from the East. The confrontation between East and West, reduced to its most simplistic terms by leading combatants as morals education versus science education, marks the early modernization period of Japanese education and society. Virtually every document, every position, every policy, can best be understood from its relationship to the great struggle between these powerful ideologies and their constituencies in determining the initial aims of education in modern Japan.

With the issuance of the Gakusei of 1872, the spark for a cultural revolution was ignited. The First National Plan for Education, designed virtually in its entirety on western patterns of education and thought, represents the opening salvo. The struggle of immense magnitude was engaged: how to modernize technologically and scientifically on a western model while preserving national sovereignty and eastern cultural traditions? To many of those who participated in the ensuing battles for the control and influence of the new public school system, the Gakusei became the focus of dispute. It pitted western science against both

Japanese imperial traditions and Chinese Confucian principles of feudal social relationships that had become dominant in Japanese society.

For the remainder of the 1870s, as a result of a multiplicity of diverse influences primarily from the West, the major educational developments were implemented through repeated revisions of the Gakusei. The decade of the 1880s brought revisions of major significance; in reaction to the western influences of the 1870s, a reverse course in educational reform was charted. Promoted by imperial advisers, the reverse course in educational policy reflected traditional eastern cultural patterns as they perceived them.

Through two decades of social, ideological, and educational turmoil, the underlying struggle between western thought and that of the imperial institution and Confucian teachings determined the battle lines for control of modern Japanese education and the destiny of the nation. With a deft compromise in the form of the Imperial Rescript on Education, a sustainable national school system was finally set in place by 1890. It remained intact until World War II.

To gain a basic understanding of how the modern school system of Japan was constructed, the relevant domestic and international connections that were intertwined to form the modern Japanese tradition in education form the focus of this study. In particular, special concern has been given to those individuals, both Japanese and foreigners, who played leading roles in the transformation of Japanese education from the feudal to the modern. No country has ever constructed a national system of education in such a remarkably short period, nor relied on such a variety of uncommon individuals from throughout the world, than did Japan in the latter half of the nineteenth century.

The year of the Gakusei, the First National Plan for Education of 1872, implemented from 1873, is noteworthy for several critical reasons. First, it marks only the fourth year of the Meiji government; an extremely short interlude transpired between the end of a 250-year feudal-military regime in 1868 and the initial move toward a modern national school system in 1872. In fact, however, the modernization process had been under way well before the restoration of Emperor Meiji in 1868. Compelling forces of change were already at work during the latter part of the feudal Tokugawa regime, the so-called Bakumatsu period from 1853, marked by the uninvited entry of American warships into then-restricted Japanese waters. Elements of change during the feudal period laid the foundation for new educational ideas as the process of modernization burst into fruition under reform-minded leaders of the Meiji government.

The second factor that makes 1872 interesting is that the period of time between the old and new regimes was obviously far too brief to enable a fresh generation of postfeudal leaders to assume responsibility. That is, those who crafted the modern school system of Japan were products of the old regime immersed within feudal patterns of education. Nevertheless, those individuals who were reared in a feudal society that revered ancient Confucian social concepts, and educated in schools where Chinese classics formed the core of the curriculum, suddenly became leaders of the new western-oriented government. In effect, modern Japan emerged from a feudal society with a literate historical foundation. Ironically, perhaps no other society in the East or West encountered the modernization process better prepared for the challenge than Japan in the early 1870s.

The third factor of significance concerning the year of the Gakusei, a mere four years after the turbulent overthrow of the long-reigning Tokugawa regime, relates to the insufficient time and opportunity to carefully and thoughtfully design a comprehensive plan for a national school system. During the previous era, although there was a centralized government that determined the basic laws of the land, the central authority did not attempt to establish a national school system. A variety of social institutions, most notably the schools, were primarily operated by local clan authorities supplemented by private teachers who not only catered to the ruling samurai-warrior elite but also served an impressive number of commoners.

The factor of distance and slow communications between the Tokugawa capital in Edo (Tokyo) and the distant clans, as well as the constraints of a central government that had gained control by suppressing local clan leaders, rendered it virtually impossible for the central Tokugawa government to establish a national school system. Distance between the central seat of government and the furthermost clans was of particular importance. The clans located in the far south were the most powerful local entities, with strong clan loyalties, inherently in opposition to outside influence. It was, in hindsight, a wise policy decision to leave education in local hands. Rather than try to replace them, Tokugawa officials endeavored to influence local education by setting a pattern at the center, intended to be locally emulated, which was based on Confucian and Chinese classics as the mainstay of the educated ruling class until the revolution of 1868.

Four years later the new leaders, themselves originating overwhelmingly from the distant powerful clans in the south, educated under the old regime, and all with powerful local ties, hastily cobbled together a national plan for education that would be the responsibility of the central government. Little had changed in the four years in communications and transportation between the central government in Tokyo and the remote clans in the far south. The new government formed around Emperor Meiji was transferred from Kyoto, where the imperial family had lived for centuries. The fact that it took the emperor and his entourage three weeks to travel from Kyoto to Tokyo in 1868, a distance of three hundred miles, was indicative of the challenges and problems facing the new government.

In the Tokugawa capital of Edo, renamed Tokyo, a hastily organized Ministry of Education was formed in 1871. It faced the continuing problems of communication and transportation between the center and the distant provinces. Nevertheless, it produced a grandiose plan less than a year later for a centralized national educational system that would call for a national school system incorporating every child, a standard that no nation had achieved by that time. Under the prevailing conditions it was natural that as soon as the Gakusei was issued, continual revisions would follow as the exigencies of the day prompted changes.

The final significance of the year 1872 in relation to the beginning of the modern public school system in Japan concerns the condition of education in the West at that time. Early on, key Meiji leaders made perhaps their most critical decision concerning education. They concluded that the technical and military superiority of western countries, already painfully experienced during several episodes of coastal bombardments by foreign ships, and witnessed during awe-inspiring earlier visits by government envoys to the West, required a western-style infrastructure for Japan to modernize. However, not only was there insufficient time by 1872 to conduct a systematic investigation of western schools, there was no way for the Japanese leaders to initially distinguish which western school systems and practices would prove beneficial for, and instructive to, the Japanese.

Further complicating the task of the early Meiji educational reformers was the growing disparity in educational development among western countries. Differences among educational patterns in the continental countries of Europe and Britain and those of the new world of America were significant. The Japanese quickly developed close educational connections on both sides of the Atlantic, but the American influence took precedence during the 1870s, just as the American people were fashioning a frontier society, breaking tradition with their European roots.

European countries, with which the Japanese also developed close connections in the 1870s in various areas such as the military, were only grudgingly accepting changes in their hierarchical patterns of education. European patterns of education were characterized by high academic standards of classical curricula that catered to the ruling classes. Although the well-known European classical humanistic schools produced some of the greatest leaders of the period in many fields, it also resulted in wide gaps between the highly educated elite and the poorly educated masses. One of the major purposes of the Meiji educational leaders was to provide a public education for every child regardless of social background. To the impressionable Japanese, among western countries of the day, America appeared well on its way to achieve that goal.

Every western system of education in 1872 had enormous problems and deficiencies. Understandably, the Japanese were incapable of discerning which nation could serve as the most appropriate model for the modernization of Japanese society and education. Among the most puzzling, in the context of the Gakusei intended to establish a centralized national educational system in Japan, was the simple fact that some western countries, notably Britain and the United States, had no national system of education on the scale envisioned in the Gakusei. By 1872 France had a centralized educational administrative structure that impressed the Japanese, although there were enormous gaps in its implementation. On the other hand, America had no Ministry of Education. The fact that the Meiji leaders turned primarily to America for educational guidance in the revisions of the Gakusei during the 1870s was a clear indication of the naiveté and inexperience of their policy makers. It took nearly fifteen years for the political and educational leadership to change directions from America to Europe, recognizing Germany with its monarchical tradition and burgeoning modern sciences as the most appropriate western educational model for Japan in the 1880s.

In the process of directional change, perhaps an even more significant development involved the direct participation of the Imperial Household in forming public educational policy. During the 1870s, that is, the first decade after the Restoration, the new national educational system was primarily designed and implemented by a fledgling bureaucracy deeply impressed by the American model. In reaction, during the early 1880s, imperial advisors devised a theory of moral education for the public schools based on Japanese cultural traditions deeply influenced by Confucian concepts. It marked the first attempt to balance the purposes in education that had been predominant in the 1870s. A final compromise emerged which amalgamated both eastern and western elements in the Imperial Rescript of 1890.

In the formation of the modern educational system of Japan, with the 1872 Gakusei as the catalyst, there were many individuals who made significant contributions both from within Japan and abroad. Among them four historical Japanese figures are given major attention because of their contributions. Tanaka Fujimaro, an obscure ex-samurai from Nagoya, was given responsibility under extreme conditions for implementing the First National Plan for Education from 1873 as head of the new Ministry of Education. Mori Arinori, however, is credited with personally designing the basic structure of a truly comprehensive national school system in 1886. In addition to these two prominent bureaucrats, Takamine Hideo surfaced when the government sent him to America in 1875 to study the latest teaching methods then in vogue. In one of the great happenstances of the period, he found himself living in the home of, and studying under, the leading advocate of the most progressive form of teaching methods in the world founded by the great Swiss educator Pestalozzi. Takamine returned to Japan as the nation's first professional educator.

Ironically, the elderly Confucian advisor to Emperor Meiji, Motoda Nagazane, proved to be perhaps more instrumental than any other individual in determining the ultimate aims and purposes of education in the formation of modern Japan. It was Motoda, in the name of the emperor to whom he was deeply committed, who set the agenda that provoked a reverse course against the western influence of science and technology in the early 1880s. A consensus evolved around his ideas that ultimately emerged in the form of the 1890 Imperial Rescript on Education. A fusion of Japanese cultural patterns and western science was crafted in the Rescript that incorporated Motoda's fundamental position. Acceptable to a strategic coalition of both traditionalists and modernists, the Imperial Rescript on Education then set the pattern of modern Japanese education for the twentieth century. It appropriately brings to a close the first period of the Meiji Restoration, and the final chapter of this book.

Among the non-Japanese who played critical roles in modern Japanese education, five stand out for special consideration. In chronological order, Guido Verbeck, the Dutch-American engineer-missionary sent to Nagasaki with the opening of the ports in 1859, played an extraordinary role in modern Japan. Not only did Verbeck personally teach a large number of the first leaders of the Meiji government in his courses at Nagasaki, he opened the first channel, even during the feudal period, for eager Japanese youth to study in America at the tiny Rutgers College in New Jersey. He was brought to Tokyo after the Restoration in 1869 to head the only national institution of higher education, essentially Japan's national university. Marion Scott, an elementary school teacher from San Francisco, was given complete responsibility for setting the initial curriculum, teaching methods, and textbooks for the first public schools as the primary instructor at the first teacher training school in Tokyo in 1872. A third American, Professor David Murray from Rutgers College, was hired as the superintendent of education and influential senior advisor in the Ministry of Education during the formative years of the public school system from 1873 to 1879.

The non-American contingent was led by Henry Dyer from the University of Glasgow. He was hired by the Ministry of Works to plan and administer the Imperial College of Engineering from 1873 to 1882. This was the first institution of its kind, and produced a corps of Japanese engineers who designed the modern infrastructure of Japan. And finally, Emil Hausknecht from Berlin was employed by the Japanese government to introduce German methodology in education. An ardent advocate of the educational theory developed by the great German scholar Johann Herbart, Hausknecht's appointment as professor of pedagogy at the Imperial University in 1887 signified the rise of German influence on modern Japanese education.

There were many other individuals who also played pivotal roles in the process of launching a modern school system in Japan during the latter half of the 1800s. Together they enabled the nation to emerge successfully from feudalism to modernism in a remarkably short period. They came not only from within Japan but from Europe and America as well. In other words, an appreciation of the vital global connections between Japan, with its intimate cultural relations with China, and the western world in the nineteenth century is essential for an understanding of the formation of the modern system of Japanese education. This study, then, is designed to analyze the many connections, both domestic and international, that were established by the early leaders of the Meiji government to achieve their goal of building a modern state in the late nineteenth century.

PART I

THE FEUDAL FOUNDATION OF
MODERN JAPANESE EDUCATION

Education of the Samurai in Tokugawa Schools

NISSHINKAN

The movement for educational modernization that followed the 1868 Meiji Restoration did not begin in an educational vacuum. It emerged from a formidable foundation of schools designed to educate the hereditary samurai class, 5 percent of the population, which ruled Japan during the Tokugawa era.[1] A significant majority of those who planned and implemented the epic transformation from feudal to modern Japan originated from the ruling samurai class.whose educational background was of paramount importance in determining the course of modernization. In Bernard Silberman's study of the social background of senior ranking officers of the Meiji government during the initial five years of the modern era, a clear picture emerges of the first political and educational elite in modern Japan (see Table 1).[2]

Although the leaders of the Meiji government originated primarily from the Tokugawa governing elite of feudal Japan, there was a role reversal: in the new regime, lower-ranking samurai outnumbered upper-ranking samurai, including daimyo, the head of the han (domain), by a margin of 56 to 44 percent (Table 2).[3] This phenomenon was of considerable educational significance, since 50 percent of the Meiji leaders originating from lower-ranking samurai experienced some form of western education during the Tokugawa era, in comparison to 20 percent among the others.[4]

The educational tradition of the samurai forged during the three-hundred-year rule of the Tokugawa regime illustrates how the leaders of feudal Japan were uniquely prepared to lead the nation into the modern era. In the definitive study of the period, *Education in Tokugawa Japan* by Ronald Dore, the samurai-warrior class was characterized as broadly literate in a culture where books abounded.[5] They were educated in one of the three hundred domain (*han*) schools maintained by local clan governments in the castle towns.[6] These institutions combined the literary and military arts into the samurai tradition that was transmitted to each successive generation of leaders.

Paradoxically, in a feudal society governed by strict codes of conduct designed to perpetuate the traditional social order under-girding the Tokugawa military government, literary (*bun*) studies overshadowed military (*bu*) studies. The Chinese classics set the agenda of the literary curriculum as a means to inculcate moral and ethical values essential for good government, according to ancient Confucian teachings. The samurai value system included loyalty and obedience to one's lord, filial piety toward parents, self-discipline, diligence, adherence to duty, and frugality in one's daily life.[7] Virtually all of the leaders in the initial period of

Table 1   Social Background of Senior Officers
           of the Meiji Government, 1868–1873

Background	No. (%)
Samurai origin	161 (63)
Noble origin	72 (28)
Commoner	6 (2)
Unknown origin	14 (7)

Source: Bernard Silberman, *Modern Japanese Leadership:
Tradition and Change* (Tucson: University of Arizona
Press, 1966), 235.

Table 2   Family Background of Senior Officials
           of the Meiji Government, 1868–1873

Background	No. (%)
Lower samurai family	90 (56)
Upper samurai family	50 (31)
Daimyo	21 (13)

Source: Bernard Silberman, *Modern Japanese Leadership:
Tradition and Change* (Tucson: University of Arizona
Press, 1966), 235.

modernization of Japanese education in the Meiji era experienced some form of schooling that stressed the integral relationship between Confucius morality and public service. This schooling was the common denominator among the political elite during the transition from feudalism to modernism.[8]

Education was primarily provided by the study of Chinese writings, especially the Confucian classics; its purpose was chiefly to develop moral character, both as an absolute human duty and also to better fulfill the samurai's function in society; a secondary purpose was to gain from the classics that knowledge of men and affairs and of the principles of government which was also necessary for the proper performance of the samurai's duties.

Nisshinkan—Aizu Clan School for Samurai Youth

Among the three hundred clan schools in existence during the late feudal period, Nisshinkan of the Aizu clan exemplifies the finest tradition of samurai education. It also provides some insights to how Japanese males from the governing samurai families could virtually overnight lead their nation into the modern world. Nisshinkan, completed in 1803 by the governing Matsudaira family of Aizu located to the north of Tokyo, illustrates the vital role Tokugawa schools played in modern Japanese education.

Nisshinkan and the Aizu clan played a special historical role in modern Japan about which all Japanese children learn. The great 1868 siege of the clan's castle by vastly superior Meiji forces marks the end of major military opposition by Tokugawa-related forces. The Aizu samurai-warriors who defiantly led the month-long resistance against the Meiji besiegers received their basic education at the Nisshinkan school. In retaliation, the buildings of the school were destroyed by the victorious army.

A remarkable number of individuals who participated in Nisshinkan as well as the Aizu castle siege later made outstanding contributions in the early Meiji period. For example, during the great siege, trapped inside those supposedly impregnable walls, were three youthful defenders whose subsequent careers illustrate the magnitude of the transformation that early leaders of modern Japan underwent from the feudal to the modern. The first was Yamakawa Kenjirō, a teenage samurai enrolled in Nisshinkan who was captured in the Aizu onslaught and subsequently released by the imperial forces. He managed to secure an appointment by the Meiji government to study in America in 1871, precisely three years after he fought against the Meiji army. After completing his studies in science at Yale University, he returned to Japan to become the first Japanese professor of physics at the new Tokyo University. He later served as president of Tokyo Imperial University.[9]

The second, a boy of fifteen, was Takamine Hideo. Prior to the completion of his Confucian studies at Nisshinkan, civil war broke out. After the castle surrender he was taken to Edo (Tokyo), where he later entered the prestigious Keio Gijuku private school under Fukuzawa Yukichi. He was subsequently given a teaching assignment at the school. In 1875 he was sent by the Meiji government, upon recommendation by Fukuzawa, to study at the Oswego Teachers College in New York. He returned to Japan as the foremost progressive educator in the country, introducing the most modern educational theory in the world at that time, developed by Pestalozzi of Switzerland. He later served as president of the elite Tokyo Teacher Training School for over a decade.

The third, Yamakawa Hiroshi, brother of Kenjirō, also survived the Aizu battle on the losing side of the Meiji Restoration. Nevertheless, he was able to work his way up through the new conscript army of the Meiji government to attain the rank of general, a tribute to the wisdom of the new government in seeking capable individuals regardless of their earlier loyalties. But Yamakawa Hiroshi's critical contribution to modern Japan reached well beyond the Japanese army. He was appointed the first president of the most prestigious teacher-training institution in Japan, the Tokyo Higher Teacher Training College, in 1886, with the assignment to militarize the program. In one of the many ironies of the period, his head teacher was Takamine Hideo, former head of the Tokyo Teacher Training School, who had survived the Aizu battle with his compatriots from the Yamakawa family.

Although the Nisshinkan school catered only to samurai boys, there was a fourth survivor of the Aizu castle siege, a young girl, who cannot be ignored

Figure 1. Nisshinkan School for Samurai Youth.
From *Aizu Hankō Nisshinkan Gaidobuku* (A Guide to the Aizu Clan School Nisshinkan) (Aizu: Aizu Hanko Nisshinkan, 1994).

since she played a prominent role in higher education for women. Yamakawa Sutematsu, sister of Kenjirō and Hiroshi, was eight years old at the time. She later revealed that during the castle siege she had a dagger strapped to her waist to kill herself if captured by the Meiji forces while carrying food and supplies to the defenders holed up within the castle.[10] A mere three years later she was sent to the United States by the Meiji government at the tender age of eleven to be educated in American schools, distinguishing herself by graduating cum laude from one of

America's most prestigious colleges for women, Vassar. She was the first Japanese female to earn a college degree.

Nisshinkan has been restored in all of its original grandeur, enabling the modern visitor to experience vicariously the education that the future warrior class from the Aizu samurai families underwent during the Tokugawa feudal period. The student entered Nisshinkan at the age of ten to begin the rigorous study of a classic text entitled Rongo, the introduction to the literary training (*bun*) of their education." Every morning all beginning students studied the analects of Confucius contained in the Rongo. It emphasized the interrelationship of politics or the art of governing with morality (*seiji to dōtoku*), the basis for social harmony endorsed by

Figure 2. Nisshinkan Classroom.
From *Aizu Hankō Nisshinkan Gaidobuku* (A Guide to the Aizu Clan School Nisshinkan) (Aizu: Aizu Hanko Nisshinkan, 1994).

the Tokugawa family. Every student became immersed in the five great principles contained therein that governed their way of life: jin (benevolence), gi (justice), rei (manners), chi (knowledge), and shin (trust). They were taught that without these guiding principles, man is no better than an animal.[12]

The teaching method for reading the Rongo, called sodoku, was simple, as was the classroom. The students sat on the tatami straw-matted floor in front of the teacher, each with his copy of the Rongo, well-worn surviving samples of which are on still on display. The teacher read a passage and the students repeated it in unison. The teacher would then give an explanation of the meaning. The process was repeated until the students had achieved a standard that enabled them to pass an examination for promotion through four courses to an advanced level of Confucian studies in the higher department of the school. During these first four courses calligraphy was introduced, which initiated each student into the intricacies of writing the Chinese characters. That activity would consume much of the literary education of the future leaders of modern Japan.

The educators of the Matsudaira clan took great pride in the Nisshinkan curriculum as more progressive as well as more competitive than other han schools. For example, the teachers endeavored to instill in their students the concept that rote memorization of the Chinese classics, as difficult as they were in a foreign language, was not the way to gain a true understanding of them. They taught that the old saying—reading a passage one hundred times leads to understanding—was not necessarily true. Rather, reading fifty times or thirty times could also lead to understanding, and that the fewer the repetitions the better. Clan teachers took great pride in the fact that they even employed practical illustrations of daily life or historical incidents in clan history to teach the meaning of the great Chinese classics. In addition, there were group activities and events that encouraged competition in an attempt to develop character.[13]

Beyond the study of the Rongo and calligraphy, the Nisshinkan student underwent a broadly based comprehensive education that included, among other things, the study of astronomy. A simple observatory was built that included a celestial globe. In contrast, every student was also taught the etiquette of a samurai in order to instill the rigid social order that characterized the feudal Tokugawa era. The rules of etiquette were governed by Confucian teachings, but at a practical level the students were also taught table manners as well as the proper procedure to perform the ritual act of seppuku or hara-kiri, that is, suicide.

The following seven rules of behavior, originally conceived by the founder of the Matsudaira clan and reflecting Confucian influence, were ingrained in the minds of each student. Upon entry to the school, every student stood at attention while the rules were read aloud, one at a time. After each one, the student respectfully bowed, responding with "hai," "yes."[14] Although somewhat arcane, they illustrate the basic attitudes instilled into the leadership class of feudal Japan.

Nisshinkan Rules of Behavior

Do not disobey your elders.
Do not fail to bow (*ojigi*) to your elders.
Do not tell falsehoods (*uso*).
Do not act in a shameful manner.
Do not bully (*ijime*) weaklings.
Do not eat in public.
Do not converse with females in public.[15]

Afternoon sessions were devoted to the military arts (*bu*), which included swordsmanship, archery, riding, and the usual martial arts such as jūjitsu. Rifle training was introduced during the later years. The unusual use of a pool built on the campus stands out. Every student was taught not only swimming but also how to survive in water dressed in military armor with helmet. Each student was also taught how to ride a horse through water. Thus practical teachings characterized much of the training of the Aizu samurai during their education at the Nisshinkan.

At the very center of the splendid array of campus buildings, all resembling magnificent temples, stands the Taisei Den, the shrine to Confucius. Beautifully decorated in brilliant colors with a Chinese motif, the elegant statue of Confucius dominates the hall, as the ancient sage dominated the entire school. Written over the statue is the clarion call that "Confucius is the teacher of all" (*bansei shihyo*). The central location on campus of the Confucian statue, and the majesty of the hall itself with its rich decorations, surely engendered a lasting image of the supremacy

Figure 3. Nisshinkan Confucious Hall.
From *Aizu Hankō Nisshinkan Gaidobuku* (A Guide to the Aizu Clan School Nisshinkan)
(Aizu: Aizu Hanko Nisshinkan, 1994).

of Confucian thought among the students. This was, of course, reinforced with the years of study of the Rongo required of every student. Nisshinkan, like every clan school, posited Confucian study at the center of education (*kyōiku no chūshin*).

The Meiji government from 1868 on was led by samurai who had experienced a form of education similar to that at the Nisshinkan. The rigor and breadth of their educational experiences in premodern Japan provide some clues as to how a young samurai from Nisshinkan could enter the Sheffield School of Science at Yale University in the United States to study physics, as did Yamakawa Kenjirō. And this was accomplished even though he had not been introduced to the multiplication tables until the age of sixteen.[16] The transition from the study of the Confucian Rongo in Chinese script in feudal Japan to the study of physics in English at a premier American university was quite remarkable.

In addition to the widespread han schools provided for local samurai boys, the central Tokugawa government sponsored an advanced institution called the Shōhei Gakkō in Edo, the capital of the Tokugawa regime. With various local clans sending capable samurai youth to the school in Edo, now Tokyo, the tradition of concentrating the brightest youth in the capital city was begun. The Shōhei Gakkō curriculum drew heavily on Confucian ethical concepts from the so-called Four

Books and Five Classics from ancient China. This specialized institution served as an inspiration and model for the many han schools, including Nisshinkan.

Bansho Shirabesho—A Window to the West

In contrast to the three hundred local clan schools and the Shōhei Gakkō, the central Tokugawa government founded a special institution of foreign studies in 1856 that also catered to samurai youth, the Bansho Shirabesho, literally the Office for the Investigation of Barbarian (that is, western) Books.[17] This eventually became the most prestigious educational institution in Japan, Tokyo University. It originated from the unimpeded entry of American warships in Japanese waters in 1853 under the command of Admiral Perry. Beyond the sudden appearance of American warships, which demonstrated the inferior state of Japanese coastal defenses, the gifts brought by Perry for the Japanese "tycoon" surely baffled Tokugawa officials. They included air pumps, electric machines, model locomotives and steam engines, horseshoe magnets, mariners' compasses, and barometers.[18] The scientific devices brought by the uninvited emissaries from the West were virtually all foreign to the Japanese.

Up to that time only limited contact with the western world through the Dutch was permitted. Accordingly the Bansho Shirabesho upon its opening in 1856 concentrated on translating Dutch materials primarily relating to military matters. Japanese specialists in the Dutch language were employed to carry out the investigation, thereby opening a new "window to the West." By the second year, English was introduced. The inevitable recognition that the threatening western warships came from the United States, not Holland, compelled the school officials to revise the curriculum. Translated documents in English slowly replaced those in Dutch.

From the beginning of this special institution, the problem of staffing with qualified Japanese sufficiently versed in a western language proved challenging. Since English had not yet been widely taught, there was inevitably a lack of Japanese capable of translating materials from English to Japanese. Accordingly those who had studied Dutch were assigned to translate English materials. An official later to become well known in the modern period, Nishi Amane, undertook the study of English by using an English-Dutch dictionary to carry out this unusual assignment. By 1860, English had become the dominant foreign language at the first government school in feudal Japan to study the writings of the barbarians, that is, the westerners.[19]

With a deeper understanding of the West through the growing library of imported foreign books, an inevitable realization emerged that English was not the only western language of importance to western technological progress. The Japanese learned that France and Germany played major roles in the industrial revolution then sweeping through the West. As a consequence, the French and German languages were introduced in the curriculum, although English remained the dominant foreign language. For example, out of a total of approximately one hundred students in the early 1860s, four-fifths were enrolled in the English department.[20] Nevertheless, the French and German departments acquired teachers and translators in those languages who produced a pool of Japanese with linguistic qualifications to study in countries of the West other than United States and Britain.

The gradual expansion of the Bansho Shirabesho brought about a new and systematic effort to study the latest developments in the West through translations. There were several major consequences. First, the institution inevitably attracted progressive samurai with an interest in things western who first studied a western language. They then turned to their specific area of interest. The purpose of the institution from the outset was not language study but knowledge of western technology, initially military-related. Gradually the school was transformed from a language-teaching and translation institution to a research center. In the process a corps of Japanese specialists on the West emerged.

The graduates of the Bansho Shirabesho, who formed Japan's first corps of western specialists, called yōgakusha, were uniquely prepared in western languages and studies to play a major role in the Meiji era. The institution also provided a pool of Japanese qualified to study in the leading western nations after the Meiji Restoration.

The other major consequence of this school was that it became the primary source of information and research on the West during the Bakumatsu period, that is, the years between the entry of Admiral Perry's warships in 1853 and the end of the feudal Tokugawa era in 1868. With the name change in 1862 from Bansho to Yōsho Shirabesho, that is, from barbarian to western, it indicated a growing sophistication in the study of the West.[21] The realization that the military power of the West developed from and depended upon modern social and political institutions stimulated a more comprehensive approach. The school inexorably became deeply involved in broader investigations of the West that attracted students and faculty who had a wider perspective beyond military affairs. The emphasis on western military technology was expanded to include politics, government, economics, law, education, and so on.[22]

In the process of expansion the institution again changed its name in 1863 to Kaisejo, the School of Enlightenment.[23] It had by then grown far beyond its original purpose of learning about western military technology. It also began to import western devices including cameras and model trains for study. Even plants and seeds such as apples and tulips were brought into Japan for analysis. The window to the West through language study, translations, research, and imports was being gradually opened wider through the Kaiseijo during the 1860s, prior to the Meiji Restoration in 1868. In addition, the institution made a further contribution to the nation by providing a pool of western-oriented specialists from which came many of the sixty-five students who were sent to major western countries by the Tokugawa government during its final years.[24]

Just prior to the Meiji Restoration of 1868, the number of students enrolled in this school of foreign studies had increased to over 500, from the 100 enrolled in 1863 at the time of the name change to Kaiseijo. Enrollment in the English department jumped from 100 to 300. The French department increased to 100. And the new department of mathematics enrolled 160 students.[25] In the process, the first generation of yōgakusha knowledgeable about the West increased significantly. Among them, for example, was Katō Hiroyuki, a specialist in German studies destined to become the first president of Tokyo University in 1877.[26] That is, during the two decades from 1856 to 1877, from Tokugawa to Meiji, the school that originally investigated the writings of western barbarians became Tokyo University, using the English language and staffed primarily with western professors. The transition within higher education from the feudal era to the modern era was illustrative of the role Tokugawa institutions played in the Meiji era. They were, in a word, indispensable to the modernization process.

Private Schools during the Feudal Period—The Shijuku

Beyond the official institutions established by either local hans or the central government, a broad range of private educational schools called shijuku proliferated during the latter part of the Tokugawa period. These included around 1,500 boarding schools that also catered mostly to samurai youth.[27] Difficult to categorize, these schools offered a range from lower-level to advanced studies. The curricula varied from the traditional Chinese classics to modern western studies and language. Some were run by distinguished teachers who held a particular attraction to inquisitive samurai youth who, after studying at their clan schools, were destined for leadership in the modern era. Others, depending on the inclinations of the teacher, imparted knowledge and wisdom of a practical nature that provided the students, including increasing numbers of non-samurai, with basic skills to accommodate them to feudal society more effectively.

This unregulated sector within Tokugawa education is marked by several examples of considerable influence on modern education during the ensuing Meiji Era. One of the most notable schools was run by Yoshida Shōin, a radical thinker. He was executed in 1859 by the Tokugawa government for his subversive teachings to young samurai who were attracted by his revolutionary ideas. Such key individuals as Itō Hirobumi, a major contributor to modern Japanese education and Japan's premier political leader of the nineteenth century, and Inoue Kaoru, who became foreign minister, whetted their appetites and sharpened their instincts for social and political reform at the feet of this master teacher.[28]

An influential example of the private shijuku founded before the Meiji Restoration was the private school founded by a pioneer of western culture, Fukuzawa Yukichi. Fukuzawa's Keio Shijuku, later named Gijuku, was the preeminent private institution at the end of the Tokugawa period, and educated many of the future leaders from the samurai class recruited from throughout the country. To appreciate the role of the Keio Gijuku of feudal Japan during the first decade of the Meiji period, two critical factors are relevant. The only government institution of foreign studies in existence at that time which catered to the elite samurai class was the Kaisei Gakkō. Fukuzawa's Keio Gijuku functioned as the leading private school for samurai youth in the nation. As such it had the opportunity to greatly influence the initial standards of education for the leadership class in the Meiji period.

The second factor relates to finance. As a private school, Keio Gijuku depended upon private nongovernmental financing. From its inception, the recurring problem of generating funds to pay teacher salaries, construct buildings, buy textbooks, and so on, plagued the founder. Amid writing and translating textbooks, advising the government, and teaching at the school, Fukuzawa devoted a great deal of his precious time to the problem of financing his school.

Fukuzawa choose the teaching staff for Keio Gijuku primarily from the graduates of his first private school in the Nakatsu clan, in Kyushu, in the 1850s.[29] He obviously felt that his own students could best be entrusted with promoting the principles that he championed. These teachers, of course, were not trained to teach. Nor were they well prepared in subject matter. And perhaps most important, they were of questionable proficiency in English, which Fukuzawa adopted early on as the primary language of learning.

The recruitment of students was of necessity aimed at the samurai class since few males outside this class were prepared for such an institution. As yet the idea that girls could attend such a school was simply out of the question. This presumption ran counter to the concept of equality promoted in Fukuzawa's writings. Under the circumstances of the time, however, he had little choice. The surprising element in the recruitment of students for the first several classes, however, was the diversity in their origin. Registration records for the last class before the collapse of the feudal Tokugawa government show that out of a total number of fifty entering students, only four listed their "country" (kuni) of origin as Edo, shortly thereafter to be renamed Tokyo. Thirteen others left that section blank, leaving the possibility that they, too, came from the country of Edo. The remaining thirty-three originated from local kuni ranging from northern Honshu to the island of Shikoku to the southern island of Kyushu, that is, from the far north to the far south of the country.[30]

The fact that samurai youth from distant provinces in a country without transportation facilities enrolled in Fukuzawa's Keio Gijuku in Edo is testimony to the man's reputation, which had spread throughout the nation by 1868. His best-selling books provoked a natural interest in his school. Fukuzawa also placed recruitment advertisements in local newspapers that attracted samurai families as well as local clan leaders. At this time, fortuitously, various clans were searching for schools where they could send their young men to study English and western subjects. Many candidates walked great distances to enter Fukuzawa's private institution, paying tuition for the opportunity.[31]

Fukuzawa made a critical decision from the outset. In the *One Hundred Year History* of the institution, the purpose of his school was simply described as the pursuit of western studies through texts from America and Britain.[32] The extensive use of texts from Britain and America was indicative of Fukuzawa's personal experiences. He had already recognized English as the single foreign language essential for modernization. During travels to the United States in 1860, England in 1862, and the United States again in 1867, he had purchased hundreds of books in English for his school. This greatly influenced the education of the next generation of Meiji leaders.

The first requirement of all students at the Keio Gijuku was the ability to read English. Fukuzawa lacked sufficient funds to hire foreign teachers of English, whose salaries were customarily far higher than those of Japanese teachers. He thus began to teach elementary English using dictionaries and first- and second-grade readers that Fukuzawa had apparently purchased while in America. The purpose was not to speak or comprehend oral English but rather to read the English textbooks that he had purchased abroad. He also translated a number of English books for use as texts. In retrospect, an unusual experiment was underway at Fukuzawa's Keio Gijuku. Fifty young men from the samurai class who had been educated at their respective han schools in Chinese classics were using Webster's dictionaries from America to read elementary school textbooks in English written for American children. Advanced texts from the West culminated their education in feudal Japan.

The method of instruction at Keio Gijuku is of particular interest. After the first three months practicing the ABCs with English pronunciation drills, the students then began the study of subject matter through a mixture of Japanese and English textbooks. Fukuzawa himself had been brought up in the traditional sodoku method of learning that dominated schools in pre-Meiji Japan. Following the ancient approach to learning in China, the teacher read aloud a passage and the student repeated it until the material was memorized, often without understanding the meaning. The second stage involved the teacher explaining the meaning of each sentence.[33] Fukuzawa, unfamiliar with modern teaching methods then percolating through the West, naturally resorted to the familiar sodoku method. The Keio Gijuku teachers knew no other way. The irony of the leading proponent of modernization of Japan in the early Meiji era using the most traditional method of teaching from China in his school is of some importance. The subject matter in his classroom had been drastically transformed from Confucian studies to modern western studies. But the method of teaching and learning based on repetition and rote memorization had not.

The Keio Gijuku course lasted for fifteen months. Within that short period the students devoted much time learning to read English. In addition, the sodoku method, with the teacher reading English sentences from elementary school textbooks to university-level texts, and the students repeating verbatim, produced questionable results. The education of many future leaders of Japan during the first three years of the modern era in Meiji Japan was superficial at best. But Fukuzawa's famous school went beyond the study of western learning through English. He used the opportunity to impart his personal convictions about modernization, which made an indelible impression on Keio graduates. Both Fukuzawa and his students took pride in their perceived differences from students at other private and public schools. First, Keio boys were more studious than students at other schools, where discipline problems were not infrequent, and they set a high standard and reputation for future private schools. Although samurai youth were entitled to wear the traditional two swords and the hakama clothing style that distinguished them from nonsamurai, Fukuzawa banned both. Keio boys did not stand out in appearance as elite students, which they nevertheless were.

Keio students, however, stood out from other private and public school students through the particular influence of Fukuzawa. They were taught, either through western books chosen by Fukuzawa or through his lectures, the concepts of equality, freedom, and independence that he championed through his best-selling books familiar to all his students. They were encouraged to apply these unfamiliar concepts in their daily lives. To samurai youth, many from rural clans accustomed to their superior positions and privileges as a birthright, Keio Gijuku was a shocking experience in modern thought. The new ideas were disseminated not only through their western textbooks but through the personal influence of their respected and much beloved teacher, Fukuzawa Yukichi.[34]

The graduates from Fukuzawa's grand experiment in private education assumed leading positions in education, government, and in the private sector of feudal Japan. For example, during the final days of the Tokugawa government, graduates of Fukuzawa's school taught at the government school of western studies, Kaiseijo, and later its successor during the early Meiji era, Nankō. It also provided a pool of teachers for the various private clan schools that emerged during the final years of Tokugawa government. Wherever schools taught English, Keio graduates filled teaching positions throughout the land.[35]

These various streams of education, both public and private, illustrate that scholarship and learning occupied a special niche in Tokugawa times for the ruling samurai families. As a result Tokugawa schools in their entirety produced an impressive reservoir of talented, capable, and motivated leaders from samurai families with varying educational backgrounds, accustomed to governing. They were reared in an atmosphere of educational superiority ingrained with a mission to lead.

The influence of the feudal period on modern science introduced during the Meiji era is particularly relevant, since the focus of education in modern Japan centered on science and mathematics under the First National School System. Key leaders realized early on that the nation could not advance without achieving a scientific level comparable to that in the West. In particular the need for advanced military technology to protect the country from potential foreign invaders during the period of colonialism haunted policy makers.

The training of modern scientists became a prime objective of the Meiji government from 1877, a decade after the fall of the feudal government, with the founding of Tokyo University. The Tokugawa attitude toward western science is relevant, then, since the vast majority of students who enrolled in the new scientific disciplines in the early Meiji era received their basic education during the feudal era in han schools for the samurai. From this perspective, Tokukawa education that centered on Confucian studies exerted a negative influence on modern Japan; according to Dore's summation of the ideology of the feudal state, "All that was worth inventing had been invented by the (Chinese) Sage Emperors, all that was worth knowing had been known by Confucius. The task of later generations was simply to absorb this body of knowledge."[36] Fukuzawa Yukichi, for example, records the widespread attitude of the samurai class during the feudal era toward mathematics, the basis of modern western science. In his autobiography he recalled that his father disdained not only mathematics but money. When he learned that the teacher of the private school, where the father enrolled Fukuzawa's older siblings, taught them the multiplication tables, he was incensed. "It is abominable that innocent children should be taught to use numbers—the tools of merchants. There is no telling what the teacher may do next." The Fukuzawa children were abruptly withdrawn from the school.[37]

The Tokugawa government displayed a suspicious attitude toward science studies at this time when the leading government institution was the Shōhei Gakkō of Confucian studies. With the opening of the new school of western studies and languages in 1856, the Bansho Shirabesho, the issue of science versus nonscience studies inevitably emerged. The government's ambiguous policy illustrated the official attitude toward western science. Military science was acceptable; physical sciences were not.

> It is perfectly appropriate to deal with matters of a military nature in lectures at the [Western Studies] Institute. But whether works on science should also be presented is quite anther matter. Those captivated by outlandish theories come inevitably to resemble the Europeans and Americans in the way they look at the world. Such things also lead to unorthodox views. There seems to be some elements in physics [*kyūrigaku*] which inevitably give rise to unorthodox views. We are concerned that the study of science . . . will destroy the relations— between lords and retainers or fathers and sons—which have existed in Japan for so long. Consequently ordinary lectures [at the Institute of Western Studies] should only deal with military books.[38]

Regardless of the official position of the cautious Tokugawa government toward western science, the influence of the feudal era indirectly exerted a positive influence on the development of science in Meiji Japan. Using the Nisshinkan school from the Aizu Han as an example, the several hundred han schools for samurai youth produced a pool of thousands of literate males who were trained to become leaders. Even though few han schools included studies of science or mathematics to any level of significance, many of the graduates who despised mathematics as appropriate only for merchants were nevertheless prepared to accept the challenge that modernity presented, and that included western science and mathematics, as well as other foreign subjects such as music that were totally alien to the samurai warrior.

Western Teachers in Feudal Japan

Following the entry of Commodore Perry and his American warships into Japanese waters in 1853, the demand for western learning could no longer be contained in spite of the longstanding prohibition against foreign contacts imposed by the Tokugawa regime from the early 1600s. Military superiority of western countries such as Britain and the United States capable of operating warships in Japanese waters thousands of miles from home ports proved threatening. Their presence provoked a demand for the study of the latest science and military techniques potentially capable of preserving Japanese independence from western nations carving up the world in vast colonial empires. The confluence of influences inspired the desperately futile but well-known cry, "Revere the Emperor—Oust the Barbarians," by imperial supporters seeking to overthrow the weakening Tokugawa government, increasingly unable to contain foreign influence in the early 1860s.

As a result of the inexorable spread of western studies in the late 1850s and 1860s under the Tokugawa regime, the government increased the employment of foreign nationals from western countries. Because of the longstanding relationship with the Dutch, it was natural for Japanese government officials to negotiate with the Dutch government as they sought appropriate personnel to assist in development. The most notable contribution during this period was the famed Dutch school of naval studies in Nagasaki at the latter half of the 1850s, which attracted over 150 samurai students from several hans. Among the two-thirds who completed the two-year intensive training course in the Dutch language was the future commander of the modern Japanese navy during the Meiji era, Katsu Kaishu. He achieved early fame as the first Japanese to command a ship manned with a Japanese crew to cross the Pacific in 1860, although he was greatly aided by experienced American sailors on board.[39]

Japanese feudal leaders recognized early on that among all western nations of the day, Great Britain occupied the foremost position in international trade and influence. Industrious British merchants had already developed commercial interests with individual han governments in the south, selling ships and other industrial goods directly to them and bypassing the central government in far-off Edo. Inevitably Tokugawa and certain local han officials turned for assistance to British nationals, who quickly overtook the Dutch in importance. With the displacement of Dutch influence, the Japanese were now confronted with the English-speaking world of the West. Relations developed between Japan and England to the extent that by 1868 over 80 percent of all foreign trade, both imports and exports, was with the British.[40]

The French also staged a presence in the late Tokugawa period. Their major contribution to the advancement of Japan took the form of the construction of the dockyards at Yokosuka and Yokohama near Edo. The contract called for the French to train two thousand Japanese in modern technology to operate the facility upon its completion. A French-language school was established in Yokohama to facilitate the process. The entire operation brought to Japan from France the largest contingent of westerners during the pre-Meiji era.[41]

The dockyards in Nagasaki built by the Dutch and those in Yokohama-Yokosuka built by the French were necessary to handle the needs of a growing naval fleet during the late Tokugawa era. When the American Commodore Perry first entered Japanese waters in 1853, his presence was unwanted, but the Japanese could not prohibit it. They had no naval vessels at the time. However, by the time of the collapse of the Tokugawa regime in 1868, the central government had a fleet of forty-five vessels. The domains also operated a total of ninety-four ships, such were the technological achievements in the maritime sector at the time of the Meiji Restoration.[42]

Although the entry of American warships into Japanese waters in 1853 prompted the government to increase relations with western countries, the number of Americans employed by the Tokugawa government was minimal. The American presence was mostly in the form of Christian missionaries posted to Japan by their respective denominations on a private basis. With the ban on Christianity still in effect, they were confined to the study of Japanese or the teaching of English. The primary exception was a Christian missionary from the United States, the Dutch-American Guido Verbeck, one of the first foreigners to arrive in Japan upon the port openings in 1859. Because of his extraordinary influence on modern Japanese education, his unusual experiences as a teacher of many future leaders of modern Japan in Nagasaki during the last decade of the feudal period will be covered in the following chapter.

Education of the Samurai in the West

LONDON UNIVERSITY AND RUTGERS COLLEGE, 1863–1868

Among the samurai youth of feudal Japan, a limited number had the opportunity to study in the West. Two stand out for their contributions to the construction of the first national public school system. Originating from the most powerful clans that led the Restoration movement, Satsuma and Chōshū, Itō Hirobumi and Mori Arinori launched their careers as members of covert student missions to the West during the 1860s, the last decade of the Tokugawa era. Their careers reached fulfillment nearly thirty years later with the completion of a public school system for a modern state in the Meiji era through the initiative of Prime Minister Itō Hirobumi and his minister of education, Mori Arinori.

Although many other people made significant contributions to modern education, these two figures deserve special recognition. Itō Hirobumi, father of Japanese constitutional government, served as the first prime minister under a western-style cabinet when a modern school system was ultimately put in place. Mori Arinori, the minister of education often recognized as the father of modern Japanese education, was specifically chosen by Itō for his first cabinet to design and implemented that system.

The covert student missions to the West began when the two young samurai were smuggled out of southern Japan from their respective feudal domains. Itō left Chōshū in 1863 and Mori departed from Satsuma in 1865. Both daringly violated the central Tokugawa government's edict of self-imposed international isolation. In unrelated episodes separated by two years, each of these two youthful adventurers illegally sailed for London among a small group of students. Arriving at the center of western modernism and industrialism, both were enrolled at the University of London, the great secular British institution that contrasted with the renowned church-related medieval universities of Oxford and Cambridge. They were even assigned to the same academic tutor, a prominent British scholar in the field of chemistry, a discipline unknown in Japan at that time. Although these two important figures in modern Japanese education were not yet acquainted—since Itō returned to Japan before Mori arrived—they were both first exposed to the western world during the feudal Tokugawa period in pre-Meiji Japan.

The Chōshū Student Mission to London, 1863

Itō Hirobumi, born in 1842 and the first to be smuggled out of Japan for the West, joined a daring plan in 1863. Five young men from Chōshū hatched a scheme to sail secretly to London for study. . Among the five were a future prime minister, a foreign minister, a finance minister, and a minister of works in Meiji Japan.[1]

For Itō, an earlier encounter with his fellow clansman from Chōshū, the rebel Yoshida Shōin, provided the motivation that eventually propelled him into the center of the controversial movement advocating modern government and education for Japan. Yoshida, another uncommon figure of the time, played a unique role in Japanese history with his private academy, the Shōka Sonjuku, which Itō entered in 1857. Yoshida became an active proponent in the movement to replace the Tokugawa military regime with the imperial family as the ruling institution of the country. His advocacy was considered disloyal, and it provoked the central government to execute him exactly two years after Itō began his study with him. It was under Yoshida's influence that Itō took up the cause to "Honor the Emperor—Expel the Barbarians," one of the great slogans of the time.

The year before Itō traveled to the West, he committed his first act on the larger stage when he joined with several young Chōshū activists who devised a plot to rid Japan of the foreign barbarians. They planned to assassinate the head of the British diplomatic corps, essentially the ambassador. When this proved to be too risky, they decided to attack the British legation in Tokyo. Among the perpetrators, in addition to Itō, were Inoue Kaoru and Yamao Yōzō, later foreign minister and minister of works, respectively, in the Meiji government; these were three of the five who secretly traveled to London the following year.[2]

The provocateurs entered the compound in Shinagawa, Tokyo, where the new legation buildings were being concentrated for better protection by the Tokugawa government. Choosing the recently completed but not yet occupied British building that stood out from the others, they torched it to the ground. They all escaped undetected.[3] One can assume that the three among the group who entered the University of London the following year never revealed their involvement in the destruction of the British legation in Tokyo to their British hosts who befriended them.

The plan to go west was conceived by the young Chōshū activists, who included Inoue, the ringleader, Itō, and Yamao Yōzō, who later made a major contribution to modern engineering.[4] A total of five young samurai, the Chōshū Five, had clan approval to be smuggled out of Japan for foreign study. Funding was provided through a large loan from a wealthy Chōshū merchant then living in the capital of Edo. Yamao was able to arrange a meeting with a British merchant, James Gower, manager of the Jardine Matheson firm that had recently opened an office in Yokohama.

Jardine Matheson, one of the great British trading companies operating throughout the Far East, had previously sold a ship to the Chōshū government. The company approved the request for transportation of the five Chōshū youth to London, in spite of the central governmental ban on foreign travel, as a means of potentially improving business ties with a local progressive han government. The youthful samurai trustingly turned their funds over to Gower, who discretely forwarded the money left over from purchase of the tickets to the London office to finance their studies in England.

Since the ban on unauthorized foreign travel was strictly enforced by the Tokugawa government, the Chōshū Five were hidden in the home of another Matheson officer for a late-night boarding. They were then kept in the ship's coal storage area to avoid detection until the ship set sail on May 12, 1863. As samurai, they still wore the traditional topknot hairstyle, cutting it off the night before departure and donning ill-fitting western-style clothes for the first time.[5] The level of English among the five was abysmally low. Itō's English was virtually nonexistent. When the five were divided at Shanghai into two British ships for the long voyage to London, the officers of the ship carrying Itō and Inoue apparently misunderstood their intentions, believing they wanted to learn navigation. The ship's captain treated the boys as ordinary sailors who ate sailor's food and performed the duties of sailors while literally working their way to London. It was an extraordinary introduction to the West for the future prime minister and foreign minister of modern Japan.

Upon arrival of the Chōshū Five in London, Hugh Matheson from the shipping company took an immediate interest in them. He introduced the students to Alexander Williamson, professor of chemistry at University College, now the University of London. Williamson took an extraordinary interest in the fate of the five young samurai, making arrangements for their every need, including English lessons. Itō and Inoue were then assigned to study military affairs, politics, and law at the college from the fall semester. The other three undertook the study of science, including Yamao who was sent to Scotland for engineering studies, a decision that would prove of great value at a later date.

The relationship between Dr. Williamson and the Japanese samurai youth in 1863 is of unusual interest. At the time of their arrival in London, he was president of the Chemical Society of Great Britain. Having studied at the University of Heidelberg for three years, he then completed his degree in chemistry at Giessen, Germany, the leading institution in Europe for chemical education. Upon the recommendation of John Stuart Mill, who would later become well known in the intellectual circles of Meiji Japan, Williamson then studied mathematics under the great Auguste Comte in Paris for three years before returning to London in 1849.[6]

The academic background of this erudite Englishman is of importance in part because he took in three of the five Japanese students from Chōshū to board in his home in London. Among the three were Itō Hirobumi, to become the leading politician of the Meiji Era, and Inoue Kaoru, the future minister of foreign affairs who designed Japan's foreign policy for many years during the Meiji period of modernization. Not only were the young samurai from feudal Japan under the personal care of one of the leading scientific scholars of the West but they also experienced western-style home life under the kind treatment of Mrs. Williamson. She was an exceptional woman of great charm and artistic talent, who made the Japanese boys feel like members of the family and endeavored to make their stay in England a happy one.[7]

The radical transplantation from Tokugawa Japan to London had been swift and dramatic. The samurai boys from rural Japan had exited a land of feudalism to enter one of the most advanced technical societies in the world then undergoing the great industrial revolution. From studying Chinese classics as youth in Japan, they found themselves studying modern sciences and mathematics at one of the great institutions of western civilization. Suddenly they were riding British trains powered by steam engines, unknown in Japan. It was a rude awakening to the West.

London at that time was the factory of the world and the birthplace of a radical theory of socialism. The city had become the center of a capitalist movement, with British entrepreneurs striking out in new directions across the globe. Simultaneously, political movements were being organized in reaction. Socialist leaders from throughout the western world converged in London, where Karl Marx began writing his famous *Das Kapital* in the reading rooms of the British Museum. Charles Darwin had just published his great evolutionary thesis, *The Origin of Species*, which rocked the powerful Christian church in Europe and North America. A new era was sweeping the western world with London at the center as the samurai youth arrived to witness it.

Professor Williamson, who had taken personal responsibility for the boys, arranged for them to visit industrial sites to observe firsthand the technical achievements at the foundation of the great British Empire of the nineteenth century. It was this knowledge and perspective of the industrial and military might of the western world that provoked Itō and Inoue to make a sudden decision in March 1864. Only five months after arriving in London, they unexpectedly returned to Japan. They had learned through an article in the local *Times* newspaper of an impending attack by a British naval squadron on their home fief of Chōshū.[8]

In another of the great ironies of the time, while the five Chōshū boys were studying in England, the British Navy operating in the Far East threatened to bombard the port of Shimonoseki in their native Chōshū. It was in retaliation for an alleged shelling of British ships that had previously sailed through the straits. Aware of the inferior military capability of their native fiefdom, and against the advice of their mentor, Dr. Williamson, Itō and Inoue hastily departed London for the long trip home, and arrived in Yokohama on June 10, 1864.[9] They were intent on negotiating a peaceful solution. In another historical twist, the British ambassador to Japan, Rutherford Alcock, upon learning of their intentions, sent the two south on a British ship to act as mediators in an attempt to avert an impending catastrophe.[10]

The xenophobic sentiment within the Chōshū leadership proved too great for Itō and Inoue to overcome at the last minute. The bombardment of their beloved Shimonoseki in a display of power by Western warships was carried out in early August as Itō and Inoue watched helplessly. After recently being befriended by the British in London, the bombardment of their native fiefdom by British ships ended their first mission to the West. They were destined not to return to London to resume their studies as students. The brief but intense experience in London nevertheless left an indelible mark on them as they later began their ascendancy in the modern era of Meiji Japan.

Satsuma Student Mission to London and America, 1865–1868

The second covert student mission to the West in the 1860s included one of the principal architects of modern Japanese education, Mori Arinori. Like Itō, Mori was born into a nondescript samurai family. Nevertheless, he reached the pinnacle of international diplomacy as the first Japanese diplomat to America in 1871, and minister to the Court of St. James in London in 1880, and was then appointed by Prime Minister Itō as minister of education. Mori's achievements illustrate both the uncommon capacities of the man and the distinctiveness of his native clan of Satsuma. Although his short career was abruptly snuffed out by assassination while he was serving as minister of education, Mori Arinori stands out as one of the most significant although controversial figures in the modernization of Japanese education.

The origin of the Satsuma student mission to the West can be traced to a well-known incident during the final years of the feudal Tokugawa era. In mid-September 1862, an English businessman by the name of Charles Richardson visited foreign friends in Japan from his base in China. Four British subjects, including Richardson and a woman, went horseback riding near Yokohama on a road within the area officially designated open to foreigners. They came upon a procession of about 400 retainers from Satsuma, some walking and others on horseback, ritually transporting the father of the then-reigning clan leader on the long journey homeward after visiting the shogunate in Tokyo. When the foreigners unwittingly failed to follow the appropriate protocol under such circumstances, that is, withdrawing a respectable distance from the road in obeisance to a feudal lord, one or more chief retainers suddenly charged after the foreigners who fled on horseback for their lives. Richardson was killed in this infamous encounter, and the British retaliated.

By the time of the Richardson incident, the British Empire had reached its zenith as the world's dominant naval power. Having extended colonial rule through much of Africa, the Middle East, and South Asia, the British were vigorously projecting their influence into East Asia, with modern warships plying Chinese and Japanese waters. The stubborn Japanese with their isolationist policies who had steadfastly remained outside British influence proved a challenge to them. In a demonstration of western military superiority, British warships were shortly thereafter dispatched to Kagoshima Bay where they proceeded to bombard Satsuma coastal defenses and the city itself. The attack by foreign warships operating halfway around the world from their home base demonstrated unmistakably the superiority of western military power over samurai military technology.

The lesson intended by the British was not missed by certain Satsuma leaders who witnessed the bombardment. Among them was Godai Tomoatsu, progressive samurai who had already had the opportunity to study western naval technology at a school run by the Dutch in nearby Nagasaki, at the instigation of the Tokugawa government. Following the bombardment of his clan's major city, he realized that the only way for Satsuma to defend itself was to systematically study the technological advancements that enabled the British to project their power and influence throughout the world.

Godai devised a scheme to covertly dispatch a mission of young Satsuma samurai to London, the center of British power. The express purpose was to learn from the British by enrolling in strategic technical courses in appropriate institutions, and then apply that knowledge at home for the advancement of Satsuma. At a time when foreign travel was proscribed by Tokugawa edict except for official missions sent by the central government, Godai's grand scheme was fraught with danger. Nevertheless, following the humiliating British bombardment of their beloved capital, Satsuma realists prevailed. The bold plan to learn from their recent enemy was approved.

Godai, at the age of twenty-four, was given responsibility to organize and lead the Satsuma students to London. Mori Arinori was chosen among the fourteen students for the mission. At the time he was studying English in a Satsuma school of western studies by the name of Yōgakkō Kaiseijo. That course followed Mori's basic education in traditional Confucian studies and the martial arts at the clan school for samurai youth, the Zōshikan, where the local leadership class underwent its initial training. Godai and clan leaders chose Mori and other classmates for the mission since they happened to be among the few local youth studying English at the time.[11]

Mori was inherently an inquisitive individual who chose not to follow the normal path of samurai youth. The fact that as a teenager he chose to study English at the clan's school of western studies and languages is illustrative of his adventurous nature. It also demonstrates that at an early age he had become attracted to western ideas then gradually being introduced into Japan's closed feudal society. At that school Mori was introduced to radical concepts such as those contained in a book he encountered on national sovereignty and maritime powers by an author arrested for advocating ideas counter to the isolationist policies of the government. The theory espoused in the banned book was simple but dangerous at the time: Japan, as an island nation, should base its self-defense on a global perspective rather than on isolationist policies.[12]

The clandestine mission of Satsuma boys to London in 1865, three years before the Meiji Restoration, all traveling incognito with false names, was arranged by Godai. He negotiated with a British merchant named Thomas Glover, working with the Jardine Matheson shipping company out of Nagasaki. who had previously befriended Godai during his naval study tour in that southern city.[13] This was the same Jardine Matheson Company that had arranged for the Chōshū Five, which included Itō Hirobumi, to travel to London two years previously. This relationship provided the connecting link between the two missions. Glover dispatched a British ship to secretly rendezvous with the student mission at a secluded site off Satsuma for transfer to a larger oceangoing ship in Hong Kong on March 21, 1865.[14]

On June 21, 1865, the student mission of fourteen young samurai with two adult leaders from Satsuma arrived at Southampton, England.[15] Little could anyone

Figure 4. Satsuma Students in London.
From Benjamin Duke, *Ten Great Educators of Modern Japan* (Tokyo: Tokyo University Press, 1989), 41.

have imagined at the time that among them were two future ministers to England, the first chargé d'affaires and a minister to the United States, two ministers of education, as well as the president of Japan's only institution of higher education. Remarkably, Mori Arinori fit into three of those categories.

The first encounter with the West by the youthful Satsuma samurai, in their ill-fitting western clothes hastily made in Hong Kong during the trip westward, was the train ride from Southampton to London. The boys were astonished by their first sight of brick buildings, docks, and factories, as well as the luxuriousness of a London hotel, the Kensington. Thomas Glover was waiting for them. He briefed the boys on such important topics as housing and English-language tutors.[16]

Alexander Williamson, professor of chemistry at the University of London and president of the London Scientific Association, played the same role with Satsuma students as he previously had in 1863 with the Chōshū students. He extended generous hospitality to both groups of Japanese students by taking them on field trips and assisting in arranging housing accommodations. He even boarded the Satsuma students at his own home as well as with other faculty members of the university. For the next two years Mori lived at the home of another professor of chemistry on the university faculty. Williamson also promptly set up English lessons for the boys from Satsuma in preparation for the new semester.[17]

In October 1865, all but one of the fourteen Satsuma boys entered University College of the great London University as nonmatriculating students in the Faculty of Arts and Letters.[18] The University of London, with its core curriculum centered on science and mathematics for a new generation of industrial development, was fitting for the Japanese students who had traveled halfway around the world to learn western technology. But the relatively new subject of economics at the university was then under the powerful influence of George Maynard Keynes, and other social sciences were also burgeoning. Exposed to the social theories then circulating among the intellectual community of London, some of the Satsuma students inevitably became attracted to the social sciences within a short time. Their mentor, Professor Williamson, who was deeply influenced by John Stuart Mill's philosophy of rationalism, was actively promoting it. Mori, originally sent to London to study science and technology, soon became interested in political theories.[19] This transition from the natural to the social and political sciences would prove of enormous consequence to the future of modern Japanese education when Mori became minister of education two decades later.

Laurence Oliphant: British Parliamentarian, Friend of the Japanese Students

Meanwhile Thomas Glover, who had developed a close relationship with the Satsuma students, introduced them to a fellow Scot and distinguished member of Parliament representing Scotland, Laurence Oliphant. Because this colorful figure from the British establishment was destined to play a critical role in the lives of the Satsuma students, most notably Mori Arinori, his background is important.[20] Oliphant's experiences both at home and abroad illustrate the type of westerners that befriended the future leaders of modern Japanese education.

Laurence Oliphant lived one of the most colorful and adventurous lives of any Englishman during the global supremacy of the British Empire of the nineteenth century. Born in Ceylon under British rule, he spent much of his early life there with his father, a senior magistrate in the colonial government. Family funds enabled Laurence to travel widely in British India and throughout Europe. His family connections enabled him to travel on a diplomatic mission to the United States and Canada as an aide to the illustrious Lord Elgin, who forged various governmental ties between foreign countries and Britain. While on the mission to North America, he was hired on the spot as the Canadian inspector of Indian affairs for a year.

Upon return to England, Laurence was subsequently chosen to accompany Lord Elgin once again on a diplomatic mission, this time to China in 1859. While on this trip to the Orient, the Elgin mission was ordered to nearby Japan to show the flag before returning home. During this brief visit of less than a week, Oliphant became fascinated with Japan. He came to a startling conclusion: "It will appear that a more widely-diffused system of education exists in Japan than in our country; and that in that aspect, at all events, if in no other, they are decidedly in advance of us."[21] He wrote rather wistfully in his official report of the mission that "There exists not a single disagreeable association to cloud our reminiscences of that country."[22]

Unexpectedly, the opportunity for Oliphant to travel to Japan once again arose several years later. The British government was then in the process of negotiating full diplomatic ties with the Tokugawa government. Officials were recruited to fill the new posts in Tokyo. Oliphant, without experience as a diplomatic officer, nevertheless accepted an assignment by the Foreign Office as chargé d'affaires at the newly established British legation, taking up the post in Edo in 1862.

When Oliphant arrived in Japan this time, the country was undergoing the wrenching process of emerging from near-total isolation from the outside world. On the second night in the British legation, Oliphant experienced firsthand the wrath of anti-foreign sentiment. Conspirators entered the legation armed with knives, intent on killing the foreigners. In hand-to-hand fighting in darkened corridors, the embattled British diplomats finally forced the intruders to withdraw. Oliphant, however, received two serious wounds in the harrowing experience in which several assailants were killed. The brief but deadly encounter nearly cost Oliphant his life. The following day he was removed to a British ship in Tokyo harbor to return to England for medical treatment and recuperation.[23] As in his first experience in 1859, Oliphant spent only a few days in Japan in 1862.

Three years later in 1865, Laurence Oliphant, now a member of the House of Commons from Scotland, first met the Japanese boys from Satsuma in London. In spite of his unfortunate incident in Tokyo in 1862, he took a special interest in all things Japanese, and immediately befriended the students. They soon became attracted to Oliphant, who conveyed a sense of trustworthiness to the boys. Their relationship grew steadily deeper. Oliphant was part of the social elite of Britain, and as a member of the Athenaeum Club, Oliphant socialized with the leading figures of his country in the relaxed old-worldly atmosphere of Christian gentlemen. This has historical relevance, since Mori Arinori returned to London less than two decades later as minister to Great Britain when he spent considerable time at the Athenaeum Club. His membership as minister provided the opportunity for Mori to associate with the British establishment of that period that included Herbert Spencer, the great social critic who subsequently influenced Japanese thought.

During the summer of 1966, after one year of study in London, the Satsuma boys dispersed. Both Professor Williamson and Oliphant advised the students in planning their summer activities.[24] Six returned to Japan, while the others went on special field trips. Two of the students, Samejima and Yoshida, traveled to the United States with their new friend, Laurence Oliphant. He had intrigued the boys by revealing that he was going to America to meet a "living Confucius."[25] Their trip with him to a religious colony in the state of New York would exert an enormous influence on the Satsuma students. At the same time, Mori Arinori traveled to Russia and Hatakeyama Yoshinari, later president of the only university-level institution in Japan, visited France.

The year 1867 was an eventful period. The Paris Exhibition in April attracted exhibits and visitors from around the world, including Japan. The Tokugawa government entered a modest exhibit, as did several local fiefs including Satsuma. Godai Tomoatsu, who led the student mission from Satsuma to London, helped arrange the Satsuma exhibition in Paris before returning home. When Japanese visitors passed through London on their way to and from Paris, the boys from Satsuma had an opportunity to learn about the latest developments back home and the growing movement against the Tokugawa regime, with the active participation by their Satsuma government. By this time the Satsuma government had increased its activities in opposition to the Tokugawa shoganate, simultaneously reducing its interest in and financing of the han students in England. Jardine Matheson stepped in to loan the boys money during their financial difficulties. However the company, also facing fiscal problems, soon terminated the loans. With an impending financial crisis and the Japanese boys losing interest in their initial assignment to study technology at the University of London in favor of social and spiritual interests, they were ready for a new challenge.

Among the thousands of visitors to the Paris Exhibition, one stands out for playing a significant role in the western education of the Japanese students then in England. Thomas Lake Harris, originally from Wales, was by then leading a tiny religious colony, a sect of Swedenborgianism called Brotherhood of the New Life, located in rural New York. He had already attracted Laurence Oliphant and his mother Lady Oliphant to his teachings. Harris was the so-called "living Confucius" to whom Oliphant referred when he took two of the Satsuma boys with him on a visit to the Harris colony during the previous summer of 1866. The boys had returned to London deeply inspired by Harris and his teachings, sharing their enthusiasm with their fellow Satsuma students. This positive reaction to Thomas Harris set the stage for a meeting. Oliphant arranged for the boys to meet Harris upon his arrival in England on his way to the Paris Exhibition in April 1867. The boys were eager to meet him.[26] The regimen of Harris's Brotherhood of New Life Colony, based on self-denial, strict regulations, and severe physical labor, appealed to them. It was reminiscent of the upbringing they all experienced in Japan as samurai youth in the warrior tradition. A charismatic figure, Harris envisioned a new image of society that had a compelling attraction to the Satsuma boys growing restless in London.

The boys had by now become sufficiently fluent in English to appreciate Harris's vision for a new Japan. In his grandiose plan for a "universal rebirth of all mankind," the problem of Japan remained unsolved. Historians surmise that Harris now envisioned the boys as potential disciples for a mission to Japan. Mori's American biographer, Ivan Parker Hall, notes that Harris viewed Japan as central to his effort to carry out a global regeneration, to begin with Asiatic countries least penetrated by Christianity.[27] Whatever the motivation, Harris made a tempting offer. Aware of their financial plight in London, he invited the boys from Satsuma to join his colony in America.[28] In his *Prophecy of Japan*, Harris wrote that "I have thus solved the prophecy of Japan. It's successful outworking depends on finding a Daimyo who will carry it out."[29] Harris apparently believed that he had found his daimyos from Satsuma then studying in London.

The convergence of mutually beneficial ideas between Harris and the Satsuma boys is intriguing. The boys had originally come to England to prepare them to lead Satsuma into the new world. They, too, had an image for a new Japanese society. Impressionable in their late teens and early twenties, they were undergoing an incredible experience in London in which every influence on their thinking was now western. When Harris, a strong and forceful character, unveiled his image of a new Japan before them, he struck a sympathetic chord that raised the hopes and aspirations of the young samurai from Japan.

Meanwhile, Mori had been developing a keen interest in the relationship between the state and the individual. He was fascinated by Harris's theory of the new individual in a regenerated state. Mori envisaged Harris as someone who could lead the Japanese boys into the next stage of their western journey in search of a new Japan. To him Harris had a spiritual message with a political, social, and moral theme that proved irresistible.[30] Mori was being drawn into the Harris mystique.

In 1867, during the second year of the Satsuma student mission to England, Laurence Oliphant, by now a trusted confidant of the students, shocked the British establishment by suddenly resigning from the House of Commons. He then revealed his improbable decision to set sail for the United States in order to join the mysterious Swedenborgian sect in rural New York. Oliphant had by then become a dedicated believer in the spiritual mystic from Wales. Adding to the bizarre turn of events, Lady Oliphant, Laurence's mother, also intrigued with Harris, decided to join his tiny community in America. With the revelation of Oliphant's controversial decision to move to America, the deepening relationship between the Satsuma boys and their British confidant took on a greater urgency.

Genuinely interested in the fate of the boys, Oliphant made an unlikely proposal. He encouraged the samurai youth to join him. The decision whether to accept Oliphant's intriguing proposal divided the remaining boys from the Satsuma student mission whose adult leaders had already returned to Japan. Far from home, unable to obtain a reaction from their han, with communications taking months, and with their financial condition rapidly deteriorating, the boys were faced with a perplexing problem. Finally, disregarding Professor Williamson's opposition to Harris as a religious fanatic, the Satsuma students made a fateful decision. Six of the boys decided to leave London and join Oliphant at the Harris colony. Oliphant left England for America in August 1867. According to his biographer, he gave up "everything that had previously tempted him—his position, his prospects, politics, literature, society, every personal possession and hope."[31] The boys departed shortly thereafter.[32]

The six students along with Laurence Oliphant and his socialite mother arrived in America in late summer of 1867. Once again the young Japanese samurai were embarking on another adventure in the West, this time in the New World. America was, in its own way, as exciting a place as London had been in the late 1860s. The devastating Civil War had ended two years previously, sparking a social revolution. Simultaneously the western frontier of the United States motivated a great migration westward. The winds of change were buffeting American society as an industrial revolution was about to sweep the nation. But although they were now living in a country undergoing a great social revolution to democratize its society, the boys were not participants in it nor were they apparently aware of what was taking place outside their secluded enclave at remote Brocton in rural New York state. Not only was the secretive colony isolated geographically, it was also isolated religiously from the mainstream of Christianity in America. For all intents and purposes, the young Japanese samurai were cut off from communications with England and Japan. They were also effectively isolated from the rapidly changing society of America where they now lived.

The Brocton colony, situated on a 2,000-acre site of farmland in the western part of the state of New York far from New York City, consisted of forty members, half of them girls. It was noted for the harsh physical demands and Spartan discipline imposed on its members. In certain ways it resembled the discipline of a Japanese samurai. The daily regimen was strictly enforced. An item in one of the boys' diary graphically reveals the harsh conditions: "Mori and I got up at 4:30 to shine shoes and feed and water the cattle for two hours before breakfast." Another day Mori, Samejima, Yoshida, and Noda got up at 5 A.M. to wash dishes and clean tables after breakfast.[33]

Laurence Oliphant was treated no better. His biographer described the precarious style of life he experienced. The former distinguished member of the British Parliament "coming straight from Mayfair" slept in "a large loft containing only empty orange boxes and one mattress. . . . He often recalled in a sort of nightmare the gloomy silent labour for days and days, wheeling barrels of dirt and rubbish in perfect loneliness, for he was not allowed to speak to anyone. . . . Often after this rough work was ended, and he came home at nine o'clock, he was sent out again to draw water for household purposes till eleven o'clock, till his fingers were almost frost-bitten."[34]

Spiritual life at Brocton was also demanding not only for Oliphant but for his young Japanese friends as well. Oliphant wrote that "I cannot speak to the Japanese although I see them, dear souls, every day hard at work with their countenances beaming with delight. They feel the effects of the sphere, and of the influx that comes with labour, and they say they never knew what happiness was before."[35] The professed spiritual relationship between Harris's colony and the Christian faith has historical relevance for modern Japanese education. When Mori became the first minister of education under the cabinet system of government in 1886, bitter critics considered him a Christian unfit to direct the nation's educational policy. That reputation followed him to his death.

The relationship between the Japanese and Harris took a sudden turn in 1868 over a curious incident, the details of which vary slightly among historical accounts.[36] In May a question emerged among the boys: if war broke out between the United States and Japan, which side should the samurai boys support? Heated discussions prevailed, provoking the boys to ask Harris for his opinion. Perhaps unprepared for such a hypothetical question, he replied that they should follow the path of Christ. His answer split the boys. Those who may have already become somewhat disillusioned by Harris and his mystical beliefs decided to leave the colony promptly. Others, including Mori, remained at the colony, a sign of loyalty to their spiritual leader.

One student, Hatakeyama Yoshinari, destined to become president of Japan's only university-level institution within a few years, reacted negatively to Harris's opinion. He immediately left the colony and found his way to New Brunswick, New Jersey, to enter Rutgers College before returning home after the Meiji Restoration. Those who remained with Harris at Brocton received information that the Meiji Restoration had taken place in their homeland led by, among several others, their Satsuma han. Shortly thereafter Harris advised Mori and Samejima to return to Japan to carry out his mission to the Japanese, demonstrating the confidence Harris had in the two. They left Brocton for Japan on June 8, 1868, three years after they had first arrived in the West at London.[37]

Little could the student Mori have imagined when he sailed from the United States to Japan in 1868 that he would return to America within three years as Japan's first diplomat in Washington, with the awesome responsibility of initiating diplomatic relations with the United States. Nor could he have envisioned that he would return to London in 1880 to become Japan's minister to Great Britain, followed by an appointment by Prime Minister Itō Hirobumi as the first minister of education under a modern form of government. It was during this final assignment when he personally redesigned the modern school system of Japan in 1886, discussed in later chapters. It all dates back, however, to the covert student mission from Satsuma to the West in 1865, when Mori Arinori experienced his first encounter with the modern world.

Samurai Students at Rutgers College 1866–1868: Guido Verbeck

While Itō Hirobumi and Mori Arinori were enrolled in London University, another group of samurai youth destined for leadership in modern Japan was studying at a small college in America. Under the most unlikely circumstances, Rutgers College in the tiny community of New Brunswick, New Jersey, became the primary institution in America hosting Japanese students during the feudal period. It originated through an uncommon individual, the Dutch-American Guido Verbeck, who sent his students to Rutgers as a teacher from Japan during the closing years of the Tokugawa period.

In 1852, over a decade before the students from Chōshū and Satsuma set sail for London, Guido Verbeck left his native Netherlands for America. Like millions of other European immigrants before and after him, Verbeck sought a new life in the New World. Unlike any other immigrant in the history of the United States, however, Guido Verbeck would within a few years be sent by a Dutch-American Christian denomination to feudal Japan as a missionary. Because of his subsequent contribution to the rise of modern Japan, well beyond his role in opening the channel for Japanese students to study at Rutgers College, he would be described by a leading Japanese historian over a century later as "the father of modern Japan's formation" (kindai Nihon kensetsu no chichi).[38]

When the Americans in their Black Ships unexpectedly sailed into Tokyo Bay in 1853, a new and potentially threatening factor confronted the Japanese government. It was forced to respond to foreign demands for favorable trade and diplomatic intercourse that were backed by superior military power that could not be denied. One of the most important results of the early contacts with the Americans, who returned in 1854 and moored their menacing ships off shore south

Figure 5. Guido Verbeck.
Photo courtesy of Rutgers Seminary
Library, New Brunswick, N.J.

of Tokyo, were the treaties signed at that time. One of the provisions designated three seaports as open cities where foreigners were able to reside, beginning in five years, that is, from 1859. Among them was Nagasaki, where the Dutch had already gained a slender foothold.

During the same year Guido Verbeck, former engineer from Holland who worked for four years at his trade in the United States before entering religious studies, was about to complete the course at the Presbyterian Theological Seminary at Auburn, New York. With the already established connection between the Dutch and Nagasaki, it was natural for the Board of Missions of the Dutch Reformed Church in America to search for someone versed in the Dutch language to send to Nagasaki as a missionary. No one, however, was available in the Dutch Reformed seminary at the time with the necessary qualifications. The church leadership looked elsewhere in America and discovered that the Dutch-speaking Verbeck was about to graduate from a Presbyterian seminary.

Verbeck was immediately offered the missionary assignment to Japan by the Dutch Reformed Church in America. Disregarding his complete lack of knowledge about Japan and the Japanese, he accepted the call and received ordination as pastor of the Reformed Church. Verbeck arrived in Nagasaki on November 7, 1859, one of the first Protestant missionaries in Japan, eager to spread the gospel of Christ to the Japanese.[39] The appointment of Verbeck to Japan as a Christian missionary from the United States contrasted sharply with his original intention when he immigrated to America as an engineer in the early 1850s.

Guido Verbeck in Nagasaki, 1859–1868

Guido Verbeck's remarkable place in Japanese history began with his arrival in Nagasaki. It had taken five and a half months by ship, including one week aground and five weeks detention in Hong Kong, for Verbeck to reach Japan from New York.[40] He was one of three missionaries, two of them knowing no Dutch, sent to Japan on the same ship by the Dutch Reformed Church of America. They were separated in Shanghai, with the other two going on to Kanagawa. Verbeck, leaving his pregnant wife in China with missionaries, left for Nagasaki to secure housing.

Verbeck's initial housing arrangement reveals the problems faced by foreigners living in Tokugawa Japan. It would set him apart from other foreigners for the ten years he lived in Nagasaki, a precursor of his unique relationship with the Japanese. Since he could not immediately find housing within the quarters assigned to foreigners, he wrote that: "I was obliged to get a dwelling in the city proper; although the authorities did not directly object to my getting a house among the Japanese, yet they seemed to try to weary me out by delays and empty promises from day to day; however I persevered, . . . so that I now live in the midst of a dense population with nothing to hinder my free intercourse with them."[41]

During the first several years in Japan, Verbeck's chosen work as a Christian missionary in a land that proscribed Christianity was painfully slow. In his annual report to the missionary board in 1861, he recorded that "I have little to communicate."[42] He was nevertheless laying the groundwork in Nakasaki for his future role.

> We have by this time gained a firmer footing in the country, obtained the confidence of the people and authorities, as well as vindicated the peaceableness and disinterestedness of our aims by living among them; we have considerably enlarged the circle of our acquaintances, and consequently influence. . . . As to teaching, I continued during the year seven English pupils, three of whom were government interpreters, and the remainder officers and scholars sent, or who have come voluntarily from other principalities, for the purpose of studying the English language.[43]

During the third year of Verbeck's assignment in Japan, 1862, he reports that, "the study of language has been my chief pursuit."[44] His limited teaching, which now included a Bible class of four students, all "in consequence of having been my pupils in English," did not interfere in his language study, for he wrote that "looking to the present and future use of the language and to the fruits of that use, makes its study both important and agreeable."[45] A native Japanese teacher who later heard him lecture in Nagasaki paid this Dutchman, who already spoke four western languages, the ultimate compliment: "He knows more of the language [Japanese] than I do."[46]

Although Verbeck arrived in Japan in 1859, the opportunity to evolve from an obscure local Christian missionary, chaffing under the prohibition against Christianity, to a participant in the Japanese educational and political world did not take place until 1864 to 1865. During that period he was hired to teach at two different government schools, attracting an unprecedented number of students who would later serve in influential positions within the Meiji government. This is the very time when the covert student missions from Chōshū and Satsuma were studying in London.

In 1864 Verbeck was employed by the city government of Nagasaki, which sponsored a school called Eigosho, an English-language institution previously run by the central Tokugawa government. Verbeck obviously had gained sufficient respect and confidence of city officials by this time to warrant the assignment. Shortly thereafter, officials of the Saga han, in which the city of Nagasaki was located, learned of Verbeck's classes. They invited him to teach on alternate days at their han school, Chienkan, also located in Nagasaki. At that time the daimyo or head of the Saga fiefdom, Nabeshima Naomasa, progressive by nature, had already introduced western learning in his domain. Accordingly Verbeck was asked to teach not only English but also politics, economics, and science.[47]

As a domain school, Chienkan attracted bright samurai youth from within the han. One of Verbeck's most devoted students, who became prime minister and founder of the prestigious Waseda University during the Meiji era, was Ōkuma Shigenobu. He represented a minority of senior leaders in the Meiji government to originate from a han other than the dominant two, Satsuma and Chōshū. Verbeck received an impressive salary of $4,500 per year from the two schools, a sum far beyond that of a Christian pastor in America.[48] It marked the beginning of many years when Verbeck's salary came from Japanese governmental sources while he officially served the Reformed Church in America as a foreign missionary.

Verbeck soon attracted to his classes in Nagasaki not only local clan students but also students from other clans. His fame spread by word of mouth. One of the most illustrious groups of future leaders of modern Japan who ever studied under one teacher found their way to Nagasaki to study under Verbeck during the Tokugawa period.

There were many private schools run by Japanese that attracted samurai youth from throughout the country. Some attained wide notoriety, such as the Shōka Sonjuku in Chōshū, where Itō Hirobumi, leading statesman of the Meiji era, studied, and Yokoi Shōnan's school in Kumamoto. Although local fief schools catered to eager samurai from within the local han, it was not unusual for highly motivated students to travel great distances to study with noted Japanese teachers in another han. The peripatetic nature of an impressive number of samurai youth during the Tokugawa era was one of the more notable aspects of the late feudal period. However, Verbeck's reputation that motivated young samurai from various hans of feudal Japan to walk for weeks to the southern tip of Japan to study under a foreigner in a foreign language was unprecedented. The consequences of the teacher-student relationship between this Dutch-American and an inordinate number of leaders of modern Japan played out later when he was invited by senior government leaders, mostly former students, to move to Tokyo in 1869.

Reading like a *Who's Who* of Meiji Japan, only a few of Verbeck's many students at Nagasaki may be mentioned, selected from one of the leading histories of the period.[49] They include Etō Shimpei and Ōki Takatoo, who founded the Ministry of Education during the early Meiji Period and served as the first and second directors, essentially ministers of education, setting the initial direction toward a modern school system; Katō Hiroyuki, first president of Tokyo University; and Ōkuma Shigenobu, powerful government leader as minister of finance and later prime minister who founded the first liberal political party as well as the distinguished Waseda University. Ōkuma proved to be perhaps the most devoted of all of Verbeck's students at Nakasaki.

Verbeck went far beyond English-language teaching in his classroom. Saga prefectural authorities invited him to teach other subjects as well under their sponsorship. He offered a broad curriculum in English that included economics and politics.[50] He even included in his course the fundamentals of the American Constitution.[51] How Verbeck was capable, and inclined, to teach such a wide variety of subjects to his devoted Japanese young samurai shows the mark of the man. Considered by the Japanese as a virtual encyclopedia of western knowledge, it was Verbeck's destiny to provide a foundation in modern government to a great number of Japan's first generation of leaders during the Meiji period.[52]

Rutgers College—Pipeline to America

During Verbeck's period in Nagasaki in the 1860s, he took advantage of his unique position in Japan and his institutional contacts in the United States to make his second important contribution to modern Japan. He established a channel, a pipeline as it were, for Japanese students to study in America. His pivotal role in arranging for over three hundred young Japanese samurai, many from his classroom, to study at Rutgers College and a preparatory school in New Brunswick, New Jersey, from 1866 on rivals in importance his many other contributions to the modernization of Japan.[53]

It all began in 1866, when Verbeck sent the first two young Japanese from Nagasaki to New York City to meet John Ferris, secretary of the Board of Missions in Verbeck's adopted Christian denomination, the Dutch Reformed Church in America. They carried a cryptic letter of introduction from Verbeck dated November 6, which opened the pipeline for Japanese students to study in America.[54]

> My dear Mr. Ferris:
>   Allow this to introduce to your kind offices the brothers, Yokoi Saheido and Yokoi Daihei, two brothers from the country of Higo on this island, about which I shall further write you by mail.
>   Yours very truly,
>   Guido F. Verbeck

John Ferris recalled the moment when he met the two Japanese who appeared unexpectedly at his office in New York, and who "appeared to be Chinamen."[55] He could not have appreciated the uniqueness of the two as nephews of Yokoi

Shonan, a historical figure of the late feudal era who taught some of the most illustrious leaders of modern Japan in his private school.[56] The brothers informed him that they had come to America "to study navigation, to learn how to build big ships and make big guns to prevent European powers from taking possession of their country." Ferris explained to them that "it would be necessary to study many things" before they could build ships.[57] Accordingly he arranged for them to study at nearby Rutgers College in New Jersey, an institution founded during the colonial era in 1766 by the Dutch Reformed Church. This was a natural course for Ferris to follow since he himself was a ranking official of that Christian denomination.

The arrival in 1866 of the first two Japanese students to Rutgers College marked the opening of what would become a procession. The reaction toward the growing number of Japanese students by the residents of the small town of New Brunswick was recorded by a contemporary figure, William Griffis. Although Griffis himself went to Japan from Rutgers, an assignment also arranged by Verbeck several years later, he was on the scene when the first students arrived in New Jersey. He whimsically called it the Japanese Invasion of New Jersey.

> They arrived at first by twos and threes . . . the mystery deepened when, instead of two, there came ten, twenty, thirty Japanese lads, and still the wonder grew that they were all polite, polished gentlemen. "How strange," thought Mrs. Gunders, who kept a students' boarding house and yet, with her sister attended every meeting in the First Reformed Church. "These young men come from Japan where we send missionaries, and yet how polite they are! I still don't know what to make of it."[58]

Griffis may have been correct when he concluded that "Perhaps these lads, some of them with their top-knots hardly cut, came to the capital of the Reformed Church in America, because they did not know there were in the great United States other schools and colleges, and indeed, how should they in 1867?"[59] Without doubt they would not have known about Rutgers College if John Ferris had not directed them, upon the recommendation of Guido Verbeck, to New Brunswick, just fifteen miles from prestigious Princeton University. Perhaps envious, some Princetonians dubbed the nearby community of New Brunswick the "Japanese town."[60]

Griffis reported that often when the Japanese students found themselves in dire financial condition, local people "poured out their money unstintingly to aid the makers of new Japan to come to get their American education. . . . It was great fun and constant delight in those days to watch the ways of the future admiral of the Japanese navy, the coming envoy of the Mikado at Washington or to the European capitals, the governor of provinces, and the embryo captains and generals in the army."[61]

Griffis's mention of the future admiral of the Japanese navy deserves elaboration of the role that Rutgers College indirectly played in modern military education of Japan. Among the Japanese students studying at Rutgers in the late 1860s were several who wanted to go on for further study at the U.S. Naval Academy.

At the time Japanese were not permitted to enter the institution that prepared the officer class of the U.S. Navy such as Commodore Perry, who captained the fleet of American ships into Tokyo waters in 1853 that provoked the opening of Japan.

A delegation of Japanese students met with John Ferris, secretary of the Board of Missions of the Reformed Church in America that supported Rutgers College, imploring him for assistance in opening the Naval Academy to the Japanese. Ferris reacted favorably by contacting the U.S. senator from New Jersey who sponsored "A Resolution to admit certain persons to the Naval Academy." The resolution, which specifically stipulated that, "Students from the Empire of Japan are received for instruction," was approved by the American Congress on July 27, 1868, the same year as the Meiji Restoration.

Under the provisions of the resolution, the first two Japanese students entered the Naval Academy in 1869. Two years later the son of the ranking naval officer of the fledging Japanese Navy, Katsu Kaishu, was also accepted at the academy. During the first decade of the Meiji era a total of thirteen Japanese students studied there. Several rose to the rank of admiral in the Japanese Navy.[62] Although indirectly, Verbeck played a pivotal role in this endeavor.

The concentration of Japanese students at Rutgers College during the late Tokugawa period as a result of Guido Verbeck's efforts would have broad repercussions. As would be expected, many of the Japanese students returned home to play major roles in the modernization process during the Meiji era. The primary example was Hatakeyama Yoshinari. He became the president of Kaisei Gakkō in 1873, three years before it became Tokyo University, the leading institution of higher education in modern Japan. Ironically, Hatakeyama replaced Verbeck as president of Kaisei, his last and most prestigious governmental assignment before returning to the life of a missionary in his beloved adopted country of Japan.

3

The Meiji Restoration

REEMERGENCE OF TOKUGAWA SCHOOLS, 1868–1871

With the overthrow of the Tokugawa government in 1868, the Meiji Restoration marks the beginning of the modern era in Japanese history. The Restoration does not, however, mark the beginning of the modern era in Japanese education. During the initial three-year period after the Restoration, education for the ruling samurai classes took preference over education for the masses, as it did in the Tokugawa era just ended. After three and a half centuries of uninterrupted rule by the Tokugawa regime, revered educational institutions founded during that period of unparalleled stability predictably resurfaced under the new Meiji government.

The process began with the first educational measure taken by the new government on February 22, 1868. Three officials were appointed to an Office of Education under the newly organized Bureau of Internal Affairs charged with setting the direction of educational policy of the Meiji government.[1] Since all three were noted figures from the ranks of the Kokugakusha, specialists on Japanese history and culture centering on Shinto beliefs and customs in contrast to the new western studies, their recommendations inevitably embraced traditional educational patterns. The modern era in Japanese history was about to be launched on institutions revived from the former feudal era. There was no feasible alternative.

The Office of Education issued the first official pronouncement on March 12, 1868, declaring that the Gakushuin in Kyoto would be reopened on the 19th.[2] Both the institution and its location were fitting under the prevailing circumstances. The venerable Gakushuin was originally founded by an emperor to serve the families of the nobility. Kyoto was the city of nobility where the imperial family had resided for centuries. Accordingly, the curriculum of the school was intimately related to imperial traditions with a close relationship to indigenous Shinto ceremonies and customs. It marked the first logical step in education under the movement to restore imperial authority.

Continuing the contrasting trends under way during the Tokugawa government, exactly two days later, March 14, the Meiji government issued the well-known Charter Oath in the name of the youthful Emperor Meiji, then age sixteen. Among the five so-called oaths or declarations of intent of the new government, number five ultimately became the most important. It symbolically marked the end of three hundred years of isolation and the opening of the country (*kaikoku*) to the international community: "Knowledge shall be sought throughout the world, so as to strengthen the foundation of Imperial rule."[3] The interpretation and application of this single provision would prove highly controversial as the Restoration movement matured. In one declaration, the goal of assimilating modern western knowledge with seemingly incompatible ancient Japanese traditions epitomizes the basic scenario for the entire Meiji era. The confrontation between the two positions forms the underlying theme running through the first two decades of modern education in Japan.

Amid the haste to open schools for the nobility, coupled with the issuing of the Charter Oath seeking knowledge from "throughout the world," the Dajōkan, the highest governmental organ, called for members of noble families to become leaders of the country. They were urged to come to Tokyo, the new administrative capital, from Kyoto where most lived. Members of the nobility were also encouraged to go abroad to learn about modern western societies in order to assume leadership positions. Although only a limited number of noble families sent their youth abroad for study, it became fashionable for motivated samurai youth to study abroad in preparation for leadership positions at home. Study abroad was considered similar to visiting the Ise Shrine (O Ise Mairi), that is, once in a lifetime.[4] The number of Japanese studying abroad reached a record number of nearly four hundred by the beginning of the 1870s.[5]

Interest in the West was stimulated by the most prominent Japanese educator of the period, Fukuzawa Yukichi, highly respected among intellectuals as well as the general populace. His books on the West based on his travels to both America and England during the late Tokugawa period were widely circulated, including his best-selling Seiyō Jijō (Conditions in the West), a veritable encyclopedia of things western from politics to education. Two other writers also reached a broad audience. The great classic Self-Help by the British author Samuel Smiles was translated by Nakamura Masanao, who had studied in England before the Restoration. The oft-quoted line from the book, "Heaven helps them who help themselves," fashioned a rallying theme based on individualism for the reform of a feudalistic society. The third publication, a translation by Uchida Masao of a British publication on the unlikely topic of world geography, introduced a subject unique to the Japanese reading public.

These three publications injected unconventional perspectives into Japanese society. On the market before the Tokugawa era ended, they exerted such a profound influence on the educated classes immediately after the Meiji Restoration that they were collectively dubbed the Meiji Bible (Meiji no Seisho).[6] Within the revolutionary environment following the Meiji Restoration, the three national scholars developing educational policy at this very early stage could not ignore the far-reaching demands for western knowledge stimulated by such publications as the Meiji Bible. Consequently the Office of Education recognized a second institution of significance following the Restoration. On June 26, the Igakkō, the former Igakujo or School of Medicine, was reopened.[7] During the Tokugawa period, this institution had been conspicuously dominated by Dutch practices in medicine.

Swiftly alternating between the modern and the traditional, three days later on June 29, the government reopened the extraordinarily influential Tokugawa school, the distinguished Shōhei Gakkō, in Tokyo.[8] One of its primary purposes was to produce a corps of government officers for the feudal government. Its appeal to those in the decision-making role stems from its traditional curriculum committed to the venerable Confucian classics fundamental to the education of all samurai youth during the Tokugawa era. However, it also included courses related to kokugaku or Japanese cultural studies imbedded in Shintoism, dear to the nationalist officers then in charge of educational policy. During this early period of the Restoration, imperial tradition was of paramount concern among many government officials. They were orienting education toward imperial studies (*kōdō*) in order to develop a new national identity (*kokutai*). To rekindle the study of national culture related to the imperial tradition with its intimate relationship to Shinto, the Shōhei Gakkō was consequently intended as the academic mainstay of the Restoration.[9]

The reopening of the Shōhei Gakkō represented a major factor in the realm of education, particularly as it relates to traditional teaching methods. Teaching methodology was divided into a ritualistic three-stage process. In step one, sodoku, textual orientation, the student memorized assigned passages from Confucian and Shinto classics by reading them aloud repetitively. In step two, rinkō, student orientation, the student presented his interpretation of the passage. And finally in step three, kōgi, teacher analysis, the teacher explained the meaning of the passage, reading aloud each sentence word by word to bring the lesson to a close.[10]

In the midst of the frenetic movement to reopen selected Tokugawa schools in Tokyo and Kyoto, fighting between imperial forces and diehard remnants of the loyal Tokugawa opposition continued. The last great battle of feudal warfare in Japan, denoting the inevitable demise of the Tokugawa regime, took place on August 22, 1868, in Aizu. Continuing the rapid-fire reopening of Tokugawa schools immediately following the Aizu battle, arguably the most important institution of higher education, the Kaiseijo, became operational three weeks later on September 12.[11] Founded in 1856 as the Bansho Shirabesho in reaction to the perceived threat from foreign powers, this governmental institution introduced western studies and languages at the central level.[12] By the time of the Restoration in 1868, it had gained prominence by offering English, French, and German to samurai youth attracted to things western.

Finally, also in September of year one of the Meiji Government, two other institutions favored by nationalist scholars were reopened. The Kōgakusho, the School for Imperial Studies, and the Kangakusho, the School of Oriental Studies, both in Kyoto, were officially recognized.[13] That completed a strange assortment of higher-level educational institutions revived during the first year of Meiji. They all originated from Tokugawa institutions and all catered to the educated classes overwhelmingly dominated by samurai youth and to a lesser degree the nobility. In effect they represented the three basic schools of thought competing for influence in the closing years of the Tokugawa era: the kokugaku school of national studies (Shinto), the kangaku school of Chinese studies (Confucious), and the yōgaku school of western studies (science). Their primary purpose was to produce the next generation of government leaders.

This curious mixture of schools, all at the secondary or higher levels of education that originated during the Tokugawa era, illustrated several significant facts. First, there was little that could be considered modern among them. They served the traditional clientele that monopolized these elite institutions since their founding. Among them, with the exception of the Kaiseijo, where a few foreigners taught western languages, classroom teaching followed the traditional sodoku method from China. But perhaps of greatest importance, their rebirth demonstrated vividly that a comprehensive educational policy for the nation had not yet been considered. Excluded from the earliest Meiji schools authorized by the government to prepare the next generation of leaders was the mass of children from peasant families. They had been excluded from these schools during the Tokugawa period.

Before the first year of the Meiji Restoration ended, in November and December of 1868, major appointments were made that laid the basis for the modernization of education to begin in earnest. The government formed a Committee to Investigate the Schools (Gakkō Torishirabe Goyōgakari) similar to the Office of Education (Gakkō Gakari), which consisted of three nationalist scholars who had set initial policy. In contrast, the new organ was led by individuals who were specialists on the West including several who had studied in western countries during the feudal period. Among them were Mitsukuri Rinshō, who had spent a year in France during the Tokugawa era, and Mori Arinori, who had studied at the University of London for two years followed by one year at a Christian sect in rural America. Among the others were Kanda Kōhei, a Dutch specialist, and Fukuzawa Yukichi, a leading western authority who had been to America and Europe on three occasions. He chose to remain out of official government service. Their appointments were a signal that educational policy in the near future would follow a new direction.[14]

At the beginning of year two of the Meiji era, 1869, an irresistible tide of change was building. It may best be illustrated through the simple but prophetic words of Japan's most prominent political leader of the Meiji era, and primary spokesman for modern government and education, Itō Hirobumi. While heading a local unit of government later to become Hyogo prefecture, Itō submitted a thesis to the emperor that urged the basic principle of education for all; this theme would resound throughout the next decade of political and educational reform.

Since Itō Hirobumi played a major political role in the history of modern Japanese education, his early thoughts deserve recognition. His January 1869 thesis entitled "Kokuzei Kōmoku" (National Imperatives) marks one of the first proposals to introduce the grand concept of public education for every child. It also delineates the broad goals of the modernists in truly radical terms: to dismantle the constraints of feudalism through education. Conforming to the first phrase of the fifth declaration of the Charter Oath, that is, "knowledge shall be sought throughout the world," it would eventually play out in an historical confrontation over the direction of Japanese education for the next century. Itō's idealistic plan for education pitted the modernists against the traditionalists, who viewed the purpose of education primarily in terms of the second phrase of the fifth Charter Oath, "to strengthen imperial rule." He wrote,

> The purpose of education is to disseminate to all the people learning (*gakujutsu*) from throughout the world, and to introduce the knowledge of science and arts existent in other countries. Japan is now undergoing a cultural revolution (*bunmei kaika*) that western countries have already experienced. We now have the opportunity to abolish the old abuses (*kyūhei*) derived over hundreds of years, and to open the eyes and ears of the nation. If we fail to provide a basic education for all of our people, they will remain deaf and dumb, and without vision. That is why a great school system (*daigakkō*) should be established right down to an elementary school in every community. All of our people should be filled with knowledge.[15]

Higher Education

Three schools formed the core of higher education at the end of the Tokugawa period. They each served a distinct purpose. The Igakujo school of medicine employed Dutch medical practices as learned by Japanese doctors through Dutch teachers and textbooks from an earlier era. The Shōhei Gakkō functioned as the highest institution of Confucian studies that originated under the Tokugawa regime. It also included a rejuvenation of Japanese studies incorporated within Shintoism. And, finally, the Kaiseijo taught foreign languages and studies as western powers increased pressure on the Tokugawa government to eliminate strict barriers to foreign contacts.

The Shōhei Gakkō, the Kaiseijo renamed Kaisei Gakkō, and the Igakujo renamed Igakkō were reopened in mid 1868 when educational policy was being determined by nationalist scholars.[16] The intention of the government was to concentrate advanced learning at the Shōhei Gakkō on imperial studies to promote a national sense of identity based on the imperial tradition with its Shinto roots.[17] This was, after all, the moment of Imperial Restoration. In June, however, this provoked a bitter controversy within the Shōhei Gakkō between the Confucianists and the Shinto nationalists for supremacy. Nevertheless, in June 1869 the three schools were technically merged into a Daigakkō, the Great School, with the Shōhei Gakkō recognized as the central institution (*honkō*) within the conglomerate in spite of the internal dissension.

In the reorganization, Kaisei Gakkō of foreign studies and Igakkō of Dutch medicine continued under their separate names but as subdivisions.[18] This convenient but uneasy accommodation reflected the intent of the Five Chartered Oaths issued at the same time, calling for a combination of moral values of the past with modern western ideas. By this time Guido Verbeck had been called to Tokyo from Nagasaki by government officials and appointed to the teaching staff of Kaisei Gakkō in April 1869.[19]

An important decision was taken by the government in July 1869, one month after the merger of the three advanced-level institutions. To address the educational needs of the country, as the new bureaus of finance, military, and so on, were being formed within government, the Daigakkō received a special assignment. Within its responsibilities a department of education was set up as a national governmental administrative organ (Seifu no Kyōiku Gyōsei Kencho).[20] It was notably sited within the main division, the honkō that contained the old Shōhei Gakkō of Confucian and imperial studies. In hindsight we now realize that this office was the forerunner of Japan's first Ministry of Education when it was separated from the higher educational institution in 1871.[21]

An inherent incompatibility among the three institutions amalgamated into one that formed the foundation of higher education in Meiji Japan laid the basis for internal dissension. Accordingly, the next stage may be the most significant one in the early development of modern higher education in Japan. First, in September 1869, the government closed the two schools for nobility in Kyoto in anticipation of a new higher education institution in the former capital.[22] It materialized many years later, however. Then in December the Daigakkō, which had incorporated the three institutions of Shōhei, Kaisei, and Igakkō, was separated into two under the general heading of Daigaku (Great School). The new names identified the two remaining streams of higher education. One was called Daigaku Higashikō, the Great Eastern School, and the other the Daigaku Nankō, the Great Southern School, reflecting the site of each main building on campus.[23] The intent of Daigaku Higashi was clear from the beginning. It was a new name for the old school of Dutch medicine, the Igakkō.

The fundamental question still officially unanswered involved a crisis of legitimacy. Which school from the Tokugawa era, the Shōhei Gakkō of Confucianist-nationalist studies or the Kaisei Gakkō of western studies, would form the core of the curriculum of the new institution now called Daigaku Nankō? The conflict between the traditionalists, the Confucianists and Shinto nationalists, and the modernizers within the old Daigakkō for supremacy of the new school intensified. The confrontation, in historical hindsight, was a precursor of the ideological struggles that would dominate the early Meiji reforms of education.

The decision concerning institutional supremacy presented a clear signal of government policy for modern higher education that affected the nation thereafter. In February 1870, the government published new university regulations demonstrating that western specialists appointed to policy-making positions were in the ascendancy. In the major reforms to take effect in July, the Daigakkō (honkō) was closed, in effect, shutting down the old Confucian-nationalist stream of higher education, under protest especially by the nationalist scholars who had previously held great influence.[24] The old Kaisei stream of western studies was then designated as the main course (honkō).[25]

In addition, in the recruitment of new students, priority was given to candidates with a preparatory background in western studies.[26] The new direction of higher education was further solidified when, also in July 1870, Guido Verbeck was appointed head teacher (kyōtō) of Daigaku Nankō, in effect, the president.[27] Incredibly, a Dutchman from America had suddenly been placed in charge of Japan's highest national institution of education, such was this foreign missionary's reputation among the leaders of the Meiji government. Many of his former students, notably Ōki Takatō, were destined to head the first Ministry of Education.

There were enormous ramifications of this decision. It meant that the imperial studies of Japanese classics and the venerable teachings of the Confucian Analects were being overshadowed by western studies in science and language as the foundation of higher education. Predictably, the new direction was not taken lightly by nationalist critics within government and from the Imperial Household. The latest moves also demonstrated that western-oriented officials within government in the Inspectorate of Schools were now making major educational decisions. It was a severe blow to the traditionalists from the old Shōhei Gakkō stream who nevertheless continued their opposition within the new institution.

To attract capable applicants from throughout the country for Daigaku Nankō under the new administration of Guido Verbeck, a novel scheme called kōshinsei was designed.[28] The recruitment primarily attracted youth from the elite samurai families, since few commoners had achieved an educational level to qualify them for advanced western studies and languages. With the old feudal fief administrative structure still in effect, the selection of new students for the single government institution of higher education in Meiji Japan was inevitably drawn from the large pool of samurai families still responsible for local government.

An announcement by the Dajōkan, the supreme organ of the new government, was circulated to each local han asking them to recommend outstanding students from their clan for the new school. The number of nominees depended on the value of rice production in each fief—the old feudal system of evaluating wealth according to rice harvests still prevailed. There may not have been a better method, but the procedure itself epitomized the transition between the ancient and the modern. Fiefs evaluated at 150,000 koku of rice production sent three students between the ages of sixteen and twenty to Tokyo; those with over 50,000 koku sent two students, and the rest one each. The hans paid all expenses.[29]

Three hundred ten recommended students arrived in Tokyo in late 1870 from throughout Japan, continuing the tradition from the feudal era when capable local samurai youth were attracted to the capital for advanced education.[30] Among them was Isawa Shūji, who became one of the leading educators of the Meiji period, serving as president of the prestigious Tokyo Teacher Training College after studying in America.[31] His selection for higher education under this unique method illustrates that ability, although still primarily restricted to the samurai class, played a major role in recruiting the future leaders of the nation.

Daigaku Nankō was divided into three departments of foreign languages and studies, a hangover from the old days. Each student had to choose a division. Two hundred nineteen enrolled in the English Department, seventy-four in the French Department, and seventeen in the German Department. The final list of students was completed for the beginning of classes in January 1871, with Verbeck at the helm.[32] The year 1871 brought further critical changes in higher education. In July Daigaku Nankō and Daigaku Tōkō simply became Nankō and Tōkō. The new curriculum of Nankō under Verbeck's administration was divided into four departments: law, literature, science, and medical, as in western universities. Significantly, there was no department of Confucian or imperial studies.[33]

By the beginning of 1871, three years after the Meiji Restoration, the school had deteriorated academically during the internal struggles for supremacy. A leading member of government, Kido Takayoshi, claimed that "There are a great many students, and they are totally undisciplined."[34] This was a primary reason why the recruitment for a new student body was carried out. Also, in the immediate rush to provide teachers for the curriculum that included foreign studies and languages, many unqualified foreigners locally available had been hired as professors. Verbeck set out to rectify the unacceptable conditions by "ousting the butchers, the sailors, and braumeisters from the ports who had been attracted by the salaries."[35]

Guido Verbeck's emergence as the chief educational officer of the single most important educational institution under the government at this initial stage of the modernization period placed him in a critical position. In a letter to William Griffis at Rutgers College in New Jersey, who shortly thereafter became a faculty member of the school at Verbeck's initiative, the new foreign head of the school clarified his authority to bring the overdue changes: "I have the casting vote." He then revealed his plans for reforming the highest public educational institution in Meiji Japan. "Our staff, I hope, will gradually come up to my 'beau ideal.' All or nearly all of the teachers engaged at Yokohama are gradually to be replaced by regularly trained professional school teachers from home, which is an excellent thing indeed. The school goes on tolerably well."[36]

Under Verbeck's able direction, the curriculum for a student body of just over 200 youth from samurai families was revamped. Verbeck, whose native language was Dutch, became director of the English Department as well as Head Teacher for the school of seventeen teachers. Eight foreigners taught English as well as physics, chemistry, and literature, all in the English language. Five Frenchmen taught French, and physics, mathematics, and literature in French. And finally four Germans taught the identical science courses plus German literature and language.

With the appointment of new foreign faculty under the administration of the Dutchman Guido Verbeck, technically a Christian missionary from the Dutch Reformed Church of America, the die was finally cast. The old Kaiseijo of foreign studies had, for all intents and purposes, displaced the old Shōhei Gakkō of Confucian-nationalist studies at the premier public institution of higher education. In the process, imperial studies and Confucian teachings were excluded from the curriculum. The modernizers had emerged victorious during this early encounter. Nevertheless the nagging issue contrasting antagonistic purposes of education arose periodically throughout the next two decades in the inevitable struggles between tradition and modernization of Japanese higher education.

On October 5, 1871, Emperor Meiji, demonstrating a continuing interest in the modernization of education, recognized the efforts of Verbeck in rehabilitating the school. He invited several foreign teachers from Nankō to the palace. Among them was Guido Verbeck. The emperor took the unusual opportunity to recognize Verbeck's contribution to Japanese education in a simple and straightforward manner: "Since you have stayed in Japan for a very long time and have had a great influence on students, speaking Japanese very well which makes your words more effective, I am very pleased."[37] As a result of Verbeck's reforms in both the curricula and the faculty, by the end of the 1871 school year Japan finally had a national institution worthy of recognition as the first public institution of higher education in the modern era. The school, which became Tokyo University in 1877, functioned essentially as a foreign-language school of science. It was frequently referred to in the English press as a polytechnic school.[38] It was now prepared to carry out its primary purpose of educating leaders for modern Japan.

During the first three years after the Meiji Restoration, the former government school of Dutch medicine, the Igakusho, also underwent a reformation similar in magnitude to that experienced by Nankō under Verbeck. In December 1869, when Igakusho was renamed the Daigaku Higashikō, or the Great Eastern School, a major decision was taken. Officials at the school were aware of the advancements of medicine in Germany, and that some of their Dutch medical texts then in use were translated from the original in German. The question arose whether this was the opportune moment to introduce German medicine into Japan, replacing Dutch medical influence. Guido Verbeck, former mentor of many officials making the decision, was now in Tokyo not only administering western studies at the highest educational institution but also acting as an adviser to the new government. He was consulted on the question of whether German or Dutch medicine should be adopted. Although a Dutchman himself, Verbeck urged his old students now in high government positions to adopt the superior German medical studies for Japan. His advice was followed.[39]

The transfer of medical studies from Dutch to German was put in place when a request for medical specialists was promptly submitted by the Japanese government to the German government. In July 1871, two German doctors arrived to find that the facilities at the medical institution were totally inadequate for a modern system of medical studies. The reform of medical education got under way at Higashikō when German doctors were confronted with students who had little knowledge of critical subjects such as anatomy or mathematics. The foreigners had to begin at the beginning with the basics of western science in order to modernize medical education in Japan. From that moment onward modern medical education in Japan was based on the German model.[40]

When the two national schools of advanced learning underwent major, and sometimes chaotic, reforms during the initial years of the Meiji government from 1868 to 1871, the most famous private institution of the day filled the vacuum. Fukuzawa Yukichi's Keio Shijuku, newly named Gijuku, was the preeminent functioning institution during this period. It continued to educate many of the future leaders from the samurai class recruited from all areas of the country, as it did in the Tokugawa period. Continuing the tradition from feudal Japan, Keio graduates filled teaching positions in the proliferating schools throughout the country.[41]

Education of Peasant Youth: The Terakoya

At the time of the Meiji Restoration of 1868, although educational opportunities under the former feudal Tokugawa government were primarily designed for the governing samurai families, there were also limited educational opportunities for children of peasant or farm families. In the absence of a governmental policy at the national or local level to provide schools for the common people, private schools spontaneously emerged that catered mostly, although not exclusively, to the lower levels of society. They were particularly associated with the peasant class. Estimated at around 15,000 at the end of the feudal period, these unregulated private schools collectively known as terakoya operated independently from government supervision and finance.[42]

The generic name of terakoya, cherished in contemporary Japan, derived from an earlier period when dedicated Buddhist priests provided a rudimentary education for a few local children in their temples. By the time of the Meiji Restoration in 1868, the number of local private schools for nonsamurai youth, who were neglected by government and purposely excluded from fief schools, had proliferated far beyond temple compounds. The venerable name of terakoya remained, covering a broad grouping of schools for the common people.

Often run by lower-ranking samurai to generate extra income, as well as by priests, Confucian scholars, and literate commoners, this broad-based category of local schools operated unrestricted by the central Tokugawa government. They provided a basic education for countless local rural children in the three Rs, with the stress on calligraphy. At the same time many were passionately committed to morality steeped in Confucian tradition, perpetuating commonly held moral values. They were not only located in the rural areas. Towns were well served with terakoya sprinkled haphazardly around the community for parents interested and financially able to enroll their children, overwhelmingly sons. Similar to the fief schools for the ruling samurai families, a national tradition in education steeped in Confucian teachings for the commoners evolved from the terakoya, revered to this very day. An earlier historian placed special emphasis on the unique relationship developed between student and teacher in these schools reflecting Confucian tradition.

> The Terakoya were characterized by an intensely personal relationship between the master and his pupils. In many cases the pupils even lived in the temple compound, but whether as a boarder or day pupil, the boy upon entering the school presented offerings to the students already in attendance and to the master, and while begging for permission to study, promised to obey the master in all things and to submit to punishment when necessary. No regular fees were charged, the master depending upon the gratitude of the pupils as expressed in volunteer gifts, and the ties thus formed between the teacher and the student often persisted in lifelong affection and respect.[43]

The local terakoya schools of premodern Japan consequently had a powerful purpose beyond the monotony of calligraphy practice. They were respected by

Figure 6. Terakoya Classroom.
From Ronald Dore, *Education in Tokygawa Japan* (Berkeley: University of California Press, 1965), 266. Reproduced by permission.

many in the community for their moral teachings gained from Chinese classics used in the practice of calligraphy. It was often symbolized by a picture hanging from the classroom wall of the venerable Tenjinsama, the patron saint of learning. The terakoya incorporated a sense of morality considered as spiritual education (*seishin kyōiku*) and teaching proper manners (*reigi sakuhō*), as well as instilling a sense of discipline, perseverance, and respect for learning. Punishment, standing for long periods at a time, and so on, was employed to maintain discipline. The old saying, if the heart is correct, so will be the calligraphy (*kokoro tadashikereba, fude tadashi*),[44] summed up the philosophy of the terakoya school conforming to Confucian beliefs that dominated the society of Tokugawa Japan.

Terakoya played a unique role in the history of Japan that is recognized in modern Japan. The contemporary Kabuki theater periodically presents one of its most popular plays simply titled *Terakoya* (The Village School), which provokes Japanese with feelings of nostalgia for the premodern days of Japan. The opening scene paints a picture that has endured through the ages. Eight young boys ranging from about five to fifteen years old are seated on the tatami floor in the starkly bare home of the teacher. They are dressed identically in long black kimonos, hair drawn back tightly. Seated behind a small low table, each student is arduously practicing the Chinese characters with ink brush on a long paper. The narrator explains that they are taught that a written sentence is worth one thousand pieces of gold; a word (one character) worth one hundred.

Following the civil war that brought about the Meiji Restoration of 1868, many terakoya reopened with the same teacher serving the same clientele in the traditional manner. Some offered a smattering of new subjects such as elementary foreign-language training or the rudiments of mathematics. Most remained consistent with the purpose of terakoya education as morality, the primary attraction to many parents willing to pay a fee to enroll their children, mostly boys, as before. The modern era in primary education had not yet emerged. It would be launched by the new Ministry of Education, founded in 1871, with the proclamation of the Gakusei, the First National Plan for Education of 1872. Based solely on western models, the Gakusei was designed to provide an elementary education for all Japanese children regardless of social class or gender. It marks the true beginning of modern education in Japan and the demise of the traditional terakoya schools.

PART II

THE FIRST DECADE OF MODERN EDUCATION, 1870s

The American Model

4 *The Gakusei*

THE FIRST NATIONAL PLAN
FOR EDUCATION, 1872

Educational historians traditionally attribute the beginning of modern education in Japan to the Gakusei, the First National Plan for Education, issued on August 8, 1872.[1] Implemented from April 1873, five years after the Meiji Restoration, the Gakusei is the most significant historical document in the annals of Japanese education.[2] The one Japanese who more than any other laid the foundation for, and set the general purposes of, the First National Plan for Education was the towering intellectual Fukuzawa Yukichi. He thus deserves recognition as a pioneer of modern Japanese education, a characterization not infrequently attributed to him. Although not an officer of the Ministry of Education bureau that designed the Gakusei, which fell under the responsibility of Mitsukuri Rinshō, Fukuzawa's influence on early modern Japanese education nevertheless was unsurpassed, extending far beyond his private Keio Gijuku school.

Fukuzawa was born in 1834 in a comparatively low-ranking samurai family in a feudal domain of the southern island of Kyushu. It was not destined to become one of the four major clans that led the overthrow of the Tokugawa regime in 1868 ushering in the Meiji Restoration. His circumstances as a child in a lower-ranking samurai family proved to be of great significance. Although a member of the elite samurai governing class by birth, he detested the rigid social order within the samurai world that locked him into an unyielding ranking system. He particularly resented the rigid custom that compelled him to treat other samurai children his age from higher-ranking families, regardless of their ability, with deference in play, language, and study. Early on he became determined to break from the bonds of feudal tradition to become an independent human being. From early childhood, independence and freedom became an obsession in his life and in his prolific writings.

His love of, and natural ability with, foreign languages led him through the traditional study of the Chinese language and classics as a samurai youth. This was followed by an intensive study of the Dutch language during the later years of the Tokugawa era, when the Dutch were recognized as the sole connection to the outside world. He spent the year 1854 in southern Japan at Nagasaki, the center of Dutch studies. From there the peripatetic Fukuzawa spent three years in Osaka where he furthered his studies in the Dutch language and Dutch science. Clan officials then ordered him to Edo (Tokyo) to teach Dutch to clan officials stationed in the capital. He walked the three-hundred-mile stretch to get there on the famed Tōkaidō Road.[3]

Figure 7. Fukuzawa Yukichi.
From Benjamin Duke, *Ten Great Educators of Modern Japan* (Tokyo: Tokyo University Press, 1989), 19.

When the American Black Ships entered Tokyo waters in 1853–1854, Fukuzawa traveled to the open port shortly thereafter. In one of the most famous moments in modern Japanese history related in standard histories, he painfully encountered the inexorable trends of the day.

> To my chagrin, when I tried to speak with them [foreigners], no one seemed to understand me at all. Nor was I able to understand anything spoken by a single one of all the foreigners I met. Neither could I read anything on the signboards over the shops. . . . There was not a single recognizable word in any of the inscriptions or in any speech. . . . I realized that a man would have to be able to read and converse in English to be recognized as a scholar in Western subjects in the coming time. . . . On the very next day after returning from Yokohama, I took up a new aim in life and determined to begin the study of English.[4]

Following the signing of a treaty with the United States that opened several ports to foreigners in 1859, the Tokugawa government sent its first diplomatic delegation to America the following year. Through influential acquaintances Fukuzawa managed to secure an appointment on the mission. At the age of twenty-five he found himself in San Francisco in March 1860.[5] He spent the next fifty-two days in the San Francisco area witnessing some of the most advanced technological achievements available in the United States in 1860. For example, the use of steam to power engines was a marvel to behold. Fukuzawa was able to observe the American home of a local merchant, Charles Walcott Brooks, who was hired by the Japanese government as a west coast representative.[6] Fukuzawa later used him to supply American books for his private school as one source to keep up-to-date western textbooks available in Japan.[7]

There was no outstanding result from Fukuzawa's first trip to the West. He did, however, purchase a copy of *Webster's Dictionary*, the first importation of this famous dictionary into Japan.[8] Upon return home amid intensifying antiforeign sentiment swirling throughout Japan, Fukuzawa was immediately employed by the government in the translation bureau. The government then decided to send a second mission to the West in 1862. Fukuzawa eagerly sought an appointment as a translator, which was finally granted. On January 22 he departed with the embassy on a British ship scheduled to visit Britain (forty-three days), Holland (forty-three days), France (thirty-nine days), Prussia (eighteen days), Russia (thirty-nine days), and Portugal (nine days) on a trip that would prove to be the turning point in his life.[9]

In comparison to the month-and-a-half visit to one American city in 1860, the nearly ten-month trip throughout Europe in 1862 provided Fukuzawa with a prolonged opportunity to observe western societies firsthand. He took voluminous notes in every country he visited. The trip also enabled him to purchase a number of English-language texts in England. Many would within a short time appear as textbooks in his private school in Tokyo. The experience in Europe, combined with his earlier trip to America, rendered Fukuzawa Japan's leading authority on the West in the early 1860s.

The most important result of these two journeys to the West was his conviction that Japan, as a result of three hundred years of Tokugawa feudalism, had fallen far behind western societies technologically and educationally. The supremacy of the West in virtually all areas was overwhelming. He concluded that the nation was consequently in danger of losing its independence as western imperial powers gained control over backward nations throughout Asia, Africa, and Latin America. Acutely aware of the dangerous international environment that confronted Japan in the 1860, Fukuzawa viewed the period as a crisis of national sovereignty that could only be met with drastic reforms to develop a prosperous country with a powerful military component.

Once again, upon Fukuzawa's return from the West at the end of 1862, the nation was undergoing traumatic antiwestern hysteria. Disgruntled samurai carried out random acts of terror. But this time there were murders of westerners as well as shelling of foreign vessels passing near Japanese ports, which provoked retaliatory bombardments by western warships (covered elsewhere in this study). Fukuzawa himself felt endangered as a leading proponent of western studies and languages. He noted that "All students and interpreters of western languages continually risked their lives. For thirteen or fourteen years I did not once venture out of door at night."[10] In spite of the hostile environment, he organized the notes taken while abroad into his first book, which shook the very foundation of Japanese society. He appropriately titled it *Conditions in the West (Seiyō no Jijō)*, and it sparked one of the most dramatic movements in Japanese history, often called the grand awakening to the West.

The final opportunity for Fukuzawa to travel to the West during the feudal era became available in 1867. The Tokugawa government sent a mission to Washington and New York to settle the purchase of ships from an American company. The Japanese, traveling via Panama, arrived in New York on April 22 for a four-month visit in the United States. Shortly thereafter the mission traveled to Washington, where they met President Andrew Johnson. Fukuzawa used this trip to purchase a large number of books for his school.[11] He attributed the subsequent use of the books he purchased in America at his private school as the primary factor in their widespread acceptance in many schools. "Use of American textbooks in my school was the cause of the adoption all over the country of American books for the following ten years or more."[12]

A curious byproduct of the 1867 trip to America occurred when representatives of the Tokugawa government, motivated by the purchase of so many English books by Fukuzawa, hastily made a huge purchase of English books for the government. Unprepared for the endeavor, they hastily requested the American State Department to make the selection. The final shipment weighing ten tons included, among others, 13,000 copies of elementary readers, grammars, and math books, 2,500 copies of *Webster's Dictionary*, and 600 history books.[13] The episode illustrates how western books found their way to Japan during the feudal era through chance opportunities.

Of all of the results of Fukuzawa's three trips to the West in the 1860s, his initial best-selling book, *Conditions in the West*, to which he added supplements from time to time, proved the most provocative. The significance of this publication relates not only to the content, a revelation to the Japanese, but its authorship. The book is the first account of conditions in the West as observed firsthand through the eyes of a Japanese. Until this time all written accounts and images of the mysterious West available to the Japanese reading class were filtered through translations of works originally written by western authors. Fukuzawa's book appealed to the Japanese with the authenticity of a Japanese author.

Among the many areas of society covered in *Conditions in the West,* Fukuzawa reveals his particular interest in education. In a section under schools (*gakkō*) in volume 1, he makes a description that must have been startling to his Japanese readers unaccustomed to such conditions in their country.

> In every western country there is not a town or village without a school. The schools are founded both by the government and by private citizens. All children, boys and girls, enter the elementary school at age six or seven. They first learn to read and write and then study such subjects as the history of their country, geography, arithmetic, fundamentals of science, art, and music.[14]

The sales of *Conditions in the West,* which brought the author unexpected income, motivated Fukuzawa in his systematic approach to take the next step. He published his second book, which also achieved best-selling status. *The Advancement of Learning (Gakumon no Susume,* 1872), illustrates his evolving plan for the modernization of Japan. It laid out the purposes of education that would enable Japan to modernize in order to achieve parity with the West. According to his logic, the independence of the nation depended upon the development of an independent spirit of each citizen of the country. Ultimately the primary instrument to achieve that goal was education.[15]

The Advancement of Learning begins with a simple but profound statement that has become ingrained in the history books of modern Japan: "No individual is born above another." From this perspective he then repeatedly refers to the symbiotic linkage between the freedom and independence of every Japanese and the freedom and independence of the country (*kojin no jiyū dokuritsu to kokka no jiyū dokuritsu*). Without the independent spirit of the individual, the independence of the state cannot be achieved or preserved (*isshin dokuritsu shite—kuni dokuritsu suru*).[16] In effect, education has a practical purpose. Every individual must acquire through education the practical skills necessary to earn an income to live an independent life. In contrast, the feudal tradition whereby samurai devoted endless hours to the study of calligraphy and the Chinese classics, which Fukuzawa underwent, had become obsolete in a modern technical society he envisioned for Japan.

The popularity of Fukuzawa's books that introduced revolutionary western concepts was indicative of his influence on the leaders of the Meiji government. To a man, they had to have read both *Conditions in the West* and *The Advancement of Learning*, as well as Fukuzawa's later works such as *An Outline of a Theory of Civilization* (*Bummeiron no Gairyoku*). The demand for his books presumably went beyond the ruling elite. According to a local newspaper of the day, pirated editions (*nisehan*) reached such a level that Fukuzawa personally appealed to local governments to strictly prosecute unauthorized editions of his publications.[17] Consequently the assumption can be made that no other Japanese in the final years of the Tokugawa period and the opening years of the Meiji era exerted a greater influence on the literate classes, particularly the decision makers of the country, than did Fukuzawa. The writings of the central core of the Meiji leaders were sprinkled with ideas derived from Fukuzawa's writings.

Applying his basic convictions on independence to its ultimate conclusion, Fukuzawa made a major and somewhat curious decision early on in his career. In order to preserve his own independence, he decided that he would not play an official political role within government. The history of the early Meiji period is centered on the role of the Meiji government led by outstanding samurai leaders. Fukuzawa stands out among them as the most prominent figure of the early Meiji era who functioned outside the government. He cherished his role as an independent thinker who practiced the principles that he promoted. It was this unprecedented position that Fukuzawa had attained which enabled him to exert an inordinate influence on Ministry of Education officials responsible for designing the first national school system in Japan. They ritually visited his office on the Mito campus of the Keio Gijuku to seek his advice on modern education, which he generously extended.

The French Connection: Mitsukuri Rinshō

One of the Ministry of Education officials who frequented Fukuzawa's office during this critical period was Mitsukuri Rinshō, who was responsible for the preparation of the First National Plan for Education as head of the bureau that wrote it. He was Japan's first great linguist, attaining an impressive level of proficiency in five languages, including two Asian and three western. To achieve such an accomplishment by the age of twenty-one during the Tokugawa era, when Japan was officially closed to the outside world, illustrates his unusual linguistic abilities. It also demonstrates that opportunities for foreign-language study were available in feudal Japan to those inspired and positioned to take advantage of them.

Mitsukuri's knowledge of French, the last one he mastered, qualified him to represent the Tokugawa government at the great Paris World's Fair of 1867. Upon his return to Japan after the fall of the feudal regime in 1868, the French-oriented first director of the Ministry of Education in the new Meiji government, Etō Shimpei, appointed him to head the ministerial bureau commissioned to draw up Japan's first plan for a national system of education. In the history of modern Japanese education the Gakusei turned out to be the most significant connecting link with the French tradition in education. Mitsukuri was the ministry official directly responsible for that relationship.

The connection between Mituskuri Rinshō, French education, and the modern school system of Japan has its roots in Mitsukuri's childhood.[18] He was born in 1846 in Edo of a samurai family living in the house of the Tsuyama clan, of no particular significance. His father died shortly thereafter. In a twist of fate he was turned over to his grandfather, a specialist in the Dutch language. As a samurai child, however, he was first introduced to the Chinese language at the age of five. By ten, as he progressed rapidly in Chinese, his grandfather sent him to a teacher of Chinese classics and calligraphy for more advanced study.

By the time Mitsukuri was thirteen years old, his grandfather, who had already introduced Dutch to his young ward at home, then sent him for further study with a Japanese who specialized in teaching the Dutch language. At the age of fourteen he was translating Dutch into Japanese. With the boom in English studies, he then began to study English under a private tutor. In 1863 his English proficiency reached a level whereby he was assigned by the Tokugawa government at the age of sixteen to the prestigious Kaiseijo school of foreign studies, the forerunner of Tokyo University. While there he edited an English dictionary. From the age of nineteen he collaborated with the great Fukuzawa Yukichi on English translations of treaties and various diplomatic materials for the foreign affairs office of the government.[19]

A colleague in the foreign affairs office was then sent to France by the government to study the French language. Greatly impressed by the widespread use of French as the language of diplomacy throughout Europe, the friend upon returning to Japan strongly urged Mitsukuri to learn French. With that inspiration, he became determined to master the French language. Fortuitously the Japanese government had just decided to enter an exhibit at the forthcoming Paris International Exposition in 1867, the first time Japan participated in a world's fair. Mitsukuri applied to join the Japanese delegation. His acceptance further motivated him to concentrate on French-language study. On January 12, 1867, he left for France, arriving at the port of Marseilles fifty days later.

Mitsukuri was determined to make the most of the opportunity to sharpen his linguistic skills while serving the interests of the Tokugawa government. He spent much of the time translating materials at the Paris Exposition into Japanese—for example, data on the new Swiss telegraph that later took him to Switzerland for several weeks. By the time he returned to France he was reading French newspapers and even negotiated a business contract in French.

Unexpectedly, in the midst of Mitsukuri's adventures in France, the Tokugawa government, which had officially sent Mitsukuri on this mission to Europe, collapsed in January 1868. A new government in the name of Emperor Meiji grasped political leadership of the country. Like other Japanese then studying abroad, Mitsukuri experienced great anxieties over his delicate situation. Within days after the Tokugawa downfall, he sailed from France, arriving home on February 24, 1868, the year henceforth designated in Japanese history as Meiji Gannen, denoting the great transition from feudalism to modernism.

Mitsukuri's well-known linguistic skills in western languages were immediately put to work by the new government with his appointment to teach at his old school, the Kaiseijo, the center of foreign-language study.[20] He was shortly thereafter assigned as a government translator working primarily on French-language materials, earning the equivalent of the doctoral degree in languages in 1869 at the age of twenty-four.[21]

Mitsukuri's moment of historical consequence, however, occurred with his assignment, in October 1870, to the Gakkō Torishirabe Goyōgakari, the Committee to Investigate the Schools, the forerunner of the Ministry of Education.[22] In fact this group of individuals, shortly thereafter to include the equally youthful Mori Arinori, recently returned from his unusual exploits with the Harris colony in rural New York,[23] developed the initial proposal for establishing the Ministry of Education for Japan. This special group of progressive Japanese with strong connections to the West played an important role in setting the general direction of education that ultimately became official government policy. Thus from the beginning of the Meiji Period, Mitsukuri Rinshō was a prominent figure in modern Japanese education.

Founding of the Ministry of Education, July 1871

The Gakkō Torishirabe Goyōgakari, the Committee to Investigate the Schools to which Mitsukuri was appointed, drew up a proposal to establish a bureau of educational affairs. In effect, this committee served as a preparatory office for the Ministry of Education since many of its members, including Mitsukuri, became officials of the ministry when it opened on July 18, 1871. Etō Shimpei, a samurai from Saga han with French proclivities, was appointed as the temporary director of the ministry (*mumbu daisuke*) on the day it began functioning.[24]

The second key figure in the Ministry of Education during the first days of its existence was Ōki Takatō, also a samurai from Saga han. He became director (*mumbukyo*) of the ministry on July 28, 1871, following the first ten heady days under Etō.[25] In fact, the two worked together in choosing the staff since Ōki was destined to follow Etō once the initial appointments were decided. Consequently Ōki held a strategic position from the beginning. Etō and Ōki were coincidentally students of Guido Verbeck in Nagasaki during the early 1860s before the Tokugawa regime came to a close. It was this student-teacher relationship between Verbeck and top government officials such as Etō and Ōki that led to a governmental request that he move from Nagasaki to Tokyo in 1869 in order to participate in the modernization program. It was also during Ōki's term at the ministry that Verbeck was chosen to head the only higher education institution under the ministry, Daigaku Nankō, as well as serving as an advisor to the Ministry of Education.

The priority of Etō, first director of the ministry immediately followed by Ōki Takatō, was to plan a national school system under control of the government.[26] One Japanese historian described the first ten days of the new ministry as one of the most critical periods in modern Japanese education chiefly because of the appointment of Etō Shimpei as the chief officer. The vital contribution Etō made to the modern system of education within a span of ten days is attributed to his selection of the officials to staff the first educational ministry in modern Japan. He was then promptly reassigned to head the new Ministry of Justice on July 28.[27]

Etō Shimpei and his immediate successor Ōki Takatō set the fundamental direction of the Ministry of Education for its first decade by appointing fifty-four officials, the overwhelming majority classified as specialists on the West (*yōgakusha*).[28] This contrasted sharply with the first three officials appointed by the government in 1868, shortly after the Restoration, to reopen schools following the demise of the Tokugawa era. During their period of influence the bias was toward traditional education. Due to Etō's strategic choice of ministry officials, the influx of western-oriented officers effectively brought the initial period of Meiji education, with its close relationship to Japanese and Confucian studies, to a close. From 1871 western studies were in the ascendancy under the direction of the Ministry of Education.

Even though the Ministry of Education was initially staffed primarily by modernists with a western bias, their educational background should not be overlooked. At the time of their appointment they were all samurai by birth who had themselves been educated in feudal clan schools during the Tokugawa era. In their upbringing, they were steeped in Chinese classics based on Confucian teachings. Consequently the most significant characteristic of the pioneers of modern Japanese education was their common background as products of feudal Tokugawa Japan.

One of the early organizational measures taken by Ōki as the head of the ministry succeeding Etō was the establishment of a special office, the Gakusei Torishirabegakari, or the Deliberative Committee for a National School System, on December 2, 1871.[29] Its single mission was to draw up the First National Plan for

Education, that is, the Gakusei. Ōki had the critical responsibility of choosing the members. It was his decision to appoint Mitsukuri Rinshō, widely recognized as a French specialist with an impressive number of translations including a document on the administration of French education, to head the bureau.[30] That appointment placed Mitsukuri in an influential position in designing Japan's first plan for a modern national school system. Since the Gakusei represents the single most important document in Japanese educational history, Mitsukuri's central role in its formulation renders him one of the key figures in early modern Japan.

The timing of the establishment of the Ministry of Education in July 1871, should be placed in historical perspective. Of overriding importance, the government abolished the feudal han system to be replaced by a prefecture or state system of governance from August 28, 1871.[31] Each of the newly created regional units of government, the seventy-two prefectures and three large cities, were then placed under the administrative control of a chihōkan, a local governor, appointed by the central government.[32] From that moment onward the government in Tokyo was empowered with making national decisions, including those concerning education.

With the prefectural system of administration in place from 1871, the new Ministry of Education was then in a position to construct a national public school system. As long as the country remained divided among several hundred feudal clans each subservient to a local daimyo, a national plan for education was inconceivable. With the formation of a centralized form of government, a centralized system of education designed by the newly organized Ministry of Education inevitably followed.

When the ministry's internal bureau responsible for the Gakusei, the first national plan for education, began working on the original draft under the direction of Mitsukuri Rinshō, all but two of the twelve assigned officials were recognized as authorities on western studies (yōgakusha). Etō Shimpei, the first director of the Ministry of Education, and Ōki Takatō, the current director, as well as Mitsukuri had carefully screened them. Of the remaining two nonwestern officials, one specialized in Japanese studies (kokugakusha) and the other in Chinese studies (kangakusha).[33]

By this time many translations of documents from several western countries prepared mainly at the Kaiseijo, the school of western studies, were available to the government. Among them, according to the memoirs of Tsuji Shinji who worked on the original draft of the Gakusei, there was one primary source of reference in drawing up this historical proposal. Entitled the Futsukoku Gakusei, literally the French Gakusei, it described the French educational system.[34]

Although it is difficult to pinpoint the original French documents used for the translation, the Futsukoku Gakusei outlined the highly centralized, uniform administrative structure of French education. It was based on the Napoleonic imperial university that theoretically included every school and student in the land. All French teachers were subject to the University of France whose head was appointed by Napoleon.[35] The Napoleonic scheme for the administration and control of French education epitomized a highly centralized system of education that appealed to the Japanese.

At this time France was considered by Japanese leaders as a nation with high cultural standards. Among government circles the French legal system was already deemed superior to that of other western countries. Mitsukuri himself had become an authority on French law as the translator of the French penal code, the French civil law code, and the French common law code. By using France as a model, the Japanese in authority believed that Japan could rapidly become a modern state as well.[36] By choosing the highly structured, easily understood French educational administrative system as a model, the first comprehensive plan for a national school system in Japan was drawn up in the extraordinary period of less than two months.

The historical development of the French Gakusei has relevancy for the study of the Japanese Gakusei, since both grew out of a social and political revolution. Under the Napoleonic regime, the famous University of France was designed and implemented into law in 1808, giving the state a monopoly over education. The entire system was centralized and organized under government control through this one all-encompassing institution. The basic principle of state control over education for the benefit of the state reflected Napoleon's attitude toward education as stipulated in his decree: "There shall be constituted under the title of Imperial University a body charged exclusively with instruction and public education throughout the Empire. No school, no educational institution of any kind whatsoever shall be permitted to be established outside the Imperial University."[37]

In retrospect, the American, British, German, or French administrative model could have been chosen for Japan in 1872 by Mitsukuri and his team, since there were many translated materials on education for each of these leading western countries. However America did not then, nor does it now, support a national school system with central control in Washington under a Ministry of Education. The British were just testing a form of Ministry of Education, although most schools were either directly under, or deeply influenced by, the Church of England or other Christian bodies. Germanic countries prior to the German unification under Bismarck in 1870 did not have a national school system either. France stood alone among western powers at the time of the Meiji Restoration with the most developed, although far from complete, national school system growing out of the Napoleonic era. It was a natural decision by the Mitsukuri bureau to adopt the French model of educational administration for Japan's first attempt at a national school system, placing the control of education in the hands of the ministry.

Mitsukuri's team completed the first draft of the Gakusei by February 1872. The second was finished by March, only a few months after the team began its daunting assignment. It then took over four months for the Ministry of Education to secure its approval by the top decision-making organ of the government on August 2, 1872. It was officially proclaimed the following day for implementation with the opening of the new school year in April 1873.[38]

The four-month period of intensive negotiations that took place to receive official sanction illustrated the primary obstacle that would plague the implementation of the Gakusei from the day of its promulgation. The plan for a national school system to include every child was far too grandiose for a near-bankrupt government to provide adequate financing. All of the new governmental ministries were submitting budgets to drastically reform institutions under their jurisdiction. For example, the Ministry of Education's budget request for the Gakusei competed for national funding with the Department of the Army authorized to build a new conscript army, the Ministry of Public Works planning to expand communications and transportation facilities, and the Justice Ministry's plan to create new courts in every district.[39]

The Ministry of Finance, responsible for the national budget, reacted negatively to the initial Gakusei proposal submitted by the Ministry of Education. There were no concrete provisions to finance the gigantic plan to support the tens of thousands of new public elementary schools mandated in it. The financial bureau demanded revisions to meet the austere economic realities confronting the government. Negotiations caused a delay in the approval process as budgetary revisions were hastily submitted by the Ministry of Education.

Finally, in Japanese fashion, the ministries of Finance and Education forged a budgetary compromise. Inevitably the result sewed the seeds of widespread local opposition to the implementation of the Gakusei from the outset. Not only was the ministry's budget for implementing the Gakusei plan cut in half by the Ministry of Finance, the method to finance the remaining amount of the actual costs of the new schools, teachers, textbooks, and so on, was shifted to the local community. The principle that those who benefited from the new public schools should pay for them carried the day. Student tuition and local taxes must cover the major costs of the nation's first public school system.[40]

The First Plan for a National School System: A Vision of Modern Japan

The Gakusei of 1872 outlines the first public school system for the country.[41] The first factor of significance is its brevity and simplicity. The proposal in its original version covered forty-four handwritten pages with only a dozen or so lines per page. The preamble alone takes over four of the forty-four pages. Seven pages of the main text are devoted exclusively to provisions for Japanese students to study abroad, only indirectly related to the domestic school system itself. Six pages merely list names of places or curricular subjects. Perhaps in anticipation of a reaction toward the potentially enormous costs in launching the first school system for the nation, five pages are devoted to a tedious explanation of the proposed student scholarship system. The remaining two dozen pages sketch an entire school system, the ultimate in succinctness and simplicity. It was referred to appropriately as a desk plan by a leading contemporary Japanese historian.[42]

As a comprehensive plan for national education on the magnitude of the Gakusei, the original proposal is notable for the absence of a statement clarifying its purpose. In fact, that was spelled out in an accompanying preamble of four and a half of the forty-four pages signed by the Dajōkan, the unelected government body empowered to render the final decisions on official regulations. This top governing body had finally given its guarded approval after grave reservations about finances were deliberated. As noted previously, the noteworthy feature of the preamble is its similarity with Fukuzawa Yukichi's best seller *Gakumon no Susume* (The Encouragement of Learning), then ready for publication.[43] Although there is no evidence that Fukuzawa personally wrote the preamble, his influence on the Dajōkan is clearly evident in this document.

There was another source of influence on the preamble to the Gakusei that illustrates the general tone of the revolutionary spirit of the day. One of the most popular books of the early Meiji period was Nakamura Masanori's translation of *Self-Help* by the Englishman Samuel Smiles. The opening theme proclaiming that "heaven helps those who help themselves" permeates the preamble to the Gakusei. It struck a responsive chord among the leadership class. The moral value of effort and the gospel of work and industry were concepts that fit the mood of the times: "The spirit of self-help is the root of all genuine growth in the individual; and, exhibited in the lives of many, it constitutes the true source of national vigour and strength. . . . The spirit of self-help, as exhibited in the energetic action of individuals, has in all times been a marked feature in the English character, and furnishes the true measure of our power as a nation."[44] The intrinsic relationship between the individual and the power of a country, in this case Britain as envisioned by Smiles, catapulted the book into the forefront of the ideals of the Meiji decision makers.

The following preamble to the Gakusei is taken from a book in English on Japanese education published by the Ministry of Education shortly after its issuance. It can be considered as an officially authorized translation.[45]

> The acquirement of knowledge and the cultivation of talent are essential to a successful life. By education men learn to acquire property, practice learned professions, perform public services, and make themselves independent of the help of their fellow-men. Schools are designed to provide this essential education. In their various capacities they are intended to supply to all classes of men the knowledge necessary for a successful life. The simple forms of language, the methods of writing, the principles of calculation, the highest knowledge of law, politics, science and arts, the preparation of the officer for his duties, of the farmer and merchant for their occupations, the physician for his profession, all of these it is the proper function of schools to supply. Poverty and failure in the careers of life find their chief cause in the want of education. Although schools have been established for many centuries in Japan, yet so far as they have been provided by government they have been confined to the military retainers and to the upper classes. For the lower classes of society and for women, learning was regarded as beyond their sphere, and, if acquired at all, was of a limited character. Even among the higher classes the character of education was defective. Under the pretext of acquiring knowledge for the benefit of the state,

much time was spent in the useless occupation of writing poetry and composing maxims, instead of learning what would be for their own benefit or that of
the state. Recently an improved educational system has been formed, and the
methods of teaching remodeled. It is designed henceforth that education shall
not be confined to a few, but shall be so diffused that there may not be a village
with an ignorant family, nor a family with an ignorant member. Learning is no
longer to be considered as belonging to the upper classes, but is to be equally
the inheritance of nobles and gentry, farmers and artisans, males and females.

The purposes expressed in the preamble of the Gakusei, as well as the general
provisions contained in Japan's first national plan for education, can be summarized in several comprehensive statements. They reflect the official position of the
Meiji government on education at the outset of the modernization process.

1. The purpose of the new education is to develop within each student the ability to advance in life (*risshin chisan*).
2. In order to achieve this, the new curriculum must avoid the feudal teachings
   of the past that proved meaningless, to be replaced with new courses that
   will enable the individual to advance in life with the technological knowledge
   according to the chosen field of endeavor.
3. In contrast to the old schools, each serving a particular social class, all students should attend school regardless of social background so that no family
   has an uneducated member.
4. Since the local community will primarily benefit from the school, it must be
   financed by the local community.[46]

Much can be learned from this summary about the vision of modern Japan held
by the leaders of the Meiji government. It can be divided essentially into three categories. The first is individualism (*kojinshugi*), that is, education that develops the
individual for life. The new public schools were promoted as a means of achieving
enlightenment by all Japanese, not reserved for a select group as in the pre-Meiji
era, thereby eliminating illiteracy. Enlightenment, however, was not intended as
an end in itself but rather as a means of securing independence of the individual. In
the new Japan everyone needed the ability to make a living, including the samurai
class that previously gained unearned advantages ascribed by birth rather then
proven by ability.

The second theme emphasized in the preamble was utilitarianism (*jitsugakushugi*) or rationalism (*gōrishugi*). Success in life requires that each individual
acquire skills and abilities to survive in the new industrial society. No longer can
one depend on an inherited birthright according to social class. The new schools
must provide each child with the knowledge and skills to meet that requirement.[47]
Feudal education under the Tokugawa regime was branded as a waste of time for
one seeking to get ahead in the world. Calligraphy and Chinese classics, staples
of the old school, were swept away in the new school. Mathematics, science, and
foreign languages moved to the center of the curriculum. They were intended to

provide the new Japanese with technical knowledge and skills to secure a job, to earn money, and to move ahead in a capitalist society envisioned by the early Meiji decision makers.[48]

The third category relates to the great idealistic spirit of social equality among the four social classes (yonmin byōdō no seishin) carefully differentiated by the feudal Tokugawa government.[49] All children regardless of social class and gender would attend a common public elementary school together. The school becomes, in effect, an instrument of social reconstruction aimed at eliminating the economic and political disparities that characterized the rigid social class structure of Tokugawa Japan. The old feudal system divided society into four distinct classes. An entrenched samurai class that held a monopoly on government achieved its privileged status among them through hereditary rights. It would be replaced through the new school system aimed at equality of all social classes.

Finally, the first national school system in Japan introduced two comprehensive principles of education, each of revolutionary proportions. Elementary education for all inaugurated the concepts of mass education and mass literacy, a goal that no nation in the world had achieved by the 1870s. Consequently, from the first academic year 1873, the focus of education in Japan concentrated on elementary educational provisions for all irrespective of social class or gender. The second principle of major significance, the centralization of education, placed responsibility for determining educational policy for the nation in the hands of the relevant governmental organ, the Ministry of Education. It has remained so ever since.

The Administrative Structure

Of all the provisions in the Gakusei, the administrative structure of education has received an inordinate amount of attention by historians. Second in importance only to the provisions for elementary education for all, the new system posited control of education at the national level of government. "The management of educational affairs throughout the whole country (Japan) shall be in the hands of one central authority, the department of education."[50]

This single provision conforms to the French model as understood by the Japanese Ministry of Education in 1872. According to the interpretation, section one of the Gakusei outlines the administrative structure as based on the school district system (gakku sei).[51] The plan called for the country to be divided into eight national school districts called Daigaku Ku (university districts) responsible for administering educational policy emanating from the minister of education. This provision consequently established a centralized national school system from the very outset of the modernization process. Each of the eight university districts was responsible for administering thirty-two middle school districts, the Chūgaku Ku. Within each of these districts a middle school was to be established serving an area with a population of approximately 130,000 residents.

Each middle school district was then responsible for educational policy as stipulated by the university districts for 210 elementary school districts, the Shōgaku Ku. Each elementary school district was finally responsible for establishing an elementary school serving a population of 600 residents within its area. The grand total of public schools envisioned under Japan's first national school system included 256 middle, or secondary, schools and 53,760 elementary schools, all subject to the regulations of the Ministry of Education.

Administratively each of the eight university districts, the Daigaku Ku, was to establish a Bureau of Management called the Tokugaku Kyoku at the district headquarters. It was responsible for overseeing and inspecting educational affairs in compliance with Ministry of Education policy within its jurisdiction, in consultation with the appropriate prefectural governor (chihōkan). Each of the thirty-two middle school districts within each of the eight national school districts was mandated to establish a Bureau of Educational Administration called the Gakku Torishimari. Within this office ten to thirteen superintendents were to be appointed by the appropriate prefectural governor, each responsible for overseeing educational affairs in twenty to thirty elementary school districts. Finally the plan called for each prefecture to establish an office of education to carry out the educational affairs within the purview of the prefecture.[52] The scheme in its entirety represented the Japanese version of Napoleon's University of France.

The elementary school was divided into a lower division of four years for children age six to nine or ten and an upper division of four years for children age ten to fourteen. The middle school was also divided into a lower division for children age fourteen to sixteen and an upper division for children age seventeen to nineteen. Teachers for the elementary school were required to be at least twenty years old with a certificate from a teacher training school (shihan gakkō) or have completed the middle school. Middle school teachers had to be at least twenty-five years old and have received a university degree.

The elementary school curriculum began with the basic subjects of the three R's including reading (dokuhon), writing (shūji), pronunciation (tango), conversation (kaiwa), mathematics, and history. Morals (shūshin) was listed next in order among a total of fifteen subjects, ending with physical education (taisō) and singing (shōka). There was no required course for morals at the upper elementary level, where various natural science courses were introduced. At this level the course on morals was ranked number fifteen, essentially optional, among the twenty courses on the list.

Higher education was covered in a brief note. The university should include the four departments of science, literature, law, and medicine. Teacher-training schools were urgently called for. Without them it would be impossible to effectively establish a modern public elementary school system.

The final issue proved to be critical. How to finance the first national school system calling for over 53,000 new public elementary schools caused great consternation. The authors of the proposal were well aware that the government could not possibly finance such a grandiose plan of that magnitude. Conforming to the general tenor of the preamble, that the prosperity of each individual is dependent upon education, Mitsukuri Rinshō's Ministry of Education bureau conceived a solution that would, it was hoped, get the proposed system under way. The report simply stated that the local community is responsible for financing the local public school.[53] In other words, those who benefit from the school should pay for it. With that understanding, governmental approval was granted.

During the formulation of the Gakusei, an historical development of great magnitude took place. The Ministry of Education's special bureau responsible for the plan under Mitsukuri Rinshō's guiding hand began deliberations on the draft from early December 1871. Just three weeks before, the powerful Iwakura Mission departed on November 12 for a two-year study of American, British, and European institutions, the topic of the following chapter. On board the ship headed for San Francisco was the corps of the new Japanese government under the leadership of Iwakura Tomomi, titular head of government. The official purpose of one of the most unusual missions in diplomatic history was to negotiate revisions of treaties signed by the former Tokugawa government with western powers, now considered unequal. However, the major purpose was to investigate firsthand the workings of western societies for the modernization of Japan.

In addition to key cabinet members of government, ranking officials from various ministries were attached to the mission for specific assignments related to their sector of government. The future head of the Ministry of Education, Tanaka Fujimaro, was selected to represent the ministry. He and four aides were assigned to the mission to investigate all aspects of educational systems among the major western countries. Tanaka returned home nearly two years later in 1873 to assume control of the ministry in order to implement the First National Plan for Education, the preparation of which had just gotten under way in Japan when he left for America. Manifestly, no other country in the world devised a modern school system in such an unorthodox fashion as did Japan in the early 1870s.

5   The Iwakura Mission

A SURVEY OF WESTERN
EDUCATION, 1872–1873

On November 12, 1871, amid befitting pomp and circumstance, a high-powered delegation of government officials left Yokohama on board the U.S.S. *America* bound
for Washington, D.C., the first major destination.[1] Led by Iwakura Tomomi,
titular head of government, the Iwakura Mission departed on a two-year survey
of modern societies in the United States and Europe. The huge delegation of fifty
members included half of the senior-ranking members of the ruling oligarchy.
Upon their return in 1873, they were expected to apply those aspects of western
societies deemed appropriate to modernize Japanese society. The ultimate goal
was a modern state that had attained parity with, and independence from, the
western world.

Among the delegates was an obscure official, Tanaka Fujimaro, representing
the newly founded Ministry of Education. The reason why Tanaka, a lower-ranking
samurai from the Owari han, was chosen for the mission remains inexplicable to
this day. Lacking foreign language ability and having no knowledge or experience
in the field of education, Tanaka himself may have been surprised with his appointment. He departed Japan for the West commissioned with the awesome responsibility of implementing Japan's first public school system upon his return in 1873.

Iwakura Tomomi—The Court Noble

In historical perspective, the Japanese government set a precedent by dispatching
the nucleus of its ruling oligarchy overseas for a two-year study tour less than three
years after the final battle at the Aizu Castle ended the war of restoration. During
that short period the new government itself was transferred from Kyoto, the home
of the emperor for centuries, to Edo renamed Tokyo, the new eastern capital.

Leadership of the new Meiji government was quickly assigned to a tiny group
of individuals dubbed the oligarchy. Among them, Iwakura Tomomi stood out
from the others by virtue of personally having served Emperor Meiji before the
1868 Restoration. He did not, therefore, originate from the samurai class, as did all
of the other top leaders. Rather, as a member of the imperial court in Kyoto during
the Tokugawa period, he secured a privileged status among the new Meiji leadership due to his noble status, seniority in imperial service, and relationship with
Emperor Meiji. When the unprecedented proposal emerged in 1871 to dispatch a
ranking delegation of government officials to the West to gain a firsthand perspective of modern societies, it fell appropriately to Iwakura to lead it.

Figure 8. The Iwakura Mission Departure.
From Richard Sims, *Modern Japan* (London: Bodley Head, 1973), 36.

Iwakura exhibited unique qualities during the initial opening of Japan. In spite of his secluded life among the highly ritualistic traditional customs of court life in Kyoto, he sent his two sons to study under Guido Verbeck in Nagasaki shortly after the Meiji Restoration. In a truly radical decision for the times, he then followed this by sending his boys to study at Rutgers College in America in 1870, as arranged by Verbeck. As fate would have it, they developed a close personal relationship with Professor and Mrs. David Murray, later hired by the mission to

Figure 9. Iwakura Tomomi (center).
From Akiko Kuno, *Unexpected Destinations: The Poignant Story of Japan's First Vassar Graduate* (Tokyo: Kōdansha International, 1993), 112.

work in the Ministry of Education. Thus when Iwakura left for America in 1871, he was on his way to see his sons who were already there.

The origin of the Iwakura Mission is of considerable importance since it illustrates how early Meiji governmental decisions that profoundly affected modern Japanese education depended on foreign advisors.[2] One year after the Meiji Restoration of 1868, Guido Verbeck was invited by the government to move from Nagasaki, where he had lived for exactly one decade, to Tokyo. Among his unusually prestigious assignments, one was to serve as the senior advisor to the new government that included many of his former students. Concurrently he served as head of Nankō, already referred to as the Imperial University. Among the bureaucratic leadership was his most dedicated student, Ōkuma Shigenobu, who wielded considerable influence among the higher-ranking officers. Ōkuma was destined for the prime ministership during the next decade.

According to a letter to his friend, William Griffis, who was a frequent guest at the Verbeck home, Verbeck reveals how he became involved in the mission. "Influential friends spoke to me of an embassy abroad as among the probabilities of that fall or winter. This suggested to me the composition of the paper, which on or about the 11th June, 1869, I privately sent to my friend Okuma, one of the leading men at the time. . . . Satisfied with its having reached his hands, I left the matter there, never spoke nor inquired further about it, and not hearing about it from the parties addressed, I gave it up as so much matter thrown away."[3]

Although Verbeck did not receive a reaction to his proposal for over two years, he had in fact drawn up a detailed recommendation in 1869 to send a government embassy of officers to the West. He recalled that he had been frequently asked by Japanese about the forms of government, the laws, education, religion, and "similar topics concerning the civilization of the West." Rather than abstractly answering the inquiries, he concluded that "there is something in the civilization of the West that must be seen and felt; in order to be fully appreciated, personal experience is necessary to understand the theory of [western] civilization."[4] Verbeck then drew up a detailed proposal to include specified commissions of officers from the various departments of government. They were to study the constitutions, laws, finances, armies, navies, and so on, in France, England, Prussia, Holland, and the United States. "A commission of three Officers and a Secretary to examine the various systems of national and high schools, the laws in regard to popular education, the manner of establishing and supporting public schools, school regulations and branches of learning, school examinations and diplomas. The Officers of this commission ought to visit and see in full operation Universities, Public and Private schools, as well as Special schools such as Polytechnic and Commercial schools."[5]

Without responding to Verbeck's proposal, Ōkuma concealed it, "afraid to show it to any one because it might have endangered his high position, as he was already suspected by many conservatives as being a [Christian] convert."[6] He later showed it to colleagues within government where it ultimately reached Iwakura Tomomi. Iwakura then met Verbeck on October 26, 1871, to inquire about his proposal of which Iwakura had just become aware. Verbeck, in fact, had forgotten the details during the intervening two years and four months since he wrote the proposal. Three days later, October 29, 1871, Iwakura and Verbeck went over the translation "clause by clause. At the end he [Iwakura] told me [Verbeck] it was the very and the only thing for them to do, and that my programme should be carried out to the letter." The Iwakura Mission left for America two months later, recalled Verbeck, "organized according to my paper."[7]

Emperor Meiji set the stage for the Iwakura Mission in a revealing speech to the delegates chosen to travel to the West. "After careful study and observation, I am deeply impressed with the belief that the most powerful and enlightened nations of the world are those who have made diligent effort to cultivate their minds, and sought to develop their country in the fullest and most perfect manner. . . . If we would profit by the useful arts and sciences and conditions of society prevailing among more enlightened nations, we must either study these at home as best we can, or send abroad an expedition of practical observers to foreign lands, competent to acquire for us those things our people lack, which are best calculated to benefit this nation"[8]

On January 15, 1872, the Iwakura Mission arrived in San Francisco. Among the passengers on board ship, in addition to the large contingent of Japanese delegates, were five Japanese girls age seven to fifteen, unaccompanied by their parents. The youngest of them, seven-year-old Tsuda Umeko, assisted by eleven-year-old Yamakawa Sutematsu, would eventually make a major contribution to the education of girls in modern Japan with the founding of the institution that became the distinguished Tsuda College, discussed in the following chapter.

A Survey of Western Education—Tanaka Fujimaro

Although Kido Takayoshi was technically responsible for the investigation of western educational institutions during the Iwakura Mission, Tanaka Fujimaro actually undertook the day-to-day research. Kido, a representative of the oligarchy, devoted his time primarily to political and diplomatic issues as well as visiting a limited number of schools. Tanaka, in contrast, was assigned to represent the Ministry of Education in order to conduct a comprehensive survey of western educational systems. It included laws and practices governing personnel, salaries, teaching conditions, school buildings and furnishings, educational administration and financing, school fees, examinations, and so on, at the elementary, middle, and higher educational levels. His mission also included the study of libraries, museums, and special schools such as those for the handicapped.[9]

Tanaka Fujimaro was born in 1845 into a lower-level samurai family in the Owari domain around Nagoya. He underwent the usual education of a low-ranking samurai, studying Chinese writing and the classics plus the practice of rudimentary martial arts. He experienced a difficult childhood complicated by the suicide of his father when he was only sixteen years old, compelling the family to move to a tiny village where they struggled to survive. At age eighteen he was chosen to serve the Owari han government when he submitted a letter to the officials urging them to join in the movement with the Satsuma and Chōshū hans that led to the overthrow of the Tokugawa government.[10]

Tanaka remained with the Owari han government until the second year of Meiji, 1869. During this period he was involved in antiwestern activities as the social and political turmoil of the late 1860s provoked economic disorder. He promoted a local group opposing the sale of imported goods in order to improve the sale of locally made goods. Taking matters into his own hands, Tanaka led a band of angry cohorts who attacked a local store selling western goods. The enraged samurai slashed the imported products with their swords, one of the few times that, as samurai, they had an occasion to use them. Tanaka was also caught up in the split within his clan over supporting either the imperial side or the Tokugawa government. He sided with the imperials, encouraging his clan leaders to throw their support behind the emperor.[11]

In 1869, Tanaka was assigned to work in the new Meiji government in Tokyo. He joined the office of the Daigakkō, the governmental office that became the Ministry of Education in July 1871. A mere three months later, on October 12, he was appointed a senior secretary, *mumbu daijo*, in preparation for a special assignment.[12] Ten days later he was assigned to the Iwakura Mission, and two weeks after that he boarded the ship headed for Washington, D.C.[13] He was about to embark on a prolonged study of western education that would lead to his assignment as head of the Ministry of Education upon his return in 1873. As noted above, historical accounts unfortunately do not reveal why Tanaka Fujimaro was chosen by senior ministry officials to join the Iwakura Mission with such a momentous assignment. He was not a specialist on education, Japanese or Western. Moreover he could not be classified as an authority on the West, nor was he able to use any of the western languages.

Tanaka Fujimaro was surely one of the most colorful unorthodox Japanese educational officials to emerge in the Meiji era. In one of the many unusual episodes in his dramatic lifetime, he fell in love with and later married a local geisha from Nagoya, breaking the taboo of mixing the social classes. Moreover, he remained faithful to her throughout his life, taking her with him on several overseas assignments, a rarity among government officials. Among the stories illustrating the unusual nature of Tanaka, we learn from his wife's memoirs, for example, that he attended the enthronement ceremony for the Restoration of Emperor Meiji in 1868 in Kyoto in peculiar attire. He wore western-type shoes that did not match, and a traditional red hakama coat that surely made him stand out from the others.[14]

Tanaka's unprecedented career as an international educator began with his arrival in San Francisco with the Iwakura Mission in January 1872, at the age of twenty-seven. After extensive welcoming ceremonies, the Ministry of Education representative, accompanied by a translator, set out on his first visit to an American school, a nearby Oakland public elementary school. The fact that Tanaka required a translator is worthy of note since his understanding of western education from that day onward was funneled through an interpreter

Tanaka took copious notes during his many school visits covering all aspects of western education, not only transcribing what was translated for him but what he personally observed. Among the remaining records of the mission, a note recorded during his first school visit speaks volumes about Tanaka and the simplicity of his initial impressions of American education. He carefully noted that boys and girls attended the Oakland public elementary school together. This was contrary to the tradition in Japan where few girls attended school, and rarely in the same classroom with boys.

Tanaka was also intrigued by another American custom that caught his eye. He recorded that the children carried their lunches to school with them. An indication of the thoroughness of this Japanese observer was his curious reaction to the type of food the pupils brought to school. Among the details indicating that Tanaka must have inspected the lunch boxes of the children, he recorded that some brought slices of buttered bread in their lunches. Others, in contrast, brought slices of bread with pieces of meat between them.[15] He was, of course, describing a western innovation, a simple sandwich that was obviously a curiosity to this foreign visitor. But the odd combination of meat between two slices of bread in the lunch pails of American children attracting the attention of the Japanese who would head the Ministry of Education into the modern world may be a lesson in itself. Commenting that even adult Americans eat simply, Tanaka's notes reveal the naiveté of the senior government bureaucrat responsible for Japan's first public school system.[16]

Following the initial stopover in San Francisco, the Iwakura Mission boarded the transcontinental railroad bound for Washington, D.C., making several stops on the way. The completion of this 3,000-mile long landmark achievement in

American ingenuity and technology had taken place several years earlier when the famous golden spike was driven in at Promontory Summit, Utah, in 1869. It reduced the arduous trip across the continent from months in a covered wagon to one week on a train. In sharp contrast, the first railroad in Japan, running twenty miles between Tokyo and Yokohama, was finally completed in 1872 while the Iwakura Mission was in the West.

Mori Arinori—Chargé d'Affaires in Washington

Waiting at the Japanese legation in Washington for the arrival of the Iwakura Mission was Japan's first diplomatic representative to the United States, Mori Arinori. One year previously, Mori, at the extraordinarily youthful age of twenty-four, was appointed chargé d'affaires. As we recall, this adventurous Japanese as a teenager had defied the ban against unauthorized foreign travel, sailing off to London in 1865 to begin his studies at the University of London, and after two years had hastily decided to travel to America to join a local Christian sect under Thomas Harris. After one year in the austere religious colony he returned to Japan in 1868, shortly after the Meiji Restoration, to join the new government. Experiencing a tumultuous period in and out of various government posts for the next several years, he was suddenly assigned in 1871 to head Japan's first diplomatic mission to the United States. At a time when Satsuma men played a dominant role in the Meiji government, the choice of Mori from Satsuma, who had lived in America and spoke English, a rarity of the day, was not incomprehensible even though he was only twenty-four. This was, after all, an extraordinary moment in the history of Japan.

Upon the arrival of the Iwakura Mission in Washington on February 29, 1872, Mori, aided by his American secretary Charles Lanman whose recorded account of the mission was published as *The Japanese in America* (1872), was thrust into the position of hosting his nation's senior political leaders, all of them older than he was. It was Mori's responsibility not only to make the necessary arrangements but to translate both from Japanese into English and vice versa between the senior Japanese and American government officials. For a young man of twenty-four, it was a daunting task that began with the first meeting with President Ulysses S. Grant.

Within a week of the mission's arrival in Washington, Mori took his Japanese guests to the White House to meet the president of the United States. Just seven years previously he had accepted the surrender of General Robert E. Lee, ending the great American Civil War. The meeting with senior Japanese leaders was propitious since it brought together a former American commanding general with the Japanese officials, all but Iwakura brought up in the samurai-warrior tradition of Japan, however diluted by that time. The relationship proved to be cordial and lasting.

A letter from the emperor of Japan presented to President Grant at this initial meeting reconfirms the importance to Japan of learning from the United States: "It is our purpose to select from the various institutions prevailing among enlightened nations such as are best suited to our present condition, and adopt them, in gradual

Figure 10. Chargé d'Affaires Mori Arinori in Washington.
From Benjamin Duke, *Ten Great Educators of Modern Japan* (Tokyo: Tokyo University Press, 1989), 38.

reforms and improvements of our policy and customs, so as to be upon an equality with them."[17] No official statement from the Japanese government better describes the underlying purpose of educational reform during the first half of the 1870s.

Shortly thereafter Tanaka Fujimaro, representing the Ministry of Education, separated from the main body of the mission that remained in Washington, to embark independently on his educational mission. This also separated him from Kido Takayoshi, vice ambassador of the mission technically responsible for education. Kido, ranking officer of the Meiji government, remained with the mission to conduct political and diplomatic matters. Tanaka, meanwhile, launched the study of American education on his own. Although he had already visited schools at several stops on the trip across America, Tanaka's educational mission took shape with visits to Washington-area schools.

Niijima Jō—Christian Translator and Guide to American Education

Since Tanaka Fujimaro could not understand English, he needed a capable translator as well as a guide. Mori, responsible for making the necessary arrangements for the mission members, called upon another most unusual Japanese living in America at the time to serve in that capacity, Niijima Jō. Well known in Japanese history as the founder of the great Christian university Dōshisha in Kyoto, Niijima had left Japan illegally during the Tokugawa era to find his way to America to learn about Christianity. His escape from feudal Japan was reminiscent of Mori Arinori's clandestine departure for England during the same period.

The extraordinary life of Niijima Jō was fortunately made known through a collection of his letters written in English. Originally published in 1891, *The Life and Letters of Joseph Hardy Neeshima* reveals the fascinating story of another pioneer of modern Japanese education.[18] Educated in the Chinese classics and rudimentary military arts followed by the study of Dutch, the young samurai learned about Christianity through Dutch books. He became determined to go to America to learn more about the religion of the West. He cunningly arranged to be hidden on an American merchant vessel, agreeing to work for his passage from the far northern island of Hokkaido, whose port city of Hakodate was one of three open to foreign ships in 1864. Purely by chance, the boat that departed in July 1864 with Niijima aboard was headed for Shanghai and then to Nagasaki, another open port. As an illegal Japanese on a foreign ship in foreign waters, a position punishable by death, Niijima could not go on to Nagasaki.

The ship captain, who befriended Niijima, giving him the common American name of Joe, was able to find another American ship in Shanghai that was owned by a shipping merchant in Boston. The captain accepted the Japanese runaway on his boat, which remained in Chinese waters throughout the winter. The ship finally reached home port in Boston in September 1865, over a year after Niijima left his native country.

The Boston ship owner, Alpheus Hardy, happened to be a magnanimous American businessman who took an immediate interest in the adventurous Japanese boy. In an act of kindness by an American toward a Japanese acquaintance that characterized the early relationships between the two countries, Niijima's newly found American benefactor decided to educate the resourceful young man in the finest schools in Massachusetts at his own expense. The American merchant and his wife thereby began a personal relationship with the Japanese fugitive that grew into a family tie with strong loyalties. The significance of Niijima's unexpected arrival in the port of Boston cannot be underestimated. In the 1800s Massachusetts was at the forefront of innovation in American education. The leading American university, Harvard, was located at nearby Cambridge. Moreover, several of the other leading private American colleges of the day, for example Amherst and Williams, were founded in the state of Massachusetts. A network of prestigious private preparatory secondary schools that catered to intellectual and business families had been founded in Massachusetts to supply well-qualified candidates for the nearby colleges, and remain in place today.

Niijima unexpectedly found himself living in the home of a well-to-do American merchant who recognized the unique qualities of his young Japanese ward. Moreover, Niijima's benefactor had personal contacts with the educational elite and the necessary finances to provide Niijima with the very finest educational opportunities available in America in the 1860s. He was first enrolled in the prestigious Philips Academy in Andover, Massachusetts, in 1865, for a two-year study mostly of English. His presence among some of the most capable students from the finest families primarily from the American East had to be inspiring. From there Hardy arranged for Niijima to enter Amherst College, among the foremost private institutions of American higher education then and now. About half of all Amherst graduates entered the Christian ministry, the ultimate goal of Niijima.

It was at Amherst that Niijima enrolled in a course with Dr. William Clark, the founder of the Sapporo Agricultural College nearly a decade later in 1876, the topic of chapter 12. It was also during his Amherst days that Niijima struck up a unique relationship with one of the leading Christian intellectuals on the faculty, Dr. Julius Seelye. He and his wife invited Niijima to leave the dormitory and stay at their home during vacation periods and illnesses, where he was treated like a son. Seelye became president of Amherst in 1876.

Graduating in 1870 from Amherst, Niijima then entered the prestigious Andover Theological Seminary in preparation for the Christian ministry with the ultimate aim of becoming a missionary in Japan. It was during his course at the theological seminary that he first met Mori Arinori, chargé d'affaires of the Japanese legation in Washington, responsible for all Japanese students studying in America. Recognizing the advanced level of education in New England, he was on an official trip to Boston in 1871 when he first met Niijima, and offered to help him get a passport since he had left Japan without permission seven years previously. In other words, Niijima was an illegal alien. Nevertheless it was a cordial meeting between the fugitive from Japan and Japan's top diplomat in the United States, a commentary on Mori's broadminded character.

By the time the Iwakura Mission arrived in Washington on February 28, 1872, Mori Arinori had struck up a cordial relationship with Niijima Jō. Shortly before the Iwakura Mission arrived, Mori sent a request to Niijima to come to Washington "to inform the Japanese Embassy about the system of American education."[19] This was an unusual recognition of Niijima by Japan's senior diplomat in America. However, Mori was planning to ask Niijima to accompany Tanaka Fujimaro as translator on his survey of American schools.

With the understanding that Niijima, upon his insistence, would not be recognized as a government-sponsored student with official obligations, he accepted the offer. That decision placed the devout young Japanese Christian, who had lived in America for seven years without his government's approval, in daily contact for the next year and a half with the senior Japanese bureaucrat empowered to set educational policy throughout the decade of the 1870s. It was, to say the least, an exceptional situation. By this time Niijima had become acclimated to American society and its elite educational opportunities. He was living a lifestyle both at home and in school enjoying advantages available only to well-to-do Americans. Moreover, he had become quite critical of his own country, believing that his mission in life "may be some service for opening the country [Japan] to the light of truth and light."[20] Niijima had understandably become so enamored and comfortable with American culture as he experienced it at the elite level that he seriously considered becoming a naturalized American citizen. He finally rejected the idea only because it could potentially become an impediment to his goal of returning to Japan as a Christian missionary.[21]

An early indication of the relationship between Tanaka and Niijima that went far beyond that of translator and guide occurred several days after they first met in Washington. Tanaka invited Niijima to dinner at his hotel. After dinner they "spent nearly three hours in conversation on the subject of national education." Although Niijima had no experience with regular American public schools then proliferating throughout America serving the masses, he assuredly promoted the American school system to Tanaka as the ideal. He also revealingly added in his report to his American parents that "I did not speak to him on the subject of religion thus far, but I could no longer keep down my burning zeal."[22]

Following initial welcoming ceremonies, Tanaka set out for his first visit to schools in Washington, D.C. He was escorted by the highest educational official in the United States government, Commissioner of Education John Eaton.[23] Coincidentally, Commissioner Eaton was an ordained Christian pastor who had graduated from the Andover Theological Seminary, the same institution where Tanaka's translator, Niijima Jō, was then a student. The cordial relationship between the two Andover seminarians may have been a factor in Eaton's personal interest in the Tanaka mission. For example, Eaton gave Tanaka a small collection of school laws, official reports, and writings of such distinguished American educators as Henry Barnard and Horace Mann.[24]

Commissioner of Education John Eaton was a former general in the Union Army of the Civil War under General Grant, now president. Volunteering as a chaplain, he rose to the rank of brigadier general by the end of the war. General Eaton, as he was often referred to thereafter, was involved in a campaign to save his Bureau of Education, then functioning within the Department of the Interior, from members of the Congress who wanted to eliminate it.[25] It was the only office in the U.S. government that faintly resembled a ministry of education. Appropriately, Tanaka was accredited to the bureau by the State Department at the request of Iwakura.

Eaton graciously went out of his way to accommodate Tanaka. He first took his Japanese guests, including Niijima, to a private girl's school in the Washington area. Tanaka, brought up in the samurai-warrior tradition of feudal Japan, must have been impressed with his first school visit in the capital of the United States in the company of a senior government officer, a former American general no less. It can be assumed that Eaton chose a school worthy of a visit by foreign guests. He spent another day with his Japanese guest on a visit to nearby Columbia College in Washington, D.C. Indicative of the schedule maintained by Tanaka and his group, Niijima reported that they had a "very enjoyable time, though it was [the] busiest day I ever had since I came here. I kept talking partly in Japanese and, partly in English, from 9 A.M. till 5 P.M. It was [a] long eight hours' pulling. We returned to Arlington House at half past eight." Because of the intimate relationship emerging between Niijima and Tanaka, Tanaka asked Niijima, even before they left Washington for a lengthy trip to the north, to accompany him to Europe upon completing the American survey.

Tanaka Fujimaro was by now surely enjoying himself to the fullest. He was able to visit schools in the capital of the United States, although carefully selected, in the company of the highest educational official in the land. He had the service of a sophisticated bilingual translator from Japan experienced in the ways of American intellectual life. In addition, Eaton had supplied Tanaka with many official reports on education in the United States that were later translated and printed in Tanaka's final report. Eaton also contacted educational officials in Harrisburg, Pennsylvania, to make arrangements for the next stop on Tanaka's educational mission. Tanaka had to be pleased with the way his educational survey in America had begun.

From the initial Washington visit onward, Niijima introduced Tanaka to his American hosts as the Japanese commissioner of education. This was obviously based on the official title General Eaton carried in the American government. Niijima wrote that "We are going to leave Washington next week to visit the schools of Philadelphia and New York, and we may possibly reach the hub of the universe within three weeks."[26] In that revealing aside, the hub of the universe to Niijima was Boston, an attitude that was surely conveyed to Tanaka during the many opportunities he had with his new friend over the next two years.

Tanaka's educational survey, however, did not go directly from Washington to Philadelphia, as Niijima's letter indicated. In a letter home to his father we learn indirectly of a stopover in Harrisburg, the small capital city of Pennsylvania.[27] The most likely reason for the visit was to meet James Wickersham, state superintendent of education, whose office was located in Harrisburg. The three-day meeting between Wickersham and Tanaka marked the beginning of a unique relationship between an American superintendent of a state school system and a senior official of the Japanese Ministry of Education.

James Wickersham had been a professor at a Pennsylvania teacher training college when he wrote a book entitled *School Economy* published in Philadelphia. Somehow the Japanese Ministry of Education had obtained a copy and found it interesting enough to translate it under the title of *Gakkō Tsūron* [General Theory of Education].[28] It was widely circulated to those in educational circles, particularly within the Ministry of Education. Tanaka undoubtedly came across Wickersham's translated book before he left for America. It is within reason to conclude that he wanted to meet the author, located within hours of Washington.

As U.S. commissioner of education, Eaton sent the following letter to Wickersham, the Pennsylvania superintendent of education, on March 30, 1872, listing the purpose of the impending visit by the Japanese commissioner of education and his translator. "Mr. Tanaka desires to obtain a correct and full idea of education in the United States—the legislation, organization, methods of taxation, of expending money, of conducting State, city and district systems of education, and also information in regard to architecture, furniture, methods of instruction, textbooks, discipline, etc."[29]

Tanaka arrived at Wickersham's office in Harrisburg on April 2, 1872. Wickersham recalled that Tanaka "remained several days, each morning being spent in listening to an explanation of our system . . . and in taking notes on the most important points."[30] This was the first opportunity for Tanaka to interview a senior American educational officer responsible for the public schools of an entire state. This was important to Tanaka, since he knew that he would be responsible for the administration of education for his country. It was also critical to him, since he learned from his month in Washington that the federal government in America had no legislative or administrative control over local education. For example, Commissioner of Education Eaton, senior educational officer in the U.S. government, was merely the head of a bureau within the Department of the Interior, and was far removed from President Grant's cabinet.

Commissioner Eaton was also far removed from local American schools. Rather, in lieu of a national Ministry of Education, each of the American states determined the laws for schools within their respective borders. Tanaka was apparently sufficiently knowledgeable to appreciate that, for example, the great American cities of Philadelphia and New York were not the centers of administrative power in their respective states. Rather, the administrative control of American education was legally vested in the small capital cities of each state such as Harrisburg, Pennsylvania, and Albany, New York.

In a further degree of decentralization of American education, each state delegated certain educational powers to the local school boards, along with taxing authority to finance the schools, made up of locally elected lay representatives. To a foreigner observing the system for the first time, it presented a formidable challenge to understand the positive and negative features of the American tradition of local control of education. Consequently when Tanaka, with no background in American social institutions, arrived in Harrisburg to meet Wickersham, he was endeavoring to untangle the web of interrelated administrative powers within the American education system.

To Tanaka, scheduled to implement the first national school system in Japan upon his return to Japan, educational administrative patterns in America were of supreme importance. Accordingly he methodically collected documents and reports on the subject from as many states as possible. He planned to have them translated into Japanese for a more thorough understanding of the issues involved. One wonders how much Tanaka understood when Wickersham explained through a translator how even his administrative power, as superintendent of a state system of public education, was restricted by laws that delegated certain powers to local school boards. In turn, school board members themselves were restricted by the necessity to please the public to regain their seats in local elections—precisely how grassroots democracy works in the American tradition. In Tanaka's report of his visit with Wickersham, published after his return to Japan, he included a simple description of the interrelationships between the various administrative levels in the Pennsylvania system of education as he understood them.[31]

An explanation of the administration and financing of American education that Tanaka encountered during his first several weeks in America in 1872 in Washington with Commissioner Eaton and in Harrisburg with Superintendent Wickersham turned out to be critical. His reaction to the Wickersham visit as explained by his translator was a precursor: "Pennsylvania has the best school law for an intelligent people of any of which he [Tanaka] has been acquainted."[32] When Tanaka became the de facto minister of education during the first decade of a national system of education in Japan, he set out to decentralize administrative control with Pennsylvania as the model. It brought about the first bitter confrontation over educational policy in modern Japan, leading to Tanaka's downfall in 1879.

From Harrisburg, Tanaka and Niijima moved on to visit schools in Philadelphia, and from there to New England where Niijima had spent the previous seven years as a student. Taking advantage of his contacts in the area, Niijima went far beyond the role of a translator. He seized the opportunity to arrange wherever possible accommodations in Christian homes during stopovers. For example, when they visited Boston, Niijima asked Alpheus Hardy, his benefactor, to accommodate them in his home, which he did. When they visited Amherst, Professor and Mrs. Seelye invited them to stay at their home.

Niijima was understandably pleased with the visit to the American northeast that he had personally helped arrange for Tanaka. He expressed his pleasure in a letter to his American father revealing the comfortable environment that Tanaka enjoyed during his survey of education in that part of the United States. "Since we were invited to your house [Hardy's home in Boston], we have found friends here and there, and feel so thankful to you for your first opening the pleasant home for us. It is so pleasant for me to be in such a Christian family as President Porters [of Yale University]. I am glad Mr. Tanaka had such a good opportunity to see so many Christian families, and the ways and means of Christian living."[33]

The extremely favorable image of American education and society gained by Tanaka Fujimaro during his three-month trip through the northeast of America had to be influenced by his traveling companion on whom he relied, and to whom he treated as a friend and colleague. Niijima's positive attitude about his adopted country where he enjoyed the finest education available at the time could not have escaped Tanaka's notice. It is particularly relevant when at a later time Tanaka adamantly refused to compromise in his reforms of Japanese education based on the American model. His inordinate admiration for American educational practices provoked senior officers among the Ministry of Education to mockingly dub him the "American worshiper" (America kabure).[34] It eventually cost him the top position in the Ministry of Education.

To appreciate the hectic schedule that Tanaka maintained during his travels in America, and the variety of educational institutions he visited, Niijima's description of their short visit to New Haven is indicative. "You may be interested to know how much we have seen during our brief stay in New Haven. Monday we visited Yale College, Cabinets, History and Art Gallery, and Sheffield Scientific School. Tuesday we visited Deaf and Dumb Asylum, one high school, Brown School, Insane Asylum in Hartford, one normal school in New Britain and State Reform School and gold plating factory in Meriden. Wednesday we were guests to the inauguration ceremony of the new governor of the State, riding in an open carriage for four hours. Today we visited three public schools in this city. It has been pretty hard pull since we came here."[35]

In one of Tanaka's stopovers, he made a contact that would have a major impact on modern agricultural education in Japan during his tenure as director of the Ministry of Education. This connection illustrates how the original purpose of the Iwakura Mission designed by Guido Verbeck was achieved. When Tanaka, accompanied by his translator Niijima, visited Amherst College in Massachusetts from April 23 to 27, 1872, he was hosted by the well-known Christian scholar and later president of the institution, Julius Seelye.[36] It was during this visit that Seelye invited them to stay at his home, familiar to Niijima who often stayed there during his college days at Amherst.

Indicative of Tanaka's broad interest in American educational practices, he took the opportunity to visit a local agricultural school where Professor Seelye introduced him to a graduate of Amherst College, William Clark. Clark, by then an authority on agricultural education, was in the midst of establishing the Massachusetts Agricultural College, an early innovator in agricultural education in America. Three years later, Dr. Clark was invited to Japan by the Japanese Ministry of Education under Tanaka to establish the nation's first agricultural college in Hokkaido, covered in a later chapter.

Dr. David Murray—Superintendent of Education in the Empire of Japan

Of all the educational connections established with Americans by the Iwakura Mission, the series of events that led to the introduction of Dr. David Murray, then on the faculty of Rutgers College, to mission officials proved of perhaps greatest importance. It all began during the Tokugawa era when Guido Verbeck, involved in so many connections, advised the Japanese students enrolled in his classes in Nagasaki to go to Rutgers College for further study. Many did so. As a result of this connection, Rutgers College and a local preparatory school in New Brunswick became the primary institutions in America to receive Japanese students before the Meiji Restoration. Among them were many who returned to Japan to assume responsible positions of leadership in the institutions of the new government.

With little or no orientation, these young samurai, some in their teens, from Tokugawa Japan found themselves on the unfamiliar but charming campus of Rutgers College. Not only were they far from home, they were often inadequately prepared to use the language of the college classroom. Bright and motivated, the Japanese students were in dire need of personal assistance and friendship. Dr. Murray, professor of mathematics at Rutgers, and his wife provided that by inviting the Japanese students to their home where close personal friendships between this kind and generous American couple and the youthful samurai from Japan were forged.

The official connection between David Murray and the Japanese government began with a letter circulated by Mori Arinori from the Japanese legation in Washington in 1872. Mori, who had arrived in Washington less than a year earlier as Japan's first diplomat to establish relations between the two countries, extended his mandate well beyond diplomatic matters. Although he had no idea that a decade and a half later he would become minister of education, Mori became directly involved in educational modernization at this stage. The following letter

Figure 11. Dr. David Murray.
Photo courtesy of Griffis Collection,
Rutgers University Library, New Bruns-
wick, N.J.

addressed to leading American educators reflects his keen interest in educational matters that led to David Murray's position as the superintendent of education in the empire of Japan.

Legation of Japan for the United States of America, Washington D.C. Feb'y 3d, 1872

Dear Sir:

Having been Especially Commissioned, as part of my duty in this country, to look after the Educational affairs of Japan, and feeling personally of great interest in the progress of that Empire, I desire to obtain from you, a letter of advice and information bearing upon this subject, to assist my countrymen in their efforts to become instrumental in advancing civilization in the East. In a general way, I wish to have your views, in reference to the elevation of the condition of Japan intellectually, morally, and physically, but the particular points to which I invite your attention are as follows:

The effect of Education -

lst. Upon the material prosperity of a country,

2d. Upon its Commerce,

3d. Upon its Agricultural and Industrial interests,

4th. Upon the social, moral and physical conditions of the people; and -

5th. Its influence upon the Laws and Government.

Information on any one, if not all of these points, will be gratefully received and appreciated by me, and the same will soon be published both in the English and Japanese languages, for the information of the Japanese Government and people.

Figure 12. Dr. Murray's Students from Japan.
Photo courtesy of Griffis Collection, Rutgers University Library, New Brunswick, N.J.

Very respectfully
Your obd't Servant,
Arinori Mori[37]

One can only imagine the reaction of the presidents of Harvard, Yale, Amherst, and, of course Rutgers College with whom the Japanese were so familiar, upon receipt of this formal letter from the Japanese embassy in Washington in 1872 with its complex questions. Predictably the responses varied greatly; some took it quite seriously, responding with long and detailed explanations. Others, such as Harvard president Charles Eliot, merely forwarded pertinent reports available to him at the time.

Of all the responses to Mori Arinori's letter, the reply that had the greatest impact on the modernization of Japanese education resulted from the reaction of Rutgers College president William H. Campbell. He passed the letter on to a member of his faculty, Professor David Murray. President Campbell's action not only relieved him of the task of answering such broad questions as Mori posed but it was also a natural reaction to turn the letter over to Murray for a response. At a memorial service held years later, the local church pastor fondly recalled that the Murray home was "in reality a social center for the Japanese students here. . . . Their home was the symbol of hospitality."[38] On a small campus such as Rutgers, the entire community had to be aware of the special relationships being forged between the Murrays and the Japanese students. Hence President Campbell naturally requested Professor Murray to reply to Mori's letter on his behalf. Murray, unaware that his response in March 1872 would lead to his appointment as superintendent of educational affairs in Japan, neverthelesswent to great lengths to answer Mori's letter.

Reply to the Queries of Hon. A. Mori, Chargé d'Affaires of Japan, on the Subject of National Education[39]

. . . The problem of education is justly regarded by statesmen as the most important in all the circles of their duties. All other functions of government, such as of the repression and punishment of crime, the encouragement of national industries, the development of commerce, the defense against enemies, all are inferior in importance to the training of the young which determines the character of the nation. . . .

The nations which have in modern times exerted the greatest influence on the world's history, those which have made the most rapid progress and wealth and power, are those which have made education their special care and have furnished the most general and the most thorough culture to their citizens. The two nations which in the past century have advanced most in wealth, population, fame, and influence, are the United States and Germany. . . .

In these nations, if there is any one feature in which their systems of government excel, it is in the variety and profusion with which the means of education have been provided. Differing widely in other circumstances, they still have shown this common aim in their efforts to render education universal, and to leave no human soul within their territory without the opportunity for development.

Having directly and in great detail responded to the main topics listed by Mori in his letter, Murray then takes the opportunity to make several profound conclusions in the form of a warning to the Japanese.

Every nation must create a system of education suited to its own wants. There are national characteristics which ought properly to modify the scheme of education which would be deemed the most suitable. The culture required in one nation is not precisely required in another. There are traditional customs which it would be unwise to subvert. There are institutions already founded which are revered for their local and national associations, which without material change may be made the best elements of a new system. Every successful school system must be a natural outgrowth from the wants of a nation. If, therefore, changes are to be made in the educational system of any country, wisdom would suggest the retention, so far as admissible, of those institutions already in existence. This is but a proper concession to national self respect, and will go far to make any new features acceptable.

On the basis of this reply by Murray, Mori invited Murray to Washington for an interview at the Japanese legation. Murray did not know at that time that the Ministry of Education had planned to invite four foreigners from the West, one each from the United States, England, France and Germany, as advisors in the modernization of Japanese education. Obviously impressed, Mori arranged for another meeting for Murray to meet with Kido Takayoshi, technically in charge of Ministry of Education affairs on the Iwakura Mission, before he left for England. The meeting, which took place in Boston, apparently also went well. Kido then met Tanaka Fujimaro, already in England, arriving at a final decision to invite Murray to take the position. With that, plans to fill the other three positions for foreigners were dropped. David Murray signed an agreement with the Japanese government to "take charge of all affairs connected with Schools and Colleges."[40] He was scheduled to arrive in Japan to take up his challenging duties in the spring of 1873, when Tanaka planned to return from Europe following his lengthy survey of western education.

Before returning to Japan, however, Tanaka and his confidant Niijima left New York for England on May 11, 1872.[41] The second stage of Tanaka's mission, which would take him all over Europe for the next nine months, got under way. Japanese students studying in Europe at the time provided translation services for the party as it moved from one continental language area to another. Regardless of Tanaka's impressions gained from his prolonged visit to England and Europe, the critical decision had apparently been set. American education would serve as the model for Japan's first national school system.

From May 1872 to January 1873, Tanaka and Niijima visited schools and related institutions in major cities from London to Moscow, traversing the continent on a seemingly unlimited budget. It was an exhaustive experience, as seen from a few excerpts from Niijima's letters from Europe to his American benefactor.[42]

Since writing you from Macon I have been to Geneva, Berne, and Zurich and arrived here last night via Augsburg and Leipzic. We leave for St. Petersburg this evening and may possibly remain in Russia for a week. Then we will return and begin to study the Prussian system of education.[43]

We did not stay long in St. Petersburg, only five days, visiting there the University, a training school, the Founding Hospital, Museum, Hermitage, etc. . . . We came back to Berlin on the 16th. Finding all schools unopened there, we thought time might be better spent visiting other parts of Europe. Accordingly we started for Holland via Frankfurter-on-the-Main. We came down the Rhine by steamer as far as Rotterdam. Without stopping in that busy city we proceeded to The Hague, where we were kindly received by the Minister of Public Instruction, and a fine opportunity was given us to visit all schools in the capital. . . . We visited the Royal Palace and also the House in the Woods, the Queen's private residence, and had there a fine opportunity to see the

Queen. . . . We stopped at Leydon a couple of days on our way to Amsterdam, and visited the University, Botanical Gardens, a fine Ladies' school and museums. . . . We came to Copenhagen yesterday and called on the Minister of Public Instruction this morning.[44]

Of all the systems of education in Europe, Tanaka was most deeply impressed by German education. However, he rejected it as a model for Japan as too developed and highly organized for a nation in transition from feudalism to modernism.[45] Curiously, during his lengthy European visit Tanaka stayed for a relatively short time in France, although he collected many reports. The significance of Tanaka's apparent lack of interest in French education as a model for modern Japanese education should not be overlooked. The first public school system in Japan, for which Tanaka was responsible upon return home, is often characterized as profoundly influenced by the French school system. By this time, however, Tanaka had become deeply attracted to American education. Niijima Jō's influence may have been a factor, as revealed by his bias in a letter from Holland: "The American system is far superior to the Hollanders."[46]

Many reports were gathered from the various stops in Europe that placed a heavy burden on Niijima. As the trip came to an end, he wrote to his former teacher at Amherst College, Professor Julius Seelye, that "Since last September I settled down in Berlin and engaged to the work of translation, i.e. translating the school systems in the different countries in Europe into the Japanese."[47] Those translations became part of Tanaka's final report, the *Riji Kōtei*, on his mission to the West.

One vital factor became clear during Tanaka's research trip throughout the West. There can be no misunderstanding of his purpose which he was aware of from the day he left Japan for San Francisco. Although considered a junior member of the Iwakura Mission when it departed from Yokohama in late 1871, Tanaka knew that his responsibility upon returning home sometime in 1873 was of momentous import to the future of Japan. Niijima Jō reveals that during the trip, Tanaka repeatedly asked Niijima to return to his native country "to assist him in establishing a new school system in Japan."[48] Niijima, however, decided not to return to Japan with Tanaka. Rather, he was determined to complete his theological studies in America in order to return to his homeland as a Christian minister.

After one year, three months, and twenty-one days abroad, Tanaka Fujimaro finally returned home in March of 1873.[49] His wife recalled that her husband suddenly arrived at the front door of their Tokyo home after his long absence without previously notifying her.[50] That thoughtlessness toward his wife, a rarity in their relationship, may have been caused to some degree by what was on his mind. From the moment he returned to the Ministry of Education on March 27, he assumed responsibility for establishing Japan's first modern school system.[51] As an experienced comparative educator who had surveyed the educational systems throughout the West, he was uniquely prepared for the momentous task of laying the very foundation of Japanese education in the modern era, the focus of the following chapter.

6

The Modern Education
of Japanese Girls

GEORGETOWN, BRYN MAWR,
VASSAR, 1872

The year 1872 marks the dawn of the modern era in the history of education for Japanese women. During that year, just four years after the Meiji Restoration, two seeds were planted that gradually blossomed into movements that eroded centuries of feudal attitudes toward female education. The first stems from the nation's initial attempt to implement a national school system, the Gakusei of 1872. The intent was to provide a public elementary school education for all children regardless of gender. The second was the dispatch of five Japanese girls to the United States in 1872 to receive an American education. Upon return home as young women, they were to transmit modern American principles of education for females to Japan. The focus of this chapter concerns the second of the two.

Once again, a truly unique set of circumstances led to the unlikely scenario of five Japanese girls from seven to fifteen years old being dispatched to the United States in late 1871 with the Iwakura Mission. With no facility in the English language and virtually no preplanning, it was hoped that they would be brought up as American girls in American homes, attending American schools. After ten years they were then expected to return home and, as educated Japanese women, introduce an American-style education for Japanese girls on the basis of their American experiences. As improbable as it appears, this long-range plan actually played out as originally envisioned.

No other sector of education remained in such a backward condition as that available for girls at the beginning of the Meiji period in 1868. The common attitude toward females in general, which governed their educational opportunities, was profoundly influenced by a book written in the early seventeenth century titled *Onna Daigaku*, a cruel title literally meaning Women's Great Education or Greater Learning for Women. It was written by one of Japan's historical moralists, Kaibara Ekken. In a feudalistic agrarian society immeasurably influenced by Confucian concepts of social stratification and harmony between the higher and lower strata, Japanese women were locked in a subservient position. *Onna Daigaku* codified their status.

Prior to the spread of Confucian thought into Japan from China, a few women held exalted positions in society. For example, among the 122 emperors before Meiji, there were several female emperors, a status not available to women today. There were also several female authors who achieved distinction, most notably

Lady Murasaki with her well-known *Tales of Genji* memorialized by magnificent contemporary Kabuki performances. With the official adoption of Confucian ideology by the Tokugawa regime from the 1600s, male supremacy became more rigidly applied than ever. It was during the reign of the samurai that Kaibara wrote his powerful thesis laying out the precepts that governed the relationships between men and women. It was intended to codify the accepted lifestyle of a female first as a daughter and then mother in the household of a Japanese family in the 1600s.

Kaibara Ekken

Kaibara Ekken was born in Fukuoka on the southern island of Kyushu in 1630, at the early stage of the Tokugawa era of the samurai.[1] Son of a medical man, he was brought up in the studies of Confucian classics, later teaching in local han schools. He traveled throughout Japan writing travel accounts that were widely circulated, along with many moral commentaries that established him as an intellectual moralist of the early Tokugawa period.

The underlying thesis of Kaibara's *Onna Daigaku* was female subservience governing a woman's life from birth to death. At each stage of life she must follow the rules that prevail in the household. The wife was always to address the father and then husband as "master and lord," either shujin or danna. The Three Obediences of every girl—obedience to her parents while at home, obedience to her husband when married, and obedience to her son as head of the house when she is widowed—prevailed.[2] The primary purpose of female education, imparted by the family, was to instill the concepts of subservience and obedience as a "good mother and faithful wife" (*ryōsai*). This well-known adage remains, usually in jest, in the vocabulary of contemporary Japan. The following excerpt from a translation by Basil Chamberlain, a leading scholar on Japanese social institutions who resided in Japan during the Meiji era, sets the tone.[3]

> Seeing that it is a girl's destiny, on reaching womanhood, to go to a new home, and live in submission to her father-in-law and mother-in-law, it is even more incumbent upon her than it is on a boy to receive with all reverence her parents' instructions. . . .
>
> From her earliest youth, a girl should observe the line of demarcation separating women from men. . . . It is written likewise, in the Lesser Learning, that a woman must form no friendship and no intimacy, except when ordered to do so by her parents. . . .
>
> In China, marriage is called returning, for the reason that a woman must consider her husband's home as her own, and that, when she marries, she is therefore returning to her own home. However humble and needy may be her husband's position, she must find no fault with him. . . . The sage of old [Confucius] taught that, once married, she must never leave her husband's house. . . .
>
> It is the chief duty of a girl living in the parental house to practice filial piety towards her father and mother. . . . But after marriage, her chief duty is to honour her father-in-law and mother-in-law. . . .

A woman has no particular lord. She must look to her husband as her lord, and must serve him with all worship and reverence, not despising or thinking lightly of him. . . . The great life-long duty of a woman is obedience. . . . When the husband issues his instructions, the wife must never disobey them. . . .

Let her never even dream of jealousy. If her husband be dissolute, she must expostulate with him, but never either nurse or vent her anger. A woman must be ever on the alert, and keep a strict watch of her own conduct. In the morning she must rise early, and at night go late to bed. While young, she must avoid the intimacy of familiarity of her husband's kinsmen, comrades, and retainers. . . .

The five worst maladies that afflict the female mind are: indocility, discontent, slander, jealousy, and silliness. . . .

Parents! Teach the foregoing maxims to your daughters from their tenderest years! Copy them out from time to time, that they may be read and never forget them. . . . How true is that ancient saying; A man knoweth how to spend a million pieces of money in marrying off his daughter, but knoweth not how to spend an hundred thousand in bringing up his child. Such as have daughters must lay this well to heart.

General Kuroda Kiyotaka

Upon the overthrow of the Tokugawa regime in 1868, a major challenge in promoting the modern education of women was how to liberate them from the all-pervasive influence of the classic *Onna Daigaku*. One of the first to make the effort was a high-ranking military officer, Kuroda Kiyotaka, a general in the new army who realized the importance of female education in the modernization of the nation. As a former samurai warrior, Kuroda was an unlikely figure to pioneer the western education of Japanese girls.

Kuroda Kiyotaka is seldom recognized for his contributions to female education. He is best known as a general, short-lived prime minister, and the individual most closely related to the development of Japan's last frontier, the northern island of Hokkaido. This last, his position in the early 1870s as director of the Bureau of Frontier Development (Kaitakushi) responsible for the advancement of Hokkaido, enabled him to make his most consequential contribution to the field of female education.

Born in a lower-ranking samurai family of the Satsuma clan in the town of Kagoshima in 1840, Kuroda witnessed the attack on his birthplace by the British Navy in 1863.[4] He ultimately became involved in the intrigue surrounding the Meiji Restoration of the late 1860s. During the final days of the conflict in 1868, remnants of the defeated Tokugawa forces fled north to the sparsely inhabited island of Hokkaido. At that time this northernmost frontier island had received little attention by the Tokugawa government. In a final encounter that ended military resistance to the new government, the fugitives surrendered to the Meiji forces under the command of Kuroda.

Perceiving the Russian threat as increasingly serious, the Meiji government in July 1869 opened the Kaitakushi, the Frontier Development Bureau responsible for the advancement of Hokkaido. Kuroda was appointed to the bureau and took control of it from 1870. He promptly devised a twofold plan for the development of the island. He recognized the necessity of hiring foreign specialists in surveying, mining, and so on, and particularly agriculture, that would attract immigrant farmers to the inhospitable region. Second, he recommended that Japanese youth be sent abroad to gain developmental skills necessary to accomplish his formidable goal.

In order to find foreign specialists to work in Japan, Kuroda traveled to Europe and America in 1870–1871. When he visited the Japanese legation in Washington in January of 1871 on his way home from England, the secretary serving Mori Arinori as chargé d'affaires was Charles Lanman, who recorded the event that brought together the two samurai from Satsuma. It was a firsthand account of Kuroda's visits with Mori that reveals his revolutionary attitude toward the education of Japanese girls.

> During his [Kuroda's] two brief visits to this country, he became so deeply impressed with the happy condition of the American woman, that he began to inquire into the cause of such a state of things, and was told that it was because the women of the country were educated, treated with the highest consideration, and are regarded equal to men in all the higher qualities of humanity. With his friend, Mr. Arinori Mori, he held several long discussions on the subject, took the advanced ground that the Japanese ought to intermarry with the people of the more enlightened foreign nations, and in his zeal, went so far as to insist that Mr. Mori should marry an American lady without delay. To this the youthful minister replied that he considered himself a true patriot, and would like to oblige his friend, but did not think it necessary for him to go into the marrying business so suddenly. From that time, however, Mr. Kuroda thought and talked unceasingly about the importance of educating the women of his native land.[5]

Returning home in July 1871, Kuroda presented a memorial to the government to the effect that the work of pioneering was not confined to the opening of rivers and mountains, nor even to the augmenting of population, but that it must take cognizance of the all-important labor of fostering human talents, of training youthful minds—in other words, that the first great aim never to be lost sight of in founding a new colony must be to provide itself with men and women properly equipped to become the leaders of a pioneering population. He closed his memorial with a suggestion to send abroad some young girls who might someday become mothers in the infant colony.[6]

Under Kuroda's proposal submitted to the government, Japanese girls would be sent to the United States for a period of ten years to receive the finest education available in America. Kuroda's department held a recruitment effort that resulted in no applications. The second recruitment produced five applicants, all originating from samurai families, ranging in age from seven to fifteen. Among them, two would become leading proponents of modern education for Japanese girls.

Tsuda Umeko and Yamakawa Sutematsu

Tsuda Umeko, a mere seven years old when she departed Japan for the United States for an American education, was born in 1865. Her father, Sen, who made the monumental decision to apply to the government for a scholarship for his daughter, originated from a samurai family in an obscure han. Exhibiting a progressive nature, he had learned English in difficult times, securing an assignment with an official diplomatic mission to the West in the late 1850s. With an interest in western agriculture, he developed a relationship after the Meiji Restoration with Kuroda's Bureau of Frontier Development, which had by then embarked on modern agriculture programs for Hokkaido. He consequently became aware of the bureau's recruitment of girls for study in America. Concerned about his own daughters' educational opportunities in Japan, he submitted an application for his second daughter, Umeko, which was approved.[7]

The background of Yamakawa Sutematsu is far more dramatic; she was to become Japan's first female university graduate.[8] She was the daughter of a ranking samurai from the Aizu clan that fought the Meiji military forces to the bitter end in 1868. In the final classic siege in feudal Japan, Sutematsu was trapped inside the doomed castle with her two older brothers, Kenjirō, who was to become president of Tokyo Imperial University, and Hiroshi, later an army general and first president of the Higher Tokyo Teacher Training College.

At the time of the castle siege in 1868, Sutematsu was eight years old. Her personal account of the episode, recollected as an adult in Japan and composed in English, stands as a tribute to her courage as well as the education she received in the United States. It is surely the only recorded account originally in English by a Japanese who was on the scene of a castle siege in feudal Japan.

> We women and children were divided into bands of workers, those who washed and cooked the rice, those who did the housework, and those who made the ammunition for the men at the front. I was too young to be trusted with the making of cartridges, so the work allotted me was to bring the leaden balls from the storehouses, and after they had been made up into cartridges to carry them back to another storehouse, whence they were sent to the men. . . . The last month of the siege, the imperial troops planted guns on the hills around us, and not a day passed when cannon-balls did not whiz over our heads, dropping into the castle and crushing into the keep itself. It was then part of my work to roll them together in piles, out of the way. My mother, sister, sister-in-law and I expected death at any minute but none of us liked the idea of being mutilated instead of killed outright. So we made our mother promise that if any of us should be mortally wounded she would cut off our heads in true samurai fashion. A few days after this, while we were snatching a mouthful of food, a shell fell into the room, and bursting, wounded my sister-in-law in the breast and me in the neck. My wound was nothing to speak of, and I was up and at work again at the end of the week. It was different with my sister-in-law. We saw that she must die. . . . Strange as it may seem, my

future husband was one of the attacking forces and was wounded during the night assault. Little did I dream that I should be the wife of one of the enemy whose cannon-balls I so carefully rolled into heaps.[9]

Following the surrender of Aizu forces in September 1868, Sutematsu's family along with the bulk of her clan were forced by the victorious Meiji government to move north for resettlement in an isolated district assigned to them. They suffered terribly under harsh conditions. Her brother Hiroshi, who would later rise to the rank of general in the new Meiji army, was placed in charge of the clan. Meanwhile other remnants in opposition to the new government had fled north to the island of Hokkaido where they were shortly thereafter subdued by government forces under Kuroda Kiyotaka.

In 1871 Sutematsu's other brother Hiroshi, responsible for the family and the Aizu clan in exile, learned of Kuroda's plan to send young girls abroad for a modern education to promote the development of Hokkaido. Apparently concerned over the future of his sister, Hiroshi submitted an application to the Frontier Bureau on behalf of Sutematsu.[10] With only five applicants, the bureau approved Sutematsu's candidacy along with the other four. Under this unusual set of circumstances, Tsuda Umeko, age seven, from Tokyo unexpectedly met Yamakawa Sutematsu, age eleven, from Aizu preparing to board a ship in late 1871 bound for the United States. The plan called for them to attend American schools for the next ten years at government expense. They had no preparation in the English language nor any introduction to American customs.

The five girls were invited to the palace for a private audience with the empress before their departure, an indication of the Imperial Household's interest in the child mission. In itself, the event epitomized the position of females in Japan at the beginning of the modern era, including that of the empress herself. It marked the first time that she met with girls from samurai families. In the arcane imperial ritual of the period, it is clear that the empress, in fact, never saw the five little girls. Umeko's memories of the event confirm this. "All that remains in my vision—the memory of a child of six—is a vision of strong, stone-walled enclosures, broad gates, and wondrous passageways, with the rustling silks and gorgeous dresses of the court ladies, and then a large room with a heavy hanging screen, through which we could see nothing even if we had dared to raise our bowed heads, but behind which we knew was seated the sacred presence."[11]

In a farewell message to the Iwakura Mission, Emperor Meiji indirectly recognized the purpose of including the contingent of five girls among the fifty ranking government officers. He added a unique twist by encouraging Japanese women to travel abroad with the specific goal of modernizing Japanese society. "We lack superior institutions for high female culture. Our women should not be ignorant of these great principles on which the happiness of daily life frequently demands. How important the education of mothers, on whom future generations almost wholly rely for the early cultivation of those intellectual tastes which an enlightened system of training is designed to promote. . . . Liberty is therefore granted

Figure 13. Departure of the Japanese Children for America. From Akiko Kuno, *Unexpected Destinations: The Poignant Story of Japan's First Vassar Graduate* (Tokyo: Kōdansha International, 1993), 112.

wives and sisters to accompany their relatives on foreign tours, that they may acquaint themselves with better forms of female education, and, on their return, introduce beneficial improvements in the training of our children."[12]

The girls departed with the Iwakura Mission on December 21, 1871, on the steamer *America* amid a colorful ceremony with a fanfare of gun salvos. In addition to the Iwakura Mission of about fifty members, the United States minister to Japan, Charles DeLong, and his wife were on board, returning to Washington. Mrs. Delong had agreed to chaperone the five Japanese children, although she did not speak Japanese and the girls only knew a smattering of English words.

The Iwakura Mission with the five little girls in tow arrived in San Francisco on January 15, 1872, after a rough sailing across the Pacific Ocean. Since the diplomatic mission took precedence wherever it went, little attention was given to the girls. They had to persevere through the various welcoming ceremonies and the long train trip across the United States to Washington, which included several stopovers at major cities such as Chicago. Upon the arrival of the mission, referred to as the Japanese embassy, in Washington on February 29, 1872, the *Evening Star* reported that none of the five girls in the party could speak a word of English. In a curious misinterpretation of their presence in the capital of the United States, the article explained that "Their mission is to be educated here, and to return to Japan and assist in rearing female wall flowers to adorn the court of the Mikado."[13]

The American reporter who wrote that story was obviously unaware of the purpose for sending the girls to America. The *Evening Star* also reported that in response to the announcement that the girls would accompany the embassy, many Americans had contacted the Japanese legation offering to "take them in and educate them." Before any arrangements could be made, they were placed under the supervision and care of Mr. and Mrs. Lanman in Georgetown.[14]

From this simple announcement in a local newspaper, no American reader could have imagined that a new era in the modern education of Japanese women was about to unfold. And at the heart of it was, once again, an uncommon American. Charles Lanman by chance became intimately involved in the modern education of Japanese women from the moment the girls arrived in Washington. The year before the mission's arrival in the United States, Joseph Henry, director of the Smithsonian Institution and a distinguished physicist, introduced Lanman to Mori Arinori.[15] As Japan's first envoy to Washington, Mori was looking for help to prepare a treatise on American life. Mori hired Lanman to compile that work, entitled *Life and Resources in America*, published in the latter half of 1871.

Charles Lanman, secretary of the Japanese legation when the Iwakura Mission arrived in Washington in 1872, lived in the Georgetown area of the capital. In contrast to his fashionable city life, throughout much of his life he spent his vacations exploring wild regions in a canoe, "being one of the earliest white men to introduce it as a pleasure craft."[16] The great author Washington Irving once characterized the adventurous Lanman as "the picturesque explorer of our country." Two of Lanman's best-known books at the time reflect his love of adventure: *A Tour to the River Saguenay* (1848) and *Adventures in the Wilds of America* (1854).[17]

Mori Arinori, an unmarried diplomat only twenty-four years old when the five young girls arrived at the Japanese legation in Washington, was overwhelmed with the responsibility of taking care of them. Accordingly the girls were first sent to the Lanman home in Georgetown under Mrs. Lanman's care until permanent arrangements could be made. They were then placed in a house rented by the Japanese legation, and tutored by hired governesses. Niijima Jō, who had been summoned from his studies in Massachusetts to serve as a translator for Tanaka Fujimaro from the Ministry of Education, was staying nearby. His visit with the girls illustrates the strange environment in which the Japanese girls had been suddenly placed. "I saw two of them yesterday. One is them is about fifteen years old and another is only eight years old, the daughter of my old classmate, who is now a prominent officer in the country. She is a little cunning and a cute thing I ever saw. I had pleasant conversation with them and dined with them too. They don't understand what the ladies in the families speak to them; so when I go there to see them they are delighted to see me, and ask me ever so many questions. . . . They make such graceful Japanese bow each time when I speak to them."[18]

The destination of the five girls was finally decided in the fall of 1872 after months of temporary arrangements. In fact, the oldest two were sent back to Japan partly for health reasons. A family in New Haven, Connecticut, agreed to accept Yamakawa Sutematsu and Nagai Shige, considered later in this chapter. Tsuda Umeko, by now seven years old, was the major challenge. The Lanmans, who were childless, quickly became attached to her and asked that they be allowed to keep her with them. In this happenstance manner, Mr. and Mrs. Charles Lanman of Georgetown, Washington, became the surrogate parents responsible for the education of Tsuda Umeko, who would eventually establish the first private college for women in modern Japan. "As our house was the one she [Umeko] first entered on her arrival in Washington, and my wife had become much interested in the child and felt that she was then too young to be sent to a boarding school, it was decided that she should come to us from a temporary home in Washington on the first of November, 1872."[19]

The American Education of Tsuda Umeko and Yamakawa Stematsu

From 1872 to 1882, Tsuda Umeko and Yamakawa Sutematsu experienced an American education that few American girls could have dreamed of. Umeko grew up as the adored child of devoted sophisticated foster parents wise in the ways of the American government, living in the elegant Georgetown section of Washington, D.C. Ironically the setting could not have been more propitious for the future of female education in Japan for two major reasons. The Lanmans were totally committed to providing Umeko with the finest educational opportunities available for upper-class girls in Washington. And Umeko proved to be the ideal student. She was bright, devoted, and eager to learn.

The Lanmans entered Umeko at age seven into the prestigious private Georgetown Collegiate Institute where she excelled in her academic studies. Simultaneously Charles Lanman supplemented formal lessons by teaching composition to his "sunbeam from the Rising Sun" at home, constantly encouraging her to read and write. As the author of Daniel Webster's biography published in 1852, former librarian to the War Department, State Department, and House of Representatives, and host to Charles Dickens and Washington Irving in his home, Lanman personified the ideal tutor of English composition. Umeko indeed mastered the English language with an impressive writing style. It was exhibited throughout her life by the many letters she sent her American friends after returning to Japan, especially the huge number written to her American mother, Mrs. Lanman.[20]

During her elementary school days in America, several experiences undoubtedly influenced Umeko. Perhaps the most important was her baptism into the Christian faith. Although the Lanmans were apparently not overly religious, they were active members of the Episcopalian faith. It may have been an inevitable consequence that Umeko would come under the influence of Christianity and become baptized while living in America. The other was the opportunity to meet distinguished Americans. For example, on a trip to New England with her foster parents, she met two leading intellectuals of the day, Henry Wadsworth Longfellow and John Greenleaf Whittier. During the summer of 1876, she also visited the Philadelphia Centennial with her Japanese girlfriends, Yamakawa Sutematsu and Nagai Shige, who came down from New Haven, Connecticut. The three spent several weeks in Philadelphia accompanied by the Lanmans and the Japanese minister to America.

Even at home, Umeko had the opportunity to meet such distinguished American personalities as Daniel Webster, frequent houseguest of the Lanmans. Webster once held the reputation as "the most commanding figure in the United States Senate."[21] As secretary of state, Webster had engaged Lanman as his personal secretary. Ironically he held that position when Webster developed American foreign policy that sent the American naval fleet under Commodore Perry on the expedition into Japanese waters in 1853. That turning point in Japanese history led to the enforced opening of diplomatic relations between Japan and America that enabled Tsuda Umeko as a child to travel to America less than a decade later.

In June 1878, upon Umeko's completion of the Georgetown Collegiate Institute, the Lanmans enrolled her into the Archer Institute, a private finishing school for girls from the better families of Washington in preparation for college entry. She excelled not only in mathematics and languages but, according to a final report from the school, "Her progress in Latin, Mathematics, Physics, Astronomy and French, has been much in advance of her class, she having a clear insight into all the branches to which she has devoted herself."[22] Charles Lanman and his wife could not have asked for a more rewarding result from their efforts to provide their Japanese daughter with the finest education available in Washington in the 1870s.

Meanwhile, the educational experience of Yamakawa Sutematsu during her decade in America was as unusual as those of her childhood friend Umeko. In contrast to Umeko's American education in Washington, Sutematsu received her early American education in New England. Chargé d'Affaires Mori in Washington contacted friends in New Haven for assistance in locating someone to take care of both Sutematsu and the third remaining girl, Nagai Shigeko. Among those consulted were Sutematsu's brother Kenjirō, then studying at Yale University, former Yale president Theodore Woolsey, and the superintendent of education for Connecticut, Birdsey Northrop. Through a coincidental set of relationships with these three, Reverend Leonard Bacon agreed to accept both of the girls as his own children into his home in the charming town of New Haven. At the age of seventy-one, his commitment to provide an education for two Japanese children for the next ten years, at Japanese government expense, illustrated the unusual nature of the man. A graduate of Yale University, Bacon served a local Congregational Church for many years as a pastor noted for his powerful sermons.

Like Umeko in Washington, Sutematsu, at age eleven in 1872, was suddenly placed within an environment closely related to leading American educators of the period. Many were deeply influenced by one of the great American colonial universities, Yale. Sutematsu's foster father Bacon himself lectured in the theological department of Yale.[23] In other words, Sutematsu in New England, like Umeko in Washington, was about to undergo an educational experience in the United States that few American girls could dream of. Moreover, the family of Reverend Bacon included a young daughter from his second marriage nearly the same age as Sutematsu. Alice Bacon would become not only a foster sister of Sutematsu but a lifelong cherished friend of both Sutematsu and Umeko. The other Japanese child, Shigeko, was quickly placed in the home of another influential citizen of New Haven so that the two girls would not speak Japanese to each other on a daily basis.

Figure 14. Yamakawa Sutematsu at Vassar College.
From Akiko Kuno, *Unexpected Destinations: The Poignant Story of Japan's First Vassar Graduate* (Tokyo: Kōdansha International, 1993), 205.

Following intensive tutoring by Mrs. Bacon, Sutematsu entered the local Hill House High School in the college preparatory curriculum. She excelled in her academic studies from the beginning of her American education. Her brother Kenjirō, a student at nearby Yale University, supplemented her formal schooling in English with Japanese lessons each week. Indicative of the style of life Sutematsu led, in 1874 the superintendent of Connecticut education, Birdsey Northrop, close friend of Mori Arinori, personally escorted Sutematsu and Shigeko to Washington. They stayed with Umeko at the Lanman house in Georgetown.[24]

On completion of her high school studies at Hillhouse, and upon recommendation of Northrop, the chief educational officer of Connecticut, Sutematsu visited various well-known colleges for women in the New England area. She finally chose Vassar, located in Poughkeepsie in the state of New York. Her close friend Nagai Shigeko entered Vassar at the same time.

Shigeko would leave the school one year before graduation to return to Japan, where she married a naval officer she met while at Vassar when he was a cadet at the U.S. Naval Academy. He became an admiral in the Japanese navy. Sutematsu, however, remained for the full four-year course at Vassar, living in the dormitory and enjoying every moment of her American education. Joining in many extracurricular activities while maintaining high academic grades, she was elected class president during her sophomore year. Finally, in 1882 Sutematsu graduated from this elite American college for women as valedictorian. Dressed in Japanese kimono, she gave a valedictorian address entitled "British Policy toward Japan."[25] It was, of course, given in English.

In 1881, when the ten-year experiment by General Kuroda's Frontier Development Bureau ended, the Japanese government notified the three scholarship recipients in America to come home. Shigeko returned immediately. In order to graduate from the Archer Institute, a college preparatory school, Umeko was allowed to remain for an additional year before returning home in 1882. Lanman, writing in his report *Leading Men of Japan* published under the sponsorship of the Japanese legation, summed up his attitude toward his Japanese daughter when writing about her father Tsuda Sen as one of the leading men. Without revealing his personal relationship to Umeko as her American father, Lanman meant his comments more as a tribute to her than her Japanese father, an agriculturalist, and his experimental garden distinguished for its flowers and vegetables from the West. "In his style of living and the adornments of his house, Mr. Tsuda has adopted many of the ideas gathered by him in foreign lands; and the extensive garden which surrounds his dwelling is said to be one of the most beautiful in the city of Tokyo. Nor will a more interesting flower be seen in the coming years, than the form of his daughter Ume Tsuda, who has for the last ten years been receiving a judicious education in the city of Washington, which was given to her by the Japanese government as a tribute of respect for her distinguished father."[26]

Umeko, upon completion of the Archer finishing school in Washington at age seventeen, and Sutematsu at age twenty-two upon graduation from Vassar College, departed for Japan in October of 1882. The first grand experiment in modern education for Japanese women had come to an end. As originally envisioned by General Kuroda Kiyotaka in 1871 as a means to develop the last frontier of Japan, the proposal to educate Japanese girls in America resulted in producing several young women with impeccable western academic credentials. One overriding question confronted Umeko and Sutematsu as they arrived in Japan in November 1882: How could they contribute to the modern education of Japanese women as a result of their prestigious American education?

During the decade that Sutematsu and Umeko had spent in the United States, conditions had drastically changed in Japan. Although the two young ladies were the most educated Japanese women at that time, they could not read, write, or speak the Japanese language like their contemporaries. Having received the finest education available for women in America, they were culturally separated from their Japanese cohorts. To complicate matters further, the Frontier Bureau for the Development of Hokkaido that had financed their American education had been closed by the government the year before they returned home. Umeko and Sutematsu were essentially foreigners not only in their own homeland but within their own families, without any plans for the future.

Within the year Sutematsu's life underwent a sudden change. Although courted by progressive Japanese boys, Sutematsu unexpectedly received an offer of marriage by a ranking Japanese army officer whose young wife had suddenly died. General Oyama Iwao, minister of war and nearly twenty years older than Sutematsu, and who had studied in France for several years, made a proposal of marriage. In an excruciating decision, Sutematsu decided that she could best make a major contribution to the modern education of Japanese women as the wife of a senior member of the Japanese government. One year after she graduated from Vassar College in America she became the wife of the Japanese minister of war and subsequently the mother of his three children. As noted previously, General Oyama had served with the Meiji forces that laid siege to the Aizu castle in 1868 when Sutematsu at age eight aided in the defense of the castle.

Meanwhile, Tsuda Umeko searched for a position where she could use her American education for the benefit of Japanese women. Unfortunately when she returned from America in 1882, the Ministry of Education had come under the influence of conservative leaders who were promoting moral education based on Confucian classics. Consequently there was little interest by the ministry in promoting modern higher education for Japanese girls. Umeko bided her time in frustration, teaching here and there while tutoring on the side.

Umeko's tutoring jobs brought her into contact with ranking government officials including Itō Hirobumi, head of government, and Minister of Education Mori Arinori. Itō invited her to live in his household while teaching English and western customs to his wife. When Mori, chargé d'affaires in Washington when Umeko arrived with the Iwakura Mission, returned to Japan in 1884 from his position as minister to England, he hired Umeko to tutor his children in English so they would not lose their foreign language skills gained from four years in London.

In September 1885, Umeko finally found a teaching position. At the age of twenty, and with only a college preparatory education in America, she was appointed to the faculty of the new Peeress School for girls from the upper classes. However, with the appointment of a general as president of the school by the Ministry of Education, Umeko accepted the fact that her ideas on modern education for Japanese women on the American model would have little recognition at the school. Her biographer succinctly describes Umeko's attitude: "Before long Ume too realized how hard it would be to teach these girls any intellectual independence. She was working not only against all their previous training but against the school's own policies."[27] Growing increasingly restless and struggling to readjust to the Japanese language, especially its written form, which she had never been taught, Umeko became at times discouraged with her life in her native country as expressed in many letters to her American mother, Mrs. Lanman.

By 1889, Umeko had decided to continue her western education by enrolling in an American college for women. Although she had completed eleven years of schooling in Georgetown at outstanding private schools, she had not received any education beyond the secondary level. Through friends in America, she was able to enroll at Bryn Mawr College near Philadelphia in September 1889. She was given a two-year leave of absence from the Peeress School, which was extended for a further year at her request. For the next two and a half years Umeko experienced life as a student at one of America's premier institutions of higher education for women. She majored in biology. Since the school was located only a few hours from Washington, she was able to maintain close contacts with her American foster parents, the Lanmans. A friend later characterized Umeko's choice of Bryn

Figure 15. Tsuda Umeko, Alice Bacon, Nagai Shigeko, and Yamakawa Sutematsu.
From Yoshiko Furuki, *The White Plum: A Biography of Ume Tsuda* (Tokyo: Weatherhill,
1991), 119.

Mawr as another instance of the right Japanese being in the right place at the right time. "The college was a fortunate choice. Bryn Mawr was only four years old, with a young Dean and faculty eager for experiment, zealous to present the highest standards of scholarship [for women] before a still somewhat skeptical masculine world."[28]

Umeko thrived as a dormitory student at Bryn Mawr. Her academic accomplishments warranted special recognition by the president who cited her high grades especially in biology and chemistry. He also noted that Umeko had an "extraordinary command of the English language, both in speech and writing, and is peculiarly fitted to teach it." The school made an exceptional offer to her to remain at the institution to continue the scientific research she had become involved in, collaborating with a distinguished faculty member in the field of genetics. She declined the offer and decided to return home once again with a goal that could be characterized as establishing a Bryn Mawr in Japan. Her model for herself may have been the female dean of Bryn Mawr at the time, Martha Carey Thomas, a leading educator of women in America.[29]

The seeds of modern education for Japanese women that were planted when five young Japanese girls arrived in the American capital of Washington in 1872 finally took root many years later, well beyond the focus of this book. In September 1900, Tsuda Umeko, with the never-wavering assistance of Yamakawa Sutematsu and Sutematsu's American sister Alice Bacon, as well as the other Japanese girl who went to America with her, Nagai Shigeko, founded the "first school to offer higher education to women" in Japan.[30] It was simply named Eigaku Juku (Women's Institute of English Studies). Ten students were enrolled for a three-year course primarily involved in English language education that reflected the education of its primary founder. It would become known as Tsuda College for Women, a leading institution of higher education for Japanese females in the twentieth century.

7 The Modern Japanese Teacher

THE SAN FRANCISCO METHOD,
1872–1873

The year 1872 marked the beginning of teacher training in modern Japan. Through an unusual set of circumstances, an obscure elementary school teacher from San Francisco made one of the most decisive contributions to Japanese education. Marion McDonnel Scott was given the responsibility by the Ministry of Education in 1872 to set the curriculum, determine the textbooks, and develop the teaching methods for the nation's first national system of modern public elementary schools scheduled to open in 1873. It was a remarkable opportunity for an unpretentious American, the vice principal of an elementary school in San Francisco, to teach English at Japan's only institution of higher education, Nankō, in 1871. One year later he unexpectedly found himself at the very center of the nation's first teacher-training school. Ironically, Scott may not have been trained as a teacher himself since research into his background in America has not yet revealed such training.

When Scott was suddenly transferred from Nankō to the newly opened Tokyo Teacher Training School in 1872, he accepted a mandate to teach eighteen Japanese young men, nearly all from the samurai class, how to teach Japanese children in a modern elementary classroom. He was expected to teach his warrior-students, in English, exactly how he taught American children in California using the same curricula, the same textbooks, and the same teaching methods. Scott's classroom in downtown Tokyo marked the first time that any Japanese had been trained in teaching methodology, to follow a prescribed curricula, and to use textbooks designed for the elementary classroom, in this case for American children. It served as a model for all public elementary schools in Japan prescribed by law from 1873.

The opportunity for Scott to assume such a critical position in Meiji Japan in September 1872 resulted from the issuance of the Gakusei, the first national plan for education, by the Ministry of Education in August of the same year.[1] The primary provision of the new ordinance stipulated that each local community must build a public elementary school to accommodate all children within the proper age range with the opening of the school year in April 1873. Ministry officials realized that at this initial stage of educational modernization, no reform of education could be effective if classroom teachers for the new schools were not trained in modern teaching methodology. Accordingly, in the same month as the Gakusei was promulgated, May 1872, the fifth year after the Meiji Restoration, the Ministry of Education published a formal notification of its plan to open the first training school for elementary teachers in Tokyo.[2]

The preface stipulated that the purpose of the new school to train teachers was specifically designed to meet the requirements of the Gakusei. It reiterated the intent of the Gakusei to develop personal independence without discrimination according to social class through a national public school system. Therefore, one of the most urgent demands was the training of teachers for the new public elementary schools. Foreign countries, it noted, already had teacher training schools. Thus it was deemed necessary to follow their examples by hiring a foreign teacher and employing a foreign curriculum and school regulations as the model for Japan. The following provisions were included:

1. One foreign instructor will be employed on the faculty.
2. One translator will be employed to translate the foreign teacher's lectures.
3. Twenty-four students from age twenty-four, who studied Japanese and Chinese classics, calligraphy, and basic mathematics, will be selected by examination for the first class.
4. The lectures and curriculum will be based on foreign practices in order to develop the curriculum for the new public elementary schools.
5. Ninety pupils will be chosen for an attached elementary school to be taught by the twenty-four teacher trainees using the methodology taught to them by the foreign instructor.
6. Each student-trainee will be paid 11 yen per month from the national budget.
7. Upon graduation each student will be awarded a license to teach, and will become a certified teacher according to a written pledge made at the time of entry.[3]

The key figure in the plan was the foreign instructor since the success or failure of the entire project depended primarily on this one individual. In one of the most unlikely developments in the modern history of Japanese education, Marion McDonnel Scott, employing the so-called "San Francisco Method," set in motion a revolution in Japanese education in the early 1870s.[4] From then on, no other individual figured so prominently in the great transformation of the Japanese elementary school classroom from the feudal to the modern.

The underlying purpose in hiring Scott was not restricted to the training of teachers in modern methodology. Ministry of Education officials had far more grandiose goals than that. They were searching for a new curriculum, new teaching materials, and new textbooks, all from California, to accompany the latest teaching techniques. It was an enormous responsibility placed upon this young American who was hired by the Japanese government at the impressive sum of 200 yen per month, the equivalent of about $200, considerably more than he earned as a public school teacher in San Francisco in 1870.[5]

The connection between Marion Scott and modern Japanese education in a sense began when Scott left his home in Virginia in 1864 at the height of the American Civil War. History does not yet reveal the motive that led this young American from a small town in the eastern part of the United States to the rapidly growing frontier town of San Francisco in the far west. One could speculate that the Civil

Figure 16. Marion McDonald Scott.
From Hirata Muneyoshi, *M. M. Sucotto
no Kenkyū* (Tokyo: Kazama Shoten, 1995),
preface.

War that raged up and down Virginia from 1861 to 1865 may have been a factor in the mind of a young Virginian male eligible for military duty. Nevertheless, the fact that Scott chanced the long and dangerous journey as a southerner picking his way through the war zone and on through the volatile western frontier to the turbulent society of San Francisco brands the young man as a true adventurer.

Scott never envisioned that west for him would become the Far East of Japan, a mysterious country to the Americans of the 1870s about which Scott had little if any knowledge. Rather, he was on his way to California where he would become an elementary school teacher in a typical public school in San Francisco. Again historical evidence has not been uncovered revealing why or how he became a teacher. Records in the San Francisco Public Library list him first as an assistant teacher, and in 1871 just prior to his departure for Japan, as vice principal of the South San Francisco Grammar School.[6]

Scott's Japanese biographer claims that he was a graduate of the University of Virginia, in spite of the fact that Scott's name does not appear on any student records of the institution. That could have been a result of the chaotic Civil War. Since that university only had three departments during the Civil War—law, medicine, and engineering—the conjecture is that Scott graduated from the law department. A post-Japan article on law published by Scott, and the conferring on him of an honorary doctorate of law by the University of Hawaii, lends some credence to this speculation.[7] If Scott did in fact graduate from the law department of an American university, an unproven assumption, he was therefore not formally trained as an elementary school teacher.

Scott's official translator at the Tokyo Teacher Training School was Tsuboi Gendo, who studied English at Kaisei Gakkō; he played an important role in the early modernization process as a translator. Recollecting fifty years later the startup of the school where he was assigned to Scott's classroom, translating both student questions and Scott's answers, Tsuboi claims that Scott was a graduate of an American teacher training school.[8] Regardless of his formal schooling, which remains historically unverifiable, Scott had passed the first-in-the-nation California state teacher's qualification examination. With that he had settled into the routine life of a public school teacher in the rough-and-tumble American West of the late 1860s. The fact that Scott may not have been trained as a teacher is obviously significant. The irony was that the Japanese entrusted the responsibility for modernizing their public school classrooms to an American without known formal teacher training, and with only five years of on-the-job experience. It illustrates not only the truly unique situation in which Scott was suddenly placed. It also exemplifies the condition of education in Japan at the time. The success of Scott's endeavors also speaks to the uncommon traits of this obscure American public school teacher.

Although California had been historically as well as geographically far from the mainstream of American educational developments, which were centered mostly in New England, there were certain educational innovations taking place in this frontier state. For example, the California superintendent of education, in his Second Biennial Report in 1867 when Scott was teaching in San Francisco, boasted that "California is the only State in the Union in which teachers have gained the legal right to be examined exclusively by the members of their own profession."[9] It was this state qualifying examination that Scott passed which enabled him to teach in a San Francisco public elementary school, perhaps without a certificate from a state normal school.

Upon entering the teaching profession, Scott was guided by, and subject to, the Rules and Regulations of the San Francisco Public Schools of California passed in 1866. In order to gain some understanding of, and appreciation for, the modern teaching methods Scott introduced into Japan from California, we turn to the provisions of the Rules and Regulations that he followed in his San Francisco classroom. He faithfully passed on to his Japanese teacher trainees these very practices, dubbed by Japanese historians simply the "San Francisco Method" (Sanfuranshisuko An).[10]

> Teachers shall daily examine the lessons of their various classes, and make such special preparation among them, if necessary, as not to be constantly confined to the textbook, and instruct all their pupils, without partiality, in those branches of school studies which their various classes may be pursuing. In all their intercourse with their scholars, they are required to strive to impress on their minds, both by precepts and example, the great importance of continued efforts for improvement in morals and manners, and deportment, as well as in useful learning; Teachers should only use the textbook for occasional reference, and should not permit it to be taken to the recitation to be referred to by the pupils, except in such exercises as absolutely require it. They should assign many questions of their own preparing, involving an application of what the

pupils have learned to the business of life. Teachers should endeavor to arouse and fix the attention of the whole class, and to occupy and bring into action as many of the faculties of their pupils as possible. They should never proceed with the recitation without the attention of the whole class, nor go round the class with recitation, always in the same order, or in regular rotation. Teachers at all times should exhibit proper animation themselves, manifesting a lively interest in the subject taught, avoid all heavy plodding movements, all formal routine in teaching, lest the pupil be dull and drowsy, and imbibe the notion that he studies only to recite."[11]

While teaching under the Rules and Regulations of the San Francisco public schools, Marion Scott was unexpectedly invited by the Japanese government to teach English at the most advanced educational institution in Japan, Nankō, in 1871. Guido Verbeck had been appointed to head that institution in October of the previous year with the intention of replacing nearly every locally hired teacher.[12] They had been hastily chosen from the ranks of foreigners who happened to be in Japan at the time, and many were totally unqualified. According to Verbeck's letter to his old friend, William Griffis, recently returned to America from teaching at Nankō, he was expecting Scott on the next ship: "The school goes on tolerably well. By this month's steamer two American teachers (Professor Scott and Mr. Wilson) come out for here."[13] Verbeck's use of the term "Professor Scott" is interesting since Scott came to Japan directly from an elementary school teaching position.

According to Scott's private correspondence written years later to the most prolific foreign chronicler of the period, the same William Griffis, he "was engaged to go to Japan through the agency of Arinori Mori, Minister at Washington, and Charles Walcott Brookes, Japanese Consul at San Francisco, and went to Tokyo in 1871."[14] It has been impossible to learn how or why Brookes chose Scott for this fateful mission.

Walcott Brookes, former merchant in San Francisco, had originally been employed by the Tokugawa government as a resident consul. He befriended Fukuzawa Yukichi during the Tokugawa mission to America when it stopped in San Francisco in 1860, later sending books to the prolific and influential Fukuzawa.[15] When the Iwakura Mission stopped over in San Francisco on its way to Washington in early 1872, Brookes joined the mission, accompanying it across America to Washington, where he met Mori Arinori, head of the new Japanese legation in Washington. It was this connection that led Mori, obviously on the basis of a request from Tokyo, to contact Brookes, who had returned to San Francisco, for assistance in choosing someone to teach English at Nankō. From Verbeck's letter quoted above, it can be assumed that Verbeck originated the request for an American teacher of English for Nankō.

From some undiscovered motivation, Scott reacted favorably to Brooke's invitation to teach English in Japan. He promptly resigned his post at a local San Francisco elementary school and departed for Tokyo with his wife, arriving in August of 1871. One factor may have been financial since his salary in Japan was quite attractive. However, he could never have imagined that just one year after his arrival he would be transferred from Japan's only national higher educational institution, Nankō, to the new Tokyo Teacher Training School at the center of the faculty.

Scott's arrival in Japan during the summer of 1871 was fortunately timed. One month earlier, on July 18, the Ministry of Education was established under the directorship of Etō Shimpei. He was shortly succeeded by Ōki Takatō. Their primary responsibility involved the development of a plan for the nation's first national school system. A special bureau was established by Ōki in December 1871, under the leadership of Mitsukuri Rinshō, to draw up the original plan called the Gakusei, the first national plan for education in the nation's history.

Within four months after Scott arrived in Japan, Mitsukuri's committee began the task of drawing up the Gakusei within the newly organized Ministry of Education. Scott, of course, had no relationship to the committee and may not have known its assignment at that time. Recognizing that the central recommendation to create 52,000 new public elementary schools would require an enormous number of new teachers, the Gakusei specifically called upon local prefectures throughout the country to establish elementary teacher-training schools as quickly as possible.[16]

To bring about a genuine reform of the traditional classroom and textbooks of the old terakoya schools, a simple clause was inserted in the instructions for implementing the Gakusei: in order for the new educational plan to succeed on the basis of western concepts, both the teaching methods and the curricula content should be based on western models. Accordingly, a new teacher-training school was hastily scheduled to open in Tokyo in August 1872 to train a nucleus of teachers in modern teaching methodology from the West.

From September 1871, Scott taught English at Nankō, the name being shortened from Daigaku Nankō, the Southern School. Nankō was a curious institution. The student body numbered 440, with half enrolled in the English Department and the remainder split between the French and German departments. Each section had a Japanese translator for the all-foreign faculty under Guido Verbeck.[17] Nankō served as the premier national school of higher education with advanced-level course work for the most able students solely in foreign studies and languages. In 1877, Nankō would become Tokyo University, discussed in a later chapter.

With the imminent opening of the Tokyo Teacher Training School in August 1872, filling the two key posts of principal and one foreign instructor around which the school was centered became critical. One of the few key figures in the Meiji Restoration who did not originate from the samurai class, Morokuzu Nobuzumi, was appointed principal. No particular reason can be discovered to explain this crucial appointment. Morokuzu had studied English at the Kaisei Gakkō from 1869 before joining the Ministry of Education in 1871. He was originally appointed by the first minister of education Ōki Takatō to the elementary and secondary education department at the age of twenty-one. At the age of twenty-three he was transferred from the ministry to the Tokyo Teacher Training School as the first principal from May 1872. His initial duty was to prepare the entrance examination for the first class to begin in September.[18] The Gakusei, which provided the motivation for the teacher-training school, was not officially proclaimed until August.[19]

Morokuzu suddenly found himself responsible for the new teacher training school as a young man in his early twenties with no experience in teacher training. No Japanese, of course, had any knowledge or experience in this field since there had never been a school for training teachers in modern methodology. The choice of Scott to fill the other critical post, with responsibility for introducing modern western teaching methods, was even more critical. According to Tsuji Shinji, a member of Mitsukuri's bureau within the Ministry of Education that drew up the Gakusei, Scott was chosen for the post for one primary reason. Ministry officials believed that Scott was a graduate of an American teacher-training college.[20]

Ministry of Education officials were surely aware of Scott's background as an elementary school teacher before coming to Japan. It was through the ministry that Scott had been originally recruited as a teacher of English for Nankō, a national institution under ministry control. Under the circumstances with the imminent opening of the school and the strategic position of a qualified foreign specialist in teaching methodology unfilled, it is understandable why the ministry invited Scott, already under contract with the ministry, to take the position based only on his previous position in San Francisco. He was transferred from Nankō after one year of his two-year contract was up, with a salary increase of 50 yen per month.[21] It is also conceivable that Guido Verbeck, Scott's principal at Nankō and an advisor to the ministry, may have recommended him for the new position.

The team of Principal Morokuzu, age twenty-three, and his head teacher Scott, twenty-nine years old, assisted by the young translator Tsuboi Gendo, then twenty-one, proved to be a dynamic one. The site for the new Tokyo Teacher Training School was in itself bursting with symbolism. The venerable Shōhei Gakkō, located in a Confucian temple in Tokyo, the most prestigious Confucian school during the Tokugawa period, was chosen for the site.[22] Not only was the intention of the new school to wipe out the old school; it literally did.

Demonstrating a deep sense of duty and responsibility, Scott immediately undertook to replicate an American classroom complete with American-type desks and chairs. The traditional straw-matted tatami flooring, on which students previously sat for Confucian lessons, was removed to make room for regular wooden floors. The renovation was necessary to accommodate the new desks and chairs imported from America. The old walls were replaced by blackboards. Charts and graphs were hung on the remaining wall space. The main hall of the old school became a replica of Scott's San Francisco elementary school classroom.[23] Students sat on chairs behind a desk in a style widely used in America, where the top lifts up to get at the books and writing materials inside. It was reminiscent of a typical classroom in many public schools in America in the 1870s, exactly as was intended.

Three hundred applicants sat for the first entrance examination of the new Tokyo Teacher Training School. Fifty-four, ranging in age from eighteen to thirty-six, were successful, the overwhelming majority coming from the samurai-warrior class.[24] Thus the first class of mainly samurai-warrior teacher trainees in Japan's history set a pattern for elementary school teachers in the early modern era. For example, during a five-year period from 1873, the second year of Scott's contract, to 1878, out of a total of 240 graduates of the Tokyo Teacher Training School, 164 came from former samurai families.[25] With the abolition of the formal feudal system in the early 1870s, eliminating the privileged ascribed status of the samurai within the society, samurai were suddenly confronted with securing a livelihood dependant upon individual ability. Teaching proved attractive to many samurai youth whose Tokugawa education centered on the literary arts, including the study of Chinese classics along with the military arts. Scott's first class, therefore, consisted mostly of teacher-trainees who, as former samurai-warriors, were in fact most familiar with the traditional classroom and the literary arts.

Tsuboi Gendo, English student at Nankō, was also transferred to the new training school with Scott from Nankō. He presumably was well acquainted with the American as a student in the English Department, where Scott taught. Tsuboi would become one of the most famous English translators for foreign teachers during the first decade of the Meiji educational reforms. It was through Tsuboi, who personally witnessed Scott's classes, that a picture of what transpired during those momentous days at Japan's first teacher training school is still available. According to him, the top class of eighteen students entered Scott's classroom to experience life in an elementary classroom exactly as Scott taught his San Francisco elementary children two years previously. They each received a monthly stipend of 10 yen. The remaining students were relegated to a separate class, receiving 8 yen a month to cover their expenses.[26] Students in the first group, upon receiving instruction from Scott in English, with Tsuboi providing the necessary translation, were then assigned to teach the lower section of students what they had learned. This time, Japanese was the primary language of communication since the English ability of even the top class of trainees was limited.

Beyond the basic course in teaching methods in the main division of the school (*honka*), in which Scott taught his students how to teach English and mathematics at the elementary level, the trainees also studied other subject matter in the supplemental course (*yoka*) under regular Japanese instructors. These courses included physics, chemistry, Japanese, and Chinese classics.[27] Thus there were two divisions in the school divided not only by subject matter but also by method; it can be assumed that the courses taught by regular Japanese instructors conformed to the traditional patterns of lecture-memorization-examination teaching methods. The Japanese instructors, however, also used translated western textbooks wherever available.[28]

Scott employed several notable features in his teaching methods. From a present-day perspective, his classroom methods appear anything but revolutionary. However, by comparing them to the classroom of the terakoya, the prevalent private elementary school during the feudal era, it can be more fully appreciated how and why Scott's teaching methods from California were truly revolutionary to the Japanese in 1872.

A brief review of how a Japanese child in a terakoya classroom during the feudal period learned his lessons, taken from the records of a typical rural school, is revealing.[29] Japanese educational historians characterize the terakoya teaching method as individualistic on the basis of the role of the teacher and student in the learning process. The student sat on the tatami floor behind a low table. On the right of the table were placed a writing brush and ink stone, in the middle writing paper, and on the left a handbook with model Chinese characters. During the morning session that began at eight o'clock, the student devoted the entire time practicing calligraphy by copying the characters monotonously over and over again, six to twelve per page. The sample was then displayed to the teacher for correction. Each child progressed at his own pace, beginning with the i—ro—ha, the ABC's of the Japanese language. The student first learned how to write each character, then how to read it, and finally memorized its meaning.

The teaching method was simple. Working with each student individually, the teacher corrected the writing by placing small circles at the end of a stroke indicating that the brush did not come off the paper properly, attempting to instill a natural touch like that of an artist painting a picture. The emphasis with each student was on precision, correctness, and conformity, while the other students went about practicing their calligraphy. Upon completion of this process with one student, the teacher then turned to the next student and repeated the procedure until every student had individually demonstrated his skill at writing the venerable Chinese characters. In the afternoon the students, one at a time, sat before the teacher and read aloud from some passage that often contained a moral message.

In contrast, the first factor in Scott's transformation of the terakoya classroom to the San Francisco classroom related directly to the following clause in the California regulations for teachers: "Teachers should endeavor to arouse and fix the attention of the whole class. . . . They should never proceed with the recitation without the attention of the whole class."[30] The California teaching method, recognized by the Japanese as perhaps Scott's major contribution to the modern classroom, centered around the key concept of the "attention of the whole class."[31] It was the teacher's responsibility to make every effort to "fix the attention of the whole class" on the teacher and on student response as the class was led through the lesson together. The teacher's role in the terakoya classroom was to "fix the attention" of one student at a time while the other students went about their individual preparation until their turn came. To the Japanese it was the contrast between the individual teaching method of the terakoya and the group teaching method employed by Scott that distinguished the modern classroom from the feudal.

The difference between handling the class as a whole or as individuals had ramifications of great significance. First, the number of students in the class was critical. In the terakoya classroom, student numbers were traditionally small. A typical village terakoya in Gumma prefecture, for example, was opened in 1838 and closed down in 1872 with the launching of the Gakusei. During the thirty-five years in operation, the total number of students numbered about 150, all from

Figure 17. A Terakoya Classroom in Feudal Japan.
From Hamada Yōtarō, *Kindai Kyōku no Kiroku* (Tokyo: Nihon Hōsō Shuppan Kyōkai, 1978), 1:19.

local farm families.[32] In the one-room terakoya school with only five students or so, the teacher went around the class, with each student reciting or demonstrating a writing lesson while the remaining students, working independently, were still within the teacher's notice. Orderliness and discipline were more easily maintained with a small number of students. In contrast, the group teaching method from San Francisco allowed one teacher to accommodate many more students than in the terakoya classroom, a significant factor in launching a national public school system.

The differences in teaching between the individualistic approach of the terakoya and the whole-class approach of the San Francisco classroom also meant that the California teacher had to prepare a lesson. The teacher could not simply make an assignment one day, and the next day go methodically from student to student listening to each one recite what he had memorized, or correcting the calligraphy samples. Rather, the modern teacher had to prepare a lesson for the whole class that involved a procedure for introducing new material in a comprehensible form, explaining new concepts to arouse the interest of the student, and reinforcing the learning process with a set of prepared questions. The answers demonstrated to the teacher the depth of understanding by the students.

The use of a dialogue between teacher and student in the form of questions and answers, the so-called mondō method, was the second innovation of Scott's

Figure 18. An Early Modern Classroom in Meiji Japan.
From W. G. Beasley, *The Modern History of Japan* (London: Weidenfield and Nicolson, 1963), 180.

classroom. An example is illuminating. The following first-grade lesson on the persimmon (*kaki*) from Scott's classroom was circulated throughout the nation in a text for teachers published by Scott's principal, Morokozu Nobuzumi.[33] It can be assumed that many local teachers dutifully followed it in their classrooms, with the teacher asking the questions and then writing the student's answers on the blackboard to be repeated by the entire class.

QUESTION BY TEACHER: What is a persimmon?
ANSWER BY STUDENTS: A fruit that grows on a persimmon tree.
QUESTION: How do we use this fruit?
ANSWER: We eat it.
QUESTION: How do we eat it?
ANSWER: We usually eat it raw.
QUESTION: How does it taste?
ANSWER: It tastes sweet.
QUESTION: What color is it?
ANSWER: Red
QUESTION: Is it always red?
ANSWER: No. It is first green but turns red when it ripens.

From today's perspective this classroom dialogue appears simple, certainly not innovative. But from the historical perspective of a nation emerging from feudalism to modernism, it was considered progressive. The local elementary teacher who followed this technique had the aura of a modern teacher in a modern classroom interacting with the students.

The third feature of Scott's modern teaching methods introduced into Japan derives from a continuation of the same clause underlying the first reform utilizing the whole-class method: "[Teachers should endeavor to arouse and fix the attention of the whole class], and to occupy and bring into action as many of the faculties as possible."[34]

"To bring into action as many of the faculties as possible" was undoubtedly intended by the California state school officials to break away from the traditional learning process that consisted primarily of memorizing written texts. Under this age-old approach to learning, the single faculty of reading written texts precluded other means of learning. Scott introduced the use of other faculties in the learning process by using so-called "object lessons." At that time, a new book on the American scene was causing ripples in the educational world. Samuel Calkins's *Primary Object Lessons,* published in 1861, was the forerunner of the modern methods of using audio-visual teaching materials in the form of concrete objects. Indicative of Scott's interest in the latest theories in teaching, he brought Calkins's book with him from California.[35]

According to the most modern theory of learning in the West at that time, Calkins claimed that teaching materials, that is, objects, charts, graphs, and so on, must be carefully chosen by the teacher according to the developmental growth of the student. The teaching lesson does not begin with opening the book to page one when the student begins to read. Rather, it begins with the teacher observing what the student already knows and interests him or her. The first principle of teaching was observation (*kansatsu*). Reinforcing Calkins's theory, Scott introduced *A Manual of Elementary Instruction* by Edward Sheldon, then principal of America's most progressive teacher training school at Oswego, in the state of New York. In effect Scott brought with him to Japan the earliest forms of progressive educational theory being developed by the great educational innovator, Pestalozzi of Switzerland, and adopted at the Oswego school.[36]

In essence, Scott employed a modern approach to the old method of transmitting knowledge from teacher to student. Rather than relying on textbooks and the written word, Scott employed pictures, graphs, charts, and other concrete materials in his classroom, all new to the Japanese.[37] The use of graphs in the teaching of mathematics, for example, was a novel approach. Pictures of objects with their names attached proved novel in the teaching of English, until then based on the memorization of written vocabularies. But the old memorize-repeat approach remained basic to this new method of teaching the class as a whole. It, too, was aimed at more efficiently and effectively transmitting knowledge.[38] Nevertheless, Scott attempted to encourage critical thinking in his own classes which, inevitably, proved difficult to disseminate to local teachers through written reports and publications on his teaching methods.[39]

Scott's personality was another factor that contributed to his success as a model teacher. According to Tsuboi Gendo, his translator who witnessed the demonstration classes, Scott sometimes made mistakes during the mathematics lessons. He never got flustered or became arrogant. Rather, standing in front by the blackboard with chalk in hand, he responded accordingly: "Let's try to solve this problem together." He would then follow the students' direction in seeking the proper solution. It was a problem-solving atmosphere unheard of in the Japanese classroom before Scott arrived on the scene.[40]

The modern approach to teaching introduced by Scott incorporated a methodology that required the would-be teacher to undergo a training course. No longer, as with the terakoya, could anyone so inclined open a school, recruit students, and instantly become a teacher. Modern teaching required qualifications based on proven ability to teach. To become a teacher in the new public school system, the teacher had to meet certain standards for teacher certification. The role of the Ministry of Education was to set national teaching standards that grew out of Scott's classroom, ideally to be met by every public school teacher in modern Japan.

Beyond the new teaching methods introduced by Scott, his other contribution of great consequence was the introduction of American elementary textbooks into the Japanese curriculum. At the time of the Gakusei, there were no appropriate textbooks available in Japan. These had to be quickly imported and hastily adapted for the new public schools. Scott was instrumental in this process for he, too, needed modern elementary textbooks for his own demonstration classes. To meet that need he either used books brought with him to teach English at Nankō, or he ordered textbooks that were commonly used in America.[41]

Among the imported texts used by Scott for teaching reading, the venerable *Wilson Reader* is invariably considered by historians as an example of how the textbook problem was dealt with during the initial period of modernization. Considered in some detail in a later chapter, suffice it to note here that Scott first introduced the *Wilson Reader*, designed to teach American children how to read English, into his Japanese classroom. With Scott's stamp of approval the American elementary reader underwent immediate translation into Japanese. It will forever be recorded in the history of modern Japanese education as the first reader (*dokuhon*) to teach Japanese children how to read their language in the public elementary schools of Meiji Japan.[42]

With the introduction of the *Wilson Reader*, the issue of morals education inevitably arose. One of the major criticisms of the overwhelming American influence on the modernization of Japanese education during this early period concerns its lack of morals education (*shūshin*). For example, the curriculum that grew out of Scott's teachings at the Tokyo Teacher Training School had no specific course on morals which traditionally played an important role in feudal Japan. The reason for its absence is attributed to Scott's dominant role focusing strictly on teaching methods.[43]

Ironically, the *Wilson Reader* used by Scott in his classroom was full of moral and religious concepts that were considered essential for American children of the period. For example, in the Introduction to [American] Teachers using the book, it noted that, "No pains have been spared to give all the readers not only a moral but a Christian influence." The book included several lessons of a religious nature. It ends with a poem entitled "God Is Love." Perhaps to Scott, his teaching was immersed in morality. But moral education to the Japanese critics of modern education meant traditional Confucian morality, alien to the young American teacher from San Francisco.

Scott's influence spread nationwide even before he completed his first year at the school. Of the many books and reports that grew out of his work at the Tokyo Teacher Training School, Principal Morokuzu Nobuzumi's *Essentials for Elementary School Teachers (Shōgaku Kyōshi Hikkei)* was one of the most important. Circulated from December 1872, only three months after the opening of the training school, the publication was the first book on the modern principles of teaching in the Japanese language.[44] It was designed for first- and second-grade teachers. Based solely on Scott's methods and principles of teaching, it stressed the revolutionary concept that teachers must motivate the student's interest as the basis for effective learning. Teachers should encourage students not only to study but to play and enjoy themselves as well; excessive study, it claimed, harms the sensitivity of the child. The teacher must reduce mental stress by introducing short periods of physical activity to refresh the spirit; learning is not sitting passively at the desk all day memorizing facts and figures.[45] The Pestalozzi influence on Scott was evident through these concepts.

The second publication of importance, also compiled by Scott's principal, *Elementary School Mathematics (Shōgaku Sanjutsu Sho)*, was published by the Ministry of Education as a textbook in March 1873.[46] It was intended to meet the challenge of teaching modern mathematics, which formed the core of the new curriculum. Scott, who concentrated on how to teach both mathematics and reading, also brought elementary school mathematics books from America for use in his class. His methods and course content were immediately compiled in Morokuzu's *Elementary School Mathematics* for distribution throughout Japan.[47]

In the process of introducing teaching methods and textbooks from San Francisco for use in the Tokyo Teacher Training School, Scott naturally followed the elementary school curriculum he employed while teaching in California. This was precisely as intended by the Ministry of Education. Since the ministry had no experience at curriculum development or time to develop one, there was no other choice but to rely completely on Scott's model classroom and materials he brought from San Francisco.

During Scott's first year at the Tokyo Teacher Training School, he developed a complete model elementary school curriculum based on his courses called the Katō Shōgakkō Kyōsoku, the Elementary School Curriculum for the Lower Grades. Pressed for time, as the first national school system, the Gakusei, was scheduled to begin in April 1873, the Ministry of Education published it in September 1872. Titled simply the *Shōgakkō Kyōsoku* (Elementary School Curriculum), it included a literal translation of the San Francisco elementary school regulations.[48] The official issuance of this document marks an historical milestone that represents the first modern curriculum for Japanese elementary schools.[49]

Eager to disseminate modern teaching methods in time for the new schools, the ministry also published, in May 1873, the *Shōgaku Kyōju Sho* (Elementary Teaching Methods) for national distribution. It was simply a compilation of Scott's teaching practices. The publication also included sketches of many of Scott's visual materials he used in his teacher training classroom. This provided local teachers with an opportunity not only to emulate Scott's methods in their own classrooms but also to duplicate the visual aids he employed. Combined with the *Elementary School Curriculum*, the *Elementary Teaching Methods* provided the new public schools with a national standard in what to teach, with recommended textbooks mostly in translation, and how to teach it. It was all based on Scott's model classroom in Tokyo and the San Francisco school regulations.

How teachers in the provinces reacted to the spate of materials and instructions being distributed by the Ministry of Education was of critical importance. It had to be a confusing and difficult period for them. Without the opportunity of a firsthand observation of Scott's classroom in far-off Tokyo, it would be virtually impossible to fully grasp the essentials of his teaching methods and textbooks imported from San Francisco. Modern theory applied in an elite teacher training school in the capital city of Tokyo was carried out in a contrived atmosphere. To apply it as described in books and reports at the local level to peasant children by untrained teachers was an entirely different matter.

The second stage of development in the Tokyo Teacher Training School during Scott's brief but crucial two-year service took place in 1873. In May an elementary school was added with seventy-eight carefully selected students.[50] Essentially an experimental school, the addition provided Scott's students with the opportunity to apply his teaching methods in an actual classroom environment, however contrived. And indeed it was contrived, hardly a typical public school classroom setting. The new elementary school attracted children from highly placed families such as the son of Tanaka Fujimaro, director of the Ministry of Education responsible for the school itself.[51]

The attached elementary school not only catered to the influential families of Tokyo but it also employed Scott's methods that originated from the great progressive educator, Pestalozzi from Switzerland. His theories were then in vogue at the Oswego Teacher Training College in the state of New York, as mentioned above. As a result, the experimental elementary school classrooms where Scott's students applied the new methods took on a highly progressive character.[52] In the circuitous route from Switzerland to Oswego to San Francisco and on to Japan, and finally to the attached experimental school in Tokyo, surely some of the originality of modern educational theory was lost. But the fact that the Japanese in 1872 were suddenly experimenting with the most modern educational concepts available in the West less than five years after the feudal Tokugawa era ended is a story in itself.

David Murray, in his capacity as a senior officer in the Ministry of Education, visited the school during the last day of 1873. In his official report to the head of the ministry, Tanaka Fuimaro, he expressed his unequivocally favorable evaluation of Scott's work. "From my observation of the operations of this institution and the wide field of usefulness in this direction, I unhesitatingly pronounce it the most promising work in which the department of education is engaged."[53]

Emperor Meiji became aware of, and took an interest in, Scott's work at the Tokyo Teacher Training School. Reflecting his personal concern for educational progress, which later took him all over the country, the emperor paid a special visit to the school on May 18, 1874. Following his usual procedure, Emperor Meiji visited classes in session. Scott was then given the unusual privilege of making a short speech before the royal guest. The significance of this former elementary school teacher from San Francisco addressing the august emperor of Japan on educational matters once again illustrates the uniqueness of the period. It also demonstrates the unusual role that foreigners played in the modernization of Japanese education. Scott used the opportunity to advance the cause of national self-assertion, and particularly the vital role of teacher training in it. Emperor Meiji must have been impressed with the sincerity and genuine commitment to the modernization of Japanese education by this dedicated American teacher. "For a country to become strong and prosperous, its people must possess a high level of knowledge," Scott said. "In order to achieve that goal schools must be developed. Large expenditure of funds is not the critical factor. Rather, the preparation of a corps of capable teachers is the most important prerequisite. In today's world, the leading nations are well aware of this. The first step for Japan, then, is to develop teacher training schools. Our Tokyo Teacher Training School is ultimately aimed at enlightening all Japanese, the first stage for Japan to become a great and prosperous country."[54]

Several months after the imperial visit, Scott's two-year contract with the Japanese government at the training school ended. Tanaka Fujimaro, head of the Ministry of Education, however, recommended that he continue teaching English in Japan. Scott promptly accepted a teaching position at the Tokyo English School, the preparatory school for Nankō, Japan's leading public institution of higher education and the forerunner of Tokyo University. The Tokyo English School was later renamed the Tokyo Daigaku Yobimon, the Tokyo University Preparatory School.[55] This appointment took Scott back to the English classroom for which he was originally brought to Japan in 1871. Since there was only one national institution of higher studies at the time, those students who entered the elite preparatory school were on the way to the leadership class of the society.

Tanaka Fujimaro's remarks at Scott's farewell ceremony indicate that his relationship with the Tokyo Teacher Training School ended amicably. As the senior officer of the Ministry of Education, Tanaka extended the nation's appreciation with a simple but appropriate evaluation of Marion Scott's contribution to the modernization of Japanese education: "The Tokyo Teacher Training School is the first institution to train teachers in our country. Its success has depended on your efforts and your many contributions. You introduced new teaching methods that you personally developed. I firmly believe that they will be essential in the development of our country."[56] With that poignant farewell, Scott left the Tokyo Teacher Training School. However, his contribution to the modernization of Japanese education was not yet completed.

During his two-year tenure as the head teacher at the teacher-training school from 1872, Scott was directly involved in the mainstream of educational reform. From 1874 on, his contribution to modern education took a more indirect form. Again it was an unprecedented opportunity for a foreigner. In one of the most fortuitous developments in Scott's career, among his first class at the elite preparatory school where he was assigned to teach English were two particularly assiduous students. They were destined to become outstanding intellectuals of modern Japan. Both went far beyond English fluency, mastering the foreign language as few Japanese then or since have been able to do. What renders their English accomplishments important in this context is that they both attributed their love of the English language to their teacher, Marion Scott.

Japan's leading Christian scholar of the late nineteenth and early twentieth centuries, Uchimura Kanzō, was a student in Scott's first-year class after he left the Tokyo Teacher Training School. He identified Scott's method of teaching as the basis of his foreign language learning. He was overwhelmed by Scott's moving spirit. He recalled with great fondness how he felt when entering Scott's classroom for the first time as a teenager. It was a new world that contrasted sharply with Uchimura's English classes up to then, for Scott avoided rote memorization. Rather, he taught his Japanese students to understand the meaning of English sentences in the context in which they were written.

Uchimura also recalled with great appreciation how Scott encouraged his students to write short sentences in English. The purpose was not to achieve mechanical perfection in written composition, but rather to express one's ideas. At last, Uchimura concluded, Scott's students were freed from memorization of grammatical rules and vocabulary. They were finally able to express themselves in a foreign language.[57] Few Japanese have done so more ably than Uchimura Kanzō who went on to graduate from one of the most prestigious institutions in America, Amherst College in Massachusetts. That was followed by the completion of theological studies at the Hartford Theological Seminary. He returned home from America to become one of the great intellectual pillars of the Christian church in Japan, launching a new movement in Protestant Christianity that survives to this day.

The other student in Scott's classroom who distinguished himself, Niitobe Inazo, authored the enduring classic that introduced to the West in eloquent English the great Japanese spirit of Bushidō, the Way of the Warrior. After graduate study in America and earning a German doctorate, Dr. Niitobe later served as president of two Japanese colleges and was appointed undersecretary of the League of Nations. Niitobe recalled in equally glowing terms Scott's lasting influence on him as his English teacher. The following English passage in the original stands as a tribute by Niitobe to Marion Scott's ability to teach Japanese how to write English movingly.

> I owe to Mr. Scott my taste and love of literature. He encouraged me to write. . . . No teacher at whose feet I sat either before or after him inspired me with such love of learning as did Mr. M. M. Scott. I dare say that many of my school mates will share with me the feelings of heartfelt gratitude to this veteran of education. He was an educator in the highest sense of the term drawing out of each boy what lay latent in his little soul. He often times showed that he could not do sums correctly, or rightly grasp algebraic formulae; but he never appeared embarrassed when he showed ignorance or made mistakes. He never for one moment pretended to much knowledge; but he was possessed of something greater—namely, wisdom.[58]

The personal testimony of two of Scott's Japanese students who became leading intellectuals of the twentieth century reinforces the ultimate conclusion that Scott was a master teacher, whether formally trained in teaching methodology or not. Ministry of Education officials were fortunate that their hasty and unexpected decision in 1872 to assign him to one of the most responsible positions in the new school system turned out so well. Without doubt, Marion M. Scott from San Francisco was the right individual at the right time at the right place when the Japanese government entrusted him with the central role of introducing modern teaching methods in Japan.

8

Implementing the First
National Plan for Education

THE AMERICAN MODEL,
PHASE I, 1873–1875

With the proclamation of the Gakusei, the First National Plan for Education, on August 3, 1872, the Ministry of Education faced an enormous challenge.[1] It was charged with implementing a truly ambitious plan at the opening of the following school year in April 1873. The responsibility for enforcing the primary provision, which called for an elementary school in every community to accommodate every child, was suddenly placed upon the ministry that had been organized for only a year. Two unlikely individuals were placed in charge of the ministry to carry out its unprecedented mandate. Tanaka Fujimaro, former samurai from Nagoya, Japan, and Dr. David Murray, mathematics professor from Rutgers College in America, were brought together in Tokyo on an historic mission in mid-1873. Tanaka, as head of the Ministry of Education, and Murray, his senior advisor, were destined to work together for the next five years endeavoring to bring about the great transition from feudal to modern Japan through education.

To review the background circumstances briefly, Tanaka Fujimaro had been dispatched by the Ministry of Education on the Iwakura Mission in 1871 to survey western systems of education. It was during this mission that David Murray signed a contract as senior advisor to the Ministry of Education from the summer of 1873. After traveling throughout North America and Europe on a year-and-a-half tour of education in twelve western countries, Tanaka returned to Japan in March 1873, several weeks before the Gakusei became effective.[2] During his prolonged study of western systems of education, Tanaka had become deeply impressed with the American system. Upon his return home, he immediately assumed the senior administrative position at the Ministry of Education, and was responsible for the nation's educational policies from 1873 to 1879.[3]

Four months after Tanaka returned home from the West, Dr. David Murray arrived in Japan to assume his duties as a ranking official of the Ministry of Education. According to his contract with the Japanese government of March 15, 1873, Murray was to "take charge of all affairs connected with Schools and Colleges."[4] In his words, he served the Japanese Department of Education as the "Superintendent of Schools and Colleges."[5] As the highest paid official in the Ministry of Education, Murray's salary of 600 yen per month, nearly the equivalent of $7,000 per year, was far higher than he received as a professor at an American university in 1872.[6] It also surpassed the salaries of both Tanaka Fujimaro and Hatakeyama Yoshinari, president of the nation's premier institution of higher education, Kaisei Gakkō, who was Murray's former student at Rutgers College.

The relationship between David Murray and the Japanese government originated with the letter that Mori Arinori, first Japanese diplomat assigned to Washington, sent to leading American educators in 1871. Mori solicited their advice on the proper role of education in the modernization process. David Murray, then professor of mathematics at Rutgers College, went to great lengths to answer Mori's letter on behalf of the college president. Little could he have imagined that as a result of his thoughtful and reasoned reply of March 1872, he would become a senior official of the Japanese government the following year.

Since Murray's contract placed him in an extraordinarily influential position directly under the director of the Ministry of Education, his character, his attitude toward the Japanese, and his depth of knowledge about educational affairs proved crucial. Murray's farewell address before the New Brunswick Historical Club clarified his basic attitude toward his unusual assignment. It revealed not only his personal commitment to the task but the influence of the Japanese students he befriended at Rutgers College during the Tokugawa era.

> Those who have regarded Japan from an outside viewpoint have supposed it to be an uneducated nation and that consequently the whole fabric of education would require to be revised from the foundation. Nothing could be more erroneous. On the contrary Japan stands today among the nations where education is held in the highest regard, and where it is nearly universal. . . . I have been most deeply interested in the efforts of the nation to connect itself with the great march of modern progress. . . . I go with an earnest purpose to use whatever experience I have gained in my previous labors in education for the best of the nation. But I go not only to impart to Japan the results of our system so far as I can, but I humbly confess that I go there to learn from them what is good in theirs.[7]

From the very beginning of their challenging assignment, Murray and Tanaka forged a cooperative working relationship devising policies to modernize Japanese education under adverse circumstances. They often discussed educational administration, teacher education, curricular matters, universities, financing, and so on, that is, the entire gamut of education. Murray deeply influenced Tanaka's thinking with his thoughtful, practical advice on all these topics.[8]

Their contacts, moreover, extended far beyond the workplace and well beyond Japan itself. The wives of both men became deeply involved in this relationship. The couples developed a close personal bond, and although absorbing interpersonal relationships characterized not a few contacts between Japanese and non-Japanese in the modernization process, the Murrays and the Tanakas forged a social as well as professional relationship that surpassed others of the period. Reminiscent of the hospitality extended by the Murrays to the Japanese students who studied at Rutgers College during the Tokugawa era, Mrs. Tanaka, former geisha from Nagoya, was invited to live with the Murrays in their Tokyo home for months.

During the weekdays she learned western ways and customs, returning to her family on weekends. She also assisted Mrs. Murray in adjusting to life in bustling Tokyo. Tanaka's son fondly recalls how the two families frequently visited each other's homes and toured local sites together, such was their warm friendship.[9]

By the time Tanaka and Murray assumed their respective posts in mid-1873, the Ministry of Education had already published critical guidelines and taken several decisive measures that set the stage for their arrival. In September 1872, just one month after the Gakusei was issued, the ministry published a document entitled the *Elementary School Regulations* (*Shōgaku Kyōsoku*). This historic document contained the first modern curriculum in the history of Japan designed for the naion's new public school system, beginning the following school year in April 1873. It was meant to implement the Gakusei.[10] Based on western models drawn from translated materials mostly from America, the *Elementary School Regulations* introduced many new subjects beyond the basic three R's through western textbooks. To ministry officials in charge, this document conforming to the broad provisions of the original Gakusei was intended as the foundation for the cultural revolution (*bunmei kaika*) envisioned from the very beginning of the Meiji Era.[11]

The second pivotal document took the form of a publication by the Tokyo Teacher Training School under Marion Scott's direction entitled *The Instructional Manual for Elementary School Teachers* (*Shōgaku Kyōshi Kokoroe*). It was issued in May 1873, one month after the Gakusei came into force. The Ministry of Education, which commissioned the publication, intended it to serve as a teacher's guide throughout the nation.[12] It thus represents the first official attempt to standardize teaching methods based on a national curriculum outlined in *The Elementary School Regulations*. The two documents were designed to launch the new public elementary school system with a uniform curriculum and a standardized method of teaching it. Tanaka and Murray were responsible for implementing its provisions.

Although it was all on paper, with limited influence during the first year of the national school system, a highly significant aspect of these first two documents intended to get the Gakusei off the ground cannot be overestimated. Both were deeply influenced by American education. First, the curriculum briefly outlined in the Gakusei of 1871, and codified in the *Elementary School Regulations* of September 1872 (*Shōgaku Kyōsoku*), was based on Marion Scott's curriculum at the Tokyo Teacher Training School and documents obtained from several American cities.[13] The second document, the *Instructional Manual for Elementary School Teachers* (*Shōgaku Kyōshi Kokoroe*), was also based on Marion Scott's teaching methods that he followed in his San Francisco public school classroom. It was transmitted to his Japanese students at the Tokyo Teacher Training School from 1872. Commissioned by the Ministry of Education but published by the Training School, this detailed teacher's guide even included a dress code. It circulated throughout the nation, with prefectural education offices publishing their own versions for local teacher training schools, precisely as the ministry intended, as a national standard for teachers.[14] Consequently the American influence on early modern Japanese education through these two critical documents was potentially enormous. That bias was further magnified in the hands of the American-oriented head of the ministry, Tanaka Fujimaro, and his American advisor, David Murray.

Further evidence of the influence American educational practices exerted during the implementation of the first national school system emerged shortly thereafter. First, Tanaka himself had little input into the preparation of this important document, the Gakusei. He was traveling all over the western world for over a year and a half when the report was drawn up in Tokyo. Thus he returned to Japan in 1873 with the task of implementing a plan over which he personally had little direct influence, and he was not happy with certain provisions of the plan he was supposed to put into action. The Gakusei had been drawn up in Tokyo on the basis of translations of reports about western education. Tanaka, in contrast, observed western education firsthand. Inevitably conflicting differences between the two perspectives emerged.

During Tanaka's western sojourn with the Iwakura Mission, he collected many reports and took copious notes, devoting day after day to visiting schools in a dozen countries from kindergarten to the university. It was truly a remarkable experience that perhaps no other contemporary comparative educator could match from east or west. During this extended journey, Tanaka naturally formed his own ideas on ways to reform Japanese education that ran counter to the Gakusei he was ultimately assigned to implement. Consequently he set out upon his return to Japan to revise the Gakusei, which had only been officially in force a month after he arrived home.[15] Tanaka's plan for the modernization of Japanese education was deeply influenced by American practices in education.

As the senior official in the Ministry of Education, Tanaka had his bureau publish a document entitled *American School Laws* (*Beikoku Gakkō Hō*). This report was merely a translated compilation of school laws that he personally collected from Massachusetts, New York, New Jersey, and Pennsylvania.[16] Tanaka had taken a special interest in regulations governing the administration and supervision of American education as he traveled through the eastern states, constantly aware of his position-to-be as head of the Ministry of Education. Tanaka's other critical report from his western trip was published in November 1873, under the title of *Riji Kōtei*; it was intended to provide useful information about the West. It represents the first public document of a survey of western education undertaken personally by a Japanese official. The significance of the *Riji Kōtei* was that Tanaka used portions of it as the basis for his effort to modernize Japanese education. Although his assignment was to administer the implementation of the Gakusei, the individualist that he was, he often followed his own instincts when they went counter to the Gakusei provisions, relying on the *Riji Kōtei* as a guide.

This lengthy document of sixteen volumes included reports on both private and public education in twelve western countries collected during Tanaka's exhaustive trip to the West, which lasted for one year, nine months, and twenty-one days. It covered the entire gamut of education from school laws and regulations, school management and administration, finance, buildings, universities, high schools, middle schools, and elementary schools, teacher education, teacher salaries, libraries, fees, exams, special education, and museums.[17] Judging from the length of time that he spent in each country and the depth of the report devoted to each nation he visited, Tanaka was obviously impressed with German education of the day, to which he devoted 380 pages in four of the sixteen volumes of his report, and education in America, where he spent the most time, with 220 pages. British education covered 116 pages. Beyond Germany, his continental tour took him to Belgium, Holland, France, Russia, Denmark, Sweden, Italy, Austria, and Switzerland. As previously mentioned, he apparently had little interest in French education, spending about a week in the country. He did, nevertheless, collect many French publications that he included in his report.[18]

The irony in Tanaka's lack of interest in French education is that the Gakusei has since its inception often been characterized as French-oriented since the French model of educational administration was adopted in the Gakusei. Tanaka claimed that there was an understandable reason why the authors of the Gakusei such as Mitsukuri Rinshō turned to the French administrative design for Japan in the early 1870s. France of the late nineteenth century had a well-defined organized educational administrative structure. It was easily understood by the Japanese through documents. Consequently, the French model appeared appropriate for Japan during this period when the first national school system was in its theoretical stage.[19]

Tanaka had formed a different perspective through his lengthy comparative educational research in the West. Although impressed with the German model where a centralized system of compulsory education had reached its highest level in the West, he felt that Japan was at a different level of development. The nation was not prepared for such an advanced stage of education. Further, with the lack of a sufficient budget allocated to the Ministry of Education, an ideal, efficient compulsory national system of education as in Germany was far too costly to employ as a model for Japan emerging from centuries of feudalism.

In contrast to European traditions in education, Tanaka looked to the United States with its decentralized structure of education for his primary model. He felt that American education reflected the will of the people, and that local educational policy originated from the bottom up rather than the reverse, as in Germany.[20] For the remainder of the 1870s, Tanaka's conviction that American education would best serve Japan as a model for the reform of the Gakusei shaped his policies.

Problems in Implementing the Gakusei

The first year of the Gakusei, 1873–1874, under the direction of Tanaka and his chief advisor Murray, proved predictably chaotic. The modernization of Japanese education envisioned in the Gakusei sketched out a national plan calling for elementary education for all children. No other country in the world had attained that standard of education. The magnitude of it defied description. Among the innumerable problems, there were no appropriate textbooks for the new curriculum under experimentation, no classroom teachers trained to teach the new courses, and few buildings adequately equipped to handle the huge numbers of anticipated students.

Shortly after Dr. Murray arrived in Tokyo in 1873, reflecting his interest in the local implementation of the Gakusei, he was sent off to the provinces on a lengthy tour of the schools. It was considered essential for him to gain some understanding of the problems he and his new friend Tanaka faced as they undertook their mission. His translator was none other than Hatakeyama Yoshinari, former student of Murray at Rutgers College in America. Hatakeyama had by this time become president of Kaisei Gakkō, the only national institution of higher education. Murray's assignment to tour the provinces called for a report of his findings to the director of the Ministry of Education. Its importance to Tanaka became evident when the entire report covering eight pages in translation was printed in the first annual report of the ministry, *Kyōiku Nenpō,* for the year 1873, issued in 1875.[21]

The condition of education in the countryside when Murray took his first inspection trip through rural Japan in 1873 fascinated him. For example, he described one classroom visit that he found intriguing. A Buddhist priest served as the teacher in the new local public school. Amazingly, the priest taught three classes simultaneously, including mathematics, calligraphy, and reading. Throughout the lesson, the teacher frequently glanced at a fan in his hand, commonly carried by priests. After class Murray inquired about the fan. The priest explained to the American visitor that he had written the main points of the lesson on the back of the fan, using it as a teaching aid. Murray came away impressed with how well the three-in-one lesson was conducted by a Buddhist priest pressed into service as a classroom teacher in modern Japan.[22]

The first crucial problem confronting Ministry of Education officials was an administrative structure to implement the uniform curriculum. The Gakusei, prepared under the guidance of the French specialist Mitsukuri Rinshō, outlined a centralized administrative structure on the French pattern. It neatly divided the country into eight university districts, each with general administrative power over education within their jurisdiction. Directly under the university district Mitsukuri set a quota of thirty-two middle school districts, each administratively responsible for 225 elementary school districts within its jurisdiction. Not only was it simplistically grand in design, it represented an administrative nightmare, with various levels of management assigned at nonexistent sites, administering huge numbers of schools at differing levels. In a word, the administrative structure of Japan's first national school system as originally designed was itself unmanageable.

The Ministry of Education attempted to sort this out before Tanaka returned from the West. The revisions were set in motion from July 1873. The administrative unit listed in the Gakusei, the Bureau of Management (Tokugaku Kyoku), located at each of the eight university districts, was relocated to the Ministry of Education as the Central Bureau of Educational Administration.[23] That action amalgamated the eight regional university administrative offices into one within the ministry, effectively placing control of educational administration at the center of government under the ministry. This strategic revision was necessitated by the obvious: there were no institutions resembling universities except one in Tokyo.

The remaining District Offices of Educational Administration, the Gakku Torishimari, located according to the Gakusei at each of the middle school districts, was intended to organize and administer public elementary schools within an area covering 130,000 residents per district. Each elementary school serving a population of 600 came under this administrative unit.[24] However, this provision never got off the drawing board. Rather, when the old feudal clan system was replaced by the prefectural structure in late 1871 and early 1872, seventy-two new local administrative units were organized as prefectures or states, based loosely on the old fiefs, in addition to three major cities treated essentially as prefectures. This was a move to streamline government administration from the central government through the new prefectures, each assigned to administer government within its jurisdiction. A governor, chihō chōkan, was then appointed by the central government as the chief prefectual administrative officer. It was this civil administrative reform that provided the first opportunity for a national school system to be launched, however imperfect.

In order to implement the Gakusei, the ministry had little recourse but to recognize a role for the new prefectural offices physically in place in lieu of the nonexistent middle school districts. It consequently empowered the newly appointed prefectural governor to organize and appoint officials of the District Offices of Educational Administration (Gakku Torishimari) within its jurisdiction. They were each responsible for all public elementary and middle schools serving 130,000 residents. With the power to appoint the officials in charge of local educational administration, the prefectural governor essentially became the key individual, in a sense the chief educational officer of local public schools.[25] Again this action was necessitated because the middle school districts did not physically exist at the time. Accordingly the ministry provided subsidies to hire personnel to set up prefectural education offices in January 1873, designed to implement the Gakusei from April of that year.[26]

To retain some semblance of the original provisions of the Gakusei that called for the country to be divided into eight university districts (daigakku), the new prefectures were initially divided on a regional basis into seven university districts, not eight. One prefecture or major city within each region, although devoid of a university except Tokyo, served as the central office (hombu) of education for them all. The actual site of the district headquarters was most often located at a teacher-training school or a foreign language school under Ministry of Education control.[27] Each was assigned a number of prefectures, which continued for years, accordingly: first university district (daiichi daigakku): Tokyo (10 prefectures); second: Aichi (9); third: Osaka (12); fourth: Hiroshima (8); fifth: Nagasaki (9); sixth: Niigata (7); seventh: Miyagi (8).[28]

Prefectural reports, including much statistical data requested by the ministry, were drawn up at each prefectural education office. They were then compiled for the entire university district at the regional headquarters located at one of the prefectures and sent on to the ministry. Conversely, ministry directives were circulated through each university district headquarters to the prefectural offices within its jurisdiction.

The result of this initial reform of the Gakusei before it got underway to conform to the realities of the day produced the first national organization of educational administration in the nation's history. The line of educational administrative control ran from the Ministry of Education to each prefecture and three major cities through a university district office, then finally to the local school through the middle school district offices effectively under the prefectures. With major administrative authority resting in the eight university district offices, it is most remembered as French-oriented. The revised structure, which essentially bypassed the seven university district units except as information-gathering offices, nevertheless preserved the critical Napoleonic feature of central control of education. The revisions conformed to the original intent of the Gakusei calling for a centralized school system with a standardized curriculum under the Ministry of Education.[29]

Finance proved to be a constant source of instability as the most immediate impediment to the new public school system. Distant government officials in Tokyo had decreed in the Gakusei that the costs of the new schools will be borne primarily by the community in which they existed; that those who benefited from the schools, that is, the parents and the local citizenry, should consequently pay for them. There were reasons of principle for the Ministry of Education to place the burden for financing local public schools squarely on each local community. But the principle that those who benefited from the new schools should pay for them masked the economic realities: there were not sufficient funds available to the central government to provide adequate subsidies to the 20,000 plus public elementary schools called for during year one of the Gakusei. A heavy burden was consequently placed on local villagers to finance the new schools for their children (see Table 3).

Table 3　　　Income Sources for Local Education, 1873

Source	% of budget
Local taxes	43.2
Student fees	6.3
National subsidy	12.6
Prefectural subsidy	0
Funds carried forward	0
Educational fund	19.1
Interest income	13.4
Miscellaneous	5.4

Source: Ichikawa Shōgo, *Kyōiku Zaisei* (Educational Finance) (Tokyo: Tokyo University Press, 1972), 90.

Further exacerbating an already desperate financial situation, the Ministry of Finance reduced by more than half the budget requested by the Ministry of Education to launch the new public school system in 1873.[30] At that time, the Ministry of Finance, itself struggling to establish a modern taxation system to finance government programs, could not approve such a huge expenditure requested to launch the Gakusei. There were, realistically, no alternative sources to local financing of Japan's first public school system.

One expenditure that particularly strained the budget of the Ministry of Education at the time of the Gakusei was the huge expense to support Japanese students studying abroad, mostly in England, France, Britain, and the United States. By 1872 the number had reached 330, increasing to 382 by the following year.[31] About one-third of them had been sent to western countries for a variety of reasons by local feudal hans during the Tokugawa era that ended in 1868, or before the prefectural system was initiated in 1871 abolishing the hans. After the Restoration various bureaus within the new central government also sent candidates abroad for study. The Meiji government assumed financial responsibility for all of them regardless of their origin. It was unplanned, uncoordinated, and prohibitively expensive, consuming 11 percent of the Ministry of Education's total budget for 1873.[32]

Figure 19. A Modern Public Elementary School in Early Meiji Japan.
From Nihon Kindai Shi Kenkyū Kai, ed., Nihon Kindai no Rekishi (Tokyo: Sanseido, 1985), 4.

Among the most immediate problems beyond financing confronting the government in the launching of the first public elementary school system was the huge, and inevitable, shortage of school buildings to accommodate the anticipated number of students. Even with fewer than 30 percent of the eligible students enrolling in the elementary school during the first year, many local officials in charge of education in 1873 had only one recourse at the outset.[33] When the central government ordered local communities to open local public elementary schools, it was natural that many of the temple classrooms, the old terakoya village schools, would be conscripted as new schools, making up the majority of the total during the first year. Often there were few if any other places available. Local Buddhist temples in many communities, which served as the center of social and cultural life of the people, were also employed as public schools. Local Shinto shrines were not as readily employed as schools simply because the configuration of the shrine did not lend itself so readily as did the Buddhist temples, with their large open worship spaces easily adapted for classroom use. Although the Gakusei was designed specifically to replace the old terakoya schools, stipulating that they be closed immediately, many were reopened as quickly as possible as public elementary schools.[34] Only the names were changed.

The number of terakoya schools available in each community was often insufficient to provide an elementary education, regardless of its nature, to accommodate all school-age children. The scramble was on. Beyond the wide use of temples, other facilities such as private homes, rice warehouses, old barns, stages of Shinto shrines where rituals were performed, and so on, were also brought into the curious mixture to meet the demands of the central government. The use of private homes as public schools would appear even more incongruous than using temples or shrines. However at this initial stage, the number of students in tiny villages who enrolled in the new local public elementary school was so small that the total enrollment could often be accommodated in a private home. In many instances where the old terakoya school was held in a teacher's private home, it was simply recognized as a new public elementary school.[35]

Table 4   Buildings Used as Public Elementary Schools, 1876

Type of building	No. (%)
Buddhist temples	8,333 (35.95)
Private homes	7,383 (31.85)
New school buildings	5,965 (25.73)
Others (warehouses, barns, etc.)	1,064 (4.59)
Unknown	245 (1.06)

Source: Tsuchiya Tadao, *Meiji Zenki: Kyōiku Seisaku Shi no Kenkyū* (The History of Educational Policy in the Early Meiji Period) (Tokyo: Kōdansha, 1962), 141.

One of the earlier statistical reports available concerning school buildings shows that only a fourth of all schools, even a few years after the Gakusei was started, were housed in facilities designed as schools (Table 4). Nevertheless, the fact that nearly six thousand new schools were constructed at local expense during the first three years of the national system is impressive. Some were handsomely designed.

New Curriculum and Textbooks

It was also a natural consequence that at the very beginning of the Gakusei in 1873 the old curriculum and the old methods of teaching by the old teachers were continued.[36] The key elements in effectively modernizing the schools involved two factors: (1) a modern curriculum with its associated modern textbooks, and (2) newly trained teachers capable of implementing the modern curriculum. As we have said, the new curriculum was spelled out in the Ministry of Education publication in 1872 entitled the *Elementary School Regulations* (*Shōgaku Kyōsoku*). It listed the following subjects to be taught in the new public elementary schools in the following order: reading, writing, recitation, history, geography, science, arithmetic, health, and morals.[37]

Textbooks for the new curriculum proved to be a major problem. When the ministry published the *Elementary School Regulations* in 1872, it was unprepared to meet the immediate need for appropriate textbooks covering the new courses. There were several options. The old texts used in the terakoya and other private juku schools of the recent feudal regime were still available, and were being used by teachers from terakoya schools now teaching in the public schools. Although the old materials had been effective in teaching calligraphy and reading, there were no textbooks in the fields of the new sciences and mathematics. Moreover, the traditional texts did not convey modern ideas of enlightenment intended by governmental reformers in their zeal to modernize feudal Japanese society.

The second option was to produce new textbooks in each subject area. The problem with that solution was the total absence of Japanese authors capable of writing appropriate textbooks for the new courses. This was especially apparent in science and mathematics. The third possibility was to import foreign textbooks. This option was really the only feasible solution to meet the immediate need for modern elementary school textbooks with the imminent opening of the first public school system in April 1873.

The specter of untrained teachers from the old feudal schools using any material available as textbooks in an unregulated environment in the new public schools haunted the Ministry of Education. Accordingly in October 1872 it hastily set up an in-house textbook department exclusively devoted to translating foreign textbooks. A month later it authorized a textbook translation department at the Tokyo Teacher Training School where the American, Marion Scott, exerted an overwhelming influence. This had the identical function as the textbook department within the ministry, such was the feverish activity to fill the textbook vacuum for the opening of the first public school year in 1873.[38]

Between the two departments, translated textbooks in all subjects considerate appropriate for a modern curriculum gradually became available. The ministry then provided a subsidy to local schools to buy textbooks, including some from abroad, as well as other teaching materials and equipment imported mostly from the United States.[39] Many western books, especially American and British due to Marion Scott's influence and the increasing availability of English translators, were published as textbooks from 1873 onward for the next several years. Consequently historians have appropriately dubbed this period as the "textbook translation era" (*honyaku kyōkasho jidai*).[40] It could also have been branded the "American textbook era" due to the large number of American elementary textbooks under translation.

When the first public elementary schools opened in April 1873, a baffling array of textbooks was employed by teachers. It varied according to the area, that is, rural or urban, the relative progressiveness of the individual teacher, and the availability of school funds to buy whatever was locally available. The textbooks at this initial stage of modernization included materials from the old terakoya-type schools, translations of foreign textbooks produced by the ministry and the Tokyo Teacher Training School, mostly from America, and a strange combination of commercial books published for a general audience by Japanese authors. Since the textbooks published by the Ministry of Education were intended as samples, not required texts, each local school district was free to choose its own materials. It was a wide-open, fluid situation where virtually anything available could be used as teaching materials.

The *Elementary School Regulations* circulated by the Ministry of Education only listed recommended readers (*dokuhon*) for the new schools. Among them were recent publications by the most popular writer of the time, Fukuzawa Yukichi, whom we discussed earlier.[41] Among his books included on the list as elementary readers were two of his classics, *Seiyō Jijō* (Conditions in the West) and *Gakumon no Susume* (The Advancement of Learning).[42] Both are currently well known outside Japan in translation.

Obviously these texts were not intended as materials to teach reading to children, since they were written for the literate adult population. In fact, Fukuzawa's *Conditions in the West* became an adult best seller. It was one of three books jointly characterized as the Bible of the Meiji Era (Meiji no Seisho), which included the popular translation of Samuel Smiles's *Self Help*.[43] Rather, they were intended to be read to the students by the teacher as an introduction to the western world. This was considered essential for enlightenment of the masses through imparting new values and new knowledge in the same manner that Confucian classics were used to teach morality in the old schools.

Curiously, a foreign book on physics titled *Butsuri Kunmō* (Enlightened Physics) was also included in the recommended list, demonstrating that the ministry had little sense of appropriate materials and subject matter for a mass elementary school system.[44] It simply used what was available at the time. Not only was the subject matter far too difficult for elementary children, the translation was not geared to the elementary Japanese level. At this time, however, government leaders were convinced that science was the very foundation of western economic and military power. The inclusion of science courses at the elementary level was not intended to develop a scientific way of thinking among the masses, but rather to provide a basic knowledge of facts and concepts in western science for all as part of enlightenment for the modern era.

According to the availability of translated textbooks, children in the new public schools were introduced to a confusing array of foreign concepts, ideas, perspectives, places, and so on. The new textbooks in history, geography, and science introduced western ideas considered essential to break down the old feudal society in order to usher in modernization. An interesting example concerns a theory new to the Japanese about the world's races. In the first elementary reader in the modern era, the translated version of the American *Wilson Reader* series, the text begins with a lesson concerning the five races existent in the world. Five faces—crude but recognizable—illustrated the different facial characteristics associated with each race as commonly understood in the West. Japanese children, and their parents as well, learned for the first time the concept that they, as Japanese, were members of a race classified by westerners as oriental.[45]

In the new science classes at the elementary school level, an alien world unfolded before the children. They were introduced to the concept of universal natural laws learned through experimentation and reasoning. They were also introduced to the principles of vacuums, electricity, and magnetism. In the better-equipped schools, students learned how to read thermometers and barometers. The favorite textbook for elementary science in the new schools of 1873 was Fukuzawa Yukichi's *Illustrated Course in Science* (*Kunmō Kyūri Zukai*), adapted from western books. The new scientific teachings in the public schools were implemented as the government adopted the western calendar and the standard twenty-four-hour day, all part of the technological revolution.[46]

Even at the elite Tokyo Teacher Training School, bizarre concepts were introduced to the future teachers through translated texts used in the specialized courses. In the history course, for example, a book from the West called *The Common School History of the World* included a description of Japan as a land of barbarians (*yaban*).[47] Although this was not an uncommon belief among westerners at the time, it was without doubt inappropriate to include it in a course for prospective Japanese teachers.

The preponderance of western books selected for translation as texts for the new public elementary schools understandably related to the field of science and technology, where there was an effort to meet an urgent need. Moreover, to fill the gap in morals education, of less urgency at this time, all titles recommended by the ministry were also exclusively foreign texts. The haphazard method of choosing texts was evidenced by one in particular. It seems that Fukuzawa Yukichi came across a second-hand copy in a local bookstore of the *Elements of Moral Science* by Francis Weyland. How such an obscure book reached a bookstore in Japan at this time remains unknown. Fukuzawa used the book in courses at his private school in Tokyo, the forerunner of the now-famous Keio University. Among his students was one Abe Taizo who shortly thereafter entered the Ministry of Education, where he translated the book into Japanese. It was then listed as a morals text for the new public elementary schools—such was the eclectic approach to textbook selection.[48]

Other examples of inappropriate textbooks for Japan's first public elementary schools included Fukuzawa's translation of Robert Chambers's *Moral Class Book* from England, and a translation by Mitsukuri Rinshoo of Hubbard Winslow's *Moral Philosophy*. Two of the most popular books of the period, Nishimura Masanao's translation of Samuel Smiles's *Self Help* and Fukuzawa's original book, *Seiyō Jijō* (Conditions in the West), also made the recommended list for the elementary course in morals education.[49] It is questionable how elementary school teachers could make use of any of the difficult morals texts recommended by the Ministry of Education in the urgency of opening the new schools on schedule. Officials did not have the time or experienced personnel to choose appropriate textbooks, especially at the lower elementary school level.

Since morals education was superceded in importance by science and technical education, the Ministry of Education did not follow a strict policy on the use of its recommended translated morals textbooks. Accordingly they were used sparingly in the new classrooms, and then only as reference materials in the better districts. Because the western morals texts were foreign to local teachers, many who came from the old terakoya schools accustomed to traditional Confucian moral teachings, large numbers of them continued their old traditional teachings in the new morals class. Other schools offered no morals course. The result was a diverse picture in morals education at the beginning of the modern school system, with each local school district setting its own curriculum and choosing the texts.[50] This state of affairs, in which morals education was officially relegated to the bottom of the new curriculum amidst great confusion and shortage of appropriate texts, caused consternation among critics of the period.

Among the official textbooks of the period, the one that has drawn most attention from historians was the first elementary school Japanese reader, the *Shōgaku Dokuhon,* published in four volumes available from 1873. It was, in fact, a direct translation by Tanaka Yoshikane from the Tokyo Teacher Training School of a contemporary American textbook to teach elementary reading to American children.[51] The Reader of the School and Family Series by Marcius Wilson, published by Harper and Brothers in 1860 and known as the *Wilson Reader,* was brought to Japan by Marion Scott for use at the Tokyo Teacher Training School.[52] In the translation published by the Ministry of Education widely used throughout Japan for the next decade, there were many pictures of the daily life of American children appropriately modified in clothing and facial features for the Japanese version. The childhood scenes depicted kite flying, fishing, boat rowing, and a game similar to baseball, all dutifully carried in the translated edition. One can readily imagine the associated issues in using a reading text specifically designed for American children of the late nineteenth century translated for the first Japanese public elementary schools in 1873 following three hundred years of feudalism.

The issue of religion posed an immediate difficulty with translated readers from the United States. Unregulated by the federal government in the decentralized American context, textbooks of that day in the United States inevitably included a fair number of Christian stories to be popular, that is, acceptable as well as profitable. The *Wilson Reader* was no exception. However, the leaders of Japan assumed that the religious issue would not prove insurmountable. Their thinking was based on the popular slogan of "Tōyō no Dōtoku—Seiyō no Gakumon," essentially "Eastern Morality—Western Knowledge." Japan would be able to modernize through western science while preserving its ethical foundation derived from a unique blend of Confucianist-Buddhist-Shintoist moral beliefs. In other words, it was believed, Christian values sprinkled throughout translated American textbooks used in the Japanese classroom would not replace traditional values of Japan, a confidence that Emperor Meiji and his advisors would openly question before the decade of the 1870s ended.

The *Wilson Reader* illustrates the problems confronting the translators. For example, in one lesson a child is pictured at bedtime kneeling in prayer. A word-for-word translation of the following prayer in English was made.[53] "O God, I thank thee that the night, / In peace and rest hath passed away, / And that I see in this fair light, / My father's smiles which make the day, / Be Thou my guide and let me live, / As under thine all seeing eye, / Supply my wants and sins forgive, / And make me happy when I die."

Among the formidable problems in translating this prayer into Japanese, with its stilted English phrasing commonly used in prayers, was the precise word in Japanese to translate God of the Christian religion. There were several possibilities with different shades of nuances. The most common word was Kamisama, the one used in the Japanese Christian Church of today. However the translator of the *Wilson Reader* in 1873 chose a different word, Amatsukami, a term commonly associated with the mythical gods of ancient Japan in the indigenous Shinto faith. That translation rendered the Christian prayer in the *Wilson Reader* as if the child were praying to a Shinto god rather than the Christian god. The second translation in 1874 revised the text to simply use the word kami, more neutral than Amatsukami, but still commonly associated with Shinto spirits. Such were the challenges facing the harried translators as the country moved to hastily produce modern textbooks.[54]

At the same time that the *Wilson Reader* was translated and published as a Japanese reader, specialists on Japanese studies (*kokugakusha*) within the ministry prepared the first Japanese reader written by Japanese authors. The contrast with foreign texts was striking. Whereas the translated reader from America compiled stories and homilies about children's daily life and activities such as flying kites or fishing, exemplifying everyday activities in daily language, the first Japanese-authored reader began with the well-known i-ro-ha sounds of the Japanese language followed by basic vocabulary. It then moved into traditional stories based on Confucian moral teachings and the tales of the first Emperor Jimmu Tenno of an ancient era, similar to the old texts from feudal Japan. These were intermingled with a sprinkling of stories from the West. Even they involved feudalistic-type themes.[55] Again, it was much too difficult for children to read, and fell into the category of texts to be read to children rather than texts to teach reading skills.

From an historical perspective, perhaps of greater importance than the new Japanese readers was the first textbook for the history course. This provided the Meiji government with the initial opportunity to interpret the history of Japan in modern terms. With the intention of the first national public school system to reach every child in the nation, an entire generation of Japanese youth could learn about the origins of Japan and the Japanese people, a goal never achieved before. The first history textbook of modern Japan recommended by the Ministry of Education reflects the general trends under the new leadership. Entitled simply *Shi Ryaku* (Abridged History), it was divided into four parts for grade four, where history as a formal subject was first introduced in the elementary curriculum.[56] Part one concerned Japan, titled Kōkoku (Imperial Japan), and covered nineteen pages. Part two covered China in eighteen pages. Parts three and four on western history extended over eighty pages. The division of the world into three areas for historical teachings, as well as the disproportionate coverage between Japan and the West, were significant.

The first attempt at teaching Japanese history at the elementary level in the public schools following the great Restoration of the imperial system is a lesson in itself. It began with several brief stories of the early gods. Then, without interpretation or analysis, a listing of the names of each emperor followed. Historically the most famous emperor was the mythical Emperor Jimmu of 666 BC. Accordingly, the list began with a simple story of Jimmu. From then onward, the 122 emperors were listed in chronological order followed by a simple statement about their reign. This short section on Japanese history ended with Emperor Meiji, number 122, with the simple statement that the Meiji Restoration took place. With that cryptic description the history of Japan in the first modern curriculum was completed.

The fact that Emperor Meiji received only one line in the first history textbooks obviously has critical ramifications. Until the Meiji Restoration of 1868, few Japanese children knew anything about their emperor other than the name. The terakoya schools of Tokugawa Japan which catered to a minority of rural youth placed primary emphasis on reading and writing Chinese characters and learning Confucian ethical teachings. The clan schools that catered to the ruling samurai class had the same emphasis at a more advanced level, along with the martial arts. During the Tokugawa regime, the emperor was confined to his royal capital in Kyoto under supervision of military units loyal to Edo (Tokyo). Therefore the imperial tradition in premodern Japan was purposely underplayed by the Tokugawa government and its supporting samurai class, preserving their dominant position as the rulers of Japan for nearly three hundred years. With the sudden turn of events that produced a samurai-led restoration of the imperial institution overthrowing the Tokugawa family, the initial history books under the new government nevertheless did not place great emphasis on the imperial tradition. The early modern leaders looked to the West, not the Japanese past. The first history textbook under their regime reflected this mindset.

The lengthy history of the West in part three begins with a description of the Assyrians, followed by the Babylonians, the Persians, Greeks, and Romans. Part four begins with Europe and ends with four pages on America, about one-fifth the length devoted to Japanese history. In contrast to a simple listing of Japanese emperors in the section on Japanese history, American history begins with Columbus discovering America in 1492. This is followed by a brief analysis of the causes of the American Revolution, even including the decisive Battle of Lexington. The role of George Washington and Thomas Jefferson in the formation of the United States and its Constitution is also included. The great Civil War, which had taken place a decade before this history book was written, included a picture of Abraham Lincoln. It ends with a brief description of the sitting president, Ulysses Grant.[57]

The textbook for the first history course in modern Japanese elementary schools is of significance for several reasons. The superficial coverage of Japanese history, simply listing the emperors in chronological order and neglecting analysis and interpretation of the recent Meiji Restoration, is a prominent feature. Although a non-issue at the time, critics especially within the Imperial Household were aware of the orientation and proclivities of the new government. Their opposition to the cursory teachings of Japanese history, or the absence of it, emerged within the decade as a primary source of contention. It provoked a reorientation in the direction of the modernization of Japanese education and society characterized as the "reverse course," the topic of a later chapter.

The insertion of a picture of the American president in the first history text for the Japanese elementary school concisely illustrates the issue. There was no picture of the Japanese emperor. Since few Japanese children had even a superficial knowledge about Emperor Meiji, this would have been a golden opportunity to acquaint all Japanese youth with their emperor in whose name the Meiji Restoration was undertaken. However, those officials in the Ministry of Education implementing the first national school system decided that Abraham Lincoln would be honored with a picture, not the emperor of Japan. The curious result was that many Japanese children at the beginning of the modern school era were familiar with the image of a president of the United States, Abraham Lincoln, with his distinctive beard. Few knew what the emperor of Japan looked like.

In spite of the new texts mostly translated from western sources with their strange stories and curious pictures of unfamiliar people, Japanese children outside the new schools acted little differently than before. For example, the songs they sang and the games they played on the way home from the new public schools were not much different from the songs and games that children from the old terakoya sang and played after school. Outside the school in a familiar environment, tradition prevailed. Inside the school in a nontraditional setting, a revolutionary change was under way. It was all part of the transition from the feudal to the modern in Meiji Japan.[58]

The Modern Teacher

At the beginning of the modern period in education, when many terakoya schools were pressed into service as public schools, inevitably many of their teachers, mostly samurai along with priests, were retained in position as the corps of local public school teachers. There were few other individuals available to undergo hastily arranged short-term teacher training courses taught by teachers untrained themselves. Those few who completed the questionable local training courses were recognized as qualified to teach.

Listing new courses in an official curriculum and publishing translated textbooks represented only half of the equation. Applying them effectively by teachers in the classroom was the other half. The problem was that the old teachers from the terakoya-type schools, the majority of them samurai who were educated mostly in Confucian studies and the martial arts, had little knowledge about the science and mathematics included in the new curriculum. Even the old approach to adding and subtracting traditionally taught through the abacus was outdated; the modern way of teaching calculation used the blackboard. In addition, teachers had no skills to teach the new and unfamiliar subjects of geography or music.

To meet this need, as we have seen, the Tokyo Teacher Training School had been launched in 1872. A major step forward by the Ministry of Education then took place with the founding of regional elementary teacher-training schools in 1873 and 1874, patterned after the Tokyo model. Six new regional schools were opened throughout the country in the following locations: Osaka and Miyagi in August 1873, and Aichi, Hiroshima, Nagasaki, and Niigata in February 1874.[59] These locations conformed to the seven university districts called daigakku that included the preeminent Tokyo Teacher Training School. Each daigakku was assigned one teacher training college. The first graduates from the Tokyo Teacher Training School, who completed the one-year course in July 1873, had not yet influenced the local public schools.[60] The Training School's *Instructional Manual for Elementary School Teachers*, which came out a month after the Gakusei started, had also not yet reached the local level.

Among the ten first-year graduates of the Tokyo Teacher Training School, most were recruited to staff the new regional colleges that were launched a month later. Even the principal, Morokuzu Nobuzumi, who worked with Marion Scott as head teacher, was assigned as principal of the new Osaka Teacher Training School in 1874. Combining the six regional institutions along with the original Teacher Training School in Tokyo under Scott's supervision, formal teacher training was henceforth spread, however thinly, throughout the nation by these seven institutions that trained male elementary teachers in modern classroom methodology. The graduates, however, were destined not for the new public elementary school classrooms. Rather, they filled positions not only at the nationally sponsored teacher-training schools but also at the gradually increasing number of prefectural training schools all over the country.[61]

A significant aspect of all teacher-training schools was the type of student attracted to them. Among the first graduating class of ten students from the most prestigious Tokyo Teacher Training School, eight came from samurai families, whereas only about 5 percent of the general population were classified as samurai. The lopsided ratio remained consistent for years. The identical situation existed at the regional level. For example, available statistics from local newspapers reported that in 1875, of the twenty-two graduates from the Hiroshima Teacher Training School, nineteen originated from samurai families. The following year among graduates from the Niigata Teacher Training School, eight out of nine fell into the same category.[62] In other words, from the very beginning of the modern school system, elementary teacher training was overwhelmingly dominated by males from the former ruling samurai warrior class educated in Confucian studies and the martial arts.

Former samurai prevailed not only at the elementary teacher-training schools. At the local public elementary school level the same condition existed. Many of the premodern terakoya schools as well as the private juku schools were taught by samurai. When those feudal-type schools were pressed into service as public schools, many of the teachers, themselves samurai, of necessity continued to teach in their old schools. In fact, a solid majority of the first public school teachers originated from the samurai class.[63] The major exception was in the city of Tokyo, which often did not conform to the patterns prevailing in the rest of the country. For example, statistics from the first public elementary school in the new capital city showed that thirteen teachers out of twenty-seven were commoners, an exceptionally high proportion.[64] At the same time, all senior officials at the Ministry of Education, with the notable exception of Dr. David Murray from America, also originated from the samurai class. From top to bottom in the first modern school system in Japan, samurai played the predominant role.

In spite of the new regional teacher training schools, the demand by local communities for trained teachers could not be met for many years. For example, even by 1876, three years after the modern system of public schools was launched, there were only 8,768 graduates from teacher training schools among 52,262 elementary teaching posts throughout the nation, a ratio of about one to six.[65] Various means were used to fill the huge gap. Graduates of the training colleges were in considerable demand to visit local communities, presenting lectures on modern teaching methods. In addition, the practice of sending representative local teachers to the nearest training college for short periods to observe demonstration classes, then returning home to conduct demonstration classes for fellow teachers, also helped to fill, however superficially, the tremendous need for trained teachers at this time.[66] Even though girls were obviously available, their educational opportunities were too restricted, rendering them unacceptable as teachers. Elementary teaching was a man's world that continued well into the post–World War II era.

David Murray recognized the urgent need for trained teachers as a result of his first provincial tour of schools in 1873, shortly after his arrival in Japan. As senior

Table 5   Gender Gap among Elementary School Teachers during the First Years
of the Gakusei, 1873–1874

Year	Male teachers	Female teachers	Total
1873	26,696	411	27,107
1874	36,204	662	36,866

Source: Ogata Hiroyasu, *Gakusei Jisshi Keii no Kenkyū* (Implementing the Gakusei), (Tokyo: Kōsō Shobō, 1963), 171.

advisor to the director of the Ministry of Education, he submitted a recommendation to Tanaka Fujimaro that represents one of his major contributions to the modernization of Japanese education.

"As it has always been found in all Western nations that females are the best teachers of children, it seems very desirable to make use of their agency in carrying forward the education of the country. They have more tact and patience than men in dealing with children and know better how to render them the assistance they need in their education. But, in order that women may be fitted to undertake the work of teaching, they must first be trained for it. And hence it becomes a duty of the department of education to provide some adequate means of preparing a corps of female teachers."[67]

Tanaka, the progressive that he was, responded instantly, an indication of his impulsive character and personal convictions. Murray submitted his proposal to Tanaka on December 31, 1873. Five days later, on January 4, 1874, the ministry submitted a formal proposal for a teacher training school for women to the head of the Dajōkan, the highest decision-making organ of government. The Dajōkan granted approval on January 20. One month later, the ministry issued a formal announcement of the decision to begin the formal training of female teachers. The facilities were completed for the opening of the first female teacher-training school in modern Japan, the Tokyo Teacher Training School for Women (Tokyo Joshi Shihan Gakkō), on October 31, 1875.[68] The distinguished western scholar and translator of *Self Help* and Mill's *On Liberty,* Nakamura Masanao, was appointed by the ministry as the first president of the school.[69]

For a government bureaucracy to act so decisively under the severe financial restraints then in effect speaks volumes about the period, the influence of David Murray, and the attitude of Tanaka Fujimaro. The major English newspaper reported that the empress, who had donated "5000 rios to the Ministry of Education for female education" that was used to finance the new building, inspected the facilities and visited classes. The paper also quoted from Tanaka's opening remarks that "If we consider well the words of the western proverb, that girls are the mothers of education, we sum up in a few words the reason female education is so weighty a matter."[70]

Figure 20. First Trained Female Teachers in Modern Japan, 1875.
From Ministry of Education, *Gakusei Gojūnenshi* (Tokyo: Ministry of Education, 1922). vol. 1, preface.

Tanaka's role was pivotal in the founding of the first teacher training school for women in modern Japan. His lifestyle reflected his attitude. After he became director of the Ministry of Education upon his return from the West with the Iwakura Mission in 1873, he was often seen riding through the streets of Tokyo or in the nearby countryside in his carriage accompanied by Mrs. Tanaka. It was a rare sight among high government officials. It was Tanaka who encouraged his wife to learn about western customs from Mrs. Murray by living in the Murray home during weekdays. Tanaka's wife emulated Mrs. Murray in many ways.[71] For example, Mrs. Murray followed the custom of riding in her buggy to the Ministry of Education in the afternoons, where she waited for Dr. Murray in the waiting room of the ministry.

Mrs. Tanaka then followed suit. She also rode her buggy to the ministry to pick up her husband, the two ladies passing the time together at the ministry waiting room. It provoked critical comments in a contemporary magazine. But the very fact that Tanaka, as director of the Ministry of Education, rode home from the office beside his wife, or took his wife to official parties, a rarity among bureaucrats, characterized him as one of the most progressive figures in Meiji Japan. His wife felt that he was always endeavoring to educate her since she had no formal education as a child.[72] This attitude was surely a factor in Tanaka's prompt action to begin the first teacher-training school for girls in modern Japan in 1874.

Table 6 Teacher Salaries at a Local Elementary Public School District (Eighteen Elementary Schools in Toyohashi) in Early Meiji Japan

Rank	Salary per month	Prescribed no. of teachers by law	Actual no. of teachers
1	15 to 30 yen	18	5
2	7 to 12	0	2
3	3 to 6	0	18
4	2.5	0	0
5 (Ass't.)	0.25	30	49

Source: Tamaki Hajime, *Nihon Kyōiku Hattatsu Shi* (Developmental History of Japanese Education) (Tokyo: Sanichi Shobō, 1954), 26–28.

With the lack of a secure financial foundation for the public schools, teacher salaries were pitifully low. They varied from school to school depending on the economic conditions of the local community. Teaching as a vocation proved financially unattractive in many districts. Revealing statistics are available for a local public school district somewhat after the new system was put in place: the highest-level teacher, in grade one, received 30 yen per month. Each school was to have one teacher at that level, presumably the principal. However, the vast majority of teachers was placed in the bottom grade as assistant teachers, receiving one-fourth of one yen per month, a salary 120th of grade one teachers.

School Attendance

In the absence of other means to measure the progress of the new schools, attendance rates became a barometer of success. Since the government had in reality little means to compel school-age youth to attend the new schools, statistics reveal the degree of success of government policy aimed at convincing parents to send their offspring to the new schools, many with pitiful facilities such as no desks. Available data show that a majority of families had little motivation to send their kids to the new schools even though the Gakusei stipulated that all children should attend. In some communities the pressure to attend school resulted in a wide range in the ages of elementary school students, some over twenty years old, producing an odd mixture in the classroom.[73] School attendance rates during the first year of the Gakusei demonstrated a degree of success. It also revealed to ministry officials how far they were from their stated goal of elementary school attendance for all.

School attendance was predictably low under the prevailing conditions. The central government launched a major campaign to induce local education officials to encourage if not coerce parents to send their children to the new schools. Great efforts were made to convince parents of the importance of the new schools with their new kinds of knowledge and revolutionary courses in science and technol-

Table 7   Elementary School Attendance during the First Year of the Gakusei, 1873

Eligible children	Attendance at school		Rate of attendance (%)		
	BOYS	GIRLS	BOYS	GIRLS	TOTAL
4,205,341	880,335	302,633	39.9	15.1	28.14

Source: Tsuchiya Tadao, *Meiji Zenki: Kyōiku Seisaku Shi no Kenkyū* (The History of Educational Policy in the Early Meiji Period) (Tokyo: Kōdansha, 1962), 115.

ogy. Local campaigns were carried out in many communities. In some, officials visited the homes of all parents attempting to persuade them to cooperate. In others, when the police came across children on the streets during school hours, they exhorted them to get to school or personally escorted the students to school. Students in Kyoto were given uniquely designed badges to wear as a mark of honor to encourage other kids to attend, provoking the selling of imitations to those who preferred to stay out with a minimum risk of punishment.[74]

Nevertheless, assuming that these early governmental figures are fairly accurate, although their validity cannot be adequately determined, the hyperbole of the Gakusei authors stipulating that every child should attend school proved far from realizable. On the other hand, that a country emerging from feudalism just five years previously could induce nearly 40 percent of male children to attend the new schools in spite of the added financial burden is often rightly interpreted as a remarkable achievement. In other words, the first sip of educational modernization drunk from a glass half full or half empty depends on how the evaluation is construed.

Regardless of how the analysis is made, there was obviously a great deal of reluctance, if not outright hostility, to the new public elementary schools. Local opposition movements were led mostly by farmers who were directly affected by the schools. The next chapter focuses on the peasant opposition to the schools in some detail. Farmers, however, were not the only ones opposed to the new schools. Even local samurai and intellectuals were dissatisfied with them, yearning for the old fief schools that catered to samurai families, teaching the Chinese classics in the traditional manner. To fill the void, some samurai quietly opened private classes to cater to like-minded families, employing the traditional style of curriculum and teaching methods.[75]

Higher Education—Kaisei Gakkō

A broad category of schools roughly categorized as post-elementary, left over from the Tokugawa period, proved to be a valuable asset to the modernization process. At varying levels of academic development, this conglomerate of institutions was classified as semmon gakkō, or specialized schools. Some were private or semiprivate, while others naturally continued under government control when the Meiji government came into power. Among the eight on record by 1875 were four medical schools, two law schools, one agricultural school, and one comprehensive school. The number increased to eleven by 1876, catering to over five hundred students.[76] Because the Gakusei was devoted overwhelmingly to public elementary schools, the introductory level of education has received most historical attention. Simultaneously however, the specialized schools at the higher level that also developed both in numbers and importance played a significant role in modern Japanese history.

The key institution in this category was the Kaisei Gakkō. It was so named in April 1873, when the new district system was implemented. Henceforth the institution was officially called the Kaisei Gakkō First Middle School of the First University District (Daiichi Daigakku Daiichiban Chūgaku Kaisei Gakkō).[77] The critical importance of this school in spite of the official "middle school" designation is that it formed the foundation for the nation's first university, the preeminent Tokyo University, four years later in 1877.

To review the historical development, Kaisei Gakkō originated in the late Tokugawa period as a school of western studies and languages. The new Meiji government in 1869 brought together three former Tokugawa schools, the old Shōhei school of Confucian studies, the Kaisei school of western studies, and the Igakkō school of medical studies. The amalgamation was given the name of Daigakkō, literally the big school. Six months later the name was changed by separating the old Kaisei stream of foreign studies into the Daigaku Nankō, or Southern School, and the Igakkō stream of medicine into the Daigaku Higashikō, the Eastern School. In effect, the old school of Confucian studies was subordinated by the school of western studies.

The next major change took place in July 1871 when the names were simplified to Nankō and Higashikō. It was during this period that Nankō underwent a major transformation under the new directorship of the Dutch-American Guido Verbeck, appointed head teacher in July. An unusual number of senior government leaders had studied under Verbeck in Nagasaki several years before the Restoration of 1868. That experience obviously had a strong influence on them illustrated by their urgent request that Verbeck come to Tokyo to serve as their advisor shortly after the Restoration. With his arrival at the seat of the new government that contained many of his students, he was appointed to head the most advanced government institution of higher studies. Verbeck moved quickly to upgrade the institution. As a result of Verbeck's reforms in both the curriculum and the faculty, Japan finally had an institution worthy of recognition as the first public institution of higher education in the modern era. The school became essentially a foreign language school of science.

In April 1873, when Tanaka Fujimaro returned from Europe from the Iwakura Mission to take charge of the Ministry of Education, Nankō was renamed Kaisei Gakkō. Guido Verbeck then resigned as head of the school in September to become advisor to the highest organ of government.[78] Virtually all of the Kaisei students, originating from samurai families, represented nearly every province in the country. Their daily schedule included five hours of foreign languages and learning, one of Japanese and Chinese reading, and one of gymnastics. They were "strictly forbidden to drink any kind of distilled or fermented liquors, to go out at night, to visit the Yoshiwara [brothels], or to go to tea houses and amuse themselves with singing girls."[79]

In a circular distributed at the opening ceremony of the renamed school in October, the purpose of Kaisei Gakkō, referred to as the Imperial University in the English press, was officially translated accordingly: "The college devoted to the revival of learning and the reformation of knowledge in which the sciences hitherto unknown in Japan shall be studied." The reporter for an English newspaper editorially contrasted the new facilities with the former by noting that "the buildings heretofore in use were mere sheds ranged in rows."[80]

The opening event was a royal affair. In attendance was Emperor Meiji himself, arriving for the occasion at seven o'clock in the morning. He spent the day visiting classes, observing science experiments, and watching a physical education class in session. His presence was another demonstration of the extraordinary interest the Imperial Household had in education, including the empress, who visited the Kaisei Gakkō in November.[81] Government officials in attendance along with the emperor included Tanaka Fujimaro and David Murray from the Ministry of Education.[82] The presence of Murray at this ceremony, a few months after he arrived in Japan, is evidence that he had already become an integral part of the Japanese educational establishment. From then on, as a ranking official of

Figure 21. Kaisei Gakkō (Imperial University).
From Nihon Kindai Shi Kenkyū Kai, ed., *Nihon Kindai no Rekishi* (Tokyo: Sanseido, 1985), 146.

the ministry, he provided historians with new insights and information about the modernization procedures as they unfolded from a foreigner's perspective. He was given a translation of the emperor's remarks on this occasion titled "Address of the Emperor to the Foreign Teachers at the Opening of the Kaisei Gakkō, October 9, 1873."[83] "The construction of the new buildings of the Kaisei Gakkō having been completed, I have come hither with many officers of my household to preside over the ceremony of their opening. It [is] a great pleasure to me to learn of the rapid progress of sciences and arts in this school. I attribute this progress largely to your zeal and industry. I look for a more rapid enlargement [sic] among my people. May all these teachers understand this."

David Murray was then given the unusual opportunity to respond to the emperor's remarks by speaking on behalf of the foreign teachers who made up the faculty of the highest-level national institution in Japan.[84] From this ceremony onward, Dr. Murray took a great interest in the Kaisei Gakkō. His former student at Rutgers College, now close friend and confidant upon whom he relied heavily, Hatakeyama Yoshinari, was appointed president two months later on December 19, 1873.[85] The ministry depended upon Hatakeyama to deal with the foreign teachers on its behalf. During Hatakeyama's tenure he, in fact, developed a close personal relationship with the foreign staff that greatly respected this gentle Japanese educator.[86]

An incident recorded by an American teacher under Hatakeyama, Warren Clark from Rutgers College, illustrates the cordiality between the new Japanese president and his foreign faculty. It incidentally reveals the delicate position of a devout Japanese Christian holding a high administrative post in early modern Japan. Hatakeyama had been baptized in the First Reformed Dutch Church in New Brunswick while studying at Rutgers College in the 1860s. It was during this time that he developed a close relationship with the Murrays as well as with his fellow student, Warren Clark. By 1873, even though the official ban against Christian teachings had been lifted, a Christian president of Japan's only institution of higher education had to be circumspect.

Clark, invited by Hatakeyama to teach at the Kaisei Gakkō, privately offered two Bible classes for students in the "Legal and Scientific departments of the Tokio University" (Kaisei Gakkō). He recalled that President Hatakeyama, upon learning of the unauthorized lessons from Clark, quietly reacted accordingly: "Of course I cannot officially give you permission; but," he added, with a knowing look, "go ahead, and God bless you, and I will be diplomatically blind to your doings."[87] Even though Hatakeyama held the important post as president of the only university-level institution in Japan at the time, he was assigned to accompany David Murray as his interpreter on a second regional tour of schools in 1874. The trip took him to distant Nagasaki by boat, followed by stops at Kyoto and Osaka.[88] He also translated official reports from the Ministry of Education for Murray.[89] The two formed a virtual father-son relationship.

Under the administration of Hatakeyama, the name of the institution was changed in July 1874, to Tokyo Kaisei Gakkō.[90] The following year a major revision of the curriculum was again carried out. The costs of operating a school in three foreign languages taught exclusively by foreigners proved a financial burden too severe to continue. Accordingly, in 1875 the courses in French and German were phased out. The students in those departments were transferred to the English department, setting a pattern that continued into the 1880s. Moreover, the curriculum itself was divided into law, science, and engineering, all taught in English. With the concentration on science courses, the institution fit even more than before the category of an English-language polytechnic school. Henceforth all examinations, including the 1876 entrance examination, were conducted only in English.[91] It was all part of the transition of Kaisei Gakkō to Tokyo University that took place in 1877.

Emperor Meiji's visit to the Kaisei Gakkō was indicative of his growing interest in the progress of modern education during the early years of his reign. The visit was a continuation of his rounds of higher educational institutions in Tokyo such as the Tokyo Teacher Training School the year before. From the beginning of his reign in 1868 to 1875, the emperor visited many schools at various levels. On each occasion he offered a few general remarks of satisfaction and support. Otherwise the Imperial Household made little effort to influence the course of modern educational reforms being carried out by Tanaka and Murray in the emperor's name.

Before the end of the 1870s, however, the emperor became profoundly concerned with the direction that modern education was taking. Rather than approving the reforms that he observed during the earlier school visits, his imperial advisors reported that the emperor was deeply troubled by what he observed from the very beginning of the modern system of education. What disturbed him was not only the policies that the American-oriented head of the ministry and his American advisor promoted. Of greater importance was what they ignored—the absence of morals education reflecting what the Imperial Household considered to be traditional values and customs of Japanese culture. The emperor's criticism of modern education suddenly burst forth at the end of his first decade in the form of the Imperial Will on Education, 1879, ushering in the second decade of the modern period in Japanese education, characterized as the reverse course.

The Meirokusha—An Association of Meiji Intellectuals, 1873–1875

During the initial period of modern education in Japan, 1873 to 1875, marked by the first public school system and the emergence of the first university-level institution, a short-lived but notable development took place. A group of Japanese intellectuals representing the leading western-oriented figures of the time organized the Meirokusha, literally men of the sixth year of the Meiji era, that is, 1873 when the idea first emerged. Although the group disbanded within a relatively short time, the Meirokusha provided a forum for the most outstanding thinkers of the day to formulate, present, and debate their ideas about the future of modern Japan. Through their magazine, the *Meirokusha Zasshi*, the opinions of the most outstanding figures of the day were made available to the reading public. Moreover, since they were recorded they have enabled future generations to analyze the evolution of thought of the early Meiji intellectuals.

The origin of the first academic association of Meiji samurai men is attributed primarily to one of their most colorful and innovative members, Mori Arinori. Once again the American influence comes into play since Mori had just returned from America after serving in Washington, D.C., as the senior diplomat representing Japan. Mori's two-year tenure brought him into close personal contacts with the leading intellectuals of American society. Taking advantage of his diplomatic position, he purposely sought out American decision makers beyond the political sector concentrated in the nation's capital. With unbounded energy, he struck up acquaintances with American academics then concentrated in the New England area, where he traveled on various occasions visiting university and college campuses. Through these experiences Mori became familiar with American academic societies.

Shortly after returning to Japan from America in July 1873, Mori approached several well-known individuals, notably those who had already staked out a reputation as progressive thinkers, about organizing a Japanese association of like-minded intellectuals. His position represents another example of the deep influence America exerted on Japan during the initial period of modernization: "There is something we can learn from scholars in America. They form scholarly societies which do joint research on academic subjects and hold discussions for the benefit of the general public. Scholars in our country are isolated, without mutual intercourse, and do little to benefit the general public. I would like to see our country's scholars follow the example of the Americans and join together to form a scholarly society that would meet for discussion and research."[92]

Among those Mori contacted was Fukuzawa Yukichi, arguably the most powerful thinker of the moment, who exerted an enormous influence on intellectual thought of early Meiji Japan. His private school, the Keio Gijuku, was already producing graduates who took up teaching positions in all of the leading schools of the day. His books on the West became bestsellers. And his indirect influence on Ministry of Education officials when they launched the first public school system in 1873 is legendary, sparking rumors that he ran the ministry from his private office on the Keio campus.

Others who joined the group, having already made significant contributions to educational modernization, included Mitsukuri Rinshō. He was the prime compiler of the Gakusei, and had attained an advanced level of fluency in three western languages unmatched by any other member. Tanaka Fujimaro, head of the Ministry of Education responsible for implementing the Gakusei, joined the Meirokusha upon his return home after nearly two years in America and Europe with the Iwakura Mission. In contrast to the linguist Mitsukuri and virtually all of the other members who studied a foreign language, Tanaka learned about the West through observation and translation. Hatakeyama Yoshinari, president of Kaisei Gakkō and David Murray's intimate friend from the days when he was a student of Murray's at Rutgers College, also joined the society.

Although membership of the Meirokusha was eclectic in many aspects, it was also in many ways homogenous. . All the members originated from the samurai class brought up during the Tokugawa era as warriors educated in Confucian teachings from an early age. At some stage of their education, for a variety of reasons they became interested in western ideas. Nearly all learned one or more western languages. Many of them studied in the West—the United States, England, Holland, France, and Germany. And one, Mori Arinori himself, had served as Japan's leading diplomat in a western country. They were all among Japan's most distinguished thinkers of the early Meiji period. Of considerable interest and a sign of the times, most were government officials with the conspicuous exception of Fukuzawa Yukichi.

With the formation of the Meirokusha and the decision to publish a magazine with articles by the members for "the exchange of opinion, the spread and popularization of knowledge, and the development of discriminating minds,"[93] a vehicle for disseminating the latest ideas by the most prominent thinkers of Meiji Japan became available. It produced a torrent of new ideas that were all deeply influenced by western ideas. The Meirokusha had a profound influence on the reading public during the short period of its existence, setting trends and opinions toward the future of the nation.

The articles that grew out of the discussions and personal research covered an unusually broad area of interests. They included government, politics, economics, law, religion, philosophy, education, and literature. Among the more unusual topics was the four-part series on "Wives and Concubines" by Mori Arinori, delineating the rights and obligations of each marriage partner, presumably as he understood the relationship in the West. He became well known for his advocacy of western-style marriage ceremonies. Following his own advice, he threw a rather lavish reception for one hundred guests at his own wedding, the first western-style ceremony with western dress recorded in modern Japan. Fittingly, Fukuzawa Yukichi served as witness. The gala event made the newspapers of the day.[94] Other topics ranged from "Writing Japanese with the Western Alphabet" by Nishi Amane in the first issue in early 1874, to a series on "The Outline of Western Culture" by Nakamura Masanao in issues ten to twelve, to "On Change" by Nishimura Shigeki in the final issue in November 1875.[95]

The Meirokusha and its journal came to an abrupt end in 1875 after a year in operation. The government had recently placed restrictions on private publications. In view of that, Fukuzawa recommended that the journal be stopped.[96] With the demise of the Meirokusha, a unique chapter in modernization came to an end. Nevertheless the public exchange and discourse on new ideas by the most prominent Japanese intellectuals represented another milestone on the road to modernization. Reflecting the times and circumstances, it was profoundly influenced by western thought and practices from the design and operation of the organization itself to the issues pursued by the enlightened members.

The initial period of modernization of Japanese education and society from 1873 to 1875 came to an end as both Tanaka and Murray, principal figures in the

Ministry of Education, prepared for a forthcoming major event overseas. The American government had invited the Japanese government to participate in the great centennial celebrations of American independence at Philadelphia from July 4, 1876. A huge exhibition was planned to open on Independence Day, with a special section set aside for educational displays.

The Japanese Ministry of Education welcomed the opportunity to participate in the forthcoming Philadelphia Centennial. Both Murray and his wife, and Tanaka and his wife, along with a small retinue of ministry officials including Hatakeyama Yoshinari, president of Kaisei Gakkō, were scheduled to attend the event. It would take them out of Japan for an extended period. Because of the American centennial's importance to the 1877–1879 period in modern Japanese education, chapter 13 is devoted to it. It proved to be a stepping stone to the second phase of American influence on modern Japanese education under Tanaka Fujimaro and his American advisor, David Murray.

Rural Resistance to
Modern Education

THE JAPANESE PEASANT, 1873–1876

When the First National Plan for Education, designed to serve every Japanese child of elementary school age, became official in 1873, 80 percent of the population consisted of peasant farmers. Many lived in isolated rural communities in mountainous areas where every member of the family was brought into the rice growing process at planting and harvesting time. Young children were not exempt. For a typical farmer, there was no need for their offspring to learn to read, write, and calculate in a full-time formal school in order to plant and harvest rice. What children learned informally at home was sufficient to meet the needs for survival of a typical peasant family in Japan in the early 1870s.

With the implementation of the Gakusei from April 1873, the venerable village terakoya schools were officially closed, to be replaced by western-type schools mandated by the central government. The demise of the terakoya was particularly painful to peasant families as grassroots institutions that grew out of the needs of rural communities and, in turn, responded to local conditions. Parents sent their children to the schools voluntarily on the basis of their ability to pay, their own level of education and interest, and the expectations of the value gained by participating in them. The terakoya were consequently closely related to rural values. For example, they catered to boys, reflecting the longstanding tradition of girls being brought up for motherhood, best learned in the home. Second, terakoya primarily taught reading and writing sufficient for the student to get along in the local community. In some the abacus was also taught, rounding out the three R's.

Finally, the terakoya schools reflected local financial conditions and cultural patterns. They charged modest fees adjusted to the local economy in order to attract enough students to support the teacher who had no official credentials to teach. Since terakoya were all private, low fees as well as the fundamental goals of the school steeped in cultural traditions of morality served as attractive features to village parents. Their sudden closure in 1873 by edict from far-off Tokyo predictably provoked anger and frustration throughout the countryside.[1] If ever there was a school that uniquely reflected Dr. David Murray's profound thought in his reply to Mori Arinori in Washington in 1872 that brought him to Japan a year later, it was the Japanese terakoya village school of premodern Japan: "There are traditional customs which it would be unwise to subvert. There are institutions already founded which are revered for their local and national associations, which without material change may be the best elements of a new system. . . . If, therefore, changes are to be made in the educational system of any country, wisdom would suggest the retention, so far as possible, of those institutions already in existence."[2]

The modern Japanese public elementary school under the Gakusei was specifically intended to replace the terakoya, with its unstructured curriculum and untrained teachers, by a modern national curriculum taught by trained certified teachers. Ironically, the process violated the very essence of Murray's earlier advice. By closing down the neighborhood terakoya school, replacing it with a local public elementary school mechanically assigned to a population of 600, the old village and town patterns were often ignored. Many school districts did not conform to the arbitrary boundaries where 600 people lived. If a village fell considerably short of the magic number, it was combined with another to conform to the regulations. In drawing up the new elementary school districts, not only were unfamiliar combinations of villages cobbled together but the elementary school district did not always conform to other administrative civil units that had evolved naturally on the basis of local village borders. The new elementary school districts in some areas were effectively isolated from the traditional unit of local organization.[3]

There was an ulterior motive behind the separation of local elementary school districts from traditional village boundaries. Progressives within the government were highly critical of social patterns that had evolved within rural communities, considered the very core of the feudalism they were dedicated to eradicate. To avoid the influence of those feudal customs that bound the villagers in hierarchical relationships, the government implemented the new school districts and purposely ignored traditional social units. It was all part of the modernization process employing education as an instrument to reconstruct local Japanese society.[4]

Moral education proved to be a major obstacle to the new school system. To many rural parents, a disproportionate emphasis was placed on the new technical subjects, science and mathematics, in a policy objective by the government to lay the basis for a modern industrial society. Conversely, there was little concern for traditional morals education fundamental to the terakoya schools that endeared them to the local community. For example, only during grades one and two of the new curricula was a smattering of morals taught for one hour a week. The subject itself was listed at the bottom of the curriculum. From the third grade on there were no morals courses at all. The new public schools were thus often regarded as appealing only to the intellect. In contrast, the old terakoya schools, according to the prevalent attitude of the day, appealed to the heart.[5]

In place of the traditional morality of respect for elders, parents, superiors, and so on, based on Confucian teachings, the modern curriculum was meant to impart a new spirit of enlightenment based on social equality. The Gakusei had declared a modern spirit of social equality, equality of educational opportunity, and a spirit of individualism. These vague concepts were to be imparted to the students by teaching that the old traditional Japanese society, in contrast, was based on feudal patterns of discrimination among the social classes. Modern Japan would be based on equality of the sexes and social equality for all.[6] Understandably, such teachings in Japan of the 1870s were treated with disdain by many Japanese, notably those who were most affected by it in rural Japan.

Many of the village terakoya, however, were promptly reopened as public elementary schools with the same teachers teaching in the traditional manner. In contrast, the new Ministry of Education under Tanaka Fujimaro set out to drastically revise the local educational environment. As quickly as possible the old teachers were replaced or retrained in the new methodology using new textbooks introduced by Marion Scott at the Tokyo Teacher Training School. Scott modeled his training course, which included teaching methodology, curricula, textbooks, and teaching materials, precisely after his former San Francisco elementary school. Consequently the Ministry of Education issued the new curriculum based on the curriculum of a standard American elementary school, replacing the traditional subjects of the old terakoya schools. Japanese children, both rural and urban, were about to experience a new world designed for American children.

In some communities the old cherished terakoya was destroyed to make way for the new public school building. In others, the old schools were simply closed and new buildings constructed at different sites with new and strange subjects such as health and singing. Moreover, the local community, including desperately poor peasant parents, was primarily held responsible to finance the expensive changes that included student fees.[7] The decision to replace the old school with the new, compelling peasant farmers to pay for it, made by unknown government bureaucrats in distant Tokyo with no relationship to or understanding of local conditions, proved unsettling. A social revolution was under way aimed directly at the peasants and their children.

Typical of rural societies, the Japanese farm family and village constituted a traditional conservative influence with change begrudgingly accepted. For example, the Gakusei's stipulation that each family was responsible for sending every school-age child to the nearest public elementary school, by itself, introduced an alien situation in every rural village that was bound to provoke a negative reaction. Until the Gakusei, nonsamurai parents decided whether they would send their children to a local private school. Government officials were not involved in that personal assessment. There were, of course, no public schools for commoners before this time so private education was strictly a family choice. To further exacerbate the situation, the government decreed that parents must send female children to the same school with their sons, a revolutionary idea in a feudal society.

Government policy reached far beyond public school attendance in its intrusion in local affairs. Just as the Gakusei was being implemented in 1873, the government passed two other laws that also impacted deeply on village life. The first was a conscription bill to draft local youth into the new army, raising the anxiety of peasant families confronted with the loss of farm hands. The other was a detested land tax of 3 percent of assessed value. The government set the rate, considered excessive by farmers, to finance the costly programs to modernize the nation. The tax had a debilitating influence on the lives of farmers causing some to give up farming and leading to a detested landlord system.[8]

These three laws were, in one sense, a package of bills inextricably related to the entire modernization process. A new school system was essential to develop human resources for the industrial modernization with its accompanying proliferation of factories. Modern military capability was equally essential. The nation had to protect its borders as it entered the international arena where colonialism had already brought much of the underdeveloped world under the control of powerful western nations. The government also needed military forces to counter internal opposition to its revolutionary policies. To finance these programs designed to bring about a transformation of a feudal society required huge sums. Government leaders felt compelled to enforce a national tax system to pay the proliferating bills.

The new package of laws imposed by a distant and unknown central government had a decidedly negative impact on peasant life. Families with children of school age lost their help on the farm during both morning and afternoon school sessions, particularly critical during planting and harvesting seasons. Those with draft-age sons lost strong bodies from farm work, breaking up the family as sons were taken away for military training and potentially placed in life-threatening situations. And those who owned farmland had to pay the new government a burdensome land tax to meet the costs of national programs about which they knew little of and understood less, in addition to local school fees.

Peasant reaction toward the first attempt at a modern school system in Japan is best understood by dividing the many issues into different categories. Arguably the most critical was the financial factor. Japanese farmers were, from the Tokugawa era, intimately familiar with having their rice production taxed to finance the domain's governing apparatus. They were also long accustomed to the nonproductive ruling samurai class existing on peasant productivity. Governing policy of most local domains assessed an annual tax on each village as a unit and placed responsibility on the village headmen to determine its implementation. This method granted some degree of local autonomy as long as the taxes were paid.[9]

Regardless of the method of calculating the government's share of rice harvests or the means of collecting it, Japanese peasant communities resented the taxation system long before the Meiji Restoration. They carried out widespread acts of protests that date back hundreds of years. For example, one of the largest Tokugawa peasant uprisings took place in 1764 with an estimated 200,000 farmers participating. At that time the government decided to increase the number of post stations on the main road from Edo to Nikkō, site of the great Tokugawa mausoleum, for a major ceremony. The government substantially raised taxes on local communities along the way, which provoked a three-month uprising led by peasants from the entire northern Kanto district who were most affected by the increase. Although the government was ultimately forced to abandon the increase by the violent opposition from farmers, six hundred of the leaders were punished. The primary instigator was executed.[10]

Peasant uprisings, including large-scale violent protests, continued to the end of the Tokugawa era and contributed to the unrest that finally brought the three and a half centuries of one-family rule to a close in 1868. Under the new Meiji government, the national policy of rebuilding every sector of the society on a western model, from education to the post office to the army, required enormous funding. Since it was virtually impossible to borrow the necessary funds for such infrastructure from abroad, the government necessarily turned to the traditional form of financing national expenditures. From 1868 through the end of the decade, nearly 80 percent of all ordinary revenue to finance the modernization of Japan came from the onerous land tax.[11]

Meiji leaders found themselves in a financial predicament. On the one hand, the government was dependent on farm production to generate a taxable base to finance national expenditures. At the same time, Ministry of Education policy antagonized farmers by requiring their children to attend the new public elementary schools financed by local taxes assessed on farmers. For the modernization of education, farming had to be productive. One historian summed it up succinctly. To make farming pay for industrialization, it must pay to engage in farming.[12] On the other hand to build a strong nation in the future, political leaders realized early on that every child, including peasant children, must be educated regardless of the costs or peasant reaction.

By the time the Gakusei was initiated in 1873, local taxes had already become a major source of unrest among the peasants, literally a time bomb waiting to be detonated. The basic principle stipulated in the Gakusei, that those who benefited from the new public schools must finance them, was severely undermined when many local parents were convinced that rather than benefiting from the new public schools, they were being penalized by them. The new schools snatched their able-bodied sons from the fields. Student fees then ate into family finances already ravaged by the detested land tax imposed by the same central government. In addition, new laws now compelled farm families to pay for the local school beyond individual student tuition through school taxes (Table 8).

Table 8   Financing the First Public Elementary Schools, 1873

Sources of income	% of budget
Local taxes	43.2
Local fund	19.1
Local gifts	13.4
National subsidy	12.6
Student fees	6.3
Miscellaneous	5.4

Source: Ichikawa Shōgo, Kyōiku Zaisei (Educational Finance) (Tokyo: Tokyo University Press, 1972), 90.

Many examples demonstrate how dramatically, and drastically, financial policy affected local communities, requiring extraordinary sacrifices by the ordinary Japanese farmer. Nara prefecture was a good example. In order to finance the new school in one village, the total amount required came to 602 yen. Of that, student fees brought in 198 yen, nearly a third of the new budget. Almost all of the rest was derived from various local taxes. In several rural villages in northern Aomori prefecture, school officials demonstrated a degree of ingenuity to cover the short-fall by cultivating rice paddies to generate income. The subsidy from the central government that ordered the new school was minimal.[13]

The second major irritant provoking widespread opposition was the nature of the new schools themselves. The new schools posed a threat to local customs and values as well as to the traditional way of thinking. For example, Japanese social behavior places great emphasis on the dominant role of the group. The new schools placed great concern on the development of the individual, in part because of the powerful influence of Fukuzawa Yukichi.

The dominant role of the unfamiliar subjects of science and mathematics in the new curriculum provoked opposition by the peasantry. Conversely, there was too little concern for traditional morals education fundamental to the old terakoya schools. In place of the traditional morality of respect for elders, based on Confucian teachings, the modern curriculum taught, in contrast, that the old traditional Japanese society was based on feudal patterns of discrimination among four social classes. Modern Japan would be based on equality of the sexes and social equality for all.[14]

The Gakusei also stipulated that elementary children attend the new public schools in coeducational classes. That provision violated longstanding tradition in rural Japan, where the content of learning for girls differed sharply from that of boys. The educational opportunities available for girls were purposely tailored to fit the expectations for females in a traditional society—to become respectful daughters and good mothers. Sewing and flower arrangement fit that category rather than mathematics and science, the very core of the new western-type curriculum of the public schools. Many conservative farm families were already troubled with the new fashion for girls with hairstyles on the shorter western model. The new schools were a forceful reminder that unwanted change was under way, heightening parental anxieties.[15]

The modern curriculum set by the Ministry of Education for all elementary schools throughout the nation had little attraction to a rural population. The stipulated courses, including geography, history, and science, appeared irrelevant to farm families. The old terakoya offered the basics in reading and writing, which attracted certain parents who believed their offspring should be able to read and write. But the new schools went far beyond that by introducing peculiar subjects foreign to the Japanese peasant such as singing (*shōka*) and physical education (*taisō*).

The new curriculum for the elementary schools also presented a clear distinction between the old and the new, the familiar and the unfamiliar. Ministry of

Education officials concluded, and rightly so, that the modernization of western societies depended on technological achievements. To attain that level, science education must take precedence. Fundamental to all science was basic mathematics. Hence mathematics became the central subject of the new schools in combination with science, the two consuming an inordinate proportion—about half—of the weekly timetable. Mathematics played a limited role in Japan before the Meiji Restoration. The simple, easily learned, and inexpensive abacus derived from China served the average farmer well. Suddenly western mathematics became basic to the new school system, and the preoccupation with science and mathematics underscored the contrast with traditional education in feudal Japan that focused on calligraphy and morality. Predictably, the curriculum of the modern school provoked widespread opposition among farmers.

The revolutionary educational policy implemented from 1873 antagonized the peasants in a variety of other ways. The Gakusei stipulated that all children should attend the local public elementary school, regardless of social or family circumstances. Traditional patterns of education had strictly separated children of the samurai in domain schools, purposely separating them from the rest of the social classes. Terakoya schools catered to those commoners who were inclined to educate their children. Most rural youth from farm families received little or no formal education. Suddenly children from the different classes in a society that previously segregated its people into four social classifications, in addition to the outcast Burakumin who worked with, among others, dead animals such as butchering, were brought together by government decree in a public school. They were all to sit side by side in a common classroom. It was the first great attempt at social engineering in Japan, employing the schools as an instrument of social reform. However, the very foundation of the society, the peasants, were unprepared for it.

The new schools became symbolic of the changes that local farmers were experiencing precisely when their subsistence living underwent further erosion with new taxes. Their livelihood depended precariously on the price of rice in which, unfortunately, the market deteriorated during the first three years of the Gakusei from 1873 to 1876. That coincided with the peak of violent acts against the new schools. Simultaneously other foreign influences such as western clothes and western hairstyles, along with the increasing presence of westerners, many hired by the government to introduce western technology, provoked widespread angst among the peasants. The school became a visible and available target of local frustration against change in the guise of modernization. To some farmers the very word *school* (*gakkō*) evoked anger. Reports of parents purposely beating their children so they physically could not attend the new schools illustrated the extreme reaction among peasant families in the first stage in the modernization of Japanese education.[16]

Local opposition erupted not only against the new educational policies but toward the multiplicity of changes under way. For example, the reading public was surely startled when the headlines of a local newspaper of the period proclaimed that "one day contains twenty-four hours." Further, the article explained that each day was divided into two equal parts, separating the morning from the evening; that each hour was divided into sixty parts, and that each minute was further divided into sixty units called seconds (*byō*).[17] This had to be a baffling revelation to many farmers used to the lunar calendar. Demands to return to the old calendar from the new western calendar imposed by the government, abolish military conscription, forbid foreigners to travel through local areas, reduce the land tax— among other grievances—all became intertwined in the campaign against the new elementary schools. Progressive central leaders, determined to transform a feudal society into a modern one, had struck particularly sensitive nerves, provoking a predictable peasant reaction to the effects of the new policies on their daily lives.

Violent Reaction toward the New Public Schools, 1873–1876

With the issuance of the first national plan for education in August 1872, new schools were built or the old terakoya schools reorganized to implement the new system from the following April. Even before the new system got under way, riots broke out around the nation led by farmers, and continued from 1873 for the next three years. Although the unrest was a reaction against various innovations such as conscription and taxation as well as educational reforms, the new local schools and their teachers often took the brunt of the antimodernization movement. For example, in Okayama prefecture, twenty to thirty thousand farmers protested against the introduction of the new official category of *shin heimin*, the new commoners, in which all Japanese except nobility were henceforth classified. Farmers opposed being grouped in the same category with the traditionally outcast burakumin people who labored in detested work such as handling dead animals. But the demonstrators also opposed local school fees and destroyed forty-six public elementary schools to express their general opposition to government policy.[18]

That was only the beginning. Unrest boiled over spontaneously at various locations. Again, in the same year of the Gakusei, ten thousand farmers in Tottori prefecture demonstrated against the new school system while demanding that foreigners be required to receive local permission before entering the prefecture.[19] During the same year, over one hundred telegraph poles were demolished by protestors in another area of the country, an act clearly aimed at modern technology since the telegraph had recently been introduced into the country from the West.[20]

The new schools established under the Gakusei had become symbols not only of change but also of government intrusion and, as such, fell victims to mob psychology. In one two-month period alone, May and June 1873, farmers in Kagawa burned down thirty-four elementary schools.[21] During the whole year in that prefecture, 20,000 protestors destroyed a total of forty-eight schools. Violence spread even into the ancient capital of Kyoto where 2,000 protestors demanded an abolition of the draft and of school fees. The army was called in to break up the demonstrations. Schools were also burned in Aichi, Mie, Saitama, and Chiba prefectures.[22]

In June 1873, on the southern island of Kyushu in the old Fukuoka prefecture, amid a severe drought that destroyed crops, 300,000 farmers participated in a demonstration demanding the abolition of the new local elementary schools as well as conscription. In their anger they destroyed twenty-nine schools.[23] During the same month in Tottori prefecture, a peasant group attacked local elementary school teachers. They then proceeded to burn down two elementary schools.[24] In various other communities, the results of protest movements were equally destructive.

In June 1873, a bizarre incident took place in Tottori prefecture. A rumor swept a local community when two teachers at the new local public elementary school were accused of being "blood squeezers" (ikichi shibori) and were physically attacked with agricultural tools. Somehow in the translation of the French legal code in which the term l'emport du sang or blood tax became "blood squeezers," the weird concept was applied to the two new teachers, former samurai obviously detested by local provocateurs. They were specifically accused of sucking blood from humans. In the frenzy that ensued, one teacher escaped the mob. The other was left to die from wounds inflicted by disgruntled farmers. The campaign mushroomed to include about 12,000 angry demonstrators. They rioted for five days during which the elementary school was burned down, along with the teacher's homes, the community hall, the village headman's house, and even the local police station.[25]

In Fukui prefecture members of the Jōdo Shinshū Buddhist sect protested against the introduction of Christianity. They also demanded that foreign-language teaching, meaning English, be forbidden in the new schools. Ten thousand followers took up the cause and attacked government buildings, symbolic of the changes under way in every aspect of local society. The new school was destroyed on the grounds that the current school system imposed by the central government was based on Christianity.[26] Often anything new became associated with the West and was, in turn, not infrequently associated with Christianity, thereby posing a threat to traditional beliefs. The new schools became convenient and visible targets through association to all things new which included such trends as the new western hair styles for females and eating beef.[27] In education, it involved such innovations as the introduction of the western alphabet and could lead to the destruction of buildings including local teacher training schools.[28]

Peasant unrest that began in 1873 continued for several years. Even in 1876, three years after the Gakusei was first implemented, schools were still being burned by local mobs. For example, in December 1876, schools were attacked in every administrative unit of Mie prefecture. A total of twenty-nine elementary schools were destroyed and a further twenty-nine damaged. A major newspaper, the Tokyo Nichi Nichi Shimbun, reported that throughout the prefecture a record number of 58,300 protestors were arrested.[29] The unrest moved to Aichi prefecture the same month, where seven more schools were burned down. In some cases classes were returned to local Buddhist temples, similar to the old outlawed terakoya, or private homes as substitute classrooms.[30] In most of the violent incidents throughout the country during the three-year period from 1873 to 1876, protest movements against various modernizing influences included attacks on the new public schools.

In retrospect, the opposition to modern schools by many Japanese farm families during the first half of the 1870s was provoked by the disruption of their traditional feudal practices. It was not a political or social revolution such as the French, British, and American revolutions that overthrew dictatorial governments under the banner of freedom and equality. Japanese peasants knew little of western democracies that had already been put in place throughout the West. Rather, the typical farmer who participated in the demonstrations did so to preserve his traditional way of life, that is, one dominated by feudal patterns and customs being threatened by western ideas and government tax policies.

Although farmers formed the heart of the opposition to the new schools, many ex-samurai were also antagonistic toward the educational reforms. Traditional Confucian education based on the Chinese classics was completely abandoned by the new public schools. Confucian teachings were pointedly derided in the intro-duction to the Gakusei as useless. In direct opposition to the new public schools of western learning, according to the annual report of the Ministry of Education, some former samurai established private schools to teach Chinese classics in the traditional manner to those who still respected the teachings of the venerable Chi-nese sage Confucius.[31]

In contrast to the violent acts of resistance, passive resistance among the peas-ant classes took the form of ignoring the regulations in the Gakusei that stipulated that parents were responsible for sending their children to the new elementary schools. Farm families disregarded the central government's specific appeal that all children when they become seven years of age should enter elementary school, the place where everyone—samurai, farmers, artisans, and merchants alike—should study and be taught.[32]

The government was painfully aware of peasant opposition. To counter nega-tive attitudes toward the new schools, and in lieu of any means financially or oth-erwise to enforce school attendance, the Ministry of Education conducted a public relations campaign to encourage parents to send their children to the new schools. It was designed especially to convince the rural population of the importance of the new school and the new knowledge provided therein to their lives. Directives went out to local prefectures to exert a major effort to support the campaign.

A variety of means was employed to encourage school attendance. For example, prefectural officials in charge of school attendance in Akita methodically visited every home to explain the benefits of the new school. In Fukushima pre-fecture, officers carried a flag through the streets heralding the message of school attendance. In Saitama, police officers who encountered school-age youth on the streets during school hours personally escorted them to school. In Kyoto, each child enrolled in school was given a badge identifying him or her as a student in a certain public school. In a variety of other areas, students wore badges that simply read "school attendance" (*shūgaku shō*) as a means to encourage other school-age youth to attend school.[33]

School attendance is often used as an indicator of government success as well as failure. Since there were no effective methods to enforce compulsory attendance at the local level, the degree of voluntary compliance by parents was to some extent indicative of their approval, however begrudging, of the new local school. And since the population was overwhelmingly peasant-farmer, school attendance rates thereby best illustrated community penetration of the centrally planned western-oriented education on a national scale. Because of the novelty of this grand experiment in educational modernization, it is appropriate to consider the first three years of school attendance to judge the initial effects of the first national school system in the modern era (Table 9).

Amid the confusion and turmoil in some areas of the country, overall attendance rates increased by over 6 percent during the initial three years of Japan's first national system of education. Although modest gains were achieved, statistics also demonstrate that approximately two-thirds of all eligible elementary school children were not enrolled in school. Manifestly the number of parents who opposed the new public schools far outnumbered those who participated in active demonstrations against them. In other words, a silent majority of Japanese parents were not yet convinced that they should send their children to the nearby public school, regardless of government decree.

The data also illustrate the enormous gap between attendance rates of boys and girls. Whereas the rate of attendance by boys increased to 50 percent during the first three years of the new system, attendance by girls during the same period increased only to 18 percent. In other words, the gap between the educational standards of boys and girls was widened during the initial period of educational modernization. Even though the Gakusei specifically stated that all girls of elementary age must attend school, the prevailing attitude that girls should be educated in the home continued.

In addition, the national figures fail to show the high dropout rates during the year, or the great variation from community to community. As could be expected,

Table 9   Elementary School Attendance during the First Three Years of the Gakusei, 1873–1875

	Eligible children	Attendance at school		Rate of attendance (%)		
		BOYS	GIRLS	BOYS	GIRLS	TOTAL
1873	4,205,341	880,335	302,633	39.9	15.1	28.14
1874	4,923,272	1,183,731	408,384	46.2	17.2	32.09
1875	5,167,667	1,365,305	463,169	50.5	18.6	34.99

Source: Tsuchiya Tadao, *Meiji Zenki: Kyōiku Seisaku Shi no Kenkyū* (The History of Educational Policy in the Early Meiji Period) (Tokyo: Kōdansha, 1962), 112.

attendance rates were higher in the cities than in the countryside, highly significant in a country where the vast majority of the population was engaged in farming. In addition, the more remote from the great Tokyo-Kyoto metropolitan regions, the greater the discrepancy between female and male attendance rates. For example, in northern rural Akita prefecture in 1874, 23.6 percent of eligible boys attended school. In contrast. only 3.5 percent of eligible girls were enrolled.[34] In both categories, the difference between peasant and urban opposition to the new public schools was significant.

The rash of violent protests against the new school system peaked in 1876. There were several reasons for the sharp decline thereafter. One was the increased effectiveness in suppressing organized civilian protests by the conscript army. Ironically, the expanding military forces were financed by the land tax that was instrumental in provoking peasant uprisings in the first place. In other words, the government during the later half of the 1870s was in a position to exert military power to enforce its policies. A prime example was the suppression of the famous Satsuma Rebellion of 1877 led by one of the four major leaders of the original Meiji government, Saigo Takamori. Government military forces operating in the distant southern prefecture were able to overpower his determined forces, ending with Saigo's ritual suicide before his beleaguered position was overrun. The conscript army had come of age, proving too powerful for peasants to confront when it was called into service against local unrest.

The second factor that brought an end to local rioting against the new schools was the rise of a political movement, the Jiyū Minken Undō, the Peoples' Movement for Freedom or the Movement for Freedom and Popular Rights. It was led by disaffected samurai when it was first organized during the mid-1870s, but progressive farmers were attracted to its campaign for human rights and representative government by the latter half of the decade. Previously peasant uprisings against the new national school system occurred in part because there were no other means actively to oppose government policy. With the rise of the Jiyū Minken Undō, a new form of protest became available for the first time in the history of Japan in the form of a grassroots political movement. From 1877 on, educational policy was framed within the context of the reaction of the Jiyū Minken Undō, bringing to a close the most violent period of opposition to the modernization of education in Japan.

10

The Imperial University
of Engineering

THE SCOTTISH MODEL, 1873–1882

The main focus in modern Japanese education during the early Meiji period was elementary education, and the Ministry of Education concentrated its resources primarily at that level from 1873. But meanwhile, major educational developments were taking place independently of the ministry. Among them, one of the most important was an institution that trained the first corps of Japanese engineers, who served the country by engineering an infrastructure of the nation's roads, buildings, water plants, and so on, for the modern era. The school was designed by a Scotsman, Henry Dyer, who dubbed it the Imperial University of Engineering.[1]

Japanese interest in engineering after the Meiji Restoration of 1868 was greatly motivated by astonishment at the advancements in western civilian and military engineering. The Meiji leadership, especially those like Itō Hirobumi and Yamao Yōzō who studied in the West during the Tokugawa era, recognized early on the necessity to modernize the nation's outdated defense capability. But the nonmilitary infrastructure of Japan, the roads, bridges, docks, and railroads, were also nonexistent or totally inadequate to meet the growing demands of the time.

One of the glaring inadequacies was transportation in a mountainous country such as Japan with its abundance of rivers. A prime example of the challenge surfaced during the transfer of the Imperial Household from the old capital of Kyoto to the new capital of Tokyo upon the Restoration in 1868. It took the imperial entourage nearly a month to make the trip of about three hundred miles over the rugged mountains and across the rivers on the famous Tōkaidō road between the two major cities.[2] At many places along this most heavily traveled route in the country, it was little more than "a broad footpath."[3] At that time, when Americans could travel three thousand miles across the United States in a week on the transcontinental railroad, the Japanese had to walk or ride a horse to travel the twenty miles from Tokyo to Yokohama. The first railroad in Japan linking the two was completed four years after the Meiji Restoration, in 1872.

In the absence of qualified Japanese engineers, the Meiji government had no recourse but to hire foreigners to design and oversee the construction of basic engineering projects. Among the earliest was Henry Brunton from Scotland, who was originally employed by the Tokugawa government in February 1868 as a lighthouse engineer to plan and build a network of such facilities. Arriving in Japan during the summer shortly after the Meiji Restoration, Brunton found himself working with the new government, which was committed to carrying out the original contract approved by the overthrown Tokugawa regime. He encountered a dangerous and challenging assignment in an island country with a long and craggy coastline, and had to use a British ship to carry out the initial survey. The machinery had to be imported from England, most of it coming from Scottish companies.

The Meiji government established the Ministry of Works (Kōbusho) in October 1870.[4] It included departments for railroads, mining, lighthouses, telegraph, and manufacturing. In September 1871, Itō Hirobumi, although officially vice minister, assumed responsibility as head of the ministry in the absence of a minister, with Yamao Yōzō his chief deputy.[5] Both had studied illegally in England the previous decade as members of the Chōshū Five. Yamao studied engineering at a Scottish institution for several years in the mid 1860s. No one understood better than he how grossly inadequate the infrastructure of Japan was at that time.

Yamao and Itō, recognizing the urgent need for a school to train Japanese engineers in the latest techniques in western engineering, acted promptly. As ranking officials in charge of the Ministry of Works, the two organized an internal course in engineering called the Kōbu Gakkō, the Engineering School. Without teachers in modern technology, however, it proved inadequate. In April 1871, they submitted a formal request from the Ministry of Works to the Dajōkan, the highest governmental organ, proposing the formation of a university (*daigakkō*) of engineering attached to the ministry. Reflecting the realities of the state of engineering in Japan, a specific provision called for the employment of one foreigner in charge of the institution in addition to six foreign teachers to form the faculty.[6] The Dajōkan granted swift approval. The Ministry of Works set out immediately to implement the project.

Coincidentally, the government at that time decided to send senior government leaders to the United States and Europe on the Iwakura Mission in December 1871, as discussed previously. The various government ministries selected representatives for the mission to investigate western institutions and achievements in their respective areas. Itō Hirobumi joined the mission from the Ministry of Works. Among his assignments was the responsibility to search for appropriate candidates in the West to launch an engineering school.

After a prolonged visit in Washington, the Iwakura Mission then traveled to England in 1872. Upon arriving in London, Itō sought out his old friend from the 1860s, Hugh Matheson, head of the Jardine Matheson company's London office. Itō sought his help in locating someone capable of undertaking the responsibility for planning an engineering school in Japan. Matheson, a Scot by birth with close ties to his native land, as was his business partner, Sir Robert Jardine, immediately contacted McQuorn Rankine, professor of engineering at Glasgow University.[7]

Turning to Scotland for this critical assignment proved to be one of the most productive and timely developments in the entire modernization process in Japan. Japanese exposure to the West by this time was sufficient to enable the leadership to recognize and appreciate the level of engineering education the famed Scottish universities had attained by 1872. Yamao Yōzō, ranking officer of the Ministry of Public Works, had studied technology in Scotland during the Tokugawa era. In spite of the enormous influence America exerted on the Japanese at this time, while in Washington Itō did not look for an American to introduce western engineering to Japan. Rather he patiently waited until arriving in London to begin his special assignment.

By the 1870s, the Scots had achieved an international reputation in engineering education. The first chair of engineering had been set at the University of Glasgow in 1840, thereby recognizing engineering as an academic discipline. It brought together "theoretical training in engineering and scientific subjects and marrying them to practical work experience as well as laboratory work."[8] The Scottish universities of Glasgow and Edinburgh were perhaps the leading universities in engineering in the world in the 1870s. Distinguished scientists like James Watt, developer of the steam engine that sparked the industrial revolution, were on the staff of Glasgow University. He exemplified the practical nature of the engineering program at the institution. On the same faculty was the great scholar Adam Smith, professor of moral philosophy and author of the classic *Wealth of Nations*; such was the diversity of distinction of this Scottish institution.

When Hugh Matheson contacted his fellow Scot, he ignored Oxford and Cambridge. The two most famous British institutions with close historical ties to the Church of England were deemed inappropriate for the needs of Japan in the 1870s. Matheson wisely turned to his native Scotland on behalf of the Japanese.

Responding to Matheson's unusual request for a Scot to introduce engineering in Japan, Professor Rankine at Glasgow University also made a fortuitous choice. Deeply impressed by one of his senior students about to graduate, Rankine informed Henry Dyer, aged twenty-four, about the Japanese inquiry. Itō, busily engaged in contacts in London, sent his aide from the Ministry of Works to Glasgow to meet Professor Rankine who arranged a meeting with Dyer. Before completing his final examinations at the university, Dyer promptly accepted the challenge to plan an engineering school for the Japanese Ministry of Works. It was a courageous decision since Dyer was unfamiliar with Japan.

An indication of the determination of the Japanese government to initiate the project, and the confidence they placed in Scottish intermediaries, Dyer was offered the exceptionally high salary of 660 yen per month to induce him to take the position. The generous amount contrasted with the salary of a senior Japanese government leader such as Itō Hirobumi at 500 yen per month. Moreover it surpassed the salary of 600 yen earned by David Murray at the Ministry of Education, who was a full professor when hired by the Japanese government at the same time. It was an offer that Dyer could not refuse. He departed Scotland for Japan in April 1873. On board his ship were five other graduates from Britain, mostly trained in Scotland, as part of Dyer's engineering mission to Japan.

Shortly thereafter, Dr. David Murray and wife departed from Rutgers College in New Brunswick, New Jersey, to take up his assignment as senior advisor to the Japanese Ministry of Education. Murray and Dyer would meet fairly often in Tokyo in the intimate world of foreign employees of the Japanese government. But they would not serve as ministerial colleagues. Engineering education in Japan was first introduced as a theoretical course in the mainstream of higher education at the Kaisei Gakkō, which became Tokyo University in 1877. Ministry of Works officials, obviously not satisfied with the existing course under the Ministry of Education, opened a second route to engineering education under the leadership of Itō Hirobumi and Yamao Yōzō. Dyer was hired by the Ministry of Works to accomplish this goal. Inevitably it would compete with engineering education under the Ministry of Education.

In the history of modern Japanese education, the two-month voyage from Glasgow to Tokyo by Henry Dyer in late spring of 1873 played an unusually significant role. Accompanied by Itō's assistant from Japan, Dyer effectively employed his time on the ship to prepare a detailed proposal that he entitled "The Calendar for the Imperial University of Engineering." It was in this document by Dyer that the English title of the institution originated. By the time the party arrived in Yokohama on June 3, 1873, the future of modern Japanese engineering was sealed. It would be based primarily on the Scottish model. The Ministry of Works now led by Yamao Yōzō, who incidentally learned that Dyer had also studied at Andersonian College in Scotland when Yamao himself was enrolled there, embraced Dyer's proposal without modification. Dyer and his team immediately began the challenging task of introducing engineering education in Japan.

Although the task was daunting, to be sure, Dyer had certain inherent advantages in carrying out his awesome responsibilities. First, he literally began his assignment from scratch. There were no traditional issues to overcome since there was no precedent in Japan for such an undertaking. Second, he was empowered to enforce his ideas with the complete support from the government. Itō, then gaining bureaucratic ascendancy, and Yamao, in charge of the Ministry of Works, were totally dependent on the Scot. Third, even though a recent graduate in his midtwenties, Henry Dyer had a remarkable depth of technical knowledge, a tribute to the state of engineering education in Scotland. And finally he had the dedication, energy, and deep commitment to carry out his assignment effectively. Supported by a faculty of competent engineers, mostly trained in Scotland, who were equally dedicated to the task, he was able to undertake the demanding assignment with unusual confidence for a young man his age.

The final element in the equation concerns the type of Japanese student who studied the most advanced level of engineering in the world in the early 1870s under foreign instructors. Once again the foundation of modern education laid during the feudal period of Tokugawa Japan deserves special recognition. Virtually all of the students in the entering class of this great experiment in western science education came from samurai families. Only five years had passed since the feudal era ended with the Meiji Restoration of 1868. The applicants for the first class of Japanese engineers in 1873 had received their basic education as samurai warriors during the Tokugawa era. Even more remarkable, mathematics, fundamental to engineering, was given little attention in feudal domain schools for samurai youth. Nevertheless the ultimate success of the first class of engineering students was a tribute not only to their thirst for knowledge but their ability to grasp the fundamentals of western mathematics. Consequently Henry Dyer and his colleagues were capable of effectively teaching and motivating Japanese youth from the warrior class of feudal Japan, a vast unexploited resource, to become modern engineers.

In June 1873, several weeks after Dyer submitted his proposal to then-Minister of Works, Yamao Yōzō, the ministry began recruiting the first class of students. A total of eighty applied. The number was somewhat restricted since most Japanese of the period were unfamiliar with the word "engineering," *kōgaku*. It was not infrequently misunderstood as "carpentry," *daiku*, since the same Chinese character was used in both words. Forty students were finally accepted after passing an entrance examination in English, in itself indicative of the role of English among the educated elite.

The Kōgakuryō, the School of Engineering that Dyer referred as the Imperial University of Engineering, opened in August 1873. It included departments of civil engineering, mechanical engineering, architecture, chemistry, and metallurgy and mining engineering, with state-of-the-art laboratories.[9] A six-year course was divided into three two-year courses: an introductory course, the specialized course, and the practical course. Among the unique features of the program were the famed Akebane Works located in northern Tokyo equipped with modern workshops for practical training. A corps of hundreds of engineering technicians was subsequently trained at that complex, filling a vital role essential for modern engineering. The Akebane Works was attributable to the experience of Dyer. He had completed a workshop apprenticeship as part of his practical training in Scotland that involved engineers and technicians working closely together.

The Imperial University of Engineering followed the Scottish tradition far beyond the curriculum. The school became a western-style institution throughout. The faculty was completely foreign, placing a heavy burden on the budget of the Ministry of Works. In 1874, one-third of the entire budget went for foreign salaries.[10] The buildings were designed on the western style. The ornate main hall became the finest auditorium in Tokyo. The engineering students who attended class throughout the day ate western food and dressed in western clothes with distinctive Glasgow caps. The Japanese language was banned from the classroom, where only English, with a Scottish accent, was allowed. Those who couldn't adjust to this Scottish-style institution dropped out.[11]

Virtually every aspect of the Imperial University of Engineering reflected the personal attributes of Henry Dyer. He had been broadly educated at the University of Glasgow. Not only was he well trained as an engineer he was also required to study Greek and Latin along with modern languages. Philosophy rounded out his course for the master's degree in engineering.[12] He was, in every sense, not only a committed engineer but a devoted teacher as well. Completely in charge of the Imperial University of Engineering from the beginning, his contagious enthusiasm for hard work and discipline proved attractive to serious students from samurai families.

To Dyer, engineering represented a mission. He preached to his students that engineering is revolutionary; that engineers are true revolutionists. Therefore students should commit themselves as missionaries dedicated to the transformation of Japanese society through engineering. It was a novel idea that appealed to young men with a samurai upbringing. His approach to engineering as an instrument for social good fit into the vast reforms taking place during the Meiji period.

Moreover, Dyer's fundamental approach to engineering education as an applied discipline rather than the transmission of knowledge from teacher to student contrasted sharply with most disciplines in Japanese schools at the time. In his book about the school written later, he noted that, "In the college itself mere book-work was made of secondary importance, and by means of drawing offices, laboratories, and practical engineering works the students were taught the relations between theory and practice, and trained in habits of observation and original thought."[13] Dyer's personal convictions and his ability to articulate them effectively set a unique tone and atmosphere at the Imperial University of Engineering.

Underlying the Imperial University's undoubted success was Dyer's principle that the latest theories in basic engineering would be taught in the classroom and then applied at the work site. In a letter to the English newspaper, the *Japan Weekly Mail* of September 25, 1875, Dyer explained his theory of practical engineering education: "The course of training will extend over six years. During the first four years, six months of each year will be spent at college, and six months in the practice of that particular branch which the student may select. The last two years of the course will be spent wholly in practical work. By this alternation of theory and practice, the students will be able during each working half year to make practical application of the principles acquired in the previous half year. The system of instruction will be partly what is usually called professorial, and partly tutorial, consisting in the delivery of lectures, and in direction and assistance being given to the students in their work."

The consummate practitioner, Dyer took advantage of state-owned companies from Hokkaido to Kyushu. Accordingly he was able to place his students in responsible positions for their practicum in basic industries including mining, construction, railroads, communications, port development, and urban planning during the final two-year course. For example, the graduating thesis of one of Dyer's students became the master plan for the water system of the great municipality of Kyoto.[14] It was on-the-job training away from the classroom that set Dyer's students apart from students at the other national institution, the Kaisei Gakkō under the Ministry of Education. In the Department of Engineering (Kōgaku) at Kaisei, students concentrated on theory.

In order to prepare his Japanese students for a demanding engineering course taught in English by a dedicated and heavily burdened corps of fellow countrymen, Dyer brought with him a scholar from Aberdeen University in Scotland to teach English language and composition to first- and second-year students. The course included dictation as well as exercises in writing essays. "A careful course in grammatical analysis" was part of the English requirements.[15] A firsthand description of the classroom atmosphere by a professor at the institution speaks for itself:[16]

Again, I am in my classroom in the college. Before me are nine ascending rows of students with black hair, pale or sallow faces, and black and generally narrow eyes. All wear a blue uniform with brass buttons. . . . Whenever anything is written on the blackboard, there is a straining of eyes, many of which look through spectacles, and a quick writing on notebooks. Evidently, no effort whatever is required to maintain discipline . . . And so the lecture proceeds, every one of the teacher's words being drunk in with such avidity, that his prevailing feelings can hardly but be gratification and a sense of responsibility. When such consideration is being shown for his teaching, it behooves him to take heed to his every word. How different this from similar work at home! No energy wasted in preserving order, full opportunity to use every talent in the work of instruction, and even stimulation to this in the eager and ingenuous countenances before one. Such teaching is not a task, but a delight. The hour and a half are over, and the class is quietly dismissed.

In 1874, during the second year of the Imperial University of Engineering under the Ministry of Works, the Ministry of Education decided to reform engineering education under its jurisdiction at Kaisei Gakkō. David Murray contacted Dr. Alexander Williamson of University College, London, inviting him to recommend an appropriate individual to undertake the assignment. By 1874, Kaisei Gakkō was the highest-level national institution under the Ministry of Education ranking at the pre-university level on its way to university status. Once again Professor Williamson contributed to modern Japanese education, adding to his services extended to the Chōshū Five and Satusma Fourteen, the students who came to study in London in 1863 and 1865, respectively. He recommended Henry Smith to the Ministry of Education as the first professor of engineering at Kaisei Gakkō from 1874.

Professor Smith later wrote that "I was selected by Professor Williamson of University College, London, on behalf of the Japanese government for the post of Professor of Civil and Mechanical Engineering in the Imperial College in Tokyo, Japan. I had to organize the whole course of engineering instruction in the University."[17] The Imperial College Smith referred to was, of course, the Kaisei Gakkō under the administration of David Murray's dearest Japanese friend and former student at Rutgers College, Hatakeyama Yoshinari. According to Smith, his plan for the Engineering Department was met with "the great satisfaction of the Principal."[18] While the Scot, Henry Dyer, was diligently setting up the Imperial University of Engineering under the Ministry of Public Works, the Englishman Henry Smith was setting up the Department of Engineering at the Imperial College under the Ministry of Education.

With the Imperial College (Kaisei Gakkō) and the Imperial University of Engineering (Kōgakuryō) both offering engineering education under two foreigners from Great Britain, the two institutions contended for qualified students. Nevertheless, the Imperial University outside the mainstream of public education under the Ministry of Works prevailed both in facilities and accomplishments. It was Henry Dyer that set a national standard for engineering in Japan in the 1870s.

Testimony to the standard of the institution was given by a distinguished British scientist at the inaugural ceremony at Glasgow University's James Watt engineering laboratory. Lord Kelvin described Dyer's engineering institution in Japan as "the most advanced institution of its kind in the world."[19] This was truly an exceptional plaudit before an audience at a university with a world-renowned engineering program. It could also be taken as an indirect compliment to Glasgow University, from which Dyer was graduated.

An American engineer passing through Tokyo in 1876 corroborated Lord Kelvin's evaluation. William Wheeler from the Massachusetts Agricultural College was on his way to Hokkaido to serve as professor of civil engineering, mechanics, and mathematics at Sapporo Agricultural College. He, too, was clearly impressed by the engineering facilities in Tokyo that, according to his trained eye, equaled and even surpassed in certain aspects standards of engineering education in the United States.

> Last Friday we visited the Imperial College of Engineering, connected with the Department of Public Works and designed to fit Civil and Mechanical Engineers, Architects, Chemists, mechanics, manufacturers, etc., for actual service in this department of the government. We were conducted by the Principal, Henry Dyer, a Scotchman, (most of the faculty are from Great Britain), and although the institution is but three years old, it is equal in design, as it undoubtedly will be in accomplishment, to any in the United States—, superior in fact, in a practical point of view, for connected with the College are large foundries, machine shops, woodworking shops, etc. in which all forms of machinery are constructed by the actual labor of the students of the college, who spend one half of their six years course in practical field or shop work.[20]

The first class successfully completing the six-year engineering course graduated in 1879. Three years previously the name of the school was officially changed to the Kōbu Daigakkō, the University of Engineering. By that time there were three hundred students. The entire faculty came from Great Britain, among the one hundred engineers and technicians hired from that country by the Ministry of Works.[21] Indicative of the importance the institution had achieved, Emperor Meiji attended the first graduation ceremony, addressing students and faculty. Henry Dyer gave a graduation address to the assembled audience that included the distinguished imperial guest.

Among the first graduating class from the Imperial University of Engineering, the top eleven students academically ranked were immediately sent to England for advanced training. Three of them ranked among the highest students enrolled at Glasgow University, a special honor to Dyer who graduated from this prestigious institution. One of them became the leading engineering student at Glasgow during the next two years. A Scottish professor on the faculty claimed that the Japanese was "the best student he has ever taught." The second-ranking student enrolled at Andersonian College where both Dyer and Yamao Yōzō studied. The rest entered Manchester and London universities. Some of the first-year graduates returned to Japan to teach engineering at their alma mater, indirectly continuing the Scottish tradition in engineering in modern Japan. They were living proof that Dyer's Imperial University of Engineering for Japan had achieved its lofty goal.

The graduates of Dyer's Imperial University played a major role in the development of Japan's infrastructure. Some became educators. Others became practical engineers contributing to the modernization of Japan's roads, bridges, railroads, canals, and so on. A prime example was the design and engineering of Tokyo Station by a graduate, Tatsuno Kingo.[22] The original building remains to this day amid the most modern structures incorporating the latest technology in earthquake resistance, of vital importance to a nation prone to earthquakes. The cherished Tokyo Station was one of the few buildings that survived the great Kanto Earthquake of 1923 that leveled the city.

The Imperial University of Engineering achieved historical acclaim not only through the training of Japanese students to become competent engineers in Meiji Japan. It also left a mark on modern Japan through contributions rendered by its foreign faculty outside the classroom. One of the most illustrious professors was Josiah Condor who taught architecture. A modern historian of the period claimed that "no foreign architect who worked in Japan, not even Frank Lloyd Wright, was as influential as Condor."[23] His mark in Japanese history, beyond training the first generation of Japanese architects, derives from his designs for the famed Ueno Museum and the ornate Rokumeikan building. This structure, built in the early 1880s with its unique ballroom and banquet halls, was planned by Condor specifically for government parties. The period, with its western excesses that centered on western ballroom dancing, became identified as the Rokumeikan era, covered in a later chapter.

Josiah Condor holds an additional distinction in modern Japan equaled by no other foreigner. He introduced brick buildings throughout the Marunouchi district around Tokyo Station for the Mitsubishi Corporation. Among the distinctive red brick Condor buildings was the Industrial Club (Kōgyō Club), an ornate five-story building that survived World War II and the postwar economic miracle that replaced the old buildings with high-rise structures. Because of modern earthquake regulations for buildings, Condor's original Industrial Club was torn down at the dawn of the twenty-first century. A modern foundation was laid and a new red brick building patterned exactly on the original Condor design, both the interior and exterior, was constructed on the same site. Josiah Condor, professor of architecture at the Imperial University of Engineering in the nineteenth century, lives on in Japan of the twenty-first century through this five-story red brick Industrial Club. Few contemporary Japanese are aware of Condor's unique building in the heart of Tokyo now surrounded by forty-story high-rise steel and glass buildings.

Another prominent professor on the faculty of Henry Dyer's Imperial University of Engineering was the British seismologist John Milne who taught mining and geology. He was instrumental in founding the discipline of seismology and the Seismological Society of Japan. He and his his fellow countryman and teaching colleague, Thomas Gray, became keenly interested in the study of Japanese earthquakes. The subject curiously had received little attention of the academic community until then. Through a collaborative effort, Milne and Gray developed the first seismometer in Japan, stimulating student interest that resulted in the construction of seismological stations. He devoted twenty years of his academic career to Japan.

Finally, among other contributors to modern Japanese engineering, the Englishman William Edward Ayrton deserves recognition. He introduced electrical engineering to the Japanese through his courses. An inspiration to his students, he may be classified as the first professor of electrical engineering in the world, joining the faculty of Cambridge University after his Japanese experience.[24] Ayrton, according to one Japanese historian of the period, "stressed theory together with the cultivation of scientific attitudes over the memorization of facts, noting Japan's need for generalists able to solve many different problems."[25] His students were responsible for creating the Japanese Electrical Research Institute in 1891.[26]

Ayrton's attitude toward modern engineering education was typical of the faculty of the Imperial University of Engineering. The foreign professors were preparing their students to engineer the infrastructure of modern Japan. Well aware of their mission, they were devoted to sowing the seeds for future generations of Japanese scientists. Accordingly, their accomplishments came to fruition through their students long after they left Japan.

Dyer departed Japan for his homeland of Scotland in 1882, apparently for family reasons related to the education of his children. His position, notably, was filled by another Scot. In his farewell lecture he delivered what he surely considered the ultimate compliment to the Japanese. Expressing a deep sense of pride and accomplishment, Dyer characterized Japan as the "Britain of the East," as he did in his recollections published years later under the title *Dai Nippon: The Britain of the East*. In retrospect, at the time when Japan embarked on the road to modernization, Britain was undeniably among the most technically advanced nations in the western world.

11 *Pestalozzi to Japan*

SWITZERLAND TO NEW YORK
TO TOKYO, 1875–1878

Until 1875, three years after the First National Plan for Education was launched, the primary method for introducing modern ideas from the West depended upon foreign specialists classified as oyatoi gaikokujin, hired foreigners, as a necessary stopgap measure to be revised as soon as feasible. The government made a critical decision in 1875 that set a new policy in motion. In contrast to hiring foreigners to introduce western ideas into Japan, it carefully chose Japanese students to study the latest western ideas in various western countries. It was a coordinated effort to fill specific positions upon their return, replacing the foreign specialists. Just two years earlier, all of the 380 Japanese students previously studying abroad were recalled.[1] They were a disorganized lot. Some had been originally sent overseas by various Tokugawa hans before the Meiji Restoration. Others were hurriedly dispatched abroad in an uncoordinated policy by the Meiji government in the heady days following the Restoration. They had become an enormous financial burden to the new Ministry of Education which assumed responsibility for virtually all of the Japanese students abroad regardless of their original sponsors. Nearly 11 percent of the ministry's budget was spent to cover their costs.[2]

Two years later the government was ready to renew its study abroad program. The policy to renew overseas study in 1875 coincided with the Ministry of Education's emphasis on the preparation of elementary teachers in the implementation of the First National Plan for Education. In tandem with the sudden increase in elementary schools, teacher preparation had become a priority during the first half of the 1870s. As we have seen, the entire teacher training system depended primarily on American teaching methods introduced by Marion Scott; now the plan was to replace him as soon as possible with Japanese qualified in western methodology, teaching in the native language. Three scholarships designated for the study of teacher training in America in 1875 were intended to meet that goal.

Although the aim of the Ministry of Education was to place teacher education under the direction of Japanese specialists, teaching methodology would continue in the American tradition, reflecting the convictions of Tanaka Fujimaro. As director of the ministry, he clarified his intentions in a letter of August 10, 1875, to his American friend, President Julius Seelye of Amherst College. "In order to establish the system of our normal school after the model of your country, three students were sent to your country."[3]

When the Ministry of Education began its search for candidates to study teaching methodology in America, Takamine Hideo was teaching English at Fukuzawa Yukichi's private Keio Gijuku school in Mita, Tokyo. Since Fukuzawa was extremely influential with Ministry of Education officials, he took the opportunity to recommend Takamine for one of the three special scholarships.[4] The plan to appoint the recipients to administrative posts in teacher training upon their return demonstrated the confidence ministry officials placed in both Takamine and Fukuzawa who recommended him.[5]

Born in 1854, Takamine received his basic education in the tradition developed in Aizu, the present prefecture of Fukushima, during the feudal Tokugawa era. As a child of a samurai family, he entered the han school for samurai boys, the Nisshinkan, introduced in chapter 3, to be educated as a bushidō warrior. Matsudaira clan leaders were immensely proud of the school, which they considered more progressive than the typical han school.[6] Nevertheless the curriculum concentrated on the ancient Chinese classics featuring Confucian principles of loyalty and filial piety that characterized all han schools.

However, in the Aizu school there were many group activities and even play groups. Competition was also encouraged in an attempt to develop character and individualism.[7] The martial arts included such skills as horsemanship, archery, shooting, kendo, and jūjitsu. Academic courses included Japanese studies, some western studies (*yōgaku*), and, of course, calligraphy. Although the normal entering age was ten,[8] Takamine was accepted by the clan school at the age of eight, beginning with the main study of the five Chinese classics, a study intensifying from age eleven. By the age of fourteen he was the top student in his class.[9]

The following year the last great battle of feudal Japan took place, the 1868 siege of the Tsuruga Castle in Aizu, with Takamine and his family trapped inside. When the Aizu lord Matsudaira and his beleaguered defenders faced imminent disaster from starvation, lack of medical supplies, and so on, women and children were forced into service preparing food and moving supplies. According to Takamine's brother reminiscing several years later, their grandfather was prepared to take drastic measures rather than face anticipated massacre by imperial forces if the castle were overrun. He intended to kill every member of the family with his sword and then commit ritual suicide (*harakiri*).[10] That fortunately was not necessary when the family, without Hideo who was then serving with the daimyō in battle, was able to flee the castle before it fell.

The inevitable surrender took place on September 22, 1868. Although there was enormous bloodshed in the month-long battle, the defending survivors, including the fifteen-year-old Takamine, were taken prisoner.[11] In October they were moved to Tokyo by the Meiji forces and magnanimously released the following year.[12] That battle effectively ended major opposition to the Meiji imperial forces. The entire episode of the castle siege epitomizes the enormity of the challenges facing the educational reformers of the Meiji era like Takamine when they set out to construct a public school system on western models several years later.

Figure 22. Takamine Hideo.
From Mizuhara Katsutoshi, *Kindai Kyōin
Yōsei Shi Kenkyū* (Tokyo: Kazama Shobō,
1990), 418.

In July of 1869, shortly after being released, Takamine entered a private school in Tokyo to study Chinese. For the first time after the great Aizu battle, he located his mother and younger brother, still secluded in a northern village where they had fled during the siege.[13] In retrospect, Takamine's major decision in 1871 to transfer from the Chinese course to the private English school Keio Gijuku, the forerunner of Fukuzawa Yukichi's distinguished Keio University, would prove decisive.[14] Consequently Takamine was on the road to success as a student of Fukuzawa in the early 1870s. Simultaneously he was then serving as an English instructor at the prestigious Keio institution at the meager salary of 6 yen per month when Fukuzawa recommended him to the Ministry of Education for the scholarship to study teaching methodology in the United States.[15]

Isawa Shūji

Isawa Shūji was the second of three scholarship students chosen by the government in 1875 to study the latest principles in teaching training in America. In 1870, Isawa entered the Daigaku Nankō, the only national institution of higher education, then headed by Guido Verbeck from America. Shortly thereafter Verbeck reformed it into a respectable school of foreign studies. In 1874, one year before Isawa was selected to go to America, he was appointed the first principal of the Aichi Teacher Training School, a regional institution established by the Ministry of Education.[16] It was, as were all seven in this new category, patterned after the Tokyo Teacher Training School under the dominance of Marion Scott.

Isawa exhibited a progressive inclination, unique among local Japanese administrators in teacher training schools of the mid-1870s. Remarkably, he had located

Figure 23. Isawa Shūji.
From Naka Arata, *Nihon Kyōkasho Kyōshi Shiryō Shūsei* (Tokyo: Tokyo Shoseki, 1982), 1:225.

a rare copy of David Page's book, *Theory and Practice of Teaching,* a modern text on teaching methods by a professor at an American teacher training school. While serving as principal, Isawa managed to translate Page's book and published it in 1875 as *Kyōjū Shimpo* (The Modern Teacher). He used the textbook in his class to introduce Page's theories into the curriculum of the Aichi Teacher Training School.[17] It supplemented the materials being circulated among the regional training schools that originated from the Tokyo Teacher Training School.

In addition to Isawa's early attraction to modern educational theory from America, his special interest in music education distinguished him from other educators of the time. Japanese music was primarily associated with the traditional instruments of koto and shamizen played by females. It had no place in the life and education of the samurai class which dominated the educational world. In 1874 the heretofore unknown subject of singing was introduced by Isawa at his Aichi training school even though Izawa himself could not read music. It marks the first time in modern history that singing was formally taught in a Japanese classroom. To Isawa's teacher trainees, overwhelmingly males from samurai warrior families as was Isawa, the experience must have been unsettling.

Isawa's music class also proved especially interesting to a visitor to the school, Dr. David Murray, senior advisor in the Japanese Ministry of Education. According to Isawa, Murray visited his music class while on a tour of provincial schools for the ministry. Impressed by what he observed, Murray recommended to the director of education, Tanaka Fujimaro, that Isawa be sent to the United States as one of three Japanese to study the most modern teaching methods available in America at the time.[18]

Dr. David Murray, as senior advisor to the director of the Ministry of Education and former headmaster at the Albany Academy in the capital city of the state of New York, initiated the official contact to send Takamine and Isawa to America. The modernization of Japanese education might have taken a different course if Murray himself had not been familiar with education in the state of New York. Acting on behalf of the ministry, Murray sent a letter to his acquaintance, the superintendent of public instruction of New York in Albany, Niel Gilmore. He requested permission to send two Japanese students to study the latest teaching techniques at two outstanding state teacher training schools in the state. He asked Gilmore to choose the institutions. The reason for this unusual request, Murray explained, was based on the ministry's long-range plan for the reform of Japanese education. Upon return to Japan, the two would play a critical role.[19]

Gilmore recommended as one institution the Oswego State Normal and Training School in rural New York, located on Lake Ontario, known for its fierce winters with deep snows. The other was the normal school at Albany. In one of the most crucial decisions made by the Ministry of Education in the 1870s, Takamine was chosen to attend Oswego. Records do not reveal precisely why he was sent to this institution rather than the one in Albany. Regardless of the motive, no one could have foreseen at the time that a new movement in education in Japan would result from this decision.

Isawa Shūji was assigned to study at the Bridgewater Teacher Training School near Boston, Massachusetts.[20] Murray may have been involved in that process as well. This decision was as crucial as Takamine's assignment to Oswego. It placed Isawa in the vicinity of America's leading music educator, Luther Mason, destined to introduce western music education to Japan through Isawa. The third scholarship student, Kozu Sensaburō, was sent to the Albany State Normal School in New York.[21] He made no notable contribution to modern Japanese education.

Takamine Hideo and Isawa Shūji left for the United States on July 18, 1875. In addition, eleven scholarship students from the Kaisei Gakkō of foreign studies were on the same ship destined for study in the United States.[22] Indicative of the importance the Ministry of Education attached to the student mission, Takamine recorded that the head of the ministry, Tanaka Fujimaro, personally saw them off at the port of Yokohama.[23] Shortly thereafter Dr. and Mrs. Murray also departed Japan to prepare for the 1876 Philadelphia Centennial, to be followed by Director and Mrs. Tanaka Fujimaro. They would all meet in Philadelphia the following summer during the grand celebration of American independence of 1776.

The Oswego Movement in Education and Edward Sheldon

Since Takamine Hideo returned to Japan to play a vital role in teacher education as the first professional educator of the modern era, the choice of Oswego Normal School for his professional training in education assumes unusual significance. It was not by chance that the superintendent of New York schools recommended this particular institution to Dr. Murray as an appropriate venue to study the latest methods in teacher education. Oswego was not only the leading institution in the state of New York to study the most advanced theories of teaching methodology, developed by Johann Heinrich Pestalozzi of Switzerland, but it also offered arguably the most innovative course in teacher education existent in the United States in 1875. Consequently the young Takamine Hideo, who had defended his feudal lord in a castle siege seven years previously, was about to be introduced to the most revolutionary as well as controversial theory of education in the world.

Edward Sheldon, principal of the Oswego Normal and Training School when Takamine arrived in 1875, was instrumental in developing the so-called "Oswego Movement in Education" in which Takamine became intimately involved and subsequently introduced in Japan.[24] It all began in 1853 when Sheldon became the first superintendent of schools in Oswego. As the first year progressed he felt that the schools were, according to his daughter's recollection of her father, "a long way off from the real world of matter and force; that children were naturally and righteously interested in the objective world, in their own bodies, [and] in their vital relations to things and each other."[25] With average daily school attendance running at less than 40 percent, not much different from Japan at that time, Sheldon was determined to reform the schools of Oswego.[26]

In 1859, the first year the feudal Tokugawa government opened several ports to foreigners, Sheldon found precisely what he was looking for on an inspection tour of the schools of Toronto, Canada, directly across Lake Ontario from Oswego. He encountered a display of teaching materials at the Canadian National Museum that greatly impressed him. The exhibition had been sent from the Home and Colonial School in London, run by a former student of the leading educational innovator of the 1800s, Johann Pestalozzi from Yverdon, Switzerland.[27] This chance encounter in 1859 of an American visiting Canada attracted by an exhibition from London that originated in Switzerland eventually played out in Japan in the 1880s through Takamine Hideo.

The society that sponsored the London Home and Colonial School from where the exhibit originated employed the following Pestalozzi principles, which Takamine Hideo was destined to introduce in Japan. They illustrate the extent of the challenge Takamine faced in his homeland where education had been dominated by Confucian teachings for centuries.

> That, as the different faculties of children are developed at different periods, care should be taken to adapt their lessons to the state of their minds, in order that all the faculties may be called out in the right order.
>
> That the education of the mind must begin when the exercise of the mind begins and should follow precisely, both in degree and amount, the natural order of this development.
>
> That education consists, not in the amount which you can put into the mind from without, but in the amount which it can gain from its own development and exercise from within.[28]

Sheldon was so deeply inspired by the philosophy of the London school based on Pestalozzi's work, and with its materials on display at the Canadian museum, that he immediately imported samples from London. His daughter recalled the "delight with which he returned from his visit, importing samples of what he wanted, colored balls and cards, bright-colored pictures of animals, building blocks, silk-worm cocoons, cotton bolls, specimens of pottery and glass."[29]

By 1860 Sheldon had designed an epoch-making curriculum for the schools of Oswego. It contained "conversational exercises, moral instructions, physical actions and employments, lessons on form, color, size, weight, and number, animals, human body, common objects, gymnastics, singing and drawing, as well as reading, writing, and spelling."[30] Moreover, each unit of instruction conformed to the "mental, moral and physical development of the child."[31] It was, in fact, to become known alternatively as the Oswego Movement or the Oswego Plan that Sheldon promoted vigorously from that moment onward. He outlined the basis of his plan, founded clearly on the London school, that "embodies his whole ideal and philosophy of practical education" that Takamine Hideo would eventually encounter. "In this plan of studies the object is not so much to impart information as to educate the senses, and awaken the spirit of inquiry. To this end the pupils must be encouraged to do most of the talking and acting. They must be allowed to draw their own conclusions, and if wrong, led to correct them. The books should only be used for reference, and as models for lessons to be given. The children should be allowed to have two short recesses of ten minutes each, morning and afternoon, and gymnastics and singing exercises should be frequently introduced, to give change of position and rest to the children, and keep up an animated and pleasant state of feeling."[32]

Sheldon's plan provoked much anxiety among teachers, parents, and the local board of education that courageously supported it at the outset. After the first experimental year it was decided that teachers required special training to implement the highly innovative curriculum. Sheldon contacted the Home and Colonial School Society in London, from where the educational exhibition in Toronto originated, for assistance. He asked for one of their staff members to come to America to head the newly organized Oswego Primary Teachers Training School founded by the community. An Englishwoman with many years experience on the staff was dispatched for one year to teach Pestalozzi's theories at a local Oswego school used for practice teaching. Upon her departure from Oswego after a successful year, she recommended a friend, Hermann Krusi from Switzerland, to replace her.[33]

Again, in a critical moment in western educational history that would influence modern Japanese education, in 1862 Sheldon hired the Swiss educator Krusi who had formerly taught at the Home and Colonial School in London. He was the son of Pestalozzi's earliest assistant; Johann Heinrich Pestalozzi was, in fact, the godfather of Krusi, whose given name at baptism was Johann Heinrich Hermann Krusi.[34]

By 1865 the Oswego training course had been incorporated into the Oswego Normal and Training School. Sheldon was appointed principal. Krusi was the most distinguished faculty member as a "living link between him and Pestalozzi." The primary texts were Sheldon's *Manual of Elementary Instruction and Lessons on Objects*, published in 1862–1863.[35] Object lessons, a departure from the traditional method of teaching using written symbols, employed real objects in the classroom. According to Krusi, "This method, which seemed to indicate a new departure from the ordinary way of beginning with symbols instead of realities, attracted a great deal of attention in educational circles, and brought many visitors to Oswego in order to study the working of the system, with a view to having it introduced to their schools."[36]

In 1872, three years prior to Takamine's arrival, the Oswego State Normal and Training School faced a crisis. As Sheldon dubbed it, a "big fight" broke out. The local board of education entertained a resolution "That we discontinue Object teaching in our junior schools and substitute instead Cornell's *Primary Geography* and Appleton's *Elementary Arithmetic.*"[37] This was, in reality, a clarion call to "back to the basics" of the traditional three R's, and the end to Sheldon's reforms.

For the next year a bitter debate took place over Sheldon's Oswego Plan. Although accustomed to defending Pestalozzian principles underlying the new curriculum, the sarcastic personal attacks stunned Sheldon, who was dubbed the "Pope" due to his overwhelming influence in designing and implementing the plan. The local paper scathingly editorialized that "We have yet to hear of a person outside of the Pestalozzi Ring who does not believe that Objective Teaching in Oswego Schools has failed."[38]

Amid the bitter controversy over the Oswego Plan, the young Japanese Takamine Hideo arrived on campus on August 20, 1875.[39] The practical application of the most advanced theory of education in the West was coincidentally undergoing a severe test just as he arrived from Japan.

Hermann Krushi, Takamine's Swiss Father

The arrival of Takamine Hideo in Oswego, New York, in 1875 at the age of twenty-one, after the long and arduous trip from Yokohama, Japan, was not without incident. The office of the superintendent of public instruction of New York, after approving David Murray's official request from the Ministry of Education to send two Japanese students for study at state normal schools, apparently failed to notify Principal Sheldon of the impending arrival of one of them. Unprepared, Sheldon invited Takamine to stay at his home the first evening.[40] Thus the young Japanese destined to become Japan's first professional educator in modern times spent his first night at an American college campus at the home of one of the leading proponents of progressive theories of education. It was indeed a propitious and unexpected moment in the life of Takamine.

In another providential act, Sheldon hastily called upon his foreign faculty member, Hermann Krusi, to accommodate the young Japanese student in his home.[41] Generously, Krusi graciously accepted this young Japanese into his home. It was the beginning of an intimate two-year relationship between the Krusi family and Takamine Hideo, and later his brother Sase, which was to have a lasting influence on modern Japanese education.

The personal encounter between Hermann Krusi from Switzerland and Takamine Hideo, the young samurai from Aizu, Japan, living together in a tiny town in upstate New York in the mid 1870s, marks the turning point in Takamine's life. It also provides the primary connecting link between the most famous Swiss educator, Pestalozzi, and the modernization of Japanese education. Krusi's recollections of that moment provide revealing insights into the relationship that Takamine developed with this Swiss scholar and his family in 1875–1877.

> The most interesting accession to our household was the Japanese, Hideo Takamine, who, in 1875, was sent by his government to enter our normal school. His coming was quite unexpected, even to Mr. Sheldon, who, however, knew of no better place to have a person of this description taken care of and assisted in his studies than our house. I have [elsewhere] told the story of this young man Takamine, and his younger brother Saze, who came a few years afterward. Both belonged to the class of Samurai, and had passed through very exciting scenes during the reconstruction of the Empire, through prison or exile, during which the members of the family were separated and finally reunited after the declaration of peace. Takamine, the oldest of the sons, distinguished by his intelligence and moral character, received notice from Government that he was appointed to proceed to the United States, in order to study the plans and methods of instruction in a Normal school, with a fixed salary and an expectation to be promoted to the principalship of a school of the same kind. I confess that in studying the character of this young Japanese, his earnestness for improvement, faithful disposition, and absence of frivolity, I obtained a higher idea of principles—whether proclaimed by Confucius or Buddha—which had been able to manifest themselves in actions, and not, as is the case with many so-called Christians, in words and professions alone. If this remark is considered to denote a too hasty generalization from the example of one or two individuals, I can only say that this testimony tallies with that given by other parties who were entrusted with the teaching of Japanese students. As for politeness and docility, they were far ahead of scions of the Anglo-Saxon race, who, however, may be superior in energy and a practical spirit of enterprise. Our Takamine, for instance, besides doing his work at school (which, to one struggling with the English language must have presented additional difficulties), employed his spare time chiefly with the study of the modern theory of Evolution, reading with intense interest the works of Darwin, Spencer, Huxley, etc. It was from a spirit of duty as well as from eagerness for knowledge that [he] made the utmost use of [his] time and opportunities.[42]

Hermann Krusi was born in Yverdon, Switzerland, in 1817, the son of the first assistant to Pestalozzi. After serving with Pestalozzi for seventeen years, Krusi's father became principal of a normal school where Pestalozzi's theories were applied. His son Hermann received his early education at that school. According to his son, Hermann Krusi, "owing to his relations with great men in all the various branches of learning, and to his extensive travels, together with an inquiring mind and an insatiable appetite for study and the acquisition of knowledge, was led to become expert in a most amazing number of different and widely separated branches of learning." With such a broad range of knowledge he was assigned a diverse teaching load including "methods in number, form and drawing, geometry, philosophy of education, mental and moral philosophy, French and German." Krusi was the foremost authority on the great Swiss educator in the United States at that time. His book, *The Life and Work of Pestalozzi,* was widely used among educators drawn to the most innovative ideas in education of the 1800s.[43]

The relationship between Professor and Mrs. Krusi with their Japanese son during the two years that Takamine lived in their home proved lasting. Mrs. Krusi was a well-educated woman in her own right. In a history of the Oswego normal school, she is described as "talented and wise and a student herself, and hence not only as a wife and mother, but intellectually of aid and comfort and a companion to her husband. Without her, Professor Krusi's usefulness would have been seriously curtailed, and hence the School is indebted to her as well as to her husband."[44] The Krusi home, noted for its warmth and intellectual stimulation, exerted a deep impact on Takamine as expressed in a letter from San Francisco on his way home. "When I think of your home, I long so much to go back again. I would not think that I am a stranger who is going away from your house but as a member of your family who is just now going far from house for a work, but is to come back again to his old house."[45]

Takamine registered as a regular student in the teacher training course of two years, including five months of teaching practice. He was one of four males among a total enrollment of forty-five students. As a samurai youth brought up in a single-sex school for warriors, the experience of attending classes in America overwhelmingly dominated by Caucasian females must have been challenging. His grades for the two years reveal his ability in science. Courses in mathematics and zoology, botany, and physiology were completed with nearly a 100 percent grade average. He ranged from 80 to 90 in the other courses.[46] Takamine's interest and ability in science proved so advanced that, upon his return to Japan, he was temporarily appointed as an assistant to the distinguished American scholar from Harvard University, Edward Morse, then taking up a position as professor of zoology at the new Tokyo University.

During the two years at Oswego, Professor Krusi devoted a great deal of time to his Japanese protégé. Takamine's presence at Oswego during the golden years of the Pestalozzian influence extended beyond his close personal relationship both in the classroom and at home with one of the world's leading authorities on Pestalozzi. The Oswego movement attracted famous educators to the campus who either lectured on the new movement in education or studied it as interpreted at Oswego. Among the outstanding visitors to Oswego who befriended Takamine in the Krusi household, and who would exert a powerful influence in Japan through Takamine in the next decade, was James Johonnot. At that time he was one of the foremost American authorities on the new theory in education that grew out of the Pestalozzi movement. According to Krusi's recollections, Johonnot spent so much time at the school that he "became temporarily a resident of Oswego."[47] The reputation of Oswego as a center for Pestalozzi studies was such that Johonnot enrolled his own daughter in the Oswego Normal School when Takamine was a student. The relationship between Johonnot and Krusi was further strengthened when Johonnot offered to revise and edit Krusi's celebrated book, *The Life and Work of Pestalozzi*.[48]

Through the relationship between Johonnot and Krusi, including many visits to the Krusi home by Johonnot, Takamine became intimately acquainted with the famous American educator both personally and professionally. At that time Johonnot was writing a book on the Pestalozzi movement that eventually became a classic on the topic, widely used at American teacher training schools. Takamine was privileged to read the manuscript. He was so taken by it that he later translated it into Japanese and published it in 1885 under the title of *The New Educational Theory* (*Kyōiku Shinron*). It became the basic textbook for Takamine's popular course at the Tokyo Teacher Training College, of which by then he had become president. This text, as it turned out, served as the theoretical foundation of the new movement in Japanese education initiated by Takamine in the 1880s in his unswerving effort to modernize teacher education, discussed in chapter 16.[49] It all began in the home of Hermann Krusi in Oswego, New York, in 1875.

Luther Mason, Pioneer of Modern Music Education in Japan

While Takamine settled down in the home of Hermann Krusi in Oswego, Isawa Shūji, his fellow scholarship recipient from Japan, entered the Bridgewater Normal School near Boston in 1875. As a rare Japanese from the samurai class with an interest in modern music, Isawa faced an interesting challenge at the outset of his studies. In a gesture of compassion, the president of the Bridgewater school advised Isawa not to take the music course required for elementary teachers since it was foreign to Japanese culture. Isawa countered that as a scholarship student appointed by his government, he felt obligated to enroll in every mandatory course. In view of Isawa's inability to read music, this encounter motivated him to search for someone to teach him how to read music.

Through friends of another Japanese student then studying at Harvard University near Boston, Isawa was able to meet a local music educator by the name of Luther Mason. By the mid-1870s, Boston had become the foremost school district in music education in America under the inspiration of Mason. His unique methods were then spreading throughout the country. When Isawa met him in the mid-1870s, he had become America's leading music educator, with an international reputation through his sequential song series, *The National Music Course*, used in Boston's public schools.[50] Once again in the annals of modern Japanese education, a prophetic moment of historical consequence transpired during the early Meiji era. The choice of Isawa, a rare Japanese from the samurai tradition interested in music education, being sent to Massachusetts in 1875 where he would meet America's leading music educator in Boston set the stage. Little could the two of them have realized that their unforeseen historic meeting would lead to the introduction of western music in Japanese schools within several years.

At that time there was no other Japanese student in America interested in music education. In fact, in the mid 1870s there was no one in Japan concerned with the subject. The First National Plan for Education of 1872, the Gakusei, listed music within the curriculum taken from American sources as the fourteenth subject in elementary schools. It was translated as ongaku (music).[51] Nevertheless, since there were no qualified teachers, it was not taught in the new elementary schools mandated under the Gakusei. In retrospect, Isawa's introduction of music at the Aichi Teacher Training School in 1874 when he headed the institution was extraordinary.

Isawa could not have known at the time of his meeting with Luther Mason that years before, Mason's father Lowell, a music educator, had spent time with Hermann Krusi at the Oswego Normal School. He was also unaware that Mason's father had a deep interest in Pestalozzi's theories as they relate to music education. In a letter to Krusi from Lowell Mason in 1862, the first year that Krusi joined the Oswego faculty, he replied to an invitation by Krusi to come to Oswego. Exactly ten years later a letter to Krusi reveals that Lowell Mason had been to Oswego and taught a course of instruction in music to the teacher trainees. And, of considerable relevancy, Lowell Mason reported to his friend Krusi that he had published a work entitled "Pestalozzian Music Teacher."[52] His son Luther, therefore, was brought up in a musical family deeply influenced by Pestalozzi. Although records do not specifically reveal it, Luther Mason surely told Isawa of his father's relationship to Krusi, especially when he learned that Isawa's colleague, Takamine, was living at the home of Krusi at that time.

Isawa asked Mason to teach him the fundamentals of music. Apparently challenged with the idea of teaching an adult Japanese male how to read music, Mason welcomed the opportunity. He may, however, have harbored a motive unknown to Isawa. Recent historical studies indicate that Mason, a committed Christian, was deeply interested in spreading the gospel to unbelievers. Japanese music historians speculate compellingly that Mason seized upon the opportunity of meeting with Isawa to pursue his desire to further the Christian faith among the Japanese through music. According to this interpretation, Mason envisioned Isawa as a conduit to achieve that goal.[53] Regardless of the motive, Mason set up a weekly schedule for Isawa at his home every Friday for private music lessons. Mason even arranged to take Isawa on local school visits to Boston schools to observe music lessons. It was the beginning of a relationship between the two that would within several years carry over to Japan.

Knowing that he would be assigned an influential position in teacher education upon returning home, and having an interest in music education for Japan, Isawa asked Mason to collaborate with him in collecting songs for Japanese elementary children. Mason immediately accepted the challenge. As a devout Christian, according to the research noted above, Mason may have viewed the opportunity presented by Isawa not only from a professional but also from a religious motivation. In the latter half of the 1880s Christian hymns became powerful means to spread the Christian faith in America. The result was a proliferation of new hymns during that period, many of which are included in most hymnals of American Protestant churches today.

Regardless of the underlying motivation, among the tunes that Mason chose for Isawa's collection, a disproportionate number originated from American

Christian hymns of the day. The importance of his choices derives from the fact that his selections subsequently formed the basis of the first collection of Japanese songs (*Shōkashū*) for the public elementary schools published by the Ministry of Education in 1882. Although this publication later became involved in the bitter controversy between progressives such as Isawa and traditionalists, several of the songs that Mason recommended remain in the national curriculum, including those which were taken from Christian hymns, that are cherished by Japanese children today.

Acutely aware that music education in the new school system of Japan was nonexistent, Isawa then sent a letter from America to Tanaka Fujimaro, director of the Ministry of Education. Tanaka, who sent Isawa to America to study modern teaching methods, may have been surprised to receive a letter from Isawa proposing that singing be included in Japanese elementary schools, since music education was not part of Isawa's original assignment. Tanaka, continually reacting with a receptive mind to new ideas from America, was nevertheless impressed with the idea even though there was no specific word for singing (*shōka*) in the Japanese vocabulary at that time.[54] It is likely, however, that Tanaka had observed elementary school music classes during his visit to the Boston public schools during his trip to America in 1872 as a member of the Iwakura Mission.[55] Regardless of the motive, Tanaka reacted positively to Isawa's proposal to introduce western music from America. Upon returning to Japan, Isawa was immediately authorized by Tanaka, as head of the Ministry of Education, to invite Mason to Japan. Mason's arrival in March of 1880 marks the beginning of modern music in Japanese schools, considered in chapter 16.

Quite by chance Takamine and Isawa were in the United States during the great Philadelphia Centennial of 1876 celebrating the first one hundred years of America as a nation, the focus of the following chapter. This special event took place during the summer vacation following their first year of study in America. The Japanese sponsored one of the largest educational exhibitions on display that brought the director of education, Tanaka Fujimaro, and his senior advisor, David Murray, along with their wives to Philadelphia for six months. Since the Japanese exhibit required knowledgeable English-speaking guides, Tanaka summoned Japanese students studying in the American east to Philadelphia to assist. Among them were Takamine Hideo and Isawa Shūji. The summer of 1876 in Philadelphia strengthened the relationship between the two students and the senior officers of the Ministry of Education, who had plans for them to assume responsible positions in teacher education upon their return home.

Immediately after the Centennial, both Takamine and his close friend Isawa joined the Krusi family in the Catskill Mountains of New York. This provided an opportunity for Isawa to become familiar with the great Swiss educator. They immediately developed a warm relationship that continued for years as Isawa was drawn into the Pestalozzi fold. In turn, Krusi and his wife developed a keener interest in the character of the Japanese young men to whom they had become attached.[56]

Both Takamine and Isawa completed their teacher training courses in 1877. Each stayed on in America for an extra year with the approval of the Ministry of Education which financed their American studies. Indicative of the breadth of interest of each of them, Isawa wrote Krusi that he had completed a science course in geology at Harvard University during the 1877–1878 academic year.[57] That kept him in the Boston area, where he continued to work with Luther Mason on a collection of songs for Japanese elementary school children. Takamine continued his interest in science by spending the extra year at Salem, Massachusetts, on a research project.

After three years in America, Takamine and Isawa returned home in 1878. Takamine, at twenty-four years old, had become a bilingual authority on modern western educational theory. Moreover, he had developed a close personal as well as a professional relationship with the three most knowledgeable authorities on Pestalozzi in America in the 1870s, Hermann Krusi, James Sheldon, and James Johonnot. Not only was Takamine confident in the knowledge that he had undergone a special education in the United States, he was well aware that he was now Japan's leading authority on modern education. As Japan's first professional educator he was eager to reform Japanese education based on the Oswego Movement.

Takamine and his traveling companion and close friend Isawa accepted an assignment upon returning home that would place them in the forefront of the educational modernization process well underway. The two were immediately appointed by the Ministry of Education as senior administrators of the Tokyo Teacher Training School, the premier teacher training institution in the land. Isawa, former principal of the local Aichi Shihan Gakkō before going to America and older than Takamine at age twenty-seven, was appointed president of the school. The youthful Takamine was shortly thereafter appointed his vice president.

Isawa and Takamine promptly secluded themselves in the resort town of Atami south of Tokyo for several weeks. They revamped the curriculum of the school, patterning it after the curriculum at the Oswego school where Takamine had studied, and, to a lesser extent, Bridgewater Teacher Training School where Isawa had studied. Isawa, who maintained contact with Hermann Krushi in Oswego, reported to the Pestalozzian scholar on the progress of educational reform in Japan. His letter from Japan of September 17, 1879, illustrates indirectly the influence of Pestalozzi in the revisions of the curriculum carried out by him and Takamine. "We [Isawa and Takamine] have recently undertaken the task of revising the Course of Studies in our training school, and the general plan being now made, is to be submitted to the Minister of Education for his approval. When this system is practically introduced, then we Japanese can say we have such thing as Education even in the little corner of the world. This is only my view of the question, and I know not what others may think or dream of, but we shall use all our power and energy to introduce the true principle of education."[58]

Isawa's letter reveals the influence of Pestalozzian studies on the two senior Japanese responsible for the reform of teacher training as the first decade of the Meiji Restoration came to an end. His reference to the "true principle of education" unmistakably refers to the teachings of Pestalozzi that he and Takamine had studied in America. The letter also shows the depth of their convictions and determination to apply the theories they learned in Japanese schools. To these two figures who would henceforth play significant roles in elite national institutions, the modernization of Japanese education must be based on Pestalozzi's theories. Japan could then boast of an educational system in its "little corner of the world" commensurate with that of the West.

Takamine also wrote his Swiss father a revealing note on June 16, 1878, about his efforts to apply Pestalozzian theory at his new post. He implies that perhaps Isawa was not quite as enamored with Pestalozzi's theories as was Takamine.

> How many times I wish that I could converse with you, as we used to do, on many topics, especially on those with which I am now concerned. I want the counsel of your long experience and good judgment. I think Saze [Takamine's brother then living in the Krusi home] has already told you that I am at work in Tokio Normal School. . . . The teachers in the school are, in the main, young and liberal in their views, but without much interest for education and teaching. There are also a few old teachers who are only versed in the Chinese and Japanese literature who have no idea of education except book reading, and who would not listen to any innovation whatsoever. But fortunately I have a principal who was my old friend, and sufficiently educated in English that he can understand the works written in that language. Therefore I gave him your work on Pestalozzi, hoping that after he has read it he will understand me better and will sympathize more with me.[59]

The revision of teacher training in 1878–1879 under Isawa and Takamine marks two important developments that will be considered in greater detail in later chapters. First, this is the first time in the modern era that Japanese, not foreigners, instigated a revision of teacher training based on their interpretation of western methodological theories. The second important issue stems from the opposition these reforms provoked. Most prominent among those who were critical of the reforms were officials within the Imperial Household and their supporters.[60] Until this time Emperor Meiji on his many visits to schools primarily in the Tokyo area indicated a positive attitude toward the progress of modern education that was so heavily influenced by the American model. Within a year, however, the opposition to western innovations in Japanese education led by the Imperial Household would become a crescendo. Chapters 15 and 16 are devoted to that episode.

One further anecdote illustrates the changing times within the tiny world of modern Japanese educational pioneers. Shortly after Takamine returned from the United States, he met his old teacher and renowned educational reformer, Fukuzawa Yukichi. They had previously developed a close relationship when Takamine studied and taught English at Fukuzawa's private school before going to America. It was a great distinction for Takamine when Fukuzawa recommended to the Ministry of Education that his student be sent to America for further study. At that time Fukuzawa exerted a prominent influence on the modernization process with his books on the West and personal influence on the Ministry of Education.

In a revealing role reversal, Fukuzawa's former student, Takamine, upon return from America emboldened with his modern Pestalozzian ideas on education, formed a different opinion about his Japanese benefactor. In a letter addressed to "My dear Vater Krusi" in Oswego, Takamine disparaged this towering Japanese figure whose name was then, and remains to this day, synonymous with western modernization. He clearly distanced himself from what he now perceived as his former mentor's old-fashioned ideas. To Takamine, the modernization process had passed Fukuzawa by. In contrast, he displayed the new concepts in education he had learned from his Swiss benefactor in America, Hermann Krusi, to whom the letter is sent. "I have had several conversations with him [Fukuzawa] about education, but do not think his views are either correct or beneficial to its elements of natural sciences in common schools. He thinks that [the] old curriculum, reading, writing, spelling and number—is sufficient. This is quite different from my views. I think the prime end of education is the cultivation of the mind, and for this purpose, the above curriculum is quite inadequate. I wish so much to talk with you [about] these questions as they come up, but they slip off as the occasion passes away."[61]

Fukuzawa, the self-educated intellectual of the late Tokugawa and early Meiji eras and a pioneer of modern Japanese education, now appeared traditional, bordering on the feudal, to his protégé. Trained in the latest and certainly most radical educational theory in the West in the 1870s, Takamine had by then become an authoritative professional educator. He was, consequently, in a position to reevaluate his former teacher's attitudes toward education. Takamine Hideo, as Japan's first professional educator, was poised to achieve historical distinction in the 1880s when he founded a new movement in western education, discussed in chapter 16.

12 Scientific Agriculture and Puritan Christianity on the Japanese Frontier

THE MASSACHUSETTS MODEL,
1876–1877

In 1876, while Takamine Hideo and Isawa Shūji were in America studying the latest methods in teacher education, the Japanese government set in motion a project to introduce modern agricultural education from America. Dr. William Clark, president of the Massachusetts Agricultural College in Amherst, was employed to open a college of agriculture in the northern island of Hokkaido. He was destined to leave an indelible mark on modern Japanese history with a simple challenge to his students, "Boys, be ambitious!" It became one of the most recognizable injunctions in prewar Japan. William Clark also became one of the most recognizable foreign names in Japan ever since. The fact that Clark taught in the remote frontier island of Hokkaido for only eight months in 1876–1877 renders his famous departing words to his devoted students even more noteworthy.

The legacy of William Clark extends far beyond his farewell challenge. His contribution to modern Japan encompasses two areas normally unrelated. Clark introduced to his Japanese students modern scientific studies in agriculture then being taught at the most advanced agricultural colleges in the United States. Through his Puritan lifestyle and extracurricular teachings, he also stimulated his students to study the Bible, leading to their mass conversion. Through their commitment to Christianity, Clark's students in agricultural studies eventually emerged as the nucleus of one of the three historical pillars of the Protestant Christian movement in modern Japan.

General Kuroda Kiyotaka, Director of Frontier Development

The connection between William Clark and modern Japanese education was originated by an unlikely Japanese figure, an army general who made it all possible. Kuroda Kiyotaka remains one of the least recognized leaders of the Meiji Restoration. Yet he traveled throughout the West, including the United States and Europe; was promoted to general in the Japanese army; and finally attained the position, although short-lived, of prime minister. His initial connection to the northern island of Hokkaido took place when he was assigned to a military mission to overcome the remaining military opposition to the Meiji Restoration that had taken refuge in the isolated northern territory of Hokkaido. Leaders of the new Meiji government, recognizing the threat from nearby Russia, dispatched military forces under Kuroda to rout the renegades. The brief struggle led to the final surrender of opposing elements to the imperial forces commanded by Kuroda.[1]

General Kuroda was then appointed to the new Bureau of Frontier Development (Kaitakushi) with the goal of bringing the nation's last frontier of Hokkaido into the mainstream of modern Japan. He faced an inevitable question as posed later by one of the great figures who benefited from his foresight, Niitobe Inazo. "But where would he [Kuroda] seek for wisdom? In General Kuroda's mind there was one source whence he could expect wisdom and knowledge pertaining to the settlements [in Hokkaido]; and that was America. . . . He studied the rapid and wonderful progress of colonization in that country, and thought that the modus operandi at work there might produce similar results in Japan."[2]

Kuroda drew up a proposal to the government recommending that Japanese students be sent to the West to study modern ideas, and that foreign advisors be hired to work in Japan. Modern specialists, for example in agriculture, were not available in Japan. With government approval, Kuroda left for America and Europe in January 1871 with the responsibility of hiring foreign employees to fulfill his mission. Kuroda's first destination was Washington, D.C., where his fellow samurai from Satsuma, Mori Arinori, had recently arrived as Japan's first diplomat to the United States.

General Horace Capron, U.S. Commissioner of Agriculture

Through Mori's assistance, Kuroda met the president of the United States, former commanding general of the Union Army during the Civil War, Ulysses S. Grant. The president, upon learning of Kuroda's mission, recommended that he meet Horace Capron, former brigadier general of the Union Army during the Civil War under then General Grant. Capron was now serving as commissioner of agriculture in President Grant's government. Capron took an inordinate interest in Kuroda, particularly his search for an advisor in the development of Hokkaido, personally escorting him on a tour of relevant sites around Washington.

In an unexpected turn of events, the sixty-seven-year-old Capron expressed an interest in the position of advisor to Kuroda that the latter was attempting to fill. Capron promptly resigned as commissioner of agriculture and immediately signed a contract to become an official of the Japanese government with the munificent salary of $10,000, compared to his U.S. government salary of $3,000.[3] The decision sent ripples through government circles. President Grant, nevertheless, gave his blessings, an early indication of his positive attitude toward Japan that characterized his administration. The following presidential statement indicated a surprisingly visionary perspective. "I look upon the department [of agriculture] as a very important one, and full of benefit to the country if wisely administered. But with all its importance it is not equal in value to our country to your new mission. From it I expect to see early evidence of increased commerce and friendly relations with a hitherto exclusive people, alike beneficial to both."[4]

Capron became an officer of the Kaitakushi, the Frontier Development Bureau, from May 1871, under Kuroda, who was responsible for overseeing the plan to develop Hokkaido. It was, of course, a region of the world totally foreign to Capron. Kuroda in fact had pulled off a spectacular international and diplomatic feat by hiring the highest agricultural officer in the U.S. government to serve as his advisor to work in one of the most inhospitable regions of Japan. Capron left San Francisco for Japan on August 1, 1871. His work for the Kaitakushi included the development of experimental farms in both Tokyo and Hokkaido. Not unexpectedly, there were many problems involved in his efforts to introduce modern farming techniques from America that included plants, animals, and equipment. One of the most revolutionary concepts employed by the American advisor was not the cultivation of rice, the standard product for farmers of Japan. Rather he replaced rice cultivation with the introduction of wheat on the experimental farms. It led to the introduction of bread into the diet of the Japanese, competing for the first time with rice as the main staple. Capron also promoted fruit farming, importing various species from America, most notably apples.

With no Japanese familiar with the new farming techniques, the distinguished former general and senior agricultural officer literally worked with his hands to get the farms started. It was an unforgettable experience for this American in his late sixties to prepare the fields for seeding by walking behind a horse-drawn plow—one of the few agricultural implements available. It was also exasperating, since Capron not only faced shortages in skilled manpower and equipment but the brutal winters of Hokkaido rendered successful farming an enormous challenge.

Capron assisted Kuroda in hiring dozens of Americans including mining and railroad engineers, agricultural specialists, and fish processors, who were attracted in part by salaries often double their American incomes. The first endeavor included surveying the area in order to plan developmental policies. Roads, mines, and even a railroad were designed and put into operation, often under American advisors, with a sprinkling of specialists from other countries. Amid the enormous challenges, the relationship between the Japanese bureaucrats in the Kaitakushi and their foreign employees was not always amicable. Nevertheless, under the circumstances of language problems, cultural differences, remoteness, lack of communication facilities, and so on, the results were impressive. Under General Kuroda, promoted to the senior military rank in 1874, as director of the Kaitakushi, along with his distinguished and committed American advisor, General Horace Capron, the modern development of Hokkaido under the Meiji government was finally under way.

It was clear to both Kuroda and Capron from the very beginning of the project that the agricultural development of Hokkaido could only be sustained through a long-range plan. Accordingly, they proposed that a school of agriculture be founded by the Japanese government in Sapporo, the largest town in Hokkaido. Capron's report to the Kaitakushi in 1872 set the stage for the first modern school of agriculture in Japan three years later. It may have been his most important single proposal during his tenure with the Japanese government which ended in May

Figure 24. Dr. William Clark.
From Hamada Yōtarō, *Kindai Kyōku no Kiroku* (Tokyo: Nihon Hōsō Shuppan Kyōkai, 1978), 1:220.

1875. "It should be the endeavor of this Government to establish by every possible effort, scientific, systematic, and practical agriculture. In no way can this be done more effectively or economically than by connecting with the gardens at this place [Tokyo] and also with the farms at Sapporo, institutions at which shall be taught all the important branches of agriculture science. These instructions should have well appointed laboratories and should be supplied with professors of acknowledged ability in their several specialties."[5]

Kuroda set out to fulfill the mission. In 1872 he launched the first school of agriculture in Tokyo under an American chosen by Capron. With the difficulty of attracting appropriate students, the initial attempt at agricultural education in the capital city proved a failure. The first class was dismissed in 1873 after a year's misadventure. Reorganization took place later that year with a new group of students who proved more capable than the first class.

The experience provoked another report by officers of the Kaitakushi in consultation with Capron. It recommended that a new school for agriculture be founded, citing as the best example the Massachusetts Agricultural College in the United States.[6] That specific recommendation by the former U.S. commissioner of agriculture illustrated Capron's regard for the Massachusetts institution and its president, William Clark. It also laid the basis for the founding of the Sapporo Agricultural College under Clark three years later—the fifth institution of higher education in modern Japan.

Founding of the Sapporo Agricultural College

The background of William S. Clark is essential to an understanding and appreciation of his contribution to modern Japanese education. Since the details are available in various English sources, only the relevant issues are mentioned here drawn primarily from two of the major works on Clark. They include the definitive but unpublished biography by John Maki entitled *William Smith Clark: A Yankee in Hokkaido*, made available by the library of the University of Hokkaido. A more intimate firsthand account is taken from *A Fifty Year History of the Tokyo Chapter of the Alumni Association of Hokkaido University*.[7]

First, Clark's birth and education in the state of Massachusetts in 1826 is critical in itself. Massachusetts set the standard for education in America from the beginning of the nation's short history. With the first public school system and the first university, Harvard, Massachusetts was the primary source of educational innovation from the beginning of the country.

Second, Clark was able to enter Williston Seminary, a preparatory school with close relations to one of the most prestigious liberal arts schools in New England, Amherst College. Clark entered Amherst College in 1844 during an era when many of the elite private colleges in New England maintained close relationships with Christian denominations. For example, when Clark studied at Amherst, half of all the graduates entered the Christian ministry. Moreover, one out of twenty entered the foreign mission field of the various Protestant Christian churches.[8] Although Clark's education at Amherst was biased toward modern science, he was educated in an environment immersed in the Christian tradition. Graduating in 1848, Clark returned to Williston as a science teacher in the Amherst mold.

Third, from the beginning of the Meiji era Japanese officials stationed in America learned early on that New England with Massachusetts at the core provided the most attractive model in the western world for Japan to emulate. Those Japanese who traveled to America invariably found their way to the northeastern region of America where they were attracted to many educational practices, some old and some new. Mori Arinori, the first Japanese diplomat assigned to Washington after the Meiji Restoration, is reported to have recognized educational practices in New England as a model for modern Japan. He visited Amherst early on in his assignment, returning on occasion thereafter.[9]

In addition, the Japanese were treated respectfully by their New England hosts who responded positively to requests for advice, assistance, and personnel in educational modernization. As we have seen, Japanese educational and cultural leaders quickly developed close relationships with their American counterparts primarily from New England, most notably Massachusetts. The close relationship between Japanese educational leaders of the early Meiji era with many American educational leaders from Massachusetts set the stage for William Clark's intimate relationship with Japan.

Prior to the first contact between Clark and Japanese officials, Clark resigned from Williston Seminary to enroll in the Georgia Augusta University in Gottingen, Germany, in 1850. After a two-year course he received a Ph.D. in chemistry. Returning home, he joined the Amherst College faculty as a professor of analytical and agricultural chemistry, reestablishing an intimate relationship with his alma mater, where he taught through the 1860s. It was during this period that he met his "first Japanese student," Niijima Jō, enrolled at Amherst.[10] The two would meet several times both in Japan and America, as Niijima played a unique role in modern Japanese education.

When the American Civil War broke out in 1861, Clark responded by resigning from Amherst to volunteer for the Union Army under President Abraham Lincoln. During the rapid mobilization of the military, influential individuals organized local military units for the regular army. Clark worked diligently to recruit Amherst students for his unit in the campaign to preserve the Union. Without any military background or training, Clark was commissioned a major in his newly organized Massachusetts 21st Volunteers and sent to Washington to join other new units of the Union Army for training. Promoted to colonel as commander of his unit from Massachusetts under the highly heralded Burnside Division, Clark then led his men into battle against the Confederate army. In a series of early battles, most went against the northern forces. Clark lost many men in the brutal fighting. Tragically, among them was his adjutant, Lieutenant Stearns, son of the president of Amherst College. Exhibiting valor in battles such as Antietam, notorious for the heaviest loss of men in one day in the history of American warfare, Clark was recommended for promotion to brigadier general by his commander, General A. E. Burnside. He was even reported killed in battle at the brutal encounter at Chantilly when he was lost for several days before he was able to locate remnants of his unit. However, with the decimation of his Massachusetts unit, he suddenly resigned his commission as colonel just over two months before the decisive battle of Gettysburg that turned the tide of war against the South. He returned to Amherst.

Clark, recognized not only as a scholar of chemistry, was henceforth heralded as a distinguished retired colonel of the Union Army who had fought with valor to preserve the United States. He immediately rejoined the faculty of Amherst College as professor of analytical and agricultural chemistry. For the remainder of the decade of the 1860s, Clark performed his duties admirably as a teacher at his beloved alma mater. He was popular among his students and active in college life. He also reveled in the attention he received as a Civil War hero in which he took great pride.

The next stage in Clark's life grew out of the 1862 Morrill Land Grant Act, passed by the U.S. Congress while Clark was on active military duty. For the first time the American government, devoid of a ministry of education, entered the field of education in a major way. The act was the result of an attempt to provide advanced-level education in practical studies to serve the country. It was the beginning of the so-called A&M (agriculture and mechanical) colleges, many becoming the great American state universities of today. They are acclaimed for their pioneer research that brought about the agricultural and industrial revolution that catapulted the United States into a leading position in the world. By 1866 the state of Massachusetts had yet to take advantage of the opportunity provided by the 1862 act which, incidentally, called for the study of military tactics by all students. This was not an unusual provision during wartime. For some reason Clark personally accepted the challenge presented by the Morrill Act. He campaigned to have a

Massachusetts Agricultural College founded in Amherst under terms of the Morrill Land Grant. Ultimately successful in competition with several other local communities vying for the prize, Clark then devoted his seemingly endless energies to the planning and implementing the new college that was opened on a campus in Amherst in October 1867. Clark was appointed president. This was exactly one year before the Meiji Restoration that overthrew the Tokugawa government.

As president of the Massachusetts Agricultural College, Clark devoted the next eight years to planning and implementing one of the first successful agricultural colleges in America. On the basis of his experiences as a student and teacher at Amherst College, his doctoral studies in chemistry at a German university, and his harrowing wartime adventures as a ranking officer in the Union Army, Clark possessed unique qualifications for an American college president. They enabled him to achieve recognition as an able administrator of the new college. He was also a prominent lecturer in botany and horticulture, reflecting his lifelong interests in these academic disciplines.

During the early years of the Meiji government, through various routes Japanese officials learned about the success of the Massachusetts Agricultural College under Clark. For example, Japan's first diplomat to Washington, Mori Arinori, visited the campus in 1872 as a guest of President Clark. Mori had sought entry to the institution of a Japanese youth under his wing, upon the recommendation of General Horace Capron, former U.S. commissioner of agriculture then working in Japan; the boy later became Clark's translator in Japan. Indicative of Mori's respect for Clark, the young diplomat included Clark among the dozen or so college presidents from whom he sought advice on the future of Japan in a letter sent by his office in 1872. During this period several other Japanese students were also sent to the Massachusetts Agricultural College.

At this time Kuroda Kiyotaka, director of the Bureau of Development for Hokkaido, submitted a proposal to find a suitable American to plan and establish Japan's first college of agriculture, to be located in Sapporo. With government approval in 1875, he contacted the head of the Japanese legation in Washington, Mori Arinori's successor, Yoshida Kiyonari, to carry out the search. By virtue of the previous contacts both formally and informally between the Japanese and the Massachusetts Agricultural College, it was natural to offer the position to Clark, then president of the college. Accepting the challenge, Clark reacted positively and entered into negotiations for the position. He signed a one-year contract at a salary of $7,200, nearly double his presidential salary, and applied for a year's leave of absence from his college. Clark's farewell speech clarified the historical developments behind his departure for Japan, and the challenge that he had accepted. "Several years ago the Japanese minister [Mori Arinori] visited this college, went to the barns, to the plant-house, and to the armory and remarked that Japan needed just such an institution; for the people must be fed and the government needs a means of defense. And it is in view of these principles that an agricultural college is going to be established in that most promising empire, modeled as nearly as possible after ours, selected from all the institutions in the world."[11]

Clark left Amherst for Japan on May 15 to assume the position of president of the Sapporo Agricultural College, although there was some confusion over the exact title. The contract in Japanese differed from that in English. To the Japanese, the director was an official of the Kaitakushi, the Bureau of Frontier Development. Clark was, in Japanese bureaucratic nomenclature, the kyōtō or "head teacher." To Clark, however, it was perfectly clear that he was the president. In his handwritten "Memorandum of Contract between the Japanese Government and W. S. Clark in reference to the College at Sapporo," he agreed to serve as assistant director, president, and professor of agriculture, chemistry, mathematics, and English language.[12] From that moment forward he signed all formal reports simply as "president." Nevertheless, the different interpretations of his position continued throughout his tenure. For example, a surviving document included below shows that he wrote out the regulations for the school in longhand and signed it as president. However in the precise word-for-word translation into Japanese, his English title of president was translated as kyōtō, head teacher.

In addition to Clark, the Japanese also hired two of Clark's faculty members who had recently graduated from the Massachusetts Agricultural College. William Wheeler was employed as professor of civil engineering, mechanics, mathematics, and English. David Penhallow was hired to teach chemistry, botany, agriculture, mathematics, and English. The two young teachers proved as dedicated in their assignment in Japan as did President Clark. Clark's selection of them proved critical, since each became president of the college in turn, following Clark's one-year assignment. They faithfully carried out the policies and programs that Clark carefully designed after their alma mater.

The Japanese government could not have found a better-qualified American for its purposes than William S. Clark. He was a graduate of, and former professor at, the prestigious Amherst College in Massachusetts. He held a Ph.D. in science from a German university. He was a retired colonel in the victorious American army of the North and an acclaimed war hero of the American Civil War. He was president of a leading agricultural college in the state of Massachusetts renowned for its academic institutions. Finally, although not a qualification for the position in Japan, he was a devout Christian exemplifying a spirit of devotion and commitment to his religious beliefs that had an enormous appeal to his devoted students. One recalled Clark with great fondness accordingly: He was a genuine Puritan in his religious behavior.[13] William S. Clark, president of Japan's first agricultural college, was truly an American in a class of his own.

At the first meeting in Tokyo with the man who hired Clark, General Kuroda, the two began their relationship with a common understanding. Kuroda expressed his deep concern with the threat that Russian expansion into the Far East posed to the northern Japanese territory. He considered Hokkaido development as a means to preserve the security of Japan. Clark sympathized with that position, citing his experience as an officer in the U.S. Civil War a decade earlier. He, too, fought to preserve his country deeply divided by the institution of slavery. Kuroda, recently promoted to general in the Japanese army, was pleased to learn from Clark that military training was part of the education of his students in Massachusetts in order to prepare them to defend their country. The two agreed that military training should be included in the education of the Japanese students at the new school in Hokkaido. The amicable relationship between the two that grew out of their initial meeting proved lasting.

Clark used the opportunity to explain to Kuroda in detail his plan for the school. Since Kuroda was not an authority on agricultural education, and Clark was president of a leading college of agriculture in America, Kuroda deferred to Clark on all matters concerning education. That is, Clark was given a free hand to run the first school of agriculture in Japan as he saw fit. In a letter to his wife written later, he noted with some pride that "Governor Kuroda consults me constantly and always follows my advice."[14]

Shortly after Clark's arrival in Japan, the entrance examination for the first class of students for the Sapporo College of Agriculture in Hokkaido was held in Tokyo for local applicants during the summer of 1876. An entrance examination for candidates in Hokkaido would follow shortly thereafter. Since English was the language of the school, the examination included written translation exercises from English to Japanese and an oral English test. Consequently only candidates with English training were eligible. That precondition limited the qualified applicants primarily to students at the two advanced English-language schools in Tokyo taught by foreigners, the Tokyo English School (Tokyo Eigo Gakkō) and Kaisei Gakkō. Since the Tokyo English School prepared students for the more advanced Kaisei Gakkō, scheduled to become Tokyo University the following spring, the recruitment concentrated on students from the preparatory school. This assured the quality of the students as possessing the highest academic qualifications.

Clark and his two colleagues conducted an oral examination precisely as they did at their Massachusetts school, on a one-to-one basis, during their visit to the Tokyo English School. They asked each applicant basic questions in English with the response necessarily given in English. Through this exacting process eleven students, nine from the Tokyo English School and two from Kaisei Gakkō, were finally chosen by Clark in Tokyo. In a revealing comparison, Clark estimated that the successful Japanese candidates for his Sapporo Agricultural School stood academically at about the average level of his American students at the Massachusetts School of Agriculture. His assessment of their English ability went even further when he wrote home that the candidates "read and understand English very well and write it better than most of our students."[15]

The leading English teacher at the Tokyo English School when Clark interviewed the candidates was Marion Scott who had come from San Francisco in 1871 to teach English at the Kaisei Gakkō. However after one year he was transferred to the newly organized Tokyo Teacher Training School, and after two years there, he was transferred to the Tokyo English School, where he was teaching when Clark arrived from America. Scott was preparing students for the Kaisei Gakkō, an English-language institution that attracted highly qualified motivated students, overwhelmingly from former samurai families.

Among Scott's preparatory students at the Tokyo English School were two who were to become among the most outstanding intellectuals of the late 1800s and early 1900s. Uchimura Kanzo, founder of the Mukyōkai (Nonchurch) Christian movement and Niitobe Inazo, author of *Bushidō* and undersecretary of the League of Nations, had originally entered the Tokyo English School to prepare for the first class at Tokyo University. As noted earlier, they both attributed their love of learning and fluency in English to Marion Scott's composition and literature classes. Scott was clearly an exceptionally inspiring teacher.

Clark, of course, was unaware of Uchimura and Niitobe as young students at that time. He probably did not know of the unique contribution that their teacher Scott had already made to modern Japanese education. Nevertheless he was most fortunate that an officer of the Kaitakushi, the Bureau of Frontier Development, had already come to this school to recruit students. Although it is not clear, it may have been General Kuroda himself, director of the bureau, since the appeal to the students was reminiscent of his idealism. Niitobe recalled that he was attracted to the new school by the call to serve his country. The graduates would, according to the visiting representative from the bureau, "enter the administrative service of the state and they would be doing reclamation work on a grand scale, for it was they who would be opening new lands and in creating a new society." Niitobe applied immediately and passed the examination administered by Clark. However, because of his age he was compelled to wait one year.[16]

Clark's initial evaluation of his Japanese students for the first class of the Sapporo Agricultural College was a critical one. In Japan of 1876, there were only four major institutions of advanced learning, all of which were in Tokyo. The government sponsored the Kaisei Gakkō, a polytechnic institution under the Ministry of Education with courses entirely taught in English, that became Tokyo University in 1877. The Ministry of Education also sponsored the Tokyo Teacher Training School, originally under Marion Scott. The third government-run institution, the so-called Imperial University of Engineering under Henry Dyer from Scotland taught in English, was controlled by the Ministry of Works. The fourth, the private school run by Fukuzawa Yukichi, the Keio Gijuku, taught general western studies and English as a foreign language.

William Clark was about to launch the fifth advanced school of learning in Japan during the modern era, specializing in agricultural science. And even though it was located in the most remote area of the country, the nucleus of students recruited from the Tokyo English School formed an elite class equal to their counterparts in the other institutions of advanced learning in Tokyo. Consequently the new agricultural school in Hokkaido had the potential to rival in academic performance the four leading institutions in Tokyo. It would also be taught in English under foreign professors precisely as were the three governmental institutions in Tokyo. Higher education in Japan in the mid 1870s was dominated by English and foreign faculty. Only students at the private Keio Gijuku were taught by Japanese faculty, although the texts were overwhelmingly in English and English proficiency was required. From any aspect, General Kuroda had set a formidable goal before William Clark and his carefully selected Japanese students in far-off Hokkaido.

The adventure in modern agricultural education in Japan did not begin without trouble. The first untoward incident, often related, took place on a boat that left Tokyo on July 25 for Hokkaido. On board were the eleven successful candidates from Tokyo for the first class of students at the Sapporo Agricultural College, President Clark and his two colleagues from Massachusetts, plus General Kuroda Kiyotaka. Only Kuroda had been to Hokkaido. In addition, there were several female passengers. The details differ but the boys reportedly became rowdy during the voyage through some combination of girls and alcohol. Their vulgar songs particularly aroused the anger of General Kuroda who threatened to expel the most rowdy before they ever arrived at the school.

Concerned about the moral standards of the new students, Kuroda discussed with Clark on board the boat how to discipline the students at the school. With his strong Christian convictions, Clark seized upon the potential opportunity to spread the Christian faith. Deeply pious, he responded that the way to impart morality was through the Bible, the road to life. He proposed to Kuroda the use of the Bible for morals teaching. Kuroda reacted with reservations, however, since the longstanding ban on Christianity had only been lifted several years previously. In addition, he reminded Clark that the new school was a government-sponsored institution where sectarian religious teachings would be inappropriate. Although Clark protested that Kuroda had promised him a free hand in running the school, Kuroda explained that this was the single exception. With that the issue was dropped for the time being.

Shortly after Clark arrived in Sapporo upon his fiftieth birthday, two inter-related events of importance took place. First, the second entrance examination was administered to applicants from the area. This time the examination took the form of a two-and-a-half-hour written procedure followed by an English interview. Incredibly, nineteen local candidates passed the examination to join the eleven successful candidates who arrived with Clark and Kuroda from Tokyo. The school started, then, with the entering class divided between those who entered from Tokyo and the remainder who entered from Sapporo. This explains the separate organization of alumni from Tokyo (Hokudai Tokyo Dōsōkai) which published the historical narrative of the first fifty years of the Sapporo school from which much of this account is extracted.

Second, Clark by now had obtained thirty English Bibles. There is some disagreement concerning the exact process. What is in agreement is that an American living in Yokohama as a missionary or Bible agent had learned of Clark's mission to Hokkaido, perhaps through Clark himself when he arrived at the port city. As part of his Christian mission to the Japanese, he presented the Bibles to Clark with the simple request to distribute them to his students. Clark wrote each student's name in them and had them delivered to their dormitory. It marked the first step in an apparent effort to proselytize his Japanese students for the Christian faith.

At the opening ceremony of the new school, General Kuroda appealed to his youthful audience that the study of advanced agricultural science was necessary not only for the development of Hokkaido but that the purpose reached far beyond that. The new agricultural school was intended to play a fundamental role in the advancement and security of Japan. It was part of nation-building, a confirmation of Kuroda's basic mission in life as a samurai from Satsuma, now a general in the Japanese army. It underlay his indefatigable efforts to develop Hokkaido. To the new students, who nearly all came from samurai backgrounds, it had an irresistible appeal as an opportunity to serve their country. Greatly appreciated by Kuroda, as well as the Japanese people ever since, Clark and his two colleagues from America made every effort to reinforce that underlying motivation.

In contrast to Kuroda's welcoming speech to the new students, Clark took a different approach in his opening address. Reminding them of his position as president of the Massachusetts Agricultural College, his specific challenge remained in the memory of the graduates as representative of the character of their American president. It also revealed his Puritan spirit, which he endeavored to impart to his students with pronounced success. "Preserve your health and control your appetite and passions. Cultivate habits of obedience and diligence, and acquire all possible knowledge and skills you may have an opportunity to study."[17]

Although the Sapporo Agricultural School of 1876 in remote Hokkaido was intended to promote modern agricultural techniques, Clark designed it as a school of modern science. The course of study can be divided several ways. First, a command of the English language sufficient to take a full course load in science courses taught in English by the three American professors was basic. The American faculty knew barely a word of Japanese and made little attempt to learn it. This school was intended from the outset as an English-language institution. To complete the course successfully, an advanced level of English ability, both spoken and written, was required.

Second, mathematics, the foundation of science studies, was given a dominant role in the curriculum. It also became the primary cause for failure—and there were failures. This is an important factor in appreciating the magnitude of the demands placed on the Japanese boys enrolled in Clark's school. They had very little preparation in basic mathematics before they applied for the school. Moreover, they got little support from home since their fathers; almost all brought up in the samurai tradition during the Tokugawa era, had little exposure to or knowledge of mathematics. Clark's students were dealing with two foreign languages, as it were, English and mathematics. In addition to these academic demands the students were then plunged into a rigorous course in science that included chemistry, biology, and botany.

Clark personally wrote the Plan of Organization and Regulations in longhand which remains in his records. Illustrative of the enormous academic challenge placed before these twenty-four youths of Japan in the mid-1870s, they are brief enough to include them in their entirety.

Sapporo Agricultural College
Plan of Organization and Regulations

Respectfully submitted for approval
W. S. Clark, President
Sep 2nd 1876

1. The Sapporo Agricultural College was founded by the Kaitakushi for the education and practical training of young men who are expected to become its employees after graduation and to serve under the direction of the department for the term of five years. The course of instruction will occupy four years. And those students who complete it in a satisfactory manner will receive the degree of Bachelor of Science.

2. The following branches of knowledge will be regarded as important parts of the College curriculum; The Japanese and English languages, Elocution, Composition, Drawing, Book-keeping and Forms of Business, Algebra, Geometry, Trigonometry, Surveying, Civil Engineering so far as required in the construction of ordinary roads and railroads and of works for drainage and irrigation; Physics with particular attention to mechanics; Astronomy, Chemistry with special regard to Agriculture and Metallurgy; Botany, Structural, Physiological and Systematic; Zoology, Human and Comparative Anatomy and Physiology, Geology, Political Economy, Mental and Moral Science, and the most thorough instruction in the theory and practice of Agriculture and Horticulture, the various topics being discussed with constant reference to the circumstances and necessities of the farmers of Hokkaido.

3. Each collegiate year will begin on the fourth Thursday of August and close on the first Wednesday of July. It will be divided into two terms.

Terms of Admission

Candidates for admission to the freshman class will be examined orally and in writing upon the following subjects; Japanese and English Languages, which they should be able to read, write and speak with facility; Arithmetic, Geography and History, the knowledge required being equal to that contained in the common higher textbooks for public schools

General Rules

Members of College are expected to devote at least four hours of each afternoon or evening to the preparation of their college exercises.[18]

Clark also personally wrote out the daily schedule, presumably based on the course offerings at the Massachusetts Agricultural College. It was a demanding student load with a full morning schedule of academic courses. Only the three Americans from Massachusetts did the teaching, all in English. The standards were also demanding on both the student and teacher. For example, students were required to take copious notes, virtually verbatim, in pencil, and hand them in to the professor each day. That evening the professors carefully checked them, marking errors with red pencils. The next day the student had to rewrite them in ink for final inspection for accuracy by the professors. One student recalls that: "Our notes were full of blunders owing to our insufficient knowledge of English. He [Clark] carefully corrected the mistakes in every note. It was painstaking labour, and took a great deal of time."[19]

Student notes illustrating the daily routine are on display at the library of the University of Hokkaido, the successor to Clark's school. Student notebooks heavily marked up in red by their teachers exemplify the heavy demands placed on both students and the American faculty. Not only did this procedure assure correctness of content but it also enabled the students to achieve an advanced standard of English writing. Letters from the students to Clark after he left Japan, included below, are testimony to the level of English that the students achieved during Clark's eight months at the school.

The evening chore of correcting student notes by the American professors added to their heavy teaching load. For example, in addition to his administrative responsibilities, President Clark also taught two hours of English and two hours of botany every day except Sunday. His assistants had a similar schedule. Professor Wheeler taught two hours of algebra daily while Professor Penhallow taught two hours per day of chemistry. They each also taught two hours of English six days a week in the preparatory section.[20]

Clark wrote out the first daily schedule for each section, one of which is still available among his papers.

First Term, 1876–7
Exercises of Freshman Class

At 8:30 A.M. Botany Prest. Clark
9:30 Algebra Prof. Wheeler
10:30 English Language Prest. Clark
11:30 Chemistry Prof. Penhallow[21]

President Clark and his two American assistants enforced strict academic standards at the school through measures other than homework assignments. Although nineteen students passed the entrance examination administered at Sapporo, five soon failed out. None of the eleven who came from preparatory schools in Tokyo failed. Clark's letter to the Kaitakushi reveals the reason for the expulsion of the first five. It was based purely on academic deficiencies in mathematics.

Sir:
In view of the policy to be adopted in regard to the number and qualifications of students in the College, I recommend the dismissal of Messrs Fujita,

Hioto, Naito, Shimasu and Takabayashi. This course is rendered necessary by the fact that they are clearly unable to do the work of their class, especially in mathematics.

W. S. Clark[22]

With classroom concentration on English, basic mathematics, and science every morning, farming techniques were taught in the afternoon on a model farm. General Kuroda had approved a large budget for a well-equipped experimental farm patterned after the modern experimental farm at the Massachusetts Agricultural College. William Brooks was brought to Japan in 1877 from the home campus to manage the farm as professor of agriculture and botany. Of the four faculty members from Massachusetts, he remained the longest, also serving as president of the college. Not only did the farm experience provide the students with the latest farming techniques available in America and with on-the-job practical experience but it also involved every student in manual labor. Clark felt this was an essential ingredient in their education.

The farm also provided an opportunity for the American staff to import new varieties of farm products such as onions, cabbages, corn, and sugar beets as well as animals for breeding. Modern farm machinery was also imported from America. In addition, Clark and his staff conducted many field trips to gather specimens and to study the actual conditions of plant life and soil for future farming development. Balancing the heavy academic demands, the field trips were enjoyable events that the graduates recalled with nostalgia.

Among the contributions to modern Japanese agricultural education, perhaps the best known to contemporary Japanese was Clark's introduction of the American-style barn. Designed after the barn on his Massachusetts campus, the first floor held the livestock. Feed for the livestock was stored on the second floor, an important provision in the cold northern area like Hokkaido. The Japanese had never seen anything like it before. Clark's barn design, based on the American model, still dots the landscape of Hokkaido, giving it a tourist attraction that no other area in Japan has. Beyond the college program itself, Clark traveled widely in Hokkaido, dispensing advice and answering questions on a wide variety of issues beyond agriculture. He reveled in the attention he received, taking his responsibility for advising Kuroda on the development of Hokkaido seriously.

Kuroda Kiyotaka, whose foresight and initiative enabled Clark to carry out the mission assigned to him so effectively, took pride in his experiment in modern agricultural education. He invited government leaders to visit the school to see for themselves the progress made by Clark and his students. In Clark's *First Annual Report of the Sapporo Agricultural College*, published by the Kaitakushi in 1877, he reported with great pleasure on the most prominent officials who made the long trip to the far north. "In August last the College was visited by His Excellency Prime Minister Sanjo [Sanjō Saneyoshi], Minister of Foreign Affairs Terashima [Munenori], Minister of War Yamagata [Yoritomo], Minister of Public Works Ito [Itō Hirobumi], and many officers of their party. The Prime Minister was graciously pleased to express in writing his satisfaction with what he saw, and generously presented a testimonial of his approval to each of the five best scholars."[23]

This was indeed a powerful group of officials who personally observed Clark's school. For example, Minister of Works Itō Hirobumi became prime minister at a later date. Yamagata Yoritomo, general of the army and ranking officer to General Kuroda, also become prime minister, ironically replacing Kuroda, who served as prime minister from 1888 to 1889. In addition, Terashima became minister of education within three years. With such powerful leaders giving their stamp of approval, continued government support for the school was assured.

The Sapporo Band of Christian Converts

General Kuroda remained deeply concerned over the moral standards of the students that he initially discussed with Clark on the boat to Hokkaido before the school was opened. Shortly after the opening ceremony he once again broached the subject with Clark. Whether he was aware of the distribution of the Bibles to each student by Clark is not clear. Nevertheless Clark once again seized upon the opportunity to urge approval for the use of the Bible as part of the curriculum. Again Kuroda balked at the request, as he had aboard ship. But this time Kuroda took a different stance. In educational matters, he had promised to defer to Clark's wishes. Concerning the Bible, he would also defer to Clark's request on condition that it would be used as a shūshinsho, literally a "book of ethics."[24]

Clearly Kuroda was splitting linguistic hairs, perhaps to appease his persistent American professor on whom he was totally dependent for the successful operation of the school. He apparently believed that the Bible could be used for moral purposes to achieve his goal, but without a Christian appeal. Regardless of the motivation, the informal understanding between Clark and Kuroda that the Bible could be used in the classroom at the Sapporo Agricultural School, in spite of the preconditions, provided Clark with the opportunity to promote his religious beliefs to his Japanese students. It would have profound consequences for the future of the Christian movement in Japan.

About a month after classes began, Clark initiated a new classroom procedure. Before his academic lectures began he gave a short commentary on Christianity followed by a reading from the Bible. At first his students, according to the recollection of the graduates, showed little interest. Gradually however, in response to the sincerity and conviction of their teacher for whom they were growing ever fonder, a spark of interest was ignited. Small groups of students began meeting in the dormitory after dinner to exchange opinions and reactions to Clark's commentaries on Christianity. Inevitably questions about faith and the meaning of life arose for which the students sought answers. They began to read their Bibles provided by Clark in search of the answers to their questions. The boys perhaps inevitably began to question the traditional samurai values espoused by their parents. As some recalled later in life, the philosophical questions that provoked believers for centuries such as "my encounter with Christianity [*jibun to Kirisutokyō to no deau*]" stimulated increased interest in Clark's religious teachings.

By now the students increasingly appreciated the unique character of their American president not just through the classroom encounters but also during informal meetings in his room. He often related Civil War stories of a Union colonel that fascinated them. He may have intrigued them with a description of the most famous battle in which he participated, when over 20,000 American Civil War soldiers were killed and wounded in a single day at Antietam. Clark was most fortunate to survive that horrendous day of infamy in American history.

Amid the growing interest in Christianity by the students, Clark, gaining confidence in his position, was determined to maintain a strict puritanical moral standard on campus. His most notable attempt to set moral standards that would meet Kuroda's concern for student morality was a "statement of abstention" drawn up by Clark himself. He convinced all of the students plus his American colleagues to join him in taking the pledge. "The undersigned, officers and students of the Sapporo Agricultural College, hereby solemnly promise to abstain entirely from the use, in any form, except as medicines, of opium, tobacco and alcoholic liquors and also from gambling and profane swearing, so long as we are connected with this institution."[25]

Clark realized that the opportunity to spread the Christian faith among his students had reached a critical stage. They were now seekers, that is, seeking the eternal truths of the Christian faith. He responded by announcing that he would hold a meeting in his home on Sunday mornings, the day off from school, for Bible reading and discussions where he encouraged the students to read the Bible in search of the truth. The number of students who attended gradually increased. Clark expanded the Sunday meetings into full-scale Sunday services. Graduates recalled with nostalgia the long prayers by Clark followed by a commentary on Christianity, essentially a sermon. One student described the services in the following manner. "Sometimes he sat still for a few minutes, and then burst out into a strong prayer, so impressive as to penetrate the heart of every one present. Sometimes he read sermons and essays from newspapers, journals and books. Sometimes he stood up and spoke himself. He was naturally an eloquent speaker. His speech was always full of fire. When he spoke, it was so powerful that we felt as if the whole building were shaken by his energy."[26]

The Sunday meetings were dubbed by his students as Kuraaku no Kyōkai, Clark's Church. And it was indeed Clark's Church. The American professor of agriculture had become literally a Christian missionary with a growing band of youthful Japanese followers of Christ. He advised them that "To be Christian, you must become upright, diligent students. Your calling is to improve this world and make it the Kingdom of God."[27] The students eagerly responded to Clark's exhortations, ready to commit themselves to the Christian faith. They each went to him and personally "made confessions to be followers of Christ."[28]

Judging that the moment of commitment had arrived, Clark wrote out a statement that reflected his Christian beliefs entitled "The Covenant of Believers," one of the most cherished historical documents of the Japanese Christian Church. Sixteen students who had by now expressed their belief in the Christian faith signed it as an act of commitment. By signing that oath, the Japanese students were essentially undergoing baptism into Christianity. However, since Clark was not an ordained minister, he could not administer Christian baptism. Nevertheless it served the same purpose.

In hindsight, "The Covenant of Believers" laid the foundation for the formation of what came to be known as the Sapporo Band, one of the three pillars of Protestant Christianity in Japan. It represented another event in the modernization of Japan with unforeseeable consequences.

Covenant of Believers in Jesus

[Excerpts]

The undersigned, members of Sapporo Agricultural College, desiring to confess Christ according to his command, and to perform with true fidelity every Christian duty in order to show our love and gratitude to that blessed Savior who has made atonement for our sins by his death on the cross; and earnestly wishing to advance his kingdom among men for the promotion of his glory and the salvation of those for whom he died, to solemnly covenant with God and with each other from this time forth to be his faithful disciple, and to live in strict compliance with the letter and the spirit of his teachings, and whenever a suitable opportunity offers we promise to present ourselves for examination, baptism, and admission to some evangelical church.

We believe the Bible to be the only direct revelation in language from God to man and the only perfect and infallible guide to a glorious future life.

We believe in one, everliving God who is our merciful Creator, our just and sovereign Ruler and who is to be our final judge.

We believe that all who sincerely repent and by faith in the Son of God obtain the forgiveness of their sins will be graciously guided through this life by the Holy Spirit and protected by the watchful providence of the Heavenly Father, and so at length prepared for the enjoyments and pursuits of the redeemed and holy ones; but that all who refuse to accept the invitations of the Gospel must perish in their sins and be forever banished from the presence of the Lord.

For mutual assistance and encouragement we hereby institute ourselves an association under the name "Believers in Jesus." Sapporo, March 5, 1877 . . . W.S.C.[29]

Among the historical features of this celebrated "covenant" are, in the handwritten original, three tiny barely visible letters following the date: W.S.C. Not only was the handwriting and native English proof that Clark himself wrote the covenant, but he also left his signature on it as he did on Christianity in Japan. His elation was expressed in a letter to his wife. "Today they [students] have signed a paper, which I have prepared for them, which is the nearest I can come to organizing them into a Church. I enclose a copy. . . . Who would have thought I would become a successful missionary! To God is all the glory. He can save by many or by few."[30]

"The Covenant of Believers" marks the final event of significance during Clark's eight months in Japan. He had been given a year's leave of absence from the presidency of the Massachusetts Agricultural College, and it was time to return home. His farewell letter to the official of the Kaitakushi responsible for the new agricultural school was a heartfelt expression of his true feelings toward Japan and the Japanese with whom he had become associated, however briefly. William Clark departed Japan with a well-deserved sense of satisfaction in his accomplishments.

> Sapporo, April 14, 1877
> Sir:
>
> In retiring from the service of the Japanese Government I find it to be impossible to refrain from expressing my most hardy thanks to yourself and all other officers with whom I have had business inter-course for the uniform courtesy and confidence with which I have been treated. This treatment has been of great advantage both to myself and to Japan, since it has enabled me to accomplish my mission in a manner satisfactory to the Kaitakushi and most agreeable to myself.
>
> I can truly say I have enjoyed my work here very much and I earnestly hope for valuable results in the years to come. If the education of the cadets at the College can be carried on with the liberal spirit which has characterized its management in the past year, I am confident the graduates will not disappoint the great expectations of its founders. They will be men distinguished for their integrity, earnestness and practical knowledge, such as are required for the important enterprises of the Department in developing the resources of Hokkaido.
>
> With best wishes for your highest prosperity in the enjoyment of a long and happy life, I have the honor to remain,
>
> Your Excellency's most obliged and most obedient Servant
> W.S. Clark[31]

His final departure from the Sapporo Agricultural College is engraved in Japanese history. One of his students described the moment, at the time of seemingly inconsequential significance, which would nevertheless become familiar to most adult Japanese to this day. Although there are variations of his final challenge to his students, "Boys, be ambitious!" it became part of modern Japanese history and folklore, as did the name William Clark.

> We escorted him on horseback about five miles. We dismounted and rested a while. The anticipated time of parting came at last. He stepped forward and shook hands with every one of us. All of us could not look up. We felt as if we were being bereaved of our dear old father. When we were parting it certainly gave us inward pain. He mounted again on horse back and taking reins in one hand, and a whip in the other looked back toward us and called aloud: "Boys, be ambitious like this old man." He gave one whip to his horse, and straightly went off. No more, President Clark! We never met him again.[32]

Although Clark left Sapporo on April 16, 1877, a letter to him from one of his students three months later reveals that he continued to serve the Kaitakushi even after he left Hokkaido. His final assignment for the Japanese government before leaving the country for home ultimately proved to be of great importance: he chose the second class of students for the Sapporo Agricultural College. Two of them, Ota (Niitobe) Inazo and Uchimura Kanzo, became outstanding intellectuals of modern Japan, as noted previously.

> My dear Sir:
> Since you left Sapporo, three months have already passed away. . . . I have heard that you selected nineteen new pupils in Tokyo for our companions, and I think, they will arrive here perhaps next month. When I recollect that I was once living in darkness, and ignorant of Christianity, to which you were a light to me, I cannot help thanking you for your kindness. I think the new pupils are just in the same condition as I was before, and as we are elder brothers to them, it is our duty to lead them to the way of Christianity and let them live a good life.
> Yours faithfully,
> M. Oshima[33]

The legacy of William Clark, even though his exposure to Japan lasted only eight months in 1876–1877, continued through the graduates of his school to this day. As one of them wrote fifty years after the event, his disciples and their followers had been spreading his influence throughout the whole empire, some serving in government and business companies, some engaging in educational work, and others carrying on their independent enterprises.[34] However, one of the most significant legacies that has continued into the twenty-first century concerns the religious zeal Clark instilled in his students. After his departure his students, including nearly all of the first class and fourteen of the seventeen members of the second class, were baptized in the Christian church and formed the Sapporo Independent Christian Church.[35]

Among the members of the new church were two of the leading educators of modern Japan, Uchimura Kanzo and Niitobe Inazo. Uchimura went on to Amherst College, from where Clark had graduated, in preparation to become a Christian pastor. He is credited with founding one of the pillars of Christianity in Japan, the Mukyōkai, the so-called "non-church" movement that continues to particularly attract many Japanese intellectuals. Niitobe spent three years at John Hopkins University and then studied in Germany where he earned a doctorate. He returned to Japan to teach at the Sapporo Agricultural College and the University of Tokyo, followed by serving as the first president of the Tokyo Women's Christian College. Fulfilling a lifetime goal as "a bridge over the Pacific," he then served in Geneva as an undersecretary of the League of Nations. He received international acclaim for his classic *Bushidō* (The Soul of Japan). Other graduates of the Sapporo Agricultural College either became Christian ministers or, as laymen, were active within the church.

In addition to the graduates of the Sapporo Agricultural College who entered the field of religion under the influence of Clark, there were others who made significant contributions to the modernization of agriculture in Japan. For example, Satō Shōsaku went on to earn a doctorate in agricultural economics from John Hopkins University when Niitobe was studying there. He returned to serve as a senior officer of the Sapporo Agricultural College. He was then chosen as the first president of Hokkaido University when the government recognized Clark's Sapporo Agricultural College as a national university. (Incidentally, the Massachusetts Agricultural College that Clark founded and served as president before going to Japan was later recognized as the University of Massachusetts at Amherst. In other words, Clark founded two academic institutions that would become distinguished universities, one in Japan and one in America. Perhaps no other individual can be recognized with that distinction.)

Finally, one of the first graduates summed up Clark's achievements in Japan succinctly: "If General Kuroda had lived long enough to see the kind of men, whom he had wanted and whom President Clark had reared up, he would have been greatly satisfied."[36] Without doubt William Clark would have felt the same way. His prediction that his Japanese students "will be men distinguished for their integrity, earnestness and practical knowledge" was ultimately fulfilled.

13 | *The Philadelphia Centennial*

THE AMERICAN MODEL REVISITED, 1876

In 1876 Tanaka Fujimaro, director of the Ministry of Education, made his second trip to the United States to attend the Philadelphia Centennial celebrating the one hundredth anniversary of American independence. David Murray, his senior advisor from America, was also sent by the Japanese government to attend the event. During his first trip in 1871–1872, Tanaka had traveled to America as a junior member of the Iwakura Mission from the Ministry of Education to investigate the educational systems of western countries, as we saw in chapter 5. Upon his return home in 1873 he assumed the top position in the ministry, devoting the next three years, in close collaboration with Murray, to implementing the Gakusei, the first plan for a national system of education. In 1876 he returned to the United States not only to attend the Philadelphia Exposition but also to further study the decentralized administrative system of American education that appealed to him.[1]

Among the tens of thousands of Americans who attended the Philadelphia celebration, Tanaka's close friend and colleague, David Murray, was one of the most unusual. He joined his fellow Americans at the Centennial as a member of Japan's bureaucratic elite, representing the country as the "Superintendent of Educational Affairs in the Empire of Japan, and Advisor to the Japanese Imperial Minister of Education."[2] This American visitor was, accordingly, a ranking official of the Japanese delegation to the exposition. Fulfilling his duty, in late 1875 he traveled with his wife from Tokyo to California by ship and across the continent by rail to New Brunswick, New Jersey, which he considered home. From that small town Murray planned to join the Japanese delegation in nearby Philadelphia. His mission was to advise the "Japanese Imperial Minister of Education," Tanaka Fujimaro, by now his dear friend as well as professional colleague, scheduled to arrive several months later.

These two senior officials of the Japanese Ministry of Education, the former samurai from Nagoya and his closest advisor, former professor of mathematics from Rutgers College, were on a special mission. Officially, the two had been sent by the Japanese government to the Philadelphia Exposition to represent Japan with its large educational exhibition. In fact they had come to Philadelphia to undertake an investigation of the latest trends in American education.

Among the features of education in the United States in which Tanaka had become deeply interested during his first trip to the United States was the administrative structure. He returned to America in 1876 determined to gain a better understanding of a country that depended primarily on the local community to finance and administer its public schools. As we have seen, the American system of decentralized control of education contrasted sharply with the highly centralized French system that served as the model for the Gakusei of 1873. The French administrative structure had been chosen as a model for Japan while Tanaka was abroad in 1872–1873. By 1876, after three turbulent years in charge of the Ministry of Education responsible for implementing the plan, he had grave reservations about the appropriateness of the French model for his country. The Japanese director of education and his senior American advisor came to Philadelphia in the mid-1870s for a refresher course in American education for the next period in the modernization of Japanese education, phase two of the American influence.

Commonly known as the City of Brotherly Love, Philadelphia was appropriately chosen for the site of the one hundredth anniversary of the Declaration of Independence. The exposition symbolized the success of a new country united by the Constitution that offered unlimited opportunities. Moving westward across the vast plains and deserts, the Americans were conquering a continent, and then some. They had already projected their influence and a fledgling navy into Asian waters with the penetration of Japan by Commodore Perry and his Black Ships twenty-three years previously. Indeed, the fact that an American educator from nearby New Jersey, David Murray, had traveled from his post in Japan as senior advisor to the Japanese Ministry of Education to attend the Philadelphia Exposition in itself illustrated the growing influence of Americans in Asia.

By 1876 many Americans were convinced that they were building not just a new nation but forging a new people radically different from their European roots. To the Americans, the new country exemplified the first truly democratic society in the history of mankind. They were flexing their muscles through the Centennial Exposition. The Americans had arrived.

The Japanese, notably the director of the Ministry of Education, Tanaka Fujimaro, were impressed by the American experience. They, too, were engrossed in building a modern country. And they, like the Americans, were endeavoring to carry out a revolution by constructing a new society with education as a fundamental instrument. To their leaders such as Tanaka Fujimaro, the United States stood out from all western countries as a guiding beacon to a modern future for Japan. According to Tanaka's son, the American Centennial was an excuse for his father to once again visit schools and interview educators to deepen his understanding of American patterns in education for the reform of Japanese education.[3]

The decision by the Japanese government to officially participate in the Philadelphia Centennial was based on several factors. First, it presented the Japanese with an opportunity to increase their visibility in an international forum. Second, and of great import, it had the potential to provide the Japanese with an opportunity to learn the latest developments in science and technology from western countries, especially the United States, that could benefit Japan in the modernization process. It could also enable the Japanese government to develop closer relations with the United States. Consequently the government appointed a special committee to prepare the Japanese exhibit, one of the largest from abroad.[4]

The Ministry of Education enthusiastically endorsed the government's decision to participate. However, it drew up its own plan separately from the general exhibit sponsored by the Japanese government, reflecting Director Tanaka's fascination with American education. He decided to enter a Japanese educational exhibit that would stand alone. The budget came exclusively from the Ministry of Education, such was the confidence that Tanaka had in his understanding of America and the benefit the ministry could gain from participating in a "showroom of modern education" (*kindai kyōiku shyōrūmmu*).[5] Tanaka eagerly accepted the challenge not only to enter an official educational exhibit from the Ministry of Education but to personally represent Japan at the international conference on education to be held in Philadelphia during the Centennial.

Tanaka's decision to go it alone was also greatly influenced by the fact that his senior advisor, Dr. David Murray, was from New Brunswick, just fifty miles north of Philadelphia. Ministry officials thus had a unique situation in the preparation of its educational exhibit for Philadelphia. They could rely on an American educational scholar with experience at both the secondary and university levels in the United States. Moreover, he had been intimately involved in the problems of Japanese education for the past three years, earning the trust and respect of his colleagues at the ministry. Murray consequently was assigned an active role in planning the Japanese exhibit and helped to choose the materials for it.[6]

Tanaka also assigned Murray the task of editing a general history of Japanese education in English for the ministry's exhibit. No general publication on Japanese education had yet been published in Japanese, so the first official book on Japanese education authorized by the Japanese government came under the general editorship of an American to be published in English by an American company. Moreover, it would begin with an introductory chapter on Japanese education by Murray himself, such was the confidence that Tanaka placed in his senior advisor from America. It posed an unusual challenge to David Murray, who accepted responsibility for introducing Japanese education to an international audience.

The book, entitled *Outline History of Japanese Education*, opened with Murray's chapter. The remaining chapters were written by Ministry of Education officials. An indication that Guido Verbeck was still active within educational circles surfaced when he was hired to translate the Japanese manuscripts into English.[7] This was a tribute to Verbeck's extraordinary skills in the Japanese language. As it turns out, after the Centennial the book was translated back into Japanese and used as a text in the teacher-training colleges.[8]

Dr. and Mrs. Murray left Japan for America in late 1875, long before the Centennial was scheduled to open the following year in May for a six-month run. His assignment went beyond arranging for the publication of the history book by an American publisher and participating in the Centennial itself. He was also commissioned to purchase materials for Japanese libraries and museums, for which he was entrusted with $20,000—a considerable sum in the 1870s. He had also been given the specific assignment to purchase $5,000 worth of educational materials for the Kaisei Gakkō, Japan's most advanced national educational institution.[9] Plans were already under way to recognize the school as Tokyo University, as discussed in the following chapter. In 1874 Kaisei Gakkō had come under the administrative leadership of Hatakeyama Yoshinari, a former student of Murray's at Rutgers College. He had developed the closest personal relationship with the Murrays among all the Japanese students who studied at New Brunswick. Hatakeyama, while president of Kaisei, served as Murray's translator during his field trips to various regions of the country.

Tanaka Fujimaro assembled a competent team from the Ministry of Education who were all capable in English to attend the Centennial.[10] Hatakeyama was a natural choice to go to Philadelphia not only because of his position as president of Kaisei Gakkō but also due to his previous experience in the West as a student at the University of London, then as a member of the Thomas Lake Harris compound in rural New York, and finally as a student at Rutgers College in New Jersey, where he was befriended by the Murrays. Because he had also become Murray's confidant as well as translator during Murray's first three-year stint in Japan, it is conceivable that Murray requested that Hatakeyama join the mission. Tejima Seiichi was chosen for the mission to Philadelphia since he was familiar with the area. A former samurai from Numazu, he had gone to America privately in 1870 entering a secondary school in Philadelphia. From there he entered Lafayette College in a nearby Pennsylvania community. When the Iwakura Mission arrived in Washington in early 1872, he offered his services as a translator, joining the mission as it went on to Europe, where he became interested in the technical advances of Great Britain. In 1873 he was sent back to England to study the railroad system, later writing an article on technical enlightenment.[11] Tejima was particularly eager to study the latest developments in American technical education, his primary field of interest, at the Centennial.[12] Finally, Abe Taizo, former student of Fukuzawa Yukichi at his Keio Gijuku school, the chronicler for the trip, and Ideura Rikio completed the team sent from Japan.

Several Japanese already studying in America were also called to Philadelphia to assist the team from the Ministry of Education. Mekata Tanetaro, in the United States as a representative of the ministry in charge of Japanese students, joined the team from Boston Takamine Hideo, studying Pestalozzian theories of education at the Oswego Normal School in New York, and Isawa Shūji, enrolled at Bridgewater Normal School in Massachusetts, were also summoned to Philadelphia to assist with the exhibition. This provided Tanaka, who planned to appoint these two to head the prestigious Tokyo Teacher Training School upon completion of their two-year study assignment in America, an opportunity to become better acquainted with them. All in all, it was an impressive team that represented the Japanese Ministry of Education at the 1876 Philadelphia Centennial.

In addition to the official team of senior Japanese educational officials, the unpredictable Tanaka made a decision that inevitably provoked considerable reaction among the bureaucracy. He took his wife, the former geisha from Nagoya, along with him to America. On the basis of his first visit to America in 1872, he decided that the 1876 trip presented a great opportunity for the Tanakas to travel abroad as a couple, as well as a chance to express his affection for his wife.[13] It was highly unorthodox, and rather courageous, for a senior Japanese government official to take his wife abroad on an official mission. But under the circumstances and the nonconformist character of Tanaka Fujimaro, it was understandable.

The team of Tanaka, Abe, Hatakeyama, Ideura, and Tejima met with the emperor on April 26, 1876, to receive royal words of encouragement for the trip. They, along with Tanaka's wife, departed from Yokohama by steamer bound for San Francisco on May 19. They finally reached Philadelphia on June 15.[14] Dr. and Mrs. Murray, with whom the Tanakas had developed a close social relationship in Tokyo during the previous three years, had already been at New Brunswick, New Jersey, for nearly six months.

Abe Taizo kept a diary of the entire trip.[15] The team first visited the Berkeley campus of the University of California at Berkeley and the Mill's School for Girls in California, described as "the best girls' school in the west." That was followed by a quick trip to Napa Valley, the famous California wine area. Abe recorded that on the transcontinental train trip to Philadelphia, they stopped at such cities as Ogden, Omaha, and St. Louis, where the members visited high schools, teacher training schools, and other educational institutions. They spent a week in New York City. The delegation arrived in Philadelphia on June 15 and visited the Centennial the following day.

An interesting revelation by Mrs. Tanaka many years later in an interview illustrates the unique circumstances she encountered while in America. Apparently there were so few Japanese in Philadelphia at that time that wherever the Tanakas went, they became the focus of attention. The locals especially gathered around Mrs. Tanaka.[16] The attraction may have been her Japanese clothes. It may also relate to Mrs. Tanaka's reputed beauty.

On June 20, less than a week after arriving in Philadelphia, the Tanakas, along with several aides including Hatakeyama and Mekata, traveled to Rutgers College in nearby New Brunswick for the graduation ceremony.[17] Several Japanese students were graduated at the 1876 ceremony. Mrs. Tanaka recalled years later that the Murrays warmly welcomed the Tanakas to New Brunswick.[18] The Murrays had settled down in the home of Mrs. Murray's relatives during the Centennial, enabling Dr. Murray to attend the events in Philadelphia. The opportunity for the Tanakas to visit the Murrays in New Brunswick was reminiscent of their good times together in Tokyo.

A week and a half later, on June 28, Tanaka once again traveled out of the city, this time to Princeton, New Jersey.[19] The first Japanese student to attend Princeton University, Orita Hikoichi, was being graduated. The university honored Orita by inviting him to give a speech at the ceremony. He spoke about Japan's past and present. Curiously, Orita gave his presentation in Japanese.[20]

Orita's graduation from Princeton University in 1876 as the first Japanese student to do so explains why the director of the Japanese Ministry of Education attended the event. The great Iwakura Tomomi, a member of Emperor Meiji's court before the Restoration and later leader of the Iwakura Mission to Washington, had arranged for Orita to accompany his two sons to Nagasaki where they studied with Guido Verbeck in 1869. Upon the recommendation of Verbeck, all three were then sent to Rutgers College in 1870 where they developed a close personal bond with Dr. and Mrs. Murray. That relationship, incidentally, would be carried back to Japan when Orita was assigned to work in Murray's office at the Ministry of Education in 1877.

At Rutgers, Orita came under the influence of a local Presbyterian minister who was instrumental in converting him to the Christian faith. His pastor recommended that Orita enter nearby Princeton University, which had a close relationship to the Presbyterian denomination rather than Rutgers College sponsored by the Dutch Reformed Church of America. When the first Japanese student graduated from one of America's premier universities, especially someone with close ties to the powerful Iwakura Tomomi family, it attracted Tanaka to the campus for the event. A decade later Orita would make his mark on modern Japanese education, following a stint as Murray's assistant in the Ministry of Education. He was appointed as the principal of the elite Third Higher Secondary School in Kyoto, the premier preparatory school for Kyoto University.

On July 4, the hundredth anniversary of the American Declaration of Independence was celebrated in Philadelphia in grand style. Parades, marching bands, cannon fire, and so on marked the occasion. The original Declaration of Independence was exhibited and read aloud. The day's activities ended with a great fireworks display at Fairmount Park.

The following day, an international conference on education was convened at a local hotel chaired by General George Eaton, U.S. commissioner of education. Tanaka and Murray represented Japan. Eton was well acquainted with Tanaka, having hosted him in Washington four years earlier as a member of the Iwakura Mission, helping to arrange his initial visits to American schools. The conference continued for the next sixty days. Off and on during the hot summer days in Philadelphia, Tanaka went to a nearby beach, probably Atlantic City, where Mrs. Tanaka stayed for a month.[21]

The Centennial exhibition was indeed a major event. In Murray's eyewitness report, he noted that eight million people attended the six-month extravaganza. Among the exhibits that covered an area of seventy-five acres, there were "models of schoolhouses and one real school brought from Sweden. There was a variety of school furniture and the equipments of a schoolroom. There were books, maps, charts, globes and all the helps with which education is carried on."[22] The scope of the educational exhibits ran from the kindergarten level to the university level, and from the sciences to the arts.

The Japanese educational exhibit at the Philadelphia Centennial was impressive as the third largest, only behind the entries of the United States and, somewhat surprisingly, Sweden, which, as Murray noted in his report, displayed an actual school building shipped from Sweden. In terms of budget, however, the Japanese devoted the second highest amount of money on their exhibit, second only to the host country, the United States.[23] The Japanese Ministry of Education shipped a total of 7,000 packages of materials for display.[24] The exhibit consisted of fifteen different sections on school regulations, textbooks, libraries and museums, models of Japanese schools, and so on.[25] Among the various exhibits were samples of essays written by Japanese students. One entry was penned by the future author of the famous classic in English, *Bushidō* (The Way of the Warrior). Niitobe Inazo recalled with great nostalgia that his English teacher's "greatest encouragement came when among a few essays selected to be sent to the Centennial Exhibition in Philadelphia in 1876, he included mine."[26] Niitobe's English teacher was none other than Marion Scott, the head teacher of the Tokyo Teacher Training School.

Beyond the educational exhibit from Japan, the Japanese government sponsored a separate exhibit of cultural treasures that received high acclaim. A reporter from the *Atlantic Monthly* magazine described one display in effusive terms. "The Japanese collection is the first stage for those who are moved chiefly by the love of beauty or novelty in their sight-seeing. The gorgeousness of their specimens is equaled only by their exquisite delicacy. . . . After the Japan collection, everything looks in a measure commonplace, almost vulgar."[27]

During the Centennial, the Japanese delegation experienced an unfortunate development. In late July, Hatakeyama Yoshinari's health rapidly deteriorated. He was sent to a private home in nearby Bryn Mawr, but he did not respond to treatment. The decision to send him back to Japan was made when Tanaka visited him on August 23.[28] Unfortunately, the gentle Hatakeyama, who had become especially close to the Murrays, and who served his nation, died at sea. The Murrays were grief-stricken. Writing to a relative, Dr. Murray realized the extent of the loss. "I miss Mr. Hatakeyama more and more. He was more useful to me than I knew. Nobody can take his place in explaining my ideas to the officers of the government."[29]

During the Centennial, which ran until November 10, Tanaka took several side trips. There was little he and his team could do in the day-to-day management of the Japanese exhibit once it was set up. In the early days of the Centennial, he visited other educational exhibits and attended the first sessions of the international conference on education, which brought together educational specialists from throughout the world. At one session he met Canadian officials who invited him to Toronto to visit the famous Toronto Educational Museum. After the major events of the Centennial were completed, Tanaka took the opportunity to make a twenty-day trip north to Canada in order to do so. There was already an educational museum in Japan that held displays collected by Japanese delegates to the Vienna Exposition in 1873, along with various materials from within Japan. They were displayed in a small exhibit called the Tokyo Museum (Tokyo Hakubutsukan). Tanaka was interested in developing this museum into a full-fledged educational museum.

Tanaka and his aides, along with Mrs. Tanaka, left Philadelphia on August 25 for Canada. They stopped at Rochester and Niagara Falls, the well-known honeymoon capital of America, a fitting stopover for the Tanakas. They then visited schools in Toronto before observing the great Toronto Museum of Education.

Tanaka was astonished with the size of the building and the scope of the educational exhibits, and became more convinced than ever that Japan needed a modern educational museum similar to the Toronto Museum.[30] Upon Tanaka's return to Japan the following year, he worked diligently to open the first educational museum in Japan, the Kyōiku Hakubutsu Kan located at Ueno, Tokyo. Tejima Seiichi, a member of the visiting team to Philadelphia, was appointed by Tanaka as director of the new facility that became known as "The Showroom of the New Education in Japan."[31] Materials brought to Japan by Marion Scott for the Tokyo Teacher Training School and by Murray from the Centennial trip were exhibited in the museum. Years later, Tanaka's son fondly recalled that when his father took him to the museum, in which he took great pride, his father explained that it was patterned after the Toronto Museum.[32]

Another unusual byproduct of the Canadian trip resulted from a visit of the Japanese delegation to a private home for tea. It seems that the host, who was in the fire insurance business, explained how his company functioned. There were no insurance companies in Japan at that time. Abe Taizo, the chronicler of the Japanese team from the Ministry of Education, took a special interest in the explanation. He returned to Japan, promptly resigned from the ministry, and pursued his interest by establishing the first insurance company in Japan, the Meiji Insurance Company (Meiji Seimei). It was patterned after the Canadian company, with Abe Taizo as its first president.[33] It is one of the largest in Japan today.

The Japanese travelers went on from Toronto to visit schools during stopovers in Montreal, Quebec, Boston, and New York before arriving back in Philadelphia on September 16. On November 10, President Ulysses Grant officially closed the great Philadelphia Centennial. Two weeks later the Tanakas went to Washington to join with the Japanese ambassador, Yoshida Kiyonari, one of the early students from Satsuma who went to London with Mori Arinori in 1865, to visit the White House. They met President Grant. Later the secretary of state, Hamilton Fish, who had befriended Mori Arinori as Japan's first diplomat in Washington just five years earlier, showed the Japanese delegation the original Declaration of Independence. They were also shown the original treaty signed between the United States and Japan.

After the Centennial closed in November, Tanaka and several of his aides again set off on a tour of educational institutions beginning with some in the southeastern part of the United States. The delegation visited schools in Virginia and the Carolinas, including a school for black children in Raleigh. Tanaka was once again searching for solutions to the educational problems he faced at home. His 1876 excursion to America was reminiscent of his lengthy inspection of American schools in 1872 as a member of the Iwakura Mission. He returned to some of the same places, such as Amherst the alma mater of Niijima Jō, founder of Doshisha University, who had served as Tanaka's translator during his first tour. In his usual manner, Tanaka took copious notes everywhere he went for reference in carrying out educational reforms upon return home. He used every opportunity on the second tour to America to gain a better understanding of American education.

A particularly interesting example of Tanaka's experiences while in the United States in 1876 concerns his fascination with American developments in physical education. When he revisited Amherst College in late 1876, he noticed the new facilities for physical education being built on campus. He observed classes in which calisthenics were conducted without the use of props. Intrigued by what he witnessed, he decided that the modern American method in physical education should be introduced into Japan. On the basis of this visit, Tanaka later invited an American authority on physical training from Amherst and Harvard University, Dr. George Leland, to introduce modern physical education in Japanese schools, as discussed in the next chapter.

Among the various outcomes of the Philadelphia Centennial was that initiated by a team member, Tejima Seiichi. Exhibiting a strong interest in technical education, he eagerly joined the team to learn about the latest developments in technical education in the exhibits at the Centennial, as well as during American school visits. Observing the exhibits by Russian technical schools from Petersburg and Moscow, Tejima became convinced that Russian technical education was at a more advanced level than that in the United States. Upon returning home, as director of the new Educational Museum in Tokyo, Tejima used the opportunity to promote technical education in Japan, just in its infancy at the time as Japan braced for the industrial revolution. Through his efforts, the first advanced school to train teachers for secondary technical schools, the Tokyo Shokkō, was started by the Ministry of Education in 1881 to meet the growing demand for advanced technical skills. It then became the distinguished Tokyo Kōgyō Gakkō (The Tokyo Industrial School) with Tejima as the principal.[34]

Tanaka and his team, along with his wife, departed Philadelphia on December 1, 1876. They again visited schools in Chicago and Sacramento on the way to San Francisco. They departed the United States on December 16, arriving in Japan on January 8, 1877.[35] They had been in America for seven months.

One of the unexpected outcomes of Tanaka's trip to Philadelphia deserves recognition as a precursor of events that ensued during the next period in the modernization process. It emerged through a deepening relationship with James Wickersham, superintendent of education for Pennsylvania. Wickersham was the responsible official for both the American educational exhibition at the Centennial as well as the international conference on education. The two educators had first met in 1872 when Tanaka, in America as a member of the Iwakura Mission, traveled to Harrisburg with his translator, Niijima Jō, to interview Wickersham about education in Pennsylvania. Wickershan's book, *School Economy,* had been translated into Japanese and used as a significant resource for educational guidance before Tanaka left Japan.

Four years later the relationship between Wickersham and Tanaka was renewed during the 1876 Philadelphia Centennial and the educational conference that followed. A memo dated October 14 that Wickersham prepared for Tanaka during the conference demonstrated Wickersham's continuing interest in the relationship. Entitled "Obstacles to Educational Progress in Pennsylvania," the memo impressed Tanaka. He personally translated it for his official report of the Centennial published by the Ministry of Education.[36]

Wickersham's motivation for this unusual memo remains unknown. It may have stemmed from his concern that Tanaka, deeply impressed with American education, failed to recognize the inherent problems with the decentralized system of administrative control in America without a Ministry of Education. How prescient Wickersham's advice proved to be surfaced during the next several years when Tanaka exerted maximum efforts to introduce the American model into Japan. It led to his removal, in part because Tanaka failed to appreciate Wickersham's warnings about the American system based on his experience as superintendent of education of an American state.

According to Wickersham, the first obstacle to the progress of education in Pennsylvania concerned the role of the locally elected school boards that had impressed Tanaka so deeply. He described the function of local boards, consisting of elected laymen, as responsible for determining the standards of teachers and their salaries, buildings, selection of textbooks, and approving the curriculum. Moreover, the boards also possessed the power to set local taxes on real estate to finance the local schools. Consequently when the local community was conscious of the importance of education to the community, the school boards could set tax rates sufficient to maintain high academic standards of the public schools. Conversely, when the local citizenry failed to appreciate the importance of education, a tax base sufficient to properly finance the local schools was difficult to achieve. The results produced inequalities in educational standards from community to community within the state of Pennsylvania.

Wickersham pointed out that Pennsylvania had a total population of 10 million people with a school population of 900,000. The total school budget for the state came to $10 million per year, about half of what was actually needed to finance the system adequately since the voting population would not support higher taxes. Consequently teacher salaries were not sufficient to attract the necessary pool of qualified teachers who made a career in teaching. The average teacher was twenty-five years old, with many positions being filled with females under twenty-five who most often resigned immediately upon marriage. Under the circumstances, Wickersham, as state superintendent of education, was powerless to solve the continuing problem of the shortage of qualified teachers in the public schools of Pennsylvania.

In a separate report, Wickersham clarified his position concerning the American school board system, comparing the positive and negative aspects that Tanaka apparently did not understand. "The policy of placing so much power in the hands of local school boards as is done by our [Pennsylvania] laws, has its weak as well as its strong points. Among intelligent citizens, alive to the interests of education, it is worthy of all praise; but where an ignorant people, or a people wanting in public spirit, elect school boards like themselves, no policy could possibly be worse."[37]

Wickersham's advice to Tanaka is relevant to modern Japanese education. He took the opportunity during the Philadelphia Centennial to advise Tanaka that without the central role of a Ministry of Education, a national standard of education in Japan providing equal educational opportunities worthy of a modern nation was impossible to achieve. As the superintendent of education for one American state similar to a minister of education for a nation, Wickersham could not ensure equal standards of education in Pennsylvania since locally elected school boards reflected the standards of the community.

When Tanaka returned to Japan in early 1877 determined to implement an educational administrative system similar to the American, he ignored all opposition both within and without the Ministry of Education. This included that of his American senior advisor, Dr. David Murray, who recommended against adopting the American local school board system for Japan. In other words Tanaka Fujimaro, accused by some of his associates as an "American worshiper" (*America kabure*), became even more enamored with the American model during his second prolonged visit to America to attend the Philadelphia Centennial of 1876, in spite of the warnings by James Wickersham and David Murray.

14 The Second National Plan for Education

THE AMERICAN MODEL, PHASE II, 1877–1879

When Tanaka Fujimaro, director of the Ministry of Education, and David Murray, his senior American advisor, returned to Japan in January 1877 from the Philadelphia Exposition, they intensified their efforts to modernize Japanese education. After spending six months in the United States visiting schools, intermittently attending the international educational conference held in conjunction with the American Centennial, Tanaka was intent on returning to his primary pursuit in life. Japanese education, in perpetual crisis under the Gakusei, the First National Plan for Education implemented from 1873, required major revisions. Inspired by his recent experiences in the United States, Tanaka was ready to launch the next phase in the modernization process, the Second National Plan for Education, based on the American model.

The second phase of American influence on modern Japanese education from 1877 can be divided into two sectors. First, the reforms of the Gakusei dealt primarily with public elementary education. In contrast, the year 1877 marks a milestone at the higher education level. During that year Japan's first modern university was founded. Following that accomplishment, Tanaka turned once again to the reform of public elementary education that had not been satisfactorily completed before he left for the American centennial.

Tokyo University, 1877

On April 12, 1877, less than four months after his return from America and in close consultation with David Murray, Tanaka Fujimaro issued orders from the Ministry of Education merging the Tokyo Kaisei Gakkō (polytechnic) and the Tokyo Igakkō (medicine) into Tokyo University.[1] After various name changes over the years, these two national institutions of higher education were finally brought together under one umbrella. It marks the first time that an institution of higher education was officially given the title of *daigaku* or "great school," translated from then on as "university."

There was much discussion and controversy among the Kaisei Gakkō faculty concerning the structure of a modern university. Faculty members frequently consulted with Murray who had maintained close relations with them. For example, he had purchased $5,000 worth of American educational materials for the school during the Philadelphia Centennial. The Japanese were eager to learn how

American universities were academically organized. Murray, a former professor at Rutgers College, was able to provide critical advice in the planning stages of Japan's first university.[2]

Tokyo Kaisei Gakkō, successor to Nankō, the Southern School, revamped and stabilized in 1871 under Guido Verbeck, had already established itself as an advanced institution of foreign studies under foreign teachers. In 1873, President Hatakeyama Yoshinari, Murray's former student at Rutgers College, revised the structure. The main courses offered in English, French, and German were reduced at the upper levels to English due to budgetary constraints. The curriculum also underwent revision, combining the courses into three departments of law, literature, and science.

Upon the 1877 merger of the Tokyo Kaisei Gakkō with the Tokyo Igakkō, the Tokyo School of Medicine under German influence, the academic structure of the new university was virtually in place. It began with the four departments (*gakubu*) of law, literature, science, and medicine, each a continuation of the faculties from the two previous schools. However, the first three from Kaisei Gakkō functioned as a unit under a single head, Katō Hiroyuki, who had replaced Hatakeyama upon his death at sea while returning from the Philadelphia Centennial. The medical department came under a different head.[3] Japan now had a national four-year institution of higher education resembling in its structure an American university.

Continuing the tradition from the previous institutions, the language of the classroom in the non-medical departments was English. The faculty was dominated by American and British professors. Candidates were prepared primarily in the attached English-language school, the Tokyo University Preparatory School (Tokyo Daigaku Yobimon).[4] In the same manner, the medical school maintained its tradition with the German language and medical studies playing the dominant role. One of the most famous German doctors on the staff, who devoted years of service to modern medical education in Japan, was Erwin Baelz. His diary, published as *Awakening Japan*, reveals the extent of German influence. After examining his Japanese students in German during this time of transition, he concluded that "I am highly pleased with the results. I could never understand how Wernich and Hilgendorf [German professors] could say that it would be impossible to make efficient medical practitioners out of the Japanese."[5]

The name Tokyo University originated from a proposal by Katō Hiroyuki, the first president. While serving as head of the former Kaisei Gakkō, he recommended a name change to Tanaka Fujimaro, director of the Ministry of Education. Katō proposed that his institution be designated as the Tokyo Kaisei Daigakkō or Tokyo Kaisei University. He felt that the institution had achieved an academic standard worthy of the new designation. However, since the decision to merge Kaisei Gakkō with the Igakkō medical school had already been made, the name of the new institution that included medical studies could no longer be recognized under the old name of Kaisei. It was then decided to drop Kaisei, and the new institution became simply Tokyo University.[6]

At the same time the Tokyo English School (Tokyo Eigo Gakkō), formerly the preparatory school for Kaisei Gakkō, was merged with the lower division of the old Kaisei Gakkō. The new institution was then attached to the new Tokyo University as the Tokyo Daigaku Yobimon, the Tokyo University Preparatory School.[7] Through this series of reconfigurations of existing governmental institutions, a streamlined structure for public university education was put in place. It was concentrated on this one national institution in Tokyo.

Since students from the old Kaisei Gakkō and Igakkō continued on under the new name of Tokyo University, those qualified to graduate during the year of transition had to be accommodated. Therefore during the first year as Tokyo University, a graduation ceremony was scheduled for those who fit into this category. This is considered the first graduation ceremony at Tokyo University even though the new institution had been operational for less than a year. In fact, only three students from the science department under the old Kaisei Gakkō were qualified to graduate in July. The ceremony was postponed until December to enable the officials to properly prepare for the event.[8]

Indicative of David Murray's influential role in the establishment of Japan's first university, he was given the honor of presenting the graduation address to the first class of three students. It was, of course, given in English. The *Tokio Times* reported that Professor Murray gave a "carefully prepared scholarly paper on the values and methods of education." He used the opportunity to make a thoughtful evaluation of the past five years of educational modernization since the First National Plan for Education was implemented in 1873. With a deep sense of satisfaction and pride, the American educator gave his unqualified endorsement of Japan's modern school system in 1877. He concluded that "This country is now prepared and qualified to furnish education to its citizens from the first primary instruction to the limit of full university training."[9]

The composition of the first entering class of students at the new Tokyo University in 1877 reveals that a social class transition was under way, however guarded. A decade had passed since the Meiji Restoration of 1868, overwhelmingly led by the samurai-warrior class. Since the primary purpose of Tokyo University was the preparation of the next generation of leaders, the extent to which samurai families were represented among the student body is of some consequence. Students from the former elite class made up 73.9 percent of the first class, with 25.5 percent coming from the new heimin (commoner) class. The remainder, 0.6 percent, originated from the nobility.[10] In other words, one-fourth of the next generation of leaders of modern Japan were no longer related to the old samurai families that had governed the nation for hundreds of years. A transformation in the leadership class of modern Japan was under way.

New Academic Disciplines from America—Edward Morse

The rearrangement of names and departments at the new Tokyo University from 1877 was accompanied by the rapid addition of new faculty members from abroad. The influx proved expensive with foreign faculty salaries suddenly catapulting.

Their costs consumed one-third of the entire university budget for the initial 1877–1878 academic year.[11] A fresh wind once again blew across the educational landscape with the introduction of new academic disciplines from the West. Similar to the modernization of the elementary school curriculum, the expansion of subject areas at the university level fell primarily within the fields of science.

Among those who exerted a profound influence on Japanese scientific thought at this time was Edward Morse, graduate of Harvard University. As the first professor of zoology at the newly named Tokyo University, he occupies an unusual niche in modern Japanese history for introducing the concept of evolution into Japan.[12] Until Morse's arrival there was no word for it in the Japanese language.[13] Morse was studying at Harvard University when Charles Darwin's epochal book, *On the Origin of Species,* was being circulated. It espoused the explosive theory of evolution considered by many then and now as contradicting the biblical account of Creation. Morse as a student witnessed the renowned intellectual thinkers on the Harvard faculty debate the basic tenets of this revolutionary theory that reverberated throughout the western Christian world. He became an ardent advocate of the controversial Darwinian theory of "survival of the fittest," the basis of evolutionary thought.

In 1877, just as Tokyo University was formed, Morse coincidentally traveled privately to Japan for the summer to collect a rare species of shells. Arriving in June, he took the train from Yokohama to Tokyo bearing a letter of introduction to Dr. David Murray, senior advisor to the Ministry of Education, for assistance in arranging travel to gather the specimens. In one of the most extraordinary chance incidents of modern Japan, Morse spotted from the train layers of shells embedded in an exposed cliff along the tracks. He immediately identified them as an ancient shell mound.

Shortly thereafter, Morse met Murray at his office in the Ministry of Education who introduced him to the director, Tanaka Fujimaro, as well as several officers of Tokyo University. Morse relayed to them with great excitement his accidental discovery of the prehistoric shells while riding the train. The Japanese were astounded with his explanation of the importance of the shells found in Japan in the evolutionary process of Darwin's theory. Although they were deeply impressed with Morse's scientific conclusion derived from a train ride, the Japanese may not have understood his scientific explanation. The American scientist's enthusiasm, however, must have influenced their surprising reaction.

Dr. Murray invited Morse on the spot to accompany him on a planned trip to Nikko, the great site of the memorial to Tokugawa Ieyasu a hundred miles north of Tokyo. While Morse was visiting Nikko with Murray, ministry and university officials hurriedly made an extraordinary decision. They were so deeply impressed by their initial meeting with Morse that, upon his return to Tokyo from Nikko, they promptly offered him a two-year contract to organize a department of zoology at the newly organized Tokyo University. In addition, he was invited to establish a museum of natural history. They offered Morse the highest salary of any foreign professor, which he could not turn down.

Within three weeks of his arrival in Japan on a private research project, Morse signed a contract as the first professor of zoology at Tokyo University. Suddenly what was intended by a young American scholar from Harvard as a leisurely summer on the Japanese coast gathering rare specimens turned into the introduction of modern zoology into Japan. A month later, in July, the Japanese government set up its first marine biological laboratory at Enoshima, just south of Tokyo, for Morse to conduct his research.

As word spread of Morse's activities, Japanese scholars visited him to inquire of his studies. His fame spread quickly throughout the academic world. With the opening of the Tokyo University semester in September 1877, Morse presented the first lecture on zoology given in Japan. No interpreter was provided since the university was essentially an English-language institution. It had all transpired within the short period of two months.

Morse relished the opportunity offered to him by university officials to introduce a subject dear to his heart, evolution, to the Japanese public. He described the first public lecture on the topic in his detailed diary published later as *Japan Day to Day*. It not only indicates Morse's pleasure with the unexpected opportunity to spread the gospel of evolution, it also reveals the trials and tribulations he faced in America when he attempted to spread the theory of evolution in his own country. "Saturday, October 6, 1877. I gave my first lecture in a course of three on Evolution tonight in the large college hall. A number of professors and their wives and from five hundred to six hundred students were present, and nearly all of them were taking notes. It was an interesting and inspiring sight. . . . The audience seemed to be keenly interested, and it was delightful to explain the Darwinian theory without running up against theological prejudices as I often did at home. . . . One of the Japanese professors told me that this was the first lecture ever given in Japan on Darwinism and Evolution."[14]

Morse quickly adjusted to his new academic environment. He thoroughly enjoyed teaching Japanese students. He wrote in his daily record that "I am in love with my students already. It is a delight to teach such good boys all greedy to learn."[15] They responded to his lectures by taking copious notes. As a result of his university course, the first book on zoology in the Japanese language was entitled *Theory of Animal Evolution as Given by the American Professor, Edward S. Morse, and Taken Down by His Pupil Chiomatsu Ishikawa.*[16]

The chance, and quite phenomenal, recognition of valuable research shells by an American scholar from a passing train near Tokyo had ramifications for modern Japanese education beyond the introduction of zoology in Japan. During the first summer at home, Morse used the opportunity to collect twenty-five hundred books and brochures for Tokyo University, adding substantially to the books collected by Morse in 1876 to became the genesis of the Tokyo University Library. His manuscript "Shell Mounds of Omori" was also released under the university imprint, in effect the first publication considered as the origin of the distinguished Tokyo University Press.[17] Omori was the site where Morse first spotted the prehistoric shells from the train.

Morse's contribution to modern higher education in Japan extended well beyond his own field of zoology. His employment opened the gates to other foreign scholars, so that Tokyo University quickly became known as Japan's "window for the importation of western knowledge," both in science and nonscience disciplines.[18] This can be characterized as the golden age of Tokyo University. Morse played a leading role in that illustrious period.

Since Morse had unexpectedly accepted a teaching position while on a summer research trip, he was allowed to return home in November following the first teaching semester to arrange for his wife to come to Japan. Ministry of Education and Tokyo University officials, however, seized the opportunity and commissioned Morse to recruit two American scholars for the faculty at the university. They were to fill positions in philosophy and physics. Morse successfully recruited Ernest Fenollosa and Thomas Mendenhall, respectively, for the posts. Each made historical contributions to modern Japanese education and deserve far more consideration than possible in a general history of the period. Fenollosa, in particular, stands out for his remarkable accomplishments in unrelated fields during his many years in Japan.

Ernest Fenollosa was hired by Tokyo University in 1878. He joined the faculty as professor of philosophy, economics, and political science. It was the beginning of one of the most fascinating episodes in modern Japan.[19] As a graduate of Harvard University in the Department of Philosophy, Fenollosa had become attracted to the teachings of the British philosopher Herbert Spencer. He also demonstrated a fascination for art, taking courses at the Massachusetts Normal Art School after graduating from Harvard in 1870.

When Fenollosa arived on the faculty of Tokyo University at the age of twenty-five, he and Morse teamed up to launch a new movement in western thought. Morse continued his special lectures on Darwin's theory of evolution. Fenollosa reinforced the theme with Herbert Spencer's scientific philosophy. Spencerian concepts of social evolution attracted a wide audience among Japanese intellectuals and leaders searching for modern theories for the new Meiji society. His classics were translated into Japanese, further enhancing the teachings of the young American professors at Tokyo University. One Japanese historian describes Spencer as "the most widely read and possibly the most influential western social and political thinker in Japan during the 1880's."[20] Thus with the beginning of Tokyo University in 1877, radically new ideas were introduced into the mainstream of higher education.

At this point, an overview of the institutions of higher education near the end of the first decade of the Meiji Restoration is informative. First, there were four national institutions and one private one that fit into this category: Tokyo University, Tokyo Teacher Training School, Tokyo Imperial College of Engineering, Keio Gijuku in Tokyo, and Sapporo Agricultural College in Hokkaido. In the four national institutions English dominated the classroom. The exception was in the department of medicine at Tokyo University where German was the dominant language with the department staffed primarily by German professors. In the teacher-training school subject matter courses were taught in Japanese. Nevertheless, English texts from America predominated. In Fukuzawa's private Keio Gijuku, the texts were in English, with Japanese faculty teaching English to all students. In other words, at this time the majority of the future leaders of modern Japan undertook their advanced level of education in a foreign language taught by foreign professors, and studied from imported English textbooks. It was truly a remarkable "era of English" never to be equaled in the history of the nation.

The Second National Plan for Education

While Tokyo University was being organized in 1877, Tanaka Fujimaro launched an ambitious campaign to reform the venerable Gakusei of 1873. It consumed Tanaka and his Ministry of Education for the next three years. Virtually all of the upper-echelon officials from Tanaka and Murray on down were absorbed with the project. It would prove to be a controversial process that provoked a split within the ministry between the Imperial Household and the Ministry of Education, and between Tanaka and his American advisor Murray.

There were two reports published by the ministry vital to the process. The first was Tanaka's four-volume *Educational Report* on the 1876 American Centennial (*Beikoku Hyakunenki Hakurankai Kyōiku Hōkoku*) that he had just attended in the United States. He included an explanatory commentary on contemporary American education as he interpreted it.[21] Although many nations had entered educational displays at the Philadelphia Centennial, Tanaka's report concentrated on the American exhibit.[22] Since Pennsylvania was the host state of the Centennial in its leading city, Philadelphia, James Wickersham, superintendent of education in Pennsylvania, was responsible for the American educational exhibit. Tanaka's extraordinary interest in the American exhibit, by far the largest housed in a separate building, may have been influenced by his deepening relations with Wickersham.

Having spent over a year in the United States on two occasions, in 1872 and 1876, visiting countless schools and interviewing innumerable educational administrators and teachers from California to Pennsylvania, Tanaka Fujimaro was by now Japan's leading authority on the state of American education. Japan's senior educational official at the Ministry of Education was not only its foremost specialist on American education but he had become the leading advocate for reforming Japanese education on the American model. Tanaka Fujimaro had indeed come a long way from his days as a youthful samurai leading an attack on a local store in Nagoya, destroying imported western goods with his sword.[23]

The second document that Tanaka had published by the ministry, a report in two volumes, was entitled simply *American School Laws* (*Beikoku Gakkō Hō*). It included a variety of articles on American education collected by Tanaka during his recent trip to the United States. One volume was a translation of a recently published report that Tanaka came across in America, a compilation of the educational laws of each of the thirty-seven states from Alabama to Wisconsin.[24] Perhaps the appeal of this publication to Tanaka was the inclusion of each state's constitution as the legal basis for education. It provided him with the very latest authoritative source of available information on the legal foundation of American education.

The importance to the modernization of Japanese education of these two publications concerning American education rests primarily on the fact that Tanaka Fujimaro relied upon them as his major source of guidance in drawing up one of the most controversial plans for the reform of Japanese education in the modern era, his Education Law of 1879 (Kyōiku Rei). History had repeated itself, with modifications. The First National Plan for Education, the Gakusei of 1872–1873, was based on the translation of the French Code of Education (Futsukoku Gakusei). In a similar manner, the Second National Plan for Education, Tanaka's Education Code of 1879, was based on the translation of *American School Laws.*[25]

In launching the campaign of educational reform to replace the First National Plan for Education, Tanaka was immediately faced with severe budgetary shortfalls. Two days after his return from Philadelphia in 1877, the ministry's budget was sharply cut by the government due, in part, to the reduced income from lowering the detested land tax that had provoked widespread civil unrest. The other budgetary factor resulted from the mushrooming military costs of containing an armed opposition. A civil war had suddenly erupted in the south of the country led by the charismatic Saigo Takamori, himself one of the prominent leaders of the early Meiji government but now in open rebellion. To help finance the conflict the educational budget reduction was so drastic that it prompted the Ministry of Education to close the seven local teacher colleges funded from the national budget, a severe blow to the upgrading of teacher training. The only remaining teacher training schools under the Ministry of Education were the all-male Tokyo Teacher Training School and the Tokyo Teacher Training School for Women.[26]

In spite of the sudden proliferation of obstacles, Tanaka promptly set the process of educational reform in motion upon his return to Japan from America in January 1877. First, he appointed Murray, now head of the Office of the Superintendent of Education (Gakkan Jimusho), to undertake a major assignment. As Tanaka's senior advisor, he was given the responsibility for independently drawing up a proposal to reform Japanese education on the basis of another observation trip through the provinces and a survey of the public schools of Tokyo. The trip was scheduled to take him by ship to Nagasaki at the southern tip of the country and to include visits to the great cities of Kyoto and Osaka on the way back to Tokyo.[27]

The second act by Tanaka as head of the Ministry of Education was the organization of a special ministerial task force of senior officers to prepare an educational reform proposal.[28] The members were dispatched throughout the country to inspect local schools, commissioned to draw up a series of reports on the current state of education after four years under the Gakusei. The two sets of reports, one by Murray and the other by the ministry task force, were intended to provide Tanaka with a broad perspective on the problems of contemporary education that would enable him to draw up the final reforms of Japanese education.

David Murray, as expected, accepted the challenge given to him by Tanaka. He recorded that since the beginning of 1877, that is, upon his return from the

Centennial celebrations in Philadelphia, "I have been chiefly employed in investigations in regard to a revision of the educational code [Gakusei] of Japan."[29] Murray had been living an extraordinary lifestyle in Tokyo with his devoted wife since
he arrived to take up his post in 1873, interrupted by ten months in America to
attend the Philadelphia Centennial with the Japanese delegation. He took advantage of his unique situation by participating in various activities for foreigners in
Japan. For example, he became very active in the Asiatic Society of Japan, serving
a term as vice president. The membership of the society read like a *Who's Who* of
foreigners in the greater Tokyo area. It included scholars on Japan such as Basil
Chamberlain, whose books remain major works of the period. Other members
who were not authorities on Japan but who made major contributions to Japanese education included Marion Scott from the Tokyo Teacher Training School,
and Henry Dyer from Scotland, founder of the Imperial College of Engineering.
Curiously, the only Japanese member during the first part of Murray's assignment
in Japan was Mori Arinori, instrumental in hiring Murray when he served as the
head of Japan's first legation in Washington in 1871. Through the Asiatic Society
of Japan, Murray associated himself with the distinguished foreign academic community of the Tokyo-Yokohama area.

Murray was not a scholar on Japan, although he made an impressive study of
Japanese art and history, according to his voluminous handwritten notes on the
subjects filed in the United States Library of Congress. Therefore Tanaka provided
an office staff at the ministry capable in English to enable Murray to carry out his
official responsibilities as Tanaka's chief advisor. It was a considerable task. Relevant Japanese materials had to be translated for him. And his detailed reports for
Tanaka as well as his various speeches, some of great length, required translation
into Japanese. He was also invited on a number of official occasions to speak as an
officer of the Ministry of Education such as the first graduation ceremony at Tokyo
University in 1877. Everywhere he went he needed a translator.

In great deference to Murray, Tanaka assigned from within the Ministry of
Education highly capable officers to work in Murray's office in order to carry out
his new assignment.[30] They became very loyal to him. Several had been students at
Rutgers College during the feudal era when Murray was on the faculty. Takahashi
Korekiyo, who briefly visited America, did much of the oral translation not only
for Murray but for Mrs. Murray as well. He also reported to Murray on educational
matters.[31] Most Japanese recognize Takahashi's name today as the one-time prime
minister who was subsequently murdered as finance minister during the infamous
attempted military coup of 1936.

Egi Kazuyuki, Murray's office manager, became minister of education at a
later date. His memoirs provide invaluable insights about interpersonal relationships within the ministry and within Murray's office itself, as Tanaka focused the
bureau toward the single purpose of developing a new national plan for education. Egi not only provided significant conservative input into the deliberations
but assisted Murray in his research, translating his final report on the reform of
the Gakusei for Tanaka.[32] Murray was fortunately surrounded by capable Japanese

officials during his entire tenure at the Ministry of Education through the thought-fulness and concern of Tanaka Fujimaro.

A Survey of the Public Schools of Tokyo by David Murray

With the assignment to prepare a report for the revision of Japanese education, Murray undertook "a systematic inspection of the Public Schools of Tokio."[33] Accompanied by Egi, Murray visited 43 of the 150 public schools in the capital city. He noted cryptically that "The Mombusho [Ministry of Education], of course, is recognized in the requirement that all plans of study shall be approved by it." This brief comment would prove prophetic when the issue of control of educa-tion shortly thereafter emerged as the central point of controversy both inside and outside the ministry.

Murray's report included revealing statistics on school attendance. The capital city of Tokyo had already become the cultural and intellectual center of the country, consequently best equipped to meet the stated goals of the First National Plan for Education from 1873. Among them, the stipulation calling for every child to attend elementary school was perhaps the most critical as well as demanding. The degree to which Tokyo met this goal was indicative of the conditions throughout the rest of the country, much less prepared than the capital city to achieve the lofty goal.

Murray's report on school attendance at Tokyo schools revealed that the objec-tive of the Meiji government in 1873 to provide schools for every Japanese child was far from being met by 1878. In particular, the glaring deficiencies between the education of Japanese boys and girls in early modern Japan were vividly illustrated. Slightly more than 50 percent of eligible girls attended school in Tokyo. Much to Murray's surprise, one of the most significant results from his survey emerged in the comparison between the number of public and private elementary and middle schools in Tokyo. He noted that "It will be seen from this how important an ele-ment in the education of the city are the private schools." This was clearly an understatement when it came to the middle school level. The city of Tokyo did not support one public school for either sex above the elementary level.

Murray was concerned with the conditions in both the private and public sectors. For example, private school classes averaged thirty-nine students while public schools

Table 10   Public and Private School Attendance in Tokyo, 1878

	Males	*Females*	*Total*
School population	66,591	63,636	130,227
School attendance	54,367	35,704	90,071

Source: David Murray, "Public Schools of Tokio: A Report by David Murray, Superin-tendent of School Affairs, July 1878" (handwritten), papers of David Murray, Library of Congress, Washington, D.C., Box 1.

Table 11   Public and Private Schools in Tokyo, 1878

	Private	Public
Elementary schools	684	142
Middle schools	209	0
Elementary school teachers	1,197	707
Middle school teachers	491	0

Source: David Murray, "Public Schools of Tokio: A Report by David Murray, Superintendent of School Affairs, July 1878" (handwritten), papers of David Murray, Library of Congress, Washington, D.C., Box 1.

contained an average of twenty-eight. Moreover, only 40 of the 707 public elementary school teachers had earned a teaching certificate from either a national or local teacher-training school qualifying them to teach. The assumption can be made that among the 1,197 private school teachers, few if any were qualified to teach. Murray described the vast majority of uncertified public school teachers in Tokyo elementary schools thus: "They are often men well educated especially in the old Japanese learning. But they lack a knowledge of many of their subjects now taught in the elementary school, and they are without experience in the method of conducting schools and instructing classes." Murray was, of course, referring to the large number of ex-samurai who had gone into teaching after they lost their special status as warriors.

Murray struck at one of the primary causes for the shortage of qualified teachers in Tokyo. Their pitiful salaries "ranging from 5 to 25 yen per month" proved unattractive. The contrast between teacher salaries in Tokyo, among the highest in the nation, with Murray's salary at 600 yen per month illustrates the vast diversity among Japanese and foreign salaries. It also reveals the life style that foreigners hired by the Japanese government were able to maintain in Meiji Japan. Murray commented in his report on the problems of attracting teachers for the public schools of Tokyo, the nation's capital city. It can be assumed that, in comparison to Tokyo, teaching conditions throughout the countryside were worse. "The salaries are so small that it cannot be expected that the best talent will be attracted or that qualified men will remain longer than they can help. The scale of salaries ranges from 25 yen to 5 yen per month. About 30 teachers from the public schools resign every month and new teachers to that extent must be supplied. The average length of service of the elementary school teachers is only seven to eight months. Such a state of things of course is to be deplored, and yet the remedy is not easy to suggest."

Recognizing that each Tokyo public school was notified when Murray and his aides from the Ministry of Education were expected to arrive at the school, he accepted the fact that a visit by a high American official from the Japanese government was an extraordinary event. Undoubtedly he was directed to the classrooms of the best teachers in each school. Even then, he noted that "The quality of this [teaching] seemed to differ widely from the bright enthusiastic instruction of the earnest and well trained teacher, to the dull and listless drudgery of the hired laborer . . . much of the instruction is done by inexperienced teachers of little education. It cannot, of course, be of a higher order." Murray was surely aware that teaching standards in the provinces had to be lower.

Ministry of Education Survey of the Provinces

While Murray visited Tokyo city schools, senior Japanese ministry officials were also dispatched throughout the country for the same purpose. Several reports illustrate the problems of modernizing Japanese schools as seen through the eyes of contemporary Japanese officials.[34] For example, Kuki Ryūichi spent sixty-six days on the road visiting schools in the Third University District of Osaka, Kyoto, Wakayama, and Shiga from May of 1877. His report to Tanaka was bleak indeed, claiming that local educational officials lacked sufficient experience and knowledge concerning educational affairs to carry out their duties responsibly. Very few elementary teachers he observed employed the latest teaching methods that Marion Scott had introduced as "object lessons" at the Tokyo Teacher Training School. He concluded that not only were the students wasting their time in classes that were poorly taught but also, under the prevailing atmosphere at public schools, students developed a dislike for learning (*gakumon*).

Another ministry official soon to be reckoned with, Nishimura Shigeki, visited schools in the Second University District of Aichi, Gifu, and Mie during an extended investigation from May 4 to July 2, 1878. He reported to Tanaka that school fees were too expensive under the poor economic conditions of rural communities. In addition, in contrast to some of the old terakoya schools that ran from 8 to 12 o'clock, enabling students to work on the rice fields in the afternoons, the new public schools were in session from 9 in the morning to 3 in the afternoon. The burden on farm families both financially and physically had become too severe under the new school system, an important factor underlying the continuing problem of high absenteeism, according to this field report.

Nishimura, a known Confucianist, then used the opportunity to remind his intended reader, director of the Ministry Tanaka Fujimaro, that morals (*shūshin*) is the very basis of education throughout the world. He noted that in western countries a major purpose of education was the moral teachings of Christianity. In other countries such as China, India, and Persia, that is, non-Christian countries, morals education derived from local religions was equally important. In contrast, Nishimura reasoned that Japan was in the process of abolishing Confucianism, not to be replaced with Christianity. He claimed that the Japanese people were, as a result, at a loss in the absence of any moral foundation as the nation faced the uncertainties of the new era. Under such conditions, he argued, moral education was essential to help solve the problems confronting Japanese society. At the time, moral education was only taught through oral presentations, in contrast to western countries where excerpts from the Bible were employed in teaching morality. Consequently, Japanese teachers, often young and inexperienced, faced a heavy burden in carrying out their moral responsibilities to their students.

Still another ministry official, Egi Kazuyuki from Murray's office, reported that in rural mountainous areas, he witnessed villagers living in poorly constructed houses resembling huts with fragile temporary roofs. In contrast, the new village public elementary school mandated under the First National Plan for Education was incongruously grand with a fancy roof. He reported cryptically that peasant children were compelled to memorize peculiar facts such as the dates of George Washington's birthday and Napoleon's death. He concluded that the costs of the new public schools required by the government were extravagant, while poor rural children were being taught irrelevancies under the first modern school system in the land.[35]

Tanaka's Controversial Second National Plan for Education

Under Tanaka Fujimaro's personal guidance, a proposal to replace the 1873 Gakusei with the Kyōiku Rei, hereafter referred to as the Second National Plan for Education, slowly emerged. In his compulsive enthusiasm to reform the Gakusei, Tanaka viewed every issue from the aspect of the American system, resolutely ignoring the increasingly vocal opposition to his proposed revisions. According to a senior ministry official assigned to the special committee to plan the reforms, Kubota Yuzuru, Tanaka was characterized among his own bureaucrats as obsessed with freedom in education that he admired from his two prolonged visits to America. In a memorial paper published many years later, Kubota recalled that critics of Tanaka during this intense period labeled him as an America worshiper (*America kabure*).[36] The derisive description revealed a growing antagonism by not a few ministry officials toward this colorful figure.

The battle lines in the struggles over the modernization of Japanese education were crystallized by Tanaka Fujimaro's proposed education law along two fronts. Although interrelated, they cut across fundamental aspects of education. The first was closest to his heart. This concerned the issue of control of the nation's schools. Should the government represented by the Ministry of Education control the nation's schools according to the provisions of the Gakusei? Or should each community represented by a locally elected council of citizens make the major decisions for the local public schools? In other words, should the control of education be centralized at the ministerial level on the French pattern or decentralized to the community level on the American pattern?

Deeply impressed by what he observed in America where the national government in Washington had little influence on local education, Tanaka incorporated the later into his reform plan. He proposed a system of local school committees elected by the citizens of each community to assume responsibility for, and control over, the local public schools. Although the Ministry of Education in principle retained broad administrative power over public education under Tanaka's proposal, it nevertheless would recognize the rights of the locally elected committee to administer (*kanji*) the public schools within its jurisdiction.

It would become responsible for setting the curriculum, selecting textbooks, hiring teachers, and determining the financing of the school.[37]

The second contentious issue in Tanaka's reforms concerned the role and content of morals education (*shūshin*) in the curriculum of the public schools. The basic problem centered on the question of whether morals education should be taught in school at all, or was a responsibility best left with the parent at home. If it's the former, a second question arises. Should moral teachings in the public schools of modern Japan derive from traditional eastern concepts based on Confucian principles? Or should morals education derive from universal principles such as honesty, integrity, and so on? Tanaka took the position that morals should be taught primarily at home. The major responsibility of the school was to impart knowledge (*chiiku*).[38] Nevertheless, he included morals education in the curriculum but relegated it to the bottom of the list.

On this front the confrontation inexorably drew the emperor himself into the very center of educational reform in the modern era for the first time. The ensuing controversy that dominated the second decade of modernization in the 1880s involved the secular modernizers such as Tanaka and Itō Hirobumi, bound for the prime ministership, on one side. They were pitted against the strategic coalition of Emperor Meiji and his chief advisor, the Confucianist Motoda Nagazane, along with their sympathizers such as Egi and Nishimura within the ministry, who promoted the primacy of Confucian morality to be taught to every child as the foundation of the school curriculum.

The irreconcilable division within the ministry among senior Japanese officials was further exacerbated by the fundamental split that ultimately surfaced between Tanaka and his senior American advisor and close personal friend David Murray. Their differences over the proposal to reform education were unrelated to the role of morals education. Rather, Murray's opposition to Tanaka's reforms concerned the proper role of the Ministry of Education in the administration of Japan's modern school system. As the two highest officials within the ministry, they confronted one of the most profound issues every country faces in the modern world. Who shall control the nation's schools, that is, where should the decision-making power lie in determining what every child is taught in the curriculum, textbook content, and the manner of financing?

The controversy over administrative control of education in Japan was illustrated through the strikingly different positions of Tanaka and Murray. In one of the great role reversals of the times, Tanaka Fujimaro, director of the Japanese Ministry of Education, supported the American decentralized approach where individual communities through locally elected school boards retain significant decision-making power over the local schools. The American senior advisor to the Ministry of Education, David Murray, himself a former secondary school headmaster and professor in the United States, recommended in his official report to Tanaka, covering fifty-nine handwritten pages, precisely the opposite. Fairly isolated from the social and political struggles under way, Murray left little doubt where he stood on the issue outlined in his report to Tanaka as his senior advisor.

Within the provisions of this [proposed] law, the administration of all educational affairs in the Empire should be vested in the Department of Education. . . . In order to secure anything like a system, properly graded and
balanced, and to keep the standard of the schools and the character of the
instruction at a suitable point, it is absolutely necessary to reserve to the
Department of Education a power to prescribe schedules of study. Inspection
is necessary because in no other way can a sufficient knowledge of the educational condition of the country be attained by the government . . . or a failure
to carry out the established regulations by the local authorities be discovered
or remedied. . . . Without proper supervision a school system however perfect
in the beginning will soon fall into endless irregularities. . . . Each locality will
pursue a plan of its own, and change the well-considered scheme of instruction according to popular or individual caprice. . . . To provide against such
danger, to keep the standard of education sufficiently high . . . the Department
of Education must be vested with sufficient powers of supervision and control.
To do less than this will go back to the feudal times, and undo much that has
been already accomplished.[39]

Murray's advice to Tanaka was unequivocal. Dubbed by historians as the grad-
ualist approach to educational reform, Murray's recommendation to Tanaka was,
in essence, to avoid major changes. In other words, rather than replace the Gakusei, modify it with gradual reforms where necessary. His report to Minister Tanaka
in 1878 reveals how strongly he felt about the strategic role of the Ministry of Education. His personal aside, "I regard this as the most important matter connected
with the Code of Education," appears as an effort to exert pressure on Tanaka. As
Tanaka's senior advisor for the past four years, this advice by Murray was meant to
be taken as the most critical one he had offered. To reinforce his position, he then
listed essential powers to be invested in the Department of Education.

To prescribe plans of study for all public schools.
To prescribe the qualifications for teachers.
To inspect all schools . . . enforcing compliance with the established
    regulations.
To appoint for each city and prefecture a superintendent over schools
    and . . . head of the school bureau in that government, but so far as
    instruction in the schools is concerned, it shall be responsible to the
    Department of Education.

The fundamental position on the pivotal role of the central government in
Japanese education recommended by Murray as an American is a curious one, to
be sure. As an experienced educator from America, he knew perfectly well that the
central government in Washington, D.C., did not "prescribe plans of study" for the
public schools. Yet Murray defended persuasively, and somewhat disingenuously,
his position in the Report upon a Draft Revision. He claimed that, "In every country where popular education has made progress, it has been brought about by the

thorough supervision of the schools by the central administration." But Tanaka, by now Japan's leading authority on education in the West, knew full well that Murray's declaration did not apply to America, which Tanaka had already chosen as his model for the reform of Japanese education.

Egi Kazuyuki, Murray's senior assistant in the Ministry of Education, who translated his report to Tanaka, recalled rather fondly his understanding of Murray's position on this crucial issue. Since Egi also opposed Tanaka's proposal, he encouraged Murray to write a critique of it. Egi then took the liberty of expanding upon Murray's brief draft into a lengthy discourse in the Japanese translation. He claimed that although Murray was considered a liberal by many since he came from America, that simply was not the case. Murray recognized the critical role of individual American state governments in local education, displaying their power by setting such state standards as compulsory education laws. In particular, according to Egi, Murray admired German education where the central government set requirements for that nation's schools similar to those that Murray recommended for Japan.[40]

With Murray's added opposition to Tanaka's major plan for the revision of Japanese education, the Ministry of Education underwent a bitter internal crisis. Not only was Tanaka's senior American advisor and close personal friend adamantly opposed to his plan but senior Japanese officials within the ministry also lined up behind the American advisor's position. According to Egi's secretary, this influential educational bureaucrat supported Murray's proposal over Tanaka's plan.[41]

Tanaka ultimately disregarded both his senior American advisor's recommendations and those of his senior Japanese officers within the ministry. Whether the irreconcilable division between Tanaka and Murray over one of the most fundamental issues in modern Japanese education was the cause for Murray's resignation within the year cannot be confirmed. It would appear that it was not. The departure from Japan was amicable. Nevertheless, it was Tanaka's uncompromising position, ignoring the advice of Murray and his own subordinate officials such as Egi, that would shortly thereafter lead to his own downfall.

The Rise of the Peoples' Movement for Freedom

At this time the rise of a new force in Japanese society would within a relatively short time play a critical role in modern Japanese education. A fledgling political movement took root that the government could not ignore. The Jiyū Minken Undō, the Peoples' Movement for Freedom, exerted an increasingly powerful influence during the latter half of the 1870s as government policy in all areas reacted to it. From this time onward, educational reform in Japan was increasingly shaped in response to the proliferating antigovernment activities led by the Jiyū Minken. It was inevitably perceived by the political leadership as a potentially pervasive internal threat to the existing political and social order.

The Peoples' Movement for Freedom brought together a curious coalition of dissident groups opposed to government policy.[42] They had little in common except opposition to government programs that affected them negatively. The core of this loose organization was first formed by disaffected samurai who were left out of the new leadership class, protesting to be brought into it under their terms. The second faction within the umbrella movement for freedom consisted of farmers, who made up 80 percent of the total population, attracted to the antigovernment stance to reduce the debilitating land tax that was making the life of the impoverished rice farmers miserable. The third faction was loosely made up of urban intellectuals attracted to the rhetoric and theoretical arguments emanating from the French and American revolutions. In a classic work on Japanese religions, the author described the activities of the protest movement accordingly. "Jiyū Minken agitators circulated facsimile reports of the English Magna Carta; the name of Rousseau was repeated like that of a savior; Patrick Henry was well known to many and his words 'liberty or death' became a slogan."[43]

Inevitably teachers became aware of the budding political movement, especially after the internal Seinan War of 1877. Although precise membership figures are not available, many teachers in nearly every region of the country participated in the Jiyū Minken movement in some form. There were even teachers who took leading roles in organizing and running local branches of the loosely run organization. In one prefecture the local branch published a journal on education in which many problems of contemporary education were analyzed. Inevitably government policy on education came under criticism. By the latter half of the 1870s, public school teachers were playing an increasingly activist role in the political opposition to the Meiji government.[44]

The influence of the Jiyū Minken Undō inexorably spread into the school system itself. For example, some teachers in local professional meetings of teachers, ostensibly organized for educational purposes, grasped the opportunity to express opinions about the lack of political rights. Although outside the classroom, it represented an indirect criticism of government policy by teachers. Students at teacher-training schools were not ignorant of the political agitation either, often politically motivated by activist professors. These critical institutions within the educational world played an important role in the Jiyū Minken movement.[45]

The People's Movement for Freedom understandably became an obsession among government leaders from the latter half of the 1870s. Antigovernment slogans and demands threatened the political legitimacy of the Meiji leaders. The very modernization process that the political elite set in motion in every sector of the society was in jeopardy. Government policy, including education, could no longer be formulated without factoring in the reactionary threat of the Peoples' Movement for Freedom. A new era in the educational modernization process had emerged.

By mid-1877, the movement had reached a stage of development that enabled it to make demands focusing on voting rights that gained widespread attention. It naturally provoked increasing concern within government circles. The Peoples' Movement for Freedom also introduced into the arena of education a new factor that would come into play from the late 1870s into the next century. In America and Europe, with the rise of democratic ideology, the inevitable question concerning the role of politics in education in a modern state emerged. In essence, that is precisely what the Peoples' Movement for Freedom introduced into Japan. As an anti-government movement demanding voting rights and a national parliament to formulate laws governing the country, it was naturally perceived as a political movement. When it turned its attention to educational reform including curriculum matters, it was viewed by powerful government and Imperial Household figures as political intervention in public education. The resulting confrontation centered around the perplexing issue of the political neutrality of the public school classroom. And, of perhaps even greater significance, it inextricably included a critical question. Who should set the limits of political expression in the school, including teacher-training institutions where public school teachers were prepared at government expense. For the first time since the Meiji Restoration, the government was confronted with a new and potentially dangerous set of circumstances provoked by the Peoples' Movement for Freedom.

Unlike many government officials who reacted negatively to the Peoples' Movement for Freedom, Tanaka Fujimaro, responsible for national educational policy, took a decidedly different course. He concluded that under the prevailing social, political, and economic circumstances, the Gakusei could not be implemented effectively in its current form. A national standard for education set by the Ministry of Education had proven unfeasible. Local opposition movements, including the Peoples' Movement for Freedom, demonstrated that sufficiently to be taken seriously. Tanaka was convinced that something drastic had to be done promptly.

Continuing economic stagnation causing widespread rural poverty, as reported by his officials from the field, was also a compelling factor in Tanaka's reform plan. Accordingly, he sharply curtailed burdensome requirements placed on each community by the Ministry of Education, thereby exposing certain inconsistencies. Although school attendance requirements were significantly reduced, the decision-making power to do so remained a prerogative of the central government under Tanaka's plan. Even to this great champion of American education, there were limitations to educational decentralization.

Tanaka's plan also called for a reduction in required student attendance from four years under the Gakusei to sixteen months, with four months per year in school attendance. Although precise statistics are not available, it can be assumed that many children attended school at this rate under the existing regulations. Tanaka was pragmatically recognizing the reality of it. In addition, his proposal banned corporal punishment which provoked critics to characterize it as excessively free (*jiyū shugiteki*). Regulations governing private schools were also loosened, reflecting the demands of the Peoples' Movement for Freedom.[46]

Tanaka's plan for minimum curriculum requirements reflected what he considered as essential for a modern nation. The required courses were listed in order, beginning with reading, writing (calligraphy), mathematics, geography, history, and ending with morals.[47] As a preview of events to come, the priority of the courses provoked what can appropriately be characterized as the "great debate" on educational reform. Emperor Meiji, with the full force of the Imperial Household, would shortly react with unusual vehemence against placing morals education at the bottom of the curriculum in the public schools of the nation. To the critics, including not a few within the Ministry of Education itself such as the Confucianist Nishimura Shigeki, the ranking of courses proposed under Tanaka's plan was disturbingly indicative of the general trends underway in the modernization process that placed science above morals.

The Organization of Teachers

During this chaotic period in modern Japanese educational history, widespread interest among teachers and administrators in Tanaka's proposed educational law increased. After all, the reforms were not only controversial but they also would significantly affect both teachers and administrators. Tanaka, promoting the liberal reforms that placed more responsibility for educational decision making at the local level, encouraged teachers and administrators to organize local meetings in order to discuss his proposals.[48]

Within this environment, activist public school teachers inevitably became attracted to the Peoples' Movement for Freedom then expanding its activities, precisely as Tanaka Fujimaro drew up his educational reform plans. As part of the freedom movement, a faction of the organization led by teachers called for freedom of education, freedom from governmental control, and diversity in education. It pointedly resembled the goals and purposes of Tanaka's education law. One of the major demands made at meetings of teachers under the guise of "educational conferences" or "teachers' conferences" (kyōiku shūkai) concerned local autonomy. It was argued that the decision-making power to determine local school curricula should be made the responsibility of the teacher. Such demands as freedom of the curriculum (kyōsoku no jiyūka) began to circulate throughout the nation.[49] Support among concerned teachers for Tanaka's liberal reform proposals contained in his Kyōiku Rei followed naturally.

In hindsight, the meetings of activist teachers, including others interested in education, whether politically, academically, or professionally motivated, formed the nucleus of Japan's first education associations in the modern era. They fell into three general categories.[50] The first involved administrators and those in educational finance who often met in prefectural offices or local teacher training schools. Frequently sponsored by prefectural educational offices, they dealt primarily with administrative and financial repercussions of the proposed reforms.

The second category of local educational meetings focused on teaching methods. This topic attracted regular teachers interested in the new methodology, developed by Pestalozzi, being introduced at the Tokyo Teacher Training School under the influence of Isawa Shūji and Takamine Hideo. Motivated teachers were eager to discuss the new methodology with like-minded colleagues.

The third type involved educational research projects sponsored by local teachers. Spontaneously organized at local areas, several teachers simply got together to discuss the results of their personal research projects. Teachers from nearby schools were invited to participate for broader representation. As the group matured, bylaws and regulations were drawn up incorporating official membership. In effect, an education association had been formed with scheduled monthly meetings of teachers reporting research results as well as other topics facing teachers. Eventually, and inevitably, as the Peoples' Movement for Freedom grew, its political views on education were presented by activist teachers at some of the meetings, thereby inserting political topics into the meetings.

An example of the development of teacher organizations at this time took place with the Tokyo Education Society (Tokyo Kyōiku Kai). This group included local education officers along with classroom teachers headquartered in an elementary school in Nihonbashi, located in downtown Tokyo. About seventy members met every month to hear pertinent lectures and reports followed by discussions. Through such voluntary associations a sense of teaching as a profession emerged among teachers during the latter half of the 1870s. Since the Tokyo Education Society developed into a national organization of teachers in the next decade, its fate will be pursued in the following chapter.

Modern Physical Education from America—Dr. George Leland

Meanwhile other significant educational developments were taking place in the late 1870s. The primary issue of the period centered around the all-consuming controversial educational reforms instigated by Tanaka Fujimaro. However Tanaka's attraction to American education as a model for Japan went well beyond his concern for administrative reform of the Gakusei. His broad interests not only demonstrated Tanaka's approach to modern education but they also revealed how interpersonal relationships between Japanese and westerners in the 1870s contributed to the modernization of Japanese education.

Tanaka had taken a special interest in physical education in American schools. Since Japan's new public school system was dominated by ex-samurai from the warrior class who underwent military training in their youth, including Tanaka himself, it was natural that some form of physical training be included in the new schools. The Gakusei of 1872 alluded to it. It was also included in a Ministry of Education publication in 1874 based on a French Ministry of Education publication. Nevertheless, modern methods in physical education had not yet reached Japan, which concerned Tanaka.[51]

During Tanaka's trips to America in 1872 and again in 1876, he expressed an interest in the physical education program conducted at Amherst College in Massachusetts. He had consulted with William Clark, who, as a graduate of Amherst introduced him to the head of the physical education department.[52] The main features of the Amherst system that appealed to Tanaka during his visits were the "light form of calisthenics, performed in a single class, every student compelled to take it . . . that everybody came and joined in the exercises, which moved in a most pleasing manner to music, occupying mind and muscle alike." This approach to physical education set Amherst College apart as the first college in America to include physical education in its required curriculum under a newly formed department with a well-equipped gymnasium on its campus. It was a pioneer in the application of physical culture as a foundation for the future health and mental strength of the Amherst graduate.[53]

On the second visit to Amherst in 1876, during a side trip from the Philadelphia Centennial, Tanaka discussed with the head of the department the possibility of hiring a specialist in physical education. Upon his return to Japan, he made a formal request as director of the Ministry of Education to President Julius Seelye of Amherst College for a physical education teacher to introduce the subject to Japan. The series of communications between the two reveal how Japanese officials relied on Americans to fill their special educational requirements.

> Monbusho
> Tokio, Nippon
> 6th March 11th year of Meiji (1878)
> Rev. Julius M. Seelye
> President of Amherst College,
> Dear Sir:
>
> When I visited you at Amherst while I was in America two years ago, I had great pleasure of seeing by your kindness the gymnastics exercises of students of your College, in which I was very much interested. Since I have returned home, I had often seen the exercises in our school, but in Japan the modes in which they are taught are not complete yet, and in addition to this, they are sometimes taught in irregular orders, and therefore any remarkable benefits can not be obtained from the exercises. I thought therefore that, to develop the said art hereafter in Japan should be an important point on Education, and I came to the conclusion that, I would employ from America to our Department of Education an experienced and skilful instructor of the gymnastic to let him teach the exercises to male and female students of our schools, colleges and other educational institutions, in a proper manner according to their ages, and I take the liberty of writing to ask you to find for me a good and competent instructor of the art, for I believe you have the most excellent system of the exercises in your College, though I am exceedingly sorry to trouble you in this matter, and if you be kind enough to do so, I shall be very much obliged to you.[54]

An indication of the close relationship that the Japanese head of the Ministry of Education, Tanaka Fujimaro, officially the senior vice minister, had developed with the president of Amherst College followed within three months. A letter from Tanaka to Seelye reveals that the American college president had acted promptly on Tanaka's request.

> 15th Aug. 11th year of Meiji (1878)
> Rev. J. H. Seelye
> Dear Sir:
>
> I have acknowledged the receipt of your favor dated June 3rd 1878, wherein you informed me that you have selected for an instructor of the gymnastic exercises for which I asked you in my letter of the 6th March Mr. George A. Leland a graduate of your College and Doctor of Medicine who was very kind to accept the position of the gymnastic instructor in Japan offered by you.[55]

As a result of these negotiations initiated by Tanaka, Dr. George A. Leland, graduate of Amherst College and Harvard University medical department with a medical degree, was chosen for the assignment in Japan. In his own words, he was hired as "instructor in gymnastics and physical culture."[56] Leland was exceptionally qualified for the position. During his undergraduate days at Amherst he was the "gym captain" during all four years. He also participated in the preparation of *A Manual of Gymnastic Exercises*. When the offer to introduce physical education methods in Japan was received in 1878, he had already completed his medical degree from Harvard College and was serving as a physician in the Boston City Hospital in the department for nervous and renal disease.[57] As it turned out, Dr. George Leland was the right man at the right place at the right time when he agreed to join the Japanese Ministry of Education. With his new bride, he arrived in Japan in September 1878.

Leland's two-year contract, to be extended by one year, stipulated that he introduce American-style physical education (*taisō kyōiku*) to the Japanese. At the instigation of Tanaka, the Ministry of Education opened a physical education training facility (*taisō denshūjo*) in Tokyo in November under the directorship of Isawa Shūji, who was serving concurrently as president of the Tokyo Teacher Training School. Dr. Leland was appointed as the chief instructor.[58] Fortunately for him, Isawa had spent several years in America in the New England area and exhibited great interest in physical education, supporting Leland in his endeavors. With the head of the Ministry of Education and the president of the elite Tokyo Teacher Training College behind him, Leland found himself in a unique position to set modern standards of physical education in Japan as he had learned them in America.

Dr. Leland introduced physical education methods to his Japanese students that he had learned not only at Amherst but also at Harvard University. The purpose of physical exercise was considered part of an overall regimen for good health.[59] In contrast to the military-type training then associated with physical education, which Leland rejected, he taught free-standing calisthenics new to the Japanese. His specially selected students in training to become physical education teachers were "drilled in the old '74 [Amherst class of 1874] dumb-bell exercise, including the Anvil Chorus, in clubs, wands, rings, and in the various exercises on the usual heavy apparatus. They were also instructed by lectures in anatomy, physiology, hygiene and the theory and principles of physical culture."[60] His translator turned out to be Tsuboi Gendo, the same official who translated for Marion Scott when he introduced elementary teachings methods from San Francisco at the Tokyo Teacher Training School in 1872.

In 1879, when the principal of the Tokyo Teacher Training School, Isawa Shūji, and his vice principal, Takamine Hideo, revised the curriculum of the school, Leland's new physical education course was formally included in the new curriculum for teachers.[61] The reforms initiated by Isawa and Takamine were based on modern Pestalozzian theories of education. Leland's course, consequently, became an integral part of a major effort to modernize teacher training on the American model. Although it provoked criticism from military interests who argued that military-style physical training was superior, Dr. Leland taught Isawa's students, as well as the students at the new Tokyo Girls Teacher Training School, how to teach physical education in elementary schools. He also taught physical education at the elite preparatory school for Tokyo University, the Daigaku Yobimon, referred to in his *Chronicles* article.

At the end of the first academic year in which Dr. Leland was employed, Tanaka Fujimaro reported on his progress to Amherst College President Seelye, who had been instrumental in selecting Leland for the position. He was clearly pleased.

> Tokio, Nippon. 10th April 1879
> Prof. J. H. Seelye
> Dear Sir:
>
> With regard to Dr. G. A. Leland who was engaged by your kindness last year in the Department of Education for an instructor of the gymnastic exercises, I am very glad to inform you that since he has arrived in Japan he was attending diligently to the proper duties of his position and proved a good and able instructor. Immediately after his arrival, he commenced to teach the male and female students of the Tokio Normal School and female Normal School both under the direct control of this Department. He was very successful in it and by his kind and good conduct, some progress was made in their exercises, which the students liked best and are attending to diligently. This is quite in accordance with the expectations of this Department. The Department of Education has established a new school of the gymnastics under its direct control for the purpose to educate the students by the support of the government expense for the teachers of the gymnastics and to send them after graduation to the different parts of the country to teach in colleges and schools and to lay by this means the foundation for promotion of Physical Education. A new building for that school was lately completed and twenty five students were admitted into it after examinations, and their instruction was commenced by Dr. Leland and his assistants. I trust and hope therefore that, in some future time there will be a remarkable improvement and progress of Physical Education in Japan. It is to be indebted to your careful selection for us of an instructor that such good results as I have just mentioned will be obtained in future.
> Your Obedient servant,
> Tanaka Fujimaro[62]

The new building referred to in Tanaka's letter included a modern gymnasium based on the Amherst gymnasium. A novel feature recommended by Leland was an attached bathhouse, which apparently had great appeal to the Japanese. In a revealing offhand comment in a letter written by him, he described the new gymnasium as "just like the Barret [Amherst College gymnasium] only a little newer and better."[63] In other words, the Japanese now had one of the finest gymnasiums in the world, a remarkable achievement for a country that had discarded feudalism a decade earlier.

An important legacy of Leland was his textbook on the *New Physical Education* (*Shinsen Taisōsho*), which was translated by Tsuboi and widely used throughout Japan.[64] The title page revealed that it was "a translation of lectures and practical exercises given at the Physical Training School by Dr. George Leland from the city of Boston in America."[65] Leland's text included many illustrations of the recommended physical exercises. It also included cuts of the apparatus he introduced in his courses—light dumb-bells, wands, Indian clubs, rings, bean bags, and crowns.

Under Leland's guidance, American-style physical education originally developed at Amherst College gradually spread throughout Japan. It became part of the official curriculum of the modern public school system in the late 1870s and early 1880s. In a speech at the Amherst College centennial, a distinguished Japanese scholar who studied at Amherst, Kanda Naibu, paid tribute to Dr. Leland as "the founder of physical education in our schools, which has had such a far reaching influence in building our rising generation."[66]

With the introduction of physical education from the United States into Japan in 1879, coincidentally the end of the second era of American influence came to a controversial end at the same time. The primary advocate of American practices in education, Tanaka Fujimaro, had become locked in an epic battle during the spring of 1879 with the Imperial Household over the future course of modern education in Japan. His abrupt removal as head of the Ministry of Education brought to a sudden end the Tanaka era in modern Japanese educational history, from 1873 to 1879, with its close connections to the American model. It also denotes the beginning of a reverse course in educational reform from 1880 to 1885. Because the outcome was of such enormous consequence, the following chapter is devoted to the series of historical events that transpired in the process.

PART III

THE SECOND DECADE OF MODERN EDUCATION, 1880s

Reaction against the Western Model

"The Imperial Will on Education"

MORALS VERSUS SCIENCE EDUCATION,
1879–1880

In the spring of 1879, Tanaka Fujimaro's grand design to modernize Japanese education on the American model hung in the balance. In spite of widespread opposition from the Imperial Household, conservative government leaders, and senior Ministry of Education officials, it was carefully structured to respond to the political, economic, and social complexities of the nation about to enter the second decade of the modern era as Tanaka understood them. Titled simply the Kyōiku Rei, the Educational Law, the revisions were sufficiently broad to consider it the Second National Plan for Education since the Meiji Restoration. Tanaka, as director of the Ministry of Education, had submitted his emotionally charged proposal to the government a year earlier on May 14, 1878.[1] The first formal step in a prolonged and highly contentious approval process was finally under way.

The procedure involved a review and approval by the Political Bureau, the Hōsei Kyoku, before submission to the Genrōin, the supreme governmental body. Final approval of the emperor was required.[2] As it turned out, the initial review by the Political Bureau was critical simply because the head was none other than the increasingly powerful figure Itō Hirobumi. Tanaka was fortunate that this influential statesman of modern Japan, empowered to reject or approve proposed bills, had already acquired formidable credentials within the government as Naimukyo, the minister of the interior.

Unexpectedly, on the day that Tanaka's proposal was submitted to Itō's office, a major government leader and member of the original oligarchy of four, Ōkubo Toshimichi, was assassinated. The tragic event provoked confusion among the remaining political leadership. Within the previous nine months, three of the four original senior leaders of the 1868 Meiji Restoration had passed from the scene. Saigo Takamori committed suicide at the end of the Seinan War. Kido Takayoshi died due to illness. With the unexpected death of Ōkubo, a leadership vacuum was created within a relatively short period. Since Itō Hirobumi was among the senior leadership alliance moving inexorably into a position of increased power, a delay in his attention to Tanaka's educational proposal was inevitable during the political turmoil.

Finally, at the beginning of the following year, 1879, Itō carefully reviewed Tanaka's draft proposal submitted eight months previously. He was well aware of the controversial nature of the content as well as the turbulent state of affairs within Japanese society. In regular consultation with Tanaka, Itō streamlined the provisions by reducing their number from 78 to 49. In evidence of his commitment to educational modernization, Itō then personally shaped the final revisions to meet the social and political exigencies of the time as he interpreted them.[3] These included the Jiyū Minken Undō, the Peoples' Movement for Freedom that had become increasingly active, pressing the government for political rights. Student attendance at the new public schools was low and dropout rates high. And the national budget for education had been severely curtailed to pay the costs for the Seinan military conflict, placing a crushing burden on peasant families to finance local schools.[4]

The Political Bureau under Itō formally approved Tanaka's proposed reforms on February 20, 1879. The draft proposal, from then on referred to as the Hōsei An, technically the Political Bureau Proposal, arrived before the Dajōkan and on to the Genrōin on April 22.[5] Itō's stamp of approval provided a powerful impetus. The significance of his personal involvement in this very sensitive and controversial reform of Japanese education must not be underestimated. As we shall see, Tanaka was held responsible for the negative consequences of his far-reaching attempt to modernize Japanese education, which sparked an intense conflict over the future of Japanese society. But Itō Hirobumi, who was to become the most powerful politician of the Meiji Era, not only fully supported the provisions based on the American model but he also helped mold them into the final version. By now they had literally become the Tanaka-Itō educational reforms.

Among the major provisions of the bill, only the following are included here since they lie at the heart of the great debate that engulfed the Tanaka-Itō proposal of 1879. Deceptively simple, they nevertheless represented intractable differences in the first great confrontation over the modernization of Japanese education since the Meiji Restoration of 1868.

The Second National Plan for Education: The Education Law of 1879

1. The Minister of Education is responsible for the educational affairs of the country.
2. The basic curriculum of the elementary school will include reading, calligraphy, mathematics, geography, history, and morals (*shūshin*). Depending on local conditions physical education, singing (*shōka*), science, etc. may be added.
3. Each community shall be responsible for organizing a public elementary school administered (*kanri*) by a committee (*gakumuin*) elected by the citizens of the community.
4. Each local public school will design its own curriculum subject to the approval of the Ministry of Education.
5. The elementary school will consist of an eight-year course. However, depending on local circumstances it may be reduced to four years with a minimum of four months of schooling per year.
6. Minimum attendance for each child during school age between 6 and 14 years old will continue for 16 months.

7. Private schools may be freely opened. The curriculum must be reported to the prefectural education office.[6]

The relevant committee of the highest governmental organ, the Genrōin, initiated deliberations on the proposal on May 20, 1879, precisely one year after Tanaka submitted it for approval. Chosen to represent the Ministry of Education in defense of the bill along with Tanaka, director of the ministry, was another senior official, Tsuji Shinji.[7] There is a certain irony in the selection of Tsuji for this assignment since he had served in the office of the newly organized ministry in 1871 under Mitsukuri Rinshō, which drew up the original Gakusei. The proposed bill he was now defending before the Genrōin was specifically designed to replace the historic plan he figured prominently in formulating years earlier. Tsuji's original involvement in designing the Gakusei may have been the reason why he was selected by Tanaka to represent the ministry in the deliberations, in effect signaling his approval of the demise of the First National Plan for Education.

Also present at the subcommittee sessions, serving as the committee chairman, was Kōno Togama.[8] At this time Kōno had little relationship with educational matters except indirectly as chairman of the Genrōin committee considering Tanaka's proposed bill. During the deliberations he made no comments that were carried in the official minutes to indicate his personal persuasion on the provocative issues under review. Nevertheless, within one year Kōno would assume the position of minister of education, replacing Tanaka as the head of the ministry, such were the unfavorable conditions surrounding Tanaka's proposal.

Between May 20 and June 25, 1879, a total of eight subcommittee sessions were convened to deliberate the Kyōiku Rei on which Tanaka Fujimaro, with the full support of Interior Minister Itō Hirobumi, had staked his career.[9] During the careful deliberations, provocative questions were raised by committee members. For example, one of the primary concerns focused on the fundamental issue that divided the Ministry of Education itself: at what level of government, local or national, should the administrative control of the nation's public schools be sited?[10]

The other question, which in retrospect overshadowed all other issues, concerned the status of morals education under Tanaka's proposed education law. Members of the committee had to be fully aware of the ongoing controversy over the role of morals in the local curriculum. They were also acutely sensitive to the growing concern by Emperor Meiji and palace critics led by Motoda Nagazane over the seemingly inexorable decline of morals education in the nation's schools. For example, when Emperor Meiji returned from one of his lengthy trips to the Hokuriku-Tokai area in October of the previous year, as noted previously, he pointedly urged Iwakura to strengthen morals education.[11]

Moreover, a coterie of senior Ministry of Education officials was adamantly opposed to the ministry's bill. Overt opposition by ministry officers exposed the internal divisions that had split the educational bureaucracy. In spite of the fissures within his own bureaucracy, Tanaka reportedly took the opportunity during committee deliberations to boldly criticize members of the Imperial Household over their position on morals education. The emperor and his personal advisor Motoda, holding Tanaka responsible for the problems of education since the Gakusei, had already discussed his possible resignation.[12] It was all indicative of the intense effort to block Tanaka's educational revisions by the Imperial Household and its loyal supporters within government.

It was no secret, evidenced by the proposed law itself, that Tanaka as the senior official at the Ministry of Education, and Itō by his approval, lacked much concern over the perceived decline in morals education. In fact, Tanaka the secularist doubted whether morals education should be included in the curriculum at all.[13] Challenging the imperial position well known to both Tanaka and Itō, official sponsors of the bill, they nevertheless relegated the morals course to the bottom of the revised curriculum.

During the Genrōin deliberations, Tanaka steadfastly reacted negatively to the revisions concerning the morals course proposed by committee members. Minutes of the deliberations clarify the opposing positions.[14] The argument before the committee in defense of the supremacy of morals education in Japan's modern public school system mirrored the rationale of the Imperial Household. Every country in the world both in the East and West, it was reasoned, must transmit to its youth not only intellectual learning (chishiki) but also moral principles (shūshin). In Japan's modern school system, it was argued, there had been an overemphasis on the former to the neglect of the latter. The "eastern tradition" (tōyō no shūkan) represents the opposite. Japanese schools, therefore, must recognize the supreme importance of morals education by placing it at the top of the curriculum. It should be introduced in the public schools as a formal course from the first grade.

Tanaka's defense of his bill, sanctioned by the powerful Itō Hirobumi, clarified the essential difference between the modernists and traditionalists concerning the role of morals in the school system. In his testimony, Tanaka conceded that the teaching of moral principles has a limited role at the elementary school. However it should not be recognized as a core subject such as reading, writing, and arithmetic, he argued. He said that the primary responsibility for imparting moral principles to children lies in the home with the parents, not with the teacher at school. Although the motion for revision was defeated after much discussion, Tanaka's success was, it later turned out, temporary. The bill was passed with minor changes on June 25, 1879, with Kōno Togama presiding.[15]

In reaction to the deliberations that took place within the Genrōin committee on the Tanaka proposal, a meeting of powerful figures occurred immediately afterward. On June 26, Iwakura Tomomi, imperial confidant and a former court noble who occupied one of the most powerful positions in government, met with the emperor to discuss the proposed education ordinance. The emperor expressed his deep concern over morals education. Emperor Meiji then informed his illustrious guest that he was about to take action. He was personally planning to formulate an imperial viewpoint on the state of morals education in the nation's schools.[16] It is now known that a position paper was under preparation within the Imperial

Household destined to drastically change the course of educational modernization in Japan.

Following the Genrōin committee sessions in June 1879, and before any further official action was taken, the Japanese government prepared a gala reception for a visiting friend from America, Ulysses S. Grant, president of the United States from 1868 to 1876. During an around-the-world tour Grant stopped in Japan for a month-long visit. His tenure as president had occurred precisely when Japanese-American contacts first developed into a cordial relationship that were greatly enhanced by him. The Japanese deeply appreciated the American president's policies toward their country during his term in office. Tanaka Fujimaro, representing the Ministry of Education, had met President Grant on two visits to the White House during Grant's tenure, once with the Iwakura Mission in 1872 and again in 1876 at the conclusion of the Philadelphia Centennial. The *Tokio Times* reported that on July 8, 1879, "a gorgeous festival was arranged for him [Grant] in the great hall of the Kobu Dai Gaku [the Imperial College of Engineering]. This was really a superb display and quite a new departure on account of the large throng of Japanese ladies."[17]

During Grant's visit to Japan, he experienced an unusual act of hospitality by Iwakura Tomomi, titular head of government. It was Iwakura's way of repaying the kindnesses extended during the Iwakura Mission to Washington in 1872. It also illustrates how by chance ancient customs of Japan survived the rush to modernize. It seems that during Iwakura's prolonged visit to the West, he was impressed by how governments in Europe used opera to entertain foreign diplomatic guests. Seeking a similar form of Japanese entertainment, he looked to the classical Noh theater that had been neglected by the Meiji modernizers as a highly ritualistic relic from the feudal past. He first arranged a Noh performance in his home in 1876 for the emperor and empress dowager. In an act of personal diplomacy, he invited Grant to his home in 1879 to enjoy the Noh performance, helping to rescue a Japanese artistic legacy from the path of modernization.[18]

After President Grant's visit, which preoccupied the government, Tanaka Fujimaro continued pressing for final approval of his education bill that at the last stage required imperial endorsement. By the end of July 1879, no word was forthcoming from the palace. Finally, at the end of the summer of 1879, the Imperial Household reacted officially and forcefully. Emperor Meiji issued one of the most important documents in modern Japanese educational history. It was simply titled "Kyōgaku Seishi," henceforth referred to as "The Imperial Will on Education."[19] A great debate on the future of modern education in Meiji Japan was, as a consequence, set in motion.

The 1879 "Imperial Will on Education"

The importance of "The Imperial Will on Education" of 1879 is such that the setting from which it emerged must be clarified before it can be fully appreciated. Its place in modern Japanese education cannot be overestimated. First, it initiated the first major confrontation over the course of educational modernization since the Meiji Restoration, setting Emperor Meiji against government policy carried out in his name. Second, it inserted the Imperial Household directly into policy decisions governing the new public school system. And finally, it sparked the great debate over the future course of educational modernization, the outcome of which profoundly influenced Japanese education and society into the middle of the twentieth century.

The most contentious issue between the western-oriented progressives and the eastern-oriented traditionalists was brought into play by Tanaka Fujimaro's intransigent position, fully endorsed by Itō Hirobumi, that relegated morals education to the bottom of the public school curriculum.[20] The controversy that ensued over morals education in the schools for the 1880s concerned nothing less than the very essence of Japanese culture in the modern world. Precisely which elements of Japanese values and customs, in particular those related to imperial ideology, should be passed on to succeeding generations in the nation's modern public schools? Beyond that profound issue was an equally vexing question: Who would be empowered to make the critical choices?

Although the debate took place during several weeks in mid-1879, it had become inevitable ever since the overthrow of the Tokugawa government over a decade earlier. Those forces seeking to modernize Japanese society through western science and technology were locked in a struggle with their opponents who believed that Japanese culture could only survive on the basis of traditional customs and beliefs. The new public school system provided the venue for a direct confrontation between these two powerful forces

Motoda Nagazane, the emperor's senior advisor and personal tutor on Confucianism, was the author of "The Imperial Will on Education." Thus his philosophical position in the development of modern Japanese education is of major importance. First, he held a strategic position within the very top echelon of the society where the major decisions were being made for the destiny of the country. Not only was he opposed to the direction that western-oriented decision makers were following but he was also well aware of his influence as a father-figure to the youthful emperor who officially had to approve those decisions. As a senior advisor to the emperor meeting with him on an intimate basis, lecturing to him as his personal tutor, and working with him in the same household privy to the reforms under consideration, Motoda realized that he had a privileged opportunity to influence the course of modern Japanese history. He was convinced that it was his destiny to do so.

Moreover, Motoda held an unwavering conviction that he had the solution to the problems Japanese society and his beloved emperor were facing following the overthrow of the Tokugawa regime and the social disruptions that ensued. The proper resolution could only be found in the age-old but time-tested tenants of the venerable Confucian classics in which Motoda was well versed, and to which he was devoted. To Motoda, Japanese society based on the enlightened rule of the emperor, where those who governed and those they governed understood and respected their mutually beneficial relationships, could best meet the challenges

Figure 25. Motoda Nagazane. From Warren Smith, *Confucianism in Modern Japan* (Tokyo: Hokuseido Press, 1959), 56.

of the new era. Motoda was, consequently, not only in a strategic position as personal advisor to the emperor where the momentous problems facing the country were ultimately considered, he was convinced that he could solve them. He took advantage on every occasion to do just that.

As a result of his position and the ability to utilize it effectively, Motoda Nagazane stands out from among all others as the leading figure opposing western trends engulfing his country during the 1870s. It was Motoda Nagazane more than any other individual who not only defined traditional Japanese moral values for the modern school system but was also instrumental in creating a new value system for Japan. Through his tireless efforts he amalgamated ancient Chinese and Japanese classical thought by positioning the Japanese imperial system within the Confucian construct, all in the name of Emperor Meiji.

Born in 1818 as a samurai in the southern town of Kumamoto, Motoda was educated in the usual manner of a samurai. He became a devoted follower of and authority on Confucius and the Chinese classics. After years of service for his clan, he was sent to Tokyo on clan affairs, where he was soon appointed to the Imperial Household in 1868, shortly after the Meiji Restoration. He had one supreme goal: to teach Emperor Meiji about the superiority of Confucius teachings. By 1871 he had the opportunity to fulfill his wishes, beginning a twenty-year career as personal tutor to the emperor on Confucianism. He would capitalize on the position to offer imperial advice that ranged far beyond Confucian virtues.

Confucianism, as Motoda lectured the emperor, "provides a complete guide in the relationships of daily life. It is the perfection of natural philosophy. It gives the individual self-control and the country peace." Motoda passionately believed that evil could be overcome by "placing all power in the hands of an absolutely autocratic emperor. . . . A ruler of such character would inevitably draw out the best side of his subjects." To attain that exalted state, he was convinced that if he were able to expound on Confucianism to Emperor Meiji, Japan would then be led by one of "faultless character."[21]

Motoda's initial lecture to the emperor on Confucianism took place in June 1871, one year prior to the First National Plan for Education, the Gakusei, which introduced western teachings and methods in education. He was then fifty-three years old.[22] His royal student was still a teenager. During the decade of the 1870s, while the Ministry of Education under Tanaka Fujimaro became engrossed in the implementation of a school system patterned after western models in the name of Emperor Meiji, Motoda presented a long series of private lectures to the emperor that stressed, among other things, the most important consideration about the future direction of Japanese education: "Education is much discussed now. We are told that it has three divisions styled respectively mental, moral, and physical. I submit however that this classification is western and unsuitable to Japan. A system of education suitable to Japan can be found in Confucius, nowhere else."[23]

Motoda then seized upon the opportunity to criticize directly to the emperor the western trends under way. "Japan promises to become exclusively an imitator of Europe and America, and all because we lack a sense of proportion in determining the aims of education. We must go back to the fundamentals at once."[24] Motoda's provocative document, "The Imperial Will on Education," was specifically aimed at achieving that goal by reversing the course of modern education on the western model. Ideologically driven, Motoda expressed his position to the emperor in plain terms. "The chief subject of study must be, of course, Confucius."[25] From Motoda's perspective, it was not, therefore, western science and mathematics that should dominate the curriculum of the modern public school system, as the great progressives of the period such as Tanaka Fujimaro advocated.

As a member of the Imperial Household, Motoda was fully aware of the policy decisions affecting the future of the nation's schools. What he witnessed year after year, as the revolutionary educational reforms of the Gakusei were implemented under Tanaka Fujimaro with the potential to destroy the social fabric, appalled him. He became convinced that the political and educational leaders of the nation were navigating the Japanese ship of state toward catastrophic disaster. Motoda was determined to use his influence on the young Emperor Meiji through the strategic role as his personal tutor to redirect the course of history.

A prolific writer, Motoda by temperament remained not only consistent but persistent throughout his life. Among his writings, his basic position was outlined in a document entitled *The Theory of National Education* (*Kokkyō Ron*) written at a

later date, in 1884. It was straightforward. The Japanese people could best be prepared to meet the challenges of the future only if they were securely anchored in
the past. He then divided education into two parts: learning (*gakumon*) and morality
(*dōtoku*). Supreme learning is found in Chinese literature and culture (*kangaku*), not
western science (*yōgaku*). Morality derives from Confucian precepts, not western
moral precepts. The advancement of the nation must be based on a national plan
for education that incorporates these fundamental principles. Ultimately modernism must be based firmly on traditional values as Motoda interpreted them.[26] He
never deviated from that moral mission.

Convinced of the superiority of Confucian teachings in meeting the inevitable
problems that Japan faced in the new era of industrialization, Motoda argued
forcefully for their unique role in the school. The cherished teachings of moral
principles contained therein would solidify and strengthen the nation for the
social and cultural revolution that modernization entails. To Motoda, westernization symbolized materialism based on technology and the teaching of scientific
information, facts, and figures. Traditional education based on the Chinese classics
meant to him the supremacy of the moral teachings of Confucius that delineated
hierarchical social relationships among individuals, and that between the emperor
and his people. The direct confrontation between modernization and tradition-
alism, then, was finally brought into focus by Motoda Nagazane a decade after
the Meiji Restoration in his resolute opposition to the educational reforms of Itō
Hirobumi and Tanaka Fujimaro.

The Imperial Tours: Emperor Meiji Visits the Classroom

The immediate provocation underlying the great debate over educational reform
grew out of a series of imperial visits to the countryside by Emperor Meiji from
1876, which Motoda seized upon to buttress his position. Surely one of the most
memorable scenes of the Meiji period were the spectacles of long imperial processions winding their slow and tortuous way over and around the spectacular
mountainous terrain and rushing rivers of rural Japan. These were not weekend
retreats from the palace in Tokyo to nearby Hakone. Rather they were well over
month-long imperial investigations to remote areas of the country by the emperor
and his retinue that reached into the hundreds.

The highly heralded events provided an opportunity for the young emperor
to learn firsthand the condition of his people, to present an image of the imperial
family as benevolently concerned with the hardships of rural Japan, and to display
the emperor as an enlightened leader during the modernization process under
way. It was also considered important that government leaders, including Ministry
of Education officers, participate. They then could gain a better understanding of
the consequences of their policies on the people confronting the changes that modernization entailed. Therefore school visits became an integral part of the itinerary,
enabling the emperor to observe firsthand how modernization was actually being
carried out in the classroom. He was, predictably, particularly interested in the role
of morals education under the new public school system.[27]

Table 12   The Imperial Tours, 1878

1876 June 2 (50 days)	Tōhoku—Hokkaido (230 members)
1878 August 31 (72 days)	Hokuriku—Tookaido (700 members)
1880 June 16 (38 days)	Yamanashi—Mie—Kyoto
1881 July 30 (74 days)	Yamagata—Akita—Hokkaido (350 members)

Source: Tōyama Shigeki, *Meiji Isshin to Tenno* (The Meiji Restoration and the Emperor) (Tokyo: Iwanami Shoten, 1992), 117.

A total of four imperial tours were conducted over a five-year period from 1876 to 1881, all during one internal crisis after another.[28] These included the Seinan War in the south, the rise of the Peoples' Movement for Freedom, and various other antigovernment protests that provoked political tensions.

The tours were also intended to help create a new image of the emperor then being forged by Motoda and others, which projected the imperial ideology as being at the historical center of the nation: that the emperor symbolized the unity of the Japanese people from ancient times. Since this interpretation runs counter to historical facts, notably during the Tokugawa period when the military shogunate ruled Japan overshadowing the imperial tradition, an effort was under way to construct a new interpretation of history. Consequently the provincial processions were calculated by some as an effort to forge a new image that "the people of the nation shared one history centering on the Imperial Household."[29]

In villages visited by the august imperial procession from Tokyo, the entire community was profoundly affected. It was indeed an unforgettable spectacle as "the grand procession radiantly ornamented with the imperial flag, the mounted officers, the shiny carriages, the trumpeters, the banners, the splendidly dressed honor guards, some of the highest officials in the land, scores of attendants of various ranks and functions, and, of course, the royal conveyance" passed through the tiny villages.[30] Although the government advised local community officials not to overdo their welcome ceremonies, many were eager to show the emperor new houses, new bridges, and new rest houses for their royal guests. Understandably it was considered by local officials a great honor to host the imperial entourage.[31]

From the educational perspective, the imperial tours took place during the critical period when the modernization policy underwent the great liberal influence of Tanaka Fujimaro as head of the Ministry of Education. The emperor, according to Motoda, became increasingly critical of the western reforms of Japanese education, particularly from America, in part from his firsthand classroom observations conducted during these trips.[32] During the imperial tours, Emperor Meiji and selected dignitaries visited public schools at every opportunity from the smallest village to the great metropolises. They observed classes in session from the elementary to the teacher-training level.

The classroom setting with the emperor of Japan in attendance created a highly formal and contrived atmosphere. Experienced teachers were chosen for demonstration classes. In some communities the top students from several schools were brought together for the royal lesson in order to present the best possible image to the emperor.[33] Students were, to be sure, on their best behavior, dressed in their finest clothes in front of the emperor of Japan. Regardless of the artificial atmosphere in the classroom, few other Japanese had the opportunity to visit local schools throughout the country as did Emperor Meiji, who witnessed firsthand how the initial decade of educational modernization was proceeding.

Motoda Nagazane shrewdly capitalized on the imperial tours for his moral cause. His writings revealed what transpired during visits to local schools as if he were present. Although this was not likely due to his age and the rigors of the exhaustive trips, he nevertheless realized the strategic importance of them. During the imperial classroom visits, according to Motoda, Emperor Meiji and his traveling companions observed the effects of the educational policies being carried out by the Ministry of Education under the guidance of Tanaka Fujimaro.[34] Officially, they were being implemented in the name of the emperor himself.

The imperial tour with particularly significant educational ramifications took place from August 31 to November 9, 1878. The long and arduous trip of two and a half months over the Japan Alps took Emperor Meiji and his entourage of seven hundred members to local communities in Nagano, Niigata, Toyama, Kanazawa, Fukui, Kyoto, and Nagoya. Included among the official delegation was no less than the titular head of government, Iwakura Tomomi, who had led the Iwakura Mission to the West in the early 1870s, on his second provincial tour with the emperor. In addition, other top officials, including Ōkuma Shigenobu, Inoue Kaoru, and, curiously, a ranking officer of the Japanese army, General Ōyama Iwao, joined the tour.[35]

Drawing from the school visits, Motoda chose a particular classroom observation of a simple nature to bolster his moralistic position. The obscure incident assumed historical importance since it subsequently became part of an educational crisis that provoked an imperial censure of the modernization process and the Meiji government itself. The example took place at a local elementary school classroom where several students were surely carefully chosen to display their ability in the use of English, considered a distinction of modern education. They carried on a dialogue in English. Emperor Meiji then asked the students to summarize in Japanese what they had just said in English. According to Motoda's memoirs, they could not. The emperor pressed the students further by asking them how the daily life of the Japanese people could benefit from the study of western ideas. This was a seemingly simple question with enormous implications that went to the very core of the educational reforms under consideration. Predictably, the students could not answer this profound imperial question. The emperor later reported to Motoda that a similar incident took place at another school.[36]

In this celebrated incident, the local elementary school students may have been tongue-tied before the intimidating presence of the emperor of Japan surrounded by his aides and local school officials in an extraordinary classroom setting. Or they may have simply memorized the English dialogue word for word without understanding the meaning. The first possibility was apparently never questioned either by Motoda or the emperor. Nevertheless, the event provoked critical historical repercussions. It was one of a number of similar experiences that took place during the imperial tours that proved to the powerful royal critics of modernization that the western educational reforms under way were not only superficial but also meaningless.

Beyond elementary education, further ammunition for the powerful skeptics from the Imperial Household was provided at the higher levels of education when the emperor paid a royal visit to Kanazawa Prefecture on one of the imperial tours. Arrangements were made for him to observe a classroom at the Kanazawa Teacher Training School where the new western methods of teaching science were being taught. The choice of a science lesson for the imperial audience had a notable importance since western science was then considered as the fundamental course of the modern curriculum being promoted by the Ministry of Education. At that time science courses used many English words and concepts foreign to the Japanese.

According to a report of the visit, two students presented in English the principles of the recently introduced telegraph as part of a demonstration lesson prepared for the emperor. One can assume that it was carefully rehearsed. As in the elementary school visit described above, the emperor then asked the students a poignant question. Could they elaborate in Japanese the gist of what they had just presented in English concerning one of the new techniques of communication imported from the West? They reportedly could not.[37]

The implication of this event was clear. Teacher trainees who could simply recite modern scientific concepts in a foreign language without comprehension would be incapable of effectively teaching them in the new public schools. It was simply further proof, verification if you will, to the emperor that the conditions of the schools were badly in need of reform from the elementary schools through the teacher training institutions; that the new educational reforms were not only ineffective but they were also dangerous to the future of the country by replacing moral education with the mere pretense of western scientific education.

The imperial visits became fundamental to Motoda's plan to reverse the direction of education reform. He now had verifiable evidence for his convictions and the support of Emperor Meiji. Motoda contended, however, that it was the other way around. He claimed in his memoirs that he was merely articulating the convictions of Emperor Meiji in "The Imperial Will on Education" that were conveyed personally to him and the court noble Iwakura Tomomi. It was, according to Motoda, the emperor himself who instructed his advisors within the Imperial Household, including Motoda, to seriously address this profound issue.[38]

The governmental procedure for approving legislation, requiring the emperor's ultimate approval, played directly into Motoda's hands. Therefore when

Tanaka submitted his final draft proposal, already mockingly dubbed the Freedom of Education Law (Jiyū Kyōiku Rei) to the Genrōin on May 14, 1878,[39] the Imperial Household simultaneously undertook a review of the contents. Tanaka's explosive draft wound itself painfully through the governmental bureaucracy for over a year. While waiting for imperial reaction to Tanaka's beleaguered education law, officials both pro and con were fully aware of the imperial reservations about morals education in the proposal.

At last, before the emperor officially acted on Tanaka Fujimaro's Second National Plan for Education, the Imperial Household circulated "The Imperial Will on Education," one of the most important documents in modern Japanese history. Written by Motoda Nagazane, the document entitled "Kyōgaku Seishi" was intended as the imperial response to Tanaka's bill. On September 10, 1879, it was presented to the hastily appointed minister of education, Terashima Munenori, who had just unceremoniously replaced Tanaka Fujimaro as head of the ministry.[40]

The official title of this document is of significance in itself. "Kyōgaku Seishi" literally translates as "the sacred words concerning education." The use of "sacred" (*sei*) refers in this context to the words of the emperor. Accordingly the title has been translated as "The Imperial Will on Education" rather than the literal "sacred words on education." The former reflects the true meaning and intent of Emperor Meiji and his advisor Motoda Nagazane.

After fifteen months of government delay, the emperor had finally acted decisively against the educational policies during the Meiji Restoration carried out in his name. Indicative of the importance he placed on the document, he met with Itō Hirobumi, then holding the powerful position as minister of the interior (Naimukyo). A copy of "The Imperial Will on Education," the first document on education ever issued under the name of the emperor,[41] was presented to Itō in the palace. He was advised by the emperor to compare the concepts contained therein with Tanaka's proposed education law that Itō had personally sanctioned.[42] The implication was clear. "The Imperial Will" should take precedence. Motoda's provocative document in the name of the emperor was unmistakably intended as an imperial stamp of disapproval of Tanaka's proposed reforms. Although purportedly reflecting the will of Emperor Meiji, whether he instigated the powerful statement emanating from the imperial household or whether he endorsed Motoda's ideas is an intriguing question whose answer remains elusive. Nevertheless, the ultimate influence of this document, not generally appreciated at the time, was incalculable.

The importance of "The Imperial Will on Education" stems from the fact that it ignited a powerful reactionary movement against the modernization and westernization of Japanese education then spreading guardedly through the nation's schools. Moreover, it marks the first formal step in the process of integrating traditional moral values in the new school system as interpreted by the Imperial Household through Motoda. And, of the ultimate significance, the essential precepts incorporated in Motoda's "The Imperial Will on Education" of 1879 ultimately reemerged in the form of "The Imperial Rescript on Education" in 1890.[43] "The Imperial Rescript on Education," in turn, represents one of the most contentious documents of modern Japan, and is the focus of the final chapter of this book. Because of its historical significance, as well as its brevity, a well-known English translation of "The Imperial Will on Education" is reproduced here in its entirety, beginning with Part I of the two-part document.[44]

Imperial Will on Education
Part I
The Great Principles of Education
(Kyōgaku Taishi)
By Motoda Nagazane

The essence of education, our traditional national aim, and a watchword for all men, is to make clear the ways of benevolence, justice, loyalty, and filial piety, and to master knowledge and skills and through these to pursue the Way of Man. In recent days people have gone to extremes. They take unto themselves a foreign civilization whose only values are fact-gathering and technique, thus violating the rules of good manners and bringing harm to our customary ways. Although we set out to take in the best features of the West, and bring in new things in order to achieve the high aims of the Meiji Restoration—abandonment of the undesirable practices of the past and learning from the outside world— this procedure had a serious defect. It reduced benevolence, justice, loyalty, and filial piety to a secondary position. The danger of indiscriminate emulation of western ways is that in the end our people will forget the great principles governing the relations between ruler and subject, and father and son. Our aim, based on our ancestral teachings, is solely the clarification of benevolence, justice, loyalty, and filial piety. For morality, the study of Confucius is the best guide. People should cultivate sincerity and moral conduct, and after that they should turn to the cultivation of the various subjects of learning in accordance with their ability. In this way, morality and technical knowledge will fall into their proper places. When our education comes to be grounded on Justice and the Doctrine of the Mean, we shall be able to show ourselves proudly throughout the world as a nation of independent spirit.

The ramifications of the 1879 imperial censure of the modernization of Japanese education extend far beyond the realm of education itself. With the emperor endorsing the document, the indefatigable Motoda Nagazane effectively projected the imperial institution directly into the growing controversy over the direction of national educational policy after a decade of imperial rule. By this time the emperor was in his late twenties, and mature enough to appreciate the highly provocative nature of the document in his name as a condemnation of the first decade of Meiji education. In essence, his seal signaled imperial rejection of official government policy for the modernization of Japanese education and, implicitly, Japanese society itself.

This concise statement deserves recognition as the single most important document that redefines the purposes of education since the modern era had begun a decade previously. It contrasts sharply with the purposes of education as defined and implemented by the government based on western models in the name of the emperor ever since the First National Plan for Education of the early 1870s. It marks, therefore, the first serious schism between the emperor and his government vis-à-vis modern educational policy.

The common understanding on both sides of the great debate, that the major purpose of education was the preservation of the sovereign state of Japan in the modern era, was not at issue. Indeed Motoda referred to it directly as the need to spread the "spirit of our country's independence" (*wagakuni dokuritsu no seishin*). However, his resolute opposition to the methods employed to achieve that goal were unmistakably spelled out. Western science and technology, referred to as "knowledge" (*chishiki*), have relegated eastern morality of Confucian teachings along with the imperial tradition to an inferior position in the schools. If continued, the bias toward western materialism in the name of modernization would lead the nation to ruin. Educational reform must be enacted so that the imbalances are reversed to reflect the supremacy of Confucian moral teachings intertwined with the respect for the imperial tradition.

To fully appreciate the determination, bordering on dogmatism, of Motoda in fulfilling his single mission in life, an accounting of the repetition of key words and concepts in "The Imperial Will on Education" is compelling. Within such a brief statement the insertion of the cherished Confucian principles of benevolence, justice, loyalty, and filial piety (*jingi chūkō*) as the foundation of education in three of the five sentences is calculated. In addition, the name of Confucius is included once, perhaps to make certain the reader does not miss the main thrust. There are also two direct references to the imperial tradition and three to the central theme of the need for Confucian morals versus knowledge and technology from the West. Obviously it was not the imbalance between eastern (morals) and western (knowledge) teachings in contemporary education to which Motoda objected. Rather, he was determined to shift the imbalance in the opposite direction. "The Imperial Will on Education" consequently signifies the opening scene of a reverse-course policy in the modernization of Japanese education.

Leading dissidents of the liberal educational reforms under way, led by Motoda, resolutely believed that rather than replace traditional moral values and teachings in the modern school, they should be more deeply implanted. It was not that Japanese cultural values were inappropriate for the industrialization process that would enable Japan to take its proper place among modern societies. On the contrary, influential critics epitomized by Motoda argued that all Japanese children attending the new schools should be more deeply ingrained with indigenous cultural patterns. And those patterns were based on Confucian moral principles of loyalty and filial piety. Simply stated, the modernization of Japan should be thoroughly grounded on a deeper commitment to, and a common appreciation of, the importance of Japanese cultural institutions.

In modern parlance, the process of modernization taking place in the 1870s provoked a major identity crisis within Japanese society. What did it mean to be Japanese in the modern world? If all Japanese children were required to attend school, what should they be taught about their own culture? The crusade led by Tanaka Fujimaro to introduce western science and technology through the new curricula and textbooks provoked deep concern within Motoda and like-minded critics. Among other factors, they feared that western values of the Christian faith could be passed on to Japanese youth.[45] As Japanese society inevitably confronted the changes brought about by the industrialization process, the issue of what commonly accepted indigenous moral beliefs could bind the people together arose. And most important, the question of who would be empowered to make the proper answers to these all-embracing questions became central to the controversy.

Motoda also employed the encounter during an imperial visit to the countryside between Emperor Meiji and several of his youthful subjects in the elementary classroom to include an addendum or Part II to "The Imperial Will on Education." It is based on the incident during the imperial tour when students carried on a dialogue in English before the emperor in a formal classroom setting. When asked to explain the meaning in Japanese, Motoda reported they were unable to do so.[46] He referred to that incident, and others similar to it during the local visits, to craft an addendum to the main text of "The Imperial Will on Education." It took the form of imperial advice sprinkled, naturally, with Confucian precepts. Obviously directed to the Ministry of Education, that is, Tanaka Fujimaro, as well as to Itō Hirobumi then rapidly ascending the political ladder, it was intended to bring about reforms of education based on the emperor's firsthand observations.

The Imperial Will on Education
Part II
Two Principles for Elementary Education
(Shōgaku Jōmoku Niken)

1. All men are by nature benevolent, just, loyal and filial. But unless these virtues are cultivated early, other matters will take precedence, making later attempts to teach them futile. Since the practice has developed recently of displaying pictures in classrooms, we must see to it that portraits of loyal subjects, religious warriors, filial children, and virtuous women are utilized, so that when the pupils enter the school, they will immediately feel in their hearts the significance of loyalty and filial piety. Only if this is done first and then other subjects taught later will they develop in the spirit of loyalty and filial piety and not mistake the means for the end in their other studies.

2. While making a tour of schools and closely observing the pupils studying last autumn, it was noted that farmers' and merchants' sons were advocating high-sounding ideas and empty theories, and that many of the commonly used foreign words could not be translated into our own language. Such people would not be able to carry on their own occupations even if they

someday returned home, and with their high-sounding ideas, they would make useless civil servants. Moreover, many of them brag about their knowledge, slight their elders, and disturb Prefecture officers. All of these evil effects come from an education that is off course. It is hoped, therefore, that the educational system will be less high-flown and more practical. Agricultural and commercial subjects should be studied by the children of farmers and merchants so that they return to their own occupations when they have finished school and prosper even more in their proper work.[47]

By attaching this addendum to the main text of "The Imperial Will on Education," Motoda Nagazane combined two principles of education. The first was that the primary purpose of public elementary education is to instill benevolence, humanity, loyalty, and filial piety (*jingi chūkō*) into the hearts and minds of the students. This inextricably relates Part II of "The Imperial Will on Education" to Part I, which proclaims that the foundation of education is embedded in these traditional Confucian teachings. The second principle is that education should be practical, preparing students with appropriate training befitting their social background. By singling out these two simple but profound concepts, the canny Confucianist integrated the traditional with the modern. Morals based on Confucian teachings that Motoda incorporated into the imperial ideology forms the basis of education. Anchored on this firm foundation, each child must then acquire the practical skills and modern knowledge, ostensibly from the West, to successfully follow in the footsteps of the father at the workplace upon completion of school.

Motoda naturally had to be delighted that the emperor endorsed his "Kyōgaku Seishi" by issuing it under the imperial seal. Verification of the persuasive power that the dedicated Confucianist exerted within the Imperial Household was demonstrated in one of his lectures that referred to the reading habits of Emperor Meiji. "Your Majesty's decision to show your confidence in the philosopher [Confucius] by making his Analects your chief textbook comes at a critical moment when the western sciences are sweeping all before them, and the Way of the Emperors, that is Confucianism, threatens to disappear from existence. No words of mine are required to mark the brilliance of this choice."[48]

It is impossible to discern the precise thinking of Emperor Meiji in this intense struggle to determine the future direction of modern Japanese education, since Motoda remains the primary source of information from within the Imperial Household surrounding the origin of "The Imperial Will on Education." The emperor, again according to Motoda, had been dissatisfied with educational policy ever since the issuance of the Gakusei in 1873, and the subsequent modernization reforms implemented by Tanaka Fujimaro based on the American model. It was that misdirected course that led Japanese education down the wrong path. In the "Kyōgaku Seishi" Motoda claimed that he served merely as the narrator for the emperor. There is, however, evidence that Motoda initiated the controversial "Imperial Will" even before the emperor carried out his tour of local areas. According to a leading Japanese historian, the original outline in his handwriting suggesting this remains available to support that conclusion.[49] Regardless of the origin, Emperor Meiji's endorsement was an official act of imperial criticism of the modernization of education. With this document, the Imperial Household exerted its authority for the first time to reverse the course of educational modernization in Meiji Japan.

"The Educational Affair" ("Kyōiku Gi") by Itō Hirobumi

The great debate sparked by "The Imperial Will on Education" unexpectedly entered an even more consequential phase. One of the most powerful political figures in the nation, Itō Hirobumi, uncharacteristically issued a retort to "The Imperial Will on Education" within several weeks. Itō's response came about when the emperor pointedly asked him to compare "The Imperial Will on Education" with Tanaka's bill to reform education, mentioned previously.[50] Although drafted by Inoue Kowashi, senior government official and Itō's confidant, the response was circulated as "The Educational Affair" (Kyōiku Gi) under Itō's name.[51] Inoue Kowashi, it should be noted, will appear in the final chapter as he emerges as the author of the controversial 1890 "Imperial Rescript on Education" that incorporated the core concepts of Motoda's 1879 "Imperial Will on Education."

Although he had avoided entanglements during the governmental deliberations of Tanaka's bill, even though he had personally endorsed it with his own modifications at the initial stage over a year previously, Itō now suddenly seized the opportunity to stubbornly defend it. Perhaps stunned by the imperial proclamation that represented an imperial censure not just of Tanaka, the educator, but of Itō, the politician, he accepted the challenge. In what could itself be interpreted as a shocking sign of modernization under way, Itō rebutted "The Imperial Will on Education." The rapid sequence of events clarifies the discourse between the emperor and Itō Hirobumi at the center of the great debate.

Because of the historical significance of the response to Motoda's "The Imperial Will on Education" by Itō Hirobumi, destined to become the preeminent statesman of the Meiji era, extensive segments are included here. It was prefaced with a personal letter from Itō to Emperor Meiji, which reveal that these two powerful figures had a private meeting concerning educational policy when the emperor presented "The Imperial Will on Education" and differing viewpoints predictably surfaced.

Table 13   Critical Sequence of Events, "The Imperial Will on Education," 1878–1879

Education code by Tanaka submitted to the government	May 1878
Imperial visit to the countryside	August 1878
Terashima appointed minister of education	September 10, 1879
"Kyōgaku Seishi," "The Imperial Will on Education"	September 11, 1879
"Kyōiku Gi," "The Educational Affair"	September 1879

Figure 26. Itō Hirobumi.
From W. G. Beasley, *The Modern History of Japan* (London: Weidenfield and Nicolson, 1963), 181.

Your Majesty:

Your Majesty granted me audience the other day and graciously referred to the need for educational reform to repair the decline in our customs. Deeply moved by the Sacred Will, which reflects profoundly the trend of our age and which holds out grand and far-reaching perspectives for the future, I have ventured to express an opinion, respectfully imploring your Imperial inspection. Since the Emperor has already expressed his views on this matter, I dare not annoy his wise ears by simply repeating his words. I hope only to supplement what he says. Let Imperial wisdom be its judge.

Respectfully,

Hirobumi

The Educational Affair (Kyōiku Gi)

[Excerpts]

Deceit is praised and profit pursued without shame. Manners have collapsed and ethics decline. This is the destruction of order. Strange ideas are warmly taken up. Pleasure is found in stirring people's minds, destroying the national policy, and brewing disorder. This is the breakdown of propriety. These are the two essential forces that bring about the destruction of our traditional customs, and it is urgent that the Way of Education be carefully considered at this time.

The destruction of our traditional ways, however, had its own cause. . . . At the time of the Restoration, an unprecedented reform took place, accompanied by changes in our customs. This was inevitable in the circumstances of the times. First the seclusion of our country was ended and freedom of association granted. Second the feudal structure was abolished and military discipline relaxed. The isolation of the country had constrained human minds in a static condition and limited the range of communication. The feudal ruler proclaimed it virtuous to cultivate simple living and to die for honor. Those who worked for their living were despised. Moreover the tradition of regional sovereignty kept each han by itself, and the people did not have the right to travel. There was no contact between the city and the countryside. These customs came to an end barely ten years ago. The world changed suddenly for us.

Our government boldly took matters in hand to correct the defects of the seclusionist, feudal past. Now for the first time our people have been able to follow their own will, go out beyond their usual bounds, and exercise freedom of action and speech. Because of the intensity of this change, many of the elegant and beautiful things in our tradition have also disappeared. This I take to be the greatest single cause of our present moral disarray.

The damage to our customs has come from the excessiveness of the change and it was inevitable. Therefore we should not blame the new educational system for everything. Since education is not the principal cause of the failure, it can be no more than an indirect cure. Education is a long-term cause; its immediate results should not be demanded of it. Since the promulgation of universal education in 1872, local sovereignties have been surrendered to the central government, but the educational system has barely gone into operation. If the government now takes the initiative in promoting and expanding education, we should attain a civilized condition within a few years. Present teaching rules should remain in effect, and those in charge of teaching ethics should select the proper textbooks. Teachers are to be self-disciplined, moderate in speech, and worthy models for their students.

Moreover our students usually come from Confucian schools, and whenever they open their mouths it is to babble political theory and argue about the world situation. Thus when they read western books, they plunge themselves into radical schools of European thought, delighting themselves with empty theory. In order to remedy this situation we should spread the study of the industrial arts. Students who wish to pursue higher studies should look forward to practical work. After all it is science that, together with politics, brings about prosperity. In law and politics, examinations should be stricter, and only the best students granted admission. The details can be worked out by the Ministry of Education.

If we are to blend the new and the old, and take the classics into consideration, and establish a single national doctrine, we are in an area that it is not proper for government to control; for this we must wait for a sage.[52]

Itō's response to "The Imperial Will on Education," although written by his close associate Inoue Kowashi, illustrates a basic difference between him and the imperial position formulated by Motoda. The problems facing Japanese society, according to Itō's document, stem from the inevitable consequences brought about by the rapid transition from feudalism to modernism. Motoda essentially agreed that the root cause of moral deterioration stemmed from the social transformation under way. Where the two antagonists differed significantly was in the solution to the problems in education that grew out of the stresses and strains of modernism. Itō reasoned that since the schools did not produce the problems, they did not deserve the blame. He argued that "since education is not the primary cause of the failure, it can be no more than an indirect cure."

The shrewdness of Motoda, on the other hand, was exemplified in his position that the institution of the school should be the very instrument to reform society. Through the school all children should be taught what Motoda considered to be the eternal truths of Confucianism; that a harmonious society is achieved through proper social relationships between the emperor and his subjects and among the subjects as espoused by Confucius. Regardless of the root cause of the problems brought about by modernism, the new school system could be employed to solve them. From this perspective, Motoda's concept of the school as an instrument of social reform was surprisingly progressive.

Characteristically, Motoda did not concede the last word in the great debate. Surely taunting Itō, he responded with a document entitled "Kyōiku Gi Fugi," essentially "A Consideration of the Educational Affair." Undated but closely following Itō's document, and circulated either in late September or early October 1879, Motoda's document explained that the emperor was dissatisfied with Itō's response that did not conform to the emperor's concerns expressed in "The Imperial Will on Education." Consequently Motoda claimed that he was directed by the emperor to prepare a response to Itō's response.[53] The implication was clear. With the imperial endorsement of Motoda's response, his "Consideration of the Educational Affair" was, in other words, another "Imperial Will on Education."

Motoda repeated his basic position that the foundation of education is embedded in morals. Western-style morals textbooks, widely used in the schools during the 1870s but devoid of cherished Confucian virtues, reflect Christian traditions that must be avoided. Confucian classics reflect eastern traditions appropriate for Japanese schools from the elementary level through the university. Motoda then criticized Itō's efforts to strengthen the nation through western-style science and technology prominent in the higher levels of education. He conceded that science should be taught at the university level. However, since the purpose of the university is to prepare leaders for the nation, morals education (dōtoku) must take precedence over science (kagaku) at the most advanced level of education as well.[54]

In spite of the direct confrontation between Itō Hirobumi and Motoda Nagazane, the progressive pitted against the traditionalist, their ultimate goal was the same. These two great figures of early modern Japan devoted their lives to their country and their emperor in the pursuit of preserving national sovereignty. Itō, the shrewd progressive politician, endeavored to achieve that goal through the development of human resources based on modern science. It was, in his own words, intended "to abolish the old abuses (kyūhei) derived over hundreds of years." The equally shrewd and resourceful Confucianist Motoda proclaimed that oriental morality based on the revered Chinese classics must form the foundation of modern Japanese society. He envisioned the emperor as the nucleus of an administrative system that governed the nation.

Between the antagonistic positions represented by these two powerful nationalists, the traditionalist ultimately carried the day. Motoda not only articulated the will of Emperor Meiji but he also represented a faction of influential officials within the Ministry of Education that opposed Tanaka's radical reforms of education. It appeared to them that Tanaka's so-called Freedom of Education Code would further incite the increasingly active Peoples' Movement for Freedom then stirring up the society.[55] These ministry officials welcomed the opportunity presented by "The Imperial Will on Education" to reverse the course of educational reform that they had heretofore been unable to derail.

Nevertheless, in spite of the powerful opposition to Tanaka's education code, it was finally proclaimed by Itō Hirobumi as minister of the interior on September 29, 1879. As the Second National Plan for Education, it officially replaced the First National Plan for Education, the Gakusei of 1872–1873.[56] It had survived the lengthy approval process essentially as Tanaka Fujimaro and Itō Hirobumi originally designed it. However, only a compromise instigated by Itō rendered this possible. Moreover, because of the deep controversy surrounding the bill, especially the minor role of morals education within the new curriculum, its implementation was further delayed for three months. Through the efforts of Itō Hirobumi and Iwakura Tomomi, close associate of the emperor as well as a colleague of Itō, Tanaka's Education Law (Kyōiku Rei) incorporating the Second National Plan for Education had officially been approved.[57]

Although Tanaka Fujimaro had seemingly won the battle over the modernization of Japanese education with the passage of his Education Law, he had, in fact, lost the war. With the controversy surrounding his bill, and the powerful opposition from within the palace that included the emperor himself, the new law on education was doomed even before it was proclaimed. Likewise, Tanaka's tenure as director of the Ministry of Education was about to end. Responding to the crescendo of criticisms of Tanaka by some of his own ministry officials and advisors to the emperor led by Motoda Nagazane, Itō was compelled to react. But as an original supporter of Tanaka, he could not simply abandon the great champion of educational modernization. The accomplished politician that he was, Itō crafted a deft compromise.

Demonstrating his increasing influence within government, Itō offered a solution in a letter of August 28 to his old colleague, Iwakura Tomomi, who wielded enormous power within government and the palace. He recommended that Terashima Munenori, then serving as head of the Ministry of Foreign Affairs, be appointed as Mumbukyo, that is, minister of education. The position had been technically vacant except for two insignificant periods when high government officials carried the title while simultaneously holding other posts. Nevertheless, Tanaka Fujimaro held the top administrative position within the ministry as director (Munbu Daisuke), not as minister of education (Mumbukyo).[58] Regardless of his official title, Tanaka had served as the ranking officer within the ministry for the past six years, recognized by all as the official in charge of, and responsible for, Japanese educational policy during that entire tumultuous period.

Although Tanaka was not technically demoted with the appointment of Terashima as minister, effective September 10, the writing was on the wall.[59] Tanaka first learned that Terashima had been appointed as minister of education with Itō's approval upon arriving at his office on the very day of the appointment, without having been consulted. He recognized that the move was intended to effectively eliminate his influence within the ministry. He was fully aware that palace and government officials, including his own subordinates within the ministry, had monitored his every movement during the recent crisis over his controversial bill.[60]

From the moment of Terashima's appointment, the Tanaka era in modern Japanese educational history deeply influenced by American education had come to an abrupt end. Compelled by circumstances beyond his control, Tanaka submitted a request to be transferred. Although his transfer was not immediately carried out, his impending departure from the Ministry of Education was inevitable. On February 28, 1880, Kōno Togama assumed control as minister of education (Mumbukyo), replacing Terashima as head of the ministry. Obviously Terashima, who had traveled to London in 1865 with the Satsuma students, had been appointed to the post as an interim measure.[61]

On the same day, Tanaka was transferred to the Ministry of Justice with the surprising position of minister.[62] Perhaps Itō Hirobumi arranged the new position for his colleague, recognizing that Tanaka had shouldered the brunt of criticism for all those who supported the disgraced reforms of education, including Itō himself. According to Tanaka's son, his father received the fateful announcement of the transfer out of the ministry by telegram while traveling on an insignificant assignment in far-off Kyushu.[63]

Remarkably resilient, Tanaka Fujimaro went on to serve the Japanese government admirably as minister of justice, and later as minister to both Italy and France before retiring from government service. He and his devoted spouse, the former geisha from Nagoya, toured Europe together as they had in America. But his failure to bring about the great reforms of education envisioned in his Kyōiku Rei, the Second National Plan for Education, had a lasting influence on this historical figure. Before his death he systematically culled his files, burning nearly all of them.[64] In the fires he destroyed one of the great sources of historical documentation on early modern Japanese education. Many years later his wife, who lived well into the twentieth century, recalled her concern with her husband burning papers in the back yard for days. When asked what he was doing, he simply replied that it was not good to keep old things too long. But his wife surmised that her husband

Table 14   Critical Sequence of Events, The Second National Plan for Education
            (Kyōku Rei), 1878–1880

Submission of the Education Law to the government	May 14, 1878
Approval by the Political Bureau	February 20, 1879
Deliberations by the Genrōin	May 20 to June 25, 1879
Emperor's discussion with Iwakura	June 26, 1879
Itō recommends Terashima as minister of education	August 28, 1879
Terashima appointed minister of education	September 10, 1879
Kyōgaku Seishi (Imperial Will on Education)	September 11, 1879
Kyōiku Gi by Itō Hirobumi	September, 1879
Proclamation of the Education Law	September 29, 1879
Kōno appointed minister of education	February 28, 1880
Tanaka transferred to Justice Ministry	February 28, 1980

wanted to destroy materials related to his controversial period at the Ministry of
Education, a sad commentary on one of Japan's most progressive educators in the
modern era.[65]

Statistical Review of the Gakusei Era, 1873–1879

With the closing of the first period in the modernization of Japanese education
from 1873 to 1879, the era of Tanaka Fujimaro and Dr. David Murray from Rutgers
College also ended. A reassessment of the progress of the first public school system to date is warranted before moving on to the great "reverse course" reforms
from 1880 that opened the second period in the quest for modern schools. First,
evidence of the achievements can be gained by analyzing attendance records at
the public elementary schools.[66] Although parents were consistently cajoled into
sending their children to the local elementary school, the government lacked the
authority and the means to enforce compulsory attendance. Compliance, therefore, indicated the relative degree of success of Japan's first attempt to construct a
modern school system.

Attendance records compiled by the Ministry of Education during the first
period of modern education can be interpreted in various ways. To begin with,
the reliability of the data derived from the village level comes into question
without an effective corps of school inspectors. In addition, records of students
who entered the school and subsequently dropped out for various reasons are
not available. Although official figures showed that 40 percent of eligible students
attended elementary school in 1879, six years after the public school system began,
the significance of the figure is difficult to assess. Assuming that the public schools
of Japan at the beginning of 1880, twelve years after the country emerged from the

Table 15   Elementary School Attendance Rates, 1873–1879

	Total population	Eligible children	School attendance (%)		
			BOYS	GIRLS	TOTAL
1873	31,253,880	4,205,341	39.9	15.1	28.1
1876	34,084,784	5,160,618	54.2	21.0	38.3
1879	35,668,242	5,371,383	58.2	22.6	41.2

Source: Horimatsu Buichi, *Nihon Kindai Kyōiku Shi* (The History of Modern Japanese Education) (Tokyo: Risōsha, 1979), 63.

Tokugawa era, effectively enrolled about a third of all children, several conflicting conclusions can be drawn.

First, illiteracy in rural Japan remained at a very high level. The preamble of the First National Plan for Education of 1873 stipulated that no family shall have an illiterate member. By 1880 that goal was far from being attained. The second conclusion interprets the same figure from a positive perspective. To achieve a rate of school attendance for rural children that started from a very low level, perhaps in the single digits, to over a third in six years is a remarkable achievement. To attain this standard in a mountainous country on four main islands without modern means of transportation and communication renders the statistics even more impressive. For example, by 1880 the primary means of transportation in the capital city of Tokyo depended on tens of thousands of jinrikisha, the two-wheeled carts pulled by human runners. The more affluent depended on the palanquin or horse and buggy. Under those circumstances, school attendance rates proved that the new system was firmly in place in spite of immense difficulties.

The sharp increase in students under the provisions of the Gakusei, motivated by the principle that no family should be without an educated member, placed an enormous demand for elementary schools. At the beginning in 1873 all kinds of facilities from warehouses to private homes were converted into classrooms to accommodate the children. At the end of the first six years, the number of schools had dramatically increased to educate perhaps a third of eligible students. However, many of the schools were woefully lacking in adequate facilities suitable to provide a modern school environment.

To meet the needs of the increasing numbers of students under the Gakusei, one of the most impressive results of the first six years of educational modernization can be found in the increasing numbers of teachers for the new schools. The Tokyo Teacher Training School, with Marion Scott as the central figure, launched a nationwide program to prepare a corps of professionally trained teachers that gradually spread throughout the country. Takamine Hideo and Isawa Shūji took over the reins of this preeminent teacher training institution near the end of the

Table 16   Elementary Schools, 1873–1879

	Public	Private	Total
1873	7,998	4,599	12,597
1876	23,487	1,460	24,947
1879	26,710	1,315	28,025

Source: Ogata Hiroyasu, "Gakusei Jisshi no Ikisatsu to Sono Hokai" (The Process of the Implementation of the Gakusei and Its Beakdown), *Waseda University Bulletin of Social Sciences* (1962): 378.

first period, boldly introducing the most progressive concepts of teaching methods in the world. Throughout the entire period, statistics show that the teaching corps was overwhelmingly male-dominated.[67] Since teaching appealed to many of the samurai who were dispossessed from their elite hereditary status, a pool of qualified males was available to fill the need for teachers. The traditional role of females in the home had not yet been overcome.

A review of the financial support for education during this six-year period is of particular importance. The policy to modernize Japanese education with the 1873 Gakusei was plagued from the very beginning by the lack of a sound financial foundation. The Ministry of Finance vetoed the original proposal in 1872 because of this very defect. It was glossed over by the tentative understanding that those who benefited from the new schools should pay for them. Statistics show that the defect was never remedied.[68] The local financial burden on struggling farmers exacerbated social and political unrest that had spread throughout the country, motivating the government to reduce the detested land tax in 1877. However, by reducing national income, the government was compelled to decrease the national subsidy for local education. As the land tax was reduced, the educational burden on farmers was increased.

Table 17   Public Elementary School Teachers, 1873–1879

	Males	Females	Total
1873	26,696	411	27,107
1876	51,014	1,248	52,262
1879	68,696	2,350	71,046

Source: Ogata Hiroyasu, *Gakusei Jisshi Keii no Kenkyū* (Implementing the Gakusei), (Tokyo: Kōsō Shobō, 1963), 171.

Table 18   Income Sources for Local Education, 1873–1879 (percentage)

Source	1873	1876	1879
Local taxes	43.2	36.4	41.9
Student fees	6.3	5.7	4.5
National subsidy	12.6	9.7	5.6
Prefectural subsidy	0	0	5.9
Funds carried forward	0	13.1	18.7
Educational fund	19.1	17.8	7.3
Interest income	13.4	9.3	9.8
Miscellaneous	5.4	8.0	6.1

Source: Ichikawa Shōgo, *Kyōiku Zaisei* (Educational Finance) (Tokyo: Tokyo University Press, 1972), 90.

Through all the trials and tribulations confronting Japanese education as the country emerged from feudalism, the first decade of modern educational reforms ended on a comparatively solid foundation. Educational modernization patterned on western, primarily American, practices, however imperfect, was well under way. Every community supported a public elementary school that attracted on average about a third of the children as the 1870s came to an end.

The major concern of the government at the beginning of the second decade of educational modernization from 1880 was not attendance rates or school facilities. Rather, policy makers had became embroiled in a confrontation over the curriculum and textbooks in the determination of what should be taught in the new public schools and who would make the determinations. The secular progressives championed the cause of western science and mathematics as the center of the curriculum. The traditionalists promoted Confucian morality and imperial ideology as the foremost concern of the school. Because the outcome had repercussions far beyond the school and the immediate period, the following chapter focuses on the Third National Plan for Education, a reverse course in educational policy that emerged at the beginning of the 1880s.

16

The Third National
Plan for Education

THE REVERSE COURSE, 1880–1885

When Tanaka Fujmaro, head of the Ministry of Education since 1873, was uncer-emoniously transferred to the Ministry of Justice in early 1880, the way was cleared for the second decade of educational modernization in the Meiji era. It was launched with a rapid succession of conservative educational reforms. They dem-onstrated that Motoda Nagazane had triumphed over Itō Hirobumi, and that his "Imperial Will on Education" was more persuasive than Itō's "Educational Affair." The reforms also revealed how widespread the opposition to Tanaka's liberal reforms within his ministry actually was.

In the transition, Kōno Togama became minister of education (Mombukyo) replacing Terashima Munenori.[1] Terashima, a moderate with experience in inter-national affairs, had been appointed as an interim minister. He accomplished little during his stint in the Ministry of Education of less than half a year. In contrast, Kōno was well aware of the sensitive issues at hand having served as chairman of the government committee that conducted deliberations on Tanaka's controver-sial education bill in 1879.[2]

Upon assuming the top position within the ministry, Kōno immediately set out to replace Tanaka's bill, following through on the direction of ministerial policy already set in place. There were various influences at work during the beginning of the 1880s, each of which provided a stimulant for reform that, when combined, unleashed a powerful force engulfing the Ministry of Education. The first derived from "The Imperial Will on Education" written by Motoda Nagazane in 1879 to recognize morals education in the Confucian mode as the foundation of the cur-riculum, with the imperial tradition given a central role.

The second was a resurgence of the antigovernment political movement known as the Peoples' Movement for Freedom (Jiyū Minken Undō). Increasingly strident in their demands, the leaders were perceived as a clear and growing dan-ger to the Meiji government, which had never been compelled to prove its raison d'être. The potential for the movement to penetrate the public schools through activist teachers dissatisfied with their pitiful salaries and lack of freedom in the classroom proved compelling to ministry officials.

Finally, the immediate motivation for educational reform emerged from the annual conference of prefecture governors, the Chihōkan Kaigi, the local officials responsible for education within their jurisdiction. Just one day before he assumed the top position in the Ministry of Education on February 28, 1880, Kōno Togama as conference chairman brought to a close the meeting of governors that had been in session since February 5. Although education was not on the official agenda, the officials were unhappy with the effects of Tanaka's liberal education law enacted from September of the previous year. The new law, as intended, effectively reduced the role of the prefectures in the public schools within their jurisdiction. The administrative decisions with which the governors were empowered before Tanaka's education law were now technically being made, or neglected as many claimed, by the locally elected school board responsible for administering the local public schools. Prefectures had played a pivotal role in the administration of education from the beginning of the modern school system. From a gubernatorial standpoint, public education was looked upon as one sector of a community administratively integrated with all the other sectors. Setting local education policy apart from general policy proved unsettling to prefectural governors accustomed to having local officials, educational and otherwise, dependant upon them.

Local political conditions confronting the governors also prompted their concern with the schools. Ever since the Seinan War in 1877, antigovernment political movements were expanding into local areas. Just three months before the conference of governors, in November 1879, the oppositional political organization called Aikokusha held a major rally in Osaka. Plans were drawn up for local speaking tours to recruit new members in a campaign to expand the movement throughout the country. Among the demands for political rights was a revolutionary call for a national parliament. Under these conditions, prefectural authorities were highly critical of Tanaka's new education bill, since they were now unable to safeguard local schools from the spreading influence of the increasingly political movement against the government. This became especially acute when local activist teachers joined the movement or sympathized with it.[3]

The theoretical position against government educational policy that attracted both activist students and teachers was formulated in part by a leading member and prolific writer of the Peoples' Movement for Freedom, Ueki Emori. In an article published in the journal *Aikoku Shinshi,* October 1880, he laid out the case opposing Ministry of Education policy.[4] It reached the reading public at a critical period when the Ministry of Education was intent on dismantling Tanaka Fujimaro's so-called Freedom of Education Law that recognized the principle of local control of education. The article was obviously timed to provoke a reaction against government policy.

Ueki's basic principle was simply stated but highly provocative. Education should be free (*kyōiku wa jiyū ni*). Essentially supporting Tanaka's rationale for replacing the First National Plan for Education due to its rigidity and uniformity, Ueki denounced the ministry's plan to return educational control to the central government. Under provisions of the original Gakusei, he argued, every child was compelled to pass through a uniform school system set by the ministry. The result: everyone wore an identical kimono or everyone was stark naked. A uniform system of education acted as an obstacle to the development of a spirit of independence.[5]

In various newspaper articles, Ueki rebuked government policy at a time when opposition forces were demanding a parliament and a constitution. He claimed that all Japanese have the freedom to learn, and that all teachers have the freedom to teach. Moreover, since each community finances local education, local residents should have the freedom to control their local schools. The key concept in the Peoples' Movement for Freedom was, of course, freedom itself. Through his writings Ueki championed the cause for jiyū kyōiku, freedom of education, which attracted not a few students and teachers. It exerted a deeply disturbing influence on conservative government officials in the new regime then in control of the Ministry of Education.

Amid growing concern that social and political unrest spreading gradually throughout the country could spill over into the schools, many governors at their 1880 conference demanded a revision of the new education law designed by Tanaka Fujimaro. Led by the governors of Kyoto and Yamanashi, that is, a major metropolitan area and a rural province, the conference was marked by widespread concern over the Second Plan for National Education. Chairman Kōno Togama was in agreement with their sentiments as he assumed the post of Minister of Education the day following the conference.[6]

Following Kōno Togama's ascendancy to the senior position in the Ministry of Education in late February 1880, the next opportunity to advance the revisionist campaign arose in March. It was announced that another imperial tour was scheduled for June 16. This would provide Emperor Meiji with the opportunity to visit schools, asking probing questions in search of defects of school policy.[7] Minister Kōno used the opportunity to hastily schedule a local tour of schools by ministry officials prior to the emperor's departure. The purpose of the ministerial tour was to provide officials with the opportunity to witness personally the immediate effects of Tanaka's education law during the six months since its approval.

Kōno's tour took on added significance due to its route and timing. Departing on June 7, it covered the same route as the forthcoming trip planned by the Imperial Household for Emperor Meiji. It enabled ministry officials to lay the groundwork for the emperor's impending visit. The imperial tour, leaving nine days later, included prefectures from Yamanashi to Nagano, Gifu, and Kyoto. The route took Emperor Meiji directly through the towering mountains of the main

Table 19   Critical Sequence of Events, End of the Tanaka Fujimaro Era

Itō recommends Terashima as minister of education	August 28, 1879
Terashima appointed minister of education	September 10, 1879
Proclamation of Tanaka Fujimaro's Education Law	September 29, 1879
Tanaka transferred out of the Ministry of Education	February 28, 1880
Kōno Togama replaces Terashima as minister of education	February 28, 1880

island of Honshu, now appropriately referred to as the Japanese Alps, to the Japan Sea, returning farther south to Kyoto and then home. It was an extremely arduous trip at that time. The schedule provided both the emperor and the new Minister of Education Kōno a timely opportunity to observe local education from the most rural areas to the great historic city of Kyoto in order to prepare a major revision of Tanaka Fujimaro's education law.[8]

In his report on the trip, Kōno solidified his position within the conservative cause. He declared that the Ministry of Education must intervene (*kanshō*), that is, control, education in the nation's public schools. In a rambling discourse on western education, he laid the rationale for a reform of Tanaka's educational reform. He specifically noted that such countries as Germany, Italy, Switzerland, France, Norway, and Denmark all have centralized systems of education. Of some curiosity, he even mentioned the historical Austrian-Prussian war.[9] Kōno's references to European history, however, were in themselves revealing. It is unlikely that he personally was aware of European patterns in education, not to mention European history. Rather, the conclusion can be drawn that Egi Kazuyuki, as the only ranking ministry official with some knowledge of European education, wrote Kōno's report. The source of Egi's knowledge about European education is of some relevance. The evidence points compellingly to the source as David Murray, in whose office Egi worked for several years. It was Murray who first recommended the central control of education to Tanaka Fujimaro on the basis of European patterns of education that he admired, most notably that of Germany. Egi picked up Murray's theme after Tanaka lost power. In other words, David Murray's influence came into play even after he returned to America in 1878 through his former subordinate Egi Kazuyuki.[10]

Upon his return from the inspection tour on July 26, Minister Kōno, now convinced that central control of education was indeed essential, immediately appointed a task force within the Ministry of Education assigned to draw up a revision of Tanaka's education law. Among the most influential members was Egi Kazuyuki, who became the primary official responsible for drafting the revisions that set the general framework for the reforms.

Indicative of the preparations well under way by ministry officials who had opposed Tanaka's bill from the beginning, the preparatory committee completed the first draft of the revisions within a very short period. In fact, it took shape during Kōno's tour, such was the certainty of the changes about to take place. The ministry's draft proposal was quickly shaped into a formal bill called the Revision of the Education Law (Kaisei Kyōiku Rei) for presentation to the Dajōkan for approval in December 1880.[11]

The state of the nation's elementary schools had evidently taken a turn for the worse, as witnessed by Kōno and his school inspectors from the Ministry of Education. Since the regulations governing school attendance had been loosened under Tanaka's educational reforms, in some instances uninterested parents refused to pay school fees. Others withdrew their children from the school. Some refused to pay taxes to finance the already underfinanced local public school. With the decreased demand for public school places, school buildings under construction in some communities were simply abandoned. Both the number of public schools and students decreased alarmingly.[12]

On the other hand, the number of private schools and students increased since the regulations governing their founding and operation were considerably relaxed under Tanaka Fujimaro's code of education. The single requirement to open a private school involved merely reporting the intention to the prefectural governor, who had no authority to reject it regardless of the circumstances. In addition, private schools became eligible for government subsidies since they contributed to the public welfare, further stimulating their proliferation at the expense of the local public schools.[13] Within a year after Tanaka's law went into effect, the number of private elementary schools in the capital city of Tokyo outnumbered public schools by 3.5 times, a trend under way before the Tanaka reforms.[14]

Examples of atrocious conditions in some private schools stood in stark contrast to many that prospered in the expanding metropolis. The Ministry of Education reported on possibly the worst private school that officials personally witnessed. In a small private house, one couple enrolled over one hundred students who stood shoulder to shoulder in tiny rooms breathing putrid air. The teachers were completely unqualified to teach. Their lessons were full of errors. The students were unruly, yelling at each other throughout the lessons. The officials reported that the education these students received in this private school was a complete waste of time.[15]

Even though the controversial locally elected school boards were intended to play the central role in the administration of schools under Tanaka's education law of 1879, the results were inconclusive. In some communities the new school board members working with teachers who played a prominent role on joint committees actually set the local school curriculum. In others the boards chose new teachers. In general, however, the vast majority of school board members were inexperienced in decision-making matters concerning curricula, course requirements, and so on, granted under Tanaka's Education Law. It was natural for many board members to turn to prefectural education offices and the Ministry of Education itself for advice and direction. Such decisions had been made at the higher levels of administration ever since the first public school system was started in 1873. As a result, the ministry retained much of its influence over the new public schools even during the short period of Tanaka's liberal education law specifically designed to curtail it.

The Third National Plan for Education, 1880

The Ministry of Education launched the second decade of the Meiji era with the Third National Plan for Education. Although officially labeled merely the Revision of the Education Law (Kaisei Kyōiku Rei) promulgated on December 28, 1880,[16] it represented a reverse course in educational reform affecting the very foundation of the nation's schools. A new era in modern Japanese education was under way.

The speed with which the new reforms received final governmental approval demonstrated that powerful forces supported them. On December 23, 1880, the bill came before the deliberative committee of the supreme organ of government, the same committee that had deliberated the contentious educational reform bill proposed by Tanaka Fujimaro a year earlier. Indicative of the rapid changes underway, Kōno Togama had chaired the final session on Tanaka's bill on June 25, 1879, representing the government. Before the same committee on December 23, 1880, Kōno presented the new bill by virtue of his new position, minister of education (Mombukyo), succeeding Tanaka as the senior responsible official.[17]

One of the fundamental reforms involving adminstration empowered the Ministry of Education to implement the ensuing proliferation of reforms of the Tanaka era. The control of Japanese education had consequently been reversed. Article 23 stipulated that local communities must adhere to the elementary school regulations set by the Ministry of Education. Any exceptions to fit local conditions required approval by the minister.[18]

A further revision of a structural nature met demands by the prefectural governors at their conference. Article 11 revised the procedure for the locally elected school committees; henceforth local communities were empowered only to nominate candidates, two or three times the required number, to the prefectural governor. The governor in turn chose the final members from among them. Even the procedure for nominating the members required Ministry of Education approval.[19]

And finally, the third major revision, arguably the most significant, concerned the curriculum. The original proposal submitted to the government for approval listed six required subjects for the elementary school, similar to the list under Tanaka's education law being revised. In Tanaka's bill, however, morals (*shūshin*) was ranked at the bottom.[20] Near the end of the deliberations by the government on the new bill, the emperor and palace officials that most certainly included Motoda Nagazane called for a major revision. The final version passed on December 28, 1880, with imperial approval, positioned the morals course at the top of the new curriculum.[21] In essence, Motoda Nagazane and the Imperial Household had prevailed, thrusting the emperor directly into national educational affairs.

With the passage of the bill, the Third National Plan for Education, a new figure entered the picture who would play a central role. On April 7, 1881, just over three months after the new education bill was approved, Fukuoka Takachika was appointed minister of education, replacing Kōno Togama.[22] For the next two and a half years, until December 12, 1883, he remained in this position. The timing of Fukuoka's tenure is critical. During that period virtually all of the education bills supplanting those put in place by the Ministry of Education under Tanaka Fujimaro were enacted.

The defining moment of Fukuoka's term arose in December of his first year in office. At a meeting of provincial governors (*chihōkan kaigi*), Fukuoka laid out his basic educational policies for these local officials primarily responsible for implementing them. Simply stated, they would be based on Confucian teachings. Schools, teachers, regulations, textbooks, and so on, would henceforth all reflect this guiding principle.[23] "A schoolteacher should not rest content with a mere knowledge of textbooks on morals. What is essential for him is a character upright, loveable, and respectable, combined with varied experiences and ability adequate to control children. Hence men of wide information and sound morals, who have untainted honour and popularity, should be selected as teachers, so that pupils may learn more and more to be quiet and orderly and to pay respect to others. The teaching of morality should be based upon the native doctrine of the Empire, and on the principle of Confucianism."[24]

In retrospect, Fukuoka's policies were clearly inspired and guided by Motoda Nagazane's 1879 "Imperial Will on Education." The two-year interim between that document and Fukuoka's assumption of office in 1881 served as a transition period, setting the stage for the reverse course from Tanaka Fujimaro's image of modern Japanese education in the American mold to Motoda Nagazane's image in the Confucian mold. From this perspective, one Japanese educational historian aptly concluded that the Ministry of Education under Fukuoka had, in essence, become Motoda Nagazane's Ministry of Education (Motoda no Mombusho).[25]

One month after Fukuoka became head of the Ministry of Education, the first order to implement the Revision of the Education Law was issued. The ministry circulated to each prefecture the Guidelines for the Elementary School Curriculum (Shōgakkō Kyōsoku Kōryō) on May 4, 1881.[26] With this document, the Ministry of Education set a national standardized curriculum for the nation's public schools with the course in morals education at the pinnacle. Tanaka Fujimaro's great plan for the liberal reform of Japanese education on the American model with its locally elected school boards determining what would be taught locally had been effectively overturned.

The Imperial Way: Egi Kazuyuki

Egi Kazuyuki henceforth assumed a position of profound influence on modern Japanese education. He played a prominent role as the officer responsible for drawing up every regulation, including the first guidelines issued during the hectic initial period of the reverse course policy of the early 1880s.[27] One among them stands out: the Regulations for Elementary School Teachers (Shōgakkō Kyōin Kokoroe) circulated to all prefectures and elementary school teachers from June 18, 1881.[28] Writing about his days in the Ministry of Education, Egi recalled vividly the intent of this historical document: to promote "The Imperial Way" (kōdō shugi). It was meant as the guiding principle to implement the Revisions of the Education Law in which he was also deeply involved.[29]

The first provision sets the parameters for the conduct of teachers and the tone of the entire document. In guiding students, it said, it is more important for teachers to instill moral standards than to transmit knowledge. Basic to the moral precepts to be taught by teachers were, among others, loyalty to the imperial family, love of country, and respect for parents and elders. Teachers must set a moral standard for their students by setting a good example through their own moral convictions and actions.[30]

Although Motoda Nagazane, Confucian lecture to the emperor, initiated the reverse course with his "Imperial Will on Education" of 1879, Egi Kazuyuki codified it into ministry regulations in the early 1880s. His primary aim, to restore the Imperial Way (*kōdō*) to its proper place in education, conformed precisely to Motoda's intentions. Originally Egi hoped that his document would be designated as a Chokuyu (imperial statement) but realized that the process would be too lengthy and complicated. Nevertheless, he took great pleasure in learning that the emperor was especially pleased when presented with his draft that spelled out the purpose of education as sonno aikoku, "respect the emperor—love the country." It also placed greater emphasis on Confucian morality than knowledge. Egi noted in his memoirs that the emperor inquired about the writer—the first time he learned the name of Egi Kazuyuki.[31] From then on Emperor Meiji would often encounter the name of Egi Kazuyuki, faithful supporter of imperial ideology, as he staked out a major position within the Ministry of Education.

Egi's background varies from the usual samurai upbringing. Born in 1854 in Yamaguchi Prefecture of the prominent Chōshū clan, he was brought up in a middle-ranking samurai family. His father rotated among local administrative posts. Consequently he was unable to attend a regular clan school for samurai youth located in the castle town or other major towns where large numbers of samurai families lived. Rather he attended various local private schools alongside nonsamurai children.

Later Egi was sent to a military school in Osaka for a short period, then to Tokyo in 1871, where he entered a private English school. He was then accepted into the Daigaku Nankō, the highest-level national school, from where he soon transferred to the newly founded Imperial University of Engineering (Kōbu Daigaku) under Henry Dyer and his team of Scottish and British professors. It was there that he met Yamao Yōzō, minister of works, responsible for the engineering school. In need of money, Egi was introduced by Yamao to the director of the Ministry of Education, Tanaka Fujimaro, who invited him to join the ministry in 1874. He was assigned to the office of David Murray.[32] Within a year after the internal upheaval in the ministry, Egi prepared a draft of the law that replaced Tanaka's educational code of 1879 that he had opposed so vigorously.

Morals Education—The Reverse Course

Of all the regulations issued by the Ministry of Education to implement the reverse course in educational policy, the Guidelines for the Elementary School Curriculum proved to be the most significant. In listing the required courses for all public schools, morals (*shūshin*) was catapulted from the bottom of the curriculum to the preeminent position.[33] Until this time morals was taught primarily through translated western textbooks. In fact, one of the major criticisms of Tanaka's Education Law concerned the absence of any guidelines for the content and textbooks of the morals course. Henceforth, however, textbooks and teachings were to be derived mainly from Confucian texts. This, then, marks the end of the era of translated morals textbooks from the West and the beginning of domestically prepared textbooks for the morals course.[34]

The head of the new Textbook Bureau within the Ministry of Education was none other than Nishimura Shigeki, well known for his Confucian convictions sympathetic to the Imperial Household.[35] Nishimura quickly escalated official control by conducting a review of textbooks in use in public elementary schools and local elementary teacher training institutions from May.[36] After careful scrutiny to determine their appropriateness, the ministry then circulated to each prefectural education office a list of those texts that should not be used in the public schools. Of particular interest, texts related to political issues such as the Peoples' Movement for Freedom were included on the proscribed list.[37]

Indicative of the times, among the books banned by the Ministry of Education in 1880 were publications that the ministry had itself translated and produced for textbook use during the Tanaka era. In effect the ministry censored its own textbooks, such was the atmosphere within the government organ now in control of the nation's schools. It is often pointed out, however, that among the publications used as texts but henceforth banned by the central authority, were those written by the most popular progressive intellectual, Fukuzawa Yukichi.[38] Clearly they were inappropriate for elementary school use and should never have been included on the recommended list in the first place.

The ministry then decided that only a morals text produced from within its ranks would suffice. Ready and presumably eager to undertake the assignment was Nishimura Shigeki who occupied the sensitive post of head of the Textbook Bureau. From his early days in the Ministry of Education from 1873, Nishimura had been an advocate of strengthening morals education with a Confucian foundation when the ministry was under the control of the liberal Tanaka Fujimaro. There was no one with better credentials than Nishimura to write a textbook for the most important course in the revised curriculum. His text entitled *Elementary Moral Teachings (Shōgaku Shūshin Kun)* was published by the Ministry of Education in April 1880.[39] The ministry then had an acceptable textbook ready to implement the new course in morals education.[40]

It could be anticipated that any morals text prepared by the Confucianist Nishimura would adhere closely to the sentiments contained in the "Kyōgaku Seishi," "The Imperial Will on Education," of 1879. This was reinforced by the fact that he consulted with Motoda Nagazane, author of that document and member of the Imperial Household, during the preparation of his text.[41] Nevertheless, Nishimura's text turned out to be less revisionist than one would anticipate. The author himself was a unique individual, having been a founding member of the distinguished group of progressive thinkers that formed the Meirokusha of 1873.

Nishimura's morals textbook reflects the dual character of this unusual figure. The publication, in two volumes, begins with a long list of proverbs and statements taken directly from Confucian and other Chinese classical texts without comment or interpretation. The author, in effect, then balanced this section with a series of quotes, proverbs, and sayings from the West, including the writings of Pestalozzi, Plato, and, at considerable length from the well-known translation of Samuel Smiles's *Self Help*. Of some curiosity, Nishimura, reflecting his eclectic nature, also included excerpts from the Bible.[42] In hindsight, Nishimura's morals textbook turned out to be transitional.

In late 1882, the Imperial Household made public a morals textbook of its own. Motoda Nagazane, Confucian tutor to Emperor Meiji, once again exerted his influence on modern Japanese education in a powerful way. Whether he was dissatisfied with the official morals textbook by his fellow Confucianist, Nishimura, which contained excerpts from the Christian Bible, cannot be determined. Whatever the motivation, Motoda personally wrote a morals textbook in 1881 entitled *Principles for Guiding Children* (*Yōgaku Kōyō*) circulated from November 1882. Motoda himself signed the preface.[43]

Motoda claimed that the content of his publication approved by the emperor was inspired by "The Imperial Will on Education" of 1879 ("Kyōgaku Seishi") that he had also written. He noted that Emperor Meiji had originally instructed him to prepare the document in the summer of 1879 in the midst of the great debate on educational reform. The emperor empowered Motoda, according to his recollections, to incorporate his thoughts into the new document with concrete examples illustrating the principles contained in "The Imperial Will on Education."[44]

Motoda's *Principles for Guiding Children* faithfully reflected the concepts contained in "The Imperial Will on Education," in a strategic tactic to resurrect Confucianism in the schools. The theme, as always, extolled the basic Confucian virtues of loyalty and filial piety (*chūkō*) by listing a total of twenty virtues to be taught in the schools. Following the first two, loyalty and filial piety, such virtues to be taught in the classroom were friendship (*yūai*) and trustworthiness (*shingi*).[45] Each virtue was then illustrated by a fable or story from ancient China or an historical event chosen from Japanese history, with visual sketches taken from Chinese classics.[46]

Motoda's textbook vividly contrasted, as intended, with the spate of textbooks translated from western sources used in morals classes of the 1870s. The emphasis from the beginning of the Meiji Restoration had been on individualism, and foreign texts that extolled individualism were chosen for translation. Fukuzawa Yukichi in his popular books deeply influenced by foreign books, some of which were recommended by the Ministry of Education as morals texts, extolled individualism as the basis for equality (*byōdō*). This was a popular concept then spreading through fledging western democracies. The Peoples' Movement for Freedom picked up this theme in its demands for a constitution and an elected parliament for Japan in the late 1870s.[47] It was perceived as a threat by the ruling Meiji oligarchy.

The egregiously missing ingredients in the morals textbooks of the 1870s, according to Motoda and like-minded traditionalists, were the great moral principles of Confucius as they applied to the relationship between children and parents and the emperor and his subjects. The new basis of morality would not be individualism but respect and loyalty of children toward parents, a fundamental principle of Confucian thought. Motoda's *Principles for Guiding Children*, however, went one strategic step further. He applied the identical relationship of respect and loyalty between parents and children to that between the emperor and his subjects. In this manner the country assumed the characteristics of a family, often referred to as the family-state. In Motoda's *Principles for Guiding Children*, moral teachings ultimately become an instrument of nationalism (*kokka shugi*).[48]

The *Principles for Guiding Children* assumed a special urgency when it was formally presented by the Imperial Household to a meeting of local chief educational officers (Chihō Chōkan Kaigi), that is, prefectural governors, on December 2, 1882. The imperial representative explained to the governors that every western country had morals education that was not appropriate for Japan. Consequently the emperor commissioned Nagazane to write this book to delineate the proper form of morals education for the nation's schools.[49] It reflected, therefore, the imperial will on morals education.

This maneuver of going directly to such an influential group not only added urgency to the document itself but also demonstrated the ability of imperial advisors such as Motoda to project the Imperial Household and the emperor himself directly into local educational affairs. Although intended for a broader audience well beyond the school, the book was originally meant to serve as a textbook for morals education for the nation.[50] In this sense it competed with Nishimura's official textbook and its successors originating from the Ministry of Education.

With Motoda's reference to the emperor as the inspiration, his *Principles for Guiding Children* carried imperial prestige. Each governor dutifully carried a copy back to his home area where it was reproduced in local newspapers, reaching the reading public from one end of the country to the other. Although it was far too difficult for elementary school children to read, since Motoda was unable to write appropriately for children, it was distributed to every school by 1884.[51] Virtually every teacher and administrator in the public schools of Japan, as well as the reading public, become well aware of the emperor's convictions interpreted by Motoda in this text. In effect, the Imperial Household functioned as a quasi Ministry of Education in an attempt to refocus the direction of modern education.

The third stage in the reform of morals textbooks was an official textbook emanating from the Ministry of Education. In June 1883, the ministry published *Shōgaku Shūshin Sho* (Elementary School Morals), based overwhelmingly on Confucian writings and Chinese classics. It completes the full reverse course from morals education in the 1870s under Tanaka Fujimaro's era. There were no longer any references or passages from western sources.[52]

Modern Music Education from America: Luther Mason

Conservative winds in the early 1880s blew across subjects beyond morals education. One of the most interesting episodes of the period concerns the latest import from America in the form of modern music education, introduced in an earlier chapter. It was initiated in 1876 when an official of the Ministry of Education, Isawa Shūji, was sent to a teacher training school near Boston, Massachusetts, to study the latest methods in teacher education. With an unusual interest in music, foreign to the samurai class, he was able to meet America's leading music educator, Luther Mason, then in charge of the music program for Boston's public schools. When Isawa returned from America in 1878, he soon became director of the Bureau of Music in the Ministry of Education, and invited Mason to Japan to introduce western music in the public schools. Mason arrived in Japan in March 1880, eager to begin the task of introducing music education to the Japanese based on his experiences in America. It proved to be a daunting mission since there were no western musical instruments available, no Japanese familiar with western music, and no basic vocabulary in the Japanese language for the translation of such simple words as singing.

There was, moreover, a decidedly negative factor in Mason's assignment in Japan. Although Tanaka Fujimaro, head of the ministry in the 1870s, had given his full support to Isawa sanctioning the official invitation for Mason to come to Japan, he had become embroiled in the bitter controversy over his proposed education law. The timing was crucial, and most unfortunate, for Mason. He was apparently unaware of the ideological turmoil within the Ministry of Education when he arrived in Japan just ten days after Tanaka had been replaced as director of the ministry.[53] Consequently, when Mason assumed his new assignment to introduce modern music education in Japan with great enthusiasm and total commitment, the great reverse course in educational policy had just gotten under way.

Nevertheless, Mason was initially given carte blanche to introduce not just music education for elementary schools but western music in general. He had neither guidelines nor restrictions placed upon him. In the absence of any Japanese knowledgeable about western music, that was understandable. He began by giving music lessons to specially selected students who would in turn teach others the basic principles of music. It turns out that his translator acting as an assistant was Mrs. Takamine Hideo, wife of the new president of the Tokyo Teacher Training School who went to America with Isawa in 1875.[54] The teaching was extremely difficult. There was no concept of the basic terms associated with western music such as clefs, notes, chords, sharps, and flats. Nevertheless, without any musical background, Mason's students underwent a rigorous course that included the theory of harmony, singing, piano, organ, and violin.

Regardless of the formidable problems facing him, the irrepressible music teacher wrote his family in Massachusetts that "I have been here just one year and I think it has been the most successful year in my life. If I have my health another year and the government doesn't get into any war, I shall establish music in the schools of Japan."[55] Mason did indeed have good reason to be pleased with his accomplishments. Working with students at the Tokyo Teacher Training School and the attached elementary school, he developed the first methodology course in music education in Japan. From Mason's work, the first specialized school of music, the Tokyo Music School (Tokyo Ongaku Gakkō) was started.[56] It eventually developed into the prestigious Tokyo Geijutsu Daigaku of today, the Tokyo University of Arts.

One of the major contributions to modern Japanese education by Mason was the publication of the first elementary school songbook in 1882. The initial compilation of tunes took place in Boston in the late 1870s when Isawa and Mason worked on the project, not realizing at that time that their efforts would ever bear fruit. Now working with Isawa in Japan, Mason's Japanese students helped compile a final version with tunes from America with which Mason was familiar. Japanese words were added that formed the basis of the first official *Collection of Elementary School Songs* (*Shōgakkō Shōkashū*) in modern Japan.[57]

Among the songs included in the first elementary school songbook was one that has survived the test of time. Every Japanese elementary student from the 1880s to this day has learned the beloved tune called "Cho Cho," or "Butterfly." When Mason taught Isawa how to read music at his home near Boston, he introduced the American school song "Lightly Row" that appealed to him. Mason urged Isawa to search for an appropriate Japanese poem or story to fit the music. Isawa applied a local verse about a butterfly which he had heard while teaching at the Aichi prefectural teacher training school before going to America. A modern song for children was born for the Japanese elementary school, a collaboration between Isawa and Mason that not only survived the ages but also transcended East and West through music.[58]

By 1882, senior officials of the Ministry of Education were carrying out a powerful reverse-course policy under pressure from the Imperial Household. Inevitably Mason could not escape its influence. Naturally he taught his new Japanese students the elementary songs then used in American schools. But the conservative officials now in charge of the ministry had a different perspective on education. Ratcheting up the pressure, Motoda Nagazane turned his focus on music education. He wanted all courses, including the new music course designed by Mason, to reflect the teachings contained in the new morals textbooks. In other words, western music listed in the curriculum as singing (*shōka*) should also reflect the moral values in the new textbooks that espoused the teachings of Confucius and the Imperial Way. This demand presented a decidedly different approach to elementary school music. In fact, as noted in a previous chapter, many of the tunes that Mason had recommended for the new songbook for the elementary school course in singing were taken from Christian hymns popular in the United States in the later half of the 1800s. Whether Motoda was aware of that fact remains unknown. Moreover, the Japanese words initially applied to Mason's tunes by ministry officials and others brought in for that work did not have a Confucian flavor.

As the conservatives gained power, Isawa found himself in a delicate position. He was personally responsible for inviting Mason to Japan through their relationship that developed during his study tour in America. In addition, he worked closely with Mason in choosing tunes from America for the first elementary school songbook. In a painful reaction to the inexorable trends under way, Isawa, by now a high-ranking officer within the ministry, found it necessary to officially notify his American colleague and friend that it was necessary to, as it were, change his tune.

To what extent Mason understood the nuances of the following letter written originally in English from his dear friend Isawa has never been clarified. In hindsight, it is clear that Isawa was reacting to the reverse-course policies under way within the Ministry of Education, indicating that he was not fully in agreement with them, and taking the consequences for his close personal relationship with Mason.

> July 1st 1880
> Mr. L. W. Mason.
> My dear friend
>   Now I am in such a position that I must write a few lines to communicate you rather a grave thought. . . . Please understand me that I am a just and sincere friend of yours always doing the best as my ability permits toward your success. . . . Up to this day, I have fought many fights to clear off the obstacles which would have stopped the progress of your work if left unchecked. Although my official influence has been injured to some extent by acting such an awkward part, I did not care the least of such effect, for I took it better to help a friend who is left helpless in a strange land than to gain my influence. I have not had the slightest wish to tell you these things. . . . If you have eyes to see, please see through my inner heart but not outward appearance. You can clearly see that our aim is not the total adoption of European or American musics, but the making of a new Japanese music. You are one of the best musicians of higher esteem in America, and every one of us is willing to conform yours opinion, and take it as an authority. But, you as an educated liberal musician must grant a proposition that music should be national . . . those pieces imported from foreign lands must be more or less naturalized.[59]

It had to be difficult for Mason to understand or appreciate that behind that carefully calculated letter from his Japanese friend and colleague was a conflict raging within the educational world. It pitted the progressives such as Isawa and the husband of Mason's music translator, Takamine Hideo, against the traditionalists such as the Minister of Education Fukuoka Takachika and Motoda Nagazane from the Imperial Household over the role of traditional morals in the nation's schools. Even music education underwent a curious intermingling with morality as the new music textbook for elementary schools in the mid-1880s was revised to reflect the elementary teacher's guide placing new emphasis on morals in the songs taught to children.[60]

Under the prevailing conditions within the ministry, Mason's contract was abruptly terminated in late 1882 at the peak of the reverse-course policy, after a two-year assignment. Although he fully expected to return to Japan under an extended contract when he departed for a short leave of absence in July of 1882, he received notice of termination in November while he was out of the country. Speculation over the precise causes for Mason's dismissal remains.[61] It would appear, though, that both Isawa and Mason, as well as western music education, were caught up in the prevailing winds of the reverse course in educational reform.[62]

Restrictions on the Political Activities of Teachers

While the Ministry of Education was absorbed in revising the curriculum, particularly the course on morals, as well as reorienting other courses such as music, it was also aggressively moving to restrict the political activities of teachers. As the Peoples' Movement for Freedom inexorably expanded its influence, employing tactics that could affect education, government officials became increasingly alarmed. Movement leaders organized lecture meetings (*enzetsukai*) for the general public to propagate their beliefs. At the same time, teachers were forming local organizations under the guise of kyōiku enzetsukai, "educational lecture meetings," at public schools in which representatives from the Peoples' Movement for Freedom were invited to speak.[63] Activists encouraged public school teachers to utilize their unique positions as teachers to solidify a grassroots movement for political freedoms.

Trends under way in local areas by the beginning of the 1880s caused consternation within the Ministry of Education. Political organizations under the broad category of Peoples' Rights Associations (Minken Kessha) operated in virtually every prefecture. They sponsored lecture meetings where current educational problems were discussed. In nearly all of these groups local teachers actively participated. It had a special appeal to younger teachers as well as teacher trainees.

The movement was particularly strong in Nagano prefecture. For example, among the founding members of the Nagano branch of the Peoples' Movement for Freedom, local teachers participated in a leadership role and continued to actively support its activities, which included many enzetsukai, the popular lecture meetings. Among the 101 graduates of the Nagano Teacher Training School from 1877 to 1882, 44 joined this local association that published its own educational journal analyzing contemporary educational issues. In one year alone, 1879–1880, 84 percent of the graduating class joined en masse. During May of that year, the local chapter sent a delegation to Tokyo carrying a petition for a national parliament resisted by the government.[64]

Under these conditions, government officials became increasingly suspicious of teacher loyalty. With antigovernment sentiment spreading throughout the country, teachers could not avoid it. A few local organizations of citizens, including teachers, were spontaneously formed to support Tanaka Fujimaro's education law associated with the cause of freedom. Some published educational journals supporting the activities of the locally elected school boards organized under the law, while criticizing government policy aimed at eliminating their authority. Articles concerning school board elections, the new methodology in education, and so on, proliferated, urging teachers to support the revolutionary concept of freedom in education that Tanaka promoted. The movement split teachers into those who were primarily politically motivated and those who were more interested in educational reform through these movements.[65] Regardless of the basic motivation, because of the sensitive position of teachers in the formation of youth attitudes toward government and the imperial tradition, government restrictions on teachers appeared inevitable.

In April 1880, increasingly alarmed by the expanding influence of political movements, the government moved to suppress general opposition by passing an ordinance placing limitations on the right of assembly (Shūkai Jōrei). Public and private school teachers and students were lumped together within the broad category of public employees, along with police and military personnel, who were henceforth banned from participating in meetings of a political nature. They were also prohibited from joining political organizations.[66]

The national crackdown on dissent prompted the Ministry of Education in June of the following year, 1881, to issue several relevant ordinances. At one end of the educational spectrum, professors at Tokyo University were classified as government employees subject to the political restrictions governing all civil servants.[67] At the other end, the ministry issued in June the Regulations for Elementary School Teachers (Shōgakkō Kyōin Kokoroe), discussed previously, written by Egi Kazuyuki. Moving quickly to strengthen political restrictions on teachers, the ministry issued a second order a month later on July 21, 1881, ominously titled the Regulations Governing the Conduct of Teachers (Gakkō Kyōin Hinkō Kentei Kisoku).[68]

The final provision in the Regulations for Elementary School Teachers, issued by the ministry under Egi's hand, reflected one of the main concerns of the government, the political activities of teachers. Based on the stipulations in the general law restricting teacher's rights to attend political meetings (Shūkai Jōrei), Egi Kazuyuki took one critical step forward. He inserted the provision in his regulations that public school teachers must be politically and religiously neutral in the classroom. No teachings of a political or religious nature, therefore, could be included in their teachings in order to preserve the political neutrality of the classroom. Beyond that, under the second regulation teachers were also not allowed to make public speeches advocating a religious or political persuasion.[69]

Amid the issuance of the ministry's restrictive directives, concern over the political activity of teachers under the influence of the Peoples' Movement for Freedom was further aggravated when its most prominent leader, Itagaki Taisuke, formed a political party in late 1881. It was appropriately named the Jiyūto, the Freedom Party. Itagaki had been an irritant to the government ever since he resigned from a major leadership position in the mid 1870s to mount the antigovernment movement that culminated in the Peoples' Movement for Freedom. In his Education Manifesto, Itagaki argued that the educated man armed with knowledge will take advantage of the uneducated. Among his demands was a western-style parliament. To participate in the modern political process in which all Japanese have equal rights, he said, educating the common man is essential to achieve independence and self-reliance. Therefore the problems of education were legitimate issues for the Peoples' Movement for Freedom.[70]

There was no widespread response by teachers to Itagaki's call for the education of the masses. However, in many local areas, the response was sufficient to provoke alarm among educational officials. In Iwate prefecture, for example, among the forty-one members of a chapter of the movement, eight were local public school teachers. When former teachers and educational staff of the local school board are included, they made up nearly half of the total membership. The chapter also published a journal to spread its influence.[71]

The vast majority of teachers abided by the new law, presumably read by them since prefectural governors were instructed to distribute a copy to each teacher.[72] The law also had its intended effect by discouraging activist teachers from remaining in the movement. For example, many teachers who were members of the Fukushima Freedom Party (Fukushima Jiyūtō), a local political party, took an active role in its activities that promoted revolutionary activities. However as a result of the new regulations, at least ten were forced to resign because of their political activities.[73] Other activist teachers, embittered by the restrictions, attempted to circumvent the intent of the law. Rather than overtly teaching about, or advocating, political rights, they assigned readings from newspapers and magazines critical of government policy, which were not uncommon. Some local educational officials strictly prohibited such measures in an attempt to suppress political teachings in the schools. They even discouraged teachers themselves from reading articles criticizing government policy carried in the press, a policy supported by the Ministry of Education.[74]

The second regulation, Regulations Governing the Conduct of Teachers, spelled out just cause for dismissing teachers. Included on the list of offenses justifying termination were a criminal record, severe alcohol problems, and others (sono ta). This bill, along with the strict provisions of the law against political activities by government employees, opened the way for local educational officers to apply them broadly against teachers involved in political activities. It also served as an intimidating influence on the teaching profession in general.[75]

There were, however, isolated instances where activist teachers provoked local government officials who applied the new laws as they concerned Emperor Meiji. A local newspaper, the Tochigi Shimbun, carried an article by an elementary school teacher indirectly critical of the emperor. He was jailed for one year.[76] In another instance, a public school elementary teacher in the city of Kobe tore up a picture of the emperor, conceivably one that had been distributed to local schools by the Imperial Household at the instigation of Motoda Nagazane. The teacher was given a three-year prison sentence for his offense.[77] Manifestly some local officials interpreted acts antagonistic to the emperor as political activities that were banned by the new laws.

Overall, government policy restricting teacher's political rights produced its intended results. In areas where teachers were active in political organizations such as the Jiyū Minken Undō, political momentum was adversely affected as local teachers learned about the new laws. Many of the activists quit the movement.[78] Since a number of teacher training schools had become sources of young political activists, the police placed local teacher training colleges under close surveillance. For example, a policeman attended every assembly of students, including those of a purely academic nature, at the Kanagawa Teacher Training College during this era of suppression.[79]

These restrictive bills represent a watershed in the history of Japanese teachers. They mark the beginning of a crackdown in the struggle that revolved around the interpretation of political neutrality of the public school. Beyond that, a basic question lay at the very heart of the issue: who would be empowered to make the critical interpretations that set limits on teacher's civil and political rights?

Simultaneously with the political restrictions on teachers, the government from 1881 took measures to curb the influence of educational associations that had evolved from teacher initiative. Concerned with the influence exerted by the Peoples' Movement for Freedom among these private organizations, some of which had taken public positions against government policy both educational and otherwise, local governments gradually applied pressure on them. In some instances local organizations of teachers, struggling to survive, accepted subsidies from local prefectural offices. There were also cases where prefectural officials served as officers of teacher associations. In the process governmental influenced increased to the extent that not a few teacher organizations came under the dominating influence of local government, thereby curtailing antigovernment activities by them.[80]

A prime example of the period was the Tokyo Education Association of classroom teachers, which originated in 1878 during the freewheeling days when the director of the Ministry of Education was Tanaka Fujimaro. Originally it included a mixture of classroom teachers and local educational officers interested in the liberal educational reforms under Tanaka. By 1882 it had changed its name to the Tokyo Education Association (Tokyo Kyōiku Gakkai) with over two hundred members, and published a professional journal on education. Shortly thereafter it boldly changed its name to the All Japan Education Association (Dai Nippon Kyōiku Kai), recruiting members from all over the country for its first general conference scheduled for September 1883.

Indicative of the influence on the association already gained by the government, at the 1883 meeting a high official of the Ministry of Education, Tsuji Shinji, was elected president. A relative liberal, well respected, he had been an original member of the committee that wrote the First National Plan for Education of 1872, the Gakusei. Nevertheless, efforts by the Ministry of Education to utilize this professional education association to counter the activities of the Peoples' Movement for Freedom were set in motion. In 1884, the association elected another senior official of the Ministry of Education, Kuki Ryūichi, as chairman. As a result, the All Japan Education Association had effectively become a support group of the government.[81]

Restrictions on the political activities of teachers were not confined to the public domain. In 1882 the predecessor of the distinguished Waseda University, the Tokyo Semmon Gakkō, was founded by Ōkuma Shigenobu. Ōkuma, it should be recalled, was a devoted student of Guido Verbeck when he taught in Nagasaki during the Tokugawa regime in the mid 1860s. By 1880 he had became a powerful member of the inner circle in the Meiji government. In one of the defining moments of government leadership, Ōkuma was forced to resign in 1881 in an incident known as the great political change of the Meiji era (Meiji Jūyonen Seihen). The result was a new government of a more conservative persuasion than that of Ōkuma, who pursued relatively liberal policies during his long government service.

The significance to modern education of the 1881 leadership crisis emerged in the form of a new private school established by Ōkuma the following year, the Tokyo Semmon Gakkō. It quickly became a hotbed of antigovernment teachings in its political courses then promoted by the Peoples' Movement for Freedom. Ōkuma recalled that "From the beginning we held to one simple proposition; the will of the people is never identical with the opinion of the government."[82] According to him, the Meiji political leaders feared the potential for social unrest of a new private institution outside its control. "The government regarded this school as a training center for conspirators and constantly sent its agents to shadow us. . . . There is no doubt that they did not favor us with satisfactory reports. Large numbers of agents infiltrated the campus, and, disregarding the sanctity of the classroom and dormitory, they waited for an opportunity to create a disturbance and to plot the destruction of the school from within. At times their interference led to trouble."[83]

With the founding of the private Tokyo Semmon Gakkō by Ōkuma, at the same time that an antigovernment political party was formed with the same political persuasion guided by Ōkuma, further evidence of an expanding threat to the government became evident. Beyond the immediate threat to the political leadership, Ōkuma's private school represented an institution that brazenly fostered independence from government control, similar to Fukuzawa Yukichi's Keio Gijuku school. One major factor, however, differentiated Keio Gijuku from Ōkuma's Tokyo Semmon Gakkō. Fukuzawa's private school provided many teachers for government schools and officers of the government itself. The outstanding example is Hamao Arata, who later became minister of education and president of the Imperial University. Ōkuma's private school went a step further by promoting antigovernment teachings. From that period onward, the school, which became Waseda University in perpetual competition with Keio University, distinguished itself from other private institutions. With varying intensity it has taken pride as a politically progressive institution preserving academic freedom ever suspicious of government policy.

The Portrait of Emperor Meiji in the Schools

During the reverse-course policy of the Ministry of Education in the early 1880s, the Imperial Household initiated a policy of extraordinary significance. It endeavored to raise student awareness of, and respect for, Emperor Meiji. This took place at the very time the Imperial Household was also promoting its own publication on morals education written by Motoda Nagazane, the *Principles for Guiding Children*. A portrait of the emperor was first distributed for display at all schools directly under Ministry of Education control such as national high schools and teacher training colleges. Since the Imperial Household was instrumental in this campaign,

Motoda Nagazane from his position within the household surely exerted considerable influence in promoting the campaign. As previously mentioned, he included a veiled warning that something like this would transpire in his famous addendum to the 1879 "Imperial Will on Education." "Since the practice has developed recently of displaying pictures in classrooms, we must see to it that portraits of loyal subjects, righteous warriors, filial children, and virtuous women are utilized, so that when the pupils enter the school, they will immediately feel in their hearts the significance of loyalty and filial piety."[84]

From 1882 onward throughout the decade, every public school in the country received a copy of an official portrait of the emperor from the Imperial Household. The purpose was to familiarize all students from the first grade through the teacher training schools with the image of Emperor Meiji. This was felt to be particularly necessary as the imperial tours to the regions came to an end by the mid-1880s. The portrait served as a substitute for the opportunity to see the emperor in person.[85]

The arrival of the august portrait from the Imperial Household was marked by ritual ceremonies of reception by local schools, some on a grand scale. In one example, officials from the prefectural office and the local community joined with several thousand residents for a two-day event. Lanterns decorated the streets, balloons were released, a fireworks display was held, and an all-school sports festival was conducted to mark the grand occasion.[86] It is well within reason to assume that the event must have particularly pleased Motoda Nagazane.

After the Ministry of Education and the Imperial Household devoted several years advancing morals education with the emperor at the center, Egi Kazuyuki, ministry official deeply involved in the process, visited a local school in 1884 to determine its effectiveness. The teacher used the approved text for the morals class. A section devoted to the filial relationship between the ruler (*kun*) and his subjects (*shin*) was read to the class. Egi then asked the students who was the kun. Their reply: the emperor. Who was the shin? Their reply: government bureaucrats. After several years of studying the new morals education that Motoda Nagazane and the Imperial Household, and Egi and the Ministry of Education, had promoted so vigorously, students could not yet relate themselves or their families to the emperor in a filial manner as intended by these powerful figures and institutions. Egi concluded that proper morals were still lacking due to the poor teaching of it in the schools.[87]

The Reverse Course versus the New Movement in Education: Takamine Hideo

The prestigious Tokyo Teacher Training School inevitably felt the conservative winds of change sweeping through the Ministry of Education in the early 1880s. However, a remarkable development took place at this elite teacher training institution during the peak of the reverse course era. A new movement in education based on the most modern theory of education existent in the West was initiated by Japan's first professional educator, Takamine Hideo. Isawa Shūji and Takamine Hideo, graduates of progressive teacher training schools in America, the topic of chapter 11, had assumed administrative control of the Tokyo Teacher Training School upon return home in 1878. They promptly revised the curriculum to conform to the one under which they had studied in America, introducing the most progressive Pestalozzian theory of education in the West. At the time, Tanaka Fujimaro was head of the Ministry of Education and not only appointed Isawa and Takamine to their prestigious positions but he also approved their overhaul of the curriculum. In contrast, Motoda from the Imperial Household and Nishimura Shigeki from within the Ministry of Education itself were highly critical of them.[88] At the time, however, they were in no position to impede them.

By 1881, Tanaka had been replaced with Kōno Togama followed by Fukuoka Takachika. They were determined to replace Tanaka's liberal education code based on the American model with a new curriculum based on Confucian teachings. Meanwhile, as the reverse course at the Ministry of Education got under way, Takamine Hideo, the leading proponent of Pestalozzian theories in Japan, had become president of the elite teacher training school. As the nation's first professional educator, Takamine faithfully applied the progressive principles of modern education that he had learned at the Oswego Teacher Training College in America.

The ministry promptly moved to change the anomalous situation. In August 1881, amid a host of interlocking directives implementing the reverse course in educational reform, the Regulations and Principles of Teacher Training (Shihan Gakkō Kyōsoku Taikō) was issued.[89] The primary provision elevated the course on morals from the bottom to the top of the curriculum for teacher trainees. This brought the training school curriculum into conformity with the Guidelines for the Elementary School Curriculum (Shōgakkō Kyōsoku Kōryō) issued four months earlier on May 4. Future teachers at the Tokyo Teacher Training School under Takamine were required thereafter to take three hours per week in morals education, the same number of course hours devoted to pedagogy. Overall, the total number of hours per week devoted to teaching methodology under the original Isawa-Takamine curriculum of 1878–1879 was sharply reduced under the latest revisions.[90] In addition, foreign texts were dropped from the morals course, including Samuel Smiles's widely circulated book Self Help. Motoda Nagazane's Principles for Guiding Children (Yōgaku Kōyō) replaced the foreign texts in local teacher training schools throughout the nation.[91] As a result of these changes, the reverse course in educational modernization had reached from the elementary level through the teacher training schools.

Regardless of the ideological persuasion of the decision makers in the Ministry of Education, Takamine Hideo, typical of Pestalozzi devotees throughout the West, harbored a missionary spirit to introduce this highly controversial foreign concept to the Japanese. He was in a prominent position to do just that precisely as the Ministry of Education came under conservative leadership of Minister Fukuoka Takachika, committed to Confucian teachings, and Egi Kazuyuki, senior official committed to imperial education. If ever there were two organizations at cross-purposes during the first half of the 1880s, it was the Ministry of Education and the Tokyo Teacher Training School.

As president of the school from 1881, Takamine embarked on his mission by first appointing a committee of faculty and in-service teachers to carry out an internal curriculum reform at the nation's premier teacher-training institution. To initiate the project, a nationwide study was undertaken to evaluate the state of teaching in Japan's public schools. The report concluded that the nation's teachers were poorly trained in teaching methods. As Japan's leading authority on Pestalozzi, Takamine then undertook a revision of the curriculum. He replaced subject-matter courses such as history, science, and so on, a mainstay of the curriculum, with integrated courses (*jitsubutsu*) centered on teaching methods. Teacher trainees, he claimed, should have studied subject matter before entering the school. The purpose of training teachers at this level was not what to teach in science classes, but how to teach science, mathematics, and so on. This interpretation of the role of the school rendered it essentially a higher teacher-training college that concentrated on the methodology of teaching, dear to Takamine's heart.[92]

Takamine introduced his students to the great classic on Pestalozzian theory, *The Principles and Practice of Teaching* by James Johonnot, one of America's foremost authorities on the topic. Takamine was convinced that the modern theory of education developed under the most advanced psychological research into learning theory carried out by the great Swiss educator should be introduced to Japan. To achieve that goal he translated Johonnot's classic, which he used as his basic textbook in his courses at the Tokyo Teacher Training College. It was published later under the title of the *New Educational Theory (Kyōiku Shinron)*.[93]

In contrast to the traditional learning process of memorization, repetition, and testing, the modern teaching theories that Takamine's students were taught involved the scientific process of inductive thinking based on the techniques of observation, comparison, and conclusion. The purpose of teaching was to instill in the student the inductive ability of how to think. This was in opposition to, and in contrast with, "what to think," which was criticized by the modernists as the primary purpose of the traditional classroom.

At the same time, the Confucianists such as Nishimura Shigeru and Egi Kazuyuki within the ministry were espousing the cause of traditional morals education in the school with equal zeal. One side led by Takamine Hideo was devoted to the study of education and how the child learns according to natural developmental stages as an active rather than passive participant in the learning process. The other side led by Motoda was primarily concerned with imparting proper ethical and moral precepts to the child based on traditional social values originally derived from the teachings of Confucius. Modern teaching methodology was of little interest to Motoda.

In order to survive the rising tide of conservatism and reaction to the modern trends within the Ministry of Education, Takamine and his students at the Tokyo Teacher Training School inevitably had to adjust. Reacting to the ministry's Guidelines for the Elementary School Curriculum that elevated morals education to the top of the curriculum, teacher training courses were accordingly revised. The major revision centered on Takamine's progressive integrated course (*jitsubutsu*) that combined mathematics, science, and how to teach them into a single course. Featured as a core curriculum requirement exemplifying the unity of learning, a concept in Pestalozzian theory, it was dropped by 1883. In its place the traditional structure of separate specialized courses in mathematics and the various science disciplines was reinstated. One of the major Pestalozzian innovations implemented by Takamine had come to a sudden end.

Accommodations also had to be made within individual lessons. For example, although the new Guidelines for Elementary Teachers stipulated the primacy of morals education, the Takamine progressives clearly attempted to circumvent the underlying purpose by designing unique lessons to conform to the overall regulations. The following simple lesson for the attached training school integrated morals into science teaching, which was meant to apply modern theory of learning based on observation of the child's immediate environment. It was the Japanese accommodation of Johonnet's book, the *Principles and Practices of Teaching* based on Pestalozzian theory, which took on a unique political and ideological meaning in Japan far beyond a simple science lesson.

> TEACHER: Holding a leaf with a drop of water on it, asks what it is.
> STUDENT: Identifies it as a leaf with water on it.
> TEACHER: How much water is there?
> STUDENT: Only a drop.
> TEACHER: But if you have many drops of water, what do you have?
> STUDENT: A river.
> TEACHER: Moral: How important one drop of water is. As a river begins with one drop of water, both good and evil deeds begin with a single act that can turn into a river of good or evil.[94]

Not only did Takamine's personality and teachings at the Tokyo Teacher Training School endear him to his students but an active movement promoting the new theory in education called *kaihatsu shugi*, "developmental education," was also launched. The number of his students slowly increased, many of them catching the fever of change. They were eager to return to their home areas to pass on the most modern ideas in education they had learned. Two of them, Wakabayashi Torasaburō and Shirai Tsuyoshi, became well known in the Japanese educational world as authorities on the modern theory of education by writing a book on the subject. Based on Takamine's teachings, and entitled *Revised Teaching Techniques* (*Kaisei Kyōju Jutsu*), it caused a stir within the educational world as the first book authored by Japanese that became a classic in the field of kaihatsu shugi.[95]

In spite of opposing trends under way at the Ministry of Education, through the efforts of one single individual, Takamine Hideo, a new movement in modern Japanese education emerged that marks him as Japan's first professional educator. A new professional self-confidence among teachers was spreading precisely as the government took action to suppress their political activities. A new interest in teaching methodology was generated and disseminated by the proliferating educational journals. For example, the influential *Kyōiku Jiron* (Educational Journal) published many articles on the new concepts from 1884. Teachers and academics formed new research groups to report on their studies.[96] A fresh wind had been unleashed in Japanese schools through the teachings of Takamine, on the basis of Pestalozzi's theories, even as educational authorities at the Ministry of Education were exerting a major effort to redirect the core of modern education from western learning to traditional morals education in the Confucian mode.

In retrospect, this unexpected progressive movement in education marks the first modern transformation of the Japanese classroom carried out by a Japanese. Moreover it was potentially more revolutionary than that brought about by Marion Scott a decade earlier at the same institution. Takamine's accomplishments were more impressive than Scott's, which were enthusiastically supported and encouraged by the Ministry of Education. Takamine's efforts, in contrast, took place at a time the Ministry of Education was carrying out a restrictive policy toward teachers. Not only were his accomplishments remarkable under the circumstances but it was also a mark of the man that powerful ministry forces did not replace him.

Developmental education (*kaihatsu shugi*) as a movement, and Takamine's translation of Johonnot's book, the Bible of the new believers, inevitably came under heavy criticism by the traditionalists such as Motoda Nagazane from the Imperial Household. The issue in contention boiled down to an age-old question: what is the purpose of education? For example, should it serve the emperor, the state, the community, the family, or the individual? Critics argued that kaihatsu shugi did not address this fundamental question. Rather, it was merely concerned with the superficial, that is, efficiency in the learning process. The primary purpose of education to those then making the decisions for Japanese schools was considered of far greater significance. It was moral—in the Confucian tradition.[97]

Fresh Winds from the West: The German Factor

While the Ministry of Education was carrying out major conservative reforms of Japanese education, fresh winds from the West were blowing across the land. During the first decade of modernization in the 1870s, western educational influence originated primarily in the United States through the efforts of Tanaka Fujimaro. From the 1880s on, German educational influence gradually replaced the American.

The political ascendancy of Itō Hirobumi and his confidant Inoue Kowashi in 1881, as a result of the great political upheaval known as the Meiji Seihen, provides the opportunity to trace the genesis of German influence on modern Japanese education. During 1881, the government bowed to the demands of the political opposition, the Peoples' Movement for Freedom, for a representative form of government. On October 12, an Imperial Rescript committed the government to establish a parliament and a constitution by 1889. A special committee was established to undertake the preparations, chaired by Itō Hirobumi assisted by Tanaka Fujimaro, the previously displaced director of the Ministry of Education. Inoue Kowashi was also appointed to the committee.[98] Inoue, already German-oriented, grasped the opportunity to recommend to Itō that, in constitutional matters, "Japan should follow the Prussian example."[99]

As deliberations progressed, it was decided to send a Japanese delegation of senior leaders to Germany to undertake a personal investigation of the German constitutional form of government. Indicative of Itō's growing interest in the German model being promoted by Inoue, he accepted the assignment to carry out an investigation of the German constitution. Itō departed for Berlin on March 14, 1882, effectively withdrawing from the field of domestic conflict for nearly a year. It was during his absence in Europe that his earlier nemesis, Motoda Nagazane, pursued the powerful campaign to promote Confucian morality in the nation's schools.

Inoue, capitalizing on his growing influence, remained in Japan, further promoting his interest in the German model. He recommended that German studies and language be given a more prominent position in the law and literature departments at Tokyo University. At that time, German influence was contained primarily to the department of medicine, partly through the influence of Guido Verbeck, as we have seen. A subtle shift in other departments within the university got underway shortly thereafter, as German professors began replacing American and British professors.[100] The movement was supported and encouraged by the Ministry of Education. It was reported that Fukuoka Takachika, then head of the ministry, met secretly with the president of Tokyo University to discuss how German influence could be expanded at the nation's only university.[101]

Until this time English was the primary language of instruction in the nonmedical fields. Even Japanese professors used English in their advanced courses. From 1881 on, German was introduced as a compulsory course.[102] However, in early February 1884, the new head of the Ministry of Education, Ōki Takatō, who ran the ministry at its very inception in 1871, decreed that Japanese would become the main language of instruction, replacing English. And of great relevance for the future, German textbooks replaced English textbooks wherever possible.[103]

German influence on Japanese education reached new levels when Itō Hirobumi returned from his lengthy study of the German constitution in Berlin.

Table 20   Tokyo University Foreign Faculty, 1881–1885

	British	American	German
1881	5	10	12 (10 medical)
1882	3	5	12 (6)
1883	3	2	10 (4)
1884	3	1	11 (3)
1885	1	1	10 (3)

Source: *Tokyo Daigaku Hyakunen Shi* (One Hundred Year History of Tokyo University), (Tokyo: Tokyo Daigaku, 1984), 1: 486.

Upon assuming the prime ministership in 1885, he was in a position to appoint a minister of education, Mori Arinori, who invited to Japan a German scholar, Emil Hausknecht, a proponent of the Herbartian theory of education developed in Germany. As professor at the Tokyo Imperial University, Hausknecht laid the foundation of a new movement in Japanese education in the late 1880s based on the German model, covered in the following chapter.

The Rokumeikan Era

The middle years of the 1880s turned out to be one of the most fascinating periods in early Meiji Japan. Although the Ministry of Education came under increasing influence of forces promoting the Imperial Way, irresistible elements of western culture continued to make inroads on cultural traditions. In a well-known history of modern Japan, the mid 1880s is aptly described: "The span of half a decade from 1883 to 1888 was a phenomenal period. It saw the eruption of a veritable rush of improvement of every imaginable type. An almost universal feeling developed among the sophisticated urbanites that everything Japanese fell far short of western standards, and that improvement was the crying need in every phase of life. No aspect, social, economic, political, religious, intellectual, or moral escaped this fetish for improvement."[104]

Evidence of the diverse influences buffeting Japanese society in the mid-1880s was the Western hairstyles that appeared on the streets with increasingly regularity. Western-style clothes became more popular, replacing the traditional kimono. Interest in the English language spread, especially among girls. Some private girls' schools with strong programs in English attracted students from age fourteen to forty, such was the growing interest in studying English. It became fashionable to insert English words in conversational Japanese. In one prominent girls' school the use of Japanese was banned on Fridays, dubbed the English Day.[105]

Ballroom dancing epitomized the trends. The most vivid example of the period was the well-known Rokumeikan, a huge ornate structure intended by the Foreign Ministry as a state-of-the-art guesthouse for foreign dignitaries built in Hibiya, Tokyo. It was designed by the most influential architect in Meiji Japan, the Englishman Josiah Condor, who introduced western architecture at the Imperial College of Engineering under the Scotsman Henry Dyer. This Italian-style building with its expansive banquet hall and dance floor for western-style ballroom dancing, with the added intriguing boast of a bathtub "such as never been seen before in the land," achieved great prominence.[106] Forever after this brief period has become known as the Rokumeikan Jidai (era).[107]

The Rokumeikan exemplified the challenges facing Japanese leaders in their efforts to lead the nation into the intimate circle of world powers then dominated by western nations. International diplomacy, they discovered, was a world unto its own. With the increasing number of foreign diplomats and male military attachés assigned to Tokyo, the government concluded that they should have available some form of entertainment that fit international customs. The Rokumeikan was built to provide that entertainment for western officials, hence western dancing

Figure 27. Rokumeikan.
From Akiko Kuno, *Unexpected Destinations: The Poignant Story of Japan's First Vassar Graduate* (Tokyo: Kōdansha International, 1993), 112.

and dress were introduced, and Japanese diplomats and other socialites could mingle on the dance floor.

The spectacle of Japan's socialites, decked out in long gowns and tuxedos or grotesque dress for the popular western-style costume balls, waltzing around the floor to western music epitomized to some critics the vulgar excesses of the day. A familiar participant, Tsuda Umeko, by now returned from her ten-year experience living with the Charles Lanmans in Washington, D.C., the topic of an earlier chapter, was impressed. She wrote her American mother, Mrs. Lanman, a vivid description of the dance floor: "old emperors waltzing with peasant girls and Dutch maidens, old daimyos [feudal lords] polka-ing with the Goddess of Liberty, and a jinrickisha man and a Japanese carpenter at the same set with Queen Elizabeth."[108]

To some Japanese the Rokumeikan dances symbolized how deeply western customs had penetrated the society, flouting accepted Japanese moral traits. The affront to traditional Japanese sensitivities was magnified when the leading political figure of the nation, Itō Hirobumi, previously returned from Germany in 1883 to assume his ascendancy in government, joined in the dancing with his wife. When he became prime minister in 1885, his first cabinet participated in the festivities, becoming known as the "dancing cabinet."[109]

It immediately became apparent that there were too few Japanese ladies, young or otherwise, who could dance with the western diplomats, converse with them in a foreign language, or mingle comfortably with foreigners in any setting. Tsuda Umeko was one of those few who met two of the "good many officers from the ships" at the ball who, perhaps predictably, "said they were coming to see me."[110] The government sponsored the Rokumeikan Dancing Society (Buyōkai) to teach socialite wives and daughters, including those of government officials, how to dance. The wife of Itō Hirobumi took the lead by joining the classes, setting off a fashionable trend for western clothes and hairstyles among females of the higher classes.

Other socialites who took dancing lessons for the balls included the wife of the minister of education, Mori Arinori, the fifth daughter of Iwakura Tomomi, leader of the famous mission to Washington in 1871, and Mrs. Oyama Sutematsu, wife of General Oyama, educated at Vassar College in America. Dancing was even introduced at the Peers School for Girls (Joshi Gakushuin), and the Girls Teacher Training School in Tokyo (Tokyo Joshi Shihan Gakkō).[111]

The Rokumeikan exposed an urgent need to educate girls from the better Japanese families in western customs and languages. In the mid-1880s, Christian missions from western countries, notably America and Britain, targeted Japan and China for special consideration. The mission boards recognized that in eastern societies the education of girls lagged far behind that of boys in the mainstream of education. Mission schools for girls filled a special niche in the modern Japanese school system at this time.

Among the more famous and successful schools for Japanese girls founded by Christian organizations from the West during this period was Tōyō Eiwa Jogakuin. Like others, this mission school catered to the better social classes in the greater Tokyo area. Indicative of the times, it became fashionable for political families to send their daughters or granddaughters to these schools where English was then, and remains to this day, a prominent attraction to upper-class families. For example, Tōyō Eiwa Jogakuin enrolled girls from the families of Itō Hirobumi, Kido Takayoshi, and Iwakura Tomomi, all senior members of the political elite.[112] In spite of, and in contrast to, the reactionary trends under way within the Ministry of Education, "English fever" and private Christian mission schools for girls increased significantly.

An episode in 1884 at the elite Tokyo Girls Teacher Training School (Tokyo Joshi Shihan Gakkō) revealed how western-style customs had penetrated the upper-class families of Tokyo. As a state institution, the school recruited girls from throughout the nation including many from rural areas. In contrast, the attached secondary training school catered to local girls primarily from the leading Tokyo families. One graduate from rural Japan recalls her astonishment when the school held a western-style ball the day after she entered. Oddly, music was provided by musicians from the Imperial Household. Males from the foreign community were invited. To the dismay of the regular female students from local areas, most of whom never learned to dance, they merely watched the younger Tokyo girls from the attached high school boldly dancing and mingling with the foreign guests.[113] It was all part of a renewed attraction of things western symbolized by the Rokumeikan.

Persistent Problems at the End of the 1880–1885 Period

During the five-year period between 1880 and 1885, when the traditionalists exerted the greatest influence on Japanese public schools since the Meiji Restoration of

1868, the continuing problem of school financing plagued the conservative reformers as it did the progressives during their heyday. It influenced the rate of school attendance with deficient school facilities and an absence of strong local initiatives to attract students. It had the inevitable consequence of increased financial burdens on the beleaguered farmers. For example, by 1882, about 40 percent of all schools charged student tuition to supplement the local school tax. However, even in those schools where tuition was not charged, many did not supply textbooks and essential supplies. Parents were expected to provide them, a factor in keeping school attendance low and school dropout rates high.[114]

Although many local governments passed on the financial burden for textbooks to the parents, the proportion of their budgets devoted to financing the public schools increased dramatically during the 1880s. It coincided with the decrease in educational subsidies from the Ministry of Education, which were actually suspended from 1882 in the face of a national budget crisis.[115]

School attendance rates illustrate the problem. Immediately after the enactment of the revision of Tanaka Fujimaro's Education Act by conservative forces in 1880, school attendance figures for both boys and girls jumped during a two-year period. However from 1883, the peak, the rates leveled off. This state of affairs reflected the deteriorating economic conditions of local communities. Even though the parents of about half of all first graders could afford to send them to school in 1883, half dropped out after three years. In other words, even during the peak of elementary school attendance in 1883, only about 25 percent of all forth grade children were actually in a fourth grade classroom. Moreover, after three years of schooling in the great metropolis of Kyoto, only 58 percent of those who entered first grade completed the third grade. Thirty-five percent entered fourth grade.[116] Finance had much to do with those conditions.

Table 21   Proportion of Local Community Budgets for Education, 1880–1884

Year	% of budget
1880	29.8
1881	32.8
1882	35.1
1883	39.8
1884	47.7

Source: *Nihon Kindai Kyōiku Hyakunenshi* (One Hundred Year History of Modern Japanese Education) (Tokyo: National Educational Research Institute, 1974), 2: 47.

Table 22   Elementary School Attendance Rates,
1880–1885 (percentage)

	Boys	Girls	Total
1880	58.72	21.91	41.06
1881	62.75	26.77	45.47
1882	66.99	33.04	50.72
1883	69.43	35.48	53.05
1884	69.28	35.26	52.92
1885	65.80	32.07	49.62

Source: *Naka Arata, Gakkō no Rekishi: Shōgakkō no Rekishi*
(The History of Schools: The Elementary School) (Tokyo:
Daiichi Hōki Shuppan, 1979), 2: 66.

Table 22 illustrates how the intent of the first public school system of 1873, the Gakusei, had fallen far short of its primary goal a decade later. "No household with an uneducated child" became the slogan of the nation's first attempt at a public school system. It was an unrealistic goal from the start, although it served as a stimulant to bring nearly half of all peasant children into the schools by the mid-1880s. That in itself was a remarkable achievement under the financial constraints that persisted throughout the period.

As the first half of the 1880s ended, that is, the middle of the second decade of the Meiji period, the great transition away from the American model of education promoted by Tanaka Fujimaro was transforming Japanese education. Although the alternative course embedded in the venerable classics of the great Chinese sage Confucius was given a rebirth in the curriculum of the early 1880s, it could not stem the tide of western modernism. Neither the laissez faire of the American educational tradition nor the rigid social order of the Confucian model fit the needs of Japanese society undergoing enormous stress in the search for an appropriate model for the future. A new leader was on the horizon who would chart a different course in the modernization of Japanese education, the focus of the next chapter.

17 Education for the State

THE GERMAN MODEL, 1886–1889

During the last half of the 1880s, the system of Japanese education in place since 1873 underwent another period of major reforms. It began with a meeting that took place in Paris in September 1882 between the future minister of education, Mori Arinori, and the future prime minister, Itō Hirobumi. A new interpretation of the purpose for modern Japanese education emerged from that historic meeting: the school was perceived by these two as an instrument of nation building, and the "Prussian notion of education" was chosen as the model.[1]

Itō Hirobumi had traveled to Germany in 1882 to undertake a year-long study of the German constitution. A long series of lectures from respected German authorities on the topic were arranged for him in Berlin and Vienna, which kept him out of Japan for a year. At the same time, Mori Arinori was serving as the Japanese minister to the Court of St. James in London from 1880. This was the second major diplomatic assignment to the West for Mori; as Japan's first chargé d'affaires in Washington, he had hosted the high-powered Iwakura Mission in 1872. Itō Hirobumi's visit to Washington as a member of that mission brought him into close association with Mori. A decade later, Mori was now making a name for himself in diplomatic circles of London, striking up acquaintance with leading British figures of the day. His most notable relationship was with one of the great influential thinkers of the nineteenth century, Herbert Spencer.

During a break from his lectures in Germany, Itō visited Paris in late August and early September 1882, to attend a diplomatic event. Mori Arinori was sent from London to the same event, providing Itō with an opportunity to meet with him.[2] During several days in late summer in Paris, two of the most colorful urbane Japanese set in motion a powerful concept in modern Japan, that is, education for nation building. The new German state that emerged in the early 1870s out of the Prussian tradition provided the basic guidelines to achieve that goal. The understandings arrived at that historic meeting in Europe were instrumental in setting the course of educational history for Japan into the middle of the twentieth century.

The Paris meeting between two leading statesmen of modern Japan provided an opportunity for them to discuss the future of the nation from a unique international perspective far from home. One of the far-reaching conclusions they reached concerned the purpose of Japanese education in the modern world. It was nothing less than the preservation and security of the nation, or nationalism (kokkashugi) based on the Prussian model. The fundamental factor in achieving that lofty aim, they concluded, was education.[3] By the end of the Paris meeting, Itō, convinced ever since he worked with Mori Arinori ten years earlier in Washington that he was the best man to develop educational policy, was now more resolute in his convictions than ever. Itō felt that he could entrust Mori to develop a national plan for education to meet the overriding goal. Japanese education must be structured to ensure the welfare of the country.[4] In essence, education was perceived by these two Japanese leaders as an instrument to serve the state.

Prussian patterns of government and education that formed the new powerful German state in 1870 held a particular appeal both to Itō and Mori. First, the centralized structure of German government, if adapted to Japan, would enable Japanese political leaders, that is Itō and Mori, to implement educational reform from the top down in an efficient manner. Germany had also developed a strong comprehensive school system that served powerful national political interests. In other words, education that served as an instrument of resurgent nationalism in Germany conformed to the goals of the Japanese political elite for their country in the 1880s.[5]

For a deeper understanding of German influence on the modern system of Japanese education at that time, Itō's appreciation of the German pattern of government and education is essential. He learned from private lectures by German scholars about the famous phrase attributed to the Prussian King Frederick that "as the state, so [goes] the school." The new state of Germany had recently been united under Bismarck, who met with Itō, extending advice to him for the future of Japan. Itō also learned that Prussian education was designed to strengthen the power and prosperity of the state; that the educational system was designed to produce a citizenry to meet that goal; and that the dual-track structure of a highly academic curriculum for the future leaders and a general education for the masses was instrumental in developing the powerful industrialized state of Germany. As a result, the schools produced a dedicated, loyal, literate society serving the interests of the state. Finally, a strong central government was essential to effectively design and enforce this system. The German approach to education as witnessed in 1882 appealed to these two Japanese policy-makers as an ideal model for Japan.[6]

After the Paris meeting, Mori and Itō deepened their mutual agreement through meetings in London and subsequent letters that spelled out the purpose of education. Increasingly concerned that the political activities promoted by the Peoples' Movement for Freedom threatened the public order, they concluded that politics must be kept out of education. The fundamental purpose of education was not only to increase knowledge and skills of the individual and to hone competitive instincts. Of greater importance was the nurturing of values for the welfare and security of the state through a spirit of nationalism. Deeply influenced by German traditions, Itō placed his confidence in Mori to develop a school system to meet that goal when Itō was scheduled to assume government leadership in the near future.[7]

Itō Hirobumi's interlude in Europe in 1882–1883 concluded with a melodramatic moment that brought to an end the career of one of the great leaders of

modern Japan, Iwakura Tomomi, whose Iwakura Mission to the West in 1871–1873
exerted an enormous influence on early Meiji Japan. According to the diary of the
distinguished German doctor, Erwin Baelz, longtime professor at Japan's premier
medical school, in 1883 Iwakura's son asked him to treat his ailing father in Kyoto.[8]
In an extremely emaciated condition, Iwakura was brought to Tokyo for treatment. He promptly asked Doctor Baelz for the true state of his condition. Baelz
frankly told him that "Your condition is hopeless." In a heart-warming moment,
Iwakura then appealed for his assistance, revealing the intensity of conviction
among the great leaders of early Meiji Japan. "Thank you. There is, however, one
thing more I have to ask you. As you know, Privy Councilor Itō is in Berlin and
is to bring back the draft for a new constitution. It is essential that I should have a
talk with him before my death. . . . Many weeks must, however, elapse before he
can be back. You must manage to keep me going by then. You will be able to do
that. . . . It's not for my own sake."

Unfortunately, Dr. Baelz was unable to meet Iwakura's impassioned request.
He died as Itō passed through Hong Kong on his way home to prepare to become
prime minister scheduled for 1885. Mori Arinori, true to his commitment to join
the first cabinet under Itō, resigned his post as ambassador to Great Britain, returning home in April 1884. A mark of the reputation this celebrated Japanese diplomat
had attained while in London, a farewell party was hosted by one of the most distinguished and world-famous personalities, the philosopher Herbert Spencer. Most
fitting, the party was held at the Athenaeum Club in London, where members of
the British Establishment and their guests mingled in the comforts befitting leaders
of the most powerful empire in the world. Mori, as an honorary member by virtue
of his diplomatic position, spent considerable time at the club, arguably the most
exclusive in the world at that time.[9]

Between Mori's first arrival in London in 1865 as a nineteen-year-old samurai
youth from Satsuma during the Tokugawa government, to his departure in 1884
as minister to the Court of St. James under the Meiji government, monumental
developments had taken place in Japanese education. Mori had been directly or
indirectly involved in some of the early ones. In others, notably those that transpired during his four years in London, he obviously had not. When he returned
home in 1884, the tides of change were swirling through Japanese society. On the
one hand, western trends were gaining momentum. The Rokumeikan was just
built. Western ballroom dancing was in vogue. Simultaneously, leading officials at
the Ministry of Education were pursuing a new direction in education centered on
Confucian studies, placing the imperial tradition at the core.

As English-language fever swept the upper circles of Japanese society upon his
return home, Mori was appropriately concerned about the English ability of his
two sons who had spent the last four years in London. Accordingly Tsuda Umeko,
recently returned from ten years in Washington, was hired by Mori, soon-to-be
Japanese minister of education, to tutor his sons in English. She recalled that the
two Mori boys could "only speak English [and] are like little English children
knowing hardly any Japanese . . . regular foreigners, restless and full of life, and can

hardly contain their fun and spirits—such cunning fellows."[10] Tsuda agreed to tutor the Mori boys in English lest they forget all they had learned in London. Once again the irony of the times is revealing. The primary architect of modern Japanese education, on the eve of becoming the minister of education, had two sons who were "like little English children knowing hardly any Japanese."

As Mori prepared to assume the post of minister of education in the first Itō cabinet of 1885, he found himself thrust into the midst of the controversy over the direction of the nation's schools centered on the role of morals education. A reactionary movement underway within the Ministry of Education was, as we have seen, characterized by the central role of the teachings of Confucian morality. Simultaneously, progressives such as Takamine Hideo were leading a new movement at the Tokyo Teacher Training School, advancing Pestalozzian principles incorporating modern psychological concepts in child development. And there were still the influential writings of Fukuzawa Yukichi and his theory of enlightenment critical of both feudalism and the rebirth of Confucian teachings in the schools. The Japanese educational world resembled a ship buffeted between powerful currents headed in multiple directions. A navigator who could chart a steady course ahead was needed. Mori was determined to fill that position as minister of education from December 22, 1885. At thirty-eight, he was the youngest member of Prime Minister Itō's first cabinet.[11]

Mori's appointment was not without its critics. Opposition had developed within the senior ranks of the Ministry of Education as soon as Mori returned from London in 1884. The director of the ministry, Ōki Takatō, was pressed by Itō to approve Mori's initial assignment to the ministry as an advisor pending his appointment as minister. Ōki lived to regret his reluctant approval when Mori criticized an educational reform plan sponsored by Ōki in June 1885. When Mori shortly thereafter replaced Ōki as the new minister of education, he promptly annulled Ōki's reforms.[12]

A reinvigorated Motoda Nagazane, Itō Hirobumi's irrepressible antagonist who had led the successful movement against the progressive reforms of Tanaka Fujimaro just six years previously, also attempted to block Mori's appointment, with the support of the emperor.[13] He realized that the reverse course of educational reform he had instigated from 1880 would be threatened by Mori serving at the helm of the Ministry of Education. Motoda's Imperial Will on Education of 1879 had prevailed over Itō, and during Itō's prolonged absence in Germany from 1882, the stage had been left open to Motoda and like-minded supporters. After Itō's return from Europe in the summer of 1883, the continuing tension between him and Motoda resurfaced. The immediate cause was sparked by Itō when he made it known that he planned to appoint Mori as minister of education in his first cabinet. With that intention, Itō signaled that he had returned to the field of battle with Motoda, and by association the Imperial Household, over educational reform.

Motoda, the leading protagonist of Confucian morality as the foundation of education, protested to the current director of the Ministry of Education, Ōki

Takatō, that Mori was a Christian. This is the same Ōki who was in control of the Ministry of Education within weeks after it was formed in 1871, and who served as senior officer when the First National Plan for Education was issued. Ōki was pressured by Motoda not to yield responsibility for the nation's school system, and Ōki consulted with Itō over Motoda's complaint that, after all, originated from the Imperial Household. Although the opposition to Mori could be considered the will of Emperor Meiji, Itō resolutely refused to reconsider the appointment of Mori as his first minister of education.[14] Itō's commitment to Mori made in Paris three years previously would be honored.

The charge that Mori was a Christian followed him to his grave.[15] From his bizarre experience as a member of the Swedenborgan sect in rural New York at the end of the Tokugawa era, there was a suspicion that he had been converted to the Christian faith as propounded by the cult leader Thomas Harris. In one of the rare personal statements on the subject, Mori refuted the charges in an interview in English years later when he was asked "Do you belong to the Christian faith?" Mori's answer went beyond the intent of the question. "I profess none of those so-called religions: the Christian, the Buddhist, the Mohammedan or anything else. I am a plain man, just as appearing now before you. The aim of my life is simply to live an honest and harmless life."[16]

Mori, perpetually restless, effectively used the interlude after his return from London in 1884 to prepare for his new duties as minister of education with a deter-mined readiness to tackle the problems of education. He was assigned temporarily as a research officer of the Ministry of Education in 1884, prior to his appointment as head of it. One of his interim assignments had him serving as the ministry official responsible for the Tokyo Teacher Training School.[17] This placed him in a strategic position to begin planning one of his primary reforms of modern Japanese education, the great revision of teacher training that would soon follow. Increas-ingly dynamic, Mori made school visits to regional districts giving speeches that indicated the direction he would take as minister. All along, and apparently unbe-knownst to Motoda Nagazane and the Imperial Household, Mori was carefully preparing a definitive comprehensive plan to reform and modernize the Japanese school system.

There were many challenges facing the new government of Prime Minister Itō and Minister of Education Mori in 1885. For example, the condition of local teach-ers was particularly difficult. Salaries, pitifully low, made it extremely difficult for teachers to support a family, resulting in a high turnover rate. Many teaching posi-tions were filled by part-timers who had regular jobs elsewhere, either on the farm or in local stores. In one Nagano community, not one elementary school teacher considered teaching as a career. The quality of teachers, especially in local villages, was consequently abysmally low.[18]

In spite of the many difficulties, within four months after Mori's appointment as the first minister of education with the title of Mumbu Daijin that continues to this day, he unveiled his plan for the modernization of Japanese education. It began with a series of four regulations issued by the Ministry of Education that

Figure 28. Minister of Education Mori Arinori.
From Benjamin Duke, *Ten Great Educators of Modern Japan* (Tokyo: Tokyo University Press, 1989), 42.

encompassed every level of schooling from the elementary through the university. It deserves to be collectively labeled as the Fourth National Plan for Education, such was the scope and magnitude of the reforms that Mori set in place that remained until World War II.

Mori Arinori streamlined an entire system of education that had every appearance if not substance of the German model designed to serve the needs of the state. One distinguished Japanese scholar, Nagai Michio, who became minister of education in the post–World War II period, characterized Mori's plan specifically as modeled after the Prussian or German school system of the early 1880s.[19] That was precisely when Itō Hirobumi studied the German constitution in Germany and Mori Arinori served as ambassador to Great Britain. It was also the time when the two held their historic meeting in Paris to set the direction of Japanese education for the next century.

The Fourth National Plan for Education: Imperial University Ordinance

Mori Arinori's educational reforms of 1886 began, appropriately, at the top of the system with the Imperial University Ordinance. From the beginning of the national system of education in 1873, the government had concentrated on elementary schools. By 1886 the elementary system had achieved a reasonably stable condition. Mori recognized that since the education of the future leaders of the country had been relatively neglected by the government, the post-elementary level required greater attention. Therefore his reforms affected the higher and secondary levels to a far greater extent than the elementary level.

The new name of the nation's only institution of higher education, the Imperial University, incorporated the old and the new by recognizing the continued central role of the imperial tradition in an institution set up primarily to teach modern academic disciplines from the West. The name Teikoku Daigaku (Imperial University) was also used in accordance with the governmental commitment for a forthcoming Imperial Constitution (Teikoku Kempō) and the Imperial Parliament (Teikoku Gikai) scheduled for 1889. As a government institution, the Imperial University fit into the overall plan for the governmental reorganization under the new cabinet system with Itō Hirobumi as prime minister.

Among the provisions of the University Ordinance, the initial one stipulating the purpose of the Imperial University is of primary importance. It reflected the thinking of the new prime minister, Itō Hirobumi, and his minister of education, Mori Arinori, who personally formulated many of the provisions of the ordinance.[20] It stated that "The Imperial University shall have for its object the teaching of such arts and sciences as are required for the purposes of the state."[21] Reflecting the meeting between Mori and Itō in Paris several years previously, Mori incorporated the concept directly into the initial provision of the Imperial University Ordinance: the needs and interests of the individual are superceded by the needs of the state, and the advancement of science and technology should relate directly to the needs of the state, not to scientific advancement per se.

The new university was divided into two. In contemporary terms, an undergraduate school merged the five separate faculties from the old Tokyo University of law, medicine, engineering, natural sciences, and humanities into a unified comprehensive unit called the Bunka Daigaku, the College of Culture (Arts). It resembled the structure of many western universities, with a president (sōchō) administering the entire institution. The role of the undergraduate school was to teach the theory and application of arts and sciences (gakujutsu gigei).[22] A research graduate school of arts and sciences topped the new university.

Among the structural changes brought about by the Imperial University Ordinance, the integration of the Kōbu Daigakkō, dubbed the Imperial University of Engineering by its founder Henry Dyer, into the Faculty of Engineering in the Imperial University, was one of the most important. The Kōbu Daigakkō did not have the status of a regular university at that time, since it was administered by the Ministry of Works, not the Ministry of Education. Nevertheless it maintained extraordinarily high academic and performance standards of engineering under demanding Scottish professors. With the demise of the Ministry of Works in 1885, the Imperial University of Engineering came under the temporary control of the Ministry of Education. As a natural transition, it was then merged into the Engineering Department of the new Imperial University the following year under Ministry of Education control.[23]

Amalgamating the two streams of engineering at the university level was difficult. The Engineering Department of the old Tokyo University was characterized by theoretical studies. In contrast, Henry Dyer, reflecting Scottish tradition, purposely stressed applied engineering at the Imperial University of Engineering. Basic to his curriculum was practical training at the work site, a practice not followed at

Tokyo University. An uneasy relationship between the two conflicting approaches to engineering education was inevitable.

Financially and administratively, the Imperial University was placed under the control of the minister of education, who appointed the president. Article 6 of the ordinance clarifies the central role of the government. The president shall superintend the whole affairs of the Imperial University under the direction of the minister of education. Further, the officers of the university beyond the president included a Board of Councilors, consisting of faculty members who deliberated on "the curricula of studies." Article 8 stipulated that the councilors be selected and appointed by the minister of education from among the professors.[24]

The overriding conclusion to be drawn from the Imperial University Ordinance of 1886 relates to its origins in the 1882 meeting in Paris between Itō Hirobumi and Mori Arinori. They agreed that the purpose of education is to preserve the independence and security of Japan; thus, education would become an instrument to serve the state. The Paris agreement fell into place exactly four years later when Mori, in his very first reform only four months after he assumed his ministerial post, set the agenda for the nation's only university. It would serve the interest of the state, to be controlled by the state under the firm direction of the state's minister of education, Mori Arinori. The intent of Mori's proposal soon became evident. Within a relatively short time, half of the students at the Imperial University were enrolled in the law department. Upon graduation nearly all entered government service.[25] The tradition of the single national university providing the nucleus of government officials who majored in legal studies was set in motion by Mori from the beginning of the institution. It has continued ever since.

Emperor Meiji demonstrated an interest in the new Imperial University, and within several months after its inauguration, he visited the campus on October 29, 1886.[26] Minister Mori welcomed him. Together they visited classes under way. The emperor was impressed with the progress in the law, medicine, and science departments. However, he was disappointed by the absence of a department devoted to the study of morals (*shūshin*). His attention was particularly drawn to the inferior facilities in the Department of Japanese and Chinese Studies, which nominally included the study of oriental morals (*wakan dōtoku*). During his one-day visit, Emperor Meiji was somehow able to detect that any morals teaching at the new university was superficial at best. The difference between conditions in the Department of Japanese and Chinese Studies and those in the science, medical, and law faculties was apparently striking.

The emperor used the visit to point out the disparities between western and oriental studies at Japan's foremost institution of higher learning. His spokesman on education, Motoda Nagazane, wrote a report on the visit a week after the event that expressed the emperor's opinion. In a severe critique of the new Imperial University entitled "Seiyuki" (Sacred Words), the Imperial Household went on record as registering deep concern.[27] The absence of an academic discipline on morals education with Confucian studies at the center at the university level had provoked

imperial displeasure, a signal that the controversy over the role of morals education in modern Japanese education was about to heat up once again.

The contentious issue of morals education at the university level about which
the emperor was troubled indicated that the pendulum under the Itō cabinet had
swung sharply the other way from the previous five years. Rather than serving the
emperor as Motoda Nagazane had intended, the new school system under Mori
was designed to serve the state. The difference between the two interpretations
would become clear as Mori's policies were implemented. Each unit in the school
system had a specific role in an integrated structure to produce loyal patriotic
citizens that would contribute to a strong and independent nation in the next century. It reflected the political thinking of both Prime Minister Itō Hirobumi and
his minister of education, Mori Arinori. Because of the enormous significance of
Mori's educational reforms as they relate to the controversy surrounding morals
education, the issue will be considered in some detail in the final chapter, forming
the background for the "Imperial Rescript on Education" of 1890.

Middle School Ordinance

Of all the sectors in Mori's plan, arguably the most important one is found at the
middle, or secondary, level, that is, between the elementary school and the university. Until this time, educational modernization was first and foremost concentrated on the development of a national system of public elementary schools, by
now firmly in place. The second concern was higher education, with one institution, Tokyo University, incorporating a preparatory school attached to the university. Since Tokyo University offered mostly foreign studies in English with many
foreign faculty, the preparatory school was essentially a language school. In fact,
it was originally called the Tokyo Eigo Gakkō, the Tokyo English School.[28] The
absence of a coherent integrated plan for secondary education beyond the public
elementary schools rendered the educational system incomplete.

Mori Arinori, as the new minister of education, wasted no time in filling that
gap by introducing a comprehensive plan for secondary education. For the first
time the public schools were integrated into a uniform design from the elementary
level through higher education, in other words a national system of public education. Further, one middle school that stands out from among the others was the
Higher Middle School, the Kōtō Chūgakkō. The similarity of this school with the
German gymnasium is so striking that the conclusion that the model was German
is inevitable. Mori was knowledgeable about these schools, having traveled widely
in Europe for four years when he was the minister to Great Britain from 1880 to
1884. As one who took an extraordinary interest in educational affairs, he could not
have been unaware of the role of the elite European academic secondary schools
such as the German gymnasium.

The University Ordinance specifically stipulated that applicants to fill the university entrance quota set by the ministry must graduate from a higher middle
school (kōtō chūgakkō). When the Imperial University Ordinance was written,
these preparatory institutions did not yet exist. Consequently, the Middle School

Ordinance stipulated that five higher middle schools would be founded. Only one, to become the First Higher Middle School in Tokyo, in actuality the former Tokyo University Preparatory School, was in place and qualified to become a higher middle school. The other four had to be established one by one to provide a nationwide network of regional preparatory schools for the recruitment of qualified students for the Imperial University.

Even though the Imperial University Ordinance was issued first, it cannot be separated from the Middle School Ordinance proclaimed a month later. Mori envisioned the two as symbiotically related. In one of his most memorable speeches, he clarified their role by drawing a clear distinction between education (*kyōiku*) and learning (*gakumon*). Education included the three R's and practical education required for the masses, that is elementary and lower middle schools. In contrast, learning was the more theoretical education required for the future leaders of the nation. And that was reserved for those select students who entered the higher middle preparatory school followed by the university, both controlled and financed by the Ministry of Education.[29] The Chūgakkō Rei, the Middle School Ordinance of 1887, set out the provisions governing the new public secondary schools.

Middle School Ordinance

Article 1: The purpose of public middle schools is to prepare students to enter the workforce or the university.

Article 2: The middle schools will be divided into two types, the Ordinary Middle School (*jinjō*), and the Higher Middle School (*kōtō chūgakkō*) under the control (*kanri*) of the Ministry of Education.

Article 3: The curriculum of the Higher Middle School will include law, medicine, natural science, technology, literature, commerce, and agriculture.

Article 4: Five Higher Middle Schools will be established throughout the country, the sites to be decided by the Ministry of Education.

Article 5: The Higher Middle Schools will be financed from the national budget.

Article 6: Each prefecture will establish an Ordinary Middle School financed by the prefectural budget.

Article 7: The curriculum for the Ordinary Middle School will be set by the Ministry of Education.

Article 8: The textbooks for middle schools will be determined by the Ministry of Education.[30]

According to the new law, each prefecture became responsible for sponsoring one lower or ordinary middle school (*jinjō chūgakkō*) within its budget. Since there were no regulations previously governing this level, a patchwork of secondary schools had already developed. Some prefectures had established one or more schools for the more qualified graduates of elementary school. Others had not. Those prefectures with more than one middle school now had to choose one to be designated as the official prefectural middle school. For example, Ibaragi prefecture already had three. Two were closed. In some instances, those not chosen for prefectural support continued as private middle schools. Where there were none, the prefectures were compelled to open one.[31] For the first time, the lower middle school level was integrated into the overall framework of a national plan for public education.

The most important institutions that emerged from the Middle School Ordinance of 1886 were, without doubt, the five regional higher middle schools, the kōtō chūgakkō. Similar to the lower middle schools, there was no previous systematic organization at this level either. The country had also never before been divided into five regions for educational purposes. With the single purpose of these schools as university preparation, the framework for an organized recruiting network for the most qualified students from throughout the country to enter the only university, the elite Imperial University, was set in place. The higher middle school, consequently, represented a new experiment in the modern Japanese public school system.

Among the five Higher Middle Schools to be sited at Tokyo, Sendai, Osaka (later transferred to Kyoto), Kanazawa, and Kumamoto, the most important by far was the Daiichi Kōtō Chūgakkō, the First Higher Middle School in Tokyo. No other middle school played such a significant role in the education of the leadership class of the twentieth century. The foundation was already in place as the Tokyo Daigaku Yobimon (Tokyo University Preparatory School), the former Tokyo English School under the Ministry of Education now attached to the university since its formation in 1877. This institution came under the provisions of the new law, maintaining the tradition of using textbooks from abroad, mostly in English.[32] Consequently Tokyo University, henceforth the Imperial University, and its attached preparatory school, now the First Higher Middle School, were both brought securely under the control of the Ministry of Education.

Although the First Higher Middle School of Tokyo was inaugurated in 1886, the nineteenth year of the Meiji Period, the overwhelming majority of students in the first class came from former samurai families.[33] Since this prestigious higher middle school was designed to prepare students for the single prestigious university, the old families that dominated the preeminent schools during the feudal era continued to dominate the leading schools during the modern era. Moreover, the old capital of feudal Japan, Edo, remained the center of educational opportunity in the new capital of modern Japan, renamed Tokyo.

Mori's extraordinary interest in the higher middle schools was evidenced by his personal involvement in launching the first of the four regional institutions mandated in the new Middle School Ordinance. The Second Higher Middle School, located in Sendai in 1887, was intended to draw the most capable students from the six prefectures in northern Honshu.[34] No doubt to ensure Ministry of Education control over the school located several hundred miles north of Tokyo, Mori appointed one of his trusted ministry officials as the first principal. The head teacher or vice principal of the First Higher Middle School in Tokyo became the first vice principal of the Second Higher Middle School. The minister of education himself traveled to Sendai during the site selection process. He walked over the proposed location, finally giving his personal approval of the exact location for the entrance gate.[35]

The difficulties faced by the regional higher middle schools were illustrated by the examination for qualified students for the first class. The recruitment area included the six surrounding prefectures covering a large northern portion of the main island of Japan. The quota was set at ninety-two students. Out of seventy-three applicants, only seven passed the first entrance examination. Later in the year, another recruitment process was conducted, followed by a second entrance examination. This time twenty more applicants were accepted to complete the first class of students.[36]

The initial examination results for the regional higher middle school exposed the vast discrepancy between the educational standards of the capital city of Tokyo and the regions. The applicants were simply not academically prepared for an examination at this level. The need became apparent for a preparatory division in order to ensure that a pool of qualified students would be available for university preparation at the regional level. Accordingly, the Second Higher Middle School in Sendai was shortly thereafter divided into two units. The first section of two years was to bring the students up to the level of the ordinary middle school run by the prefectures. The second level of three years was intended to concentrate on the preparation for the entrance examination of the Imperial University in Tokyo.[37] This, then, immediately placed local students from the new Second Higher Middle School in Sendai in competition with graduates of the First Higher Middle School in Tokyo, with its long tradition of university preparation.

The gap in academic standards between the First Higher Middle School in Tokyo and the four regional higher middle schools as they were launched one by one would continue to be a serious defect in the system. Since the major purpose of all five was the preparation of the most qualified students for the Imperial University in Tokyo, the representation of graduates from the regional schools at the university would serve as a gauge of their success. In fact, for the next decade, 90 percent of the graduates from the Imperial University originated from the First Higher Middle School in Tokyo.[38]

Since graduates of the First Higher Middle School dominated the entering classes of the Imperial University, they have understandably received most attention in historical studies. However it is of some interest to follow the fate of the first graduating class of the Second Higher Middle School in Sendai to appreciate whether the new regional institution served the nation as Minister Mori intended. Of the twenty-seven students who entered the Second Higher Middle School in 1887, ten graduated five years later; eight of them were officially listed as originating from the old samurai class.[39]

In spite of the fierce competition from the First Higher Middle School in Tokyo, all of the ten graduates from the Second Higher Middle School entered the Imperial University in Tokyo in 1892. Five graduated from the law department, three from science departments, one from the literature department, and one died before graduating.[40] Among the seven graduates whose careers are recorded, all distinguished themselves in Japanese society. In the public sector, for example, one graduate of the Second Higher Middle School in Sendai became vice minister of the Ministry of Education, another president of the second national university, Kyoto University, and the third became principal of the Second Higher Middle School from where he graduated. One of the law graduates became a prosecutor at the Supreme Court. In the private sector, one of the graduates worked up the ladder of a major pharmaceutical company to the presidency. Another became the president of a major shipping company.[41] Although Mori Arinori did not live long enough to see the results, he would surely have been pleased with the graduates of the first class of the Second Higher Middle School.

With the Middle School Law of 1886, the modern public school system was set in place. It involved a two-track structure, one for the masses and one for the academic elite. The dividing line took place at the end of the elementary school, on the German model. The mass of children entered the workforce upon completion of their elementary education. The most capable continued on to the prefectural Ordinary Middle School or the preparatory course of the higher middle school. Among the graduates of the Ordinary Middle School or various private secondary schools, a tiny fraction, the academic elite, continued on to the Higher Middle School. From there those qualified entered the Imperial University in Tokyo and into leadership positions.

The two-track system conformed to Education Minister Mori's basic philosophy concerning the Higher Middle School, which he characterized as "an important institution for the nation" (*kuni ni jūyō naru basho*) in speeches that he frequently gave throughout the country. First, he said, education must serve the national interests in order for Japan to successfully compete with foreign countries. To meet that challenge, all of the human resources of the nation must be efficiently utilized. To accomplish that goal, Mori made a careful distinction between the two tracks of his educational plan. Elementary education and the Lower (Ordinary) Middle Schools were designed to provide what he called a practical education (*futsū jitsuyō kyōiku*) that prepared the masses for the workplace. In contrast, the Upper Middle School served a different clientele. Whether the graduates entered the workforce (presumably at the administrative level) or the university, they entered into the higher levels of society (*shakai jōryū*) either as government officers, officials of business and industry, or scholars.[42]

In one of his numerous speeches at local areas, in this case Wakayama prefecture, Mori outlined his theory behind the two-tiered structure, the most distinctive element of the national school system he designed. As noted above, education (*kyōiku*) represented the general knowledge and skills for the masses provided at the elementary and lower middle schools in order to effectively serve the country. Learning (*gakumon*), on the other hand, involved advanced specialized knowledge and skills provided at the higher middle and university levels, preparing the future leaders of the country. These schools were regulated and financed by the Ministry of Education.[43] In other words, modern Japan would be governed by an educated elite with a loyal competent literate working class, all serving the needs of the state. Japanese education, as envisioned by Minister Mori, therefore functioned as an instrument of nation-building precisely as it did in Germany.

Heishiki Taisō: Military Training of Teachers

Undoubtedly the most controversial reform of Japanese education under the new minister of education involved the preparation of teachers. By 1886 every prefecture maintained teacher training schools. Setting the standard for them remained the purpose of the elite training institution in Tokyo. Until this time it was called the Tokyo Teacher Training School (Tokyo Shihan Gakkō), founded under the guidance of Marion Scott in 1872. From its inception, the Tokyo Teacher Training School was intended as a model for seven regional normal schools established in 1874–1875. Graduates from the Tokyo school passed on Scott's methods at the regional schools. Graduates of the regional schools under the ministry then taught either at prefectural training schools or became school administrators. Prefectural training schools theoretically completed the system by training the corps of elementary teachers for the new local public schools mandated by the Gakusei.

In 1878, one year after the seven regional schools were closed for financial reasons, the Tokyo Teacher Training School came under the administration of Isawa Shūji, president, and Takamine Hideo, head teacher. The two professionally trained educators arrived home fresh from their study of Pestalozzian theories of education in America. Isawa then moved into the Ministry of Education. Takamine, the leading proponent of Pestalozzi's progressive methods in Japan, became the president in 1881.[44] Dedicated to the modern theories of education he had studied while a student at the Oswego Normal School, he devoted his efforts to that cause.

When Mori Arinori became minister of education in 1885, Takamine was deeply involved in launching a new movement in education, analyzed in the previous chapter, from his prestigious position as president of the Tokyo Teacher Training School. His students were moving into positions of influence, spreading the new theory of education well beyond the Tokyo area. Several of his disciples published books based on Takamine's teachings that supplemented his translation of a leading American textbook on Pestalozzi. By 1886, when Mori Arinori renamed the institution the Tokyo Higher Teacher Training College (Tokyo Kōtō Shihan Gakkō), Takamine was at his peak of influence as the first professional educator in modern Japan. He had established a national reputation as the leading proponent of modern educational theory based on Pestalozzian principles.

In one of the most bizarre reforms of education in modern Japan, Minister of Education Mori inaugurated a radical innovation in teacher education with the inauguration of the Tokyo Higher Teacher Training College in 1886. He introduced military training (*heishiki taisō*) into the regimen of teacher education. Historians have yet to adequately understand or appreciate this controversial reform of education carried out by one of the most progressive figures in modern Japanese history. This latest and most radical reform of teacher training originated while Mori served briefly in an interim position as advisor within the Ministry of

Education from 1884, before his appointment as minister at the end of 1885. He took the opportunity to submit a recommendation to Minister Ōki Takatō for a new teacher training law, proposing that a special committee be appointed to formulate its provisions. Within the month Minister Ōki followed Mori's advice by appointing a preparatory committee for the reform of teacher education. It brought together an interesting mix that included the progressive Takamine Hideo, then president of the Tokyo Teacher Training School, which would naturally be most affected by the reforms of teacher education. He was balanced by Egi Kazuyuki, rising influential conservative within the Ministry of Education.

Mori, convinced that teacher training formed the foundation for the entire school system, was dissatisfied with the noncommittal committee report. Shortly thereafter, in his capacity as the new Minister of Education under the first Itō cabinet, he wrote his own reforms of teacher training, incorporating them within his overall revisions of the entire school system. Mori's personal ideas then evolved into the Teacher Training Ordinance of 1886 (Shihan Gakkō Rei).[45] On April 10, 1886, the same day that the Middle School Ordinance (Chūgakkō Rei) was promulgated, the Teacher Training School Ordinance was also announced.

Teacher Training School Ordinance

1. The purpose of teacher training schools is to prepare future teachers with the qualities of junryō (obedience), shinai (trust), and ichō (dignity).
2. Teacher training schools will consist of a higher teacher training school (*kōtō shihan*) under the supervision of the Ministry of Education, and the ordinary teacher training schools (*jinjō*) under the supervision of the prefectures.
3. There will be one higher teacher training school located in Tokyo and one ordinary teacher training school in each prefecture.
4. The budget for the higher teacher training school will come from the Ministry of Education. The budget for the ordinary teacher training schools will come from the relevant prefecture.
5. The Ministry of Education will determine entrance requirements and assignments upon graduation.
6. The curriculum and textbooks will be determined by the Ministry of Education.
7. The higher teacher training school will prepare principals and teachers for the ordinary teacher training schools.
8. The ordinary teacher training schools will prepare principals and teachers for the public elementary schools.[46]

Although the military training provision (*heishiki taisō*) was not included in the law itself, it can be assumed that Prime Minister Itō was aware of Mori's radical plans to reform the curriculum with a ranking military officer in command. The provocative reform could not have been instituted without Itō's approval. With the stroke of a pen, Minister of Education Mori placed the newly named Tokyo Higher Teacher Training College under the administration of a ranking Japanese army officer. Accepting a recommendation from the Japanese Army, he appointed

Colonel Yamakawa Hiroshi, promoted to major general within three months, as the first president of the nation's premier teacher training institution on March 6, 1886. This was before the ordinance was proclaimed. Japan's leading professional educator, Takamine Hideo, was shortly thereafter appointed head teacher.[47]

Mori recognized the challenges Japan faced in the world. He reasoned that if the nation is to progress from a third-rate country to a second-rate country, and then to a first-rate power, teacher training schools must produce a corps of teachers capable of rendering the new elementary schools effective instruments to develop the country. It was imperative, therefore, that teachers nurture within their students a consciousness of the state (*kokka ishi*).[48]

A public speech clarifying Mori's attitude toward teacher training for the modern era was delivered at the Saitama Teacher Training School in December 1885, just prior to his assumption of office. It has been carefully analyzed by historians ever since in an attempt to discover some indication of precisely what Mori was thinking when he drew up the provisions of the teacher training ordinance. The first section listed three characteristics (*katagi*) of a teacher. The terms are vague and it is quite difficult to analyze their meaning and intent. They began with jūjun, that is, obedience. The second was yūai, fraternity. And the third was ichō, or dignity.[49]

These three concepts were included in Mori's draft of the Teacher Training Ordinance (Shihan Gakkō Rei) sent to the Imperial Household for the emperor's reaction. Realizing the importance of the proposal, the emperor, in accordance with his routine, immediately consulted his educational advisor and personal tutor Motoda Nagazane. Once again the committed Confucianist was drawn into the modern reforms of Japanese education. Motoda criticized the first two concepts proposed by Mori and suggested revisions. The precise differences in nuance of the Chinese characters are difficult to comprehend. Several months later, Article 1 of the new Teacher Training School Ordinance of 1886 stipulated that teachers are to be instilled with the three qualities of junryō (obedience), shinai (trust), and ichō (dignity) following Motoda's advice.[50]

Concerning the first quality of a teacher, obedience, Mori explained that blind obedience is certainly not the goal. Rather the teacher must be able to relate obedience to that which is good. And that quality requires the ability to distinguish right from wrong. Concerning trust, Mori argued that the strength of a nation depends upon the depth of trust that its members cultivate among the society. If it is shallow, so will the society be. Therefore it is essential that a deep fraternal trust among the teacher trainees be nurtured, in turn to be nurtured by them among their students in the classroom. Dignity is critical for teachers in setting a standard for their students, since without it teachers would only follow instructions blindly.

In order to instill these essential qualities in future teachers, Mori turned to the model of a disciplined army as his guide. An army cannot carry out its mission without the obedience and dignity of well-trained soldiers who develop a trust based on close ties of fraternity. His purpose in introducing a military regimen into the teacher training system was not to produce warriors but rather teachers with qualities of well-disciplined soldiers who carry themselves with dignity.

Although Japan was not then at war in the sense that soldiers were fighting and dying on the battlefield, Japan was nevertheless engaged in an international competitive war over technology, commerce, and knowledge in its quest to become a modern nation. Mori, although deeply concerned about European colonial powers carving up vast areas of Asia as colonies, argued that war (*senso*) is not necessarily fought with guns and bullets or the killing of human beings. Rather, all Japanese are involved in a war of skills to preserve the independence of the nation. War in the broad meaning extends to daily activities in which each individual is involved that contributes to the modernization of the country. Teacher training consequently was basic to the war in which Mori envisioned his country was engaged.[51]

During the summer of 1887, Mori wrote a brief paper summarizing his thoughts underlying the most controversial policy of his tenure as minister of education.[52] His Proposals Concerning Military Physical Education (Heishiki Taisō ni Kansuru Kengen) divided education into three aspects, intellectual (*chiiku*), moral (*tokuiku*), and physical (*taiiku*). The three categories, it should be noted, are identical to those in the title of one of the most famous books on education by Mori's British philosopher friend, Herbert Spencer. *Education: Intellectual, Moral, and Physical* stands as one of the great classics on education widely read in the 1800s and well into the 1900s. Mori was surely aware of Spencer's theory while serving as Japanese minister to Great Britain when he developed a personal friendship with the famous author.

According to Mori, ever since the opening of the Meiji era the Japanese were eager to learn from the West. In an effort to attain modernism, intellectual education (*chiiku*) had been given the greatest emphasis in the schools. In the process of modernizing, the physical component of education (*taiiku*) had received the least concern, resulting in an imbalance. For the enhancement of the nation (*kokka fukyō*), the spirit of love of country and the emperor (*chūkun aikoku*) is essential. To attain this goal, the physical component of teacher education must also be given a fundamental role.

In order to achieve a balance between the intellectual and physical training of future teachers, the present curriculum must be reformed, Mori argued, since physical training has been neglected. This can best be achieved by employing the basics of military training. Since there are currently no effective provisions for providing military training of teachers, it is necessary to employ regular army officers to carry out this objective essential for the future of the nation. Henceforth the physical training of teachers will come under the responsibility of the Japanese army (*rikugun*), not the Ministry of Education.[53]

There is, however, an additional interpretation of Mori's controversial use of the army as a guide for the modern training of Japanese teachers. Immediately upon his return from London after resigning as minister, he was thrust into the great controversy between the emperor's advisor, Motoda Nagazane, the irrepressible

Confucianist, and the government leader, Itō Hirobumi, the consummate politician. As we have seen, Mori came under intense pressure by the Imperial Household to place morals education at the center of the curriculum based on Confucian principles of virtue, benevolence, loyalty, and filial piety (*jingi chūkō*).

To counter those demands, Mori promoted the spirit of loyalty and patriotism in love of country (*chūkun aikoku no seishin*) as the main goal of education. Rather than projecting the personality of Emperor Meiji into morals education, as promoted by Motoda, Mori turned to the imperial tradition as a symbol of nationhood.[54] According to this interpretation, Mori's purpose in employing military training in teacher education was an attempt to circumvent the Imperial Household demands that educational policy should be based on Confucian morality, and that the emperor be synonymous with morality.[55]

In order to educate teachers in loyalty and service to the state, Mori conceived the idea that military training of teachers would be the most effective method to prepare them to instill the proper attitudes and discipline among their students. Whereas Motoda argued that Confucian teachings of morality with the emperor at the center would achieve that end, Mori avoided any religious or moral entanglements. He substituted a military regimen for a Confucian regimen promoted by Motoda. Education would thus be free from doctrinaire teachings while at the same time establishing a milieu for technical and scientific advancements. That would enable Japan to modernize, thereby preserving its independence.

With the appointment of colonel, then general, Yamakawa Hiroshi as president, and Takamine Hideo as head teacher of the new Tokyo Higher Teacher Training College, Mori had crafted a unique but somewhat bizarre solution to the inconsistencies that his novel approach to teacher education produced. He was well aware of the inappropriateness of having the distinguished Pestalozzian educator, Takamine, head his new institution with its revolutionary military approach to the physical training of elementary teachers. He also realized that the career army officer General Yamakawa was unqualified to administer the academic program of training teachers how to teach children in the classroom. Consequently the professional educator, Takamine as head teacher (*kyōto*), was placed in charge of classroom teaching, applying the most progressive theories in the world. General Yamakawa as president (*kōchō*) took charge of all activities outside the classroom, applying military discipline.

In another of the great coincidences of Meiji Japan, both Yamakawa and Takamine originated from the Aizu Han during the Tokugawa era and attended the same school for the samurai, Nisshinkan. Moreover, they both served the same feudal lord in the desperate escape from the famous siege of the Aizu Castle in 1868. Later Yamakawa joined the new Imperial Army that had defeated his feudal lord. He fought against the Great Saigo Takamori in the Seinan War, rising to the senior rank of colonel. Difficult times for Takamine ensued while he shared the administrative responsibilities for the new Tokyo Higher Teacher Training College with General Yamakawa. Nevertheless the two Aizu men formed an amicable working relationship.[56]

General Yamakawa acted immediately to restrict political speeches and student discussions of political topics at his school. The new president from the Japanese Army then set out to transform the shihan gakkō (teacher training school) into a shikan gakkō (military officer school) by first organizing the student body into an army structure. Freshmen were divided into platoons of six students each. Second-year students were placed in charge of the platoons. Third-year students commanded several platoons as companies. And finally, senior students were responsible for several companies such as a battalion.[57]

From all accounts, General Yamakawa's initial policies were sanctioned by the minister of education, Mori Arinori. The general had open access to Mori's office and often visited the minister to discuss his plans.[58] If Mori had reservations about the radical reforms in teacher education under Yamakawa, he could have intervened. Perhaps Yamakawa's personality and dedication to his duties as president of the Tokyo Higher Teacher Training College convinced Mori of the correctness of his policies. For example, the general undertook visits to local elementary schools in order to carry out his duties more effectively. The sight of an army general, presumably in full uniform, visiting a community school surely provoked considerable curiosity.

General Yamakawa was clearly not a typical military man but an individual with broad interests. Nor was he without family connections to education. His brother Kenjirō, who studied at Yale University, had become the first Japanese professor of physics at Tokyo University before it became the Tokyo Imperial University. He later became president. Moreover, their sister Sutematsu, the first Japanese female to graduate from a western college, Vassar, was the wife of General Oyama Masao, commanding general of the Japanese army and the commander of her brother, Major General Yamakawa. One wonders if family connections had anything to do with the army's selection of Yamakawa Hiroshi as president of the Tokyo Higher Teacher Training College.

Recollections of those who experienced the great transition of teacher training after Mori's military training policies were implemented are vivid.[59] One graduate compared dress regulations for students and teachers as going from ordinary Japanese-style kimono of the day to regular army officer-style uniforms with insignias of rank on the shoulder. Hairstyle regulations went from optional, long or short, without cap, to short-cropped, with military cap worn on and off campus.

When the students wore army-style uniforms without the traditional double swords required by regular army officers in the old tradition of the samurai warrior, they appeared to some as officers who had surrendered in battle. The sign of a defeated officer was the absence of the swords given up in the act of surrender. The students also confused regular soldiers at times in encounters off campus. Mistakenly taken as regular army officers, the future elementary school teacher was saluted by the regular soldier on occasion.[60]

Dormitories were remodeled into barrack-like accommodations. The Japanese-style custom of sleeping on a tatami floor with futon mattress rolled up during the day was replaced with bunk beds. Bed making became a ritual strictly enforced, following carefully prescribed regulations applied in the army. Personal items had to be placed in a set fashion conforming to military barracks customs. Violation of the rules resulted in disciplinary action by the dormitory administrator.

In order to maintain army discipline in the dormitories where all students were required to live, soldiers from active military units were placed in charge. These recruits brought with them the discipline and spirit instilled in the regular army based on the Imperial Rescript for Soldiers, drawn up by Mori's old friend from the progressive Meirokusha days, Nishi Amane.[61] Friction between regular soldiers from the Japanese Army, often with minimum education but overzealous enthusiasm for military discipline, and the students who had passed a demanding academic examination inevitably arose. Incidents of bullying by the soldier in charge of students in the dormitory amplified resentment among the victims.

Regulations governing students in every aspect of their daily life were tightened. For example, the dress code was strictly enforced on every occasion from the dormitory to the classroom. Inspections were frequently carried out to maintain the required standards. One of the most detested was the unannounced inspection abruptly called in the middle of the night. Students were required to fall out in front of the dormitory fully dressed with rifle and bayonet attached. Those who arrived in their assigned place first were praised. Those who showed up at the end were reprimanded. On occasion some students actually slept in their uniforms in anticipation of a midnight inspection.

Students and teachers wore insignia according to their status. As a sign of respect as well as disciplinary training, students saluted teachers in the military style. Students were ranked in a similar manner. Their status was carefully honored. Students among the lower ranks deferred to their seniors in the infamous kohai-sempai (junior-senior) relationship on every occasion. For example, juniors bowed politely to seniors. Otherwise they would be severely reprimanded by their superiors, requiring extraordinarily deep bows of apology. Lower ranks cleaned the rooms and made the beds of seniors, shined their shoes, and carried out other menial and demeaning services to show respect and to learn their place in the ranking order.

Even the bath, of great importance in Japanese custom, was employed as a disciplinary instrument. The accepted procedure calls for the bather to wash thoroughly outside the bath itself. Only then does one immerse the body into the clean bath water up to the neck. All bathers immerse themselves in the same bath water each day. Junior students at the teacher training school were required to take their bath, that is, to immerse in the common water, at the end of the line. Seniors bathed in the preferred fresh water. Others who entered the bath last were those under disciplinary action, which also included confinement in designated disciplinary rooms or isolation in special seating areas of the cafeteria.

As an additional method of maintaining military discipline, a system employing a Confidential Reporting Rule (Himitsu Chūkoku Hō) was instituted. One student was selected from each class as a reporter. That student was given the responsibility of reporting to the senior official of the school, General Yamakawa, on the daily activities of their classmates.[62] Military discipline was accompanied by military training. The use of the rifle became part of the physical education curriculum. Students were taught how to shoot and ritually care for their weapons. Physical exercises followed the army regimen. Long marches similar to forced marches of the army were conducted. In total, the new physical education program, including marches, drilling, and shooting, consumed 14 percent of the entire curriculum, and was the most important subject in the curriculum.[63]

Beyond the training school, the attached elementary school where teacher trainees conducted practice lessons came under the military influence of General Yamakawa. A reporter from the English-language newspaper the *Japan Weekly Mail* described the environment he observed at the school. "A visitor who enters the primary department of the Normal School at the beginning of one of the school hours will hear the steady tramp of many small feet. Each class marches to its room in step, frequently to the sound of music. The teachers marshal the scholars, and see that, on arriving at the classroom, they each march with precision to their appointed desks. One, two, heads up, toes out, keep step—this is the order of the day."[64]

In a continuation of unusual combinations of priorities in teacher education, Minister of Education Mori elevated English to the second most important course in the revised curriculum. Having previously served as Japan's top diplomat both in the United States and England, and having achieved English fluency, he was aware of the importance of English texts in teacher training. But the emphasis on English also reflected his international persuasion in the midst of what many critics evaluate as extraordinarily conservative reforms in the military training of teachers. In addition, Mori doubled the weekly course hours required in physics and chemistry.[65]

Mori's reforms of teacher education produced a curious result. Inside the classroom translated foreign textbooks mostly from America were used. Takamine Hideo's influence was pronounced, with the widespread use of his translated text of the American progressive educator Johonnot, the *Kyōiku Shinron* or the *New Theory of Education*. Outside the academic classroom the trappings of an army, drills, marches, inspections, rifle training, and so on, reigned supreme as local army units supplied soldiers to train the future elementary teachers in military discipline.[66]

One can imagine how uncomfortable Takamine Hideo, head teacher, felt under these circumstances. The great progressive educator, who had studied the most advanced theories of education in America, nevertheless continued to head the academic program while General Yamakawa was responsible for maintaining the military program. Under such divided responsibilities, Takamine was nevertheless able to continue teaching Pestalozzi's modern theories in his classroom while the students experienced military life and discipline outside their academic course work. The distinguished educator made every effort to separate the two.

Takamine was compelled to make unusual accommodations to preserve some semblance of academic dignity. For example, when General Yamakawa scheduled the first long march for February 15, 1887, Takamine gave a departing speech to the students. Under supervision of five army officers, the students were lined up before him in military formation, in full uniform with weapons. He referred to the march as an academic field trip (*ensoku*), carefully defining the role of five accompanying professors as academic supervisors (*gakujutsu kyōin*).⁶⁷ Everyone knew, of course, that it was a military maneuver under the control of regular army officers. The fact that the academic staff arranged for a visit to an elementary school on route, surely provoking unusual reactions among the children, and that marine specimens were gathered at the site of the training on the Chiba coast, could not obscure the true purpose of the mission. It was military training.

Even though military influence dominated teacher education outside the regular classroom, teaching methodology continued to be deeply influenced by Takamine and his Pestalozzian theory learned in America. Moreover, by 1887 half of all textbooks used at teacher training schools originated from the Teachers Library Series published by the Barnes Publishing Company in the United States. This series served as a virtual national set of textbooks for the fledgling teacher-training schools in mid-nineteenth-century America. Nearly all of the thirty-four titles had become available in Japan by this time and exerted great influence on Japanese teacher training.⁶⁸ With the prominence of English as a major subject and the widespread use of American textbooks in the classroom, a delicate but unusual balance between the academic influence from the West and the military influence from the Japanese army was attained in teacher education.

The military influence in teacher training spread rapidly throughout the country. In the usual manner, the main institution for training teachers located in Tokyo served as the model for local teacher training schools sponsored by prefectural educational departments. Before the end of 1886, the first year of General Yamakawa's appointment as president of the Tokyo Higher Teacher Training College, twenty-nine of the forty-six local training schools had adopted the military-style program. An example of the military influence can be seen at the Saitama Teacher Training School. From January of the following year, the entire staff was replaced and the Imperial Rescript for Soldiers (Gunjin Chokuyu) was ceremoniously read aloud before all students lined up on the parade grounds once a week. It was, as intended, similar to the ceremony conducted in the regular Japanese army.⁶⁹

Evidence that Mori's reforms had penetrated distant regions became available several years later through the eyes of one of the most revered foreign reporters of the Japanese scene. In 1890 Lafcadio Hearn accepted a teaching position at the Shimane Normal School in remote Matsue. His firsthand report of conditions at the school where he taught demonstrate that Mori's reforms of teacher education incorporating military training in 1886 may have achieved the purposes intended by instilling obedience, trust, and dignity in the modern Japanese teacher.

> The discipline is military and severe. Indeed, it is so thorough that the graduate of a Normal School is exempted by military law for more than a year's service in the army: he leaves college a trained soldier. Deportment is also a requisite;

special marks are given for it; and however gawky a freshman may prove at the time of his admission he cannot remain so. A spirit of manliness is cultivated, which excludes roughness but develops self-reliance and self-control. The student is required, when speaking, to look his teacher in the face, and to utter his words not only distinctly, but sonorously. Demeanor in class is partly enforced by the class room fittings themselves, The tiny tables are too narrow to allow of being used as supports for the elbows; the seats have no backs against to lean, and the student must hold himself rigidly erect as he studies. He must also keep himself faultlessly neat and clean. Whenever and wherever he encounters one of his teachers he must halt, bring his feet together, draw himself erect, and give the military salute. And this is done with a swift grace difficult to describe.

The demeanor of a class during study hours is if anything too faultless. Never a whisper is heard; never is a head raised from the book without permission. But when the teacher addresses a student by name, the youth rises instantly, and replies in a tone of such vigor as would seem to unaccustomed ears almost startling by contrast with the stillness and self repression of the others.[70]

Elementary School Ordinance

The final level of education for reform under Mori Arinori's plan reveals his priorities, which focused on the post-elementary level. Comparatively minor structural changes were implemented at the elementary level. The Elementary School Ordinance contained the following major provisions.

1. The elementary school will be divided into the lower and upper divisions, each of four years duration.
2. Children between the ages of six and fourteen are eligible to attend this school.
3. Parents are responsible (gimu) for sending their children to complete the lower division of four years.
4. Parents are responsible for paying the fees set by the prefecture.
5. The curriculum and textbooks will be set by the Ministry of Education.[71]

One of the most critical elements in the ordinance concerned provision 5, particularly the role of morals education under Mori Arinori's reforms. The new curriculum confirmed the suspicions harbored by Motoda Nagazane, the inveterate critic of western educational reforms. Mori had rejected morals education in the Confucian tradition so passionately espoused by this elderly figure. The new minister of education argued that the Confucian classics recommended as moral textbooks were more like political texts, with little relevance to the contemporary world.[72] Accordingly, the morals textbooks prepared by the ministry prior to Mori's appointment incorporating traditional Confucian moral teachings were now prohibited. In principle, any reference to religion or morals was excluded from the classroom.[73]

The morals education pendulum had swung sharply the other way. Rather than serving the emperor, as Motoda had intended, the new school system was designed to serve the state. Each unit led by the elementary school had a specific role in an integrated structure to produce loyal patriotic citizens who would contribute to a strong and independent nation in the next century. Teachers "took pride in being rationalistic, regarding their admiration for the state as a religion, a religion of patriotism."[74] It reflected the political thinking of both Prime Minister Itō Hirobumi and his minister of education, Mori Arinori. In place of morals education as the primary purpose of elementary education, Mori at a later date clarified his position thus: "The fundamental principle of elementary common school education is that every son or daughter, no matter how poor their parents, ought to be so educated as to enable them to fulfill their responsibilities and exercise their rights as units of the nation."[75]

The Elementary School Ordinance of 1886 marks a milestone as the first school law using the word compulsory (*gimu*). According to the provisions, it was the responsibility of parents with children six years old to send their children to the elementary school for a compulsory period of four years. This provision was a painful reminder that the goal of the modern school system set in motion by the First National Plan for Education from 1873 had not yet been achieved. The statistics compiled by the Ministry of Education for the year 1885 illustrates the problems school authorities encountered in their campaign to eradicate illiteracy from every household. They show that 65.8 percent of boys and 32.02 percent of girls attended elementary school, for a total of 49.62 percent.[76]

Mori also moved forcefully into textbook authorization for elementary schools by extending trends already under way. To review the process, textbooks recommended under the original Gakusei from 1873 were translated by governmental agencies. However, due to the shortage of textbooks at the local levels, schools were free to use either the officially recommended texts or others of their choice. During the reverse-course policy of conservative reforms beginning in 1881, the minister of education approved texts from titles submitted by local school officials. With the 1886 Elementary School Ordinance, Article 13, the Ministry of Education published the list of approved texts to accompany the official curriculum. Under Mori, the government had finally achieved complete control of public school textbooks (Kyōkasho Kentei Seido) through this provision.[77]

The first elementary reader approved by the ministry in 1887 illustrates the minister's new thrust in education. The reader, arranged in eight volumes, is notable as the first attempt to systematically teach the Chinese characters used in the written form of the Japanese language. Two thousand characters suitable for the time were chosen and arranged in order of difficulty, used repeatedly throughout the eight volumes. Up to this time there was little effort to organize the language for teaching purposes at the elementary level. This text, then, marks a major effort by the government to organize the Japanese written language for teaching purposes.[78]

The contents of the new text were of special note, ranging from child's play to familiar tales. However, the lessons emphasized the theme "Iwae Wagakuni o," that is, "Celebrate Our Country." They began with Japanese history dating back to the early mythical emperor Jimmu and continuing to the emperor (*tenno*) today. The unbroken reign of 122 emperors extending for 2,550 years, it was noted, renders Japan with the longest historical tradition in the world. Therefore each Japanese child should love "our country" (*wagakuni*) and respect "our emperor" (*wagakimi*).[79]

One of the stories in the elementary textbook of 1887 also illustrates Mori's approach to morals education. It remains in contemporary elementary textbooks and has a lasting appeal to elementary children. In the story "The Ant and the Pigeon" (*Ari to Hato*), a pigeon spots a helpless ant that has accidentally fallen into a pond. To save the ant the pigeon picks a leaf from a tree, dropping it near the ant, which climbs aboard and survives. Later the same ant comes across a scene in which a hunter is quietly stalking the very pigeon that saved the ant, now searching for food unaware of the danger. The ant quickly climbs up the hunter and bites his hand just as he fires his gun. The bullet misses the mark. The pigeon escapes death through the efforts of the ant, repaying one kind act for another, the moral of the story. It demonstrates Mori Arinori's universalistic attitude toward morals education in contrast to that promoted by Motoda Nagazani based on Confucian precepts.

Herbartian Education from Germany: Emil Hausknecht

By the end of 1886, the four great educational ordinances designed by Minister of Education Mori Arinori were in place. There was, however, one major ingredient missing. A new teaching method had to be found to supplement the controversial theories of Pestalozzi that Takamine Hideo had introduced at the Tokyo Teacher Training School, now the Tokyo Higher Teacher Training College. The concern for the developmental growth rates of the child basic to the Pestalozzi discipline proved not only difficult to comprehend but demanding for the average Japanese teacher to apply effectively. Moreover, lack of concern for traditional moral values inherent in the new theory reduced its appeal to many Japanese troubled with the introduction of western ideas and customs.

When Mori assumed the position of minister of education, he made a decision to look to Germany for educational guidance and a new direction in teaching methods. German influence in Japan had been inexorably increasing ever since the governmental decision in 1881 to introduce a western-style constitution by 1889. When Itō Hirobumi was sent to Germany in 1882 to study the German constitution, he learned that Germany had an institution similar to the Japanese Imperial Household. The German constitutional form of government accommodating a monarch appealed to Itō's instincts for modern government of Japan. He and Mori Arinori were converted to the cause of utilizing education to form a national consciousness in the German fashion. German constitutional scholars were brought to Japan to guide the Japanese in the process.

With the rise in interest in German institutions, new concepts from the West were once again penetrating Japanese educational circles. In contrast to Takamine Hideo's developmental education movement, which laid stress on the individual under American influence, German influence took an entirely different approach. The goal of education was not related to individual development (*kojinteki kyōiku*) but for national development (*kokkateki kyōiku*). Concepts such as education to serve the state (*kokka no tame ni*), or the theory of national education (*kokka kyōiku ron*) appeared with increasing regularity in professional journals and academic meetings.[80]

A fresh wind of modernism from the West was once again poised to exert its influence on Japanese society. The utilitarianism of American education with its deep concern for individualism was about to be replaced by the nationalism of German influence. By the mid-1880s Germany ranked as one of the most scientifically advanced nations in the West among Japanese decision makers. Progressivism and modernism became associated with Germany, and less so with America or England. Teacher organizations, educational journals, and educational research associations increasingly turned their attention to the German approach to education.[81]

In 1885, when Mori Arinori assumed responsibility for the Ministry of Education, a high-ranking ministry official, Hamao Arata, was dispatched to Germany for an official three-year investigation of that nation's educational administration. It was reminiscent of the assignment Itō Hirobumi carried out in the field of German constitutional studies in 1882. At the same time, the president of the Imperial University in Tokyo, the German-oriented Katō Hiroyuki, applied to the Ministry of Education for three openings to be filled specifically by foreign professors. Of paramount importance, a German specialist in pedagogy was on the list, similar to previous requests for German constitutional scholars in the relevant ministry.

The original request specified that the position should be filled by a graduate from a German teacher-training institution with teaching experience at a middle school. It was later revised to stipulate a specialist in pedagogy with a university degree to teach at Japan's only national university, the Imperial University in Tokyo. Minister of Education Mori endorsed the request by submitting it to the government for final approval.[82]

The Ministry of Education instructed its official on assignment in Germany, Hamao, to present the request to the German Ministry of Education. The German minister responded that there were two types of educational specialists in Germany, the theoretical scholar in education who carried out research at the university, and the practical educator who dealt with problems of the schools. Hamao requested the latter. The process by the German Ministry of Education to fill the request by the Japanese Ministry of Education was immediately initiated.[83] Within a short period the German minister introduced Hamao to Emil Hausknecht, experienced teacher at the Leipzig Gymnasium in Berlin, as the recommended candidate to fill the post in Japan. A contract was signed, and Hausknecht left Germany in November 1886, arriving in Yokohama on January 9, 1887, to fill the post as a foreign instructor in pedagogy and German language at the Imperial University in Tokyo. He was thirty-four years old.[84]

Emil Hausknecht had an ideal background for the new position that appealed to the Japanese. A graduate of the University of Berlin in foreign languages and history, he spent a year in Paris studying French, then served as an assistant at a school near London for a short period. He later earned a Ph.D. at the University of Berlin in 1879. Shortly thereafter he received a license to teach English, French, Latin, and German, becoming an assistant teacher at a gymnasium in Berlin in 1880. A year later he was recognized as a regular gymnasium teacher of foreign languages.[85] Not only did Hausknecht fulfill the requirements specified by the Japanese Ministry of Education as a graduate of one of the most prestigious universities in the western world but he also had teaching experience at a highly esteemed German gymnasium, the counterpart of the new higher middle school (Kōtō Chūgakkō) initiated by Mori in 1886. Moreover, Hausknecht was capable of teaching in English, still the preferred foreign language at the Imperial University.

With Hausknecht's teaching experience, he was naturally interested in Japan's new higher middle schools, the kōtō chūgakkō, introduced by Mori only a year previously. His special interest in this level of schooling coincided with the ministry's goal to establish a distinct character for these schools within Mori's new system. Indicative of Hausknecht's commitment and personal inclination, during his first year in Japan he sent a personal proposal to the Imperial Household for the education of the emperor's son, the prince then seven years old.[86]

Shortly after Hausknecht's arrival in Japan, upon his own initiative he embarked on a series of school visits. As a new instructor in pedagogy at the Imperial University, he arranged the visits through the university and the Ministry of Education. His purpose was to observe the Japanese system of education before he began lecturing Japanese university students on the subject. At the time, Hausknecht had no knowledge of Japanese culture or the Japanese school system. He began with visits to several public schools in Tokyo, including the Higher Teacher Training College (Tokyo Kōtō Shihan Gakkō).[87] The school observations played an important role in Hausknecht's contribution to modern Japanese education. He formed a critical perspective of the Japanese classroom and the teaching methods he witnessed, which motivated him to devote his efforts to their reform.

Hausknecht visited the Tokyo Higher Teacher Training College in February 1887 to study school regulations, textbooks, and curriculum. Takamine Hideo, head teacher (kyōtō) of the school at the time, hosted the new German professor of pedagogy from the Imperial University. Takamine, as we have learned, was trained in Pestalozzian teaching methods at the famed Oswego Teacher Training School. He had become the foremost Japanese authority on the new progressive methods of teaching based on the principle of the child's individual natural growth developed by the great Swiss educator. Hausknecht, in contrast, was a devotee of the teaching methods noted for their rather rigid systematic five-step teaching method developed by his fellow German, Johann Friedrich Herbart. For the next three and a half years, Hausknecht devoted much of his official and unofficial time in Japan to the promotion of Herbartian theory of education in which national ethics (kokumin dōtoku) superseded individualism.[88] The meeting of the two distinguished educators representing divergent theories of education was symptomatic of a powerful trend well under way. The two great theories of western education that derived originally from European sources, Pestalozzi from Switzerland and Herbart from Germany, came into sharp conflict in Japan.

Several months after Hausknecht arrived in Japan, he began a series of lectures before influential academic associations, where he promoted the German tradition in education. He was invited to address a meeting of the Dai Nippon Kyōiku Kai, the Great Japan Education Association of teachers and administrators, in April 1887. It would be the first of three invitations to address this influential group that once included 1,500 among the audience. In the first instance, in attendance was none other than the minister of education, Mori Arinori, an indication of the respect the Japanese had for this German educator from the outset.[89]

Hausknecht used the opportunity to lecture the minister and other ranking officials on the defects of Japanese education as he had witnessed them during the school visits. Surprisingly progressive, his paper entitled "The Education of Good Secondary School Teachers" (Zenryō Naru Chūtō Kyōin Yōsei), criticized current Japanese education as he had observed it. He claimed there were too many courses and too heavy an academic load on the students. In one of his criticisms on the training of foreign language teachers that resonates throughout the Japanese educational world to this day, Hausknecht called for more emphasis on conversation. In September of the same year, before the same organization, he lectured his audience of educators on education for patriotism.[90]

During Hausknecht's public appearances, he used the opportunities to propose a system for preparing teachers for the new Japanese middle schools that included a four-year course based on the German system. He also called for a national qualification examination for middle school teachers also based on the German model. He often referred to the preparation of history teachers that emphasized the role of the teacher in nurturing patriotism (*aikokushin*) among the students. His proposals proved attractive to both Japanese teachers and educational administrators, many of whom had already become attracted to the German tradition in education.

Hausknecht's teaching assignment at the Imperial University began from April 1887, three months after his arrival from Germany. During his first year he became dissatisfied with the course arrangements. Revisions in his teaching assignment by university authorities had been made after the contractual agreement was signed by both parties in Berlin. Originally agreeing to teach pedagogy and German studies, he was unexpectedly assigned additional courses, including English literature and philosophy. Hausknecht, however, was primarily interested in teaching pedagogy. During the second year, university officials revised his teaching assignment to include more courses on education.

Meanwhile Minister of Education Mori asked Hausknecht to make recommendations for the improvement of Japanese middle school education. Hausknecht naturally accepted the challenge. With his academic background firmly imbedded in the famed German gymnasium, the university preparatory school, Hausknecht was not only an authority on the German middle school but he was also committed to the cause. He promptly drew up a report for the ministry entitled The Training of Teachers for the Higher (Middle) School (Kōtō Gakkō Kyōkan Yōsei

Gi).[91] Among the provisions, he recommended a special postgraduate course at the university level for the training of secondary school teachers. The students would automatically be eligible for a stipend from the government during their course of studies. Qualification for entry would be a university degree.

On January 14, 1889, Minister of Education Mori Arinori, obviously pleased with Hausknecht's proposal, sent an order to officials at the Imperial University to establish a new course for the training of middle school teachers under Hausknecht's supervision.[92] This was one of Mori's last official decisions before his brutal assassination less than a month later. The university immediately set up a course limited to twenty students entitled Tokuyaku Sei Kyōiku Gakka, literally the Department of Education for Special Students. It was placed within the College of Arts (Bunka Daigaku) scheduled to begin with the new academic year from April 1889, to run for fourteen months. In the official English bulletin published by the university, Hausknecht's course was translated as the Pedagogic Course. His special students were appropriately called Specialists.[93]

Hausknecht's original proposal that set the requirement of a university degree for entry into his special course coincided with the German system of a postgraduate course for the training of gymnasium teachers. However, that provision necessarily restricted entry to Imperial University graduates since that institution was the only official university in Japan, and had to be modified to meet existing conditions. Most graduates of the Imperial University entered prestigious government service at a salary of around 100 yen per month. In contrast, teachers at higher middle schools earned around 40 yen per month. Consequently the new course did not attract the original clientele envisioned by Hausknecht on the German model for gymnasium teachers. Rather, his new course proved appealing to teachers at the new middle schools or instructors at regular teacher-training schools.[94] An additional incentive to attract students to Hausknecht's course was a stipend of up to 30 yen paid to each student, depending upon their background and experience.[95]

Even with the necessary revision of the entrance qualifications, only thirteen applicants passed the entrance examination drawn up by Hausknecht, falling short of the quota of twenty. In hindsight, it was remarkable that over a dozen applicants passed his English examination that concentrated on the educational thought of Johann Comenius, the great sixteenth-century Christian thinker from Moravia. A second examination was held at the beginning of the following semester. Six more applicants were accepted to complete the first class of special students. It involved a fourteen-month program, including student teaching, at the Education Department (Kyōiku Gakka) of the Imperial University.[96] In effect, Hausknecht's specially selected students carefully recruited by the ministry constituted a graduate seminar. It was similar to the seminar system of a German university training students to teach at the university preparatory school, the gymnasium. It conformed to Hausknecht's original proposal and his personal interest.

Hausknecht's approach to the academic study of education differed from the main stream in Japan at the time of his arrival. Students studying pedagogy at the university learned that education consisted of three aspects, intellectual, physical, and moral, the focus of the British philosopher Herbert Spencer. Under Hausknecht, however, education was interpreted primarily as moral in the Herbartian tradition. At the same time, Hausknecht was very strict in the German tradition not only in his theoretical interpretations but in his course requirements as well. He held a quiz at the end of each class, frequently requiring the students to turn in their notebooks for his personal inspection. Under such demanding requirements and the fact that Hausknecht lectured and examined in English, six of the students dropped out of the course early on. A major factor may have been related to their deficiency in English.[97]

According to his students, Hausknecht devoted his lectures primarily to the Herbartian principles of education employing a German text as reference. The lectures were given in English, however. The students referred to him as an orthodox Herbartian whose teachings were based directly on translations by a German scholar from the Herbartian school. Volumes have been written in many languages on Herbart's educational theories which can be divided into two distinct parts. First, the purpose of education is virtue. Second, Herbart developed a systematic approach that became well known throughout the world as the five-step teaching method. Hausknecht laid great stress on Herbart's methodology, exhaustively analyzing each of the steps in great detail.[98] The combination of the Herbartian moral philosophy of education with the five-step scientific method of teaching had great appeal to the students, some of whom became devoted to their German professor.[99]

During Hausknecht's third year in Japan, 1889, he was invited by the founders to visit the Yamaguchi Kōtō Chūgakkō, the Yamaguchi Higher Middle School, a local institution far from Tokyo with a unique origin.[100] This middle school had evolved outside the formal channels of the Ministry of Education, which had authorized five regional higher middle schools under its jurisdiction. The Yamaguchi Higher Middle School was not chosen as one of the official five so-called numbered national higher middle schools. In response to being overlooked, local officials joined with national figures from Yamaguchi such as Egi Kazuyuki, powerful Ministry of Education official we have encountered on many occasions, who had great respect for German education, and Inoue Kaoru, minister of foreign affairs. They joined together to reorganize the Yamaguchi Middle School into the Yamaguchi Higher Middle School in 1887, one year after Mori Arinori had separated the five new higher middle schools under the ministry from ordinary middle schools under prefectural jurisdiction.

At the invitation of the school, Hausknecht traveled to Yamaguchi in June 1889. His mission was to carry out an intense inspection of the school with a request to draw up a report to revise it from a German perspective. After visiting many classes and observing the teaching methods and materials, he drew up a model curriculum. The ethics course (*rinri*) was placed at the top, which had to please Egi, who positioned the morals course (*dōtoku*) at the top of the elementary curriculum in public schools under the sweeping Ministry of Education revisions in

1881. Predictably Hausknecht also strongly recommended that the five-step teaching method of Herbart fame be followed. Reflecting Hausknecht's experiences as a teacher in a German gymnasium, his unusually detailed report of nearly four hundred pages was submitted to the school officials as well as the Ministry of Education for reference.

In retrospect, Hausknecht's graduate seminar at the Imperial University, similar to the seminar system used in Germany, marks a milestone in modern teacher education in Japan. It denotes the beginning of teacher training for the new prestigious higher middle schools. It was similar to the German gymnasium that prepared academically qualified students for the university. Up to that time no teacher training institution in Japan served that purpose. Moreover, his students, called Tokuyaku Sei, or Special Students, were enrolled in a Department of Education (Kyōiku Gakka), the first time that pedagogy as a separate discipline was offered at the university level

Hausknecht's university seminar effectively divided teacher training into two categories, conforming to the two-tier structure of education that evolved under Mori Arinori's design, similar to the German system. One tier catered primarily to the masses, educating loyal literate workers who received their basic education in public elementary schools. The better-qualified graduates continued on to the lower middle school and into the work force. The highly qualified students, including those who were privately educated in preparatory schools, continued on to the higher middle schools in preparation for the university. Finally, university graduates filled the top positions throughout society forming the leadership class.

Teacher training in Japan until Hausknecht's arrival from Germany was primarily devoted to the preparation of teachers for the elementary schools, that is, education closely related to the working classes. There were no provisions for training teachers for the new higher middle schools equivalent in Mori's plan of 1886. Hausknecht's university seminar was aimed precisely at filling that vacuum by training teachers for the five higher middle schools, preparing the future leadership class for the university. Consequently the new Imperial University department of pedagogy became related to the preparation of Japan's future leaders. In contrast, teacher training schools had a direct relationship to the education of the working classes. Each institution had its own unique purpose and constituency, similar to the German tradition.[101]

Hausknecht's three-year contract was extended by six months, enabling him to remain in Japan through the completion of the fourteen-month course at the university under his supervision. Twelve students graduated on July 7, 1890.[102] Several of them later published books based on his seminar which sparked a new Herbartian movement in education in Japan, representing a major contribution to modern Japanese education that transpired after the final period covered in this book.[103]

An indication of Hausknecht's reputation among Japanese educators occurred during his last year in Japan. He gave a lecture on December 8, 1889, before a select audience consisting of Minister of Education Mori and other high officials of the ministry. True to his reputation as an orthodox Herbartian, he outlined again the five-step teaching method of Herbart. Reinforcing the ministry's education policies, he concluded that the purpose of a nation's school is to develop love of country.[104] From an historical perspective, this speech took on added importance. It was a reaffirmation of the correctness of Mori Arinori's policy of modernization of education on the German model from a distinguished German educational scholar.

The Assassination of Mori Arinori

In one of the infamous moments in modern Japanese history, on the morning that the new Japanese constitution modeled after the German constitution was promulgated, February 11, 1889, Mori Arinori was assassinated. The nation was shocked to learn that the minister of education, while preparing to attend the august ceremony, was murdered by a disgruntled former samurai from Yamaguchi prefecture. He had come to Mori's official residence that morning, ostensibly to warn him of an assassination plot. When the minister appeared, the assassin suddenly lunged past the aide, plunging a knife through Mori's chest.

A letter written by the killer revealed the motive. In a well-known incident, Mori had reportedly disregarded custom at the Ise Shrine sacred to the Shinto belief that is intimately related to the imperial tradition. The *Japan Weekly Mail* reported that Mori violated accepted procedure by "entering the principal Shrine without removing his shoes and by raising a sacred curtain with his cane."[105] Regardless of the veracity of the accounts of the event, the assassin interpreted Mori's reported actions as an affront to the emperor.[106]

Controversy that surrounded Mori throughout his colorful life followed him in death. Dr. Erwin Baelz, long-term German doctor at the University of Tokyo, recorded in his diary on the day of the assassination his frank and disturbing conclusion. "Mori was extremely unpopular, and only a few days ago had a violent wrangle with the students at the university for which he was to blame, having been so incredibly stupid as to declare that the students themselves were responsible for the latest fire and the death of one of their numbers. Passions ran high, and perhaps this horrible murder was only to be expected."[107] The leading Tokyo newspaper, the *Nichi Nichi Shimbun,* confirmed Dr. Baelz's reaction. It reported that high government officials visited the grave of the assassin.[108] Their public display of sympathy with the murderer rather than the murdered could not be mistaken. Although Mori, minister of education in the Itō cabinet, was one of the highest-ranking officers of the government, he was obviously unpopular with some of his political colleagues.

How should Mori Arinori, Japan's first diplomat to Washington, later minister to Great Britain, and finally minister of education, be remembered in Japanese history? Two weeks before his death he held two meetings, perhaps the last recorded accounts of his thoughts, that succinctly sum up his basic philosophy underlying the greatest reforms of Japanese education in the modern era prior to World War II. In a meeting with heads of national schools at the Ministry of Education on

January 28, and with prefectural education officers on February 5, he clarified the purpose of education in Japan.

Mori explained that the government had originally set up the Ministry of Education to serve the nation (*kokka no tame ni*). Likewise, educational policy was intended to serve the nation. One example of that policy was the Imperial University. Mori concluded that among the two essential purposes of the Imperial University, the advancement of science and service to the state, the later takes precedence. Moreover, education in all schools, according to the minister of education, is not designed for the primary benefit of the student, but rather for the primary benefit of the nation. In educational matters, the state (*kokka*) is similar to the Buddhist honzon (main idol). It is the central purpose of education. Therefore the consciousness of the state is essential for all.[109]

Exactly one month before Mori's death he gave a speech carried in the English-language newspaper *Japan Weekly Mail* that revealed the stark realities in the educational standards of the masses after two decades of modern education. It also vividly illustrates the relationship between education and nationhood that Mori, by then viscount, espoused during his abbreviated tenure as minister of education.

> The most important, and indeed that which comprehends the whole, is the general recognition of the absolute value of education in promoting and securing the independence and prosperity of the state. Education should therefore always have this end in view, and should not fail to develop and cultivate a spirit of patriotism.
>
> At present [1889] the number of boys and girls who attend school does not reach one-half of the total number of children of school age. Many children whose names are on the rolls of schools only attend for a brief period and then fall off. But the expense of education, already heavy, would be almost unbearable if all the children were to attend school. . . . The majority of children who do not attend school are girls. Patriotism and national independence should be kept constantly before female pupils, with a view to impressing those qualities upon their children. . . .
>
> The fundamental principle of elementary common school education is that every son or daughter, no matter how poor their parents, ought to be so educated as to enable them to fulfill their responsibilities and exercise their rights as units of the nation. . . . Illiteracy prevails so largely among the nation that we cannot regard the independence or prosperity of the nation as at all assured.[110]

Inoue Kowashi, a central figure in the next and final chapter, who became minister of education at a later date, knew Mori well. He was chosen to give a eulogy at his memorial service. Inoue used the opportunity to succinctly characterize the basic approach to education by Japan's first minister of education under the modern form of government. The most important purpose of education to Mori was the independence of the country (*kuni no dokuritsu*). To meet that goal, the modern system of education implemented by him was intended to develop a sense of national unity. Inoue recalled a conversation with Mori while they were riding together in a jinrikisha. Mori had wondered aloud whether the Japanese man pulling these two leading statesmen in his two-wheeled vehicle had any concept of Japan as a nation. Inoue then paid final tribute to his friend Mori Arinori as the first Japanese minister of education to espouse the concept of education for nationhood (*kokutai kyōiku shugi*).[111]

Mori Arinori's prominent role in modern Japanese educational history was matched by few, if any, individuals who participated in the great revolution that transpired during the early Meiji period. Evaluation of the man, however, remains a mystery to this day. In one sense he was a liberal; in another a conservative. On the one hand he was a progressive; on the other a traditionalist. By one interpretation he was an internationalist; by another a nationalist. He was a sophisticated erudite intellectual but lacked formal educational credentials. For part of his career he was a politician; for another part an educator. During his earlier years he promoted the rights of the individual, which included those of women. As minister of education he argued for the supremacy of the state over the individual.[112] In fact, he was a unique combination of them all. Assassinated at an early age, Mori Arinori was without doubt one of the most colorful, fascinating Japanese figures during the first two decades of modern education in Meiji Japan.

18

The Imperial Rescript on Education

WESTERN SCIENCE AND
EASTERN MORALITY FOR THE
TWENTIETH CENTURY, 1890

Imperial Rescript on Education

Know ye, Our subjects:

Our Imperial Ancestors have founded Our Empire on a basis broad and ever-lasting, and had deeply and firmly implanted virtue. Our subjects ever united in loyalty and filial piety from generation to generation illustrated the beauty thereof. This is the glory of the fundamental character of Our Empire, and herein lies the source of Our education.

Ye, Our subjects, be filial to your parents, affectionate to your brothers and sisters; as husbands and wives be harmonious, as friends true; bear yourselves in modesty and moderation, extend your benevolence to all; pursue learning and cultivate arts, and thereby develop intellectual faculties and perfect moral powers; furthermore, advance the public good and promote common interests; always respect the constitution and observe the laws; should emergency arise, offer yourselves courageously to the State; and thus guard and maintain the prosperity of our Imperial Throne coeval with heaven and earth. So shall ye not only be Our good and faithful subjects, but render illustrious the best traditions of your forefathers.

The Way here set forth is indeed the teaching bequeathed by our Imperial Ancestors, to be observed alike by Their Descendants and the subjects, infallible for all ages and true in all places. It is Our wish to lay it to heart in all reverence, in common with you, Our subjects, that we may all attain the same virtue.

October 30, 1890[1]

As the second decade of the Meiji Restoration ended, one final ingredient in the construction of modern Japanese public education for the twentieth century remained inadequately addressed. Ironically, it concerned the role of traditional values and customs of Japanese society. Within the Fourth National School System designed and implemented from 1886 to 1889 by Minister of Education Mori Arinori, the role of Confucian morality as well as the imperial tradition had not been appropriately defined. Powerful interest groups remained dissatisfied with the state of educational affairs. The final piece in the mosaic of modern education in Japan had yet to be put in place.

Once again two old antagonists emerged at the center of the controversy. Motoda Nagazane, the doctrinaire Confucianist of the Meiji era, represented the Imperial Household. The constitutionalist Inoue Kowashi, with German predilections, represented the modernists. A decade earlier the two were in direct confrontation over Motoda's 1879 "Imperial Will on Education" that was refuted by Inoue's "Educational Affair" circulated under Itō Hirobumi's name, considered in previous chapters. This time, in sharp contrast, Motoda and Inoue forged an unprecedented compromise. The ultimate solution to the nagging dilemma between those who championed the centrality of Confucian morality imbedded in imperial ideology, versus the fundamental role of western science, evolved through "The Imperial Rescript on Education" of 1890. The convergence of ideas from the modernists and the traditionalists incorporated therein underlies the historical significance of the Rescript.

The movement for an "Imperial Rescript on Education" had been inexorably building from the beginning of the Meiji era in 1868. The Charter Oath taken by the teenager Emperor Meiji of the same year laid the foundation. "Knowledge shall be sought throughout the world, so as to strengthen the foundation of imperial rule."

During the 1870s, under the director of the Ministry of Education Tanaka Fujimaro, the obsessive quest for western knowledge prevailed, fulfilling the intent of the first part of this lofty oath. In sharp contrast, the role of the imperial tradition in education received little consideration by Tanaka who disregarded the intent of the second part of the Charter Oath. After nearly a decade of frustration, Motoda Nagazane, as trusted advisor to the emperor, orchestrated a reaction in the form of "The Imperial Will on Education" in 1879, which, as we have seen, assimilated the imperial tradition with Confucian morality and inserted it into the center of modern education. Motoda's document of 1879 was in essence the initial version of "The Imperial Rescript on Education" of 1890.

Until Mori Arinori's appointment as minister of education in 1885, Motoda's "Imperial Will on Education" of 1879 laid the basis for a resurgent Confucianism as the moral foundation of education with the emperor at the center. However, from the beginning of the comprehensive school system designed by Mori, Confucian teachings espoused by Motoda were relegated once again to an insignificant position. The Elementary School Ordinance, the Middle School Ordinance, the Imperial University Ordinance, and the Teacher Training School Ordinance of 1886 under Mori's hand disregarded morals education in the Confucian mode.[2]

The decision by Minister Mori to proscribe morals textbooks based on Confucian teachings in use during the previous period further exacerbated the issue. The all-engulfing ban necessarily included Motoda's own text on morals education, *Principles for Guiding Children* (*Yōgaku Kōyō*). It had been circulated to all schools and widely used through a campaign orchestrated by the Imperial Household. In spite of the book's direct imperial connection, it too was boldly rejected by the new minister of education.

Motoda and Emperor Meiji had sufficient cause for deep reservations about the future of Japanese education under Mori Arinori. The Imperial Household had attempted to block Mori's appointment from the outset, conveying the emperor's opposition directly to Prime Minister Itō. The nagging concern was that the nation's schools would fall under the control of a suspected Christian who could potentially implant Christian morality in the nation's schools. This would naturally come at the expense of Confucian morals, of supreme importance to Motoda and the Imperial Household. Nevertheless Prime Minister Itō steadfastly ignored the powerful voices of imperial opposition to Mori Arinori as minister of education in his first cabinet of 1885.

Mori carefully avoided any religious bias in his educational ordinances of 1886. With Mori's policies reversing the course of resurgent Confucianism in the nation's schools that Motoda had successfully promoted, a confrontation between the two was inevitable. To clarify Mori's educational policies, in 1887 Motoda met with the new minister of education in the palace.[3] Motoda grasped the opportunity to specifically ask Mori what the relationship was between Japanese education and the imperial institution in the modern world. Mori, as reported by Chief Secretary Yoshii Tōmomi from the Imperial Household who was also in attendance, replied that up to now the emperor had not been directly related to education. Yoshii countered that Emperor Meiji was deeply interested in educational trends currently under way as they affect the affairs of state. He was, however, especially unhappy with the conditions he witnessed during the school visits, when he discovered that the students could not explain in Japanese what they had been studying in their western-oriented textbooks.[4]

The direct reference by the imperial spokesman to Emperor Meiji's tour to the provinces nearly a decade previously is indicative of the importance the imperial visits to schools played in molding the educational policies originating from the Imperial Household. On the basis of his classroom observations, according to Motoda, the emperor concluded that the guiding motive in education should be *chūkun aikoku*, "loyalty and love of country." The implication was certainly understood by both parties that this meant loyalty to the emperor. Without doubt this was intended as a criticism of the Tanaka Fujimaro era, when the new school curriculum was overwhelmingly devoted to the adoption of western culture and technology to the perceived neglect of Japanese culture and customs.

Yoshii then made one of the most significant revelations of Emperor Meiji's attitude toward the entire process of educational reform since the beginning of the First National Plan for Education, the Gakusei of 1872–1873. It also reinforced Motoda's oft-repeated claim that he reflected the opinion of Emperor Meiji in his writings critical of the modern reforms of education based on western models. According to Yoshii, during the sixteen years that he had served as an advisor to the emperor on educational matters, he often heard his "sacred words" (*seii*) on the state of education. Emperor Meiji frequently expressed his criticism (*hihan*) of the modern school system that emphasized knowledge (*chiiku*). The implication was clear. The same misguided policies the emperor criticized in "The Imperial Will on Education," written by Motoda in 1879, were being carried out under Mori's revisions of education of 1886. In both instances the imperial advisors, Motoda and Yoshii, made it clear that the emperor's wishes were not being followed. The imperial representatives then repeated the basic position that Mori should place greater emphasis in the nation's public schools on morals (*tokuiku*) based on the Confucian principles of jingi chūkō (virtue, benevolence, loyalty, and filial piety) as traditionally defined. They should take preference over western knowledge (*chiiku*).

Mori promptly ignored the adversarial demands from the Imperial Household concerning the primacy of morals education with Confucian teachings as the foundation. Not only was he opposed to traditional moral teachings but he also opposed western Christian teachings as the basis of morality then exerting a strong influence on American education. Rather, Mori was searching for a new form of ethics devoid of religious or cultural associations befitting a modern industrial society (*kindai shakai no rinri*). In consultation with various scholars in the field of ethics, he approved a morals textbook for the schools issued in 1888. It reflected Mori's position concerning ethics in the formation of a modern society to meet the demands of the day.[5] This textbook assumed a unique role in the evolving system of modern Japanese education. The preface to Mori's text, made available to the English-speaking readers of the period, sets the general tone of the minister of education's approach to morals education.

> The object of all who teach Ethics by means of this book should be to reveal to their scholars a standard that shall suffice to distinguish between what is good and what is bad, what is right and what is wrong in such actions as result from the feelings with which human beings regard each other. . . . The object of moral teaching is the distinguishing between good and evil in the hearts of man, the enabling of men to seek virtue and to forsake vice; and, in the case of the young the cultivation of virtuous habits by the impression that the citing of real cases of virtuous living are calculated to produce.[6]

What was absent in Mori's textbook on morals is equally important as what was included. For example, there was no specific reference to filial piety among family members, respect for seniors and elders, or loyalty to the emperor. These basic teachings formed the fundamental principles espoused by Motoda Nagazane as the essential ingredients to be taught to all children as a national moral standard. Mori avoided philosophical systems from both East and West. Rather, he attempted to bridge the gap between the two by forging a simple moral philosophy that fit all ages and all peoples for all times. The term Mori used to describe his basic theory was *jita no heiritsu*. His American biographer, Ivan Parker Hall, defines it as "no more than a simple call for mutual respect and assistance among free-standing equals." It was similar to the Christian golden rule, "Do unto others as you would have them do unto you."[7] That interpretation aptly conforms to Mori's intentions. It was meant to be simple, common sense, yet universally applicable to all mankind. It denied Motoda's moral principles that applied specifically to the Japanese and the Japanese emperor.

Mori summarized his attitude toward morals education in the public schools of modern Japan in a speech shortly before his death, carried in the English press. The assumption is that his reference to religious sects includes Confucianism within that category.

> Some may ask what is to become of moral education if we preclude religious sects from entering into school education. This again is mixing up of religious sectarianism with morality. The moral training to be given in the school is to teach the pupils the relations between man and man, and the duty of conducting themselves accordingly . . . as to the relationships between man and supernatural beings as God and Amida—education should not concern itself. Such questions are quite foreign to moral teachings. Similar considerations apply to political parties. Patriotism is that quality which more than any other determines a man's fitness to be regarded as a unit of the nation. It should be cultivated as much as possible in any school, but neither political parties nor religious sects should be allowed admission.[8]

Precisely one month after Mori's speech, the assassination of Mori Arinori on February 11, 1889, dramatically transformed the conditions of the unresolved conflict. While Mori implemented his grand plan for a national school system during his reign of less than three years from 1886 to the beginning of 1889, Motoda Nagazane had endured what he considered grossly misguided policies governing education. From the moment of Mori's death, the tables were now turned. The opportunity for Motoda Nagazane and like-minded opponents of Mori's policies to reverse the direction of modern education, as he did precisely ten years earlier with "The Imperial Will on Education" of 1879, had unexpectedly reemerged.

The prolonged controversy over the direction of Japan's modern school system immediately took on a new direction. It was greatly magnified because Itō Hirobumi, who had originally appointed Mori to his ministerial position in his first cabinet in 1885, had stepped down from the prime ministership even before Mori's death. He headed the new Privy Council, the highest governmental organ responsible for the new constitution. Itō was replaced as prime minister by an army general, Kuroda Kiyotaka, who was shortly thereafter succeeded by the head of the Japanese Army, General Yamagata Aritomo. Within a short span, the two most powerful proponents of educational modernization on the western model, Mori Arinori and Itō Hirobumi, were removed from their strategic positions in government. The stage was now set for the final and definitive imperial connection to Japanese education in the nineteenth century, "The Imperial Rescript on Education." It would prove to be one of the most influential documents of prewar Japan, which remains controversial to this day.

The Formation of "The Imperial Rescript on Education," 1890

There were four prominent figures in the five-month deliberations of preparation of "The Imperial Rescript on Education." Yamagata Aritomo, the prime minister; Inoue Kowashi, senior government official and author of the Meiji Constitution of 1889; Yoshikawa Akimasa, minister of education; and Motoda Nagazane, elder tutor to the emperor, were all deeply involved in the process.[9] In addition, behind the scenes but actively participating and keenly interested in the outcome was Emperor Meiji himself. A strategic coalition of fervent proponents of educational reform had emerged, advocating the superiority of Japanese cultural traditions and customs over western learning.

The general histories of the period follow a common analysis of events that transpired, with minor deviations.[10] The immediate instigation for an "Imperial Rescript on Education" was the appointment of General Yamagata Aritomo as prime minister in December 1889. His distinguished military career began when he built the conscript Japanese army into a formidable force in the early 1870s. He later served as the powerful home affairs minister in Prime Minister Itō's first cabinet of 1885, when Mori became minister of education. He dealt forcefully with the Peoples' Movement for Freedom during that appointment, deeply concerned about the social instability that he attributed to the movement. Of considerable relevance, "The Imperial Rescript to Soldiers and Sailors" (Gunjin Chokuyu) of 1882 that called for loyalty to their commander, the emperor, was initiated by him as head of the Japanese Army. He favored a similar imperial oath for education.[11]

Yamagata's predilections were well known. As a student of the famous Yoshida Shōin in Chōshū during the later Tokugawa period, his loyalty to the imperial institution was finely tuned. In 1889, Yamagata visited European parliaments where the pros and cons of a given issue were publicly debated, sometimes in a way he considered unseemly. He was determined to avoid such a western approach to critical issues at home. As prime minister, among his immediate agenda for action was the reform of morals education. He was convinced that social and political unrest stemmed from the absence of a proper moral foundation of the youth based on Japanese ethics and culture.[12]

As the new prime minister, Yamagata promptly convened a meeting of local governors (chihō chōkan kaigi) in late February 1890. One of his major concerns, the state of morals education, dominated the deliberations. Its very presence on the agenda reflected the position of influential local government officials who were dissatisfied with the current situation. Yamagata recalled in his memoirs that the emperor had personally urged the government to strengthen morals education.[13] The powerful body of prefectural governors expressed deep concern over the lack of morals education in local public schools. To rectify the situation the governors advocated the supremacy of morals education, with the emperor at the center, over intellectual studies. After a long and serious debate on the issue, the governors, all appointed, issued a petition to the government expressly calling for the strengthening of morals education in the schools for the sake of nationhood.[14]

On February 26, a delegation of governors personally met with Minister of Education Enomoto Takeaki with their petition. Pressed by the aroused governors, the minister admitted that there were no particular guiding principles for morals education in the nation's public schools. The governors, reflecting the tone of their conference and personal unease over the first impending elections under the new constitution, then demanded that morals education be reformed and strengthened. In addition, they strongly urged that morals textbooks from the elementary school through the teacher training schools be approved by the Ministry of Education. Minister Enomoto responded to the determined governors by agreeing to initiate the preparation of an official guide for morals education. It represents the first concrete step in the actual formulation of "The Imperial Rescript on Education."[15]

In understanding the preparation of this document, consideration of its precise authorship and timing are of critical importance. At the initial stage, Education Minister Enomoto assigned a well-known figure and accomplished writer, Nakamura Masanao, to prepare a draft for use as the guiding principles for morals education. The choice of Nakamura for this sensitive and emotionally charged task was a curious one. He had exhibited a special interest in Christianity that could be expected to draw criticism from imperial proponents. To critics, the assignment of Nakamura demonstrated that the minister of education lacked commitment to the imperial cause on morals education in contrast to his deep interest in science. Nakamura had studied in Europe even before the Restoration of 1868. His early claim to fame was the translation of Samuel Smiles's *Self Help* in 1871. He was by now on the Faculty of Literature at the Imperial University, recognized as a distinguished scholar.[16] Concurrently he held the position of president (kōchō) of the Girl's Higher Teacher Training School (Joshi Kōtō Shihan Gakkō).[17]

According to a leading post–World War II Japanese scholar on religion, Anesaki Masaharu, Nakamura was "a Confucianist" who translated a book titled *Evidences of Christianity* that "inspired Confucianists with enthusiasm for Christianity."[18] Another researcher claims that he became a Protestant Christian in 1871 in spite of the proscription against Christianity.[19] When Reverend Warren Clark first taught in Japan in the early 1870s, he recalled that "Nakamura was my most intimate friend at Shidzuoka. He gave up an offer to go round the world with the Iwakura Embassy in order to come with me to Shidzuoka and search the Scriptures."[20] Nakamura's intimate relationship to Christianity was sufficiently known among leading political and intellectual circles to provoke mistrust by ardent proponents of moral education on the Confucian model.

Nakamura titled his thesis "The Basic Ideas on Morals Education" (Tokuiku no Taishi).[21] It was a rather vague philosophical treatise on the general principles of morality. Reflecting the eclectic interests of the author, it combined general moral principles drawn from various teachings from both East and West that included Christianity. As author of the popular translation of Samuel Smiles's *Self Help* in the early Meiji period, Nakamura advocated independence of the individual, reflecting Smiles's basic thesis.[22] An obtuse approach to morals such as that was bound to provoke harsh criticism from morals advocates in the Confucian mold.

On May 17, Minister of Education Enomoto, considered inadequately concerned with the state of morals education in the schools while overly influenced by western science, was hastily replaced. Prime Minister Yamagata appointed Yoshikawa Akimasa, a Yamagata loyalist closely aligned with the conservative cause, to head the Ministry of Education. There is some speculation that the emperor himself influenced this appointment.[23] As minister of education,

Yoshikawa automatically became deeply involved in the preparation of an "Imperial Rescript on Education" already under way, undoubtedly one of the major reasons for his appointment.

The stage was now set for concentrated action on the persistent problem of the role of morals education in Japan's modern school system. By the end of May, Nakamura's draft was circulated among interested parties. It drew immediate and heavy criticism. Conservatives rejected it as inappropriate for the occasion. Motoda Nagazane, by now elderly Confucian confidant of the emperor, predictably rejected it. In his usual fashion he prepared his own draft intended to supersede Nakamura's version.[24] Motoda obviously realized that the situation provided him with a golden opportunity once again, as in 1879 when he wrote "The Imperial Will on Education," to set the direction not only of morals education but also of the very future of the nation.

In contrast to Nakamura's general principles of morals, Motoda's version focused directly on morals education for the school. His title, "Kyōiku Taishi" (Principles of Morals Education), was similar to the one he used when drawing up "The Imperial Will on Education," Part One, ten years earlier. He included the five ethical relationships of Confucianism, beginning with love and respect for the emperor. To realize them, the three basic values were represented by the sacred ornaments preserved in the Ise Shrine of the Shinto religion. The mirror represented knowledge (*chi*), the comb affection (*jin*), and the sword courage (*yū*). The five relationships and the three moral principles formed the foundation of moral education as interpreted by Motoda.[25]

In a rambling discourse, the purpose of education according to Motoda was the development of spirituality (*seishin*) and morality (*tokusei*) of the people in the form of loyalty to the emperor and love of country. He claimed that the imperial ancestors founded the country and continued to rule Japan uninterrupted ever since. The long imperial reign was based on the special relationship between the emperor and his people that formed the nation (*kokutai*).[26] This basic theme also ran through Motoda's private lectures to the emperor during his long tenure as personal tutor.

Inoue Kowashi: Author of "The Imperial Rescript on Education"

A powerful figure in government at this time, Inoue Kowashi, then serving as head of the Legal Affairs Bureau (Hōsei Kyoku) responsible for governmental regulations, was in a position to read the Nakamura draft. Inoue ultimately played the pivotal role in the formation of "The Imperial Rescript," and a brief sketch of his background may shed some light on his fundamental approach to this critical document. As a lower-ranking samurai from Kumamoto, from where Motoda Nagazane also originated, he entered the domain school usually reserved for boys from higher-ranking samurai families. Completing his studies at the age of twenty-two, Inoue was sent by his han government to Tokyo to enter the leading institution of foreign studies under the Tokugawa regime, the famous Kaiseijo, in the French Department.

After the Meiji Restoration, Inoue was again assigned to Tokyo by his clan in 1870 to become an officer of the Daigaku Nankō, the central institution of higher education. From there he entered the Ministry of Justice. On the basis of his French studies at the Kaiseijo school, in 1872 he was sent for a year to Europe where he made a study of the French and Prussian, or German, constitutions. He returned to Japan to translate a book on that subject. In the process he became a specialist on western constitutional law, particularly the German, which he ultimately used as a model when he wrote the Meiji Constitution of 1889.[27]

Inoue, who later served as minister of education, possessed exceptional writing skills employed with great expertise on several occasions during this period under review. His most significant contribution to modern Japan by 1890 was the very recent Meiji constitution, drawn up by him the previous year under close supervision by Itō Hirobumi and constant advisement by a German scholar. It survived until World War II. However, in another of the great ironies of early modern Japan, Inoue also drafted the "Kyōiku Gi" (Educational Affair) for Itō Hirobumi in 1879. It was this document that refuted the celebrated "Imperial Will on Education" written by Motoda, previously analyzed as the most important declaration of the imperial cause in education by that time. In other words, Inoue had already clashed with Motoda Nagazane and the Imperial Household, although in the name of Itō Hirobumi, over educational reform in 1879. He specifically refuted imperial opposition to educational reform under Tanaka Fujimaro. In effect, Inoue in 1879 endorsed Tanaka's liberal policies of the 1870s.

In correspondence by Inoue to Prime Minister Yamagata in June 1890, he criticized Nakamura's original thesis on moral principles for the schools. He was concerned, for example, that the use of the word *kami* (god) could complicate the process, and that the general tenor of Nakamura's thesis exhibited a Christian flavor. He argued that an "Imperial Rescript" should not sow the seeds of religious controversy by supporting or criticizing any particular religion. Nor should it have a political bias favoring any political party. In addition, it should not indicate a bias toward East or West. Rather, an imperial edict must embody the emperor's desires, reflecting a broad prospective.[28]

Upon receiving Inoue's criticism of Nakamura's document on morals, Prime Minister Yamagata promptly responded by asking Inoue to submit a draft of his own to the minister of education. Within a remarkably short period Inoue complied. On June 20, 1890, he sent his first draft of an "Imperial Rescript" to Yamagata.[29] This act set in motion an intense process of revisions running through twenty-three drafts over a four-month period before a final version was approved.

History repeated itself in 1890 with an intriguing twist. As noted above, Inoue Kowashi, a specialist in German constitutional law, had opposed Motoda, the Confucianist, a decade earlier over "The Imperial Will on Education" in which moral education was defined in terms of the imperial tradition. Ironically, among the few individuals who initially had access to Motoda's "Imperial Will" of 1879, not distributed widely at the time, were Itō Hirobumi and his confidant Inoue Kowashi.[30] In an opposing commentary Inoue crafted the "Educational Affair" ("Kyōiku Gi") under

Itō Hirobumi's name. A decade later Inoue found himself once again responding to a document on morals education, this time written by Nakamura Masanao. Inevitably Inoue would have to deal with his old antagonist Motoda who still exerted a powerful influence at the Imperial Household. In this instance, however, their previously adversarial relationship took a decidedly different course.

Because Motoda Nagazane and Inoue Kowashi played preeminent roles in the preparation of the "Imperial Rescript" of 1890, a comparison of their educational backgrounds is of particular interest. Both were born in the southern city of Kumamoto into samurai families. They attended the same clan school, the Jisshukan, to receive a standard samurai education steeped in Confucian studies.[31] Inoue would go on for further studies in the French language that led to a year's study in Europe and into government service. Motoda went on for further Confucian studies leading to an appointment to the Imperial Household, where he tutored the emperor on Confucianism. Fate brought them together again in 1890 during the final stage in the preparation of "The Imperial Rescript on Education."

Recognizing the importance of Motoda's influence, Inoue brought him into the process by sending him a copy of his original draft on June 26. Three days later Motoda responded, noting how important Inoue's project was. This initiated a series of letters between the two, beginning with Inoue's note of appreciation for Motoda's reaction to his initial draft. Motoda, continuing his decade-old campaign, seized the opportunity to include a draft of his version of the principles of morals education mentioned above, soliciting Inoue's advice and reaction.[32]

Inoue rejected Motoda's draft of a "Rescript" as typical of the old Chinese school of Confucian thought inappropriate for a modern state. In a strategic move that deserves historical recognition, Motoda then withdrew his own version, deferring to Inoue's draft. Inoue and Motoda immediately entered into a rapid exchange of marked-up revisions that are still available. In the process the two former antagonists now found themselves collaborating, in part from their mutual concern over the political instability instigated by the Peoples' Movement for Freedom.[33]

In a definitive study to determine exactly which of these former antagonists was primarily responsible for writing "The Imperial Rescript on Education," a leading Japanese educational historian, Kaigo Tokiomi, carefully followed the progression of the twenty-three drafts that passed between Motoda and Inoue during the summer and early fall of 1890.[34] From the original through the final version, they are all in the handwriting of Inoue and Motoda. Inoue sent each draft to Motoda for a reaction, which he gave freely in the form of revisions and additions penciled in at the margins. By comparing each of Motoda's recommended changes with any subsequent revision by Inoue, the researcher was able to determine precisely how much influence Motoda exerted on Inoue in the tedious process.

Kaigo's conclusion is irrefutable. The original version of "The Imperial Rescript on Education," independently written by Inoue although revised nearly two dozen times, ends up essentially unchanged. A comparison of the two versions reproduced in this chapter substantiates that analysis. Even though Motoda recommended many revisions personally inserted, they were either sufficiently minor that Inoue ignored them, or they were incorporated without altering the original meaning. For example, several Chinese characters that had no influence on the meaning were substituted by Motoda and accepted by Inoue. In the twelfth draft, for instance, Motoda recommended the word kōen for Inoue's kuon, both meaning "everlasting." Motoda's choice subsequently appears in a later version without altering the meaning.[35]

In spite of the general coalescing of ideas between Motoda and Inoue, the conflict between eastern morality and western legalism emerged in the preparation of "The Imperial Rescript." An interesting as well as symbolic disagreement pitted the modern constitutionalist against the traditional Confucianist. Inoue, consistent as author of the Meiji constitution enacted the previous year, inserted the phrase to "respect the constitution and observe the laws." Motoda objected to that seemingly innocuous statement, arguing that a "Rescript" in the name of the emperor should only call for traditional moral principles.[36] Motoda pressed his opposition to Inoue's inclusion of the reference to the constitution by personally seeking support from the minister of education. Egi Kazuyuki, increasingly influential within the ministry, recalled that the emperor himself considered the issue and concluded that the reference to the constitution should remain.[37] This was evidence that Emperor Meiji was personally involved. The new minister of education, Yoshikawa Akimasu, strong defender of the imperial tradition, also supported Inoue's draft in the face of criticism by several other cabinet officers.

With Prime Minister Yamagata's approval, a compromise was finally accepted. Both traditional and modern sentiments from East and West would be included in "The Imperial Rescript on Education." Inoue's phrase concerning the constitution remained as originally written.[38] The final draft was completed on October 24, 1890. Less than a week later, on October 30, it was officially proclaimed.[39]

On the basis of modern scholarship, the conclusion can be made that Inoue Kowashi deserves recognition as the author of "The Imperial Rescript on Education." That judgment provokes the question of whose ideas ultimately prevailed. Motoda indirectly revealed the answer by deferring to Inoue's draft early on with minor reservations. He was apparently convinced that he essentially achieved the goals he had fought for so rigorously, with one variation concerning the constitution. In fact, the elderly Confucianist had finally attained his primary aim in life through his old antagonist, who incorporated Motoda's basic position in "The Imperial Rescript on Education."

The approval of Inoue's draft of "The Imperial Rescript on Education" of 1890 by Motoda illustrates perhaps the most significant transition that transpired among the government leadership of the great Meiji Restoration by the beginning of its third decade in power. The modernizers such as Inoue and Itō Hirobumi, who had studied in the West and had undertaken studies of western languages and societies, had undergone a transformation, exemplified by their attitude toward educational policy. From the initial introduction in the 1870s of textbooks, curriculum, and teaching methods overwhelmingly based on the American model, to "The Imperial Rescript on Education" of 1890, educational modernization had taken on a new meaning and purpose for them. An appreciation of that radical change provides us with the opportunity to understand why the history of modern education during the Meiji era is commonly divided into two distinct periods. "The Imperial Rescript on Education" completes part one (1868–1890), the focus of this book, and initiates part two (1890–1912). By comparing Inoue's "Educational Affair" ("Kyōiku Gi") of 1879 designed to counter Motoda Nagazane's "Imperial Will of Education," with Inoue's "Imperial Rescript" of 1890 in collaboration with Motoda, the magnitude of the transformation can best be appreciated. The following pertinent excerpts are juxtaposed in chronological order to illustrate the transition.

The Educational Affair, 1879 [Excerpts]
Inoue Kowashi

The destruction of our traditional ways, however, had its own cause. . . . At the time of the Restoration, an unprecedented reform took place, accompanied by changes in our customs. . . . The isolation of the country had constrained human minds in a static condition and limited the range of communication. The feudal ruler proclaimed it virtuous to cultivate simple living and to die for honor. . . . These customs came to an end barely ten years ago. The world changed suddenly for us.

Our government boldly took matters in hand to correct the defects of the seclusionist, feudal past. Now for the first time our people have been able to follow their own will, go out beyond their usual bounds, and exercise freedom of action and speech. Because of the intensity of this change, many of the elegant and beautiful things in our tradition have also disappeared. This I take to be the greatest single cause of our present moral disarray.

The damage to our customs has come from the excessiveness of the change and it was inevitable. Therefore we should not blame the new educational system for everything. Since education is not the principal cause of the failure, it can be no more than an indirect cure. . . . Present teaching rules should remain in effect, and those in charge of teaching ethics should select the proper textbooks.

Moreover our students usually come from Confucian schools, and whenever they open their mouths it is to babble political theory and argue about the world situation. . . . In order to remedy this situation we should spread the study of the industrial arts. . . . After all it is science that, together with politics, brings about prosperity. If we are to blend the new and the old, and take the classics into consideration, and establish a single national doctrine, we are in an area that it is not proper for government to control; for this we must wait for a sage.[40]

Imperial Rescript on Education, 1890
Inoue Kowashi

Know ye, Our subjects:

Our Imperial Ancestors have founded Our Empire on a basis broad and everlasting, and had deeply and firmly implanted virtue. Our subjects ever united in loyalty and filial piety from generation to generation illustrated the beauty thereof. This is the glory of the fundamental character of Our Empire, and herein lies the source of Our education.

Ye, Our subjects, be filial to your parents, affectionate to your brothers and sisters; as husbands and wives be harmonious, as friends true; bear yourselves in modesty and moderation, extend your benevolence to all; pursue learning and cultivate arts, and thereby develop intellectual faculties and perfect moral powers; furthermore, advance the public good and promote common interests; always respect the constitution and observe the laws; should emergency arise, offer yourselves courageously to the State; and thus guard and maintain the prosperity of our Imperial Throne coeval with heaven and earth. So shall ye not only be Our good and faithful subjects, but render illustrious the best traditions of your forefathers.

The Way here set forth is indeed the teaching bequeathed by our Imperial Ancestors, to be observed alike by Their Descendants and the subjects, infallible for all ages and true in all places. It is Our wish to lay it to heart in all reverence, in common with you, Our subjects, that we may all attain the same virtue.

These two documents appear as if they were written by different authors. From an historical perspective, they were. During the first decade of the Meiji Restoration, the political leadership eschewed the past viewed as feudal and therefore considered detrimental to a modern society. Inoue directly refers to this in his 1879 document. To Inoue the foundation of modern Japan and the prosperity of its people should be embedded in and dependent upon western science together with politics and "the study of industrial arts." That symbolized Inoue's reasoning in 1879. By 1890 he had undergone an historical transformation in thought, evidenced by his writings that would influence the course of the nation for decades.

This leads, then, to the final comparison of critical documents between the traditionalist, Motoda Nagazane, and his "Imperial Will on Education" of 1879, and the modernist, Inoue Kowashi, whose "Imperial Rescript on Education" of 1890 we have just quoted.

Imperial Will on Education, 1879
Motoda Nagazane

The essence of education, our traditional national aim, and a watchword for all men, is to make clear the ways of benevolence, justice, loyalty, and filial piety, and to master knowledge and skills and through these to pursue the Way of Man. In recent days people have gone to extremes. They take unto themselves a foreign civilization whose only values are fact gathering and technique, thus violating the rules of good manners and bringing harm to our customary ways. Although we set out to take in the best features of the West, and bring in new things in order to achieve the high aims of the Meiji Restoration—abandonment of the undesirable practices of the past and learning from the outside world—this procedure had a serious defect. It reduced benevolence, justice, loyalty, and filial piety to a secondary position. The danger of indiscriminate emulation of western ways is that in the end our people will forget the great principles governing the relations between ruler and subject, and father and son. Our aim, based on our ancestral teachings, is solely the clarification of benevolence, justice, loyalty, and filial piety.

For morality, the study of Confucius is the best guide. People should cultivate sincerity and moral conduct, and after that they should turn to the cultivation of the various subjects of learning in accordance with their ability. In this way, morality and technical knowledge will fall into their proper places. When our education comes to be grounded on Justice and the Doctrine of the Mean, we shall be able to show ourselves proudly throughout the world as a nation of independent spirit.[41]

The similarities between Motoda Nagazane's "Imperial Will on Education" of 1879 and Inoue Kowashi's "Imperial Rescript on Education" of 1890, quoted above, are compelling. Both took the form of short imperial messages by the emperor to his subjects. The focus in both was placed on Confucian virtues and the imperial tradition, the later especially prominent in the "Rescript." And both used nearly identical Chinese characters to emphasize the primary themes that run throughout them. Although the characters for benevolence, justice, loyalty, and filial piety (*jingi chūkō*) were used in different combinations of words or variations in the two documents, the meaning was essentially the same. Motoda employed them three times in "The Imperial Will on Education" in 1879. Inoue incorporated them into "The Imperial Rescript" of 1890. In contrast, Inoue never mentioned either Confucian virtues (*jingi chūkō*) or the imperial tradition in his 1879 "Educational Affair" opposing Motoda's 1879 "Imperial Will on Education," which did.

The primary difference between Motoda's "Imperial Will" of 1879 and Inoue's "Imperial Rescript" of 1890 concerns the modern western principles of nationhood (*kokutai*) in the "Rescript," based on the German model. However, Motoda ultimately accepted Inoue's western concept of constitutional government for the nation. Even that aspect conformed to his thinking, since the new governmental structure was aimed at social stability in order to preserve the imperial throne. Consequently Inoue's Constitution of 1889 and his "Imperial Rescript on Education" of 1890 that embedded the imperial institution into the fabric of modern government and education fulfilled a primary goal of Motoda.

A comparison of the documents demonstrates how Motoda's traditionalist thought had become incorporated into the thought of western-oriented leaders. Although the English versions above were translated by different individuals, "The Imperial Will" by a distinguished foreign scholar in 1965 and the "Rescript" by the Japanese government in the early 1900s, the evidence is convincing. Inoue Kowashi's "Imperial Rescript" is not original in content or intent. It resembles Motoda Nagazane's "Imperial Will on Education" of 1879 and his other writings to an extent that cannot be dismissed as coincidental.

The surviving written evidence indicates that Motoda Nagazane was, in essence, the originator of "The Imperial Rescript on Education" of 1890. In other words, even though Inoue was the author of the "Rescript," Motoda was the mastermind behind it. If Inoue's ideas in the "Rescript" had not conformed to Motoda's basic position, Motoda would never have accepted them. We know that a decade earlier in 1879, when Inoue's "Educational Affair" did not conform to Motoda's "Imperial Will on Education," he immediately countered with his critique of the "Educational Affair" ("Kyōiku Gi Fugi"), outlined in chapter 15. Motoda did not find that necessary with Inoue's 1890 "Rescript."

The coalescing of thought between the modernist and the traditionalist explains why Motoda quickly withdrew his own version of an educational rescript. His reaction was understandable since Inoue's "Rescript" reads in the most part as if it were written by Motoda himself. Moreover, with Inoue including the phrase in the "Rescript" that "The way here set forth is indeed the teaching bequeathed by our Imperial ancestors," Motoda had won the supreme prize. The fundamental role and integrity of imperial ideology amid the modernization and westernization of Japanese education was unequivocally and officially recognized by the modernizers.

The convergence of ideas in Motoda Nagazane's "Imperial Will on Education" of 1879 and Inoue Kowashi's "Imperial Rescript on Education" of 1890 poignantly illustrates two conclusions. First, it further clarifies the prominent role that Motoda, archconservative in the traditional Confucian style, played in the first two decades of modern Japanese education. Of equal significance, the juxtaposition of the two documents illustrates how western-oriented government leaders underwent a decisive transformation of policy during the first two decades of the Meiji period. Although the "Imperial Rescript" of 1890 written by the modernist Inoue Kowashi reflects the thought of the Confucianist Motoda Nagazane in compelling ways, Inoue's theoretical basis stems, ironically, from a modern western interpretation. For example, his position on religion is of particular import since a reading of the final version indicates that religious-like thought closely aligned to Shintoism forms an integral part of it. His purpose, however, was to avoid any religious connotations that could provoke divisions among society, reflecting modern western theory of the separation of church and state. The Meiji government had already declared that Shinto was not considered a religion. Consequently the phrases in the "Rescript" referring to beliefs and customs commonly associated with Shintoism that posited the imperial tradition as the core of moral teachings were apparently not considered by Inoue as relating to a religious creed. To the author, the "Rescript" was neutral in religious matters.[42] It was years later after the death of Motoda that the "Rescript" became the basis of a pseudo religion.

On the other hand, Inoue viewed the "Rescript" from a political perspective. Along with the constitution of 1889, also penned by him, he looked upon the "Rescript" as one of the two major pillars on which Meiji bureaucrats could effectively govern the nation in the name of the emperor. He was well aware of the role of Christianity as the moral basis of western monarchies. In designing the Meiji constitution, however, he employed imperial ideology as the basis of the Japanese moral code as well as the constitutional system. Likewise, the imperial tradition was central to "The Imperial Rescript on Education," as the government viewed education as an instrument to stabilize and maintain the Meiji state.[43]

Inoue Kowashi was attracted to the German model, and particularly its constitution, as a model for Japan in part because of the political stability of the country. France and England had experienced political revolutions. Prussia, then Germany, had not. Inoue was also deeply impressed with the central role of the German monarch, an institution similar to the Japanese Imperial Household, which was given broad powers within a constitutional form of government. This held great significance to the Japanese since the German state had developed into a mighty industrial power. Inoue was advised by a distinguished German legal advisor to the Japanese government, Herman Roesler, who advocated that "the institution of the Emperor had to be the center of the new constitutional system."[44]

Inoue, in collaboration with Itō Hirobumi, the most powerful figure in government, followed the German mentor's advice, reportedly sought "on every single point" in drawing up the Meiji constitution.[45] He designated broad powers to the Japanese emperor in the constitution, which was promulgated without a referendum in 1889. In a constitutional monarchy, the pivotal role of the emperor was a means to maintain political stability of the government through a constitution that the Peoples' Movement for Freedom had demanded for a decade.[46] In other words, Inoue devised a means to counter the pressure from the opposition for a western-style parliament and constitution patterned after one of the great western powers, while preserving the Japanese imperial tradition and cultural values. "The Imperial Rescript on Education" conformed to and reinforced this grand design.

As celebrated author of the Meiji constitution and a specialist on the German legal system, Inoue had already concluded that Japan must establish a constitutional form of government appropriate for a modern state. However, amid growing political instability within Japan, he also arrived at the conclusion that morality must play a major role in modern societies. Man is not primarily a legal but a moral being. The modern state must be based firmly on a moral foundation.[47] As Christianity provided the moral basis of western societies, Inoue turned to the imperial tradition as the center of the people's morality (*kokumin dōtoku*) in Japan.[48] This ultimately brought Inoue in line with Motoda's long-held position.

Inoue struggled with the problem of reconciling the position of the emperor in an "Imperial Rescript" with the new German-type constitution for Japan that he had so recently designed. He noted in a letter to the prime minister, for example, that in a modern constitutional form of government, the emperor or monarch (*kunshu*) must not interfere (*kanshō*) in the people's freedom of conscience (*ryōshin no jiyū*). Therefore he decided that a "Rescript" should not take the form of a political order issued by the emperor, but rather as a public statement.[49] Clearly the modern lawmaker faced a dilemma in attempting to merge East and West in the final draft of the "Rescript," symptomatic of the Meiji period from the very first day of its existence.

Inoue utilized the opportunity through "The Imperial Rescript on Education" of 1890 to further his goal of building a sense of nationhood. In a manner similar to his Meiji constitution of 1889, Inoue turned to the imperial tradition as the foundation of the nation (*kokutai*). He was influenced by several scholars who specialized in national studies (*kokugakusha*) based on the ancient classics Nihon Shoki and Kojiki. He referred to these classical works on ancient Japan while working out the details of the Meiji constitution. This thought pattern was carried over to "The Imperial Rescript," which attributed the "fundamental character of our nation [*kokutai*]" and the "source of our education" to the foundation laid by "our imperial Ancestors."[50]

Motoda Nagazane could not have expressed it more persuasively. By symbiotically relating the imperial institution with the nation, the "Rescript" in a few carefully selected words engraved the image of the Japanese nation-state as a family. The emperor was pictured as the benevolent father guiding his children in the ways of moral living. And that imperial guidance was firmly based on the moral teachings of the Chinese sage, Confucius. The trinity of the nation, the emperor, and Confucian teachings shaped the image of Japan in the modern world as envisioned by Motoda Nagazane. It was incorporated into the thought of the political leadership epitomized by Inoue Kowashi in his "Imperial Rescript on Education" that extended far beyond the realm of the schools. It was intended as a national ethic.

A significant question about the great transition in thought between the first and second decade of the Meiji Restoration among Japan's political elite remains. What was the motivation? Perhaps the most persuasive evidence underlying the transformation in the thought of Inoue Kowashi is contained in a letter written by him to leading government officials including Iwakura Tomomi on November 7, 1881.[51] This comes immediately after the momentous political change that took place only a month previously known as the Meiji Seihen. The political leadership underwent a sudden change that effectively removed those who favored Britain and America as the model for governmental reform of Japan and their supporters such as the famous Fukuzawa Yukichi. The vacuum was quickly filled by Itō Hirobumi and his confidant Inoue Kowashi.

In Inoue's 1881 letter to top governmental leaders now in charge of policy, he attempted to set a new direction for government policy from the Anglo-American influence toward the German model. The letter itself exposed a split among the modernists such as Fukuzawa favoring the Anglo-American tradition emphasizing the individual in modern society, and Inoue campaigning for the German tradition placing primary concern on the state. It also revealed Inoue's deep concern over the social unrest sparked by the Peoples' Movement for Freedom. Their demands, which included a constitution and parliament to guarantee basic freedoms were in themselves criticisms of the existing political order. Inoue noted that the general population may be influenced by the escalating political demands that could instill a spirit of revolution (*kakumei no seishin*) similar to that which took place in Britain and the United States.

The mounting threat of internal revolution to overthrow the present government posed by the Peoples' Movement for Freedom reveals perhaps the most prominent motivation underlying the transition in the thought of Inoue and many of his colleagues. Antigovernment political movements had not yet reached that critical level of concern when Inoue wrote the "Educational Affair" in 1879 defending the educational policies of the 1870s greatly influenced by the American model. By 1881, however, the political environment had changed to the extent that governmental leaders felt compelled to accede to the demands of the Peoples' Movement for Freedom. They agreed to a constitution and parliament by 1889. It was a major concession by the political leadership under increasing pressure to bow to the bold demands of the opposition.

Consequently, the primary factor underlying the transformation in the attitude toward educational reform of leading Meiji figures during the 1880s concerns events outside the schools. As the 1870s drew to a close, the Jiyū Minken Undō, the Peoples' Movement for Freedom, mounted an opposition movement toward the government that could not be ignored. By the early 1880s it had expanded to the degree that a political consensus emerged among the established leadership deeply concerned over the ability to continue in power. It increasingly influenced policy decisions. The bureaucracy ultimately became obsessed with suppressing antigovernment movements in order to maintain political stability and control over policy formation. The educational world was consequently drawn into the political trends that could not be avoided.

In order to preserve the integrity of the nation and the Meiji government under its current leadership from the threat of internal revolution, Inoue made two recommendations in his 1881 letter to the new political leaders, with whom he had close relationships. First, Inoue reasoned that in order to compete with western ideas, Japan must employ western ideas.[52] Since, in his mind, among all western countries only Prussian traditions resembled Japanese traditions, the government should henceforth look to Germany with its Prussian foundation of government as the most appropriate model for Japan to emulate. It was in part through Inoue's influence that Itō Hirobumi went to Germany in 1882 for a year's study of the German constitution and government.

In contrast to the first recommendation based on a modern western model, that is, Germany, the second recommendation in Inoue's letter was the encouragement of traditional Confucian studies. Confucian learning was not foreign to Inoue. As a samurai youth in feudal Japan, he studied Confucian classics, as did all samurai of the Tokugawa period. He knew them well since he was Confucian-educated, ironically in the same Kumamoto clan school as was Motoda. Nevertheless, in his "Educational Affair" of 1879, he avoided Confucian thought as not having any constructive role in education. Two years later he recommended it. Under the perceived political threat of internal revolution, he concluded that the ancient teachings from China instilled such concepts as loyalty and obedience (*chūai kyōjun*). In a word, Confucian studies would promote social stability, thus preserving the integrity of the nation in a time of political crisis.[53]

Inoue's position from 1881, clarified in his letter to government leaders, was marked by its appeal for a combination of the new and the old. The modern took the form of the German model. The ancient was based on Confucian teachings and imperial tradition. This letter, therefore, represents one of the most convincing pieces of evidence revealing a change of thought and the primary reason for it among the political elite that took place during the early 1880s. Within the decade it would exert an enormous influence on the course of modern Japanese education. Moreover, Inoue Kowashi's letter of 1881 portends the dichotomy incorporated in his "Imperial Rescript" of 1890. It, too, combines the old, that is, Confucian thought with imperial ideology embedded within it, and to a lesser extent the new, the constitution and the laws therein based on the German model. The combination of modern German political institutions with traditional Confucian teachings in the 1890 "Imperial Rescript," originally contained in Inoue's writings of 1881, resulted from his deep concern for the potential threat of internal disorder and potential revolution.

Regardless of the political motivation behind Inoue's ideological transformation, "The Imperial Rescript on Education" of 1890 primarily reflects the earlier ideas of Motoda Nagazane. Perhaps more than any other individual of the period, Motoda early on realized the potential of modern education as an instrument for nation-building by transmitting traditional values to each generation in the public schools. He also stands out from among his contemporaries as the most prominent figure who defined or, as some critics characterize it, "invented" precisely what constituted traditional values of Japanese society of the 1880s.[54] In effect, Motoda was instrumental in crafting a new value system for modern Japan. Confucian virtues derived from ancient China, interfused with traditions associated with the Japanese imperial family, formed the moral foundation for the study of western science and technology in the nation's modern school system.

Analysis of "The Imperial Rescript on Education"

Among the various interpretations of "The Imperial Rescript on Education" over the years, one of the most important was an officially authorized interpretation prepared for use at teacher training schools well after the Rescript's promulgation. The distinguished philosopher of the Meiji Era, Inoue Tetsujiro, summarized the essential themes of the Rescript as virtue and a spirit of patriotism and love of country.[55] Within this general framework, the Rescript can be essentially divided into three parts. The introduction sets the historical background of Japan and its people with the emperor at the center. It begins, "Our Imperial Ancestors have founded Our Empire on a basis broad and everlasting, and have deeply and firmly implanted virtue." According to Inoue Tetsujiro, the first phrase, "Our Imperial Ancestors," refers to the celebrated but mythical god Amaterasu Omikami and the first mythical emperor of Japan, Jimmu Tenno. The ancient Shinto classics Nihon Shoki and Kojiki ascribe the founding of Japan in 660 B.C.E. to these two ancient figures. The phrase implicitly includes the two hundred plus emperors who followed, thus associating the entire history of Japan directly to the imperial tradition conforming to Shinto beliefs.[56] The symbiotic relationship between the foundation of Japan and the imperial institution contained in this statement is attributed to the nationalist scholars who influenced the thinking of Inoue searching for a theoretical basis of the nation-state (*kokutai*). It firmly implants the imperial institution within the historical tradition of the country.[57]

The second part of the opening sentence incorporates a major theme that Motoda championed throughout his life, virtue as it relates to the imperial tradition. As Confucian lecturer to the emperor, Motoda began his very first lesson to his exalted student on "The Duty of an Emperor" with the historical basis for virtue. "The High Path of Supreme Virtue handed down by the Heavenly Ancestress" originated as the Supreme Command passed on in turn by successive emperors.[58] It was, therefore, the Emperor Meiji's turn to carry out this great Imperial tradition referred to in "The Imperial Rescript." The nucleus of the "Rescript," beginning "Ye, Our subjects, be filial to your parents, . . ." delineates the traditional Confucian moral principles governing relationships among family and friends, and that between the emperor and his subjects, which form the social basis of eastern morality.

Here again Motoda refers to this general concept in his lecture to the emperor. He relates Confucian morality to the concept of virtue derived from Japanese gods, thereby assimilating Japanese mythical teachings with Chinese Confucian classics. The method adopted by an ancient Japanese emperor "of developing and expanding the High Path of Supreme Virtue handed down by the Heavenly Ancestress" was to "use the [Confucian] Analects as his text book." It was, according to Motoda's lecture to the emperor, the Confucian teachings of benevolence, justice, loyalty, and filial piety that has "given our Empire its position of sublime independence before all the world, [and] is an inheritance which we owe to the never failing piety of the whole line of our sainted emperors."[59] Emperor Meiji should, consequently, depend upon these cherished Confucian principles to follow the Imperial Way.

The notion of improving oneself through education is associated with morality. The two are inextricably related. This section appeals not only to social development but also to individual development that comes through education. However the concept "to develop intellectual faculties" is coupled with "perfect moral powers." Even here the modern and the traditional are intimately related, overcoming the criticism of things western with materialism. It relates the individual to the state and society at large, incorporating the modern principles of statehood built on laws rooted in western-style constitutionalism. Although one is urged to "offer yourselves courageously to the state," the purpose is to preserve the imperial tradition. The closing section is based on the Way (Michi) "bequeathed by our Imperial Ancestors." This is taken from the Chinese sage Lao Tse.[60] The ending, "that we may attain to the same virtue," returns to the Confucian texts.[61] Virtue is the ultimate purpose of existence. It applies both to the emperor and his subjects. The closure ultimately conforms precisely to the fundamental position of Motoda Nagazane.

Another interpretative approach is to compare the similarities between "The Imperial Rescript on Education" of 1890 with that of "The Imperial Rescript to Soldiers" of 1882. Both take the form of the emperor speaking to his subjects, members of the army and students in school. Both define morality of the individual as loyalty to the emperor and the country that defines a loyal soldier and a loyal student. And both aimed at developing a strong and united modern nation (kokutai) under the emperor. It was a utopian society based on Confucian concepts and imperial traditions.[62]

A final analytical approach to the Rescript divides it into three main elements that reflect the thought of the two architects of the document, Inoue Kowashi and Motoda Nagazane.[63] The first is the Confucian factor (jūkyō shugi). The basic Confucian virtues of benevolence, humanity, loyalty, and filial piety (jingi chūkō) are repeated several times. This can be attributed to Motoda's influence and has been referred to as the family-centered morality (kazoku shugi dōtoku), emphasizing respect for elders.

This leads to the second element, imperial ideology (kōdō shugi). The emperor is seen as the epitome of Confucius morality and the virtuous head of the family, that is, the nation. It is this factor that gives the Rescript a Shinto relationship, since Imperial Household ceremonies are closely related to Shinto traditions. The first two factors that dominate the Rescript, therefore, can be attributed very much to the efforts of Motoda, who endeavored through his lectures to the emperor to enlighten him on the unique role he should play as Japan entered the modern era.

The final element, the German factor, represents an original contribution of Inoue Kowashi. Japan entered the modern world of western constitutionalism the year prior to the 1890 Rescript on Education, employing the German constitution as the model for Japan. Inoue was the principal author of that legislation. By inserting the western concept of constitutionalism in the Rescript however briefly, he placed Japan on an equal footing with the most advanced western nations governed by the rule of law. In effect, feudalism had finally been replaced by constitutionalism, the ultimate in modern enlightened government.

The unity of the three factors in the Rescript is based on the centrality of the imperial institution. Not only is the emperor the perfection of ancient Confucian virtues but he is also the head of the nation based on modern German constitutionalism. Accordingly, both "The Imperial Rescript on Education" of 1890 and the Meiji constitution of 1889 begin with the same phrase, "Know ye Our subjects" (Chin omou ni). They both took the form of the emperor presenting his ideas to his subjects, his family. Consequently both documents are characterized as "imperial centered."

The final procedural act in issuing the Rescript is in itself instructive. The deadline for the Ministry of Education was the late October 1890 session of the new parliament. Inoue intended that it would be proclaimed by Emperor Meiji himself. The minister of education preferred that it be proclaimed at the prestigious Tokyo Higher Teacher Training School. Others urged that it receive official approval by the parliament under the new constitution rendering it into law. However due to scheduling conflicts and the personalities of those involved, a hasty decision was made to speed up the process, avoiding legal entanglements. Following the example of "The Imperial Rescript to Soldiers," "The Imperial Rescript on Education" was ceremoniously presented to the emperor at the imperial palace by Prime Minister Yamagata and Minister of Education Yoshikawa on October 20, 1890. An official reading of it followed at, of all places, St. Nikolai Catholic Cathedral in Tokyo.[64]

With the promulgation of "The Imperial Rescript on Education" in 1890, the modern school system of Japan finally achieved a sustainable balance. The academic curriculum biased toward western science and mathematics continued from the early days of the Gakusei, the First National Plan for Education of 1872–1873. However, the moral foundation of the school based on "The Imperial Rescript" of 1890 would henceforth stem from Confucianism, with imperial ideology at the core. The amalgamation of western academic studies and eastern moral virtues became the hallmark of Japanese education as it entered the twentieth century. "The Imperial Rescript on Education" of 1890 consequently brings to an end the first two decades of modern education in Japan, characterized by the struggles between the modernizers and the traditionalists. It was, moreover, a vindication of Motoda Nagazane and his ceaseless efforts to carry out the second phrase of the Charter Oath declared by the emperor in 1868. With the fulfillment of this oath, the initial period of modern Japanese history comes to a close. "Knowledge shall be sought throughout the world, so as to strengthen the foundation of imperial rule."

Notes

CHAPTER I — EDUCATION OF THE SAMURAI IN TOKUGAWA SCHOOLS

1. *Nihon no Seichō to Kyōiku* (Education and the Development of Japan) (Tokyo: Ministry of Education, 1962), 35.

2. Bernard Silberman, *Modern Japanese Leadership: Tradition and Change* (Tucson: University of Arizona Press, 1966), 235.

3. Ibid.

4. Ibid., 238–239.

5. Ronald Dore, *Education in Tokugawa Japan* (Berkeley: University of California Press, 1965), 2.

6. Nobuo Shimohara, *Adaptation and Education in Japan* (New York: Praeger, 1979), 46.

7. Aoki Michiko, "Popularization of Samurai Values," *Monumenta Nipponica* 31, no. 4 (Winter 1976): 393.

8. Dore, *Education in Tokugawa Japan*, 59.

9. Masao Watanabe, *The Japanese and Western Science* (Philadelphia: University of Pennsylvania Press, 1990), 3.

10. Alice Bacon, *Japanese Girls and Women* (Boston: Houghton, Mifflin, 1891), 208–209.

11. Konno Nobuo, *Edoko Sodate Jijō* (Education of Children in the Edo Period) (Tokyo: Kikuchi Shokan, 1988), 93–103.

12. *Aizu Hankō Nisshinkan Gaidobukku* (A Guide Book to the Aizu Clan School Nisshinkan) (Aizu: Aizu Hankō Nisshinkan, 1994), 33.

13. Konno, *Edoko Sodate Jijō*, 100–101.

14. Ibid., 96–97.

15. Ibid.

16. Sakuma Hanami, *Danshaku Yamakawa Sensei Den* (The Biography of Viscount Yamakawa) (Tokyo: Danshaku Yamakawa Sensei Kinenkai, 1939), 24–25; Watanabe, *The Japanese and Western Science*, 7.

17. *Tokyo Daigaku Hyakunen Shi* (One Hundred Year History of Tokyo University) (Tokyo: Daigaku Shuppan Kai, 1984), 1: 20–43; W. G. Beasley, *Japan Encounters the Barbarian* (New Haven: Yale University Press, 1995), 46.

18. Warren Clark, *Katz Awa: The "Bismarck" of Japan* (New York: B. F. Burk, 1904), 31.

19. Takanishi Kenkichi, *Bunmei Kaika no Eigo* (English during the Enlightenment) (Tokyo: Chūō Kōronsha, 1985), 22–23.

20. *Tokyo Daigaku Hyakunen Shi*, 31.

21. Ibid., 28.

22. Ibid., 35.

23. Ibid., 28.

24. *Ishizuka Minoru, Kindai Nihon no Kaigai Ryūgaku Shi* (History of Students Studying Abroad in Modern Japan) (Tokyo: Mineruba Shobō, 1972), 104.

25. *Tokyo Daigaku Hyakunen Shi*, 38.

26. Kaigo Tokiomi, ed., *Nihon Kindai Kyōiku Shi Jiten* (Dictionary of Modern Japanese Educational History) (Tokyo: Heibonsha, 1971), 122.

27. Shimohara, *Adaptation and Education in Japan*, 46.

28. Beasley, *Japan Encounters the Barbarian*, 130.

29. Keio Gijuku, ed., *Keio Gijuku Hyakunen Shi* (One Hundred Year History of Keio Gijuku), (Tokyo: Iwanami Shobō, 1958), 1: 192–198.

30. *Keio Gijuku Nyūsha Chō* (The entering students at Keio Gijuku) (Tokyo: Fukuzawa Kenkyū Center, 1986), 1: 166–183.

31. Yoshiie Sadao, *Toyōka Han to Keio Gijuku* (Toyōka Han and Keio Gijuku) (Tokyo: Keio Gijuku Fukuzawa Yukichi Center, 2000), 82–84.

32. Keio, *Keio Gijuku Hyakunen Shi*, 257–263

33. Keio Gijuku, ed., *Fukuzawa Yukichi Zenshū* (The Complete Works of Fukuzawa Yukichi),Vol. 19, *Education* (Tokyo: Keio Gijuku,1972), 371–372.

34. Yoshiie, *Toyōka Han to Keio Gijuku* (Toyōka Han and Keio Gijuku), 91–95.

35. Keio, *Keio Gijuku Hyakunen Shi*, 563–571.

36. Dore, *Education in Tokugawa Japan*, 52.

37. Fukuzawa Yukichi, *The Autobiography of Fukuzawa Yukichi*, translated by Kiyōka Eiichi (Tokyo: Hokuseido Press, 1960), 3.

38. James Bartholomew, *The Formation of Science in Japan* (New Haven: Yale University Press, 1989), 41.

39. Hamada Yōtaro, *Kindai Nihon Kyōiku no Kiroku* (Historical Records of Modern Japanese Education) (Tokyo: Nihon Hōsō Shuppan Kyōkai, 1978), 1: 17.

40. Hugh Borton, *Japan's Modern Century* (New York: Ronald Press, 1955), 65.

41. H. J. Jones, "Bakumatsu Foreign Employees," *Monumenta Nipponica Studies in Japanese Culture* 29, no. 3 (Autumn 1974): 316–317

42. Tessa Morris-Suzuki, *The Technological Transformation of Japan* (Cambridge: Cambridge University Press, 1994), 63.

CHAPTER 2 — EDUCATION OF THE SAMURAI IN THE WEST

1. Inuzuka Takaaki, *Meiji Isshin Taigai Kankei Shi Kenkyū* (A History of International Relations in the Meiji Restoration) (Tokyo: Yoshikawa, 1987), 312.

2. Kaneko Kentarō, ed., *Itō Hirobumi Den* (The Biography of Itō Hirobumi) (Tokyo: Hara Shobō, 1943; reprint, 1970), 1: 68–72.

3. Ibid.

4. Ishizuki Minoru, *Kindai Nihon no Kaigai Ryūgaku Shi* (A History of Students Studying Abroad in Modern Japan) (Tokyo: Mineruba Shobō, 1972), 28–34.

5. Kaneko, *Itō Hirobumi Den*, 83–107.

6. J. Harris, "From Giessen to Gower Street: Towards a Biography of Alexander Williamson," *Annals of Science* 31, no. 2 (1974): 95–130.

7. Ibid., 123.

8. Watanabe Minoru, *Kindai Nihon Kaigai Ryūgakusei Shi* (The History of Japanese Students Abroad) (Tokyo: Kōdansha, 1977), 112.

9. Kaneko, *Itō Hirobumi Den*, 120.

10. Watanabe, *Kindai Nihon Kaigai Ryūgakusei Shi*, 113.

11. Inuzuka, *Meiji Isshin Taigai Kankei Shi Kenkyū*, 22–25.

12. Morikawa Terumichi, "Mori Arinori," in Benjamin Duke, *Ten Great Educators of Modern Japan*, (Tokyo: Tokyo University Press, 1989), 43–44.

13. Inuzuka, *Meiji Isshin Taigai Kankei Shi Kenkyū*, 22–23.

14. Ibid., 30.

15. Ibid., 33.

16. Inuzuka Takaaki, *Satsuma Han Eikoku Ryūgakusei* (The Satsuma Students in England) (Tokyo: Chūō Kōronsha, 1974), 52–68.

17. Inuzuka, *Meiji Ishin Taigai Kankei Shi Kenkyū*, 196–207.

18. Inuzuka Takaaki, "Mori Arinori" (Tokyo: Yoshikawa Kobunkan, 1986), 43.

19. Ibid., 47.

20. Margaret Oliphant, *Memoir of the Life of Laurence Oliphant and of Alice Oliphant, His Wife* (Oxford: William Blackwood and Sons, 1891), 1: 1–23.

21. Laurence Oliphant, *Narrative of the Earl of Elgin's Mission to China and Japan in the Years 1857, '58, '59* (London: William Blackwood and Sons, 1859), 2: 179.

22. Ibid., 50.

23. Sir Rutherford Alcock, *The Capital of the Tycoon: A Narrative of a Three Years' Residence in Japan* ([1863] New York: Greenwood Press, 1969), 1: 166–170.

24. Inuzuka, "Mori Arinori," 115.

25. Ivan Parker Hall, *Mori Arinori* (Cambridge: Harvard University Press, 1973), 96.

26. Inuzuka, "Mori Arinori," 65–66.

27. Hall, *Mori Arinori*, 101.

28. Inuzuka, "Mori Arinori," 66–69.

29. Hall, *Mori Arinori*, 104.

30. Inuzuka, "Mori Arinori," 69.

31. Oliphant, *Memoir of the Life of Laurence Oliphant*, 2: 21.

32. Inuzuka, "Mori Arinori," 73.

33. Ibid., 76–79.

34. Oliphant, *Memoir of the Life of Laurence Oliphant*, 2: 24.

35. Herbert Schneider, *A Prophet and a Pilgrim* (New York: Columbia University Press, 1942), 125.

36. Hall, *Mori Arinori*, 125.

37. Ibid., 126.

38. Umetane Noboru, *Oyatoi Gaikokujin* (Foreign Employees) (Tokyo: Nihon Keizai Shimbunsha, 1965), 70.

39. Gordon Laman, "Guido Verbeck: Pioneer Missionary to Japan," *Newsletter of the Historical Society of the Reformed Church in America* 1, no. 4 (1980): 3–5.

40. Letter from Verbeck to Isaac Ferris, January 14, 1860. Japan Mission Correspondence, Archives, New Brunswick Theological Seminary.

41. Ibid.

42. Annual Report for the Year Ending December 31, 1861, Nagasaki. Japan Mission Correspondence, Archives, New Brunswick Theological Seminary, New Jersey.

43. Ibid.

44. Ibid.

45. Ibid.

46. J.A.B. Scherer, "Recollections of Dr. Verbeck," *Japan Evangelist* 5, no. 6 (June 1898): 179.

47. Umetani, *Oyatoi Gaikokujin*, 71.

48. Miyoshi Nobuhiro, *Nihon Kyōiku no Kaikoku* (Education in the Opening of Japan) (Tokyo: Fukumura Shuppan, 1986), 36–37; Ogata Hiroyasu, "Ōkuma Shigenobu to Furubekki (Ōkuma Shigenobu and Verbeck)," in *Waseda Daigaku Shi Kiyō* (History of Waseda University), (Tokyo: Waseda University,1965), 1: 104–105

49. Ogata Hiroyasu, *Gakusei Jisshi Keii no Kenkyū* (The Implementation of the Gakusei) (Tokyo: Kōsō Shobō, 1963), 37.

50. Miyoshi, *Nihon Kyōiku no Kaikoku*, 37.

51. Ogata, "Ōkuma Shigenobu to Furubekki," 106.

52. Miyoshi, *Nihon Kyōiku no Kaikoku*, 37.

53. Willaim Elliot Griffis, *The Rutgers Graduates in Japan*, (New Brunswick: Rutgers College Alumni Association, 1885), 26.

54. Letter from Verbeck to John Ferris, November 6, 1866, Japan Mission Correspondence, Archives, New Brunswick Theological Seminary, New Jersey.

55. Griffis, "Rutgers Graduates in Japan," 30.

56. Ardath Burks, ed., *The Modernizers: Overseas Students, Foreign Employees, and Meiji Japan (Boulder: Westview, 1985)*, 170.

57. Ibid.

58. William Elliot Griffis, *In the Mikado's Service* (Boston: W. A. Wilde Company, 1901), 41–43.

59. Ibid.

60. Ibid., 44.

61. Ibid., 47.

62. *The Japanese Student* 3, no. 2 (November 1918): 58–59.

CHAPTER 3 — THE MEIJI RESTORATION

1. Tsuchiya Tadao, *Meiji Zenki: Kyōiku Seido Shi no Kenkyū* (History of Educational Policy in the Early Meiji Period) (Tokyo: Kōdansha, 1962), 5.

2. Kaigo Tokiomi, ed., *Nihon Kindai Kyōiku Shi Jiten* (Dictionary of Modern Japanese Educational History) (Tokyo: Heibonsha, 1971), 782; Tsuchiya, *Meiji Zenki: Kyōiku Seido Shi no Kenkyū*, 8.

3. Tsunoda Ryusaka, *Sources of Japanese Traditions* (New York: Columbia University Press, 1958), 643–644.

4. Ogata Hiroyasu, *Seiyō Kyōiku Inyū ni Hōto* (The Introduction of Western Education) (Tokyo: Kōdansha, 1961), 39.

5. Hideomi Tuge, *Historical Development of Science and Technology in Japan* (Tokyo: Kokusai Bunka Shinkokai, 1961), 100.

6. Karasawa Tomitaro, *Kyōkasho no Rekishi* (History of Textbooks) (Tokyo: Sōbunsha, 1956), 62–63.

7. Kaigo, *Nihon Kindai Kyōiku Shi Jiten*, 782.

8. Ibid.

9. Tsuchiya, *Meiji Zenki*, 10.

10. Okuda Shinjō, *Kyōka Kyōiku Hyakunen Shi* (One Hundred Year History of Subject Matter Education) (Tokyo: Kenjōsha, 1985), 1: 221.

11. Kaigo, *Nihon Kindai Kyōiku Shi Jiten*, 782.

12. Tsuchiya, *Meiji Zenki*, 12.

13. Ibid., 8–9.

14. Ibid., 11; Motoyama Yukihiko, *Proliferating Talent*, edited by J.S.A. Elisonas and Richard Rubinger (Honolulu: University of Hawaii Press, 1997), 119.

15. Yamazumi, Masami, *Nihon Kindai Shisō Taikei: Kyōiku no Taikei* (Outline of Modern Japanese Thought: Education) (Tokyo: Iwanami Shoten, 1990), 9–13.

16. Kaigo, *Nihon Kindai Kyōiku Shi Jiten*, 780.

17. Tsuchiya, *Meiji Zenki*, 10.

18. Tokyo Teikoku Daigaku, ed., *Tokyo Daigaku Hyakunen Shi Henshū Iinkai* (Tokyo: Tokyo Daigaku, 1984), 1: 81–83; Tsuchiya, *Meiji Zenki*, 11.

19. Kaigo, *Nihon Kindai Kyōiku Shi Jiten*, 872.

20. Ibid., 782.

21. Ministry of Education, *Gakusei Gojūnen Shi* (Fifty Year History of the Gakusei), (1992), 1: 7–8; Motoyama, *Proliferating Talent*, 129–131.

22. Kaigo, *Nihon Kindai Kyōiku Shi Jiten*, 782

23. *Tokyo Daigaku Hyakunen Shi*, 1: 83; Kaigo, *Nihon Kindai Kyōiku Shi Jiten*, 782.

24. Tsuchiya, *Meiji Zenki*, 14.

25. Ibid., 11–12; Kaigo, *Nihon Kindai Kyōiku Shi Jiten*, 782.

26. *Tokyo Daigaku Hyakunen Shi*, 1: 146.

27. Kaigo, *Nihon Kindai Kyōiku Shi Jiten*, 782.

28. Tokyo Teikoku Daigaku, ed., *Tokyo Teikoku Daigaku Gojūnen Shi* (Fifty Year History of Tokyo Imperial University), (Tokyo: Tokyo Daigaku, 1932), 1: 147–148.

29. Ibid., 148–149.

30. Ibid., 146.

31. Michio Nagai, *Higher Education in Japan: Its Takeoff and Crash* (Tokyo: University of Tokyo Press, 1971), 26.

32. Tokyo Teikoku Daigaku, ed., *Tokyo Teikoku Daigaku Gojūnen Shi*, 1: 151.

33. Tsuchiya, *Meiji Zenki*, 12–13.

34. Motoyama, *Proliferating Talent*, 121.

35. Hazel Jones, "The Formation of the Meiji Government Policy: Toward the Employment of Foreigners," *Monumenta Nipponica Studies in Japanese Culture* 23, nos. 1–2 (1968): 13.

36. Letter from Verbeck to Griffis, September 7, 1871, Griffis Collection, Rutgers University Library, New Brunswick, New Jersey.

37. *Tokyo Daigaku Hyakunen Shi*, 1: 442.

38. *Japan Weekly Mail*, October 11, 1875.

39. *Tokyo Teikoku Daigaku Gojūnen Shi*, 237–238.

40. *Tokyo Daigaku Hyakunen Shi*, 1: 217.

41. *Keio Gijuku Hyakunen Shi*, 563–571.

42. Nobuo Shimohara, *Adaptation and Education in Japan* (New York: Praeger, 1979), 46.

43. Hugh Keenleyside, *History of Japanese Education* (Tokyo: Hokuseido Press, 1937), 61–62.

44. Hamada Yōtaro, *Kindai Nihon Kyōiku no Kiroku* (Historical Records of Modern Japanese Education), (Tokyo: Nihon Hōsō Shuppan Kyōkai, 1978), 1: 17–19.

CHAPTER 4 — THE GAKUSEI

1. Tsuchiya Tadao, *Meiji Zenki: Kyōiku Seido Shi no Kenkyū* (History of Educational Policy in the Early Meiji Period) (Tokyo: Kōdansha, 1962), 3.

2. Kaigo Tokiomi, *Nihon Kindai Kyōiku Shi Jiten* (Dictionary of Modern Japanese Educational History) (Tokyo: Heibonsha, 1971), 781.

3. Eiichi Kiyōka, trans., *Autobiography of Fukuzawa Yukichi* (Tokyo: Hokuseido Press, 1960), 95.

4. Wayne Oxford, *The Speeches of Fukuzawa* (Tokyo: Hokuseido Press, 1973), 12.

5. Norio Tamaki, *Yukichi Fukuzawa, 1835–1901: The Spirit of Enterprise in Modern Japan* (New York: Palgrave, 2001), 37–43.

6. *Fukuzawa Yukichi Zenshū* (The Complete Writings of Fukuzawa Yukichi) (Tokyo: Iwanami Shoten, 1956) 19: 148–149.

7. Ibid., 17: 188.

8. Oxford, *The Speeches of Fukuzawa*, 117.

9. Tamaki, *Yukichi Fukuzawa, 1835–1901*, 47.

10. Kiyōka, *Autobiography of Fukuzawa Yukichi*, 165.

11. Tamaki, *Yukichi Fukuzawa, 1835–1901: The Spirit of Enterprise in Modern Japan*, 59.

12. Kiyōka, *Autobiography of Fukuzawa Yukichi*, 200.

13. Tamaki, *Yukichi Fukuzawa, 1835–1901*, 60.

14. Fukuzawa Yukichi, *Seiyō no Jijō* (Conditions in the West) [1869], in *Fukuzawa Zenshū* (The Complete Works of Fukuzawa Yukichi) (Tokyo: Jiji Shimpōsha, 1926), 1: 319–321.

15. Karasawa Tomitarō, *Kindai Nihon Kyōiku Shi* (The History of Modern Japanese Education) (Tokyo: Seibundō Shinkōsha, 1968), 10–11.

16. Horimatsu Buichi, *Nihon Kindai Kyōiku Shi* (The History of Modern Japanese Education) (Tokyo: Risōsha, 1959), 19–20.

17. "Tokyo Nichi Nichi Shimbun, 5–29–1873," in Suzuki Kōichi, ed., *Meiji Nihon Hakkutsu* (Unearthing Meiji Japan) (Tokyo: Kawada Shobō Shinsha, 1994), 133.

18. Otsuki Fumihiko, ed., *Mitsukuri Rinshō Kun Den* (The Biography of Mitsukuri Rinshō) [1907] (Tokyo: Kinsei Shiryō Kai, 1983), 1–25; Kaigo Tokiomi, *Nihon Kindai Kyōiku Shi Jiten* (Dictionary of Modern Japanese Educational History) (Tokyo: Heibonsha, 1971), 594.

19. Karasawa Tomitarō, *Meiji Shoki: Kyōiku Kikōshō Shūsei* (A Collection of Rare Educational Documents from the Early Meiji Era) (Tokyo: Yūmatsudō Shoten, 1980), 1: 9–11.

20. Ogata Hiroyasu, *Gakusei Jisshi Keii no Kenkyū* (Implementing the First National School System) (Tokyo: Kōsō Shobō, 1963), 134.

21. Ibid.; Karasawa, *Kindai Nihon Kyōiku Shi*, 10.

22. Kaigo, *Nihon Kindai Kyōiku Shi Jiten*, 594.

23. Ivan Parker Hall, *Mori Arinori* (Cambridge: Harvard University Press, 1973), 133.

24. *Gakusei Kyūjūnen Shi* (The Ninety Year History of the Gakusei) (Kyoto: Ministry of Education, 1964), 8; Inoue Hisao, *Gakusei Ronkō* (A Study of the Gakusei) (Tokyo: Kazama Shobō, 1963), 98–100.

25. Inoue, *Gakusei Ronkō,* 99.

26. Murakami Toshiaki, ed., *Meiji Bunka Shi* (The Cultural History of the Meiji Period) (Tokyo: Yōyōsha, 1955), 3: 41–42.

27. Inoue, *Gakusei Ronkō*, 99–100.

28. Ibid.

29. Kaigo, *Nihon Kindai Kyōiku Shi Jiten*, 781.

30. Horimatsu, *Nihon Kindai Kyōiku Shi*, 6; Karasawa, *Kindai Nihon Kyōiku Shi*, 2: 7.

31. Kaigo, *Nihon Kindai Kyōiku Shi Jiten*, 781.

32. Murakami, *Meiji Bunka Shi*, 41.

33. *Nihon Kindai Kyōiku Hyakunen Shi* (One Hundred Year History of Modern Japanese Education) (Tokyo: National Institute for Educational Research, 1973), 1: 67.

34. Murakami, *Meiji Bunka Shi*, 43.

35. Ishikawa Matsutarō, *Nihon Kyōiku Shi* (History of Japanese Education) (Tokyo: Dai-ichi Hōki, 1984), 2: 283–284.

36. Ogata, *Gakusei Jisshi Keii no Kenkyū*, 134–135.

37. H. C. Barnard, *Education and the French Revolution* (Cambridge: Cambridge University Press, 1958), 217.

38. Kaigo, *Nihon Kindai Kyōiku Shi Jiten*, 58–59.

39. Ryosuke Ishii, ed., *Japanese Legislation in the Meiji Era* (Tokyo: Pan Pacific Press, 1958), 124.

40. *Nihon Kindai Kyōiku Hyakunen Shi*, 2: 14–15.

41. Karasawa, *Meiji Shoki: Kyōiku Kikōsho Shūsei—Gakusei*, volume 2, unpaged.

42. Tsuchiya, *Meiji Zenki*, 75.

43. Ishida Takeshi, *Kyōikugaku Zenshū III: Kindai Kyōiku Shi* (The Complete Works on Pedagogy: The History of Modern Education) (Tokyo: Shōgakkan, 1968), 3: 37.

44. Samuel Smiles, *Self-Help,* 2nd ed. (London: John Murray, 1867), 35.

45. David Murray, ed., *An Outline History of Japanese Education*, prepared for the Philadelphia International Exhibition, 1876, by the Japanese Department of Education (New York: D. Appleton, 1876), 124–125.

46. Ishida, *Kyōikugaku Zenshū III*, 37.

47. Horimatsu, *Nihon Kindai Kyōiku Shi*, 44.

48. Tsuchiya, *Meiji Zenki*, 54–55.

49. Horimatsu, *Nihon Kindai Kyōiku Shi*, 44–45.

50. United States Office of Education, Washington, Circulars of Information, No. 2 (1875), 153

51. Horimatsu, *Nihon Kindai Kyōiku Shi*, 47.

52. Karasawa, *Kindai Nihon Kyōiku Shi*, 2: 9–10.

53. Ishida, *Kyōikugaku Zenshū III*, 42.

CHAPTER 5 — THE IWAKURA MISSION

1. Kaigo Tokiomi, *Nihon Kindai Kyōiku Shi Jiten* (Dictionary of Modern Japanese Educational History) (Tokyo: Heibonsha, 1971), 781.

2. Albert Altman, "Guido Verbeck and the Iwakura Mission," *Japan Quarterly* 13, No. 1 (March 1966): 54–61; William Griffis, *Verbeck of Japan* (New York: Fleming H. Revell, 1900), 255–262.

3. Griffis, *Verbeck of Japan*, 259.

4. Altman, "Guido Verbeck and the Iwakura Mission," 58.

5. Ibid., 61.

6. Griffis, *Verbeck of Japan*, 261.

7. Ibid., 260.

8. Charles Lanman, *The Japanese in America* (New York: University Publishing, 1872), 31–32.

9. Karasawa Tomitarō, *Meiji Shoki: Kyōiku Kikōsho Shūsei* (A Collection of Rare Educational Documents from Early Meiji Japan) (Tokyo: Yūmatsudō Shoten, 1982), 3: 2.

10. Nishio Hōsaku, *Shisaku Tanaka Fujimori Den* (Biography of Viscount Tanaka Fujimaro) [1934] (Tokyo: Ōzorasha, 1987), 78.

11. Yamauchi Akiko, *Tanaka Suma* (privately published, May 1980), 14; Nishio, *Shisaku Tanaka Fujimaro Den*, 7–8.

12. *Mumbu Jihō* (Ministry of Education Report) (Tokyo: Ministry of Education, 1941), 730: 106.

13. Morikawa Terumichi, *Kyōiku Chokugo e no Michi* (The Road to the Imperial Rescript on Education) (Tokyo: Sangensha, 1990), 20–21.

14. Tanaka Kaori, "Subarashii Meiji no Onna: Tanaka Suma" (A Remarkable Woman of Meiji Japan: Tanaka Suma), *Fukuso* (Autumn 1978): 72.

15. Karasawa, *Meiji Shoki: Kyōiku Kikōsho Shūsei*, 3: 3.

16. Ibid.

17. Lanman, *The Japanese in America*, 57.

18. Arthur Sherburne Hardy, *Life and Letters of Joseph Hardy Neeshima*.

19. Ibid., 115.

20. Ibid., 124.

21. Ibid., 99–100.

22. Ibid., 127.

23. Ibid., 124.

24. Robert Schwantes, *Japanese and Americans* (New York: Harper and Brothers, 1955), 130–131; Ronald Anderson, *Japan: Three Epochs of Modern Education* (Washington, D.C.: U.S. Department of Health, Education and Welfare, 1958), 6–7.

25. John Eaton Papers, Archives, William L. Clements Library, University of Michigan, Ann Arbor.

26. Hardy, *Life and Letters of Joseph Hardy Neeshima*, 135.

27. *Niijima Jō Zenshū* (Complete Works of Niijima Jō) (Kyoto: Dōshisha Shuppan, 1987), 3: 100.

28. Tsuchiya Tadao, *Meiji Zenki: Kyōiku Seisaku Shi no Kenkyū* (The History of Educational Policy in the Early Meiji Period) (Tokyo: Kōdansha, 1962), 200–201.

29. *Pennsylvania School Journal* 20, No. 11 (May 1872): 354.

30. James P. Wickersham, *A History of Education in Pennsylvania* (Philadelphia: Inquirer Publishers, 1886), 582.

31. Karasawa, *Meiji Shoki*, 30–31.

32. Wickersham, *A History of Education in Pennsylvania*, 582.

33. Hardy, *Life and Letters of Joseph Hardy Neeshima*, 138.

34. Kokumin Kyōiku Shōrei Kai, ed., *Kyōiku Gojūnenshi* (Fifty Year History of Education), (Tokyo: Minyūsha, 1922), 5.

35. Hardy, *Life and Letters of Joseph Hardy Neeshima*, 137.

36. Tsuchiya, *Meiji Zenki*, 210–211.

37. Julius Hawley Seelye Papers, Archives and Special Collections, Amherst College; Ōkubo Toshiaki, *Mori Arinori Zenshū* (Complete Works of Mori Arinori) (Tokyo: Senbundō Shoten, 1972), 3: 271–272.

38. *Daily Home News* (New Brunswick, N.J.), January 19, 1929.

39. *Mori Arinori Zenshū*, 3: 357–378.

40. Agreement between Fujimaro Tanaka, Commissioner of Education, and Professor David Murray, March 15, 1873, David Murray Papers, Library of Congress, Washington, D.C., box no. 1.

41. Morinaka Akimitsu, *Niijima Jō Sensei no Shōgai (The Life of Professor Niijima Jō)* (Tokyo: Fuji Shuppan, 1990), 281.

42. Hardy, *Life and Letters of Joseph Hardy Neeshima*, 145.

43. Ibid., 147.

44. Ibid., 145–150.

45. Karasawa, *Meiji Shoki*, 20–22.

46. Hardy, *Life and Letters of Joseph Hardy Neeshima*, 149.

47. Letter from Niijima Jō to Julius Seelye, March 10, 1873, Julius Hawley Seelye Papers, Archives and Special Collections, Library, Amherst College, Amherst, Mass.

48. Hardy, *Life and Letters of Joseph Hardy Neeshima*, 155.

49. Karasawa, *Meiji Shoki*, 3.

50. Tanaka, "Subarashii Meiji no Onna," 74.

51. Kaigo, *Nihon Kindai Kyōiku Shi Jiten*, 22.

CHAPTER 6 — THE MODERN EDUCATION OF JAPANESE GIRLS

1. Sakai Atsuharu, "Kaibara Ekken and *Onna Daigaku*," *Cultural Nippon* 7 (1939): 51–56.

2. Hugh Keenleyside, *History of Japanese Education* (Tokyo: Hokuseido Press, 1917), 231–232.

3. Basil Hall Chamberlain, *Things Japanese* (London: John Murray, 1905), 502–508.

4. Fumiko Fujita, *American Pioneers and the Japanese Frontier* (Westport, Conn.: Greenwood Press, 1994), 4.

5. Charles Lanman, ed., *The Japanese in America* (New York: University Publishing, 1872), 70.

6. Niitobe Inazo, *The Imperial Agricultural College of Sapporo, Japan* (Sapporo: Imperial College of Agriculture, 1983), 3.

7. Fujita, *American Pioneers*, 10–11.

8. See Akiko Kuno, *Unexpected Destinations: The Poignant Story of Japan's First Vassar Graduate* (Tokyo: Kōdansha International, 1993).

9. Ibid., 31–32.

10. Ibid., 54–55.

11. Fujita, *American Pioneers*, 11.

12. Lanman, *The Japanese in America*, 32.

13. *Evening Star* (Washington, D.C.), February 29, 1872.

14. Ibid.

15. Charles Lanman, *Leading Men of Japan* (Boston: D. Lothrop, 1883), 396.

16. Kartherine Knox, *Surprise Personalities in Georgetown, D.C.* (Washington, D.C.: privately published, 1958), 7.

17. Stanley J. Kunitz and Howard Haycraft, eds., *American Authors 1600–1900* (New York: H. W. Wilson, 1938), 451.

18. Arthur Sherburne Hardy, *Life and Letters of Joseph Hardy Neeshima* [1891] (Kyoto: Dōshisha University Press, 1980), 122.

19. Fujita, *American Pioneers*, 19.

20. Ibid., 22–25

21. Samuel Eliot Morison, *The Oxford History of the American People* (New York: Oxford University Press, 1965), 434.

22. Fujita, *American Pioneers*, 33.

23. Kuno, *Unexpected Destinations*, 74–75.

24. Ibid., 86–90.

25. Ibid., 96–104.

26. Lanman, *Leading Men of Japan*, 239.

27. Fujita, *American Pioneers*, 70.

28. Ibid., 84.

29. Ibid., 86.

30. Ibid., 105.

CHAPTER 7 — THE MODERN JAPANESE TEACHER

1. Kaigo Tokiomi, ed., *Nihon Kindai Kyōiku Shi Jiten* (Dictionary of Modern Japanese Educational History) (Tokyo: Heibonsha, 1971), 22.

2. Naka Arata, *Nihon Kindai Kyōiku Shi* (The History of Modern Japanese Education) (Tokyo: Kōdansha, 1973), 61–62.

3. Noda Yoshio, *Meiji Kyōiku Shi* (The History of Meiji Education) (Tokyo: Yumei Shobō, 1980), 312.

4. Mizuhara Katsutoshi, *Kindai Nihon Kyōin Yōsei Shi Kenkyū* (The History of Modern Japanese Teacher Education) (Tokyo: Kazama Shobō, 1990), 45.

5. Hirata Muneyoshi, *M. M. Sucotto no Kenkyū* (Research on M. M. Scott) (Tokyo: Kazama Shobō, 1995), 356.

6. Correspondence with the author from the Librarian, San Francisco History Room, San Francisco Public Library, April 13, 1995.

7. Hirata, *M. M. Sucotto no Kenkyū*, 342–343.

8. Kokumin Kyōiku Shōrei Kai, ed., *Kyōiku Gojūnen Shi* (Fifty Year History of Education) (Tokyo: Minyūsha, 1922), 19.

9. Sol Cohen, ed., *Education in the United States: A Documentary History* (New York: Random House, 1974), 2: 1047.

10. Mizuhara, *Kindai Nihon Kyōin Yōsei Shi Kenkyū*, 45.

11. Cohen, *Education in the United States*, 1044–1045.

12. Kaigo, *Nihon Kindai Kyōiku Shi Jiten*, 21.

13. Guido Verbeck letter to William Griffis, July 9, 1871, William Griffis Collection, Rutgers University, New Brunswick.

14. Marion Scott letter to William Griffis, January 8, 1907, William Griffis Collection, Rutgers University, New Brunswick.

15. *Fukuzawa Yukichi Zenshū* (The Complete Works of Fukuzawa Yukichi) (Kyoto: Iwanami Shoten, 1960), 17: 188.

16. Ministry of Education, *Gakusei* (First National Plan for Education) (1872), 22–23.

17. Hirata Muneyoshi, "M. M. Sucotto no Katsudō to Gyōseki" (The Activities and Achievements of M. M. Scott), *Kyōikugaku Kenkyū* (Journal of Educational Research) 5, no. 1 (March 1978): 3.

18. Kokumin Kyōiku Shōrei Kai, ed., *Kyōiku Gojūnen Shi*, 19; Kurasawa Tsuyoshi, *Shōgakkō no Rekishi* (The History of the Elementary School) (Tokyo: Japan Library Bureau, 1965), 2: 16–17.

19. Kaigo, *Nihon Kindai Kyōiku Shi Jiten*, 22.

20. Hirata, *M. M. Sucotto no Kenkyū*, 364.

21. Ibid., 357.

22. Hiramatsu Akifu, *Meiji Jidai ni Okeru Shōgakkō Kyōjuhō no Kenkyū* (Elementary School Teaching Methods in the Meiji Period) (Tokyo: Risōsha, 1975), 29–30.

23. Ibid.

24. Kurasawa, *Shōgakkō no Rekishi*, 29–30.

25. Ibid.

26. Kokumin Kyōiku Shōrei Kai, ed., *Kyōiku Gojūnen Shi*, 18.

27. Naka, *Nihon Kindai Kyōiku Shi*, 63.

28. Ibid.

29. Hamada Yōtaro, *Kindai Nihon Kyōiku no Kiroku* (Historical Records of Modern Japanese Education) (Nihon Hōsō Shuppan Kyōkai, 1978), 1: 16–19.

30. Cohen, *Education in the United States*, 1044–1045.

31. Hiramatsu, *Meiji Jidai ni Okeru Shōgakkō Kyōjuhō no Kenkyū*, 30.

32. Hamada, *Kindai Nihon Kyōiku no Kiroku*, 16–17.

33. Morokozu Nobuzumi, "Shōgaku Kyōshi Hikkei (Elementary School Teachers Guide), 1873," in Naka Arata, *Kindai Nihon: Kyōkasho Kyōjuhō Shiryō Shūsei* (A Collection of Materials on Modern Japanese Education: Textbooks and Teaching Methodology) (Tokyo: Tokyo Shoseki, 1982), 1: 20–21.

34. Cohen, *Education in the United States*, 1044–1045.

35. Kurasawa, *Shōgakkō no Rekishi*, 2: 40, 724–725

36. Ibid., 2: 726.

37. Ibid., 2: 20.

38. Karasawa Tomitarō, *Meiji Shoki: Kyōiku Kikōshō Shūsei* (A Collection of Rare Educational Documents from the Early Meiji Era) (Yūmatsudō Shoten, 1980), 1: 5.

39. Kurasawa, *Shōgakkō no Rekishi*, 2: 20.

40. Hirata, *M. M. Scott no Katsudō to Gyōseki*, 7.

41. *Kyōiku Jiron* (Educational Journal) (1922), 10; Okuda Shinpō, *Kyōka Kyōiku Hyakunen Shi* (One Hundred Year History of Subject Matter Education) (Tokyo: Kenjōsha, 1985), 1: 324.

42. Mizuhara, *Kindai Nihon Kyōin Yōsei Shi Kenkyuu*, 44–46.

43. Tokyo Bunrika Daigaku, ed., *Sōritsu Rokujū Nen: Tokyo Bunrika Daigaku—Tokyo Kōtō Shihan Gakkō* (The 60th Anniversary of the Founding of the Tokyo Bunrika University—Tokyo Higher Teacher Training College) (Tokyo: Tokyo Bunrika Daigaku 1931), 21.

44. Hirata, *M. M. Scott no Katsudō to Gyōseki*, 6.

45. Naka, *Kindai Nihon: Kyōkasho Kyōjuhō Shiryō Shūsei*, 1 ; 12–15.

46. Kaigo, *Nihon Kindai Kyōiku Shi Jiten*, 301.

47. Okuda, *Kyōka Kyōiku Hyakunen Shi*, 324–325.

48. Kaigo, *Nihon Kindai Kyōiku Shi Jiten*, 231.

49. Okuda, *Kyōka Kyōiku Hyakunen Shi*, 324–325.

50. Ministry of Education, *Nempo 1* (First Annual Report) (Tokyo: Ministry of Education, 1873), 150.

51. Tanaka Kaoru, "Subarashii Meiji no Onna: Tanaka Suma" (A Remarkable Woman of Meiji Japan: Tanaka Suma), *Fukuso* (Autumn 1978): 72.

52. Mizuhara, *Kindai Nihon Kyōin Yōsei Shi Kenkyū*, 46.

53. David Murray, *Copy of the Official Report of the Honorable Superintendent of Schools and Colleges in Japan to the Vice Minister of Education, in Circulars of Information* (Washington, D.C.: United States Bureau of Education, 1875), no. 2.

54. Hirata, *M. M. Scott no Katsudō to Gyōseki*, 6.

55. Ibid., 6–7.

56. Ogata Hiroyasu, *Gakusei Jisshi Keii no Kenkyū* (Implementing the Gakusei) (Tokyo: Kōsō Shobō, 1963), 157.

57. *Uchimura Kanzō Zenshū* (The Complete Works of Uchimura Kanzō) (Tokyo: Iwanami Shoten, 1982), 30: 551–552.

58. Inazo Niitobe, *Reminiscences of Childhood in the Early Days of Modern Japan* (Tokyo: Maruzen, 1934), 54–57.

CHAPTER 8 — IMPLEMENTING THE FIRST NATIONAL PLAN FOR EDUCATION

1. Ministry of Education, *Gakusei Kyūjūnen Shi* (Ninety Year History of the Gakusei) (Tokyo: Ministry of Education, 1964), 10.

2. Kaigo Tokiomi, ed., *Nihon Kindai Kyōiku Shi Jiten* (Dictionary of Modern Japanese Educational History) (Tokyo: Heibonsha, 1971), 781.

3. Tsuchiya Tadao, *Meiji Zenki: Kyōiku Seisaku Shi no Kenkyū* (The History of Educational Policy in the Early Meiji Period) (Tokyo: Kōdansha, 1962), 165.

4. David Murray Papers, United States Library of Congress, Washington, D.C., box no. 1.

5. Bureau of Education, Circulars of Information No. 2 (Washington, D.C.: U.S. Bureau of Education, 1875), 151.

6. Hara Yoshio, "From Westernization to Japanization: The Replacement of Foreign Teachers by Japanese Who Studied Abroad," *Developing Economies* 15, no. 4 (December 1977): 443.

7. *New Brunswick Daily Fredonian*, May 3, 1873.

8. Inagaki Tomoni, "Gakkan David Murray no Kenkyū" (Research on Superintendent David Murray), *Philosophia* 29 (December 1955): 109.

9. Karasawa Tomitaro, *Meiji Shōki: Kyōiku Kikōsho Shūsei* (A Collection of Rare Educational Documents from Early Meiji Japan) (Tokyo: Yūmatsudō Shoten, 1982), 3: 26; *Mumbujihō* (Ministry of Education Report), no. 730 (1941), 107.

10. Hiramatsu Akio, *Meiji Jidai ni Okeru Shogakkō Kyōjuhō no Kenkyū* (Elementary School Teaching Methods in the Meiji Period) (Tokyo: Risōsha, 1980), 24.

11. Naka Arata, *Nihon Kindai Kyōiku Shi* (The History of Modern Japanese Education) (Tokyo: Kōdansha, 1973), 57.

12. Ogata Hiroyasu, *Gakusei Jisshi Keii no Kenkyū* (Implementing the Gakusei) (Tokyo: Kōsō Shobō, 1963), 165.

13. Hiramatsu, *Meiji Jidai ni Okeru Shogakkō Kyōjuhō no Kenkyū*, 24–25.

14. Ogata, *Gakusei Jisshi Keii no Kenkyū*, 165.

15. Tsuchiya, *Meiji Zenki*, 180–181.

16. Karasawa, *Meiji Shōki*, 3: 26.

17. Ibid., 3: 2.

18. Ibid., 3: 14–15.

19. Tsuchiya, *Meiji Zenki*, 180.

20. Ibid., 182–183.

21. Ministry of Education, *Daichi Nenpō 1* (Annual Report Number 1), 1873 (Tokyo: Ministry of Education, 1875), 140.

22. Uetsuka Tsukasa, ed., *Takahashi Korekiyo Jiden* (The Autobiography of Takahashi Korekiyo) (Tokyo: Chūō Kōron, 1976), 141.

23. Kaneko Terumoto, *Meiji Zenki Kyōiku Gyōsei Shi Kenkyū* (History of Educational Administration in the Early Meiji Period) (Tokyo: Kazama Shobō, 1967), 63–64.

24. Chiba Shōji, *Gakku Seido no Kenkyū* (A Study of the School District System) (Tokyo: Keisō Shobō, 1962), 26.

25. Tsuchiya, *Meiji Zenki*, 117; Kaneko, *Meiji Zenki Kyōiku Gyōsei Shi Kenkyū*, 64.

26. Naka, *Nihon Kindai Kyōiku Shi*, 53.

27. Kaigo, *Nihon Kindai Kyōiku Shi Jiten*, 7–8.

28. Ministry of Education, *Daichi Nenpō I*, 140.

29. Kaneko, *Meiji Zenki Kyōiku Gyōsei Shi Kenkyū*, 63–64.

30. *Nihon Kindai Kyōiku Hyakunen Shi* (One Hundred Year History of Education in Modern Japan) (Tokyo: National Educational Research Institute, 1973), 2: 14.

31. Ishizuki Minoru, *Kindai Nihon no Kaigai Ryūgaku Shi* (The History of Students Studying Abroad in Modern Japan) (Tokyo: Mineruba, 1972), 177.

32. Ibid.

33. Horimatsu Buichi, *Nihon Kindai Kyōiku Shi* (The History of Modern Japanese Education) (Tokyo: Risōsha, 1959), 50.

34. Tsuchiya, *Meiji Zenki*, 110–111.

35. Ibid.

36. Kaigo Tokiomi, *Meiji Shonen no Kyōiku* (The Beginning of Meiji Education) (Tokyo: Rironsha, 1973), 172–173.

37. Hiramatsu, *Meiji Jidai ni Okeru Shogakkō Kyōjuhō no Kenkyū*, 25–26.

38. Ibid., 27.

39. Ogata, *Gakusei Jisshi Keii no Kenkyū*, 137.

40. Hirata Munefumi, *Kindai Nihon Kyōiku Seido Shi* (History of the Modern Japanese Education System) (Tokyo: Kitaōji Shobō, 1991), 37.

41. Benjamin Duke, *Ten Great Educators of Modern Japan* (Tokyo: Tokyo University Press, 1989), chap. 7.

42. Okuda Shinjō, "Kyōka Kyōiku Hyakunen Shi" (One Hundred Year History of Subject Matter Education), *Kenjōsha* 1 (1985): 248.

43. Karasawa Tomitarō, *Kyōkasho no Rekishi* (The History of Textbooks) (Tokyo: Sōbunsha, 1956), 62–63.

44. Okuda, "Kyōka Kyōiku Hyakunen Shi," 248.

45. Karasawa, *Kyōkasho no Rekishi*, 68.

46. Tessa Morris-Suzuki, *The Technological Transformation of Japan* (Cambridge: Cambridge University Press, 1994), 80–84.

47. Karasawa, *Kyōkasho no Rekishi*, 83.

48. Inatomi Eijiro, *Meiji Shoki: Kyōiku Shisō no Kenkyū* (Educational Thought in the Early Meiji Period) (Tokyo: Fukumura Shoten, 1956), 174.

49. Karasawa, *Kyōkasho no Rekishi*, 59–64.

50. Ibid., 752–762.

51. Okuda, "Kyōka Kyōiku Hyakunen Shi," 249

52. Mizuhara Katsutoshi, *Kindai Nihon Kyōin Yōsei Shi Kenkyū* (History of Teacher Training in Modern Japan) (Tokyo: Kazama Shobō, 1990), 45.

53. Furuta Haruyasu, *Shōgaku Dokuhon Benran* (Handbook of Elementary School Readers) (Tokyo: Musashino Shōin, 1978), 366–369.

54. Karasawa, *Kyōkasho no Rekishi*, 70–71.

55. Okuda, "Kyōka Kyōiku Hyakunen Shi," 249.

56. Kaigo Tokiumi, ed., *Nihon Kyōkasho Taikei: Kindai Hen* (A Collection of Modern Japanese Textbooks), Vol. 18, *Rekishi* (History) (Tokyo: Kōdansha, 1963), 8–57.

57. Ibid.

58. *Tokyoto Kyōiku Shi* (History of Education in Tokyo) (Tokyo: Tokyo Toritsu Kenkyūjo, 1994), 154.

59. Kaigo, *Nihon Kindai Kyōiku Shi Jiten*, 780.

60. Ibid.

61. Hiramatsu, *Meiji Jidai ni Okeru Shogakkō Kyōjuhō no Kenkyū*, 31.

62. Ishitoya Tetsuo, *Nihon Kyōiku Shi Kenkyū* (The History of Japanese Education) (Tokyo: Kōdansha, 1958), 47.

63. Ishitoya, *Nihon Kyōiku Shi Kenkyū*, 48.

64. *Tokyoto Kyōiku Shi*, 285.

65. Ishitoya, *Nihon Kyōiku Shi Kenkyū*, 47.

66. Ogata, *Gakusei Jisshi Keii no Kenkyū*, 158.

67. Bureau of Education, Circulars of Information, 146

68. Hiramatsu, *Meiji Jidai ni Okeru* Shogakkō Kyōjuhō *no Kenkyū*, 31; Tsuchiya, *Meiji Zenki*, 187.

69. *Japan Weekly Mail*, December 4, 1975.

70. Ibid.

71. Tanaka Kaoru, "Subarashii Meiji no Onna: Tanaka Suma" (Tanaka Suma: A Remarkable Woman of the Meiji Era), *Fukuso* (Autumn 1978): 72.

72. Ibid.

73. Hiramatsu, *Meiji Jidai ni Okeru Shogakkō Kyōjuhō no Kenkyū*, 33.

74. Tsuchiya, *Meiji Zenki*, 115.

75. Ibid., 155–156.

76. Asō Makoto, *Nihon no Gakureki Eritto* (The Japanese Educational Elite) (Tokyo: Tamagawa University, 1991), 118.

77. *Tokyo Daigaku Hyakunen Shi* (One Hundred Year History of Tokyo University) Tokyo: Tokyo Daigaku, 1984, 1: 284.

78. Ibid., 289.

79. *Japan Weekly Mail*, October 11, 1873.

80. Ibid.

81. Mumbusho Hōkoku (Ministry of Education Report), January 17, 1874.

82. *Tokyo Daigaku Hyakunen Shi*, 300.

83. David Murray Papers, United States Library of Congress, Washington D.C., box 1.

84. Mumbusho Hōkoku, January 17, 1874.

85. Tsuchiya, *Meiji Zenki*, 187.

86. Uetsuka *Takahashi Korekiyo Jiden*, 141.

87. E. Warren Clark, *Katz Awa, the "Bismarck" of Japan* (New York: B. F. Burk, 1904), 18, 77.

88. Tsuchiya, *Meiji Zenki*, 186.

89. Uetsuka, *Takahashi Korekiyo Jiden*, 141

90. *Tokyo Daigaku Hyakunen Shi*, 780.

91. Ibid., 286–287, 303–313.

92. Jerry Fisher, "The Meirokusha" (Ph.D. dissertation, University of Virginia, 1974), 56.

93. Teruhisa Horio, *Educational Thought and Ideology in Modern Japan* (Tokyo: University of Tokyo Press, 1988), 31.

94. *Nichi Nichi Shimbun*, February 7, 1875.

95. William Braisted, *Meiroku Zasshi* (Meiroku Journal) (Tokyo: University of Tokyo Press, 1976), vii–xiv.

96. Horio, *Educational Thought and Ideology in Modern Japan*, 31.

CHAPTER 9 — RURAL RESISTANCE TO MODERN EDUCATION

1. Ishitoya Tetsuo, *Nihon Kyōin Shi Kenkyū* (History of Japanese Teachers) (Tokyo: Kōdansha, 1958), 23–25.

2. Ōkubo Toshiaki, *Mori Arinori Zenshū* (Complete Works of Mori Arinori) (Tokyo: Sōbundo Shoten, 1972), 2: 101–102.

3. Chiba Shōji, *Gakku Seido no Kenkyū* (A Study of the School District System) (Tokyo: Keisō Shobō, 1962), 26–27.

4. Ibid.; Naka Arata, *Nihon Kindai Kyōiku Shi* (The History of Modern Japanese Education) (Tokyo: Kōdansha, 1973), 53–54.

5. Karasawa Tomitarō, *Meiji Shoki: Kyōiku Kikōsho Shūsei* (A Collection of Rare Educational Documents from the Early Meiji Era) (Tokyo: Yūmatsudō Shoten, 1981), 2: 8–9.

6. Ibid.

7. Ishikawa Matsutarō, *Nihon Kyōiku Shi* (History of Japanese Education) (Tokyo: Daiichi Hōki, 1984), 2: 317–318.

8. Tamaki Hajime, *Nihon Kyōiku Hattatsu Shi* (The Historical Development of Japanese Education) (Tokyo: Sanichi Shobō, 1954), 23–26; Roger W. Bowen, *Rebellion and Democracy in Meiji Japan* (Berkeley: University of California Press, 1980), 91.

9. Thomas C. Smith, *The Agrarian Origins of Modern Japan* (Palo Alto: Stanford University Press, 1959), 211.

10. Bowen, *Rebellion and Democracy in Meiji Japan,* 85–86.

11. Smith, *The Agrarian Origins of Modern Japan,* 211.

12. Thomas R. H. Havens, *Farm and Nation in Modern Japan: Agrarian Nationalism, 1870–1940* (Princeton: Princeton University Press, 1974), 29–30.

13. Ishida Takeshi, *Kyōiku Gaku Zenshū: Kindai Kyōiku Shi* (Complete Works on Education: History of Modern Education) (Tokyo: Shōgakkan, 1968), 3: 43.

14. Ibid.

15. Chino Yōichi, *Kindai Nihon Fujin Kyōiku Shi* (The History of Modern Education for Women) (Tokyo: Domesu Shuppan, 1979), 15.

16. Ogata Hiroyasu, *Gakusei Jisshi Keii no Kenkyū* (Implementing the Gakusei) (Tokyo: Kōsō Shobō, 1963), 256–258.

17. *Kaichi Shimpō* (newspaper), April 29, 1869, in Suzuki Kōichi, ed., *Meiji Nihon Hakkutsu* (Meiji Japan Unearthed) (Tokyo: Kawada Shobō Shinsha, 1994), 1: 80

18. Ibid.

19. Ibid.

20. Tessa Morris-Suzuki, *The Technological Transformation of Japan: From the Seventeenth to the Twenty-first Century* (Cambridge: Cambridge University Press, 1994), 73.

21. Ogata, *Gakusei Jisshi Keii no Kenkyū,* 258–259.

22. Ishitoya Tetsuo, *Nihon Kyōin Shi Kenkyū* (History of Japanese Teachers) (Tokyo: Kōdansha, 1958), 1–6; Tamaki, *Nihon Kyōiku Hattatsu Shi,* 25.

23. Ishitoya, *Nihon Kyōin Shi Kenkyū,* 1–6.

24. Hirata Munefumi, *Kyōkashō de Tsutsuru Kindai Nihon Kyōiku Seido Shi* (A History of the Modern System of Japanese Education through Textbooks) (Tokyo: Kitaōji Shobō, 1991), 40.

25. Ishitoya, *Nihon Kyōin Shi Kenkyū,* 1–3.

26. Tsuchiya, *Meiji Zenki,* 158.

27. Ishitoya, *Nihon Kyōin Shi Kenkyū,* 5–6.

28. Tsuchiya, *Meiji Zenki,* 158–159.

29. Morris-Suzuki, *The Technological Transformation of Japan,* 267.

30. Ogata, *Gakusei Jisshi Keii no Kenkyuu,* 259.

31. Tsuchiya, *Meiji Zenki,* 155–156.

32. Preamble to the Gakusei.

33. Tsuchiya, *Meiji Zenki*, 112–115; Karasawa Tomitarō, *Kindai Nihon Kyōiku Shi* (A History of Modern Japanese Education) (Tokyo: Seibundō Shinkōsha, 1976), 36–37.

34. Tsuchiya, *Meiji Zenki*, 112.

CHAPTER 10 — THE IMPERIAL UNIVERSITY OF ENGINEERING

1. Major sources for this chapter include Kita Masami, *Kokusai Nihon o Hiraita Hitobito* (The Individuals Who Opened Japan) (Tokyo: Dōbunkan, 1984); Miyoshi Nobuhiro, *Meiji no Enginiya Kyōiku* (Engineering Education in Meiji Japan) (Tokyo: Chūō Kōron, 1983); *Tokyo Daigaku Hyakunen Shi* (The One-Hundred Year History of Tokyo University), Vol. 3, *Bukyoku Shi* (Divisional Histories) (Tokyo: Tokyo Daigaku Shuppankai, 1984); Olive Checkland, *Britain's Encounter with Meiji Japan, 1868–1912* (Houndmills: Macmillan, 1989); and R. A. Cage, *The Scots Abroad: Labour, Capital, Enterprise, 1750–1914* (London: Croom Helm, 1985).

2. Edward Seidensicker, *Low City, High City: Tokyo from Edo to the Earthquake: How the Shogun's Ancient Capital Became a Great Modern City, 1867–1923* (New York: Alfred A. Knopf, 1983), 28.

3. Paul Blum, *Yokohama in 1872* (Tokyo: Asiatic Society of Japan, 1963), 12.

4. Kaigo Tokiomi, ed., *Nihon Kindai Kyōiku Shi Jiten* (Dictionary of Modern Japanese Educational History) (Tokyo: Heibonsha, 1971), 782.

5. Ishizuki Minoru, *Kindai Nihon no Kaigai Ryūgaku Shi* (The History of Students Studying Abroad in Modern Japan) (Tokyo: Mineruba Shobō, 1972), 144–145.

6. *Tokyo Daigaku Hyakunen Shi*, 1: 650–652.

7. Cage, *The Scots Abroad*, 260.

8. Ibid.

9. Ibid., 261.

10. Teijiro Muramatsu, *Westerners in the Modernization of Japan* (Tokyo: Hitachi, 1995), 26.

11. *Tokyo Daigaku Hyakunen Shi*, 3: 7.

12. Olive Checkland, *Britain's Encounter with Meiji Japan, 1868–1912* London: Macmillan, 1989), 76.

13. Henry Dyer, *Dai Nippon, the Britain of the East* (London: Blackie and Son, 1905), 5.

14. *Tokyo Daigaku Hyakunen Shi*, 3: 7.

15. Checkland, *Britain's Encounter with Meiji Japan, 1868–1912*, 83.

16. William Gray Dixon, *Land of the Morning* (Edinburgh: J. Gemmell, 1882), 356–358.

17. Checkland, *Britain's Encounter with Meiji Japan, 1868–1912*, 74.

18. Ibid.

19. Neil Pedler, *The Imported Pioneers: Westerners Who Helped Build Modern Japan* (New York: St. Martin's Press, 1990), 101.

20. John Maki, "William Smith Clark: A Yankee in Hokkaido," 1975, manuscript in Special Collection and Archives, University of Massachusetts Library, Amherst, v–32.

21. Tessa Morris-Suzuki, *The Technical Transformation of Japan* (Cambridge: Cambridge University Press, 1994), 74.

22. Miyoshi, *Meiji no Enginiya Kyōiku*, 26.

23. Seidensticker, *Low City, High City*, 68–69.

24. Muramatsu, *Westerners in the Modernization of Japan*, 32–33; James Bartholomew, *The Formation of Science in Japan* (New Haven: Yale University Press, 1989), 65–66.

25. Bartholomew, *The Formation of Science in Japan*, 66.

26. Morris-Suzuki, *The Technical Transformation of Japan*, 82.

CHAPTER 11 — PESTALOZZI TO JAPAN

1. Ishizuki Minoru, *Kindai Nihon no Kaigai Ryūgaku Shi* (The History of Students Studying Abroad in Modern Japan) (Tokyo: Mineruba, 1972), 177.

2. Ibid.

3. Julius Hawley Seelye Papers, Archives, Amherst College Library, Amherst, Massachusetts.

4. *Kibō* (Hope) 4, no. 10 (December 1957): 29.

5. Murayama Hideo, "Takamine Hideo to Osuweegō Shihan Gakkō" (Takamine Hideo and the Oswego Teacher Training School), *Shigaku Kenshū*, no. 46 (1968): 106–107.

6. Konno Nobuo, *Edoko Sodate Jijō* (Rearing Children in the Edo Period) (Tokyo: Tsukiji

Shokan, 1988), 101.

7. Ibid., 98.

8. Ibid., 96.

9. Tsuchiya Tadao, *Kindai Nihon Kyōiku no Kaitakusha* (Pioneers of Modern

Japanese Education) (Tokyo: Sekaisha, 1950), 202–203; and *Takamine Hideo Sensei

Fu* (The Biography of Takamine Hideo) (Tokyo: privately published, 1910), 11–12.

10. Hermann Krusi, *Recollections of My Life* (New York: Grafton, 1885), 249.

11. *Takamine Hideo Sensei Fu*, 17.

12. *Kibō*, 26–29.

13. *Takamine Hideo Sensei Fu*, 20–21.

14. Ibid., 25.

15. *Kibō*, 29.

16. Kaigo Tokiomi, *Nihon Kindai Kyōiku Shi Jiten* (Dictionary of Modern Japanese

Educational History) (Tokyo: Heibonsha, 1971), 387.

17. Naka Arata, *Nihon Kyōkasho: Kyōshi Shiryō Shūsei* (Japanese Textbooks: A Collection of Materials on Teachers) (Tokyo: Tokyo Shoseki, 1982), 1: 225.

18. Karasawa Tomitarō, *Kyōkasho no Rekishi* (History of Textbooks) (Tokyo: Sōbunsha, 1956), 129–130.

19. Murayama, "Takamine Hideo to Osuweegō Shihan Gakkō," 106–107.

20. Kaigo, *Nihon Kindai Kyōiku Shi Jiten*, 357.

21. Murayama, "Takamine Hideo to Osuweegō Shihan Gakkō," 106–107.

22. *Takamine Hideo Sensei Fu*, 33

23. Ibid., 34

24. Ned Harland Dearborn, *The Oswego Movement in Education* (New York: Arno Press, 1969).

25. *Oswego: History of the First Half Century of the State Normal and Training School, 1861–1911* (Oswego, N.Y.: State University College of Education, 1913), 41.

26. Dearborn, *The Oswego Movement in Education*, 7.

27. *State Normal and Training School*, 41

28. Dearborn, *The Oswego Movement in Education*, 14.

29. Oswego: *State Normal and Training School*, 41

30. Ibid.

31. Dearborn, *The Oswego Movement in Education*, 12.

32. Oswego: *State Normal and Training School*, 41–42.

33. Ibid.

34. Krusi, *Recollections of My Life*, 7.

35. Oswego: *State Normal and Training School*, 42–43.

36. Ibid.

37. Ibid., 45

38. Ibid., 46–47

39. Murayama, "Takamine Hideo to Osuweegō Shihan Gakkō," 107.

40. Ibid.

41. Krusi, *Recollections of My Life*, 232–233.

42. Ibid., 233–234.

43. Oswego: *State Normal and Training School*, 52–53

44. Ibid., 54

45. Letter from Takamine Hideo to Hermann Krusi, March 30, 1878, Archives, Penfield Library, State University of New York, Oswego, New York.

46. Murayama, "Takamine Hideo to Osuweegō Shihan Gakkō," 108–110.

47. Krusi, *Recollections of My Life*, 236.

48. Ibid., 237.

49. Tsuchiya, *Kindai Nihon Kyōiku no Kaitakusha*, 209.

50. Donald Berger, "Pioneers of Music Education in Japan: Isawa Shūji and Luther Mason," *Music Educators Journal* (October 1987): 33.

51. Yasuda Hiroshi, *Shōka to Jūjika* (Singing and the Cross) (Tokyo: Ongaku no Tomosha, 1993), 11.

52. Letters from Lowell Mason to Hermann Krusi, November 28, 1862 and January 12, 1872, in Krusi, *Recollections of My Life*, 227–229.

53. Yasuda, *Shōka to Jūjika*, 12–22.

54. Karasawa, *Kyōkasho no Rekishi*, 130–131.

55. Yasuda, *Shōka to Jūjika*, 166.

56. Murayama, "Takamine Hideo to Osuweegō Shihan Gakkō," 111.

57. Letter from Isawa Shūji to Hermann Krusi, September 17, 1879, Archives, Penfield Libraryō

58. Ibid.

59. Letter from Takamine Hideo to Hermann Krusi, June 16, 1878, Archives, Penfield Library.

60. Mizuhara Katsutoshi, *Kindai Nihon Kyōin Yōsei Shi Kenkyū* (Study of the History of Modern Teacher Training in Japan) (Tokyo: Kazama Shobō, 1990), 289.

61. Letter from Takamine Hideo to Hermann Krusi, June 16, 1878.

CHAPTER 12 — SCIENTIFIC AGRICULTURE AND PURITAN CHRISTIANITY ON THE JAPANESE FRONTIER

1. See Miyoshi Nobuhiro, *Nihon Kyōiku no Kaikoku* (Education in the Opening of Japan) (Tokyo: Fukumura, 1986), 98–101; Tsuchiya Tadao, *Kindai Nihon Kyōiku no Kaitaku Sha* (Contributors to Modern Japanese Education on the Frontier) (Tokyo: Sekaisha, 1950), 68–70; David Anthony, "The Administration of Hokkaido under Kuroda Kiyotaka: 1870–1882" (Ph.D. dissertation, Yale University, 1951); and Fujita Fumiko, *American Pioneers and the Japanese Frontier* (Westport, Conn.: Greenwood, 1994).

2. Niitobe Inazo, *The Imperial Agricultural College, Japan* (Tokyo: Imperial College of Agriculture, 1893), 2–3.

3. Fujita, *American Pioneers and the Japanese Frontier*, 10.

4. Ibid., 8.

5. Niitobe, *The Imperial Agricultural College, Japan*, 6.

6. Anthony, "The Administration of Hokkaido under Kuroda Kiyotaka: 1870–1882," 105.

7. John M. Maki, "William Smith Clark: A Yankee in Hokkaido" (unpublished, 1975); Hokudai Tokyo Dōsōkai, ed., *Hokudai Tokyo Dōsōkai Gojūnen Shi* (A Fifty Year History of the Tokyo Chapter of the Alumni Association of Hokkaido University) (Tokyo: Hokudai Tokyo Dōsōkai, 1992).

8. Ronald Story, ed., *Five Colleges: Five Histories* (Amherst: Five Colleges, 1992), 5.

9. *Amherst Record*, May 17, 1876

10. Letter from Clark to Satō Shōsuke, May 14, 1877, William S. Clark Papers, Special Collections and Archives, W.E.B. Du Bois Library, University of Massachusetts, Amherst.

11. *Amherst Record*, May 17, 1876.

12. William S. Clark Papers.

13. Ōshima Masatake, "Reminiscences of Dr. W. S. Clark," *Japan Intelligencer* 1, no. 2 (April 5, 1926): 54–55.

14. Letter from Clark to his wife, September 10, 1876. William S. Clark Papers.

15. Maki, "William Smith Clark: A Yankee in Hokkaido," vi–4.

16. J. Passmore Elkington, *Inazo and Mary P. E. Niitobe* (privately published, 1955), 14.

17. Maki, "William Smith Clark: A Yankee in Hokkaido," vi–10.

18. William S. Clark Papers.

19. Ōshima, "Reminiscences of Dr. W. S. Clark," 58.

20. John Maki, "William Smith Clark, Yatoi, 1826–1886," in *Foreign Employees in Nineteenth Century Japan*, edited by Edward R. Beauchamp and Akira Iriye (Westport, Conn.: Westview, 1990), 76.

21. William S. Clark Papers.

22. William S. Clark Papers.

23. William S. Clark Papers.

24. Miyoshi, *Nihon Kyōiku no Kaikoku*, 100.

25. Maki, "William Smith Clark: A Yankee in Hokkaido," vii–6.

26. Ōshima, "Reminiscences of Dr. W. S. Clark," 57.

27. Ibid., 58.

28. Ibid., 59.

29. William S. Clark Papers.

30. Maki, "William Smith Clark: A Yankee in Hokkaido," vii–13.

31. William S. Clark Papers.

32. Ōshima, "Reminiscences of Dr. W. S. Clark," 59.

33. William S. Clark Papers.

34. Ōshima, "Reminiscences of Dr. W. S. Clark," 61.

35. Elkinton, *Inazo and Mary P. E.* Niitobe,16.

36. Ōshima, "Reminiscences of Dr. W. S. Clark," 61.

CHAPTER 13 — THE PHILADELPHIA CENTENNIAL

1. Naka Arata, *Nihon Kindai Kyōiku Shi* (History of Modern Japanese Education) (Tokyo: Kōdansha, 1973), 60.

2. Naka Arata, "Kyōiku Gyōsei Shijō ni Okeru David Murray to Nihon Kyōiku Hō" (David Murray in the History of Educational Administration: Japanese Educational Laws), *Kyōikugaku Kenkyū* 3, no. 2 (1956): 46.

3. Tanaka Akamaro, *Mumbujihō* (Ministry of Education Report), 730 (1941): 109.

4. Ishizuki Minoru, "Philadelphia Hakurankai to Nihon no Kyōiku" (The Philadelphia Centennial and Japan), in *Jūkyū Seki Nihon no Jōhō to Shakai Hendo* (Nineteenth Century Japan: Information and Social Change), edited by Yoshida Mitsukuri (Kyoto: Kyoto Daigaku Jimbun Kagaku Kenkyūjo, 1985), 431–438.

5. Ishizuki Minoru, *Kyōiku Hakubutsukan to Meiji no Kodomo* (The Educational Museum and the Children of Meiji Japan) (Tokyo: Fukumura Shuppan, 1986), 149.

6. Tsuchiya Tadao, *Meiji Zenki: Kyōiku Seido Shi no Kenkyū* (History of Educational Policy in the Early Meiji Period) (Tokyo: Kōdansha, 1962), 5.

7. Ishizuki, "Philadelphia Hakurankai to Nihon no Kyōiku," 435.

8. Ibid.

9. Ibid., 434.

10. Ibid., 433.

11. Namerikawa Michio, ed., *Kindai Nihon no Kyōiku o Sodateta Hitobito* (Contributors to Modern Japanese Education) (Tokyo: Tōyōkan Shuppansha, 1965), 1: 150–152.

12. Tejima Kōgyō Kyōiku Shikindan, ed., *Tejima Seichi Sensei Den* (Biography of Teijima Seichi) (Tokyo: Tejima Kōgyō Kyōiku Shinkindan, 1929), 34.

13. Ishizuki, *Kyōiku Hakubutsukan to Meiji no Kodomo*, 153–155.

14. Ishizuki, "Philadelphia Hakurankai to Nihon no Kyōiku," 433.

15. *Abe Taizo Den* (Biography of Abe Taizo) (Tokyo: Meiji Seimei Hoken Sōgo Kaisha, 1971).

16. Tanaka Kaoru, "Subarashii Meiji Onna: Tanaka Suma" (A Remarkable Woman of Meiji Japan: Tanaka Suma), *Fukuso* (Autumn 1978), 73.

17. *Abe Taizo Den*, 43.

18. *Mumbu Jihō* (Ministry of Education Report), 730 (1941): 107–108.

19. *Abe Taizo Den*, 44.

20. William Elliot Griffis, *The Rutgers Graduates in Japan* (New Brunswick, N.J.: Rutgers College Alumni Association, June 16, 1885), 24.

21. Tanaka, *Mumbujihō*, 73.

22. David Murray, "Philadelphia International Exhibition," Papers of David Murray (handwritten), U.S. Library of Congress, Box 1, undated.

23. Ishizuki, *Kyōiku Hakubutsukan to Meiji no Kodomo*, 152.

24. Akira Iriye, *Mutual Images: Essays in American-Japanese Relations* (Cambridge: Harvard University Press, 1975), 28.

25. Ishizuki, "Philadelphia Hakurankai to Nihon no Kyōiku," 434.

26. J. Passmore Elkington, *Inazo and Mary P. E. Niitobe* (privately published, 1955), 10.

27. *Atlantic Monthly* 38 (July 1876): 89–90.

28. *Abe Taizo Den*, 46–47.

29. Letter of January 20, 1877, David Murray Papers, U.S. Library of Congress, Box 1.

30. Fukushima Hachijūroku, ed., *Kaikoku Gojūnen Shi* (Fifty Year History of the Opening of Japan) (Tokyo: Kaikoku Gojūnen Shi Hakkossho, 1908), 1: 738; Ishizuki, *Kyōiku Hakubutsukan to Meiji no Kodomo*, 147.

31. Ishizuki, "Philadelphia Hakurankai to Nihon Kyōiku," 442.

32. *Mumbo Jihō* (Ministry of Education Report), 730 (1941), 109

33. Ishizuki, *Kyōiku Hakubutsukan to Meiji no Kodomo*, 161.

34. Tejima Kōgyō Kyōiku Shikindan, ed., *Tejima Seiichi Sensei Den*, 35; and Numerikawa, *Nihon Kindai no Kyōiku o Sodateta Hitobito*, 1: 155–157.

35. Ishizuki, "Philadelphia Hakurankai to Nihon Kyōiku," 442.

36. Tanaka Fujimaro, *Beikoku Hakurankai Ki: Hakurankai Kyōiku Hōkoku* (A Record of the American Centennial: A Report on Education) (Tokyo: Ministry of Education, 1877), 2: 19–24.

37. James Wickersham, "Report of the Superintendent of Public Instruction of the Commonwealth of Pennsylvania for the Year Ending January 1, 1876" (Harrisburg, Pa.: B. F. Meyers, State Printer, 1876), xiii.

CHAPTER 14 — THE SECOND NATIONAL PLAN FOR EDUCATION

1. *Tokyo Daigaku Hyakunen Shi* (One Hundred Year History of the University of Tokyo), edited by Tokyo Daigaku (Tokyo: Tokyo Daigaku Shuppankai, 1984), 1: 411.

2. Tokyo Teikoku Daigaku, ed., *Tokyo Teikoku Daigaku* (Tokyo: Tokyo Imperial University, 1932), 1: 468.

3. *Tokyo Daigaku Hyakunen Shi*, 411–412.

4. Kaigo Tokiomi, ed., *Nihon Kindai Kyōiku Shi Jiten* (Dictionary of Modern Japanese Education) (Tokyo: Heibonsha, 1971), 778.

5. Toku Baelz, ed., *Awakening Japan: The Diary of a German Doctor: Erwin Baelz* (Bloomington: Indiana University Press, 1974), 26.

6. *Tokyo Daigaku Hyakunen Shi*, 413–414.

7. Ibid., 468.

8. *Tokyo Teikoku Daigaku*, 484–485.

9. *Tokio Times*, December 22, 1877.

10. Ministry of Education, *Nihon no Seichō to Kyōiku* (Japan's Growth and Education) (Tokyo: Ministry of Education, 1962), 35.

11. Hazel Jones, *Live Machines: Hired Foreigners and Meiji Japan* (Vancouver: University of British Columbia Press, 1980), 13.

12. Dorothy G. Wayman, *Edward Sylvester Morse: A Biography* (Cambridge: Harvard University Press, 1942).

13. Hideomi Tuge, *Historical Development of Science and Technology in Japan* (Tokyo: Kokusai Bunka Shinkokai, 1961), 108.

14. Edward S. Morse, *Japan Day by Day* (Boston: Houghton Mifflin, 1917), 1: 339–340.

15. Ibid., 2: 284.

16. Wayman, *Edward Sylvester Morse,* 253.

17. Ibid., 250–251.

18. James Bartholomew, *The Formation of Science in Japan* (New Haven: Yale University Press, 1989), 91.

19. Lawrence Chisolm, *Fenollosa: The Far East and American Culture* (New Haven: Yale University Press, 1964).

20. Nagai Michio, "Herbert Spencer in Early Meiji Japan," *Far Eastern Quarterly* 14, no. 1 (November 1954): 55.

21. Inoue Hisao, *Gakusei Ronko* (A Study of the First National School System) (Tokyo: Kazama Shobō, 1963), 318.

22. Tsuchiya Tadao, *Meiji Zenki: Kyōiku Seisaku Shi no Kenkyū* (History of Educational Policy in the Early Meiji Period) (Tokyo: Kōdansha, 1962), 189–190.

23. Yamauchi Akiko, *Tanaka Suma* (Mrs. Tanaka Fujimaro) (Tokyo: privately printed, May 1980), 14.

24. Inoue, *Gakusei Ronko,* 318–319.

25. Ibid.

26. Hiramatsu Akio, *Meiji Jidai ni okeru Shōgakkō Kyōjuhō no Kenkyū* (Elementary School Teaching Methods in Meiji Japan) (Tokyo: Risōsha, 1980), 31.

27. Tsuchiya, *Meiji Zenki,* 187–188.

28. Naka Arata, *Nihon Kindai Kyōiku Shi* (The History of Modern Japanese Education) (Tokyo: Kōdansha, 1973), 60.

29. David Murray, "Report upon a Draft Revision of the Code of Education in Japan to Their Excellencies The Ministers of Education, David Murray" (handwritten, unpaged), in the papers of David Murray, Manuscript Division, Library of Congress, Washington, D.C., Box 4.

30. Egi Kazuyuki Ō Keireki Dan Kankōkai, ed., *Egi Kazuyuki Ō Keireki Dan* (The Biography of Egi Kazuyuki (Tokyo: Egi Kazuyuki Ō Keireki Dan Kankōkai, 1933), 1: 36.

31. Rikken Seiyūkai, ed., *Takahashi Korekiyo Hachijūnen Shi* (Eighty Year History of Takahashi Korekiyo) (Tokyo: Rikken Seiyūkai, 1934), 47–48.

32. *Egi Kazuyuki Ō Keireki Dan,* 36.

33. David Murray, "Public Schools of Tokio: A Report by David Murray, Superintendent of School Affairs, July 1878" (handwritten), in the papers of David Murray, Library of Congress, Washington, D.C., Box 4.

34. Yamazumi Masami, *Nihon Kindai Shisō: Kyōiku no Taikei* (Modern Japanese Thought: System of Education) (Tokyo: Iwanami Shoten, 1990), 6: 45–69.

35. *Egi Kazuyuki Ō Keireki Dan,* 41–43.

36. Kokumin Kyōiku Shōrei Kai, ed., *Kyōiku Gojūnen Shi* (Fifty Year History of Education) (Tokyo: Minyūsha, 1922), 5.

37. Naka, *Nihon Kindai Kyōiku Shi,* 69–70.

38. Hayashi Takeji, *Meiji Teki Ningen* (People of the Meiji Era) (Tokyo: Chikuma Shobō, 1984), 10.

39. Murray, "Report upon a Draft Revision of the Code of Education" (unpaged).

40. *Egi Kazuyuki Ō Keireki Dan,* 39–40.

41. Ministry of Education, *Mumbu Jihō* (Ministry of Education Report) (Tokyo: Ministry of Education, 1941), 140.

42. Irokawa Daikichi, *Jiyū Minken* (Peoples' Movement for Freedom) (Tokyo: Iwanami Shinsho, 1981), 11–15.

43. Anesaki Masaharu, *History of Japanese Religions* (Rutland, Vt.: C. E. Tuttle, 1963), 354.

44. Katagiri Yoshio, *Jiyū Minken Ki Kyōiku Shi Kenkyū* (The History of the Peoples' Movement for Freedom) (Tokyo: University of Tokyo Press, 1990), 101–102.

45. Ishitoya Tetsuo, *Nihon Kyōin Shi Kenkyū* (The History of Japanese Teachers) (Tokyo: Kōdansha, 1958), 102–103.

46. Ministry of Education, *Meiji Ikō: Kyōiku Seido Hattatsu Shi* (The Development of Educational Policy in the Meiji Period) (Tokyo, 1938), 2: 161–165.

47. Ibid.

48. Ishitoya, *Nihon Kyōin Shi Kenkyū,* 117–118.

49. Hanai Makoto, *Gakkō to Kyōshi no Rekishi* (The History of Schools and Teachers) (Tokyo: Kawashima Shoten, 1979), 47.

50. Ishitoya, *Nihon Kyōin Shi Kenkyū,* 119–129.

51. Karasawa Tomitarō, *Meiji Shoki: Kyōiku Kikōshō Shūsei* (A Collection of Rare Educational Documents from the Early Meiji Era) (Tokyo: Yūmatsudō Shoten, 1983), 3: 29.

52. *Amherst Graduates' Quarterly* 15, no. 1 (November 1924): 1; Karasawa, *Meiji Shoki,* 29–30.

53. *Boston Sunday Post,* May 11, 1902.

54. Letter from Tanaka Fujimaro to Julius Seelye, March 6, 1778, Archives, Amherst College.

55. Letter from Tanaka Fujimaro to Julius Seelye, August 15, 1878, Archives, Amherst College.

56. *Chronicles of '74,* Amherst College, 28, Archives, Amherst College.

57. Ibid., 25

58. Miyoshi Nobuhiro, *Nihon Kyōiku no Kaikoku* (Japanese Education in the Opening of the Country) (Tokyo: Fukumura, 1986), 131–133.

59. Mizuhara Katsutoshi, *Kindai Nihon Kyōin Yōsei Shi* (The History of Teacher Training in Modern Japan) (Tokyo: Kazama Shobō, 1997), 484.

60. *Chronicles of '74,* 27.

61. Mizuhara, *Kindai Nihon Kyōin Yōsei Shi,* 484.

62. Letter from Tanaka Fujimaro to Julius Seelye, April 10, 1879, Archives, Amherst College.

63. Paul Phillips, "The Amherst Illustrious George A. Leland," *Amherst Graduates' Quarterly* 15, no. 1 (November 1924): 31.

64. Mizuhara, *Kindai Nihon Kyōin Yōsei Shi,* 484.

65. Phillips, "The Amherst Illustrious George A. Leland," 31.

66. Ibid., 33.

CHAPTER 15 — "THE IMPERIAL WILL ON EDUCATION"

1. Kaigo Tokiomi, ed., *Nihon Kindai Kyōiku Shi Jiten* (Dictionary of Modern Japanese Educational History) (Tokyo: Heibonsha, 1971), 778.

2. Kaneko Kentarō, *Itō Hirobumi Den* (Biography of Itō Hirobumi) (Tokyo: Tōseisha, 1942), 2: 154.

3. Tsuchiya Tadao, *Meiji Zenki: Kyōiku Seisaku Shi no Kenkyū* (The History of Educational Policy in the Early Meiji Period) (Tokyo: Kōdansha, 1962), 241–242.

4. Kurasawa Tsuyoshi, *Shōgakkō no Rekishi* (The History of the Elementary School) (Tokyo: Japan Library Bureau, 1965), 2: 77–112.

5. Ibid., 78–79.

6. Ministry of Education, *Meiji Ikō: Kyōiku Seido Hattatsu Shi* (History of the Development of Educational Policy in the Meiji Period) (Tokyo: Ministry of Education, 1938), 2: 141–165.

7. Kurasawa, *Shōgakkō no Rekishi*, 82.

8. Ibid., 82–83.

9. Ibid.

10. *Meiji Bunka Shiryō Sōsho* (A Collection of Materials on Meiji Culture), ed. Meiji Bunka Kenkyūkai, vol. 8, *Kyōiku* (Education) (Tokyo: Kazama Shobō, 1961), 124–125

11. Kurasawa, *Shōgakkō no Rekishi*, 93.

12. Ibid., 93–111.

13. *Meiji Bunka Shiryō Sōsho*, 124–125.

14. Ibid.

15. *Ibid.*, 145.

16. Kurasawa, *Shōgakkō no Rekishi*, 94–95.

17. *Tokio Times*, July 12, 1879.

18. Fujii Jintarō, *Outline of Japanese History in the Meiji Era* (Tokyo: Ōbunsha, 1958), 175.

19. Kaigo, *Nihon Kindai Kyōiku Shi Jiten*, 6.

20. *Meiji Ikō: Kyōiku Seido Hattatsu Shi*, 162.

21. *Transactions of the Asiatic Society of Japan, Lectures Delivered in the Presence of His Imperial Majesty the Emperor of Japan* 40 [1912] (Tokyo: Yushodo Booksellers, 1964), 48.

22. Ibid.

23. Ibid., 90.

24. Ibid., 91.

25. Ibid.

26. *Nihon Kindai Kyōiku Hyakunen Shi* (One Hundred Year History of Modern Japanese Education) (Tokyo: Kokuritsu Kyōiku Kenkyūjo, 1973), 1: 116.

27. Kaigo Tokiomi, *Kyōiku Chokugo Seiritsu no Kenkyū* (The Formation of the Imperial Rescript on Education) (Tokyo: privately published, 1965), 70.

28. Tōyama Shigeki, *Meiji Isshin to Tenno* (The Meiji Restoration and the Emperor) (Tokyo: Iwanami Shoten, 1992), 117.

29. Takashi Fujitani, *Splendid Monarchy: Power and Pageantry in Modern Japan* (Berkeley: University of California Press, 1998), 92.

30. Ibid.

31. Tōyama, *Meiji Isshin to Tenno*, 120.

32. Kaigo, *Kyōiku Chokugo Seiritsu no Kenkyū*, 71.

33. Ibid., 362.

34. Nagai Michio, *Kindaika to Kyōiku* (Modernization and Education) (Tokyo: Tokyo University Press, 1969), 65; and Kaigo, *Kyōiku Chokugo Seiritsu no Kenkyū*, 70—75.

35. Tōyama, *Meiji Isshin to Tenno*, 117.

36. Kaigo, *Kyōiku Chokugo Seiritsu Shi no Kenkyū*, 29; and Nagai, *Kindaika to Kyōiku*, 65.

37. Kaigo, *Kyōiku Chokugo Seiritsu Shi no Kenkyū*, 72.

38. Ibid., 70.

39. Kaigo, *Nihon Kindai Kyōiku Shi Jiten*, 25.

40. Inuzuka Takaaki, *Terashima Munenori* (Tokyo: Yoshikawa Kōbunkan, 1990), 299–300; and Kaigo, *Kyōiku Chokugo Seiritsu no Kenkyū*, 112.

41. Yamazumi Masami, *Nihon Kindai Shisō: Kyōiku no Taikei* (Outline of Modern Japanese Thought: Education) (Tokyo: Iwanami Shoten, 1990), 78.

42. Kaneko, *Itō Hirobumi Den*, 147.

43. Kaigo, *Kyōiku Chokugo Seiritsu Shi no Kenkyū*, 22.

44. Herbert Passin, *Society and Education in Japan* (New York: Teachers College Press, Columbia University, 1965), 228.

45. Yamazumi, *Nihon Kindai Shisō*, 83–85.

46. Nagai, *Kindaika to Kyōiku*, 65.

47. Passin, *Society and Education in Japan*, 228.

48. *Transactions of the Asiatic Society of Japan*, 69.

49. Ibid., 28–29.

50. Kaneko, *Itō Hirobumi Den*, 147.

51. Kaigo, *Kyōiku Chokugo Seiritsu Shi no Kenkyū*, 78; and Kaneko, *Itō Hirobumi Den*, 147–148.

52. Passin, *Society and Education in Japan*, 229–233.

53. Kaneko, *Itō Hirobumi Den*, 164.

54. Yamazumi, *Nihon Kindai Shisō: Kyōiku no Taikei*, 83–85.

55. Karasawa Tomitarō, *Kyōshi no Rekishi* (The History of Teachers) (Tokyo: Sōbunsha, 1955), 38.

56. Kaigo, *Nihon Kindai Kyōiku Shi Jiten*, 6.

57. Kurasawa, *Shōgakkō no Rekishi*, 110—112.

58. Ibid., 107–108.

59. Ibid., 109.

60. Ibid., 111.

61. Tsuchiya, *Meiji Zenki*, 289.

62. *Nihon Kindai Kyōiku Hyakunen Shi*, 106–107.

63. *Mumbujihō* (Ministry of Education Bulletin), no. 107 (1941).

64. Ibid.

65. Tanaka Kaoru, "Sofu Tanaka Fujimaro no Koto" (Grandfather Tanaka Fujimaro), *Fukuso* (Spring 1974): 74; and *Mombujihō*, 105.

66. Horimatsu Buichi, *Nihon Kindai Kyōiku Shi* (The History of Modern Japanese Education) (Tokyo: Risōsha, 1979), 63; and Ogata Hiroyasu, *Gakusei Jisshi Keii no Kenkyū* (Procedure for Implementing the Gakusei) (Tokyo: Kōsō Shobō, 1963), 174.

67. Ogata, *Gakusei Jisshi Keii no Kenkyū*, 171.

68. Ichikawa Shōgo, *Kyōiku Zaisei* (Educational Finance) (Tokyo: Tokyo University Press, 1972), 90.

CHAPTER 16 — THE THIRD NATIONAL PLAN FOR EDUCATION

1. Kaigo Tokiomi, ed., *Nihon Kindai Kyōiku Shi Jiten* (Dictionary of Modern Japanese Educational History) (Tokyo: Heibonsha, 1971), 778.

2. Kurasawa Takashi, *Shōgakkō no Rekishi* (History of the Elementary School) (Tokyo: Japan Library Bureau, 1963), 2: 82.

3. Katagiri Yoshio, *Jiyū Minken Ki Kyōiku Shi Kenkyū* (History of Education during the Era of the Peoples' Movement for Freedom) (Tokyo: Tokyo University Press, 1990), 41; Tsuchiya Tadao, *Meiji Zenki: Kyōiku Seisaku Shi* (History of Educational Policy in Early Meiji Japan) (Tokyo: Kōdansha, 1962), 257–258; Kaneko Terumoto, *Meiji Zenki Kyōiku Gyōsei Shi Kenkyū* (History of Educational Administration in the Early Meiji Period) (Tokyo: Kazama Shobō, 1967), 193–205.

4. Katagiri, *Jiyū Minken Ki Kyōiku Shi Kenkyū*, 312–315.

5. Ibid., 313.

6. Tsuchiya, *Meiji Zenki*, 282–284.

7. *Egi Kazuyuki Ō Keireki Dan* (The Career of Egi Kazuyuki) (Tokyo: Egi Kazuyuki Ō Keireki Dan Kankōkai, 1933), 1: 46.

8. Horimatsu Buichi, *Nihon Kindai Kyōiku Shi* (A History of Modern Japanese Education) (Tokyo: Risōsha, 1959), 64.

9. Yamazumi Masami, *Nihon Kindai Shisō Taikei: Kyōiku no Taikei* (Modern Japanese Thought: The Educational System) (Tokyo: Iwanami Shoten, 1990), 1: 89–90.

10. Yoshiie Sadao, *Nihonkoku Gakkan Debiddo Maree* (David Murray: Superintendent of Education in Japan) (Tokyo: Tamagawa University Press, 1998), 241.

11. Horimatsu, *Nihon Kindai Kyōiku Shi*, 64–65.

12. Ibid., 62–63.

13. Ibid.; *Nihon Kindai Kyōiku Hyakunen Shi* (One Hundred Year History of Modern Japanese Education) (Tokyo: National Institute for Educational Research, 1993), 105–109.

14. Nagai Michio, *Kindaika to Kyōiku* (Modernization and Education) (Tokyo: Tokyo University Press, 1969), 91.

15. *Mumbusho Nempō 8* (Ministry of Education Annual Report No. 8) (1880), 2: 30.

16. Kaigo, *Nihon Kindai Kyōiku Shi Jiten*, 777.

17. Ōkubo Toshikane, *Meiji Bunka Shiryō Sōsho* (Collection of Materials on Meiji Culture) (Tokyo: Kazama Shobō, 1961), 8: 152–153.

18. Yamazumi, *Nihon Kindai Shisō Taikei*, 115.

19. Ibid., 106.

20. Hayashi Takeji, *Meiji Teki Ningen* (The People of Meiji) (Tokyo: Chikuma Shobō, 1984), 10.

21. Yamazumi, *Nihon Kindai Shisō Taikei*, 98.

22. Kaigo, *Nihon Kindai Kyōiku Shi Jiten*, 777.

23. Mizuhara Katsutoshi, *Kindai Nihon Kyōin Yōsei Shi Kenkyū* (The History of Teacher Training in Modern Japan) (Tokyo: Kazama Shoten, 1990), 292.

24. Okuma Shigenobu, comp., *Fifty Years of New Japan* (London: Smith Elder, 1910), 2: 164.

25. Mizuhara, *Kindai Nihon Kyōin Yōsei Shi Kenkyū*, 295.

26. Kaigo, *Nihon Kindai Kyōiku Shi Jiten*, 777.

27. Horimatsu, *Nihon Kindai Kyōiku Shi*, 86.

28. Kaigo, *Nihon Kindai Kyōiku Shi Jiten*, 777.

29. *Egi Kazuyuki Ō Keireki Dan*, 54–55.

30. Ibid., 56–58; *Sōritsu Rokujūnen: Tokyo Bunrika Daigaku—Tokyo Kōtō Shihan Gakkō:* (Sixtieth Anniversary of the Tokyo Bunrika Daigaku—Tokyo Higher Teacher Training College) (Tokyo: Tokyo Bunrika Daigaku, 1931), 215.

31. *Egi Kazuyuki Ō Keireki Dan*, 55–62; Karasawa Tomitarō, *Kyōshi no Rekishi* (History of Teachers) (Tokyo: Sōbunsha, 1955), 37; and Motoyama Yukihiko, *Meiji Kokka no Kyōiku Shisō* (The Meiji State and Educational Thought) (Tokyo: Shibunkaku, 1998), 164.

32. *Egi Kazuyuki Ō Keireki Dan*, 3–33.

33. Karasawa, *Kyōshi no Rekishi*, 105–107.

34. Ibid., 107.

35. Ibid.

36. Kaigo, *Nihon Kindai Kyōiku Shi Jiten*, 777.

37. Horimatsu, *Nihon Kindai Kyōiku Shi*, 83.

38. Ibid., 83.

39. Mizuhara, *Kindai Nihon Kyōin Yōsei Shi Kenkyū*, 777–778.

40. Karasawa, *Kyōkasho no Rekishi*, 107.

41. Mizuhara, *Kindai Nihon Kyōin Yōsei Shi Kenkyū*, 778.

42. Kaigo Tokiomi, ed., *Nihon Kyōkasho Taikei: Kindai Hen* (A Collection of Modern Japanese Textbooks) (Tokyo: Kōdansha, 1963), vol. 2, *Shūshin* (Morals), 5–37.

43. Horimatsu, *Nihon Kindai Kyōiku Shi*, 74.

44. Ibid., 74–75.

45. Yamazumi, *Nihon Kindai Shisō Taikei*, 164.

46. Kaigo, *Nihon Kyōkasho Taikei: Kindai Hen*, 142.

47. Karasawa, *Kyōkasho no Rekishi*, 116–117.

48. Ibid., 116

49. Yamazumi, *Nihon Kindai Shisō Taikei*, 162; Horimatsu, *Nihon Kindai Kyōiku Shi*, 75.

50. Horimatsu, *Nihon Kindai Kyōiku Shi*, 75.

51. Ibid.

52. Kaigo, *Nihon Kyōkasho Taikei*, 2: 199–212.

53. Yasuda Hiroshi, *Shōka to Seijika: Meiji Ongaku Hajime* (Singing [Music] and the Cross: The Beginning of Music in the Meiji Period) (Tokyo: Ongaku no Tomosha, 1993), 162.

54. Miyoshi, *Nihon Kyōiku no Kaikoku*, 129.

55. Donald Berger, "Pioneers of Music Education in Japan," *Music Educators Journal*, October 1987, 35.

56. Miyoshi, *Nihon Kyōiku no Kaikoku*, 130.

57. Ibid., 128.

58. Karasawa, *Kyōkasho no Rekishi*, 128–129; Berger, "Pioneers of Music Education," 36.

59. *Tokyo Geijitsu Daigaku Hyakunen Shi*, 1: 93–94.

60. Kaigo, *Kyōiku Chokugo Seiritsu Shi no Kenkyū*, 112.

61. Berger, "Pioneers of Music Education," 35–36.

62. Kaigo, *Kyōiku Chokugo Seiritsu Shi no Kenkyū*, 112.

63. Ishitoya Tetsuo, *Nihon Kyōin Shi Kenkyū* (History of Japanese Teachers) (Tokyo: Kōdansha, 1958), 65.

64. Katagiri, *Jiyū Minken Ki Kyōiku Shi Kenkyū*, 101–105.

65. Ibid., 102–103.

66. Yamazumi, *Nihon Kindai Shisō Taikei*, 126; Kaigo, *Nihon Kindai Kyōiku Shi Jiten*, 26.

67. Marshall Brown, "The Tradition of Conflict in the Governance of Japan's Imperial University," *History of Education Quarterly* (Winter 1972): 892.

68. Karasawa, *Kyōshi no Rekishi*, 34.

69. Horimatsu, *Nihon Kindai Kyōiku Shi*, 78; Yamazumi, *Nihon Kindai Shisō Taikei*, 129.

70. Katagiri, *Jiyū Minken Ki Kyōiku Shi Kenkyū*, 300–301.

71. Ibid., 101.

72. *Egi Kazuyuki Ō Keireki Dan*, 63.

73. Katagiri, *Jiyū Minken Ki Kyōiku Shi Kenkyū*, 102.

74. Ishitoya, *Nihon Kyōin Shi Kenkyū*, 104–105.

75. Yamazumi, *Nihon Kindai Shisō Taikei*, 127.

76. *Tokyo Nichi Nichi Shimbun* (Tokyo Daily Newspaper), January 16, 1883, in *Meiji Nihon Hakkutsu*, edited by Suzuki Kōichi (Tokyo: Kawada Shobō Shinsa, 1994), 1: 133.

77. Suzuki, ed., *Tokyo Nichi Nichi Shimbun* (March 20, 1883): 134.

78. Katagiri, *Jiyū Minken Ki Kyōiku Shi Kenkyū*, 56.

79. Karasawa, *Kyōshi no Rekishi*, 34–35.

80. Ishitoya, *Nihon Kyōin Shi Kenkyū*, 128–129.

81. Ibid.

82. Nagai, *Kindaika to Kyōiku*, 31.

83. Ibid., 30.

84. Herbert Passin, *Society and Education in Japan* (New York: Teachers College Press, Columbia University, 1968), 228.

85. Taki Kōji, *Tenno no Shōzō* (Portrait of the Emperor) (Tokyo: Iwanami Shoten, 2002), 176–177.

86. Yamamoto Nobuyoshi, *Kindai Kyōiku no Tennosei Ideorogii* (The Ideology of the Imperial System in Modern Education) (Tokyo: Shinsansha, 1973), 72.

87. *Egi Sensuke Ou Keireki Dan*, 122–123.

88. Mizuhara, *Kindai Nihon Kyōin Yōsei Shi Kenkyū*, 289.

89. Kaigo, *Nihon Kindai Kyōiku Shi Jiten*, 777.

90. Mizuhara, *Kindai Nihon Kyōin Yōsei Shi Kenkyū*, 292.

91. *Sōritsu Rokujūnen: Tokyo Bunrika Daigaku—Tokyo Kōtō Shihan Gakkō*, 216–218.

92. *Takamine Hideo Sensei Fu* (The Biography of Takamine Hideo) (Tokyo: Takamine Hideo Memorial Committee, 1921), 80–84.

93. Tsuchiya, *Meiji Zenki: Kyōiku Seisaku Shi*, 209.

94. Kaigo Tokiomi, *Meiji Kyōju Riron Shi Kenkyū* (The History of Teaching Theory in Meiji Japan) (Tokyo: Heironsha, 1966), 100–101.

95. Inatomi Eijiro, *Meiji Shoki: Kyōiku Shisō no Kenkyū* (Educational Thought in the Early Meiji Period) (Fukumura Shoten, 1956), 299–302.

96. Hiramatsu Akio, *Meiji Jidai ni Okeru Shōgakkō Kyōjuhō no Kenkyū* (Elementary School Teaching Methods in Meiji Japan) (Tokyo: Risōsha, 1980), p. 31.

97. Ibid., 88.

98. George Beckman, *The Making of the Meiji Constitution* (Lawrence: University of Kansas Press, 1957), 69.

99. Joseph Pittau, "Inoue Kowashi, 1843–1895, and the Formation of Modern Japan," *Monumenta Nipponinca* 20, nos. 3–4 (1965): 262.

100. *Tokyo Daigaku Hyakunen Shi* (One Hundred Year History of Tokyo University) (Tokyo: Tokyo Daigaku, 1984), 1: 486.

101. Kurasawa Tsuyoshi, *Kyōiku Rei no Kenkyū* (Research on the Educational Code) (Tokyo: Kōdansha, 1975), 330.

102. *Tokyo Daigaku Hyakunen Shi*, 478–480.

103. Ibid., 484.

104. Chitoshi Yanagi, *Japan since Perry* (New York: McGraw-Hill, 1949), 97.

105. Karasawa Tomitarō, *Gakusei no Rekishi* (History of Students) (Tokyo: Sōbunsha, 1955), 59.

106. Edward Seidensticker, *Low City High City: Tokyo from Edo to the Earthquake* (New York: Alfred A. Knopf, 1983), 70.

107. Karasawa, *Gakusei no Rekishi*, 58–59.

108. Furuki Yoshiko, ed., *The Attic Letters: Ume Tsuda's Correspondence to Her American Mother* (New York: Weatherhill, 1991), 284.

109. Seidensticker, *Low City High City*, 100.

110. Furuki, *The Attic Letters*, 284.

111. *Tōyō Eiwa Jogakuin Hyakunen Shi* (One Hundred Year History of Tōyō Eiwa Jogakuin), (Tokyo: Tōyō Eiwa Jogakuin, 1977), 33–35.

112. Ibid., 35–38.

113. Karasawa, *Gakusei no Rekishi*, 60.

114. Tsuchiya, *Meiji Zenki*, 337–338.

115. *Nihon Kindai Kyōiku Hyakunen Shi* (One Hundred Year History of Modern Japanese Education) (Tokyo: National Educational Research Institute, 1974), 2: 47.

116. Tsuchiya, *Meiji Zenki*, 337.

CHAPTER 17 — EDUCATION FOR THE STATE

1. Nobuo Shimahara, *Adaptation and Education in Japan* (New York: Praeger, 1979), 55.

2. Inuzuka Takaaki, *Mori Arinori* (Tokyo: Yoshikawa Kōbunkan, 1986), 225–226.

3. *Nihon Kindai Kyōiku Hyakunen Shi* (One Hundred Year History of Modern Japanese Education) (Tokyo: National Institute for Educational Research, 1973), 1: 126–127.

4. Horimatsu Buichi, *Nihon Kindai Kyōiku Shi* (The History of Modern Japanese Education) (Tokyo: Risōsha, 1979), 138–139.

5. Nagai Michio, *Kindaika to Kyōiku* (Modernization and Education) (Tokyo: Tokyo Daigaku Shuppankai, 1969), 57.

6. Ibid., 97–99.

7. *Nihon Kindai Kyōiku Hyakunen Shi*, 1: 127; Horimatsu, *Nihon Kindai Kyōiku Shi*, 138–139.

8. Edwin Baelz, *Awakening Japan: The Diary of a German Doctor*, edited by Toku Baelz (New York: Viking Press, 1932; reprinted by Indiana University Press, 1974), 68–69.

9. Ivan Parker Hall, *Mori Arinori* (Cambridge: Harvard University Press, 1973), 289–290.

10. Furuki Yoshiko, ed., *The Attic Letters: Ume Tsuda's Correspondence to Her American Mother* (New York: Weatherhill, 1991), 157.

11. Inuzuka, *Mori Arinori*, 263.

12. Tsuchiya Tadao, *Kyōiku Seido Shi no Kenkyū* (History of Educational Policy in the Early Meiji Period) (Tokyo: Kōdansha, 1962), 438–440.

13. Ibid.

14. Inuzuka, *Mori Arinori*, 250.

15. Hall, *Mori Arinori*, 12.

16. Ōkubo Toshiaki, ed., *Mori Arinori Zenshū* (Complete Works of Mori Arinori) (Tokyo: Senbundō, 1972), 1: 178.

17. Mizuhara Katsutoshi, *Kindai Nihon Kyōin Yōsei Shi Kenkyū* (The History of Modern Japanese Teacher Education) (Tokyo: Kazama Shobō, 1990), 560.

18. Ishitoya Tetsuo, *Nihon Kyōin Shi Kenkyū* (History of Japanese Teachers) (Tokyo: Kōdansha, 1958), 310.

19. Nagai, *Kindaika to Kyōiku*, 97–98.

20. *Tokyo Teikoku Daigaku Gojūnen Shi* (Fifty Year History of Tokyo Imperial University) (Tokyo: Tokyo Teikoku Daigaku, 1932), 1: 931; Inuzuka, *Mori Arinori*, 267–269.

21. Ministry of Education, Imperial University of Japan, *The Calendar for the Year 1886–1887* (Tokyo: Ministry of Education, 1886), unpaged (original text in English).

22. *Tokyo Teikoku Daigaku Gojūnen Shi*, 934–936.

23. *Tokyo Daigaku Hyakunen Shi* (One Hundred Year History of Tokyo University) (Tokyo: Tokyo Daigaku Shuppan Kai, 1984), 1: 698–699.

24. Imperial University of Japan, *The Calendar for the Year 1886–1887*, unpaged.

25. *Japan Weekly Mail*, April 28, 1888.

26. Horimatsu, *Nihon Kindai Kyōiku Shi*, 162–163; Tsuchiya, *Kyōiku Seido Shi no Kenkyū*, 368–371.

27. Horimatsu, *Nihon Kindai Kyōiku Shi*, 163.

28. *Kyūsei Kōtō Chūgakkō Zensho* (The Complete Works on the Old Higher Middle School) (Tokyo: Kyūsei Kōtōgakkō Shiryō Hozonkai, 1985), 1: 20–21.

29. *Nihon Kindai Kyōiku Hyakunen Shi*, 1: 136–137.

30. *Kyūsei Kōtō Gakkō Zensho*, 34.

31. Fukaya Masashi, *Gakureki Shugi no Keifu* (The Genesis of Academic-Qualification Orientation) (Tokyo: Reimei Shobō, 1969), 167.

32. *Daiichi Kōtō Gakkō Rokujūnen Shi* (Sixty Year History of the First Higher Middle School) (Tokyo: Sanshūsha, 1939), 10–11; *Kyūsei Kōtō Chūgakkō Zensho*, 22, 59–60.

33. *Kyūsel Kōtō Chūgakkō Zensho*, 23.

34. Atōda Reizo, *Nikō o Kataru* (The Story of the Second Higher Middle School) (Tokyo: Daini Kōtō Gakkō Kyōsaibu, 1934), 1.

35. Donald Roden, *Schooldays in Imperial Japan* (Berkeley: University of California Press, 1980), 66.

36. Atōda, *Nikō o Kataru*, 5–6.

37. Ibid.

38. *Tokyo Daigaku Hyakunen Shi*, 1: 985.

39. *Daini Kōtō Chūgakkō Dai Ikkai Sotsugyōsei* (The Graduates of the First Class of the Second Higher Middle School), Archives, Tōhoku University, Sendai, undated.

40. *Tokyo Teikoku Daigaku Sotsugyōsei Shimeibo* (The Graduates of Tokyo Imperial University) (Tokyo: Maruzen, 1933).

41. *Nikō Meibo* (Directory of Students of the Second Middle Higher School) (Tokyo: Kōshisha, 1966).

42. *Meiji Ikō: Kyōiku Seido Hattatsu Shi* (History of the Development of the Education System in the Meiji Period) (Tokyo: Kyōiku Shi Hensankai, 1938), 3: 153.

43. *Nihon Kindai Kyōiku Hyakunen Shi*, 1: 136–137.

44. Kaigo Tokiomi, ed., *Nihon Kindai Kyōiku Shi Jiten* (Dictionary of Modern Japanese Educational History) (Tokyo: Heibonsha, 1971), 187.

45. Kurasawa Takashi, *Gakkō Rei no Kenkyū* (Research on the Educational Ordinances) (Tokyo: Kōdansha, 1978), 215.

46. *Meiji Ikō: Kyōiku Seido Hattatsu Shi*, 3: 496–497.

47. Mizuhara, *Kindai Nihon Kyōin Yōsei Shi Kenkyū*, 581.

48. *Nihon Kindai Kyōiku Hyakunen Shi*, 1: 144.

49. Horimatsu, *Nihon Kindai Kyōiku Shi*, 147–151; Shimohara, 56.

50. Terasaki Masao, "Kindai Nihon Kyōikuron Shū, Kyōshizō no Tenkai" (A Collection of Modern Theories of Japanese Education: The Development of the Image of a Japanese Teacher), *Jokudosha* 6 (1973): 63; Mizuhara, *Kindai Nihon Kyōin Yōsei Shi Kenkyū*, 510–511; Kurasawa, *Gakkō Rei no Kenkyū*, 216.

51. Mizuhara, *Kindai Nihon Kyōin Yōsei Shi Kenkyū*, 477–485.

52. Ōkubo, *Mori Arinori Zenshū*, 347–349.

53. Yamazumi Masami, *Nihon Kindai Shisō: Kyōiku no Taikei* (Outline of Modern Japanese Thought: Education) (Tokyo: Iwanami Shoten, 1990), 139–141.

54. Morikawa Terumichi, "Mori Arinori," in Benjamin Duke, *Ten Great Educators in Modern Japan* (Tokyo: University of Tokyo Press, 1989), 63.

55. Kaigo Tokiomi, *Kyōiku Chokugo Seiritsu Shi no Kenkyū* (The Formation of the Imperial Rescript on Education) (Tokyo: privately published, 1965), 390–399; and Mizuhara, *Kindai Nihon Kyōin Yōsei Shi Kenkyū*, 487–488.

56. *Takamine Hideo Sensei Fu* (Professor Takamine Hideo), edited by Takamine Hideo Sensei Kinen Jigyōkai (Tokyo: privately published, 1922), 91–97.

57. Mizuhara, *Kindai Nihon Kyōin Yōsei Shi Kenkyū*, 581–583.

58. Sakurai H., *Yamakawa Hiroshi* (Tokyo: privately published, 1967), 59–60.

59. Karasawa Tomitaro, *Kyōshi no Rekishi* (History of Teachers) (Tokyo: Sōbunsha, 1955), 40–70.

60. Machida Norifumi, *Meiji Kokumin Kyōiku Shi* (History of Education for the People of the Meiji Period) (Tokyo: Showa Shuppansha, 1928), 200.

61. Kaigo, *Nihon Kindai Kyōiku Shi Jiten*, 592–593.

62. Nagai Michio, *Higher Education in Japan: Its Take-off and Crash* (Tokyo: University of Tokyo Press, 1971), 190–191.

63. Mizuhara, *Kindai Nihon Kyōin Yōsei Shi Kenkyū*, 640–642.

64. *Japan Weekly Mail*, May 28, 1887.

65. Mizuhara, *Kindai Nihon Kyōin Yōsei Shi Kenkyū*, 640–642.

66. Machida, *Meiji Kokumin Kyōiku Shi*, 203–204.

67. Mizuhara, *Kindai Nihon Kyōin Yōsei Shi Kenkyū*, 574–576.

68. *Kyōiku Gaku Kenkyū* (Journal of Education) (December 1994): 61–64.

69. Mizuhara, *Kindai Nihon Kyōin Yōsei Shi Kenkyū*, 618.

70. Lafcadio Hearn, *Glimpses of Unfamiliar Japan* (Boston: Houghton, Mifflin, 1894), 434–435.

71. Kurasawa Tsuyoshi, *Shōgakkō no Rekishi* (History of the Elementary School) (Tokyo: Japan Library Bureau, 1965), 2: 416–417.

72. *Sōritsu Rokujūnen: Tokyo Bunrika Daigaku—Tokyo Kōtō Shihan Gakkō* (The Sixtieth Anniversary of the Founding of the Tokyo University of Culture—Tokyo Higher Teacher Training College) (Tokyo: Tokyo Bunrika Daigaku, 1931), 220.

73. Masaharu Anesaki, *History of Japanese Religions* (Rutland, Vt.: C. E. Tuttle, 1963), 365.

74. Ibid.

75. *Japan Weekly Mail*, January 12, 1889.

76. Naka Arata, *Gakkō no Rekishi: Shōgakkō no Rekishi* (The History of Schools: The Elementary School) (Tokyo: Daiichi Hōki Shuppan, 1979), 2: 66; Tsuchiya, *Meiji Zenki: Kyōiku Seisaku Shi no Kenkyū*, 337.

77. Karasawa Tomitarō, *Kyōkasho no Rekishi* (The History of Textbooks) (Tokyo: Sōbunsha, 1956), 147–148.

78. Kaigo Tokiomi, ed., *Nihon Kyōkasho Taikei: Kindai Hen* (A Collection of Modern Japanese Textbooks) (Tokyo: Kōdansha, 1964), 4: 782–786.

79. Ibid.

80. Hiramatsu Akio, *Meiji Jidai ni Okeru Shōgakkō Kyōjuhō no Kenkyū* (Elementary Teaching Methods in the Meiji Period) (Tokyo: Risōsha, 1975), 125–126.

81. Ibid.

82. Terasaki Masao, *Oyatoi Kyōshi Hausukunehito no Kenkyū* (Hausknecht, the Hired Foreign Teacher) (Tokyo: Tokyo University Press, 1991), 27–31.

83. Terasaki, *Oyatoi Kyōshi Hausukunehito no Kenkyū*, 31.

84. Ibid., 298.

85. Ibid., 297–298.

86. Ibid., 51–53.

87. Ibid., 45.

88. Horimatsu, *Nihon Kindai Kyōiku Shi*, 215–216.

89. Terasaki, *Oyatoi Kyōshi Hausukunehito no Kenkyū*, 49.

90. Ibid., 49–50.

91. Mizuhara, *Kindai Nihon Kyōin Yōsei Shi Kenkyū*, 673–675.

92. Terasaki, *Oyatoi Kyōshi Hausukunehito no Kenkyū*, 56.

93. Ibid., 58.

94. Ibid., 59–60.

95. Ibid., 55–62; Mizuhara, *Kindai Nihon Kyōin Yōsei Shi Kenkyū*, 554–555.

96. Terasaki, *Oyatoi Kyōshi Hausukunehito no Kenkyū*, 58–60.

97. Ibid., 60.

98. Ibid., 76–77.

99. Ogata Hiroyasu, *Nihon Kyōiku Tsū Shi* (History of Japanese Education) (Tokyo: Waseda Daigaku Shuppan Bu, 1971), 241–242.

100. Ibid., 99–113.

101. Mizuhara, *Kindai Nihon Kyōin Yōsei Shi Kenkyū*, 554–556.

102. Terasaki, *Oyatoi Kyōshi Hausukunehito no Kenkyū*, 66–67.

103. Ogata, *Nihon Kyōiku Tsū Shi*, 242.

104. Terasaki, *Oyatoi Kyōshi Hausukunehito no Kenkyū*, 114.

105. *Japan Weekly Mail*, February 29, 1889.

106. Suzuki Kōichi, ed., "Tokyo Nichi Nichi Shimbun, February 14, 1889," in *Meiji Nihon Hakkutsu* (Unearthing Meiji Japan) 4 (1994): 122; Inuzuka, *Mori Arinori*, 300–301.

107. Baelz, *Awakening Japan*, 82–83.

108. Suzuki, "Tokyo Nichi Nichi Shimbun, February 14, 1889," 123.

109. Ōkubo, *Mori Arinori Zenshū*, 674–675; Itō Sei, ed., *Nihon Gendai Bungaku Zenshū* (Complete Works of Japanese Literature) (Tokyo: Kōdansha, 1968), 34: 230.

110. *Japan Weekly Mail*, January 12, 1889.

111. Noguchi Isaaki, *Inoue Kowashi no Kyōiku Shisō* (The Educational Thought of Inoue Kowashi) (Tokyo: Kazama Shobō, 1994), 319; Kimura Tadashi, *Mori Sensei Den* (Biography of Mori) [1899] (Tokyo: Ōzorasho, 1987), 142–146.

112. Fukushima Masao, *Katei: Seisaku to Hō* (The Family: Policy and Laws), No. 7, *Kindai Nihon no Katei Ron* (The Theory of Family in Modern Japan), (Tokyo: Tokyo Daigaku Shuppan Kai, 1976), 229–230.

CHAPTER 18 — THE IMPERIAL RESCRIPT ON EDUCATION

1. Ryūsaka Tsunoda, comp., *Sources of Japanese Tradition* (New York: Columbia University Press, 1958), 646–647.

2. Kaigo Tokiomi, *Kyōiku Chokugo Seiritsu Shi no Kenkyū* (The Formation of "The Imperial Rescript on Education") (Tokyo: privately published, 1965), 392.

3. Ibid., 393–399.

4. Herbert Passin, *Society and Education in Japan* (New York: Teachers College Press, Columbia University, 1965), 228.

5. Kaigo, *Kyōiku Chokugo Seiritsu Shi no Kenkyū*, 387.

6. *Japan Weekly Mail*, June 29, 1888.

7. Ivan Parker Hall, *Mori Arinori* (Cambridge: Harvard University Press, 1973), 441.

8. *Japan Weekly Mail*, January 12, 1889.

9. Noguchi Isaaki, *Inoue Kowashi no Kyōiku Shisō* (Educational Thought of Inoue Kowashi) (Tokyo: Kazama Shobō, 1994), 326.

10. Kaigo, *Kyōiku Chokugo Seiritsu Shi no Kenkyū*; Yamazumi Masami, *Kyōiku Chokugo* (Imperial Rescript on Education) (Tokyo: Asahi Shimbunsha, 1991); Morikawa Terumichi, *Kyōiku Chokugo e no Michi* (The Road to "The Imperial Rescript on Education") (Tokyo: Sangensha, 1990); Iwamoto Tsutomu, *Kyōiku Chokugo no Kenkyū* (Research on "The Imperial Rescript on Education") (Tokyo: Minshūshakan, 2001).

11. Yamazumi, *Kyōiku Chokugo*, 50.

12. Ibid., 40–50.

13. Kaigo, *Kyōiku Chokugo Seiritsu Shi no Kenkyū*, 164.

14. Carol Gluck, *Japan's Modern Myths: Ideology in the Late Meiji Period* (Princeton: Princeton University Press, 1985), 115–119.

15. Yamazumi Masami, *Nihon Kindai Shisō: Kyōiku no Taikei* (Outline of Modern Japanese Thought: Education) (Tokyo: Iwanami Shoten, 1990), 6: 370; Yamazumi, *Kyōiku Chokugo*, 43–50.

16. Kaigo, *Kyōiku Chokugo Seiritsu Shi no Kenkyū*, 165.

17. Yamazumi, *Kyōiku Chokugo*, 52.

18. Masaharu Anesaki, *History of Japanese Religions* (Rutland, Vt.: C. E. Tuttle, 1963), 352–353.

19. Irwin Scheiner, *Christian Converts and Social Protest in Meiji Japan* (Berkeley: University of California Press, 1970), 17.

20. Warren Clark, *Katz Awa* (New Tork: B. F. Burk, 1904), 17.

21. Kaigo, *Kyōiku Chokugo Seiritsu Shi no Kenkyū*, 219.

22. Yamazumi, *Kyōiku Chokugo*, 51–57.

23. Ibid., 50.

24. Ibid., 62–63.

25. Ibid.

26. Kaigo, *Kyōiku Chokugo Seiritsu Shi no Kenkyū*, 219–220.

27. Kaigo Tokiomi, *Inoue Kowashi no Kyōiku Seisaku* (The Educational Policy of Inoue Kowashi) (Tokyo: Tokyo Daigaku Shuppan Kai, 1968), 3–5.

28. Kaigo, *Kyōiku Chokugo Seiritsu Shi no Kenkyū*, 251–252; and Yamazumi, *Nihon Kindai Shisō*, 375.

29. Horimatsu Buichi, *Nihon Kindai Kyōiku Shi* (History of Modern Japanese Education) (Tokyo: Risōsha, 1959), 170–171.

30. Itō Yahiko, ed., *Nihon Kindai Kyōiku Shi Saiko* (A Reconsideration of Modern Japanese Educational History) (Tokyo: Shōwa Dō, 1986), 88.

31. Morikawa, *Kyōiku Chokugo e no Michi*, 148.

32. Yamazumi, *Nihon Kindai Shisō*, 379–380.

33. Horimatsu, *Nihon Kindai Kyōiku Shi*, 171; Yamazumi, *Nihon Kindai Shisō*, 379–380; and Noguchi, *Inoue Kowashi no Kyōiku Shisō*, 258.

34. Kaigo, *Kyōiku Chokugo Seiritsu Shi*, 453–459.

35. Ibid., 299.

36. Noguchi, *Inoue Kowashi no Kyōiku Shisō*, 280–281.

37. Karasawa Tomitarō, *Kyōkasho no Rekishi* (History of Textbooks) (Tokyo: Sōbunsha, 1956), 163.

38. Noguchi, *Inoue Kowashi no Kyōiku Shisō*, 280–285.

39. Kaigo Tokiomi, ed., *Nihon Kindai Kyōiku Shi Jiten* (Dictionary of Modern Japanese Educational History) (Tokyo: Heibonsha, 1971), 9.

40. Passin, *Society and Education in Japan*, 229–233.

41. Ibid.

42. Noguchi, *Inoue Kowashi no Kyōiku Shisō*, 143–145; Itō Yahiko, *Isshin to Jinshin* (Spirit of the People) (Tokyo: Tokyo University Press, 1999), 214–215.

43. Itō, *Isshin to Jinshin*, 214–215.

44. Johannes Siemes, *Herman Roesler and the Making of the Meiji State* (Tokyo: Sophia University, 1968), 11.

45. Ibid., 13.

46. Itō, *Isshin to Jinshin*, 192.

47. Morikawa, *Kyōiku Chokugo e no Michi*, 164.

48. Itō, *Isshin to Jinshin*, 215.

49. Kaigo, *Kyōiku Chokugo Seiritsu Shi*, 251–252.

50. Noguchi, *Inoue Kowashi no Kyōiku Shisō*, 300–315.

51. Inada Shoji, *Kyōiku Chokugo Seiritsu Katei no Kenkyū* (The Development of "The Imperial Rescript on Education") (Tokyo: Kōdansha, 1971), 71–73.

52. Kurasawa Tsuyoshi, *Kyōiku Rei no Kenkyū* (A Study of the Education Code) (Tokyo: Kōdansha, 1975), 329.

53. Joseph Pittau, "Inoue Kowashi, 1843–1895," *Monumenta Nipponica* 20, nos. 3–4 (1965): 273.

54. Kenneth Pyle, *The Making of Modern Japan* (Lexington, Mass.: D. C. Heath, 1996), 127.

55. Yatsuki Kimio, "Tenno to Nihon no Kindai" (Modern Japan and the Emperor), in *Kyōiku Chokugo no Shisō* (The Thought of "The Imperial Rescript on Education") (Tokyo: Kōdansha, 2001), 2: 146.

56. Ibid., 110–111.

57. Noguchi, *Inoue Kowashi no Kyōiku Shisō*, 301–302.

58. "Transactions of the Asiatic Society of Japan, Lectures Delivered in the Presence of His Imperial Majesty the Emperor of Japan by the Late Baron Motoda," *Transactions of the Asiatic Society of Japan* 40 [1912] (Tokyo: Yushodo Booksellers, 1964), 61–63.

59. Ibid., 62–63.

60. Yatsuki, "Tenno to Nihon no Kindai," 243.

61. Ibid., 260–261.

62. Soeda Yoshiya, *Kyōiku Chokugo no Shakai Shi* (The Social History of "The Imperial Rescript on Education") (Tokyo: Yūshindōkō Bunshin, 1997), 115–121.

63. Kaigo, *Inoue Kowashi no Kyōiku Seisaku*, 935–939.

64. Kaigo, *Kyōiku Chokugo Seiritsu*, 364; *Egi Kazuyuki Ou Keireki Dan* (The Biography of Egi Kazuyuki) (Tokyo: Egi Kazuyuki Ou Keireki Dan Kankōkai, 1933), 1: 127.

Index

408 Index

Wheeler, William, 179, 205, 211
Whittier, John Greenleaf, 105
Wickersham, James, 88–90, 227–229, 236
William Smith Clark: A Yankee in Hokkaido
(Maki), 202
Williamson, Alexander, 30–31, 34–35, 36, 38,
178
Williston Seminary, 202
Wilson, Marcius, 143
Wilson Reader, 125, 143–144
Winslow, Hubbard, 143
Women's Institute of English Studies, 111
Woolsey, Theodore, 106

Yamagata Aritomo, 352–354, 356, 369
Yamagata Yorimoto, 212–213, 369
Yamakawa Hiroshi, 13, 101–102, 329, 331–332,
334–335
Yamakawa Kenjirō, 13, 18, 101, 106–107, 332

Yamakawa Sutematsu, 14–15, 80, 101–105, 108–
111, 332; American education of, 105–108
Yamao Yōzō, 29–30, 172–173, 175, 291
Yōgakkō Kaiseijo, 33
Yōgaku, 2, 49, 183, 265. *See also* western studies
*Yōgaku Kōyō. See Principles for Guiding
Children* (Motoda)
yōgakusha, 20–21, 68, 69
Yokoi Daihei, 44
Yokoi Saheido, 44
Yokoi Shōnan, 43, 45–46
Yoshida Shōin, 21, 29, 39–40, 353
Yoshii Tōmomi, 350
Yoshikawa Akimasa, 352, 354–355, 358, 369
Yōsho Shirabesho, 20. *See also* Bansho Shira-
besho

zoology, 233–234
Zōshikan, 33

About the Author

BENJAMIN DUKE is a professor emeritus of comparative and international education at the International Christian University in Tokyo. He is the author of several books on education in Japan.